Scale 1:250,000
or 3.95 miles to 1 inch
(2.5km to 1cm)

38th edition June 2015

© AA Media Limited 2015

Revised version of the atlas formerly known as *Complete Atlas of Britain*. Original edition printed 1979.

Cartography:
All cartography in this atlas edited, designed and produced by the Mapping Services Department of AA Publishing (A05309).

This atlas contains Ordnance Survey data © Crown copyright and database right 2015 and Royal Mail data © Royal Mail copyright and database right 2015.

Publisher's Notes:
Published by AA Publishing (a trading name of AA Media Limited, whose registered office is Fanum House, Basing View, Basingstoke, Hampshire RG21 4EA, UK. Registered number 06112600).

ISBN: 978 0 7495 7687 5

A CIP catalogue record for this book is available from The British Library.

Acknowledgements:
AA Publishing would like to thank the following for their assistance in producing this atlas:
Information on fixed speed camera locations provided by and © 2015 RoadPilot Ltd.
Crematoria data provided by the Cremation Society of Great Britain.
Cadw, English Heritage, Forestry Commission, Historic Scotland, Johnsons, National Trust and National Trust for Scotland, RSPB, The Wildlife Trust, Scottish Natural Heritage, Natural England, The Countryside Council for Wales (road maps).

Transport for London (Central London Map),
Nexus (Newcastle district map).

Printer:
Printed in Italy by Canale & C. S.p.A

AA

2

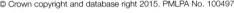

MOTORIS
ATLAS
BRITAIN

Atlas contents

Map pages	inside front cover
Route planner	II–VII
Road map symbols	**1**
Road maps	**2–115**
Britain 1:250,000 scale Some islands are shown at slightly smaller scales.	2–111
Ireland 1:1,000,000 scale	112–115
Motorways	**116–121**
Restricted junctions 116–119 M6 Toll motorway	121
M25 London Orbital 120	
Street map symbols	**122**
Town plans	**123–135**
District maps	**136–147**
Birmingham 136–137 Tyne & Wear	142–143
Glasgow 138–139 London	144–147
Manchester 140–141	
Central London	**148–163**
Central London 148–157 Central London	158–163
street map index	
Index to place names	**164–200**
County, administrative area map	164

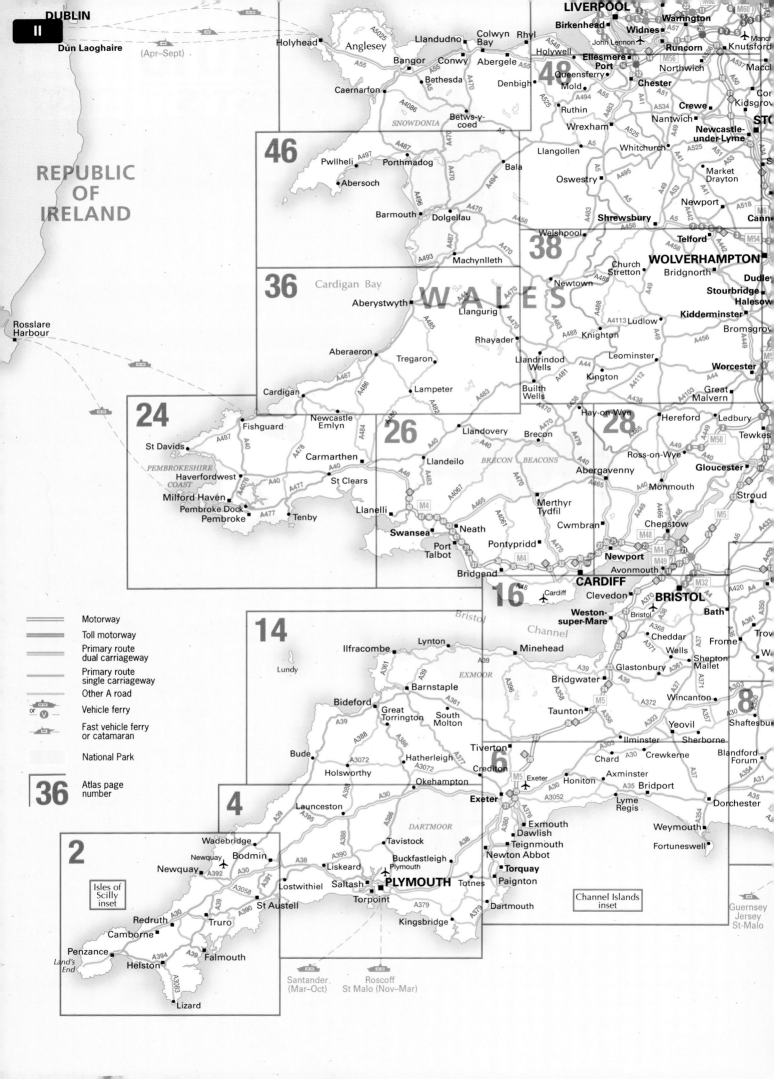

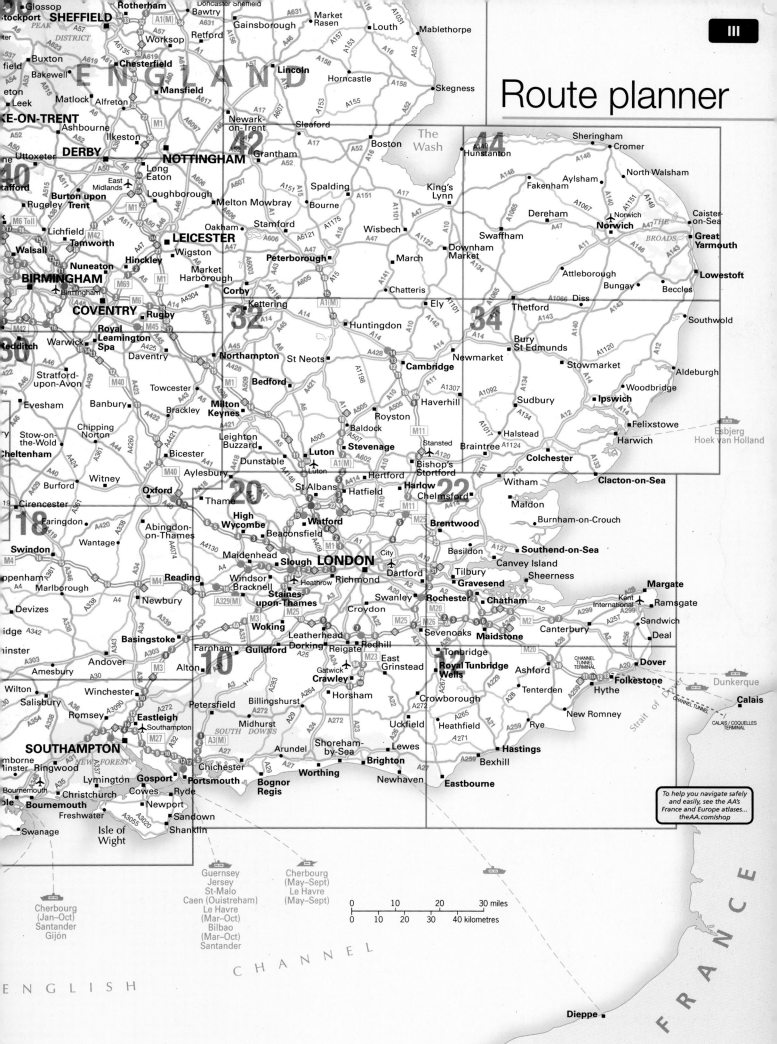

Route planner

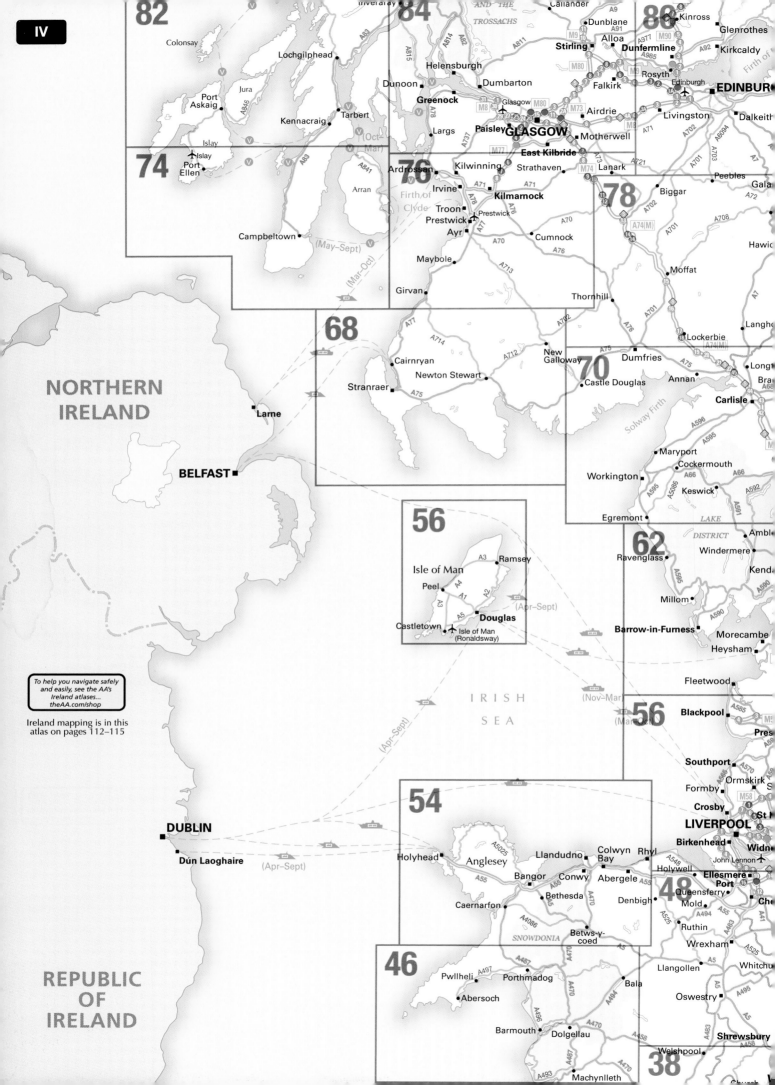

82

Colonsay

Lochgilphead

Jura

84

Inveraray

AND THE TROSSACHS

Callander

A9

Dunblane

M9

Stirling

Alloa A91

A977

Dunfermline

M90

Kinross

Glenrothes

A92

Kirkcaldy

86

Port Askaig

Kennacraig

Tarbert

Helensburgh

Dunoon

Dumbarton

Greenock

Rosyth

Firth of

Edinburgh

EDINBUR

Islay

Port Ellen

74

Arran

Largs

Paisley

GLASGOW

M8

M80

Airdrie

Falkirk

Motherwell

M73

M8

Livingston

Dalkeith

Campbeltown

(May–Sept)

(Mar–Oct)

76

Ardrossan

Kilwinning

Irvine

Kilmarnock

Troon

Prestwick

Prestwick

Prestwick

Ayr

Maybole

East Kilbride

M77

Strathaven

M74

Lanark

A721

A71

A76

A70

Cumnock

A76

A713

Firth of Clyde

(Oct–Mar)

Biggar

Peebles

Gala

A72

78

A702

A74(M)

A701

A703

Hawic

Girvan

A77

A714

A712

New Galloway

A702

A76

A701

Thornhill

Moffat

A701

A7

68

Cairnryan

Newton Stewart

Stranraer

A75

A75

Dumfries

70

Castle Douglas

Lockerbie

A74(M)

Langho

Annan

A75

Long

Bra

A68

Carlisle

Solway Firth

M

NORTHERN
IRELAND

Larne

BELFAST

Maryport

Cockermouth

A596

A595

Workington

A66

A66

A595

A5086

Keswick

A591

A592

Egremont

LAKE DISTRICT

Amble

56

Isle of Man

Peel

A3

Ramsey

A4

A2

A1

A3

A5

Castletown

Douglas

Isle of Man (Ronaldsway)

(Apr–Sept)

Ravenglass

A595

Windermere

62

Kend

Millom

A590

A590

Barrow-in-Furness

Morecambe

Heysham

(Apr–Sept)

IRISH SEA

(Nov–Mar)

Fleetwood

56

Blackpool

A585

M

(Mar

To help you navigate safely and easily, see the AA's Ireland atlases... theAA.com/shop

Ireland mapping is in this atlas on pages 112–115

Southport

A570

Ormskirk

Formby

M58

S

Crosby

LIVERPOOL

St

DUBLIN

54

Holyhead

A5025

Anglesey

Llandudno

Bangor

Conwy

Bethesda

Colwyn Bay

Rhyl

Abergele

A55

Holywell

A548

John Lennon

Birkenhead

Widn

Ellesmere Port

Queensferry

48

Ch

Dún Laoghaire

(Apr–Sept)

Caernarfon

A4086

SNOWDONIA

Betws-y-coed

A470

Denbigh

A525

Mold

A55

Ruthin

Wrexham

A525

A483

A55

A494

46

Pwllheli

A497

Abersoch

Porthmadog

A487

A470

Bala

A487

Llangollen

A5

Oswestry

A495

REPUBLIC
OF
IRELAND

Barmouth

A496

Dolgellau

A470

A458

A493

Machynlleth

Welshpool

A483

Shrewsbury

38

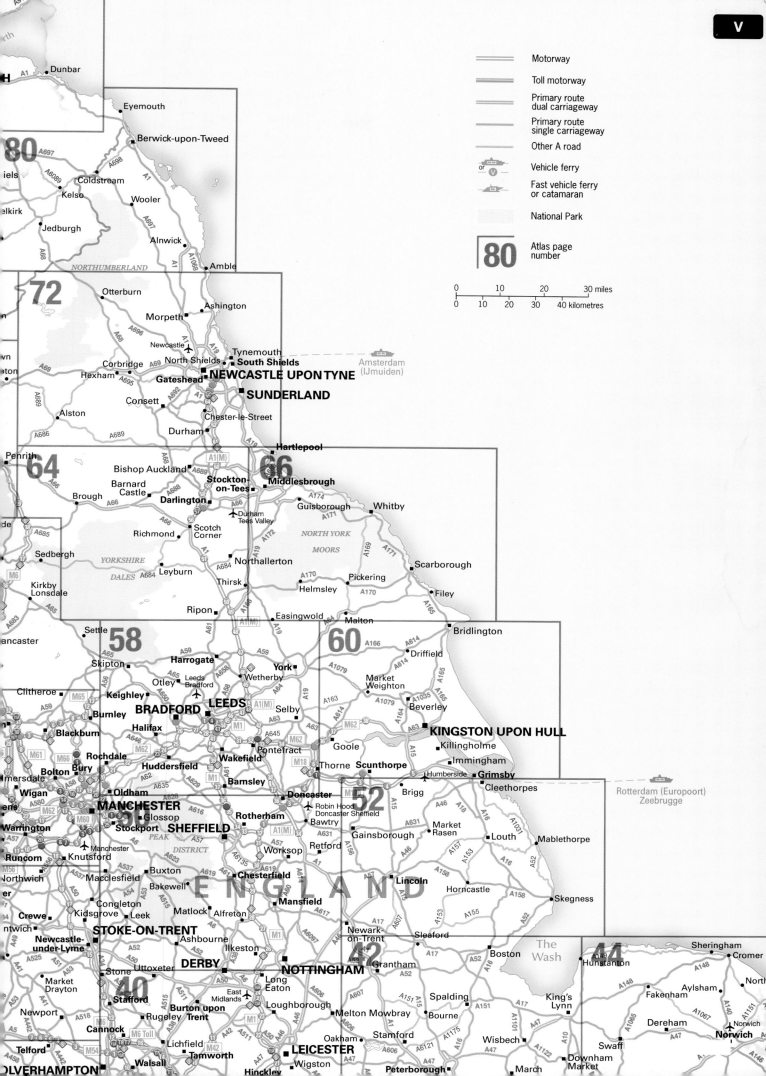

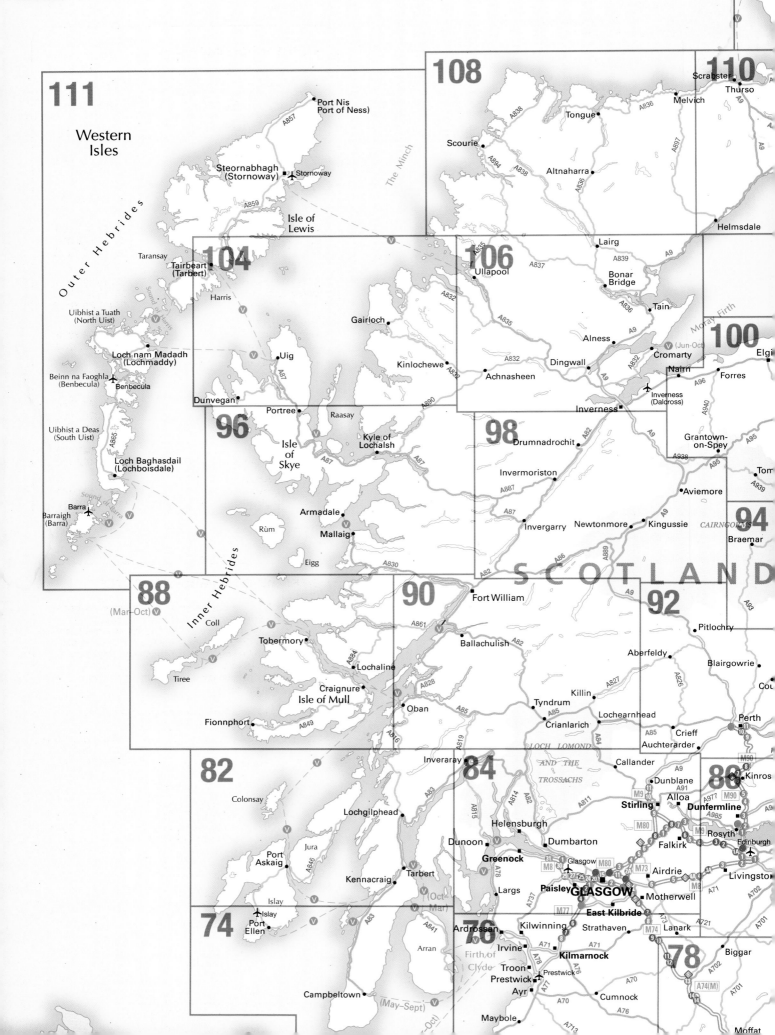

Shetland Islands are on page 111

Shetland Islands are on page 111

FERRY INFORMATION

Hebrides and west coast Scotland
calmac.co.uk	0800 066 5000
skyeferry.co.uk	
western-ferries.co.uk	01369 704 452

Orkney and Shetland
northlinkferries.co.uk	0845 6000 449
pentlandferries.co.uk	0800 688 8998
orkneyferries.co.uk	01856 872 044
shetland.gov.uk/ferries	01595 743 970

Isle of Man
steam-packet.com	08722 992 992

Ireland
irishferries.com	08717 300 400
poferries.com	08716 642 020
stenaline.co.uk	08447 70 70 70

North Sea (Scandinavia and Benelux)
dfdsseaways.co.uk	08715 229 955
poferries.com	08716 642 020
stenaline.co.uk	08447 70 70 70

Isle of Wight
wightlink.co.uk	0333 999 7333
redfunnel.co.uk	0844 844 9988

Channel Islands
condorferries.co.uk	0845 609 1024

France and Belgium
brittany-ferries.co.uk	0871 244 0744
condorferries.co.uk	0845 609 1024
eurotunnel.com	08443 35 35 35
dfdsseaways.co.uk	08715 229 955
poferries.com	08716 642 020
myferrylink.com	0844 2482 100

Northern Spain
brittany-ferries.co.uk	0871 244 0744
ldlines.co.uk	0844 576 8836

EMERGENCY DIVERSION ROUTES

In an emergency it may be necessary to close a section of motorway or other main road to traffic, so a temporary sign may advise drivers to follow a diversion route. To help drivers navigate the route, black symbols on yellow patches may be permanently displayed on existing direction signs, including motorway signs. Symbols may also be used on separate signs with yellow backgrounds.

For further information see *www.highways.gov.uk*, *trafficscotland.org* and *traffic-wales.com*

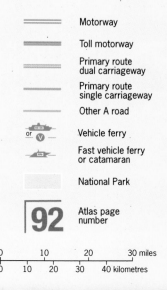

══════	Motorway
══════	Toll motorway
══════	Primary route dual carriageway
──────	Primary route single carriageway
──────	Other A road
or Ⓥ	Vehicle ferry
	Fast vehicle ferry or catamaran
	National Park
92	Atlas page number

```
0        10        20        30 miles
0   10   20   30   40 kilometres
```

Road map symbols

Motoring information

M4	Motorway with number	BATH	Primary route destination	Y 5 Y	Distance in miles between symbols	50	Safety camera site (fixed location) with speed limit in mph
Toll	Toll motorway with toll station	A1123	Other A road single/dual carriageway	or V	Vehicle ferry	60	Section of road with two or more fixed safety cameras, with speed limit in mph
1	Motorway junction with and without number	B2070	B road single/dual carriageway		Fast vehicle ferry or catamaran	50 50	Average speed (SPECS™) camera system with speed limit in mph
3	Restricted motorway junctions		Minor road more than 4 metres wide, less than 4 metres wide		Railway line, in tunnel	V	Fixed safety camera site with variable speed limit
Fleet	Motorway service area		Roundabout	○ X	Railway station and level crossing	P·R	Park and Ride (at least 6 days per week)
	Motorway and junction under construction		Interchange/junction	+++++++	Tourist railway		City, town, village or other built-up area
A3	Primary route single/dual carriageway		Narrow primary/other A/B road with passing places (Scotland)	⊕ Ⓗ	Airport, heliport	628 637 ▲ Lecht Summit	Height in metres, mountain pass
1	Primary route junction with and without number		Road under construction/ approved	Ⓕ	International freight terminal		Sandy beach
3	Restricted primary route junctions	⊨=====⊣	Road tunnel	Ⓗ	24-hour Accident & Emergency hospital		National boundary
S	Primary route service area	Toll →	Road toll, steep gradient (arrows point downhill)	Ⓒ	Crematorium		County, administrative boundary

Touring information

To avoid disappointment, check opening times before visiting.

	Scenic route	�	Aqueduct or viaduct	············	Forest drive		Horse racing, show jumping
i	Tourist Information Centre	✻ ♣	Garden, arboretum	- - - - -	National trail		Air show venue, motor-racing circuit
i	Tourist Information Centre (seasonal)	♣	Vineyard	☀	Viewpoint		Ski slope (natural, artificial)
V	Visitor or heritage centre	♈	Country park	⸰⸰⸰	Hill-fort		National Trust property (England & Wales, Scotland)
⚓	Picnic site	♈	Agricultural showground	♞	Roman antiquity	✿	English Heritage site
⊕	Caravan site (AA inspected)	⛴	Theme park	⌂	Prehistoric monument		Historic Scotland site
▲	Camping site (AA inspected)		Farm or animal centre	✕ 1066	Battle site with year	✚	Cadw (Welsh heritage) site
▲⊕	Caravan & camping site (AA inspected)	⚞	Zoological or wildlife collection	▦	Steam railway centre	★	Other place of interest
⛪	Abbey, cathedral or priory	⚑	Bird collection	⌢	Cave	☐	Boxed symbols indicate attractions within urban areas
⛪	Ruined abbey, cathedral or priory	⚓	Aquarium	✕ ▲	Windmill, monument	◉	World Heritage Site (UNESCO)
♜	Castle		RSPB site	⚐	Golf course (AA listed)		National Park and National Scenic Area (Scotland)
⌂	Historic house or building		National Nature Reserve (England, Scotland, Wales)	⚐	County cricket ground		Forest Park
⌂	Museum or art gallery		Local nature reserve	♟	Rugby Union national stadium		Heritage coast
⌂	Industrial interest		Wildlife Trust reserve	⚐	International athletics stadium	⊞	Major shopping centre

Isles of Scilly

White Island
ST. MARTIN'S
King Charles's
BRYHER
Cromwell's
Old Grimsby
St Martin's Head
Higher Town
New Grimsby
Lizard Point
Old Blockhouse
Isles of Scilly Heritage Coast
Great Ganilly
Tresco Abbey
TRESCO
Crow Bay
Crow Sound
Innisidgen Tomb
Great Arthur
Samson
North West Channel
Bant's Carn Burial
Harry's Walls
ST MARY'S
St Mary's Quay
A3110
Longstone
Hugh Town
Deep Point
Garrison Walls
Porth Hellick Downs Tombs
Old Town
Isles of Scilly (St Mary's)
Broad Sound
Peninnis Head
Annet
St Mary's Sound
St Mary's Sound
Gugh
Middle Town
ST. AGNES
Horse Point
Smith Sound
Western Rocks

0   2   4 miles
0   2   6 kilometres

a   b   c   d

New
Tow Head
Fistral Bay
West Pentire
Kelsey Head
Holywell Bay
Crantock
Penhale Point
Holywell
Trese
Ligger Point
Cubert
Ligger or Perran Bay
Rose
Perranporth
Cligga Point
Bolingey
Trevellas Downs
Perranza
St Agnes Heritage Coast
Penhallow
ST AGNES HEAD
St Agnes
Callestick
Wheal Coates
Mithian
Barkla Shop
Goonvrea
St Agnes Mining District
Goonbell
Porthtowan
Mount Hawke
Shortlane
South West Coast Path
Mawla
Wheal Peevor
Blackwater
P+R
A390
Threemi
Godrevy-Portreath Heritage Coast
Portreath
B3300
Cambrose
Chacewater
Illogan
Tuckingmill
Scorrier
A30
Mount Ambrose
St-Day
Godrevy Island
Reskadinnick
Redruth
Twelveheads
Godrevy Point
South Tehidy
Gwennap Mining District
B3301
Tehidy
Carn Brea
Carharrack
Bissoe
Navax Point
Gwithian
Kehelland
Camborne
Carnkie
Lanner A393
Perranwell
Carno Down
The Island or St Ives Head
St Ives Bay
Penponds
Connor Downs
Gwennap
Carn Naun Point
St Ives
Phillack
Angarrack
Barripper
Four Lanes
Penhalvean
Ponsanooth
A39
Zennor Head
Carbis Bay
Hayle
Copperhouse
Carnhell Green
Stithians
Gurnards Head
Zennor
Lelant
High Gwinear
Realwa
Praze-an-Beeble
Wayside
Halsetown
P+R
St Erth Praze
Carnkie
Longdowns
A30
South West Coast Path
Towednack
A30
St Erth
Leedstown
Crowan
Porkellis
Mabe Burnthouse
Pen
Pendeen Watch
Carn Galver Mine
Canonstown
Godolphin House
Wendron Mining District
Rame
A39
Lighthouse
Men-An-Tol
Mulfra Quoit
New Mill
B3311
Townshend
Godolphin Cross
Argal & College Water Park
Budock Water
Morvah
Chysauster Ancient Village
Prospidnick
Trenear
A394
Treverva
Geevor Tin Mine
Lanyon Quoit
B3309
Crowlas
Relubbus
Tregonning & Gwinear Mining District
Wendron
Seworgan
Levant Mine and Beam Engine
Pendeen
Trengwainton Garden
Guval
St Hilary
Trescowe
Carleen
Crowntown
Coverack Bridges
Brill
Penjerrick
St Just Mining District
Madron
Ludgvan
Marazion
Goldsithney
Ashton Breage
Sithney
Constantine
Trebah
Botallack
A3071
Heamoor
Longrock
Cape Cornwall
St Just
Newbridge
Chyandour
RSPB
Perranuthnoe
Helston
Gweek
Porth Navas
Ballowall Barrow
Penzance
St Michael's Mount
A394
Helford Passage
Durgan
Kelynack
Carn Euny Ancient Village
Sancreed Drift
Newlyn
Praa Sands
A3083
Mawgan
Helford
Whitesand Bay
Kerris
Paul
Cudden Point
Rinsey Head
Garras
Halliggye Fogou
Manaccan
St A
Sennen Cove
Crows-an-Wra
St Buryan
Mousehole
Trewavas Mining District
Trewavas Head
Porthleven
St Martin
LAND'S END
Sennen
MOUNT'S BAY
Gunwalloe
White Cross
Trevescan
The Merry Maidens
Lamorna
Cury
The Lizard
Porthcurno
Trethewey Treen
Merthen Point
Lamorna Cove
Poldhu Point
B3293
Porthgwarra
Minack Open Air Theatre
Cribba Head
Marconi Memorial
Mullion Cove
GOONHILLY DOWNS
B3296
Coverack
Gwennap Head
St Levan
Telegraph
Mullion Island
Mullion
Predannack Head
Ruan Major
Kuggar
South West Coast Path
Black Head
Vellan Head
Ruan Minor
The Lizard
Cadgwith
Lizard Head
The Lizard Heritage Coast
Devil's Frying Pan
Kynance Cove
Church Cove
Lizard
LIZARD POINT
Bass Point
Lizard Lighthouse & Heritage Centre

0   1   2   3   4 miles
0 1 2 3 4 5 kilometres

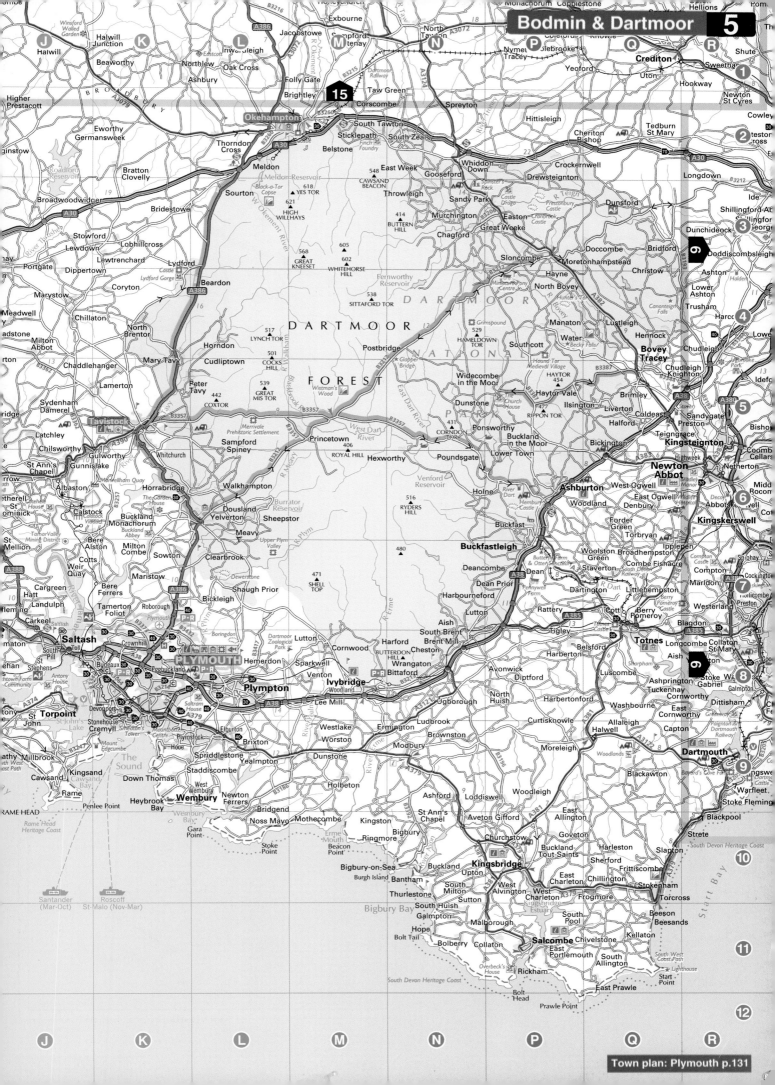

Newhaven Harbour

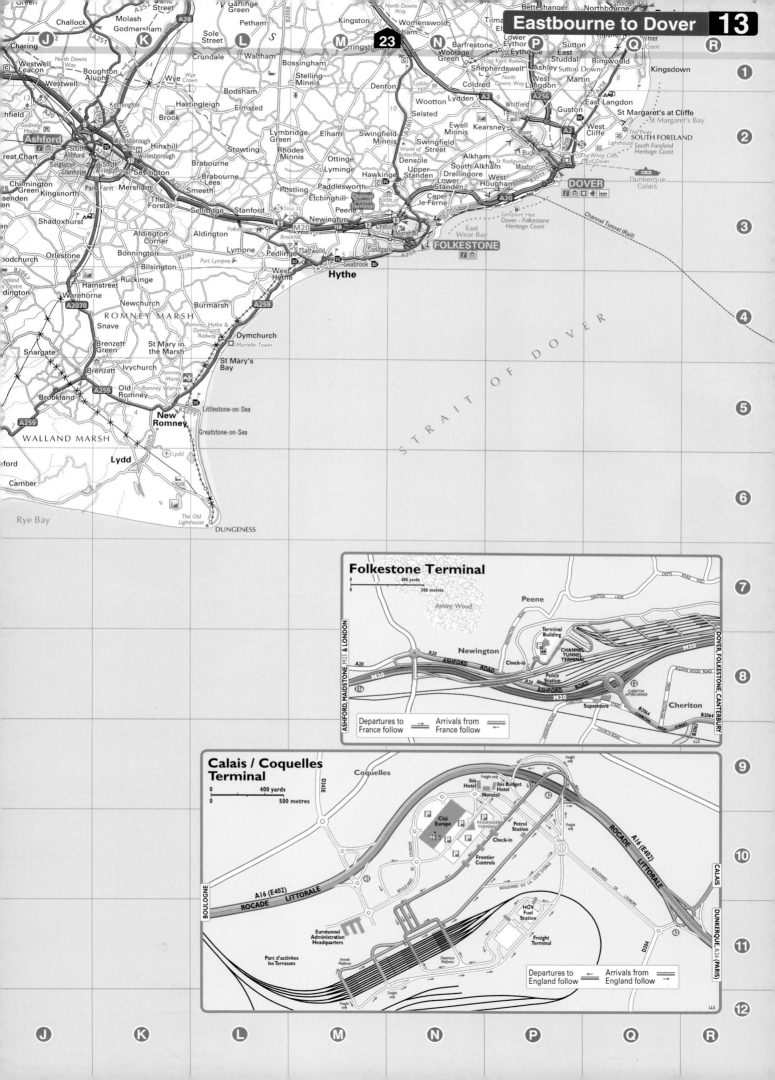

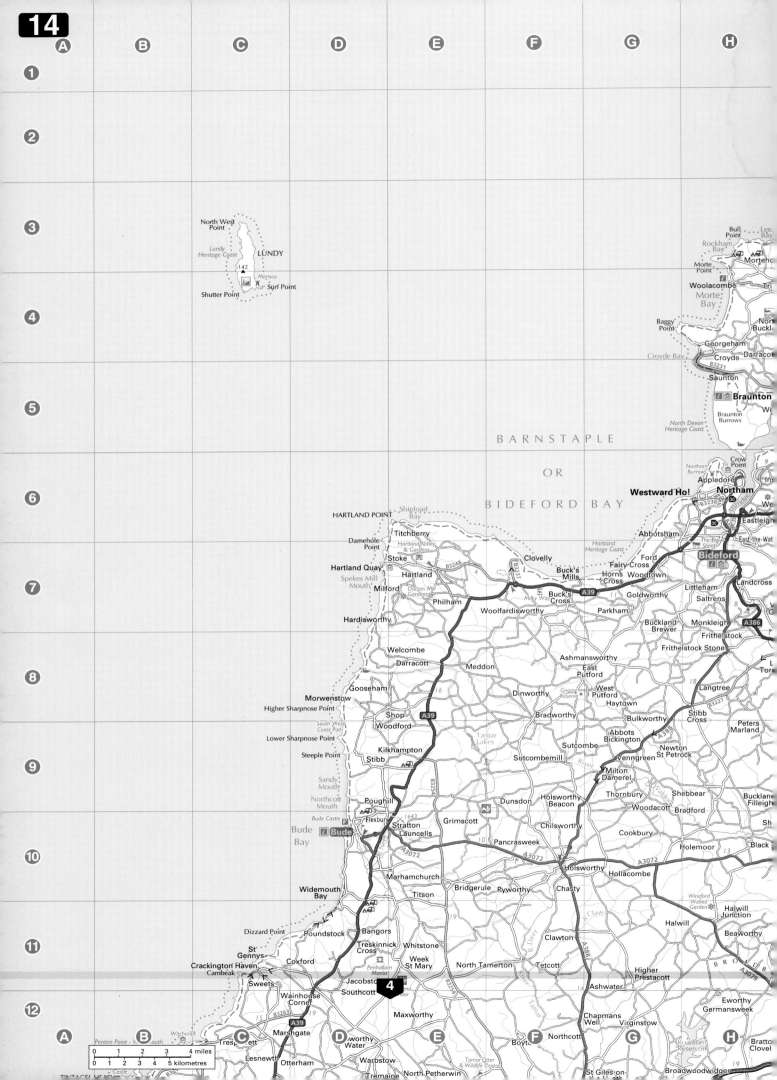

A   B   C   D   E   F   G   H

1
2
3
4
5
6
7
8
9
10
11
12

North West Point
Lundy Heritage Coast
LUNDY
142 *Marisco*
Shutter Point   Surf Point

Bull Point   Lee
Rockham Bay
Morte Point   Morteho
Woolacombe   Morte Bay   Tri
Baggy Point   Nor Buckl
Georgeham
Croyde Bay   Croyde   Darraco
B3231
Saunton
Braunton
Braunton Burrows
North Devon Heritage Coast

B A R N S T A P L E
OR
B I D E F O R D   B A Y

Crow Point
Northam Burrows   Appledore
Westward Ho!   **Northam**   Ins
Eastleigh
Shipload Bay
HARTLAND POINT
Titchberry
Abbotsham
The Big Sheep   East-the-Wat
Damehole Point
Hartland Abbey & Gardens
Clovelly   **Bideford**
Stoke   B3248   *Hartland Heritage Coast*
Hartland Quay   Ford
Buck's   Fairy Cross
Spekes Mill Mouth   Hartland   *Docton Mill Gardens*   Mills   Horns Cross   Woodtown
Milford   B3237   *Milky Way*   Buck's   A39   Goldworthy   Littleham   Landcross
Cross
Philham   Parkham   Saltrens
Hardisworthy   Woolfardisworthy   Buckland   Monkleigh   A386
Brewer
Frithelstock
Welcombe   Ashmansworthy   Frithelstock Stone
Darracott   East   Tor
Meddon   Putford
Gooseham   16   Dinworthy   West   Langtree
Putford   Haytown   18
Morwenstow   *Gnome Reserve*   B3227
Higher Sharpnose Point   Shop   A39   Bradworthy   Bulkworthy   Stibb   Peters
Woodford   Cross   Marland
South West Coast Path   *Tamar Lakes*   Abbots   Newton
Lower Sharpnose Point   Sutcombe   Bickington   St Petrock
Kilkhampton   Sutcombemill   Venngreen   Newton
Steeple Point   Stibb   *River*   Milton   Shebbear   Buckland
Damerel   Filleigh
Sandy Mouth   Dunsdon   Holsworthy   Thornbury   Woodacott   Bradford   Sh
Northcott   Grimscott   Beacon
Mouth   Poughill   B3254   Chilsworthy   Cookbury   Holemoor   Black
1643   Bude Castle   Flexbury
Bude Bay   **Bude**   Stratton   Pancrasweek   A3072   13
Launcells   A3072   Holsworthy
A3072   10   Hollacombe   *Winsford Walled Garden*
Marhamchurch   Bridgerule   Pyworthy   Chasty
Titson   Halwill
Widemouth Bay   19   Clawton   Halwill Junction
Dizzard Point   Poundstock   Bangors   B R O A D   Beaworthy
St Gennys   Treskinnick   Whitstone   A388   Higher Prestacott   A3079
Cross
Crackington Haven   Coxford   Week   Ashwater   Eworthy
Cambeak   St Mary   North Tamerton   Tetcott   Germansweek
Sweets   *Penhallam Manor*   B3254   14
Wainhouse   Jacobsto   **4**
Corner   Southcott   Chapmans   Virginstow
Maxworthy   Well   Northcott
Tamar   B R A T T O

Pentire Point - V...outh
Witchcraft
0 1 2 3 4 miles
0 1 2 3 4 5 kilometres
Castle
Tres...ett   worthy   Boyto   Bratto
Marshgate   Water   Clovel
Lesnewth   Warbstow   St Giles-on-
Otterham   North Petherwin   Broadwoodwidger
TINTAGEL HEAD...   Tremaine   *Tamar Otter & Wildlife Centre*

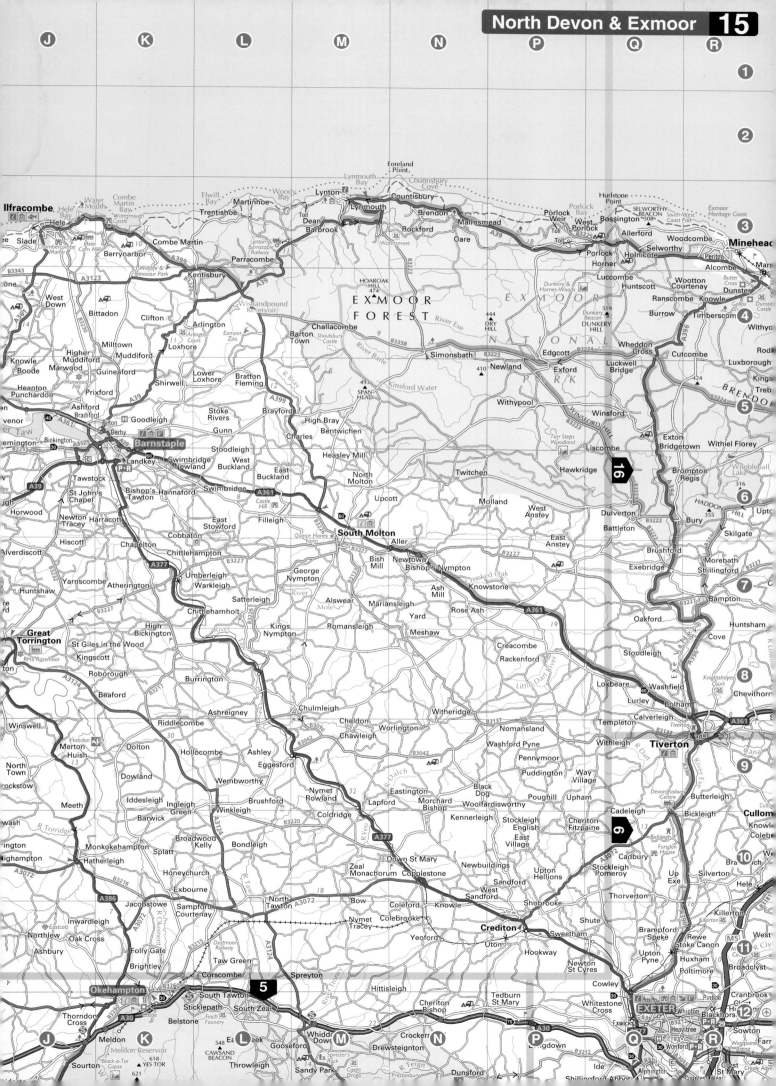

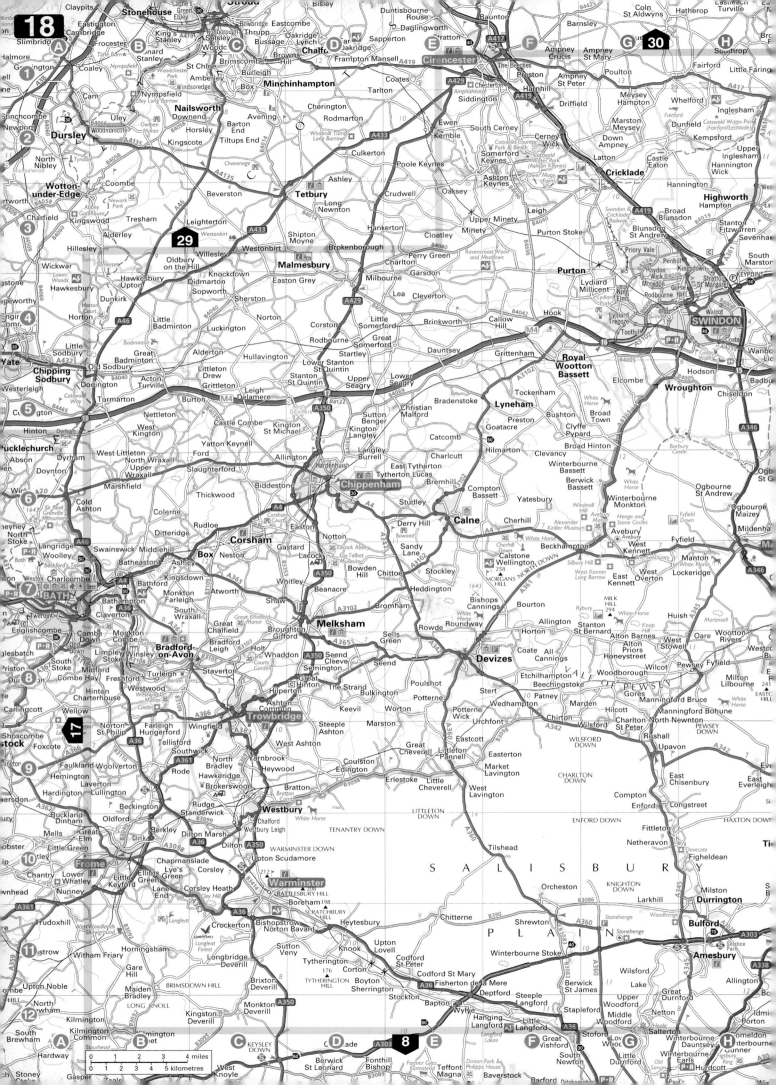

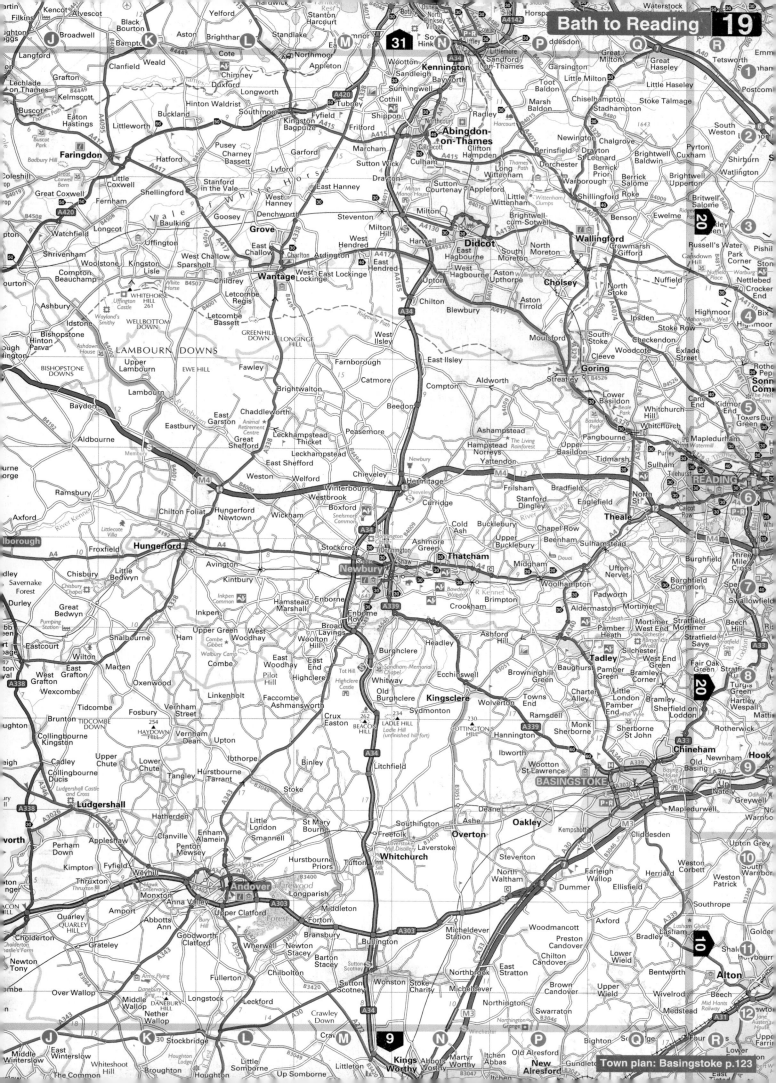

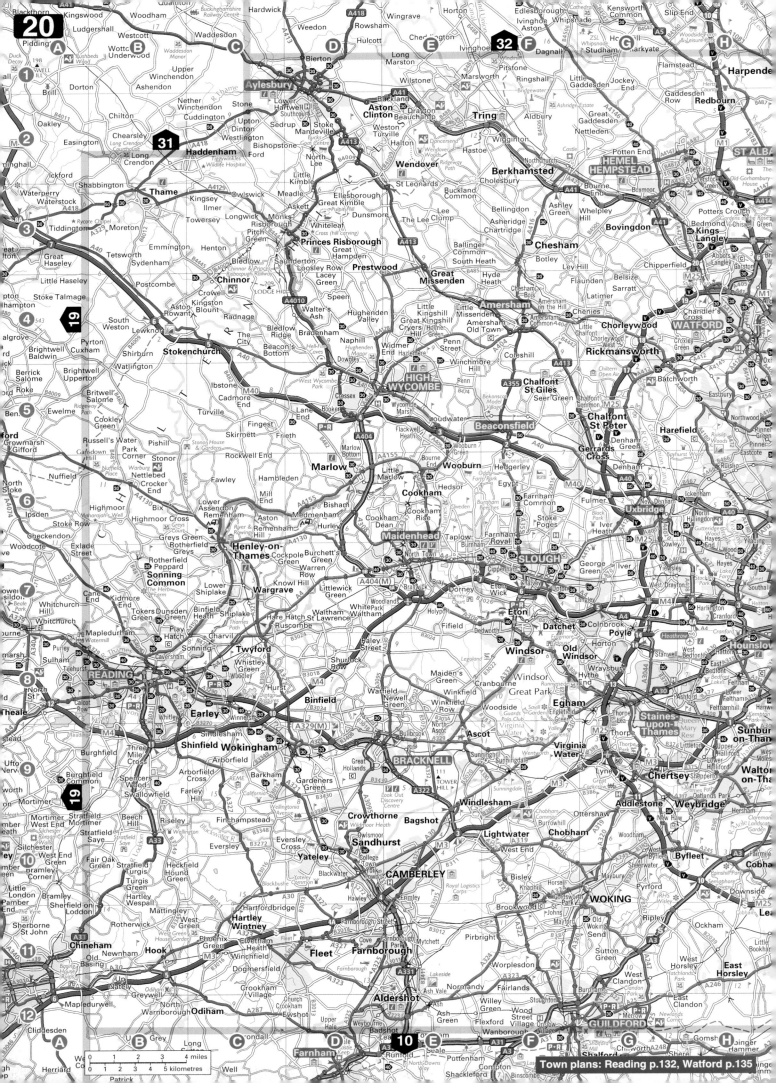

Ramsgate

BROADSTAIRS

St Ethelbert's School

MARGATE

MARGATE RD

BOUNDARY ROAD

HERESON ROAD

Granville

Ramsgate Tunnels

Bandstand

Chatham House School

St George's

Royal Victoria Pavilion (under repair)

Salvation Army

Kingdom Hall

Sports Centre

Priory School

Updown Gallery

Fire Sta

Police Sta

Maritime

Clarendon House School

Jobcentre Plus

Marina

Royal Harbour

Lifeboat Station

Ellington Park

The Old Priory School

Christchurch School

St Augustine's Abbey

LONDON, (M2), CANTERBURY

0   200 m

LLS

Map place names

Abberton, Langenhoe, Peldon, Brightlingsea, Little Clacton, Great Holland, Hurst Green, St Osyth, Holland-on-Sea, CLACTON-ON-SEA, Jaywick, Rush Green

MERSEA ISLAND, West Mersea, East Mersea, Cudmore Grove, Shinglehead Point, Colne Point, Sales Point

Great Wigborough, Bradwell Waterside, Bradwell-on-Sea, Tillingham, Dengie, Asheldham, Southminster, Burnham-on-Crouch, Holliwell Point, Foulness Point

Wallasea Island, Courtsend, Churchend, FOULNESS ISLAND, Foulness Point

Minster, Warden Point, Leysdown-on-Sea, Eastchurch, Leysdown Coastal Park, ISLE OF SHEPPEY, Isle of Harty, Shell Ness, The Swale

Whitstable, Seasalter, Whitstable Bay, Herne Bay, Hampton, Tankerton, Swalecliffe, Chestfield, South Street, Greenhill, Herne, Broomfield, Beltinge, Reculver Towers & Roman Fort, Minnis Bay

Faversham, Oare, Graveney, Yorkletts, Highstreet, Dargate, Hernhill, Denstroude, Staplestreet, Dunkirk, Blean, Upper Harbledown, Tyler Hill, Broad Oak, Sturry, Westbere, Fordwich, Hoath, Upstreet, West Stourmouth, East Stourmouth, Westmarsh

Painter's Forstal, North Street, Lewson Street, Ospringe, South Street, Sheldwich, Hogben's Hill, Selling, Overland, Harbledown, CANTERBURY, Thanington, Chartham Hatch, Chartham, Nackington, Street End, Lower Hardres, Bishopsbourne, Bekesbourne, Patrixbourne, Bramling, Ickham, Wickhambreaux, Littlebourne, Preston, Elmstone, Cop Street, Hoaden, Ash, Durlock, Wingham, Marshborough, Staple, Goodnestone, Statenborough, Woodnesborough, Worth

Eastling, Throwley Forstal, Badlesmere, Shottenden, Leaveland, Stalisfield Green, Challock, Molash, Godmersham, Chilham, Old Wives Lees, Shalmsford Street, Dane Street, Garlinge Green, Petham, Kingston, Womenswold, Barham, Woolage Green, Barfrestone, Nonington, Aylesham, Adisham, Ratling, Chillenden, Eastry, Betteshanger, Great Mongeham, Northbourne, Finglesham, Ham, Hacklinge, Sholden, Deal, The Downs, Upper Deal, Walmer, Ripple, Sutton

Charing, West Leacon, Boughton Aluph, Westwell, Crundale, Waltham, Bossingham, Wye, Denton, Stelling Minnis, Bodsham, Coldred, Shepherdswell, Lydden, Ewell, Temple Ewell, East Langdon, West Langdon, Martin, Ringwould, Kingsdown, Sutton Downs, East Studdal, Sholden

MARGATE, Westgate on Sea, Westbrook, Birchington, Garlinge, Cliftonville, Northdown, Kingsgate, NORTH FORELAND, Foreness Point, Reading Street, Minnis Bay, St Peter's, Broadstairs, Dumpton, Hereson, Ramsgate, ISLE OF THANET, Acol, Manston, Westwood, Lydden, Monkton, Sarre, Chislet, St Nicholas at Wade, Boyden Gate, Hersden, Stodmarsh, Minster, Durlock, Pegwell, Pegwell Bay, Cliffsend, St Lawrence, Richborough Roman Fort, Sandwich Bay, Sandwich, Royal St Georges, Woodnesborough, Stone Cross, Worth

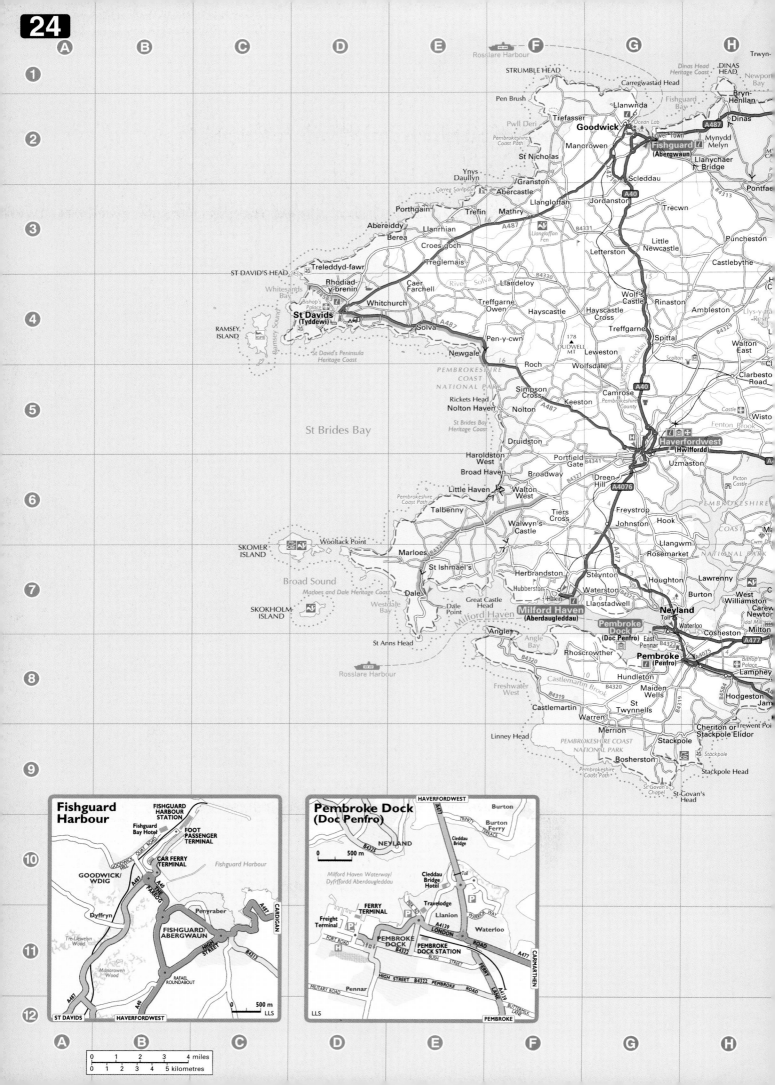

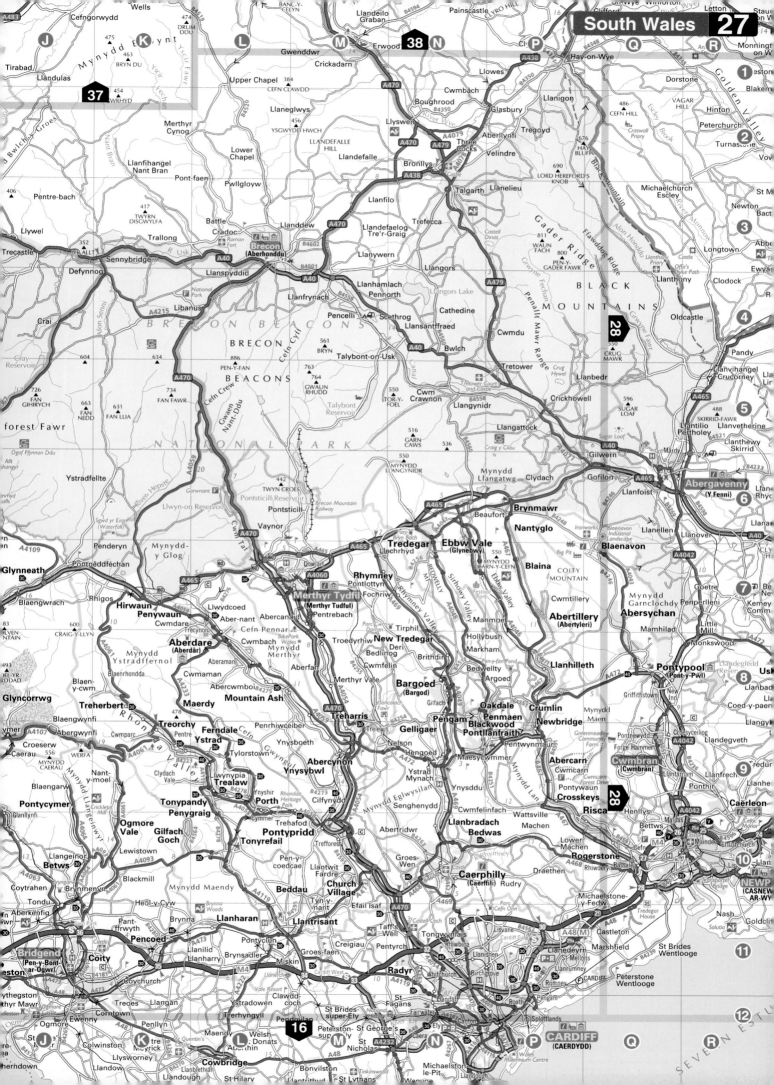

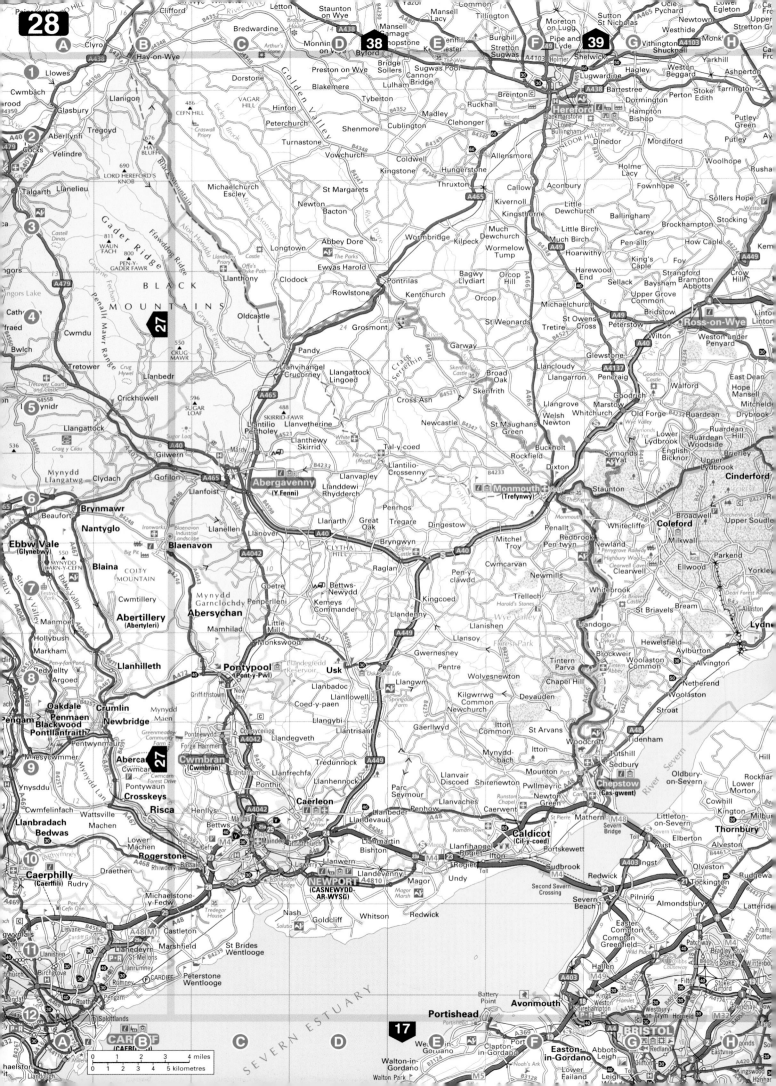

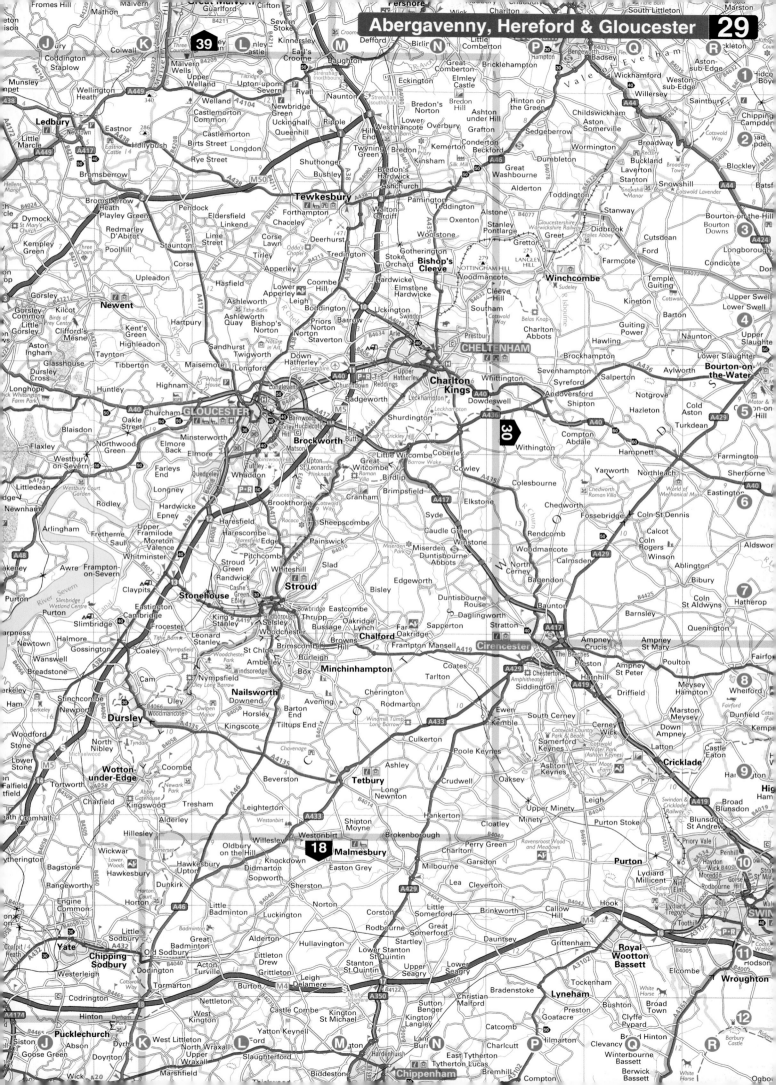

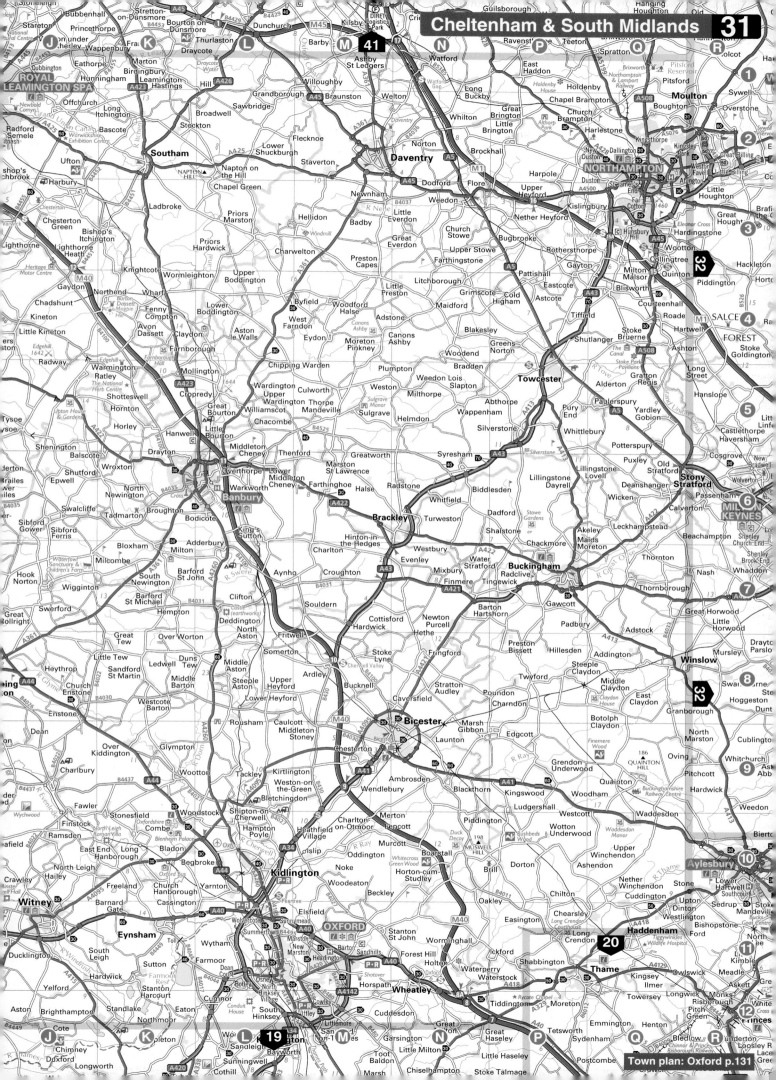

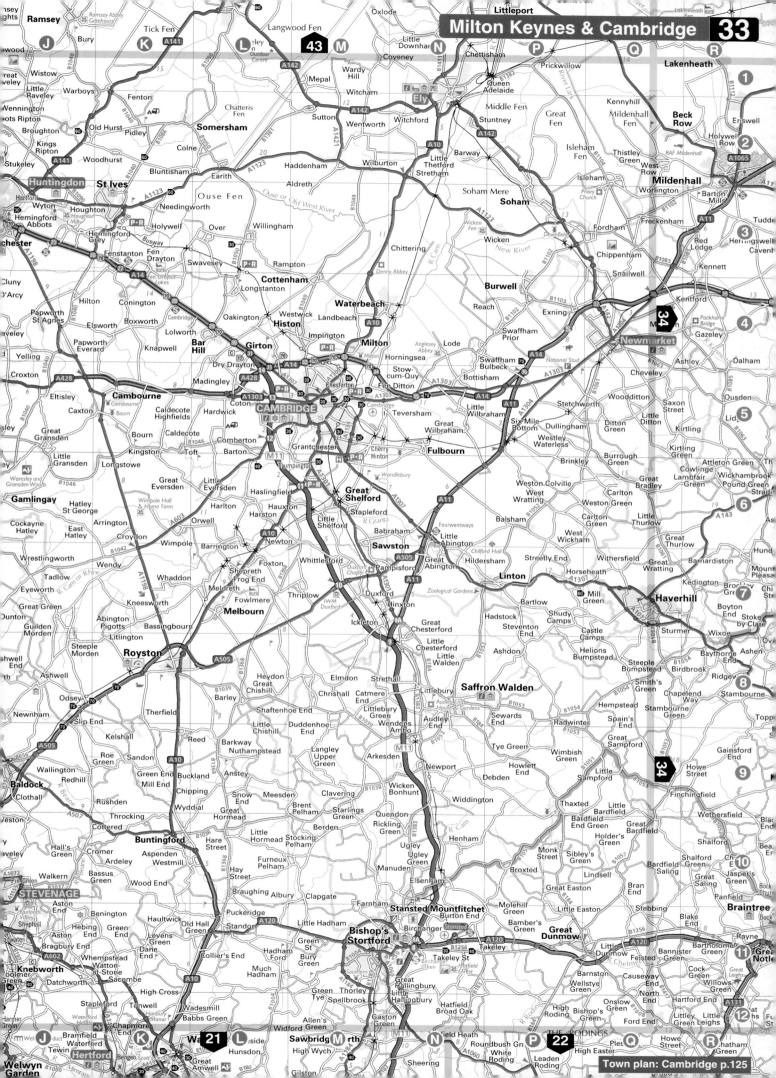

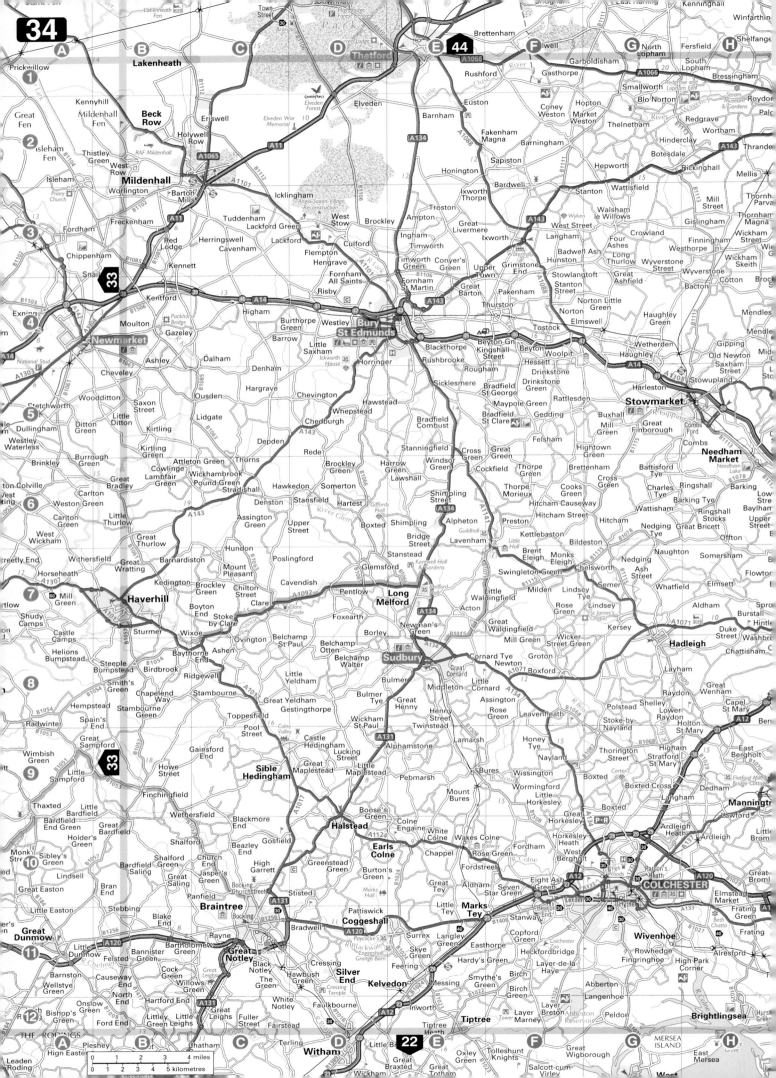

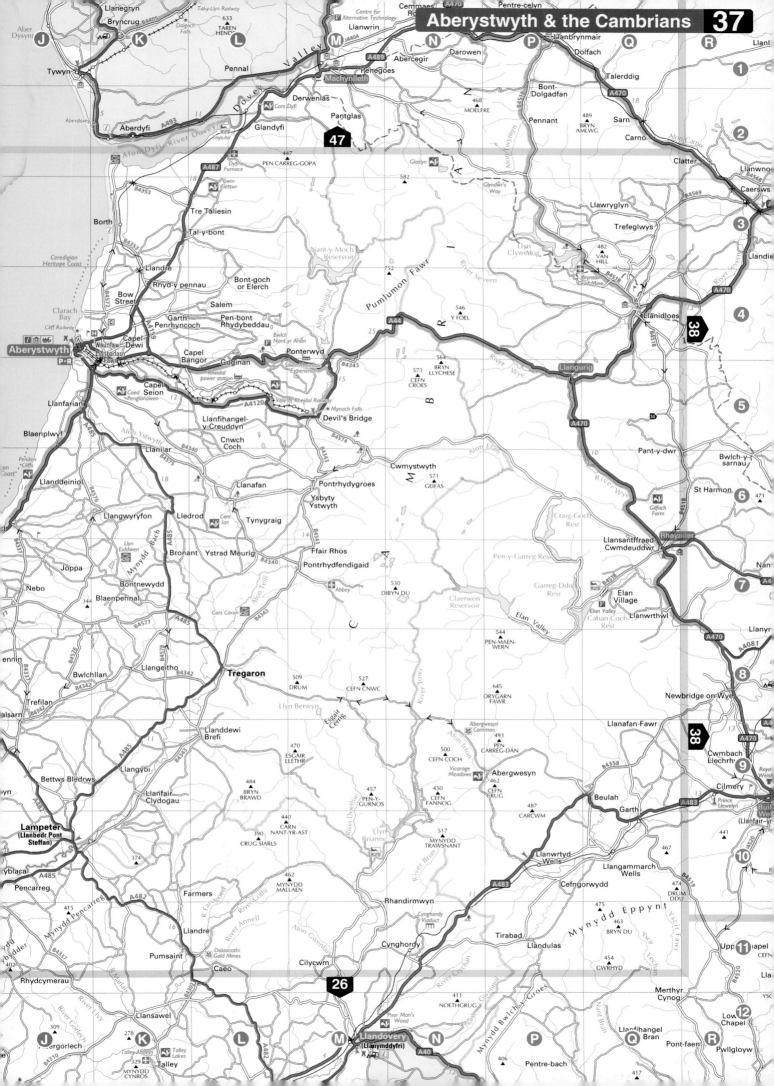

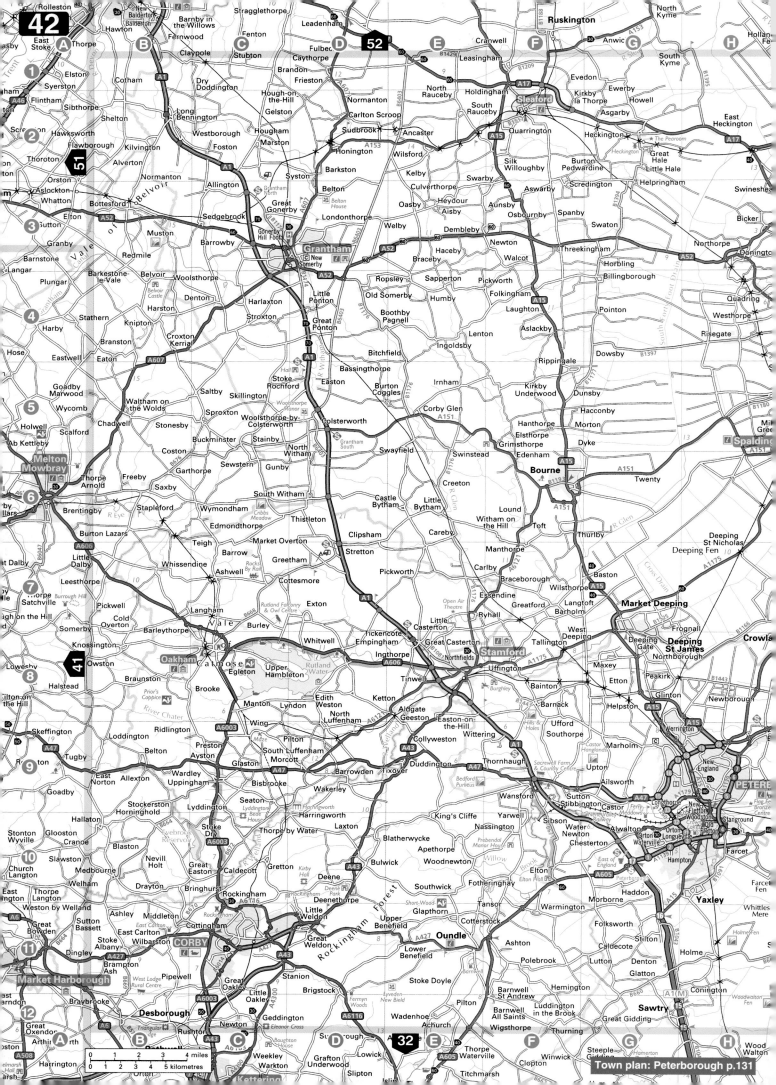

THE WASH

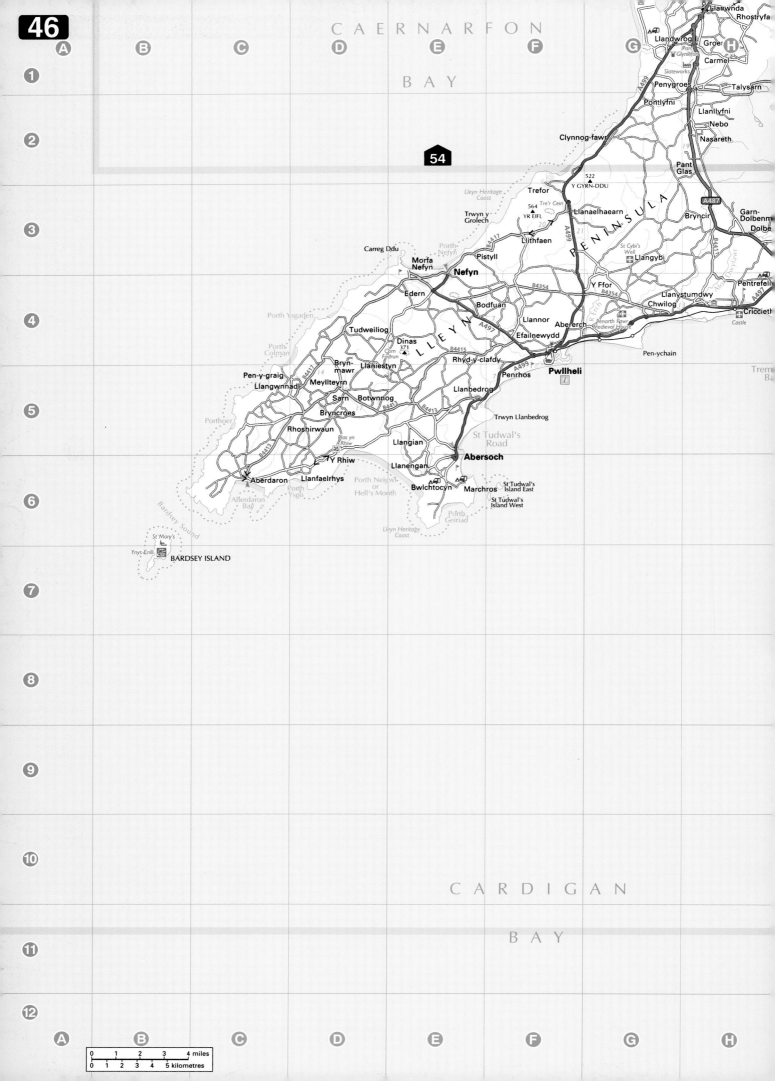

CAERNARFON
BAY

Llanwnda
Rhostryfa

Llandwrog
Groes
Carmel

Penygroes
Talysarn

Pontllyfni
Llanllyfni

Clynnog-fawr
Nebo

Nasareth

Pant
Glas

Lleyn Heritage
Coast

Y GYRN-DDU
522

Trefor

564
Tre'r Cein
YR EIFL

Llanaelhaearn
Bryncir

Garn-
Dolbenm

Trwyn y
Grolech

Dolbe

Llithfaen

PENINSULA

St Cybi's
Well

Carreg Ddu

Porth
Nefyn

Pistyll

Llangybi

Pentrefeli

Morfa
Nefyn

Nefyn

Y Ffor

Llanystumdwy

Edern

Bodfuan

Abererch

Chwilog

Criccieth

LLEYN

Llannor

Penarth Fawr
Medieval House

Castle

Tudweiliog

Dinas
371
Garn
Fadrun

Efailnewydd

Pen-ychain

Bryn-
mawr

Llaniestyn

Rhyd-y-clafdy

Pwllheli

Trem
B.

Pen-y-graig

Meyllteyrn

Penrhos

Llangwnnadl

Sarn

Botwnnog

Llanbedrog

Bryncroes

Trwyn Llanbedrog

Rhoshirwaun

Blas yn
Rhiw

Llangian

St Tudwal's
Road

Y Rhiw

Llanengan

Abersoch

Porthor

Aberdaron
Llanfaelrhys

Porth Neigwl
or Hell's Mouth

Bwlchtocyn

Marchros

St Tudwal's
Island East

Aberdaron
Bay

Porth
Ysgo

St Tudwal's
Island West

Porth
Geiriad

Bardsey Sound

Lleyn Heritage
Coast

St Mary's

Ynys-Enlli

BARDSEY ISLAND

CARDIGAN

BAY

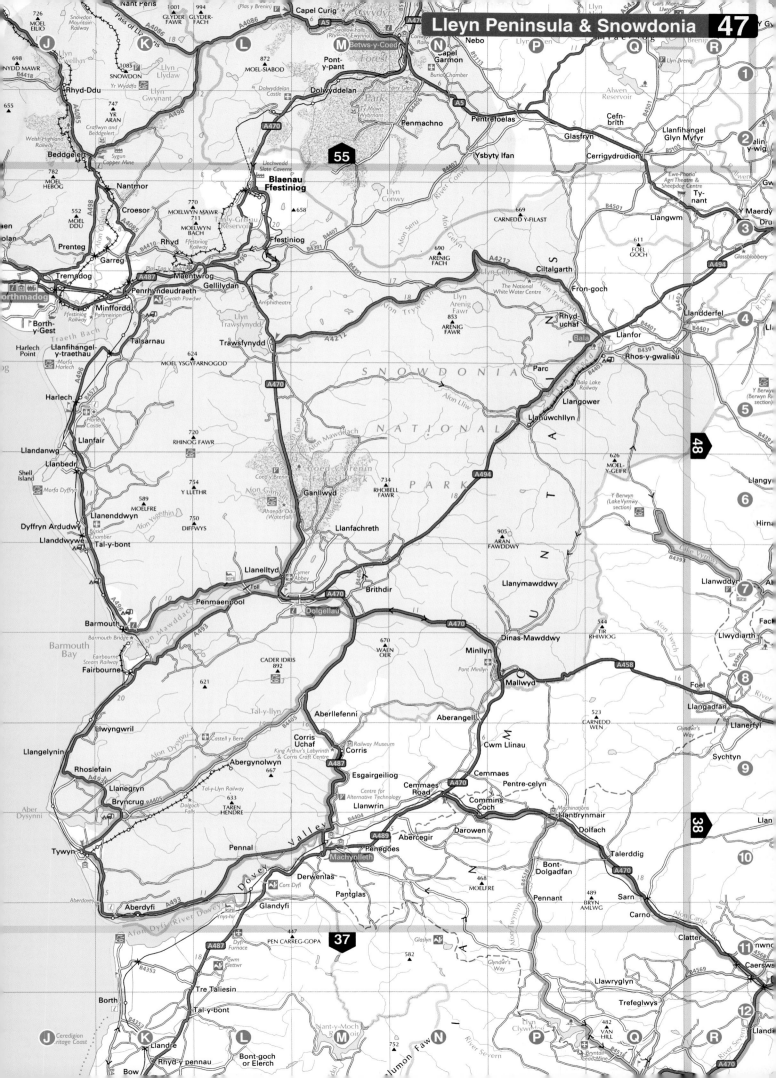

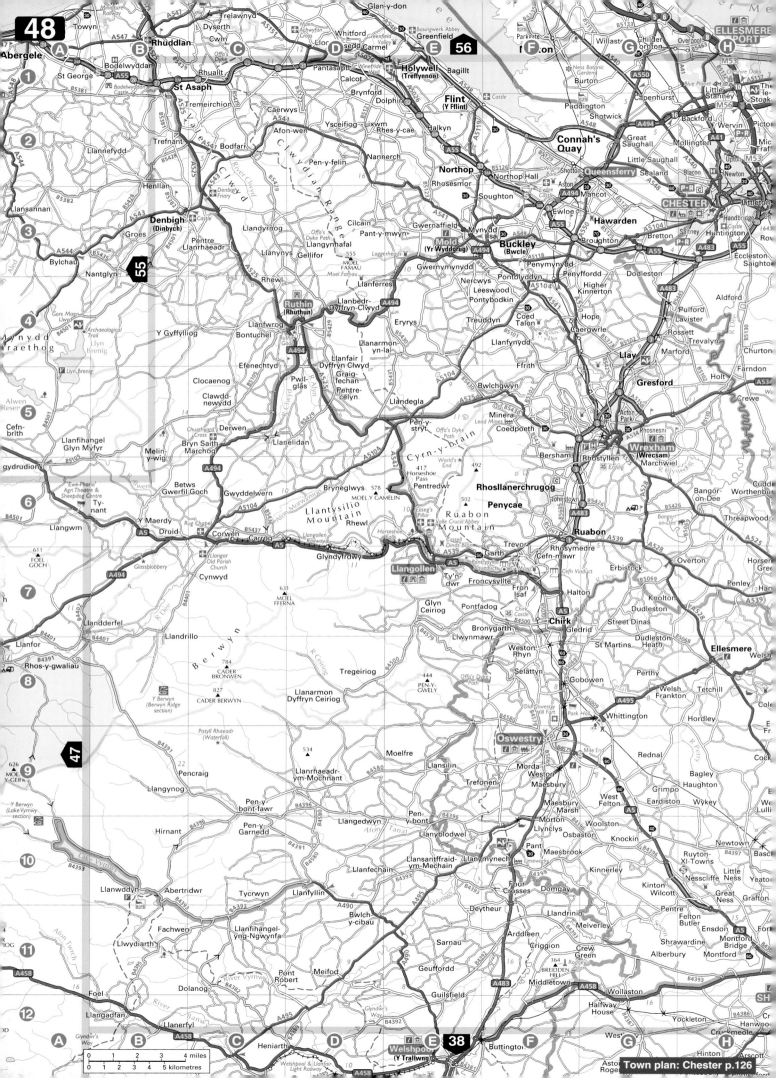

Town plan: Shrewsbury p.133

HUMBER

Skeffling

Spurn Heritage Coast
Kilnsea

SPURN HEAD
Spurn Heritage Coast

61

Rotterdam (Europoort)
Zeebrugge

GRIMSBY
West Marsh
Nunsthorpe
Scartho
A46
A16
B1219
Cleethorpes
Old Clee
Thrunscoe
The Jungle
Pleasure Island
Humberston

Waltham
Waltham Windmill
Holdby Heck
Brigsley
Ashby cum Fenby
Grainsby
Waithe
B1203
New Waltham
Holton le Clay
A1031
New Waltham
East Ravendale
Wold Newton
17
North Thoresby
A16
QB1201
Tetney
North Cotes
Marshchapel
Donna Nook

Ludborough
15
Fulstow
29
Grainthorpe
North Somercotes
A1031

North Ormsby
Covenham St Bartholomew
Conisholme
Saltfleet

Utterby
Covenham St Mary
Yarburgh
Saltfleetby St Clement
Saltfleetby All Saints

Kelstern
A631
Fotherby
Alvingham
North Cockerington
Saltfleetby St Peter
Theddlethorpe St Helen

South Elkington
South Cockerington
B1200
Theddlethorpe All Saints
A1031

Welton le Wold
A157
15
Louth
Grimoldby
Manby

Hallington
Raithby
B1520
B1200
Little Carlton
Great Carlton
Theddlethorpe All Saints
Mablethorpe

thorpe
Withcall
A16
A157
Legbourne
North Reston
Gayton le Marsh
Great Eau
A1104
Trusthorpe

Donington on Bain
Tathwell
Little Cawthorpe
South Reston
15
Withern
Maltby le Marsh
A1111
Sutton on Sea
Sandilands

OLDS
Asterby
Haugham
Muckton
Authorpe
B1373
Beesby Saleby
A52

Cadwell Park
Scamblesby
14
Oxcombe
Burwell
Belleau
Aby
Watermill & Wildfowl Gardens
Markby
A52

A153
Belchford
South Ormsby
White Pit
Swaby
South Thoresby
Bilsby Thurlby
Huttoft

Tetford
Salmonby
Brinkhill
Rigsby
Alford
B1449
Anderby
Anderby Creek

West Ashby
Fulletby
Somersby
Harrington
Sutterby
A1104
Well
B1196
Farlesthorpe
Mumby
Chapel Point

Horncastle
Greetham
Ashby Puerorum
Bag Enderby
Langton
Ulceby
A1028
Cumberworth
Hogsthorpe
Chapel St Leonards

High Toynton
A158
10
Hagworthingham
Snipe Dales
Aswardby
Sausthorpe
Partney
Scremby
Willoughby
Sloothby
Fantasy Island

Mareham on the Hill
B643
Mavis Enderby
Raithby
A16
Candlesby
Welton le Marsh
Habertoft
Addlethorpe
Ingoldmells

Hameringham
B1195
Hundleby
Spilsby
Ashby by Partney
Gunby
Orby
A158
Ingoldmells Point

Roughton
Moorby
Old Bolingbroke
Halton Holegate
Gunby Hall
Monksthorpe
Burgh le Marsh

Wood Enderby
Miningsby
Bolingbroke Castle
Toynton All Saints
Great Steeping
Bratoft
A158

Mareham le Fen
East Kirkby
Keal Cotes
Northcote
Irby in the Marsh
Skegness

A153
Revesby
Lincolnshire Aviation
Stickford
Little Steeping
Firsby
Croft

Tumby
New Bolingbroke
Keal Cotes
New Leake
Thorpe St Peter
Wainfleet Haven

Tumby Woodside
60
Stickney
40
Eastville
Fendike Corner
Wainfleet All Saints
Gibraltar Point

New York
A16
East Fen
Friskney
Wainfleet St Mary
A52

West Fen Northlands
B1183
18
Leake Common Side
23

Sibsey Trader Windmill
Frithville
Sibsey
Wrangle

Gipsey Bridge
B1192
Fishtoft Drove
Old Leake

Langrick
43
Hilldyke
Leverton
Benington

Anton's Gowt
60
40
A52

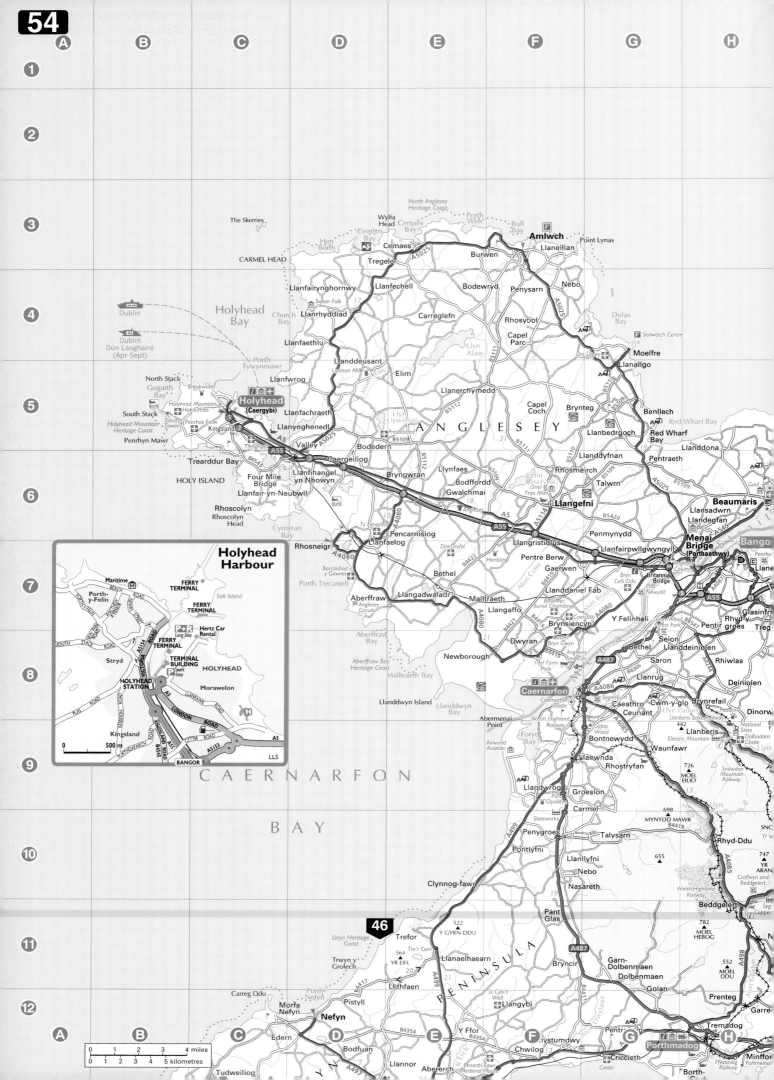

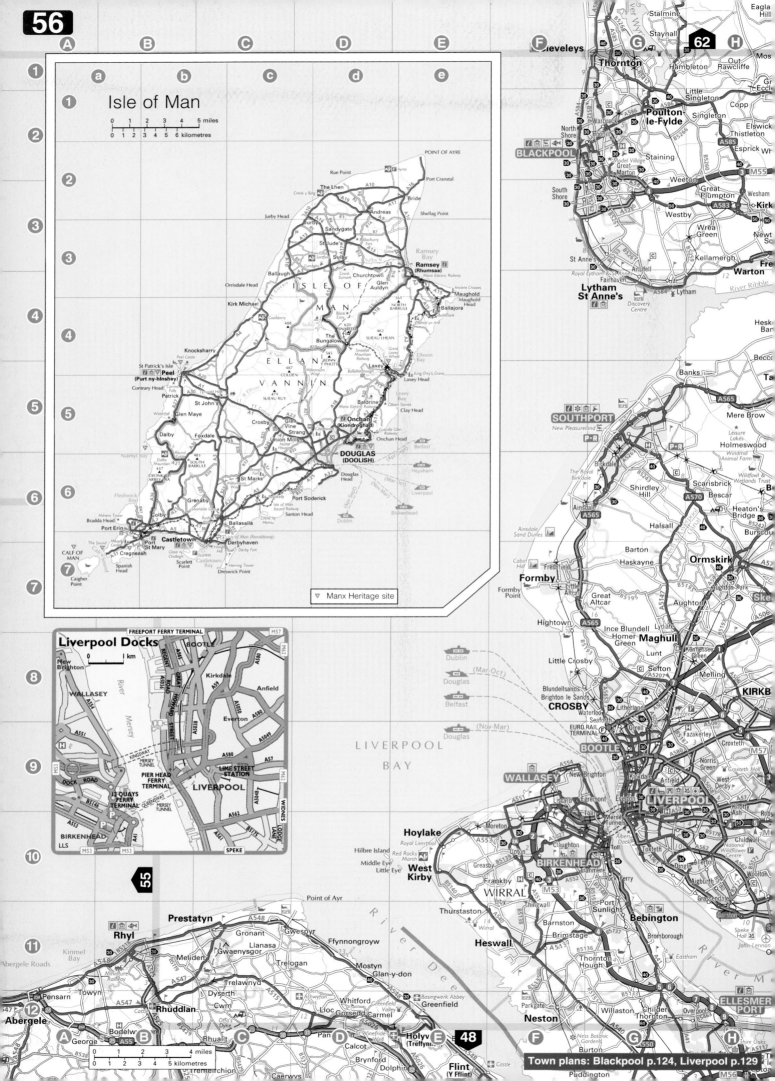

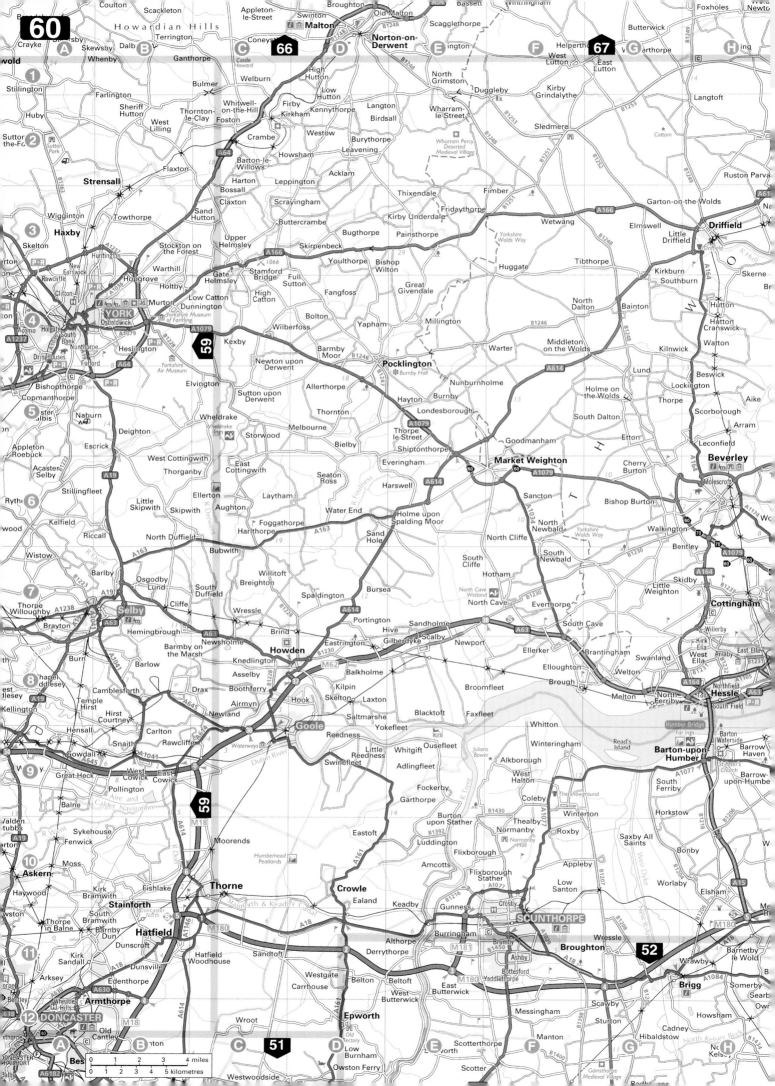

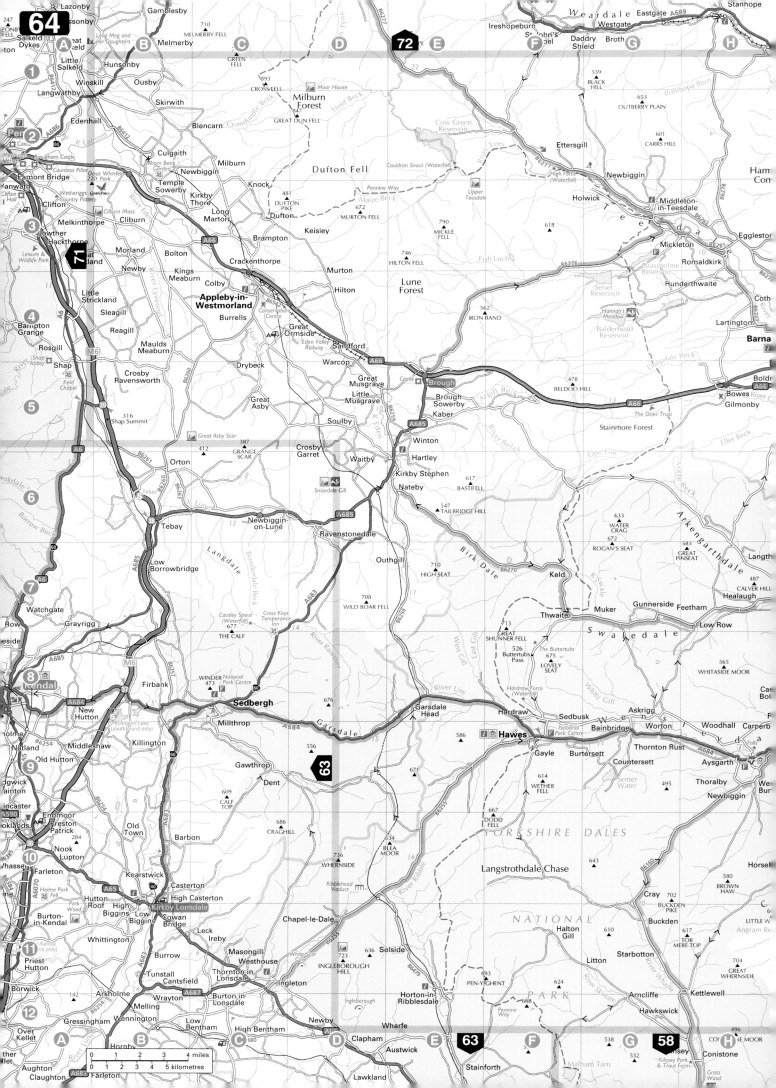

Scarborough (inset map)

North Bay

North Sands

Alexandra Gardens
Peasholm Park
Bowls Centre
Victoria Park
Cricket Ground

Trafalgar Square

Castle Hill
Castle
Coastguard Station

St Mary's
Friarage School

Fire Sta

YMCA

Council Offices

Balmoral Centre

Town Hall

Olympia Scarborough

Magistrates' Court
Police Sta
Stephen Joseph

Brunswick

Grand Hotel

Rotunda Art Gallery
Woodend Creative Workspace

SCARBOROUGH STATION

Yorkshire Coast College

South Bay

Old Harbour
West Pier
East Pier
Vincent's Pier
Lighthouse
Luna Park

South Sands

Scarborough

0   200 m

LLS

PICKERING, MALTON

FILEY

Main map

North Yorkshire and Cleveland Heritage Coast

oldsborough
Overdale Wyke
Lythe
Sandsend
Sandsend Wyke
unsley
Newholm
Whitby
Saltwick Bay
Abbey
Ruswarp
Stainsacre
Aislaby
Briggswath
Sneaton High Hawker
Sleights
Ugglebarnby
Iburndale
osmont

Ness Point or North Cheek
Robin Hood's Bay
Fylingthorpe
Robin Hood's Bay

A171

Old Peak or South Cheek

Ravenscar

292

Staintondale
Shire Horse Centre
Hayburn Wyke

Harwood Dale

Cloughton
Cloughton Wyke

Cromer Point

Burniston

Cleveland Way

Bickley
Broxa
Silpho
Suffield
Langdale End
Hackness
Scalby
Bridestones (Rock Formation)
Toll

239
North Riding Forest Park
Dalby Forest
Falsgrave
Scarborough
Castle

Oliver's Mount

Toll

Sawdon
West Ayton
East Ayton
Irton
Eastfield
Osgodby
Cayton Bay
The Wyke

Wilton
Ebberston
Ruston
Wykeham
Hutton Buscel
Seamer
Crossgates
Cayton
Filey Brigg
Allerston
Snainton
Brompton-by-Sawdon
Lebberston
Gristhorpe
Filey

Yedingham
Willerby
Folkton
Muston
R. Hertford
A1039
Filey Bay

West Knapton
Knapton
East Heslerton
Potter Brompton
Ganton
Flixton
Staxton
Yorkshire Wolds Way
Sherburn
West Heslerton
Hunmanby
Fordon

ngton
Thorpe Bassett
Wintringham
Foxholes
Wold Newton
Reighton
Speeton
Flamborough Head Heritage Coast
Bempton Cliffs
RSPB
ampton
Scagglethorpe
Butterwick
Burton Fleming
Grindale
Thornwick Bay
Buckton
Bempton
North Landing
Settrington
Helperthorpe
Thwing
Selwicks Bay
FLAMBOROUGH HEAD
West Lutton
Weaverthorpe
Flamborough
Lighthouse
North Grimston
West Lutton
East Lutton
60
Langtoft
Rudston
Boynton
Bessingby
61
Duggleby
Kirby Grindalythe
Monolith
Bridlington
BRIDLINGTON
Wharram
Miniature Village

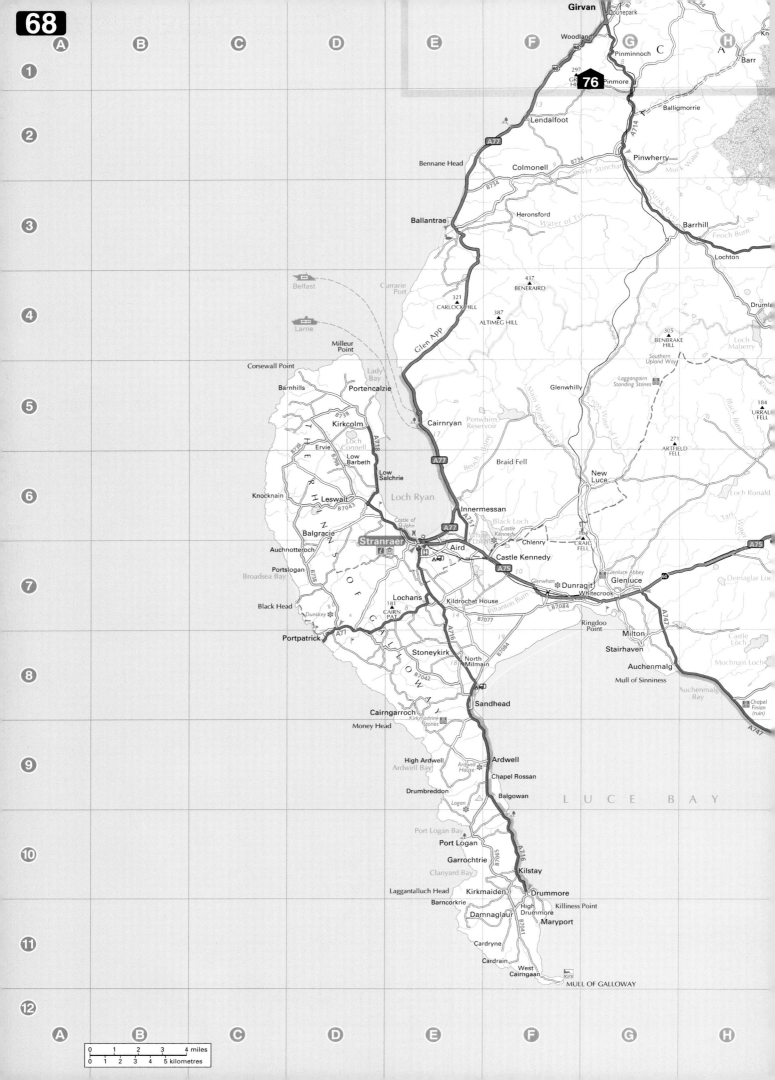

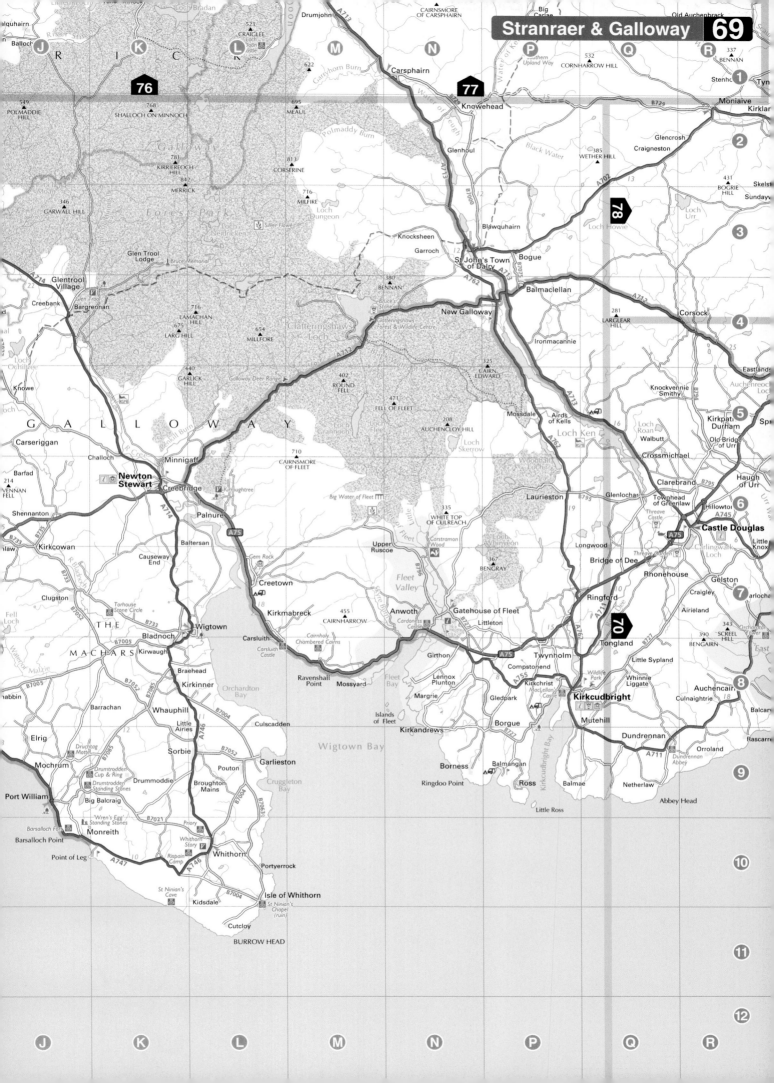

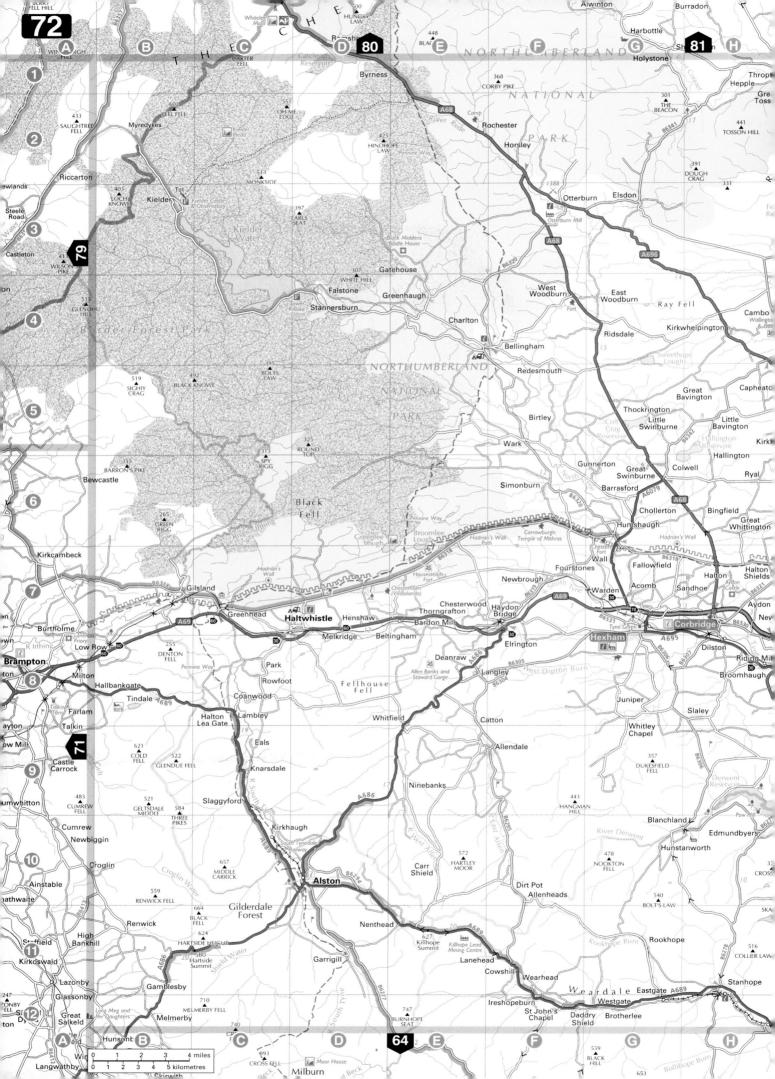

Port of Tyne

TYNEMOUTH
THE NORTH
NEWCASTLE
MEADOW WELL
PERCY MAIN
Wet 'n' Wild Water Park
Royal Quays Outlet
Premier Inn
Royal Quays Marina
Check-in
INTERNATIONAL PASSENGER TERMINAL
East Howdon
TYNE VIEW
TYNE TUNNEL
PRIORY
Jarrow
SUNDERLAND
River Tyne
0   500 m

Amsterdam (IJmuiden)

82

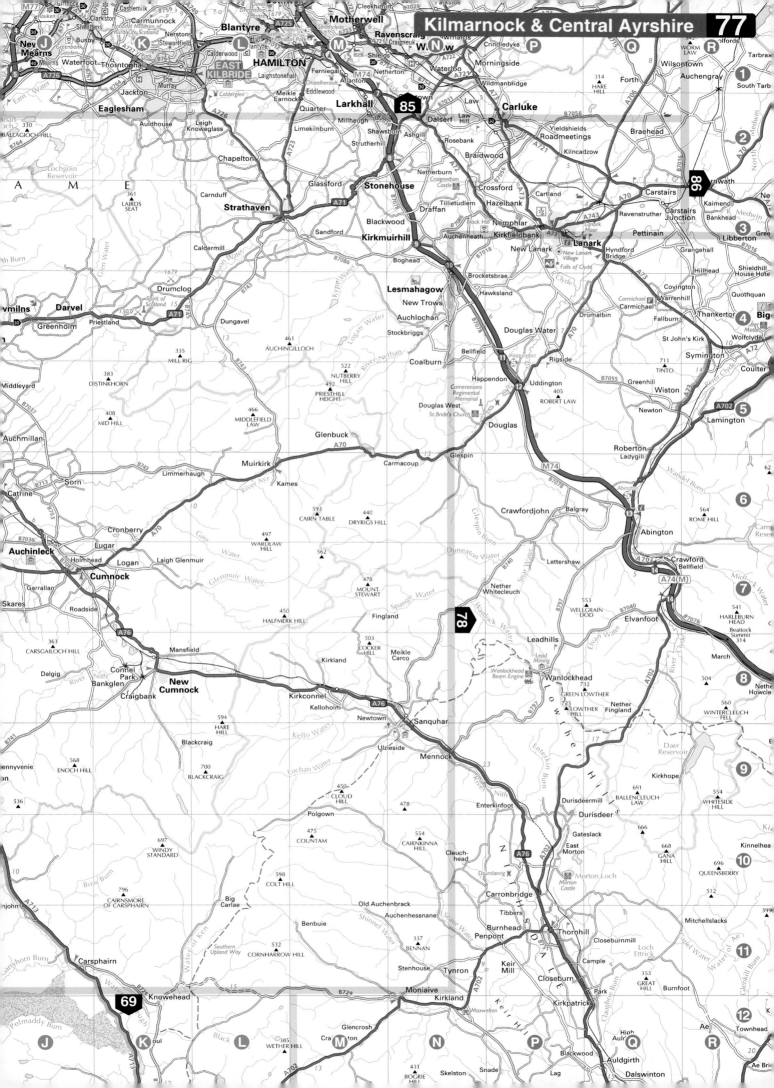

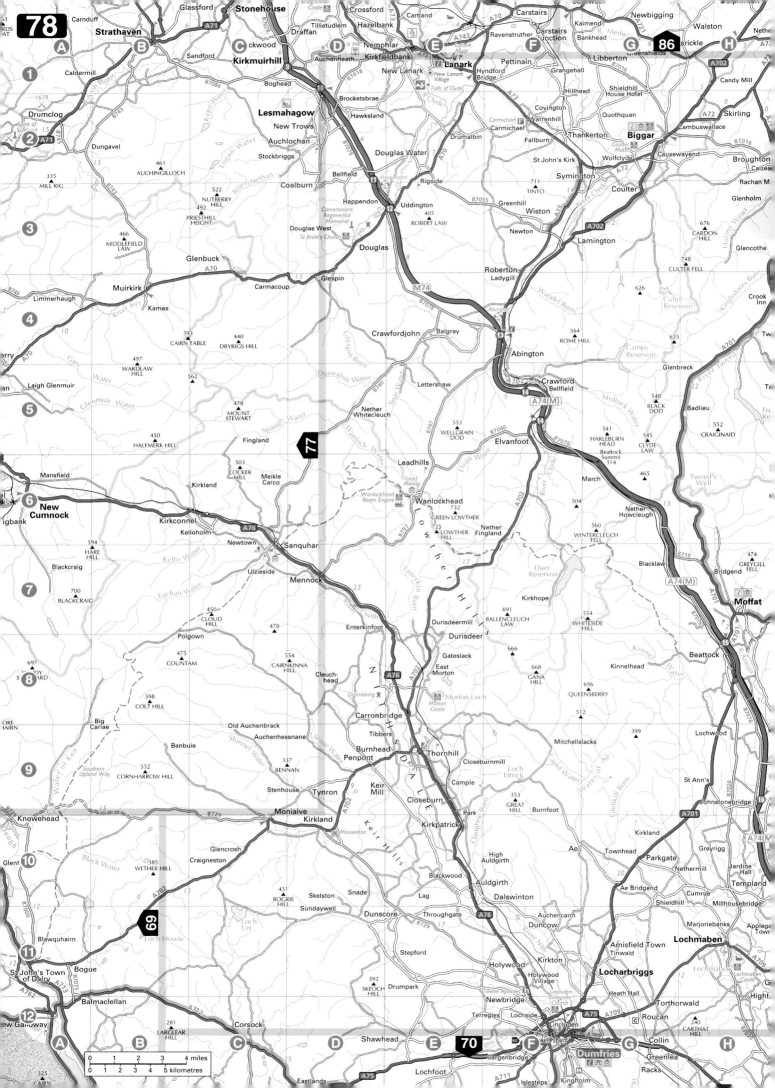

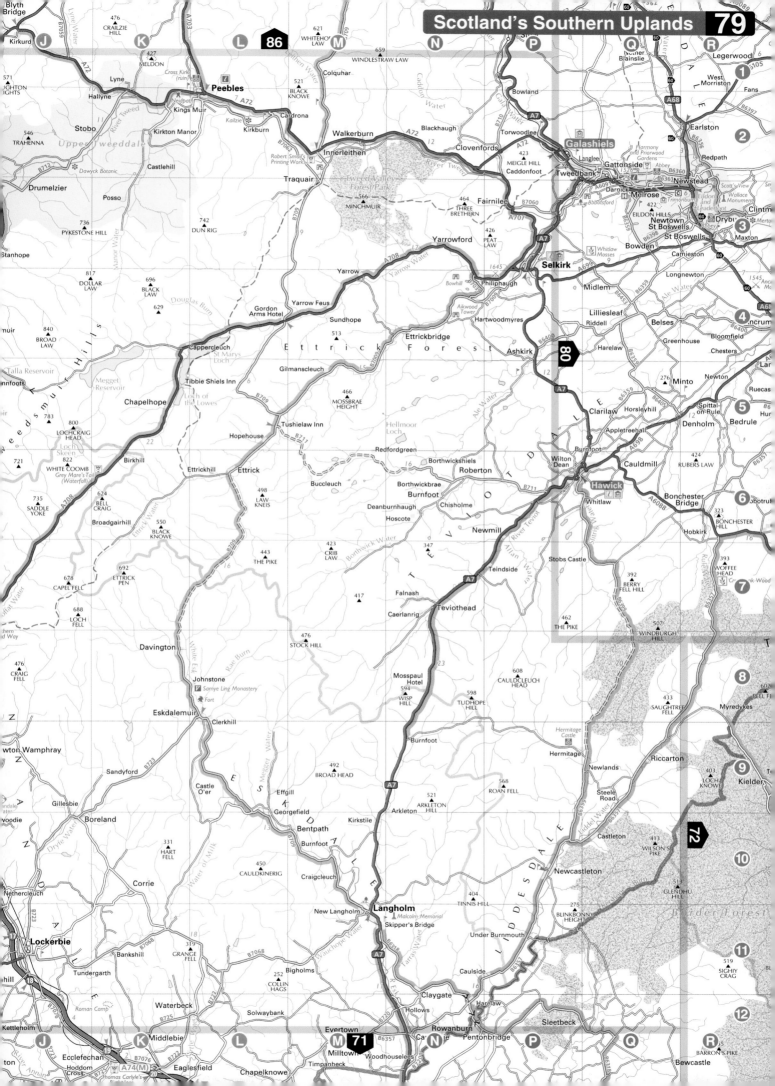

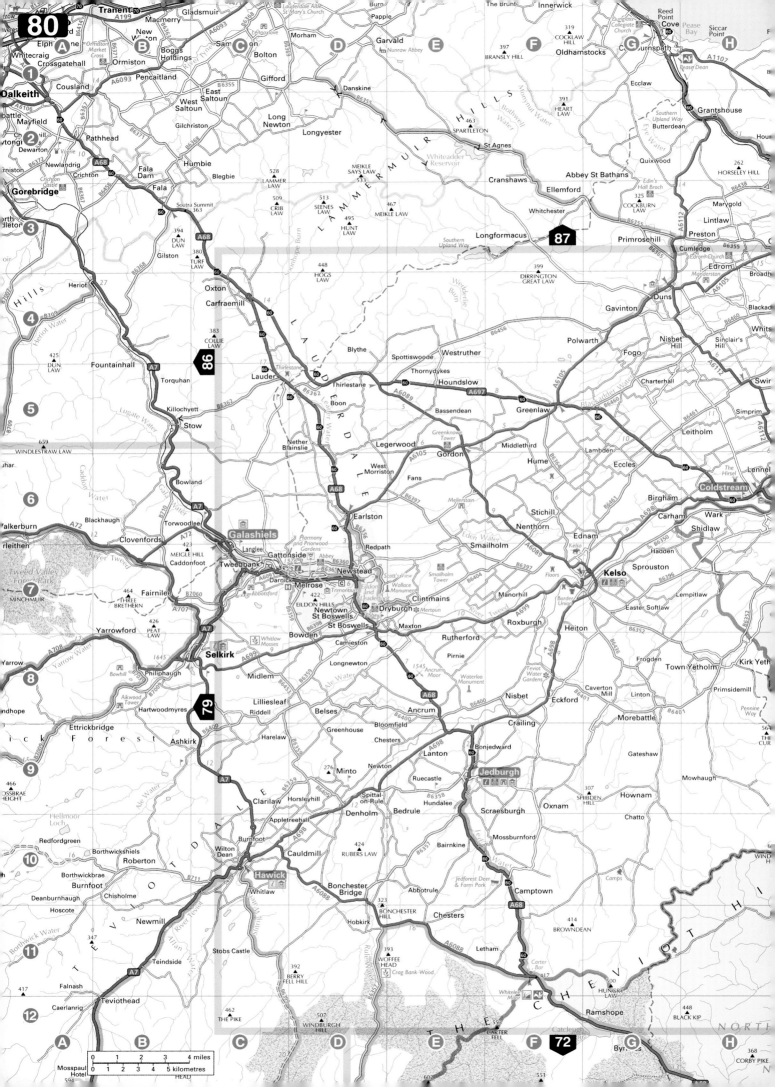

J   K   L   M   N   P   Q   R

1
2
3
4
5
6
7
8
9
10
11
12

Castle Head
Coldingham Loch
ST ABB'S HEAD
St Abbs
Coldingham
Eyemouth
Coldingham Bay
od
Heugh Head
Cairncross
Burnmouth
A1107
Reston
Ayton
A1
hencrow
Lamberton
side
Foulden
B6437
Marshall Meadows Bay
Edington
Whiteadder Water
North Northumberland Heritage Coast
Allanton
Hutton
Foulden Tithe Barn
Berwick-upon-Tweed
Barracks
A6105
Paxton
Town Ramparts
Hilton
Horndean
Tweedmouth
Spittal
B6460
B6461
Horncliffe
Murton
Huds Head
Ladykirk
Norham
Thornton
Scremerston
Upsettlington
A698
River Tweed
Cheswick
CAUSEWAY FLOODED AT HIGH TIDE
Duddo
Ancroft
B6525
Haggerston
Beal
HOLY ISLAND
Holy Island
Cornhill-on-Tweed
Bowsden
Castle Point
Etal
Lowick
Fenwick
Lindisfarne Priory
Lindisfarne Castle
Heatherslaw Light Railway
Heatherslaw Corn Mill
B6353
Guile Point
Branxton
Crookham
Ford
Lady Waterford Hall
Buckton
Longstone Lighthouse
FARNE ISLANDS
Howtel
A697
Fenton
B6525
St Cuthbert's Cave
Belford
Staple Sound
Inner Sound
North Northumberland Heritage Coast
nington
Milfield
Nesbit
B6349
Budle Bay
Bamburgh
Lanton
Doddington
B1342
B1340
Yeavering
Coupland
Seahouses
Kirknewton
B6351
Lucker
North Sunderland
YEAVERING BELL
Akeld
B6348
Chatton
Warenford
Beadnell
Wooler
A1
Swinhoe
Beadnell Bay
NORTHUMBERLAND
Newtown
Wild Cattle Park
Chathill
Tughall
Newstead
Ellingham
NATIONAL PARK
Ros Castle
Preston
Newton-by-the-Sea
THE CHEVIOT
Ilderton
Old Bewick
Preston Pele Tower
Embleton & Newton Links
Christon Bank
Embleton
Embleton Bay
CATERAN HILL
North Charlton
Dunstanburgh Castle
New Bewick
Eglingham
South Charlton
Fallodon
DUNMOOR HILL
Beanley
Rock
Dunstan
Craster
Branton
Powburn
Rennington
Stamford
Howick
Ingram
Glanton
River Aln
Denwick
Howick Hall
Cullernose Point
Bolton
Alnwick
Longhoughton
COCHRANE PIKE
Boulmer
Whittingham
Séaton Point
Alnham
Lesbury
CUSHAT LAW
Alnmouth
HILLHOPE LAW
Netherton
Shilbottle
Alnmouth Bay
A1068
Alwinton
Burradon
Edlingham
LONG CRAG
Swarland
Warkworth
Harbottle
GLANTLEES HILL
Newton-on-the-Moor
Warkworth Castle & Heritage
Amble
Sharperton
Gloster Hill
Coquet Island
MBERLAND
Holystone
Rothbury
73
Felton
Togston
uxley
TIONAL
Hepple
Longframlington
Whitton
East Thirston
Broomhill
Great Tosson
South

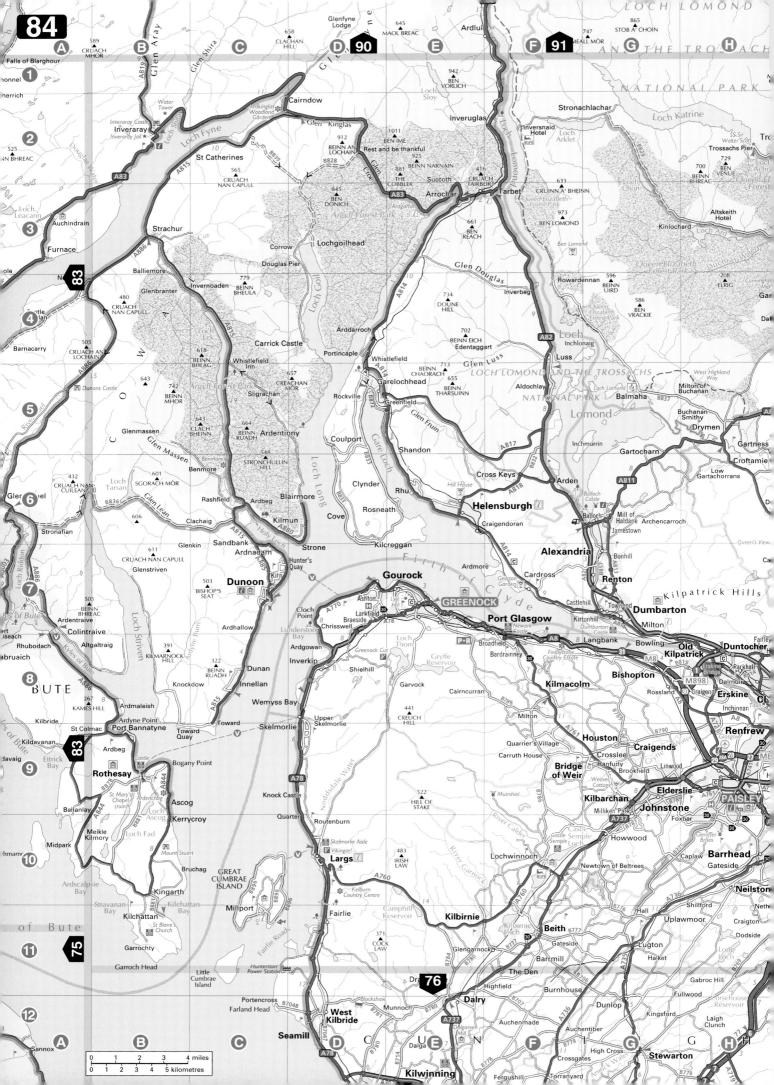

Eilean Mòr

Bagh a Chaisteil
(Castlebay)
Loch Baghasdail
(Lochboisdale)

Rudha
Mòr

Rudha
Sgor-innis

Bousd   Sorisdale

4

Cliad
Bay

Arnabost

Grishipoll
Clabhach

Loch
Cliad

Hogh Bay   Ballyhaugh   **Arinagour**

Coll-Oban

5

Bagh a Chaisteil
(Castlebay)

Totronald

COLL

Caliach Point

Feall
Bay

Coll

Acha

Calg

Arileod

(Mar-Oct)

Calgary Point

Crossapol
Bay

Uig

Eilean
Ornsay

Gunna

Rudha
Fàsachd

Calgary Bay

6

Loch Beuthachu

Treshnish Point

Caoles

Rudha Dubh

B8069

Ruaig

Rudh' a' Chaoil

Rudha Port
Bhiosd

Clachan
Mor

Balephetrish
Bay

B8068

Loch
Bhasapol

Fladda

Haugh
Bay

Ballevullin   Cornoigmore

Kenovay

Tiree

Gott
Bay

Lunga

7

Kilkenneth

B8066

Scarinish

**TRESHNISH
ISLES**

Gometra

Moss   Heylipoll

B8065

Middleton

Crossapoll

TIREE

Barrapoll

B8065

Hynish Bay

Balemartine

B8067

Mannel

Loch a
Phuill

Rinn
Thorbhais

Hynish

Balephuil Bay

Bac Mòr or Dutchmans Cap

8

Bac Beag

Staffa

Little Col

Loc
Isle

Fingal's Cave

9

10

Rudha nan Cearc

IONA

Iona Abbey
& Nunnery

IONA

Kintra

Baile Mòr

MacLean's Cross

Fionnphort

(Mar-Oct)

Aridhglas

St Columba
Exhibition
Centre

Bu

R O S S

11

Soa Island

Errald

A

12

Torran Rocks

Rudh
Arda

0   1   2   3   4 miles
0   1   2   3   4   5 kilometres

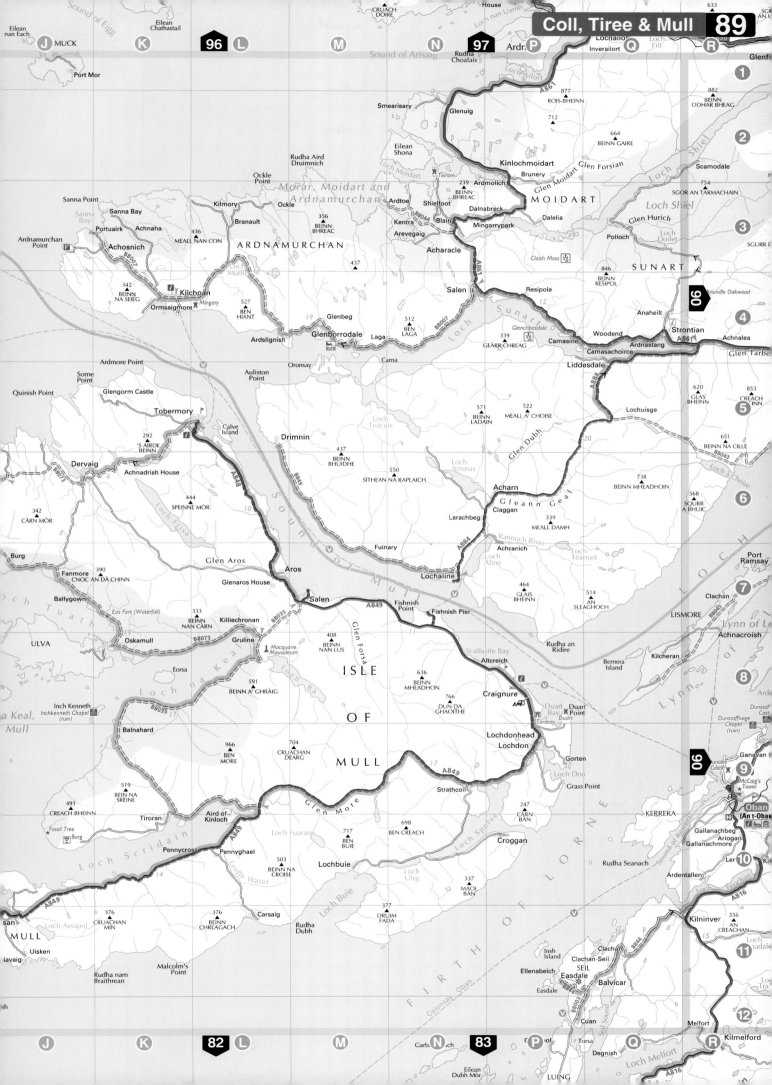

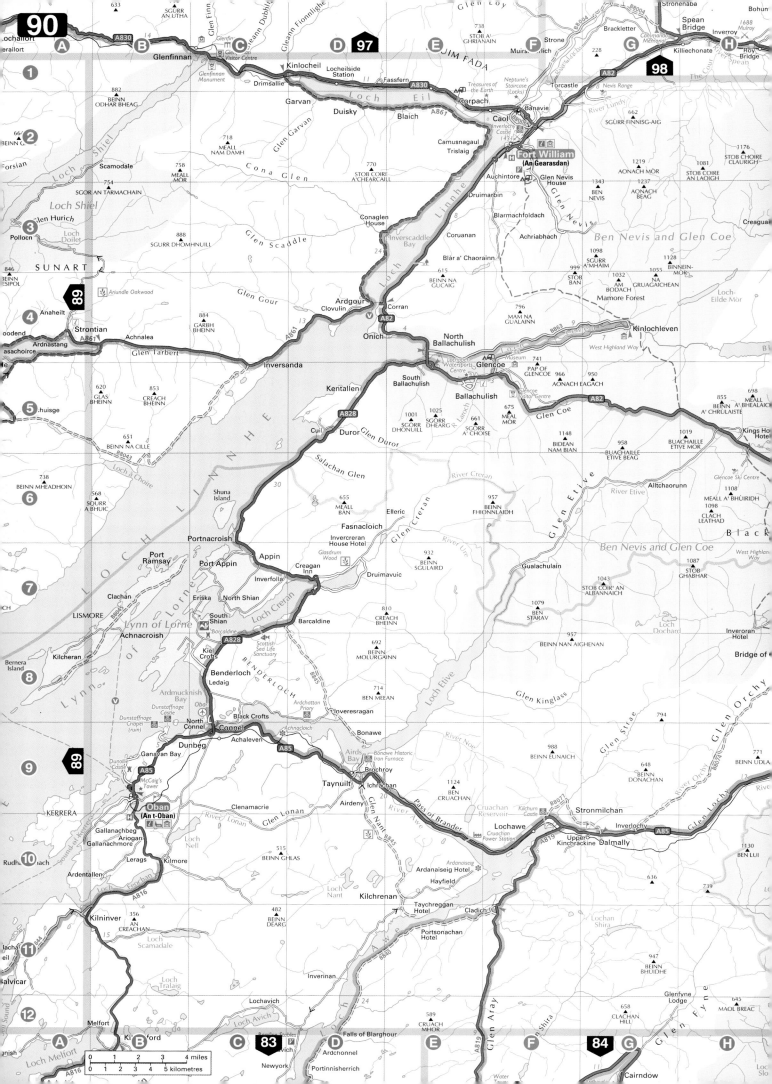

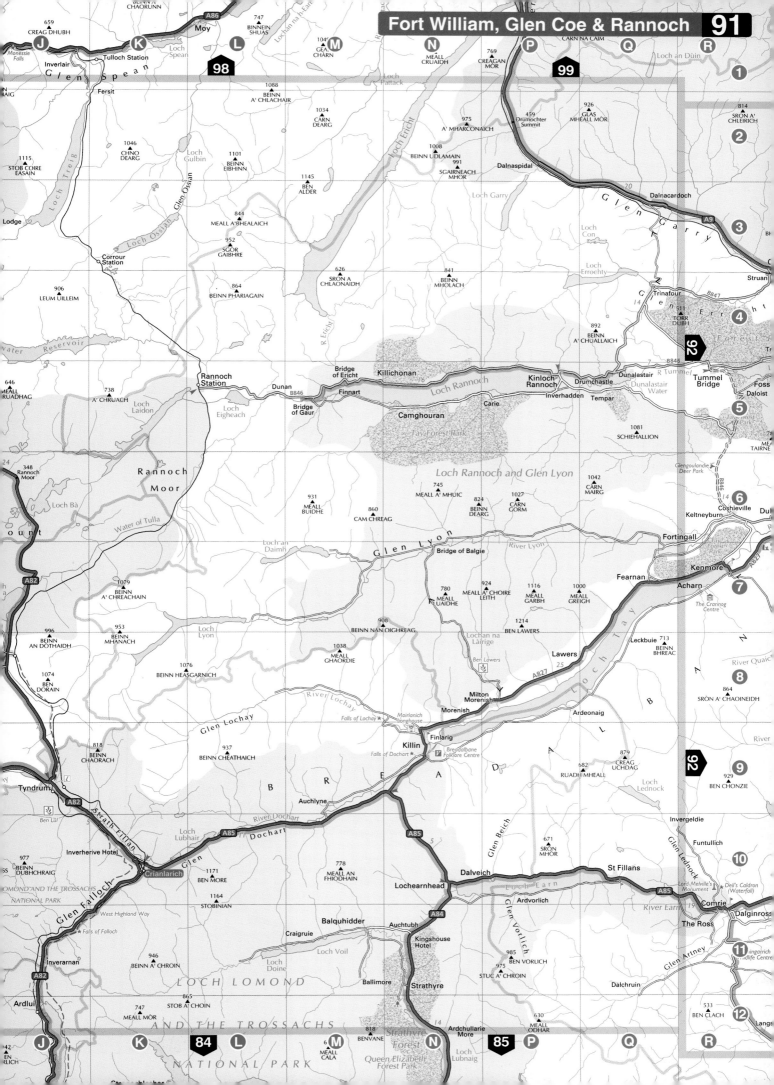

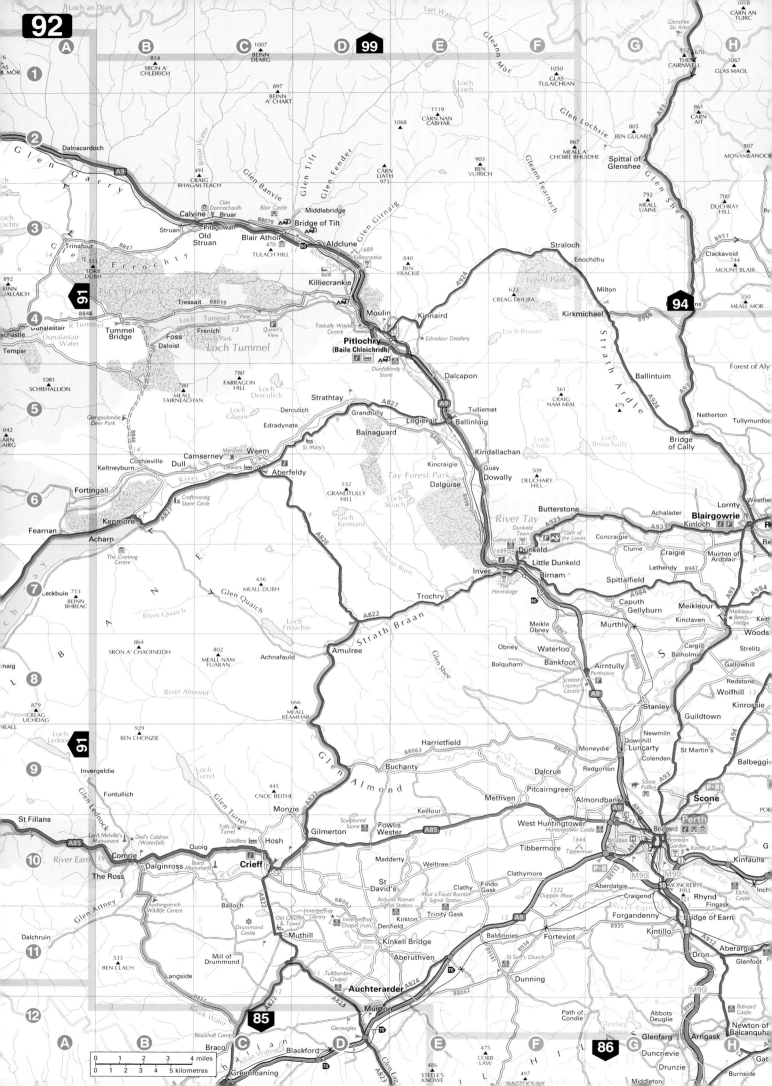

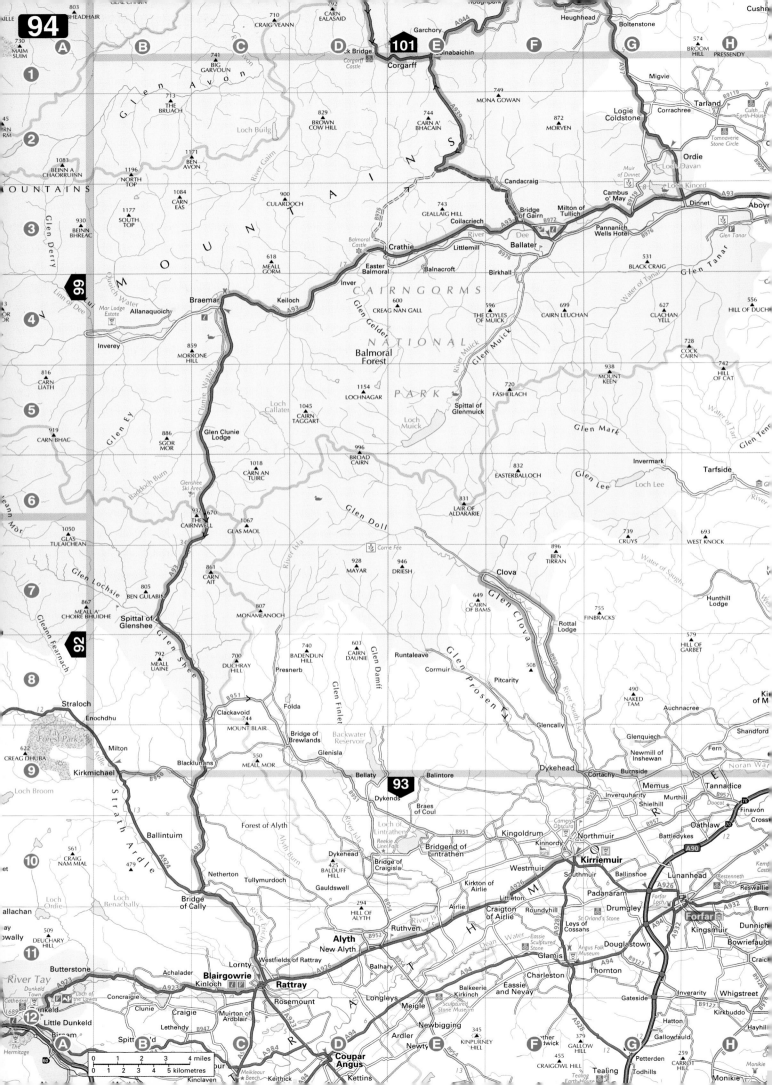

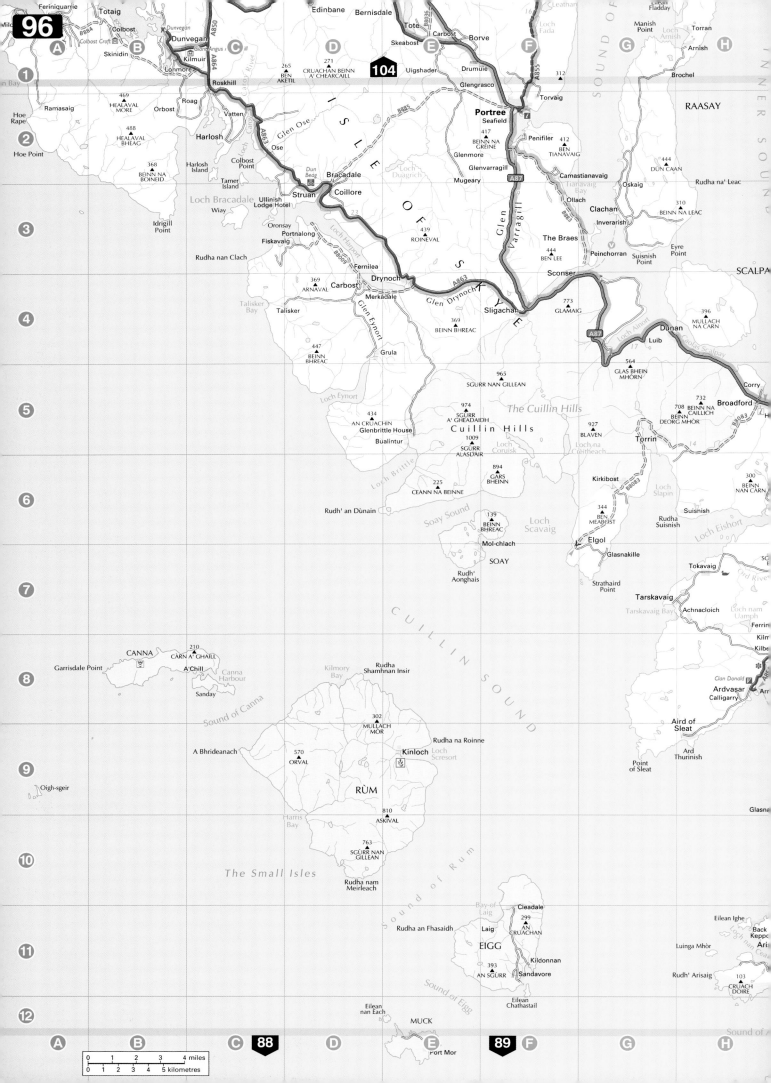

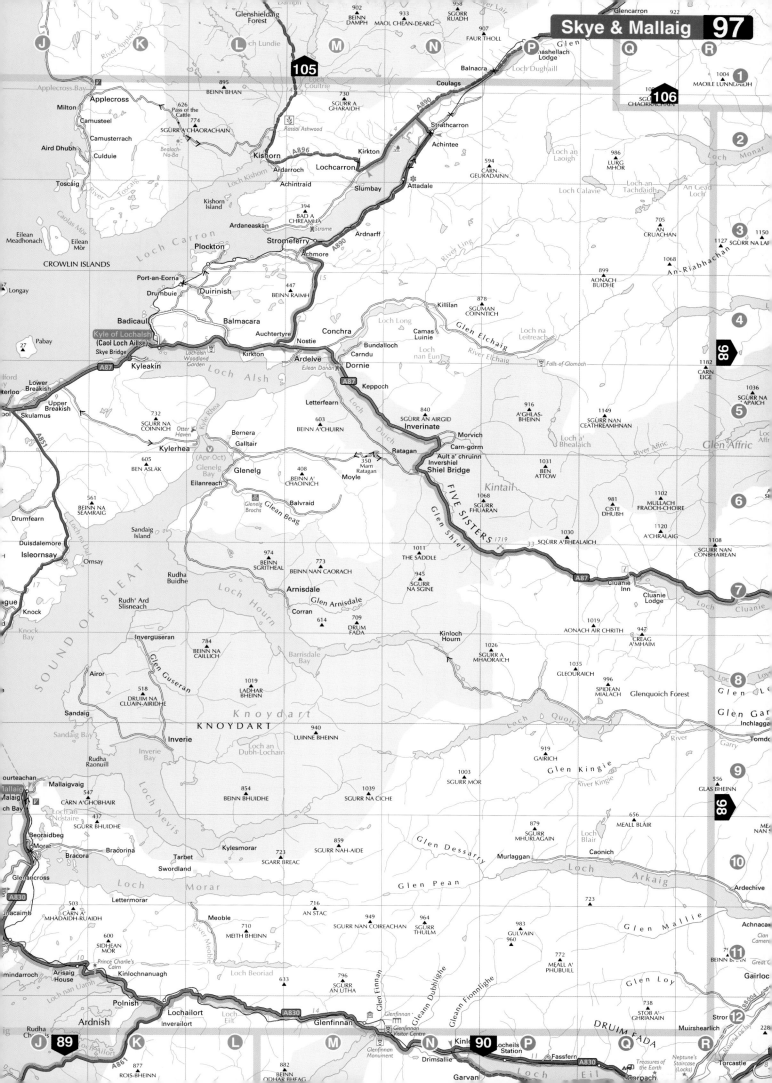

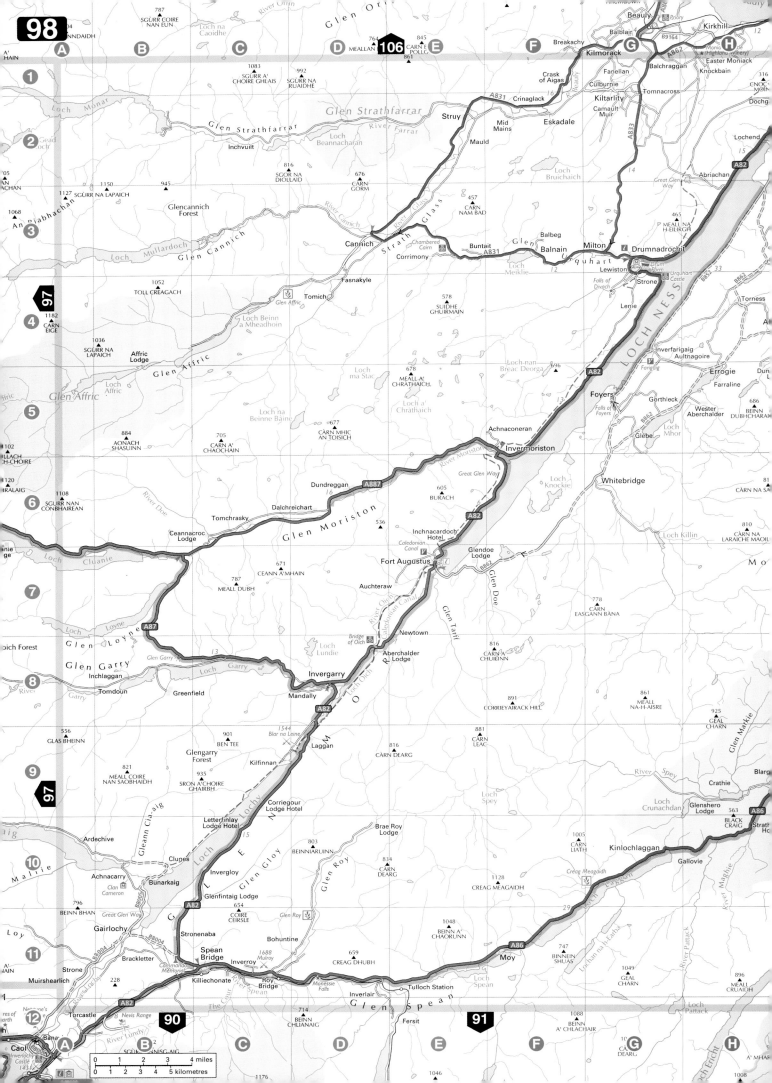

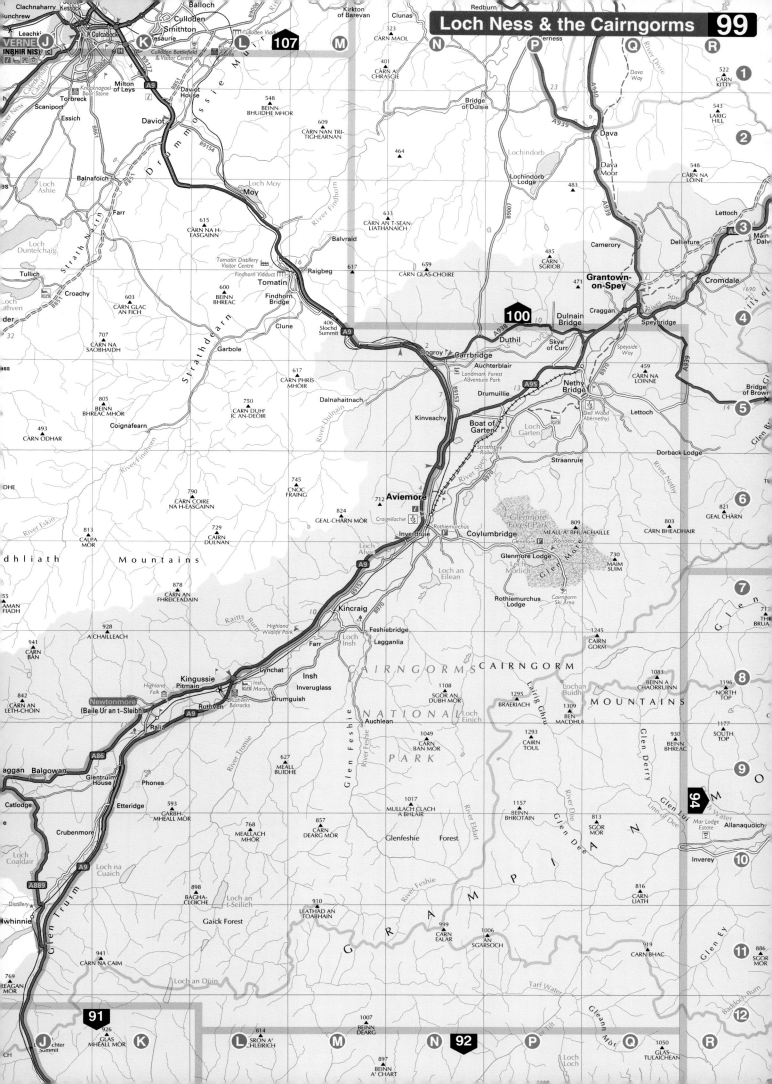

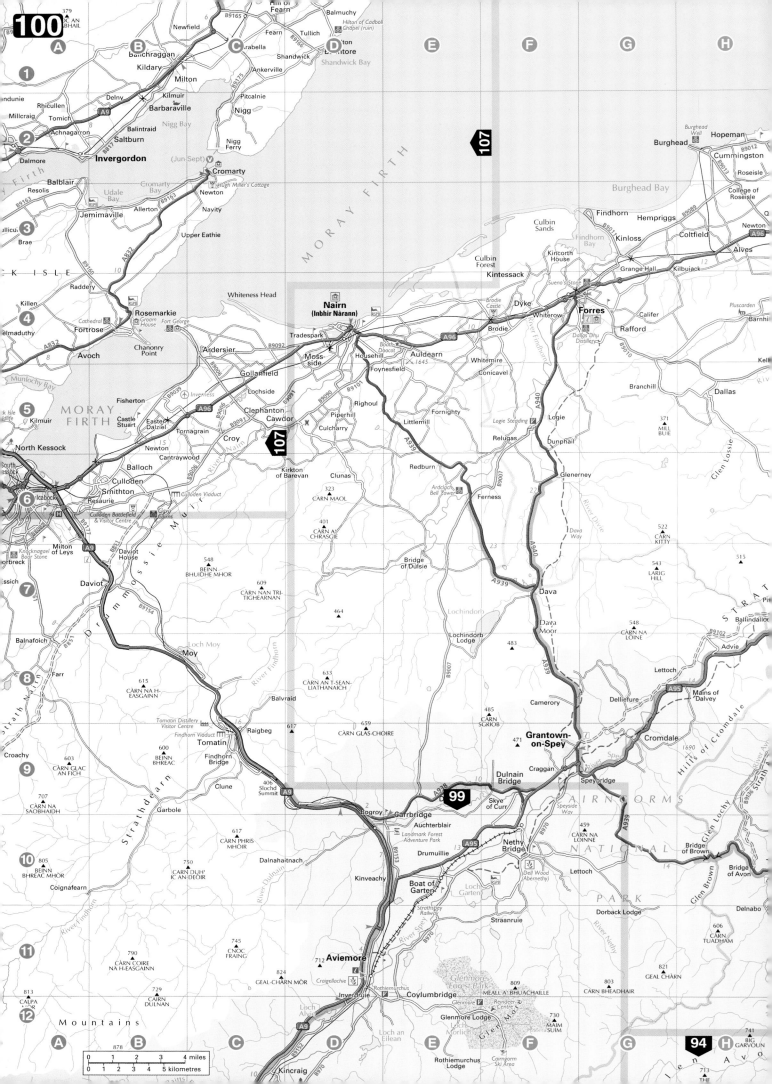

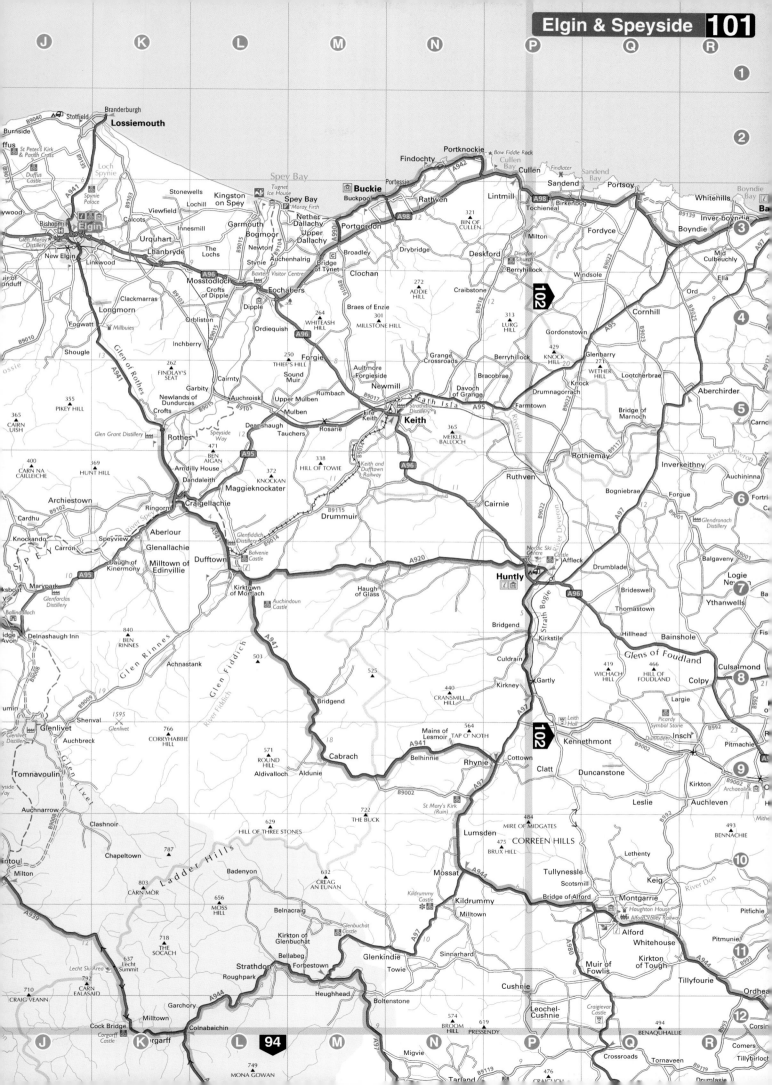

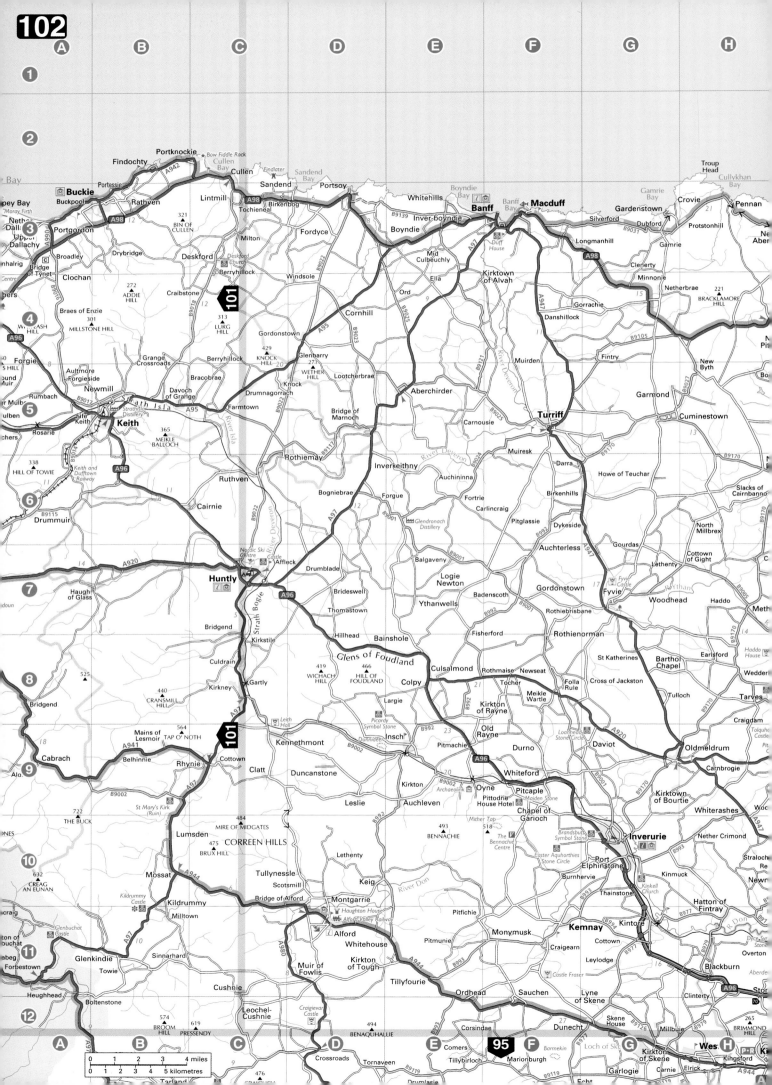

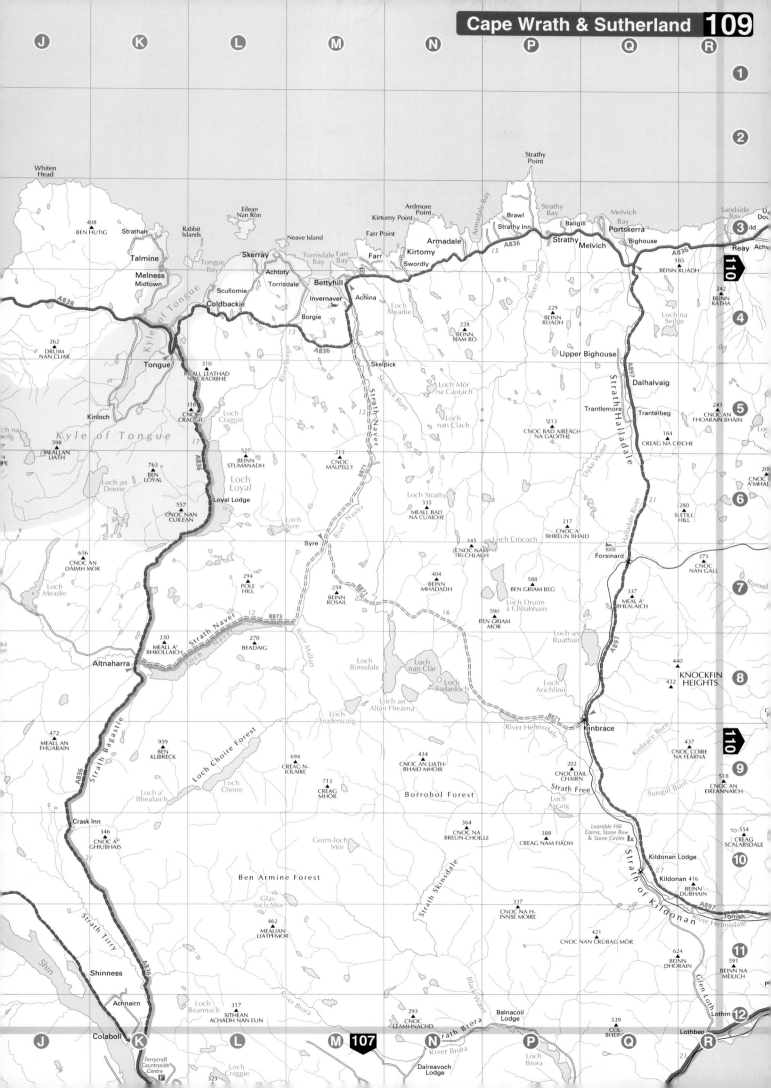

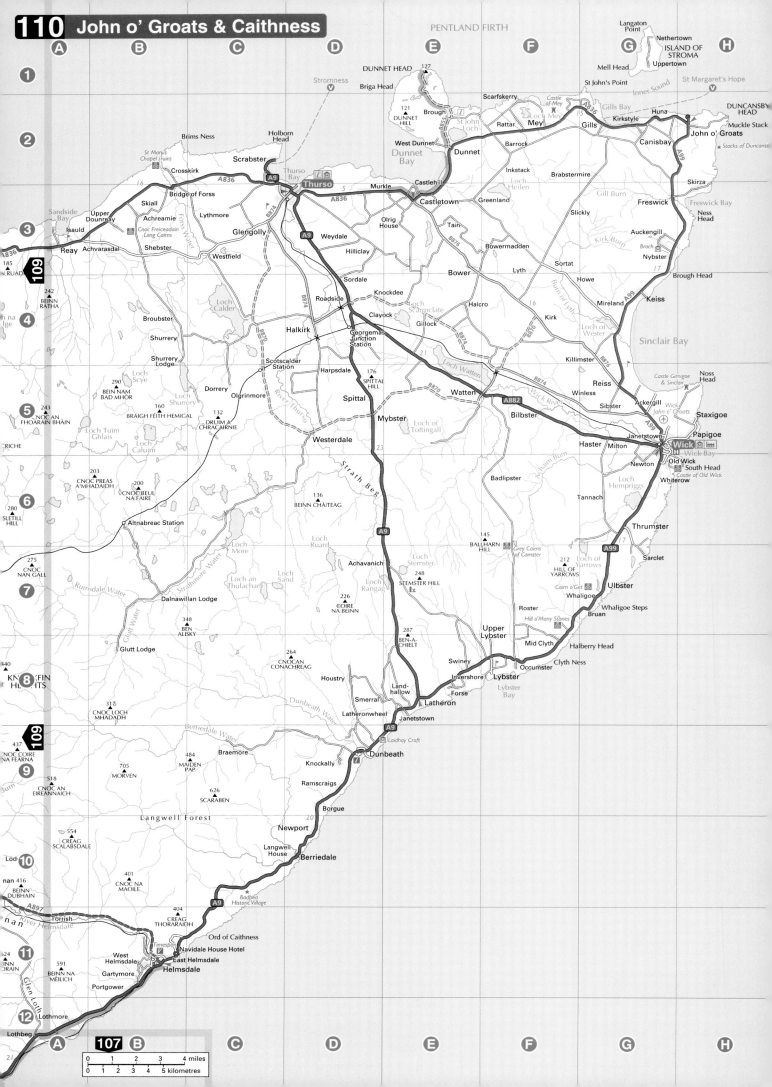

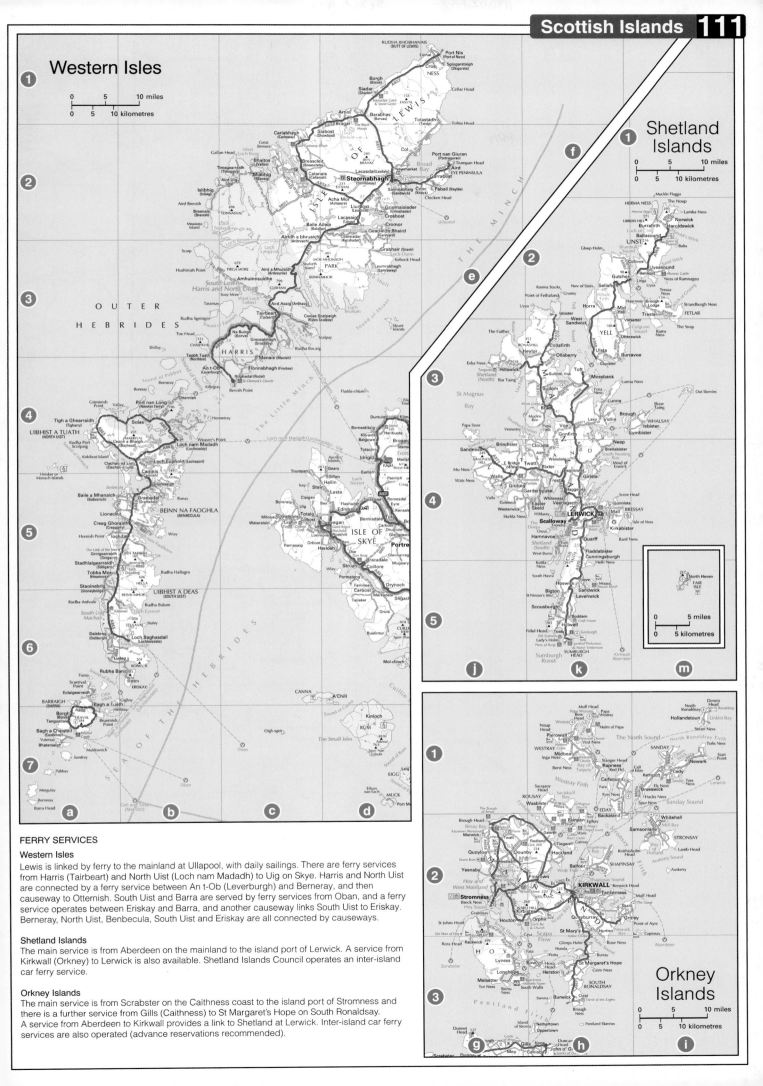

Western Isles

OUTER HEBRIDES

Shetland Islands

Orkney Islands

FERRY SERVICES

Western Isles

Lewis is linked by ferry to the mainland at Ullapool, with daily sailings. There are ferry services from Harris (Tairbeart) and North Uist (Loch nam Madadh) to Uig on Skye. Harris and North Uist are connected by a ferry service between An t-Ob (Leverburgh) and Berneray, and then causeway to Otternish. South Uist and Barra are served by ferry services from Oban, and a ferry service operates between Eriskay and Barra, and another causeway links South Uist to Eriskay. Berneray, North Uist, Benbecula, South Uist and Eriskay are all connected by causeways.

Shetland Islands

The main service is from Aberdeen on the mainland to the island port of Lerwick. A service from Kirkwall (Orkney) to Lerwick is also available. Shetland Islands Council operates an inter-island car ferry service.

Orkney Islands

The main service is from Scrabster on the Caithness coast to the island port of Stromness and there is a further service from Gills (Caithness) to St Margaret's Hope on South Ronaldsay. A service from Aberdeen to Kirkwall provides a link to Shetland at Lerwick. Inter-island car ferry services are also operated (advance reservations recommended).

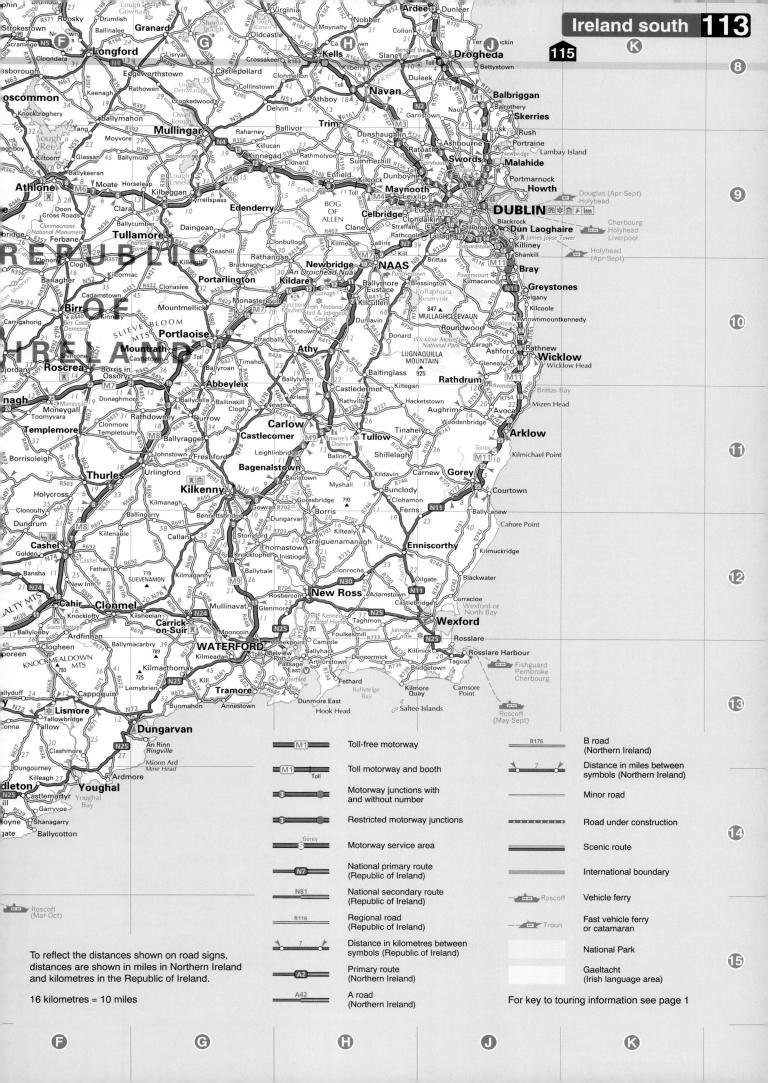

Ireland index

Abbeydorney....C12
Abbeyfeale....D12
Abbeyleix....G11
Adamstown....H12
Adare....D12
Adrigole....C14
Aghadowey....H4
Ahascragh....E9
Ahoghill....J5
Allihies....B15
Anascaul....B13
An Bun Beag....E4
An Charraig....E5
An Clochán Liath....E4
An Coireán....B14
An Daingean....B13
An Fhairche....C9
Annalong....J7
Annestown....G13
An Rinn....G13
An Spidéal....D9
Antrim....J5
Ardagh....D12
Ardara....E5
Ardee....H8
Ardfert....C12
Ardfinnan....F12
Ardglass....K6
Ardgroom....B14
Ardmore....F14
Arklow....J11
Arless....H11
Armagh....H6
Armoy....J3
Arthurstown....H13
Arvagh....G7
Ashbourne....J9
Ashford....J10
Askeaton....D12
Athboy....H8
Athea....D12
Athenry....E9
Athleague....F9
Athlone....F10
Athy....H10
Augher....G6
Aughnacloy....H6
Aughrim....J11
Avoca....J11

Bagenalstown....H11
Baile Mhic Íre....D14
Bailieborough....H7
Balbriggan....J8
Balla....D8
Ballaghaderreen....D7
Ballina....D7
Ballina....E11
Ballinafad....E7
Ballinagh....G7
Ballinakill....G11
Ballinalee....F8
Ballinamallard....G6
Ballinamore....F7
Ballinascarty....D14
Ballinasloe....E9
Ballindine....D8
Ballineen....D14
Ballingarry....D12
Ballingarry....G12
Ballingeary....D14
Ballinhassig....E14
Ballinlough....E8
Ballinrobe....D8
Ballinspittle....E15
Ballintober....F5
Ballintra....F5
Ballivor....H9
Ballon....H11
Ballybaun....E9
Ballybay....H7
Ballybofey....F5
Ballybunion....C12
Ballycanew....J11
Ballycarry....K5
Ballycastle....J3
Ballycastle....C6
Ballyclare....J5
Ballycolla....G11
Ballyconneely....B9
Ballyconnell....G7
Ballycotton....F14
Ballycumber....F9
Ballydehob....C15
Ballydesmond....D13
Ballyduff....C12
Ballyduff....F13
Ballyfarnan....E7
Ballygalley....J4
Ballygar....E9
Ballygawley....E6
Ballygawley....H6
Ballygowan....K5
Ballyhack....H13
Ballyhaise....G7
Ballyhale....G12
Ballyhaunis....E8
Ballyhean....D8
Ballyheige....C12
Ballyjamesduff....G8
Ballykeeran....F9
Ballylanders....E12
Ballylickey....C14
Ballyliffin....G3
Ballylongford....C12
Ballylooby....F12
Ballylynan....H10
Ballymacarbry....F13
Ballymahon....F8
Ballymakeery....D14
Ballymena....J4
Ballymoe....E8
Ballymoney....H4
Ballymore....F9
Ballymore Eustace....H10
Ballymote....E7
Ballynahinch....J6
Ballynure....J5

Ballyporeen....F13
Ballyragget....G11
Ballyroan....G10
Ballyronan....H5
Ballysadare....E6
Ballyshannon....F5
Ballyvaughan....D10
Ballywalter....K5
Balrothery....J8
Baltimore....C15
Baltinglass....H10
Banagher....F10
Banbridge....J6
Bandon....E14
Bangor....K5
Bangor Erris....C7
Bansha....F12
Banteer....D13
Bantry....C14
Barna....D9
Béal an Mhuirthead....B6
Béal Átha an Ghaorthaidh....D14
Bearna....D9
Beaufort....C13
Belcoo....F6
Belfast....J5
Belgooly....E14
Bellaghy....H4
Belleek....F6
Belmullet....B6
Belturbet....G7
Benburb....H6
Bennettsbridge....G12
Beragh....G5
Bettystown....J8
Birr....F10
Blacklion....F6
Blackrock....J9
Blackwater....J12
Blarney....E14
Blessington....H10
Boherbue....D13
Borris....H12
Borris in Ossory....F10
Borrisokane....F10
Borrisoleigh....F11
Boyle....E7
Bracknagh....G10
Bray....J10
Bridgetown....H13
Brittas....J9
Broadford....E11
Broadford....D12
Broughshane....J4
Bruff....E12
Bruree....E12
Bunbeg....E4
Bunclody....H11
Buncrana....G3
Bundoran....E6
Bunmahon....G13
Bun na hAbhna....C6
Bunnahowen....C6
Bunnyconnellan....D7
Bunratty....D11
Burnfort....E13
Bushmills....H3
Buttevant....E13

Cadamstown....F10
Caherconlish....E12
Caherdaniel....B14
Cahersiveen....B14
Cahir....F12
Caledon....H6
Callan....G12
Caltra....E9
Camp....B13
Campile....H13
Cappagh White....F12
Cappamore....E11
Cappoquin....F13
Carlanstown....H8
Carlingford....J7
Carlow....H11
Carna....C9
Carndonagh....G3
Carnew....J11
Carnlough....J4
Carracastle....E7
Carraig Airt....F3
Carrick....E5
Carrickart....F3
Carrickfergus....K5
Carrickmacross....H7
Carrickmore or Termon Rock....G5
Carrick-on-Shannon....F7
Carrick-on-Suir....G12
Carrigahorig....F10
Carrigaline....E14
Carrigallen....F7
Carriganimmy....D14
Carrigans....G4
Carrigtohill....E14
Carryduff....J5
Cashel....C9
Cashel....F12
Castlebar....D8
Castlebellingham....J7
Castleblayney....H7
Castlebridge....J12
Castlecomer....G11
Castleconnell....E11
Castlederg....G5
Castledermot....H10
Castlegregory....B13
Castleisland....C13
Castlemaine....C13
Castlemartyr....F14
Castleplunket....E8
Castlepollard....G8
Castlerea....E8
Castlerock....H3
Castleshane....H6
Castletown....G10

Castletownbere....B15
Castletownroche....E13
Castletownshend....D15
Castlewellan....J6
Cathair Dónall....B14
Causeway....C12
Cavan....G7
Celbridge....H9
Charlestown....D7
Charleville....E12
Cheekpoint....H13
Cill Charthaigh....E5
Cill Chiaráin....C9
Clady....G5
Clane....H9
Clara....G9
Clarecastle....D11
Claremorris....D8
Clarinbridge....D10
Clashmore....F13
Claudy....G4
Clifden....B9
Cliffony....E6
Clogh....G11
Cloghan....F10
Clogheen....F13
Clogher....G6
Clohamon....H11
Clonakilty....D15
Clonard....H9
Clonaslee....G10
Clonbulloge....G10
Clonbur....C9
Clondalkin....J9
Clones....G7
Clonlara....E11
Clonmany....G3
Clonmel....F12
Clonmellon....H8
Clonmore....F11
Clonony....F10
Clonoulty....F12
Clonroche....H12
Cloondara....F8
Clough....K6
Cloughjordan....F10
Cloyne....F14
Coagh....H5
Coalisland....H5
Cobh....E14
Coleraine....H3
Collinstown....G8
Collon....H8
Collooney....E6
Comber....K5
Cong....D9
Conna....F13
Cookstown....H5
Coole....G8
Cooraclare....C11
Cootehill....G7
Cork....E14
Cornamona....C9
Corofin....D10
Corr na Móna....C9
Courtmacsherry....E15
Courtown....J11
Craigavon....J6
Craughwell....E10
Crawfordsburn....K5
Creegs....E8
Creeslough....F4
Croagh....D12
Croithlí....E4
Crolly....E4
Crookedwood....G8
Crookhaven....C15
Crookstown....D14
Croom....E12
Crossakeel....H8
Cross Barry....E14
Crosshaven....E14
Crossmaglen....H7
Crossmolina....D7

Crumlin....J5
Crusheen....D10
Culdaff....G3
Cullybackey....J4
Curracloe....J12
Curraghboy....F9
Curry....E7
Cushendall....J4
Cushendun....J3

Daingean....G9
Delgany....J10
Delvin....G8
Derry....G4
Derrygonnelly....F6
Derrylin....G6
Dervock....H3
Dingle....B13
Doagh....J5
Donabate....K6
Donaghadee....K5
Donaghmore....G11
Donard....H10
Donegal....F5
Doneraile....E13
Doolin....C10
Doon....E12
Doonbeg....C11
Doon Cross Roads....F9
Douglas....E14
Dowra....F6
Downpatrick....K6
Draperstown....H5
Drimoleague....D15
Dripsey....E14
Drogheda....J8
Dromahair....E6
Dromcolliher....D12
Dromore....J6
Dromore....G5
Dromore West....D6
Drumcliff....E6
Drumcondra....H8
Drumkeeran....F7
Drumlish....F8
Drumod....F8
Drumquin....G5
Drumshanbo....F7
Drumsna....F7
Duagh....C12
Dublin....J9
Duleek....J8
Dunboyne....J9
Duncormick....H13
Dundalk....J7
Dunderrow....E14
Dundonald....K5
Dundrum....K6
Dundrum....F12
Dunfanaghy....F3
Dungannon....H5
Dungarvan....G12
Dungarvan....G13
Dungiven....H4
Dunglow....E4
Dungourney....F14
Dunkineely....E5
Dún Laoghaire....J9
Dunlavin....H10
Dunleer....J8
Dunloy....J4
Dunmanway....D14
Dunmore....E8
Dunmore East....H13
Dunmurry....J5
Dunshaughlin....H9
Durrow....G11
Durrus....C15
Dysart....E9

Easky....D6
Edenderry....H9
Edgeworthstown....G8
Eglinton....G4
Elphin....F8
Emyvale....H6

Enfield....H9
Ennis....D11
Enniscorthy....H12
Enniskean....D14
Enniskillen....F6
Ennistymon....D10
Eyrecourt....F10

Fahan....G4
Farranfore....C13
Feakle....E10
Fenagh....F7
Ferbane....F9
Fermoy....E13
Fethard....F12
Fethard....H13
Finnea....G8
Fintona....G6
Fivemiletown....G6
Fontstown....H10
Foulkesmill....H12
Foxford....D7
Foynes....D11
Freemount....D13
Frenchpark....E8
Freshford....G11
Fuerty....E8

Galbally....E12
Galway....D9
Garrison....F6
Garristown....J8
Garryvoe....F14
Garvagh....H4
Geashill....G10
Gilford....J6
Glandore....D15
Glanmire....E14
Glanworth....E13
Glaslough....H6
Glassan....F9
Gleann Cholm Cille....E5
Glenarm....J4
Glenavy....J5
Glenbeigh....B13
Glencolumbkille....E5
Glenealy....J10
Glengarriff....C14
Glenmore....H12
Glennamaddy....E8
Glenties....E5
Glin....D12
Glinsce....C9
Glinsk....C9
Golden....F12
Goleen....C15
Goresbridge....H11
Gorey....J11
Gort....D10
Gortin....G5
Gowran....H11
Graiguenamanagh....H12
Granard....G8
Grange....E6
Greenore....J7
Greyabbey....K5
Greystones....J10
Gulladuff....H4

Hacketstown....H11
Headford....D9
Herbertstown....E12
Hillsborough....J6
Hilltown....J6
Holycross....F11
Holywood....K5
Horseleap....G9
Hospital....E12
Howth....J9

Inch....B13
Inchigeelagh....D14
Inishannon....E14
Inishcrone....D6

Inistioge....H12
Irvinestown....F6

Johnstown....G11

Kanturk....D13
Keadew....F7
Keady....H6
Keel....B7
Keenagh....F8
Kells....J4
Kells....H8
Kenmare....C14
Kesh....F5
Kilbeggan....G9
Kilberry....H8
Kilbrittain....E14
Kilcar....E5
Kilcock....H9
Kilcolgan....D10
Kilconnell....E9
Kilcoole....J10
Kilcormac....F10
Kilcullen....H10
Kilcurry....J7
Kildare....H10
Kildavin....H11
Kildorrery....E13
Kilfenora....D10
Kilgarvan....C14
Kilkee....C11
Kilkeel....J7
Kilkelly....D7
Kilkenny....G11
Kilkieran....C9
Kilkinlea Lower....C12
Kill....H9
Kill....G13
Killadysert....D11
Killala....D6
Killaloe....E11
Killarney....C13
Killashandra....G7
Killeagh....F14
Killeigh....G10
Killenaule....F12
Killimer....C11
Killimor....E10
Killiney....J9
Killinick....J13
Killorglin....C13
Killough....K6
Killucan....G9
Killybegs....E5
Killyleagh....K6
Kilmacanoge....J10
Kilmacrenan....F4
Kilmacthomas....G13
Kilmaganny....G12
Kilmaine....D8
Kilmallock....E12
Kilmanagh....G11
Kilmeaden....G13
Kilmeage....H9
Kilmeedy....D12
Kilmichael....D14
Kilmore Quay....H13
Kilmuckridge....J12
Kilnaleck....G8
Kilrea....H4
Kilrush....C11
Kilsheelan....G12
Kiltamagh....D8
Kiltealy....H12
Kiltegan....H11
Kiltoom....F9
Kingscourt....H7
Kinlough....E6
Kinnegad....G9
Kinnitty....F10
Kinsale....E14
Kinvarra....D10
Kircubbin....K5
Knock....D8
Knockcroghery....F8

Knocklofty....F12
Knocktopher....G12

Lahinch....C10
Lanesborough....F8
Laragh....J10
Larne....K4
Lauragh....C14
Laurencetown....F10
Leap....D15
Leenane....C8
Leighlinbridge....H11
Leitrim....F7
Lemybrien....G13
Letterfrack....B8
Letterkenny....F4
Lifford....G4
Limavady....H4
Limerick....E11
Lisbellaw....G6
Lisburn....J5
Liscannor....C10
Liscarroll....D13
Lisdoonvarna....D10
Lismore....F13
Lisnaskea....G6
Lisryan....F8
Listowel....C12
Loghill....D12
Londonderry....G4
Longford....F8
Loughbrickland....J6
Loughgall....H6
Loughglinn....E8
Loughrea....E10

Louisburgh....C8
Lucan....J9
Lurgan....J6
Lusk....J9

Machair Loiscthe....E4
Macroom....D14
Maghera....H4
Maghera....H5
Magherafelt....H5
Maguiresbridge....G6
Malahide....J9
Málainn Mhóir....E5
Malin....G3
Malin More....E5
Mallow....E13
Manorhamilton....F6
Markethill....H6
Martinstown....J4
Maynooth....H9
Mazetown....J5
Middletown....H6
Midleton....F14
Milford....F4
Millstreet....D13
Milltown....C13
Milltown Malbay....C11
Mitchelstown....E13
Moate....F10
Mohill....F7
Monaghan....H6
Monasterevin....G10
Moneygall....F11
Moneymore....H5
Monivea....E9
Mooncoin....G13

112

0   10   20 miles
0   10   20   30 kilometres

Moorfields...............J4
Mountbellew Bridge....E9
Mountcharles...........F5
Mountmellick..........G10
Mountrath.............G10
Mountshannon.........E10
Moville................G3
Moy...................H6
Moynalty..............H8
Moyvore...............F9
Muckross.............C13
Muff..................G4
Mullaghmore...........E6
Mullinavat...........G12
Mullingar.............G9
Mulrany...............C7
Myshall..............H11

Naas..................H10
Naul..................J8
Navan.................H8
Neale.................D8
Nenagh...............E11
Newbliss..............G7
Newbridge............H10
Newcastle.............J6

Newcastle West.......D12
Newinn...............F12
Newmarket............D13
Newmarket-on-
  Fergus.............D11
Newport...............C7
Newport..............E11
New Ross.............H12
Newry.................J6
Newtown..............G11
Newtownabbey.........J5
Newtownards..........K5
Newtownbutler........G7
Newtown Forbes.......F8
Newtownhamilton......H6
Newtown Mount
  Kennedy............J10
Newtownstewart.......G5
Nobber................H8

Ogonnelloe..........E11
Oilgate..............H12
Oldcastle............G8
Omagh................G5
Omeath...............J7
Oola.................E12

Oranmore.............D9
Oughterard...........D9
Ovens................E14

Pallas Green New....E12
Parknasilla..........B14
Partry...............D8
Passage East........H13
Passage West........E14
Patrickswell........E12
Paulstown...........H11
Pettigo..............F5
Plumbridge...........G5
Pomeroy..............H5
Portadown............H6
Portaferry...........K6
Portarlington.......G10
Portavogie...........K6
Portballintrae.......H3
Portglenone..........H4
Portlaoise..........G10
Portmarnock..........J9
Portnoo..............E4
Portraine............J9
Portroe.............E11
Portrush.............H3

Portstewart..........H3
Portumna.............E10
Poulgorm Bridge.....C13
Poyntz Pass..........J6

Raharney.............G9
Randalstown..........J5
Rasharkin............H4
Rathangan...........H10
Rathcoole............J9
Rathcormac..........E13
Rathdowney..........G11
Rathdrum............J10
Rathfriland..........J6
Rathkeale...........D12
Rathmelton...........F4
Rathmolyon..........H9
Rathmore............D13
Rathmullan...........G4
Rathnew.............J10
Rathowen.............G8
Rathvilly...........H11
Ratoath..............J9
Ray..................G4
Recess...............C9
Renvyle..............B8

Ringaskiddy.........E14
Ringville...........G13
Rockcorry............H7
Roosky...............F8
Rosbercon...........H12
Roscommon............F8
Roscrea.............F10
Rosepenna............F3
Ross Carbery........D15
Rosses Point.........E6
Rosslare............J13
Rosslare Harbour...J13
Rosslea.............G6
Rossnowlagh..........F5
Rostrevor............J7
Roundstone...........B9
Roundwood...........J10
Rush.................J9

Saintfield...........K6
St Johnston..........G4
Sallins..............H9
Salthill.............D9
Scarriff............E11
Scartaglin..........C13
Scarva...............J6

Schull..............C15
Scramoge.............F8
Seskinore............G5
Shanagarry..........F14
Shanagolden.........D12
Shankill.............J9
Shannon.............D11
Shannonbridge........F9
Shercock.............H7
Shillelagh..........H11
Shinrone............F10
Shrule...............D9
Silvermines.........E11
Sion Mills..........D11
Sixmilebridge.......D11
Skerries.............J8
Skibbereen..........D15
Slane................H8
Sligo................E6
Smithborough.........G6
Sneem...............B14
Spanish Point.......C11
Spiddal..............D9
Sraith Salach........C9
Stewartstown.........H5
Stillorgan...........J9

Stonyford...........G12
Strabane.............G4
Stradbally..........G10
Stradone.............G7
Straffan.............H9
Strandhill...........E6
Strangford...........K6
Stranorlar...........F5
Strokestown.........F8
Summerhill..........H9
Swanlinbar...........F6
Swatragh.............H4
Swinford.............D7
Swords...............J9

Taghmon.............H12
Tagoat..............J13
Tahilla.............C14
Tallaght.............J9
Tallow..............F13
Tallowbridge........F13
Tandragee............J6
Tang.................F9
Tarbert.............C12
Templemore..........F11
Templetouhy.........F11
Termonfeckin.........J8
Thomastown..........G12
Thurles.............F11
Timahoe.............G10
Timoleague..........D15
Tinahely............J11
Tipperary...........F12

Tobercurry...........E7
Tobermore............H4
Toomyvara...........F11
Toormore............C15
Tralee..............C13
Tramore.............G13
Trim................H8
Tuam.................D9
Tuamgraney..........E11
Tulla...............D11
Tullamore...........G9
Tullow..............H11
Tulsk................E8
Turlough............D7
Tyrrellspass.........G9

Urlingford..........G11

Virginia.............G8

Warrenpoint..........J7
Waterford...........G13
Watergrasshill......E13
Waterville..........B14
Westport.............C8
Wexford.............J12
Whitegate...........E14
Whitehead............K5
Wicklow.............J10
Woodenbridge........J11
Woodford............E10

Youghal.............F14

Restricted junctions

Motorway and Primary Route junctions which have access or exit restrictions are shown on the map pages thus:

M1 London - Leeds

Northbound
Access only from A1
(northbound)

Southbound
Exit only to A1
(southbound)

Northbound
Access only from A41
(northbound)

Southbound
Exit only to A41
(southbound)

Northbound
Access only from M25
(no link from A405)

Southbound
Exit only to M25 (no link
from A405)

Northbound
Access only from A414

Southbound
Exit only to A414

Northbound
Exit only to M45

Southbound
Access only from M45

Northbound
Exit only to M6
(northbound)
No access restrictions

Southbound
Access only from M6
No exit restrictions

Northbound
Exit only, no access

Southbound
Access only, no exit

Northbound
Access only from A42

Southbound
No restriction

Northbound
No exit, access only

Southbound
Exit only, no access

Northbound
Exit only, no access

Southbound
Access only, no exit

Northbound
Exit only to M621

Southbound
Access only from M621

Northbound
Exit only to A1(M)
(northbound)

Southbound
Access only from A1(M)
(southbound)

M2 Rochester - Faversham

Westbound
No exit to A2
(eastbound)

Eastbound
No access from A2
(westbound)

M3 Sunbury - Southampton

Northeastbound
Access only from A303,
no exit

Southwestbound
Exit only to A303,
no access

Northbound
Exit only, no access

Southbound
Access only, no exit

Northeastbound
Access from M27 only.
No exit

Southwestbound
No access to M27
(westbound)

M4 London - South Wales

Westbound
Access only from A4
(westbound)

Eastbound
Exit only to A4
(eastbound)

Westbound
Exit only to M48

Eastbound
Access only from M48

Westbound
Access only from M48

Eastbound
Exit only to M48

Westbound
Exit only, no access

Eastbound
Access only, no exit

Westbound
Exit only, no access

Eastbound
Access only, no exit

Westbound
Exit only to A48(M)

Eastbound
Access only from A48(M)

Westbound
Exit only, no access

Eastbound
No restriction

Westbound
Access only, no exit

Eastbound
No access or exit

M5 Birmingham - Exeter

Northeastbound
Access only, no exit

Southwestbound
Exit only, no access

Northeastbound
Access only from A417
(westbound)

Southwestbound
Exit only to A417
(eastbound)

Northeastbound
Exit only to M49

Southwestbound
Access only from M49

Northeastbound
No access, exit only

Southwestbound
No exit, access only

M6 Toll Motorway

See M6 Toll Motorway map on page 121

M6 Rugby - Carlisle

Northbound
Exit only to M6 Toll

Southbound
Access only from M6 Toll

Northbound
Access only from M42
(southbound)

Southbound
Exit only to M42

Northbound
Exit only, no access

Southbound
Access only, no exit

Northbound
Exit only to M54

Southbound
Access only from M54

Northbound
Access only from M6 Toll

Southbound
Exit only to M6 Toll

Northbound
No restriction

Southbound
Access only from M56
(eastbound)

Northbound
Access only, no exit

Southbound
No restriction

Northbound
Access only, no exit

Southbound
Exit only, no access

Northbound
Exit only, no access

Southbound
Access only, no exit

Northbound
No direct access, use adjacent slip road to jct 29A

Southbound
No direct exit, use adjacent slip road from jct 29A

Northbound
Acces only, no exit

Southbound
Exit only, no access

Northbound
Access only from M61

Southbound
Exit only to M61

Northbound
Exit only, no access

Southbound
Access only, no exit

Northbound
Exit only, no access

Southbound
Access only, no exit

M8 Edinburgh - Bishopton

See Glasgow District map on pages 138-139

M9 Edinburgh - Dunblane

Northwestbound
Access only, no exit

Southeastbound
Exit only, no access

Northwestbound
Exit only, no access

Southeastbound
Access only, no exit

Northwestbound
Access only, no exit

Southeastbound
Exit only to A905

Northwestbound
Exit only to M876 (southwestbound)

Southeastbound
Access only from M876 (northeastbound)

M11 London - Cambridge

Northbound
Access only from A406 (eastbound)

Southbound
Exit only to A406

Northbound
Exit only, no access

Southbound
Access only, no exit

Northbound
Exit only to A11

Southbound
Access only from A11

Northbound
Exit only, no access

Southbound
Access only, no exit

Northbound
Exit only, no access

Southbound
Access only, no exit

M20 Swanley - Folkestone

Northwestbound
Staggered junction; follow signs - access only

Southeastbound
Staggered junction; follow signs - exit only

Northwestbound
Exit only to M26 (westbound)

Southeastbound
Access only from M26 (eastbound)

Northwestbound
Access only from A20

Southeastbound
For access follow signs - exit only to A20

Northwestbound
No restriction

Southeastbound
For exit follow signs

Northwestbound
Access only, no exit

Southeastbound
Exit only, no access

M23 Hooley - Crawley

Northbound
Exit only to A23 (northbound)

Southbound
Access only from A23 (southbound)

Northbound
Access only, no exit

Southbound
Exit only, no access

M25 London Orbital Motorway

See M25 London Orbital Motorway map on page 120

M26 Sevenoaks - Wrotham

Westbound
Exit only to clockwise M25 (westbound)

Eastbound
Access only from anti-clockwise M25 (eastbound)

Westbound
Access only from M20 (northwestbound)

Eastbound
Exit only to M20 (southeastbound)

M27 Cadnam - Portsmouth

Westbound
Staggered junction; follow signs - access only from M3 (southbound). Exit only to M3 (northbound)

Eastbound
Staggered junction; follow signs - access only from M3 (southbound). Exit only to M3 (northbound)

Westbound
Exit only, no access

Eastbound
Access only, no exit

Westbound
Staggered junction; follow signs - exit only to M275 (southbound)

Eastbound
Staggered junction; follow signs - access only from M275 (northbound)

M40 London - Birmingham

Northwestbound
Exit only, no access

Southeastbound
Access only, no exit

Northwestbound
Exit only, no access

Southeastbound
Access only, no exit

Northwestbound
Exit only to M40/A40

Southeastbound
Access only from M40/A40

Northwestbound
Exit only, no access

Southeastbound
Access only, no exit

Northwestbound
Access only, no exit

Southeastbound
Exit only, no access

Northwestbound
Access only, no exit

Southeastbound
Exit only, no access

M42 Bromsgrove - Measham

See Birmingham District map on pages 136-137

M45 Coventry - M1

Westbound
Access only from A45 (northbound)

Eastbound
Exit only, no access

Westbound
Access only from M1 (northbound)

Eastbound
Exit only to M1 (southbound)

M53 Mersey Tunnel - Chester

Northbound
Access only from M56 (westbound). Exit only to M56 (eastbound)

Southbound
Access only from M56 (westbound). Exit only to M56 (eastbound)

M54 Telford

Westbound
Access only from M6 (northbound)

Eastbound
Exit only to M6 (southbound)

M56 North Cheshire

For junctions 1,2,3,4 & 7 see Manchester District map on pages 140-141

Westbound
Access only, no exit

Eastbound
No access or exit

Westbound
Exit only to M53

Eastbound
Access only from M53

Westbound
No access or exit

Eastbound
No restriction

M57 Liverpool Outer Ring Road

Northwestbound
Access only, no exit

Southeastbound
Exit only, no access

Northwestbound
Access only from A580 (westbound)

Southeastbound
Exit only, no access

M58 Liverpool - Wigan

Westbound
Exit only, no access

Eastbound
Access only, no exit

M60 Manchester Orbital

See Manchester District map on pages 140-141

M61 Manchester - Preston

Northwestbound
No access or exit

Southeastbound
Exit only, no access

Northwestbound
Exit only to M6 (northbound)

Southeastbound
Access only from M6 (southbound)

M62 Liverpool - Kingston upon Hull

Westbound
Access only, no exit

Eastbound
Exit only, no access

Westbound
No access to A1(M) (southbound)

Eastbound
No restriction

M65 Preston - Colne

Northeastbound
Exit only, no access

Southwestbound
Access only, no exit

Northeastbound
Access only, no exit

Southwestbound
Exit only, no access

M66 Bury

Northbound
Exit only to A56 (northbound)

Southbound
Access only from A56 (southbound)

Northbound
Exit only, no access

Southbound
Access only, no exit

M67 Hyde Bypass

Westbound
Access only, no exit

Eastbound
Exit only, no access

Westbound
Exit only, no access

Eastbound
Access only, no exit

Westbound
Exit only, no access

Eastbound
No restriction

M69 Coventry - Leicester

Northbound
Access only, no exit

Southbound
Exit only, no access

M73 East of Glasgow

Northbound
No access from or exit to A89. No access from M8 (eastbound)

Southbound
No access from or exit to A89. No exit to M8 (westbound)

M74 and A74(M) Glasgow - Gretna

Northbound
Exit only, no access

Southbound
Access only, no exit

Northbound
Access only, no exit

Southbound
Exit only, no access

Northbound
Access only, no exit

Southbound
Exit only, no access

Northbound
No access or exit

Southbound
Exit only, no access

Northbound
No restriction

Southbound
Access only, no exit

Northbound
Access only, no exit

Southbound
Exit only, no access

Northbound
Exit only, no access

Southbound
Access only, no exit

Northbound
Exit only, no access

Southbound
Access only, no exit

M77 South of Glasgow

Northbound
No exit to M8 (westbound)

Southbound
No access from M8 (eastbound)

Northbound
Access only, no exit

Southbound
Exit only, no access

Northbound
Access only, no exit

Southbound
Exit only, no access

Northbound
Access only, no exit

Southbound
No restriction

M80 Glasgow - Stirling

For junctions 1 & 4 see Glasgow District map on pages 138-139

Northbound
Exit only, no access

Southbound
Access only, no exit

Northbound
Access only, no exit

Southbound
Exit only, no access

Northbound
Exit only to M876 (northeastbound)

Southbound
Access only from M876 (southwestbound)

M90 Forth Road Bridge - Perth

Northbound
Exit only to A92 (eastbound)

Southbound
Access only from A92 (westbound)

Northbound
Access only, no exit

Southbound
Exit only, no access

Northbound
Exit only, no access

Southbound
Access only, no exit

Northbound
No access from A912
No exit to A912 (southbound)
No access from A912 (northbound).
No exit to A912

M180 Doncaster - Grimsby

Westbound
Access only, no exit

Eastbound
Exit only, no access

M606 Bradford Spur

Northbound
Exit only, no access

Southbound
No restriction

M621 Leeds - M1

Clockwise
Access only, no exit

Anticlockwise
Exit only, no access

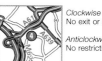
Clockwise
No exit or access

Anticlockwise
No restriction

Clockwise
Access only, no exit

Anticlockwise
Exit only, no access

Clockwise
Exit only, no access

Anticlockwise
Access only, no exit

Clockwise
Exit only to M1 (southbound)

Anticlockwise
Access only from M1 (northbound)

M876 Bonnybridge - Kincardine Bridge

Northeastbound
Access only from M80 (northbound)

Southwestbound
Exit only to M80 (southbound)

Northeastbound
Exit only to M9 (eastbound)

Southwestbound
Access only from M9 (westbound)

A1(M) South Mimms - Baldock

Northbound
Exit only, no access

Southbound
Access only, no exit

Northbound
No restriction

Southbound
Exit only, no access

Northbound
Access only, no exit

Southbound
No access or exit

A1(M) Pontefract - Bedale

Northbound
No access to M62 (eastbound)

Southbound
No restriction

Northbound
Access only from M1 (northbound)

Southbound
Exit only to M1 (southbound)

A1(M) Scotch Corner - Newcastle upon Tyne

Northbound
Exit only to A66(M) (eastbound)

Southbound
Access only from A66(M) (westbound)

Northbound
No access. Exit only to A194(M) & A1 (northbound)

Southbound
No exit. Access only from A194(M) & A1 (southbound)

A3(M) Horndean - Havant

Northbound
Access only from A3

Southbound
Exit only to A3

Northbound
Exit only, no access

Southbound
Access only, no exit

A48(M) Cardiff Spur

Westbound
Access only from M4 (westbound)

Eastbound
Exit only to M4 (eastbound)

Westbound
Exit only to A48 (westbound)

Eastbound
Access only from A48 (eastbound)

A66(M) Darlington Spur

Westbound
Exit only to A1(M) (southbound)

Eastbound
Access only from A1(M) (northbound)

A194(M) Newcastle upon Tyne

Northbound
Access only from A1(M) (northbound)

Southbound
Exit only to A1(M) (southbound)

A12 M25 - Ipswich

Northeastbound
Access only, no exit

Southwestbound
No restriction

Northeastbound
Exit only, no access

Southwestbound
Access only, no exit

Northeastbound
Exit only, no access

Southwestbound
Access only, no exit

Northeastbound
Access only, no exit

Southwestbound
Exit only, no access

Northeastbound
No restriction

Southwestbound
Access only, no exit

Northeastbound
Exit only, no access

Southwestbound
Access only, no exit

Northeastbound
Access only, no exit

Southwestbound
Exit only, no access

Northeastbound
Exit only, no access

Southwestbound
Access only, no exit

Northeastbound
Exit only (for Stratford St Mary and Dedham)

Southwestbound
Access only

A14 M1 Felixstowe

Westbound
Exit only to M6 & M1 (northbound)

Eastbound
Access only from M6 & M1 (southbound)

Westbound
Exit only, no access

Eastbound
Access only, no exit

Westbound
Access only from A1307

Eastbound
Exit only to A1307

Westbound
Access only, no exit

Eastbound
Exit only, no access

Westbound
Exit only to A11 Access only from A1303

Eastbound
Access only from A11

Westbound
Access only from A11

Eastbound
Exit only to A11

Westbound
Exit only, no access

Eastbound
Exit only, no access

Westbound
Access only, no exit

Eastbound
Exit only, no access

A55 Holyhead - Chester

Westbound
Exit only, no access

Eastbound
Access only, no exit

Westbound
Access only, no exit

Eastbound
Exit only, no access

Westbound
Exit only, no access

Eastbound
No access or exit.

Westbound
Exit only, no access

Eastbound
No access or exit

Westbound
Exit only, no access

Eastbound
Access only, no exit

Westbound
Exit only to A5104

Eastbound
Access only from A5104

M25 London Orbital motorway

Refer also to atlas pages 20–21

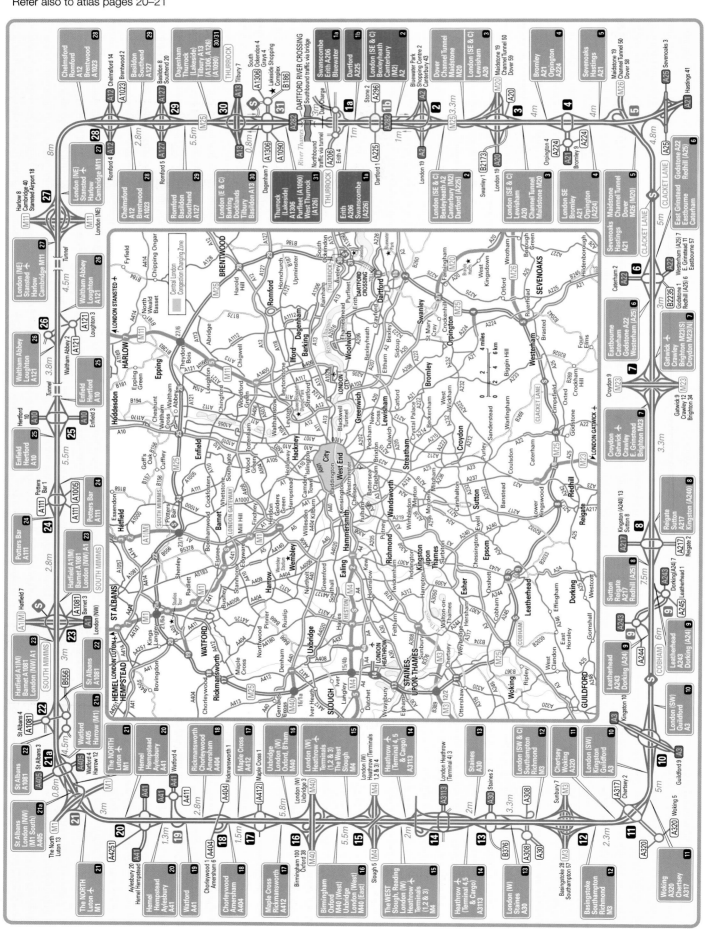

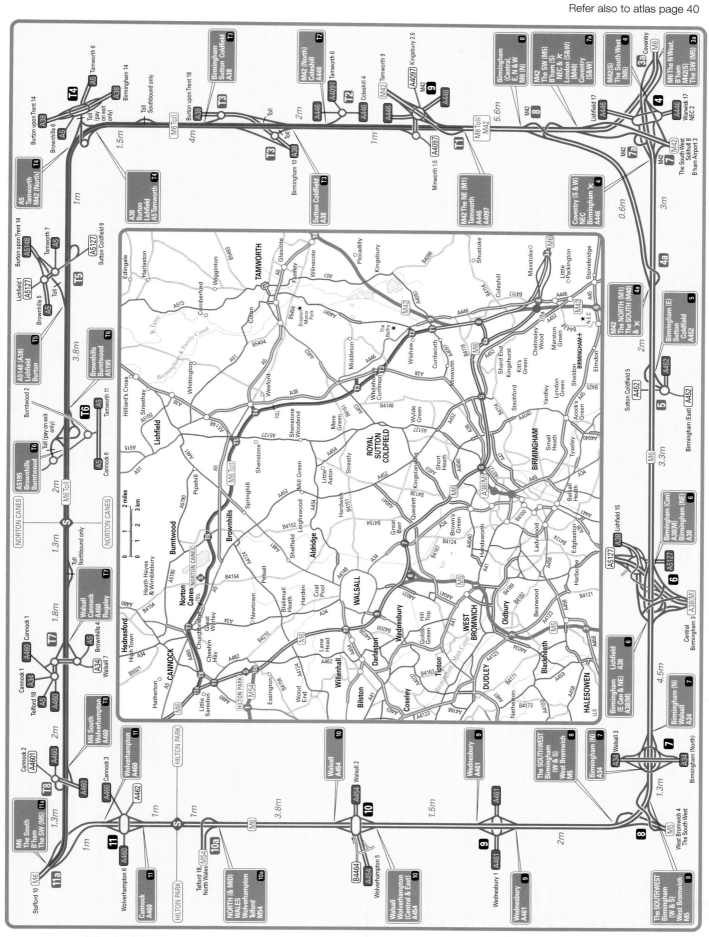

Street map symbols

Town and port plans

Motorway and junction	One-way, gated/ closed road	Railway station	P Car park
Primary road single/dual carriageway	Restricted access road	Light rapid transit system station	Park and Ride (at least 6 days per week)
A road single/ dual carriageway	Pedestrian area	Level crossing	Bus/coach station
B road single/ dual carriageway	Footpath	Tramway	H Hospital
Local road single/ dual carriageway	Road under construction	Ferry route	H 24-hour Accident & Emergency hospital
Other road single/ dual carriageway, minor road	Road tunnel	Airport, heliport	Petrol station, 24 hour Major suppliers only
Building of interest	Museum	Railair terminal	City wall
Ruined building	Castle	Theatre or performing arts centre	Escarpment
Tourist Information Centre	Castle mound	Cinema	Cliff lift
Visitor or heritage centre	Monument, statue	Abbey, chapel, church	River/canal, lake
World Heritage Site (UNESCO)	Post Office	Synagogue	Lock, weir
English Heritage site	Public library	Mosque	Park/sports ground
Historic Scotland site	Shopping centre	Golf Course	Cemetery
Cadw (Welsh heritage) site	Shopmobility	Racecourse	Woodland
National Trust site	Viewpoint	Nature reserve	Built-up area
National Trust Scotland site	Toilet, with facilities for the less able	Aquarium	Beach

Central London street map (see pages 148 – 157)

30 Safety camera site (fixed location) with speed limit in mph	London Underground station	Docklands Light Railway (DLR) station
40 Section of road with two or more fixed camera sites; speed limit in mph	London Overground station	Central London Congestion Charging Zone
50 → ← 50 Average speed (SPECS™) camera system with speed limit in mph	Rail interchange	

Royal Parks

Green Park	Park open 24 hours. Constitution Hill and The Mall closed to traffic Sundays and public holidays
Hyde Park	Park open 5am – midnight. Park roads closed to traffic midnight – 5am.
Kensington Gardens	Park open 6am – dusk.
Regent's Park	Park open 5am – dusk. Park roads closed to traffic midnight – 7am.
St James's Park	Park open 5am – midnight. The Mall closed to traffic Sundays and public holidays.

Traffic regulations in the City of London include security checkpoints and restrict the number of entry and exit points.

Note: Oxford Street is closed to through-traffic (except buses & taxis) 7am-7pm Monday-Saturday.

Central London Congestion Charging Zone

The daily charge for driving or parking a vehicle on public roads in the Congestion Charging Zone (CCZ), during operating hours, is £11.50 per vehicle per day in advance or on the day of travel. Alternatively you can pay £10.50 by registering with CC Auto Pay, an automated payment system. Drivers can also pay the next charging day after travelling in the zone but this will cost £14. Payment permits entry, travel within and exit from the CCZ by the vehicle as often as required on that day.

The CCZ operates between 7am and 6pm, Mon–Fri only. There is no charge at weekends, on public holidays or between 25th Dec and 1st Jan inclusive.

For up to date information on the CCZ, exemptions, discounts or ways to pay, telephone 0343 222 2222, visit tfl.gov.uk/modes/driving/congestion-charge or write to Congestion Charging, P.O. Box 4782, Worthing BN11 9PS. Textphone users can call 020 7649 9123.

Central London

Basingstoke
Bath

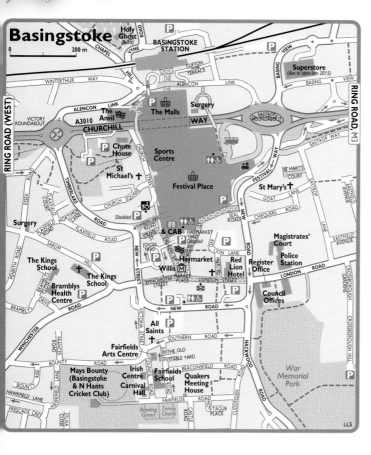

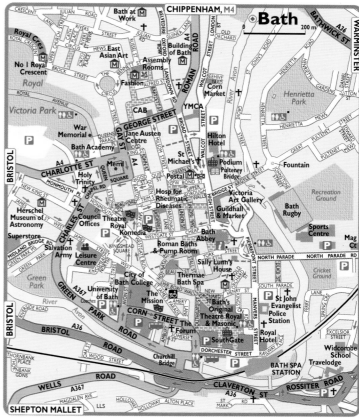

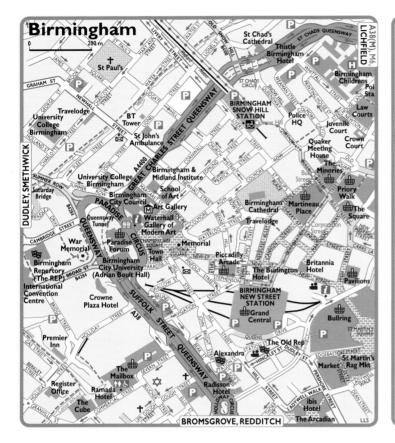

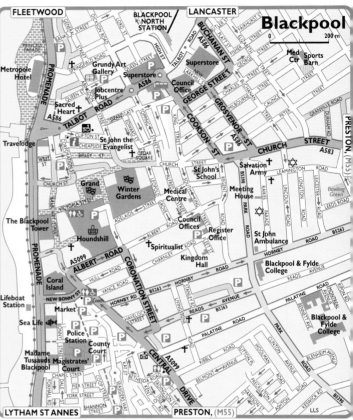

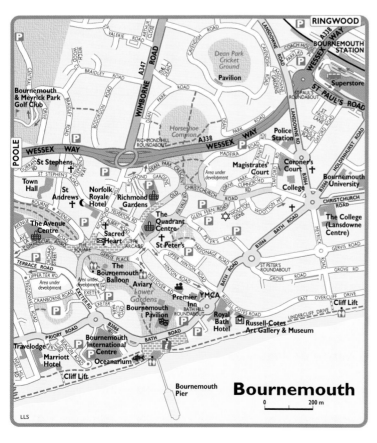

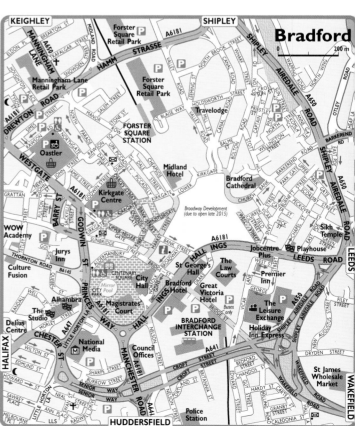

Brighton

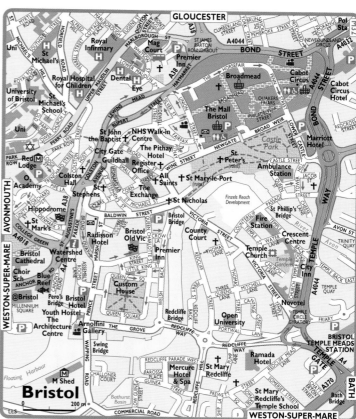

Bristol

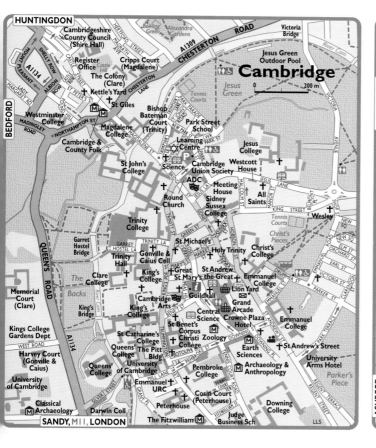

Cambridge

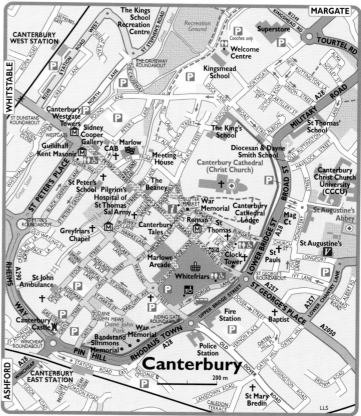

Canterbury

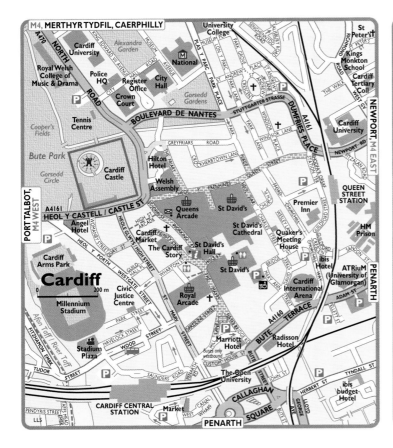

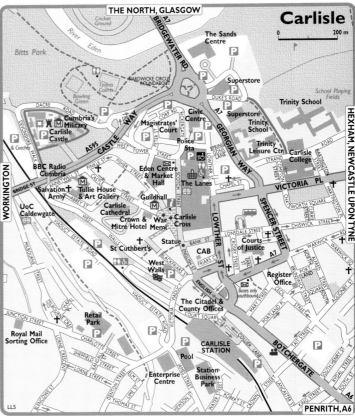

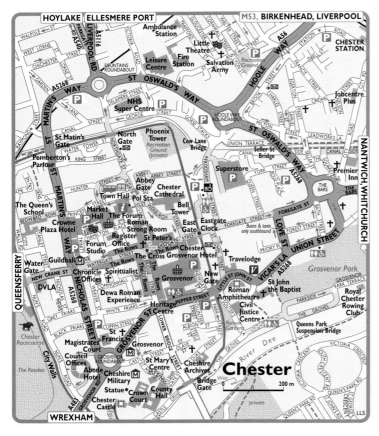

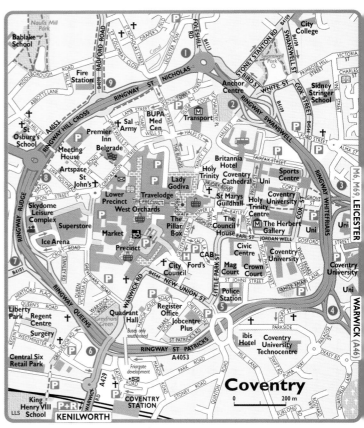

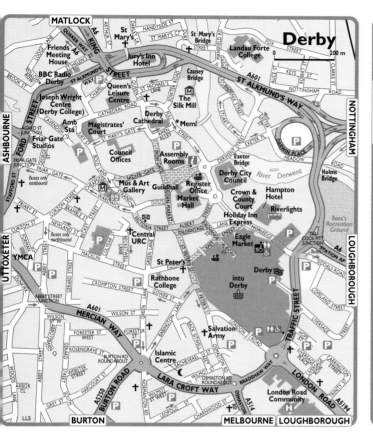

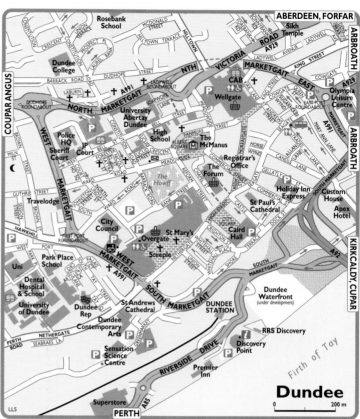

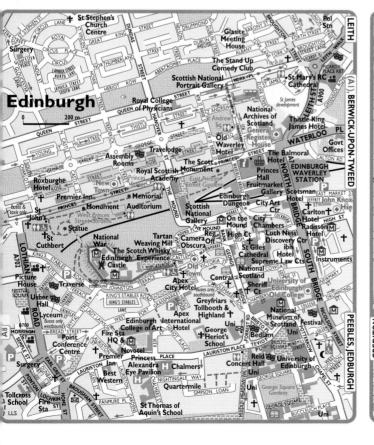

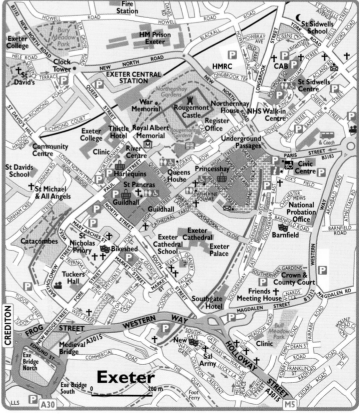

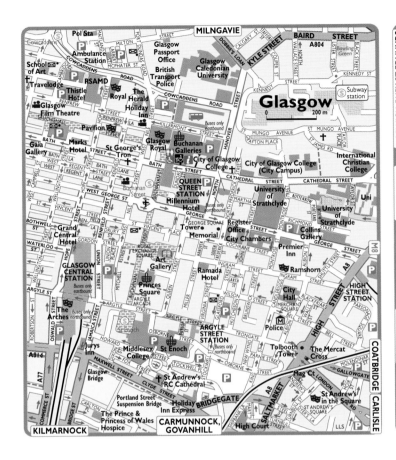

Glasgow

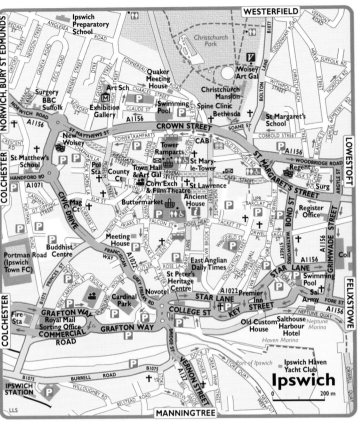

Ipswich

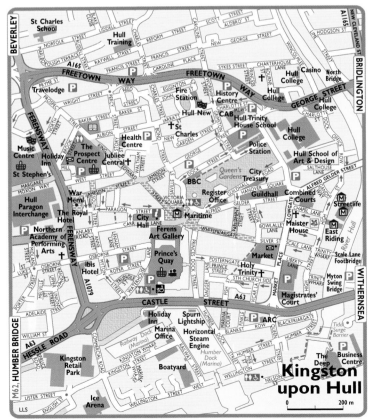

Kingston upon Hull

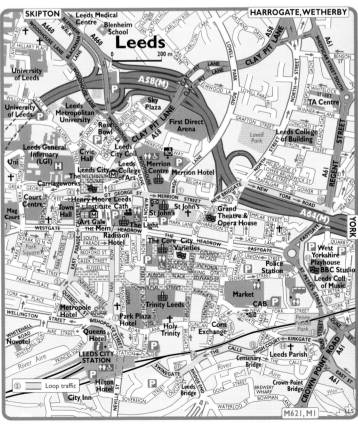

Leeds

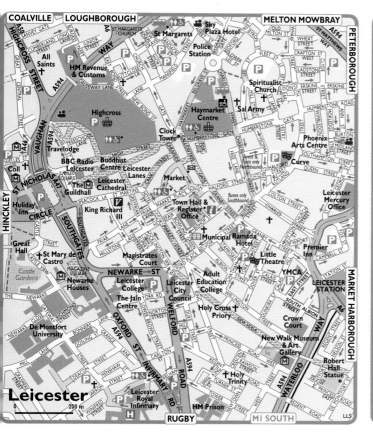

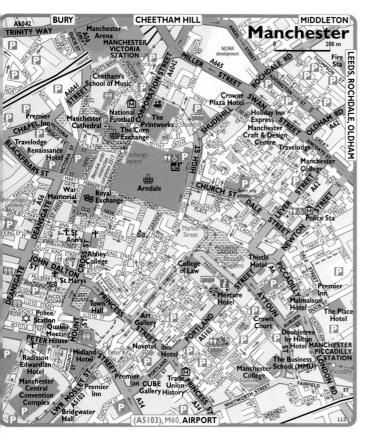

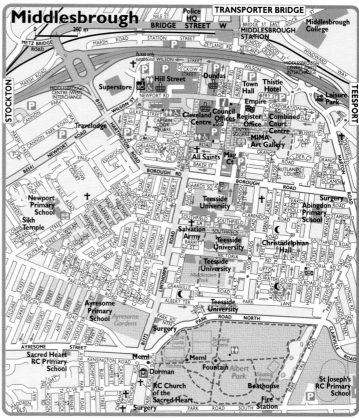

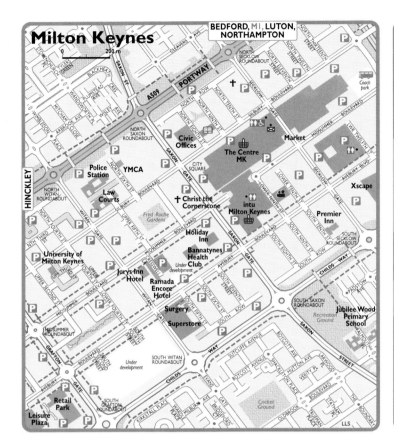

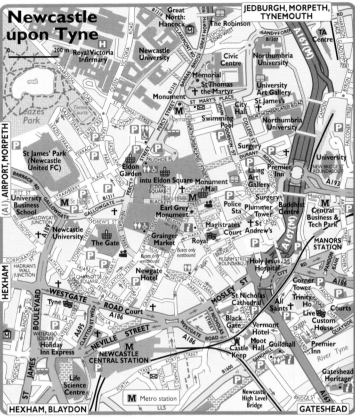

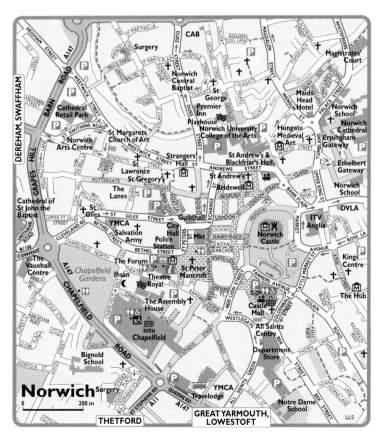

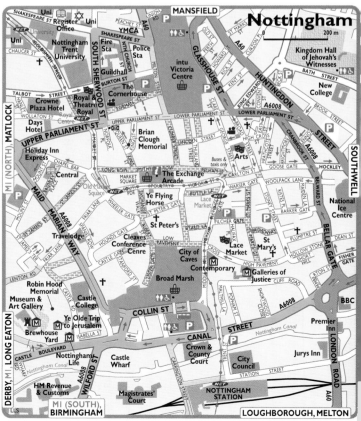

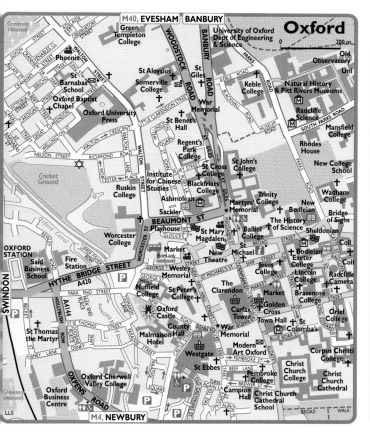

Oxford

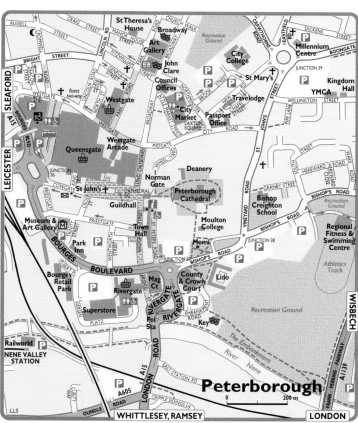

Peterborough

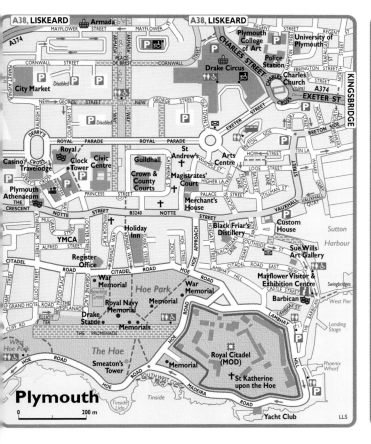

Plymouth

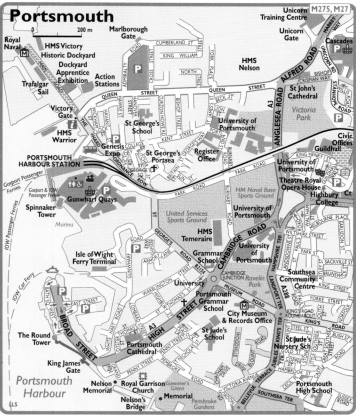

Portsmouth

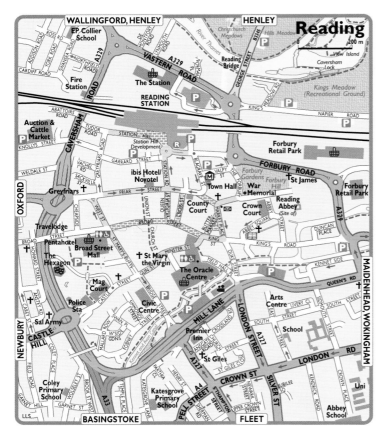

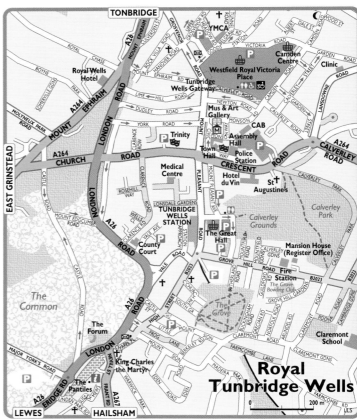

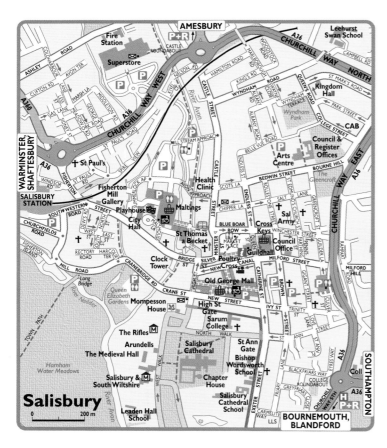

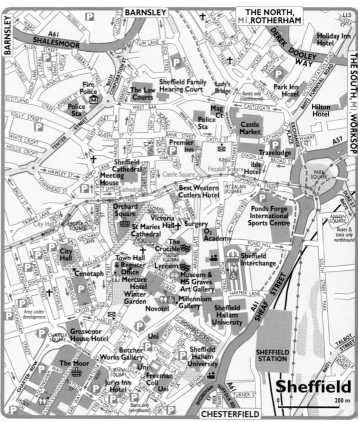

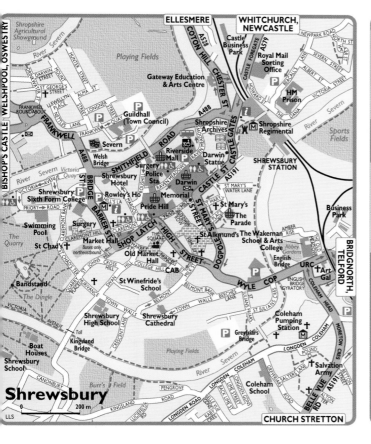

Shrewsbury

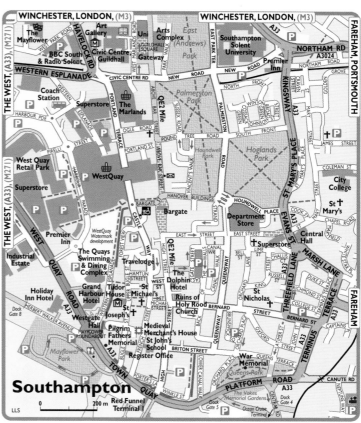

Southampton

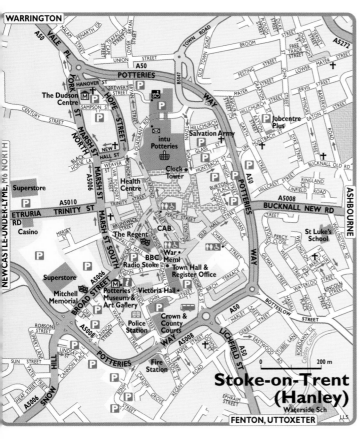

Stoke-on-Trent (Hanley)

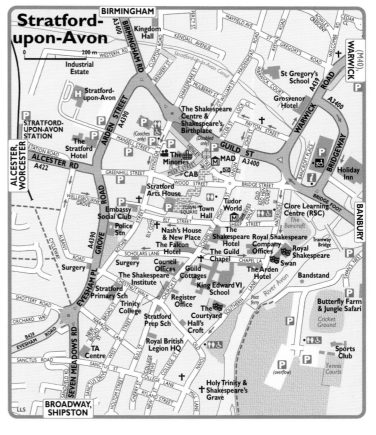

Stratford-upon-Avon

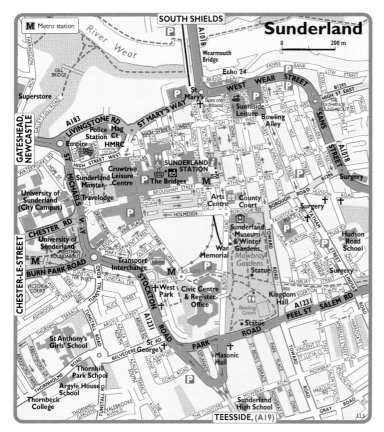

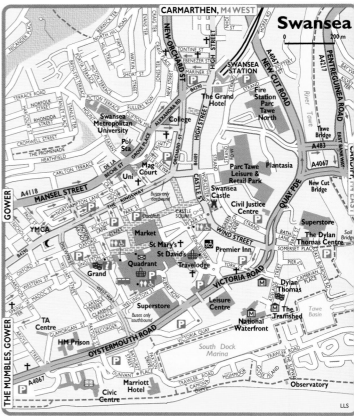

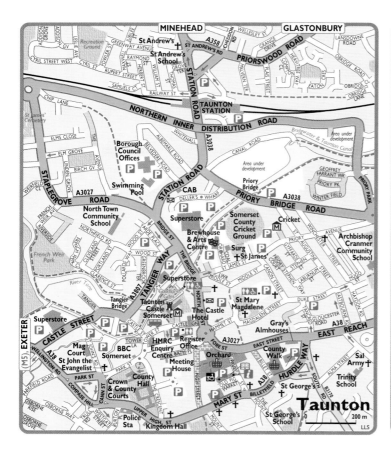

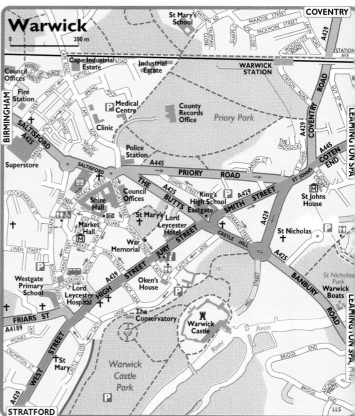

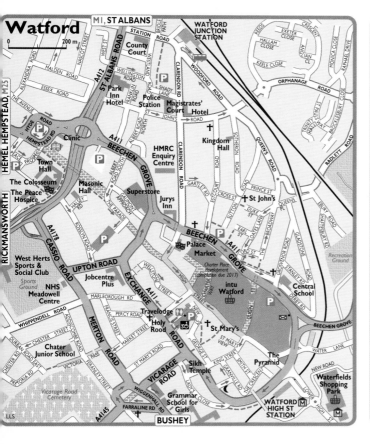

Watford

MI, ST ALBANS

0   200 m

Winchester

ANDOVER, NEWBURY   BASINGSTOKE

0   200 m

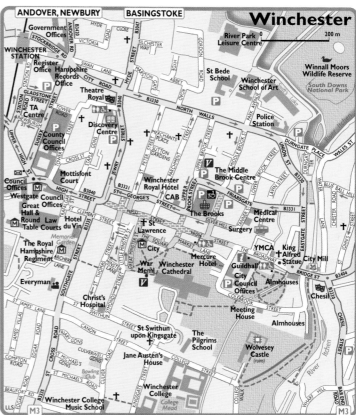

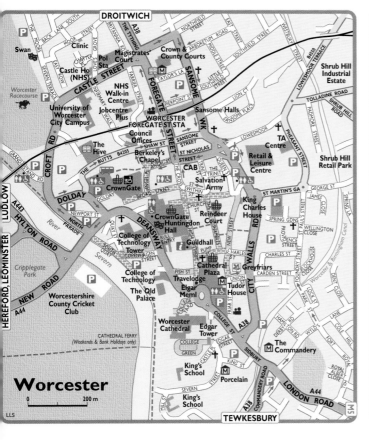

Worcester

DROITWICH

0   200 m

TEWKESBURY

York

THIRSK   HELMSLEY   SCARBOROUGH

0   200 m

LEEDS, HARROGATE

SELBY

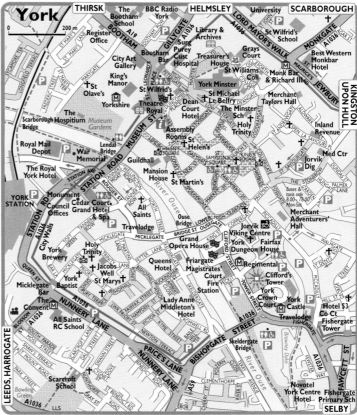

NORTH SEA

WHITLEY BAY
Seaton Delaval
St Mary's Lighthouse
St Mary's Island
Whitley Bay C
Bates Cottages
Holywell
East Holywell
Earsdon
Monkseaton
Shiremoor
WEST MONKSEATON
West Monkseaton
Murton
SHIREMOOR STATION
BACKWORTH
West Allotment
New York
MONKSEATON
CULLERCOATS
Marden
Cullercoats
Blue Reef
Marden Park Nature Reserve
North Tyneside General
TYNEMOUTH
Billy Mill
Tynemouth C
Prestone
Stephenson Railway Museum
West Chirton
NORTH SHIELDS
Tynemouth Priory & Castle
Willington Square
SILVERLINK ROUNDABOUT
HOWDON INTERCHANGE
WATERVILLE ROAD
Holy Cross
Willington
Howdon
MEADOW WELL
Arbeia Roman Fort & Museum
The Law
PERCY MAIN
PERCY MAIN VILLAGE
SOUTH SHIELDS
Amsterdam (IJmuiden)
Willington Quay
East Howdon
Royal Quays
International Passenger Terminal
Mill Dam
Westoe
CHICHESTER
Point Pleasant
Segedunum Roman Fort & Baths
River Tyne
Tyne Tunnel
Tyne Dock
Howbray Road
Grosvenor
Highfield Road
Marsden Rock
JARROW
Bede's World
St Paul's Monastery
Tyne Dock
Cauldwell
Harton
Marsden
Marsden Bay
Hebburn-Jarrow Colliery
East Jarrow
BEDE
Simonside
Harton Nook
South Tyneside General
Cleadon Park
Souter Lighthouse & The Leas
Hebburn New Town
HEBBURN
Monkton
Primrose
West Harton
Whiteleas
Brockley Whins
South Shields C
Biddick Hall
Cleadon
Whitburn
Hedworth
FELLGATE
Boldon Colliery
West Boldon
East Boldon
Cleadon
Fellgate
Wardley
East Boldon
South Bents
Folingsby
TESTOS ROUNDABOUT
NEWCASTLE ROAD
Downhill
Fulwell
Seaburn
A194(M)
Witherwack
Carley Hill
Roker
Marley Pots
High Southwick
SEABURN
Sunderland Harbour
Downhill
Hylton Castle
Castletown
Southwick
Monkwearmouth
STADIUM OF LIGHT
Sunderland Harbour
National Glass Centre
Usworth
Hylton Plantation
Low Southwick
Deptford
Stadium of Light (Sunderland AFC)
Concord
Sulgrave
Queen Alexandra Bridge
Ayre's Quay
ST PETER'S
Albany Hertburn
South Hylton
Pallion
Millfield
Bishopwearmouth
Washington Old Hall
WWT Washington Wetland Centre
SOUTH HYLTON
Ford
Sunderland Royal
MILLFIELD
SUNDERLAND
Washington Village
Barmston
Teal Farm
Pennywell
Sunderland C
UNIVERSITY
PARK LANE
Biddick
Columbia
High Barnes
SUNDERLAND
Barnes Park
Ashbrooke
Hendon
Sunderland Eye Infirmary
The Princess Anne Park
Fatfield
Mount Pleasant
Springwell
Humbledon
Hillview
Grangetown
Penshaw Monument
Herrington Country Park
Hastings Hill
Grindon
Thorney Close
Plains Farm
Silksworth Sports Complex & Ski Centre
Penshaw
Shiney Row
New Herrington
Middle Herrington
East Herrington
Farringdon
New Silksworth
Silksworth

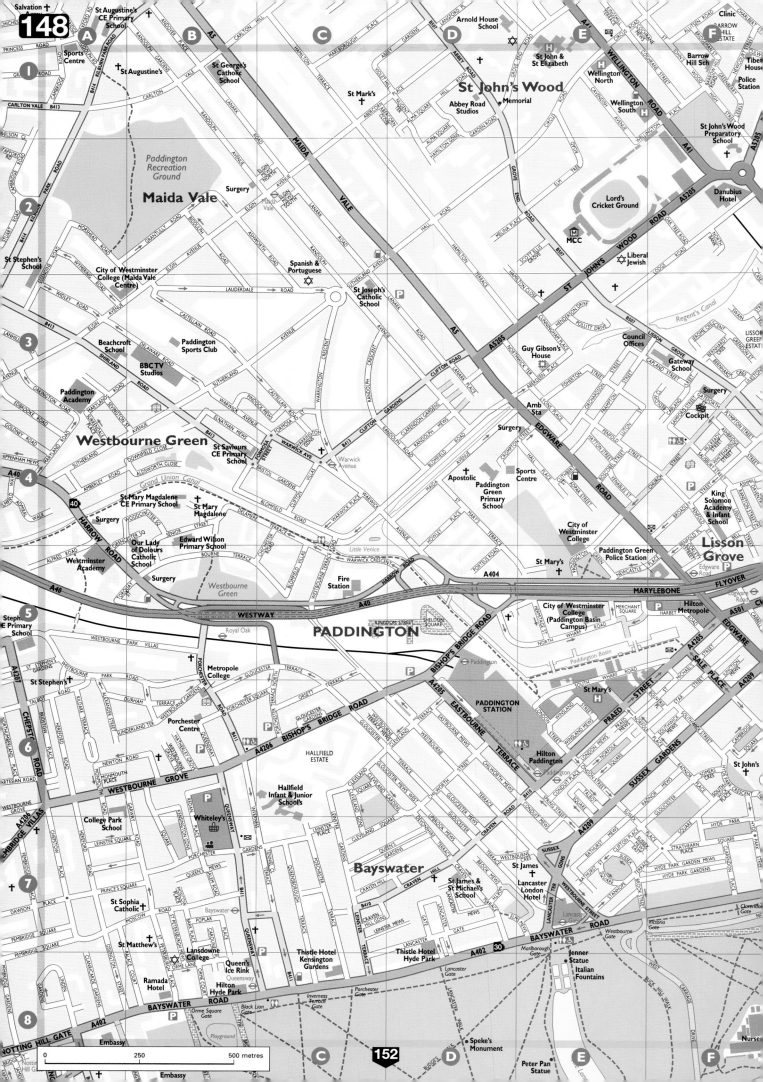

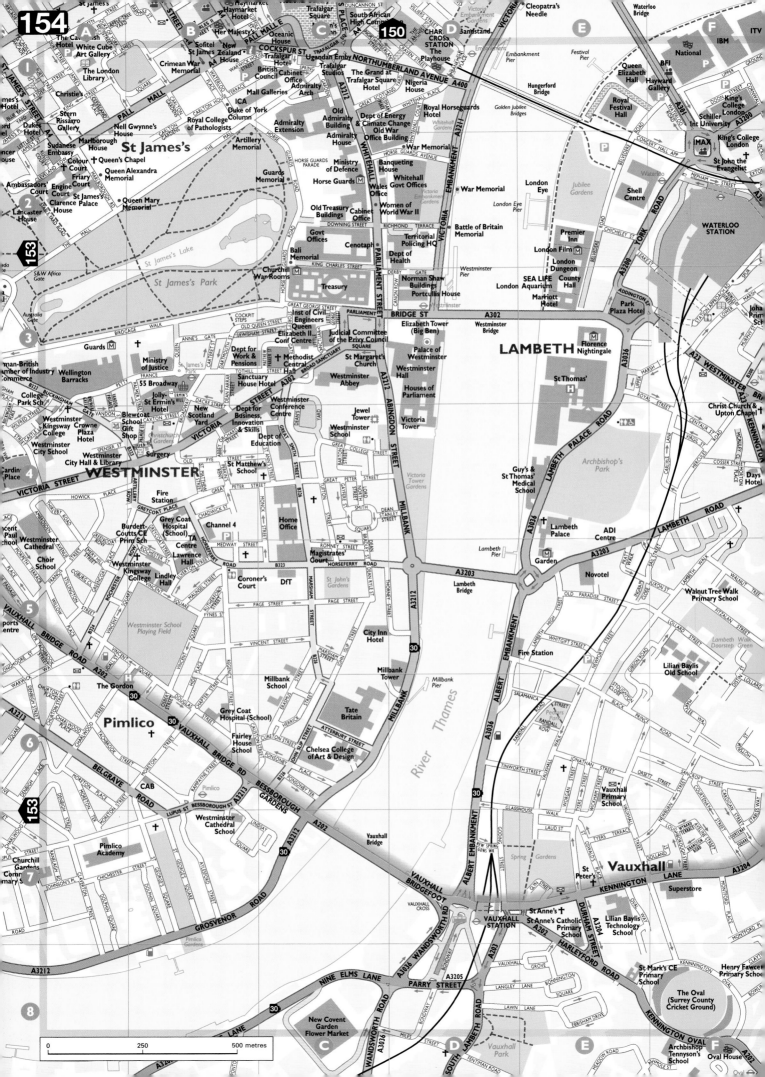

Central London index

This index lists street and station names, and top places of tourist interest shown in **red**. Names are listed in alphabetical order and written in full, but may be abbreviated on the map. Each entry is followed by its Postcode District and then the page number and grid reference to the square in which the name is found. Names are asterisked (*) in the index where there is insufficient space to show them on the map.

A

Abbey Gardens NW8 ..... 148 C1
Abbey Orchard Street SW1P 154 B4
Abbey Road NW8 ..... 148 D1
Abbey Street SE1 ..... 156 B7
Abchurch Lane EC4N 151 L7
Abercorn Close NW8 ..... 148 C1
Abercorn Place NW8 ..... 148 C1
Aberdeen Place NW8 ..... 148 E3
Aberdour Street SE1 ..... 155 M5
Abingdon Road W8 ..... 152 A4
Abingdon Street SW1P 154 C3
Abingdon Villas W8 ..... 152 A4
Ackroyd Drive E3 ..... 157 L1
Acorn Walk SE16 ..... 157 K5
Acton Street WC1X 150 E2
Adam and Eve Mews W8 ..... 152 A3
Adam's Row W1K 149 K8
Adam Street WC2N 150 D8
Addle Hill EC4V 151 H7
Adelina Grove E1 ..... 156 F1
Adeline Place WC1B 150 B5
Adler Street E1 ..... 156 D2
Admiral Place SE16 ..... 157 K5
Admiral Walk W9 ..... 148 A4
Adpar Street W2 ..... 148 E4
Agar Street WC2N 150 D8
Agdon Street EC1V 151 H3
Agnes Street E14 ..... 157 L2
Ainsty Street SE16 ..... 157 G6
Air Street W1B 150 A8
Alaska Street SE1 ..... 154 F2
Albany Road SE5 ..... 155 L8
Albany Street NW1 ..... 149 L1
Albemarle Street W1S 149 M8
Albemarle Way EC1V 151 H4
Alberta Street SE17 ..... 155 H6
Albert Bridge SW3 ..... 153 G8
Albert Embankment SE1 ..... 154 D7
Albert Gardens E1 ..... 157 H3
Albert Gate SW1X 153 H2
Albert Place W8 ..... 152 C3
Albion Gate W2 ..... 149 G7
Albion Place EC1M 151 H4
Albion Street SE16 ..... 157 G7
Albion Street W2 ..... 149 G7
Aldenham Street NW1 ..... 150 A1
Aldermanbury EC2V 151 K6
Alderney Mews SE1 ..... 155 K4
Alderney Street SW1V 153 L6
Aldersgate Street EC1A 151 J4
Aldford Street W1K 149 J8
Aldgate EC3M 156 B3
Aldgate ⊖ EC3N 156 B3
Aldgate East ⊖ E1 ..... 156 C2
Aldgate High Street EC3N 156 B3
Aldsworth Close W9 ..... 148 B4
Aldwych WC2E 150 E7
Alexander Place SW7 ..... 152 F5
Alexander Street W2 ..... 148 A6
Alexandra Gate SW7 ..... 152 E3
Alfred Mews WC1E 150 B4
Alfred Place WC1E 150 B4
Alfred Road W2 ..... 148 A5
Alice Street SE1 ..... 155 M4
Alie Street E1 ..... 156 C3
Allen Street W8 ..... 152 A4
Allhallows Lane EC4R 151 L8
Allington Street SW1E 153 L4
Allitsen Road NW8 ..... 148 F1
Allsop Place NW1 ..... 149 H4
Alma Square NW8 ..... 148 D1
Alpha Place SW3 ..... 153 G8
Alsace Road SE17 ..... 155 M7
Alscot Road SE1 ..... 156 C6
Alvey Street SE17 ..... 155 M6
Ambergate Street SE17 ..... 155 H7
Amberley Road W9 ..... 148 A4
Ambrosden Avenue SW1P 154 A4
Amelia Street SE17 ..... 155 J6
America Square EC3N 156 B3
America Street SE1 ..... 155 J2
Ampton Street WC1X 150 E2
Amwell Street EC1R 150 F2
Anchorage Point E14 ..... 157 M6
Andover Place NW6 ..... 148 B1
Angel ⊖ N1 ..... 151 G1
Angel Junction N1 ..... 151 G1
Angel Lane EC4R 151 L8
Angel Street EC1A 151 J6
Ann Moss Way SE16 ..... 156 F8
Ann's Close SW1X 153 J3
Ansdell Street W8 ..... 152 B4
Antill Terrace E1 ..... 157 H2
Antizan Street E1 ..... 156 B2
Apple Tree Yard SW1Y 150 A8
Appold Street EC2A 151 M4
Apsley Gate W1J 153 J2
Apsley House & Wellington
   Museum W1J 153 K2
Aquinas Street SE1 ..... 155 G1
Arbour Square E1 ..... 157 H3
Archangels SE16 ..... 157 J7
Archer Street W1B 150 B7
Arch Street SE1 ..... 155 J4
Arden Estate N1 ..... 151 M1
Argyle Square WC1H 150 D2
Argyle Street WC1H 150 D2
Argyll Road W8 ..... 152 A3
Argyll Street W1F 149 M6
Arlington Street SW1A 153 M1
Arlington Way EC1R 151 G2
Arne Street WC2H 150 D6
Arnhem Place E14 ..... 157 M8
Arnold Estate SE1 ..... 156 C7
Arnside Street SE17 ..... 155 K8

Artesian Road W11 ..... 148 A6
Arthur Street EC4V 151 L7
Artichoke Hill E1W 156 E4
Artillery Lane E1 ..... 156 A1
Artillery Row SW1P 154 B4
Arundel Street WC2R 150 F7
Ashbridge Street NW8 ..... 148 F4
Ashburn Gardens SW7 ..... 152 C5
Ashburn Place SW7 ..... 152 C5
Ashby Street EC1V 151 H2
Ashfield Street E1 ..... 156 E2
Ashford Street N1 ..... 151 M2
Ashley Place SW1P 153 M4
Ashmill Street NW1 ..... 148 F4
Ashmole Street SW8 ..... 154 F8
Ashworth Road W9 ..... 148 B2
Assam Street E1 ..... 156 C2
Assembly Place E1 ..... 157 G1
Astell Street SW3 ..... 153 G6
Aston Street E14 ..... 157 K1
Astwood Mews SW7 ..... 152 C5
Atherstone Mews SW7 ..... 152 D5
Atterbury Street SW1P 154 C6
Attneave Street WC1X 150 F3
Augustus Street NW1 ..... 149 L1
Aulton Place SE11 ..... 155 G7
Austin Friars EC2N 151 L6
Australia Gate SW1A 153 M3
Austral Street SE11 ..... 155 H5
Aveline Street SE11 ..... 154 F7
Ave Maria Lane EC1A 151 H6
Avenue Dock Hill SE16 ..... 157 J6
Avery Farm Row SW1W 153 K6
Avery Row W1K 149 L7
Aybrook Street W1U 149 J5
Aylesbury Road SE17 ..... 155 L7
Aylesbury Street EC1R 151 H4
Aylesford Street SW1V 154 B7
Aylward Street E1 ..... 157 G2
Ayres Street SE1 ..... 155 K2

B

Babmaes Street SW1Y 150 B8
Bache's Street N1 ..... 151 L2
Back Church Lane E1 ..... 156 D3
Back Hill EC1R 151 G4
Bacon Grove SE1 ..... 156 B8
Bainbridge Street WC1A 150 C6
Bakers Mews W1U 149 J6
Baker's Row EC1R 151 G4
Baker Street NW1 ..... 149 H4
Baker Street W1U 149 H4
Baker Street ⊖ NW1 ..... 149 H4
Balcombe Street NW1 ..... 149 G3
Balderton Street W1K 149 J7
Baldwin's Gardens EC1N 150 F5
Baldwin Street EC1V 151 L2
Bale Road E1 ..... 157 J1
Balfe Street N1 ..... 150 D1
Balfour Mews W1K 149 K8
Balfour Place W1K 149 J8
Balfour Street SE17 ..... 155 K5
Baltic Street East EC1Y 151 J3
Baltic Street West EC1Y 151 J4
Bank ⊖ EC2R 151 L6
Bank End SE1 ..... 155 K1
Bankside SE1 ..... 155 J1
Banner Street EC1Y 151 K3
Banyard Road SE16 ..... 156 E8
Barbican EC1A 151 J4
Barbican Estate EC2Y 151 J5
Barge House Street SE1 ..... 155 G1
Bark Place W2 ..... 148 B7
Barkston Gardens SW5 ..... 152 B6
Barley Corn Way E14 ..... 157 L4
Barlow/Congreve
   Estate SE17 ..... 155 M5
Barlow Place W1J 149 L7
Barlow Street SE17 ..... 155 L5
Barnardo Street E1 ..... 157 H3
Barnby Street NW1 ..... 150 A1
Barnes Street E14 ..... 157 J2
Barnham Street SE1 ..... 156 A6
Baron's Place SE1 ..... 155 G3
Baron Street N1 ..... 151 G1
Barrett Street W1U 149 K6
Barrow Hill Estate NW8 ..... 148 F1
Barrow Hill Road NW8 ..... 148 F1
Barter Street WC1A 150 D5
Bartholomew Close EC1A 151 J5
Bartholomew Lane EC2R 151 L6
Bartholomew Street SE1 ..... 155 L5
Bartlett Court EC4A 151 G6
Barton Street SW1P 154 C4
Basil Street SW3 ..... 153 H4
Basin Approach E14 ..... 157 K3
Basinghall Lane EC2V 151 K5
Basinghall Street EC2V 151 K5
Bastwick Street EC1V 151 J3
Bateman's Buildings W1D 150 B6
Bateman Street W1D 150 B6
Bath Street EC1V 151 K2
Bath Terrace SE1 ..... 155 J4
Bathurst Mews W2 ..... 148 E7
Bathurst Street W2 ..... 148 E7
Battle Bridge Lane SE1 ..... 155 M1
Batty Street E1 ..... 156 D2
Bayley Street WC1B 150 B5
Baylis Road SE1 ..... 154 F3
Bayswater ⊖ W2 ..... 148 B7
Bayswater Road W2 ..... 148 D7
Baythorne Street E3 ..... 157 L1
Beaconsfield Road SE17 ..... 155 M7

Beak Street W1F 150 A7
Bear Grove SE1 ..... 155 J1
Bear Lane SE1 ..... 155 H1
Beauchamp Place SW3 ..... 153 G4
Beaufort Gardens SW3 ..... 153 G4
Beaufort Street SW3 ..... 152 E8
Beaumont Place W1T 150 A3
Beaumont Street W1G 149 K4
Beccles Street E14 ..... 157 M3
Beckett Street SE1 ..... 155 L3
Beckway Street SE17 ..... 155 M6
Bedale Street SE1 ..... 155 L1
Bedford Avenue WC1B 150 C5
Bedfordbury WC2N 150 D7
Bedford Gardens W8 ..... 152 A2
Bedford Place WC1N 150 D4
Bedford Row WC1R 150 E4
Bedford Square WC1B 150 B5
Bedford Street WC2E 150 D7
Bedford Way WC1H 150 C3
Bedlow Close NW8 ..... 148 F3
Beech Street EC2Y 151 J4
Beeston Place SW1W 153 L4
Belgrave Mews North * SW1X 153 J3
Belgrave Mews South * SW1X 153 K4
Belgrave Place SW1X 153 J4
Belgrave Road SW1V 153 L5
Belgrave Square SW1X 153 J3
Belgrave Street E1 ..... 157 J2
Belgrove Street WC1H 150 D2
Bell Lane E1 ..... 156 B1
Bell Street NW1 ..... 148 F4
Bell Yard WC2A 150 F6
Belvedere Road SE1 ..... 154 E2
Benjamin Street EC1M 151 H4
Ben Jonson Road E1 ..... 157 J1
Bennett Street SW1A 153 M1
Ben Smith Way SE16 ..... 156 D7
Benson Quay E1W 157 G4
Bentinck Mews W1U 149 K6
Bentinck Street W1U 149 K6
Bere Street E1W 157 H3
Bergen Square SE16 ..... 157 K8
Berkeley Mews W1H 149 H6
Berkeley Square W1J 149 L8
Berkeley Street W1J 149 L8
Bermondsey ⊖ SE16 ..... 156 E7
Bermondsey Spa SE1 ..... 156 C8
Bermondsey Square SE1 ..... 156 A8
Bermondsey Street SE1 ..... 156 A6
Bermondsey Wall East SE16 ..... 156 E7
Bermondsey Wall
   Estate SE16 ..... 156 D7
Bermondsey Wall West SE16 ..... 156 C6
Bernard Street WC1N 150 D4
Berners Mews W1T 150 A5
Berners Place W1F 150 A6
Berners Street W1T 150 A5
Bernhardt Crescent NW8 ..... 148 F3
Berry Street EC1V 151 H3
Berwick Street W1F 150 A6
Bessborough Gardens SW1V 154 B6
Bessborough Street SW1V 154 B6
Betterton Street WC2H 150 D6
Bevenden Street N1 ..... 151 L2
Bevin Close SE16 ..... 157 J5
Bevington Street SE16 ..... 156 D7
Bevin Way WC1X 150 F1
Bevis Marks EC3A 156 A2
Bewley Street E1 ..... 156 F3
Bickenhall Street W1U 149 H4
Bidborough Street WC1H 150 C2
Biddulph Road W9 ..... 148 B2
Big Ben (Elizabeth
   Tower) SW1A 154 D3
Bigland Street E1 ..... 156 E3
Billiter Square EC3M 156 A3
Billiter Street EC3M 156 A3
Bina Gardens SW5 ..... 152 C6
Bingham Place W1U 149 J4
Binney Street W1K 149 K7
Birchfield Street E14 ..... 157 M3
Birchin Lane EC3V 151 L7
Birdcage Walk SW1H 154 A3
Birde Lane EC4Y 151 H6
Birkenhead Street N1 ..... 150 D1
Bishop's Bridge Road W2 ..... 148 C6
Bishopsgate EC2M 156 A2
Bishops Square E1 ..... 156 B1
Bishop's Terrace SE11 ..... 155 G5
Bittern Street SE1 ..... 155 J3
Blackall Street EC2A 151 M3
Blackburne's Mews W1K 149 J7
Blackfriars ⊖ EC4V 151 H7
Blackfriars Bridge SE1 ..... 151 H8
Black Prince Road SE11 ..... 154 E6
Blackfriars Lane EC4V 151 H7
Blackfriars Road SE1 ..... 155 H3
Blackhorse Court SE1 ..... 155 L4
Black Lion Gate W2 ..... 148 B8
Black Prince Road SE11 ..... 154 E6
Blackwood Street SE17 ..... 155 K6
Blandford Street W1U 149 H5
Blenheim Street W1S 149 L7
Bletchley Street N1 ..... 151 K1
Blomfield Road W9 ..... 148 C4
Blomfield Street EC2M 151 M5
Blomfield Villas W2 ..... 148 C5
Bloomfield Terrace SW1W 153 J6
Bloomsbury Square WC1A 150 D5
Bloomsbury Street WC1B 150 C5
Bloomsbury Way WC1A 150 C5
Blount Street E14 ..... 157 K2
Blue Ball Yard SW1A 153 M1
Bohn Road E1 ..... 157 J1
Bolsover Street W1W 149 L4

Bolton Gardens SW5 ..... 152 B6
Bolton Street W1J 153 L1
Bond Street ⊖ W1C 149 K6
Bondway SW8 ..... 154 D8
Bonhill Street EC2A 151 L4
Bonnington Square SW8 ..... 154 E8
Boot Street N1 ..... 151 M2
Borough ⊖ SE1 ..... 155 K3
Borough High Street SE1 ..... 155 K3
Borough Road SE1 ..... 155 H3
Boscobel Place SW1W 153 K5
Boscobel Street NW8 ..... 148 E4
Boss Street SE1 ..... 156 B6
Boston Place NW1 ..... 149 G3
Botolph Lane EC3R 151 M7
Boundary Lane SE17 ..... 155 K8
Boundary Row SE1 ..... 155 G2
Bourdon Street W1K 149 L7
Bourlet Close W1W 149 M5
Bourne Estate EC1N 150 F4
Bourne Street SW1W 153 J6
Bourne Terrace W2 ..... 148 B5
Bouverie Place W2 ..... 148 F6
Bouverie Street EC4Y 151 G6
Bowland Yard * SW1X 153 J3
Bow Lane EC4M 151 K6
Bowling Green Lane EC1R 151 G3
Bowling Green Place SE1 ..... 155 L2
Bowling Green Street SE11 ..... 154 F8
Bowling Green Walk N1 ..... 151 M2
Bowsell Street WC1N 150 D4
Bow Street WC2E 150 D7
Boyd Street E1 ..... 156 D3
Boyfield Street SE1 ..... 155 H3
Boyle Street W1S 149 M7
Boyson Road SE17 ..... 155 K8
Brackland Terrace SW3 ..... 153 H6
Brackley Street EC1Y 151 J4
Bradenham Close SE17 ..... 155 K8
Brad Street SE1 ..... 155 G2
Braganza Street SE17 ..... 155 H7
Braham Street E1 ..... 156 C3
Bramerton Street SW3 ..... 152 F7
Bramham Gardens SW5 ..... 152 B6
Branch Road E14 ..... 157 J3
Brandon Estate SE17 ..... 155 H8
Brandon Street SE17 ..... 155 K6
Brangton Road SE11 ..... 154 F7
Bray Crescent SE16 ..... 157 H6
Bray Place SW3 ..... 153 H6
Bread Street EC4M 151 K7
Bream's Buildings EC4A 150 F6
Brechin Place SW7 ..... 152 D6
Brendon Street W1H 149 G5
Bressenden Place SW1W 153 L4
Brettell Street SE17 ..... 155 L7
Brewers Green SW1H 154 A3
Brewer Street W1F 150 A7
Brewhouse Lane E1W 157 F6
Brewhouse Walk SE16 ..... 157 J5
Brick Court WC2R 150 F7
Brick Lane E1 ..... 156 C1
Brick Street W1J 153 K2
Bridewell Place EC4V 151 H7
Bridgeman Street NW8 ..... 148 F1
Bridge Place SW1V 153 L5
Bridge Street EC4V 151 J7
Bridge Street SW1A 154 D3
Bridgewater Street EC2Y 151 J4
Bridgeway Street NW1 ..... 150 A1
Bridle Lane W1F 150 A7
Bridstow Place W2 ..... 148 A6
Brightlingsea Place E14 ..... 157 L4
Brill Place NW1 ..... 150 C1
Briset Street EC1M 151 H4
Bristol Gardens W9 ..... 148 B4
Britannia Street WC1X 150 E2
Britannia Walk N1 ..... 151 L2
Britannia Way N1 ..... 151 K1
British Museum WC1B 150 C5
Britten Street SW3 ..... 152 F7
Britton Street EC1M 151 H4
Broadbent Street W1K 149 L7
Broadgate Circle EC2M 151 M5
Broadley Street NW8 ..... 148 F4
Broadley Terrace NW1 ..... 148 F4
Broadstone Place W1U 149 J5
Broad Walk NW1 ..... 149 K1
Broad Walk W2 ..... 148 H7
Broadwall SE1 ..... 155 G1
Broadway SW1H 154 B4
Broadwick Street W1F 150 A7
Brockham Street SE1 ..... 155 K4
Brodlove Lane E1W 157 H3
Bromley Street E1 ..... 157 J2
Brompton Road SW3 ..... 153 G4
Brompton Road SW7 ..... 152 F5
Brompton Square SW3 ..... 153 G4
Bronti Close SE17 ..... 155 K7
Brook Drive SE11 ..... 155 G5
Brooke Street EC1N 150 F5
Brook Gate W2 ..... 149 H8
Brook Mews North W2 ..... 148 D7
Brook's Mews W1K 149 K7
Brook Street W1K 149 K7
Brook Street W2 ..... 148 E7
Brown Hart Gardens W1K 149 K7
Browning Mews W1G 149 K5
Browning Street SE17 ..... 155 K6
Brownlow Mews WC1N 150 E3
Brownlow Street WC1V 150 E5
Brown Street W1H 149 G6
Brunel Road SE16 ..... 157 G6
Brune Street E1 ..... 156 B1
Brunswick Close SE1 ..... 156 A6
Brunswick Gardens W8 ..... 152 A1

Brunswick Place N1 ..... 151 L2
Brunswick Quay SE16 ..... 157 J8
Brunswick Square WC1N 150 D3
Brunswick Street WC1N 150 D3
Brunton Place E14 ..... 157 K3
Brushfield Street E1 ..... 156 B1
Bruton Lane W1J 149 L7
Bruton Place W1J 149 L8
Bruton Street W1J 149 L8
Bryan Road SE16 ..... 157 K6
Bryanstone Mews West W1H 149 G5
Bryanston Mews East W1H 149 H5
Bryanston Place W1H 149 G5
Bryanston Square W1H 149 H5
Bryanston Street W1C 149 H7
Buck Hill Walk W2 ..... 148 E8
Buckingham Gate SW1E 153 L3
Buckingham Mews SW1E 153 M3
Buckingham Palace SW1A 153 L3
Buckingham Palace
   Road SW1W 153 L5
Buckingham Place SW1E 153 M4
Buckland Street N1 ..... 151 L1
Buckle Street E1 ..... 156 C2
Buckters Rents SE16 ..... 157 J5
Budge's Walk W2 ..... 152 D2
Bulleid Way SW1V 153 L5
Bulstrode Street W1U 149 K5
Bunhill Row EC1Y 151 L3
Burdett Estate E14 ..... 157 M1
Burdett Road E14 ..... 157 L2
Burdett Street SE1 ..... 154 F3
Burgess Street E14 ..... 157 M1
Burge Street SE1 ..... 155 L4
Burlington Arcade W1J 149 M8
Burlington Gardens W1S 149 M8
Burnhouse Place SW1W 153 J6
Burnsall Street SW3 ..... 153 G7
Burnside Close SE16 ..... 157 J5
Burrell Street SE1 ..... 155 H1
Burslem Street E1 ..... 156 D3
Burton Grove SE17 ..... 155 L7
Burton Street WC1H 150 C3
Burwood Place W2 ..... 149 G6
Bury Close SE16 ..... 157 H5
Bury Court EC3A 156 A2
Bury Place WC1A 150 D5
Bury Street EC3A 156 A2
Bury Street SW1Y 150 A1
Bury Walk SW3 ..... 152 F6
Bushell Street E1W 156 D5
Bush Lane EC4V 151 L7
Butcher Row E14 ..... 157 J3
Bute Street SW7 ..... 152 E5
Butler Place SW1H 154 B4
Butler's Wharf SE1 ..... 156 C6
Buttesland Street N1 ..... 151 L2
Byefield Close SE16 ..... 157 K6
Bylands Close SE16 ..... 157 J5
Byng Place WC1E 150 B4
Byng Street E14 ..... 157 M6
Byward Street EC3R 156 A4
Bywater Place SE16 ..... 157 K5
Bywater Street SW3 ..... 153 G6

C

Cabbell Street NW1 ..... 148 F5
Cable Street E1 ..... 156 F3
Cadiz Street SE17 ..... 155 K7
Cadogan Gardens SW3 ..... 153 H5
Cadogan Gate SW1X 153 H5
Cadogan Lane SW1X 153 J4
Cadogan Place SW1X 153 J4
Cadogan Square SW1X 153 H5
Cadogan Street SW3 ..... 153 G6
Caledonian Road N1 ..... 150 D1
Caledonia Street N1 ..... 150 D1
Cale Street SW3 ..... 152 F6
Callow Street SW3 ..... 152 D7
Calshot Street N1 ..... 150 E1
Calthorpe Street WC1X 150 E3
Cambridge Circus WC2H 150 C7
Cambridge Gardens NW6 ..... 148 A1
Cambridge Gate NW1 ..... 149 L3
Cambridge Road NW6 ..... 148 A1
Cambridge Square W2 ..... 148 F6
Cambridge Street SW1V 153 L6
Cambridge Terrace NW1 ..... 149 L2
Cambridge Terrace
   Mews NW1 ..... 149 L3
Camdenhurst Street E14 ..... 157 K2
Camera Place SW10 ..... 152 D8
Camomile Street EC3A 156 A2
Campden Grove W8 ..... 152 A2
Campden Hill Road W8 ..... 152 A2
Campden Street W8 ..... 152 A2
Camperdown Street E1 ..... 156 C3
Canada Estate SE16 ..... 157 H7
Canada Gate SW1A 153 M3
Canada Street SE16 ..... 157 H7
Canada Water ⊖ SE16 ..... 157 H7
Canada Wharf SE16 ..... 157 L5
Canal Street SE5 ..... 155 L8
Canary Riverside E14 ..... 157 L4
Candle Street E1 ..... 157 K1
Canning Place W8 ..... 152 C4
Cannon Drive E14 ..... 157 M4
Cannon Street EC4N 151 K7
Cannon Street ⊖ EC4R 151 K7
Cannon Street Road E1 ..... 156 E3
Canon Beck Road SE16 ..... 157 G6
Canon Row SW1A 154 D3
Canton Street E14 ..... 157 M3
Capeners Close * SW1X 153 J3

Capland Street NW8............148 E3
Capper Street WC1E............150 A4
Capstan Way SE16............157 K5
Carbis Road E14............157 L2
Carburton Street W1W............149 L4
Cardigan Street SE11............154 F6
Cardington Street NW1............150 A2
Carey Street WC2A............150 F6
Carlisle Avenue EC3N............156 B3
Carlisle Lane SE1............154 F4
Carlisle Place SW1P............153 M5
Carlisle Street W1D............150 B6
Carlos Place W1K............149 K7
Carlton Gardens SW1Y............154 B2
Carlton Hill NW6............148 B1
Carlton House Terrace SW1Y............154 B1
Carlton Street W1J............153 L1
Carlton Vale NW6............148 A1
Carlton Vale NW6............148 B1
Carlyle Square SW3............152 F7
Carmelite Street EC4Y............151 G7
Carnaby Street W1F............149 M7
Caroline Place W2............148 B7
Caroline Street E1............157 H3
Caroline Terrace SW1W............153 J5
Carpenter Street W1K............149 K7
Carrington Street W1J............153 L1
Carr Street E14............157 K1
Carteret Street SW1H............154 B3
Carter Lane EC4V............151 H7
Carter Place SE17............155 J7
Carter Street SE17............155 J7
Carthusian Street EC1M............151 J4
Carting Lane WC2R............150 D8
Cartwright Gardens WC1H............150 C2
Cartwright Street E1............156 C4
Casey Close NW8............148 F3
Casson Street E1............156 C1
Castellain Road W9............148 B3
Castlebrook Close SE11............155 H5
Castle Lane SW1E............153 M4
Catesby Street SE17............155 L6
Cathay Street SE16............156 F7
Cathcart Road SW10............152 C8
Cathedral Walk SW1E............153 M4
Catherine Place SW1E............153 M4
Catherine Street WC2E............150 D7
Cato Street W1H............149 G5
Causton Street SW1P............154 B6
Cavell Street E1............156 F1
Cavendish Avenue NW8............148 E1
Cavendish Place W1G............149 L6
Cavendish Square W1G............149 L6
Cavendish Street N1............151 L1
Caversham Street SW3............153 G8
Caxton Street SW1H............154 B4
Cayton Street EC1V............151 K2
Centaur Street SE1............154 F4
Central Street EC1V............151 J2
Chadwell Street EC1R............151 G1
Chadwick Street SW1P............154 B4
Chagford Street NW1............149 H4
Chalton Street NW1............150 B1
Chambers Street SE16............156 D7
Chamber Street E1............156 C3
Chambers Wharf SE16............156 D6
Chancel Street SE1............155 H1
Chancery Lane WC2A............150 F5
Chancery Lane ⊖ WC1V............150 F5
Chandos Place WC2N............150 C8
Chandos Street W1G............149 L5
Chantry Square W8............152 B4
Chapel Market N1............150 F1
Chapel Street NW1............148 F5
Chapel Street SW1X............153 K3
Chaplin Close SE1............155 G3
Chapman Street E1............156 F1
Chapter Road SE17............155 H7
Chapter Street SW1P............154 B6
Chargrove Close SE16............157 H6
Charing Cross ⇌ ⊖ WC2N............154 D1
Charing Cross Road WC2H............150 B6
Charing Cross Road WC2N............150 C8
Charlbert Street NW8............148 F1
Charles II Street SW1Y............150 B8
Charles Square N1............151 M2
Charles Street W1J............153 K1
Charleston Street SE17............155 K6
Charlotte Road EC2A............151 M3
Charlotte Street W1T............150 A4
Charlwood Place SW1V............154 A6
Charlwood Street SW1V............153 M7
Charlwood Street SW1V............154 A6
Charrington Street NW1............150 B1
Charterhouse Square EC1M............151 H4
Charterhouse Street EC1M............151 G5
Chart Street N1............151 L2
Chaseley Street E14............157 J2
Chatham Street SE17............155 L5
Cheapside EC2V............151 K6
Chelsea Bridge SW1W............153 K8
Chelsea Bridge Road SW1W............153 J7
Chelsea Embankment SW3............153 G8
Chelsea Embankment SW3............153 H8
Chelsea Manor Gardens SW3............152 F7
Chelsea Manor Street SW3............152 F6
Chelsea Park Gardens SW3............152 E8
Chelsea Physic Garden SW3............153 H8
Chelsea Square SW3............152 E7
Cheltenham Terrace SW3............153 H6
Chenies Mews WC1E............150 B4
Chenies Street WC1E............150 B4
Cheniston Gardens W8............152 A4
Chepstow Place W2............148 A7
Chepstow Road W2............148 A6
Chequer Street EC1Y............151 K3
Cherbury Street N1............151 L1
Cherry Garden Street SE16............156 E7
Chesham Close SW1X............153 J4
Chesham Place SW1X............153 J4
Chesham Street SW1X............153 J4
Chester Close SW1X............153 L3
Chester Close North NW1............149 L2
Chester Close South NW1............149 L2
Chesterfield Gardens W1J............153 K1
Chesterfield Hill W1J............149 K8
Chesterfield Street W1J............153 K1
Chester Gate NW1............149 L2
Chester Mews SW1X............153 K3
Chester Place NW1............149 L1
Chester Road NW1............149 K2
Chester Row SW1W............153 K5
Chester Square SW1W............153 K5
Chester Square
 Mews SW1W............153 K4
Chester Street SW1X............153 K3
Chester Terrace NW1............149 L2
Chester Way SE11............155 G6
Cheval Place SW7............153 G4
Cheval Street E14............157 M7
Cheyne Gardens SW3............153 G8
Cheyne Row SW3............152 F8

Cheyne Walk SW3............152 F8
Chicheley Street SE1............154 E2
Chichester Road NW6............148 A1
Chichester Road W2............148 C5
Chichester Street SW1V............154 A7
Chicksand Street E1............156 C1
Chigwell Hill E1W............156 E4
Child's Place SW5............152 A5
Child's Street SW5............152 A5
Chilton Street W1U............149 J4
Chilworth Mews W2............148 D6
Chilworth Street W2............148 D6
China Hall Mews SE16............157 G6
Chinatown W1D............150 B7
Chippenham Mews W9............148 A4
Chiswell Street EC1Y............151 K4
Chitty Street W1T............150 A4
Christchurch Street SW3............153 G8
Christian Street E1............156 D3
Christina Street EC2A............151 M3
Christopher Close SE16............157 H6
Christopher Street EC2A............151 L4
Chudleigh Street E1............157 H2
Chumleigh Street SE5............155 M8
Churchill Gardens
 Road SW1V............153 L7
Churchill War Rooms SW1A............154 C3
Church Street NW8............148 F4
Church Way NW1............150 B2
Churchyard Row SE1............155 H5
Churton Place SW1V............154 A6
Churton Street SW1V............154 A6
Circus Road NW8............148 E1
Cirencester Square W2............148 A5
City Garden Row N1............151 J1
City Road EC1V............151 J1
City Road EC1Y............151 L3
City Thameslink ⇌ EC4M............151 H6
Clabon Mews SW1X............153 H5
Clack Street SE16............157 G7
Clanricarde Gardens W2............148 A8
Claremont Square N1............150 F1
Clarence Gardens NW1............149 L2
Clarence Mews SE16............157 G6
Clarendon Gardens W9............148 D4
Clarendon Gate W2............148 F7
Clarendon Place W2............148 F7
Clarendon Street SW1V............153 L6
Clareville Grove SW7............152 D6
Clareville Street SW7............152 D6
Clarges Mews W1J............153 L1
Clarges Street W1J............153 L1
Clark Street E1............156 F2
Claverton Street SW1V............154 A7
Clave Street E1W............156 F5
Clay Street W1U............149 H5
Clayton Street SE11............154 F8
Cleaver Square SE11............155 G7
Cleaver Street SE11............155 G7
Clegg Street E1W............156 F5
Clemence Street E14............157 L2
Clements Lane EC4N............151 L7
Clement's Road SE16............156 E8
Clenston Mews W1H............149 H6
Clere Street EC2A............151 L3
Clerkenwell Close EC1R............151 G3
Clerkenwell Green EC1R............151 G4
Clerkenwell Road EC1M............151 G4
Cleveland Gardens W2............148 C6
Cleveland Mews W1T............149 M4
Cleveland Place SW1Y............154 A1
Cleveland Row SW1A............154 A2
Cleveland Square W2............148 C6
Cleveland Street W1T............149 M4
Cleveland Terrace W2............148 D6
Clifford Street W1S............149 M7
Clifton Gardens W9............148 C4
Clifton Place SE16............157 G6
Clifton Place W2............148 E7
Clifton Road W9............148 D3
Clifton Street EC2A............151 M3
Clifton Villas W9............148 C4
Clink Street SE1............155 K1
Clipper Close SE16............157 H6
Clipstone Mews W1W............149 M4
Clipstone Street W1W............149 L4
Cliveden Place SW1W............153 J5
Cloak Lane EC4R............151 K7
Cloth Fair EC1A............151 J5
Cloth Street EC1A............151 J5
Cluny Place SE1............156 A8
Cobb Street E1............156 B2
Cobourg Street NW1............150 A2
Coburg Close SW1P............154 A5
Cochrane Mews NW8............148 E1
Cochrane Street NW8............148 E1
Cock Lane EC1A............151 H5
Cockspur Street SW1Y............154 C1
Codling Close * E1W............156 D5
Coin Street SE1............155 G1
Coke Street E1............156 D2
Colbeck Mews SW7............152 C6
Colebrook Row N1............151 H1
Coleherne Road SW10............152 B7
Coleman Street EC2R............151 L6
Cole Street SE1............155 K3
Coley Street WC1X............150 F3
College Hill EC4R............151 K7
College Street EC4R............151 K7
Collett Road SE16............156 D8
Collier Street N1............150 E1
Collingham Gardens SW5............152 B6
Collingham Place SW5............152 B5
Collingham Road SW5............152 B5
Colnbrook Street SE1............155 H4
Colombo Street SE1............155 H1
Colonnade WC1N............150 D4
Coltman Street E14............157 K2
Commercial Road E1............156 D2
Commercial Road E14............157 K3
Commercial Street E1............156 B1
Compton Street EC1V............151 H3
Concert Hall
 Approach SE1............154 E2
Conder Street E14............157 K2
Conduit Mews W2............148 E6
Conduit Place W2............148 E6
Conduit Street W1S............149 L7
Congreve Street SE17............155 M5
Connaught Close W2............148 F7
Connaught Place W2............149 G7
Connaught Square W2............149 G6
Connaught Street W2............149 G6
Cons Street SE1............155 G2
Constitution Hill SW1A............153 L3
Content Street SE17............155 K5
Conway Street W1T............149 M4
Cookham Crescent SE16............157 H6
Cook's Road SE17............155 H8
Coombs Street N1............151 J1
Cooper's Lane Estate NW1............150 B1

Cooper's Road EC3N............156 B3
Copenhagen Place E14............157 L2
Cope Place W8............152 A4
Copley Court SE17............155 J8
Copley Street E1............157 H2
Copperfield Road E3............157 K1
Copperfield Street SE1............155 J2
Copthall Avenue EC2R............151 L6
Coptic Street WC1A............150 C5
Coral Street SE1............155 G3
Coram Street WC1H............150 C3
Cork Square E1W............156 E5
Cork Street W1S............149 M8
Corlett Street NW1............148 F5
Cornhill EC3V............151 L6
Cornwall Gardens SW7............152 C4
Cornwall Mews South SW7............152 C5
Cornwall Road SE1............155 F1
Cornwall Road SE1............155 G2
Cornwall Street E1............156 E3
Cornwall Terrace
 Mews NW1............149 H4
Cornwood Drive E1............157 G2
Coronet Street N1............151 M2
Corporation Row EC1R............151 G3
Corsham Street N1............151 L2
Cosser Street SE1............154 F4
Cosway Street NW1............149 G4
Cottage Place SW3............152 F4
Cottesmore Gardens W8............152 B4
Cottons Lane SE1............155 M1
Coulson Street SW3............153 H6
Counter Street SE1............155 M1
County Street SE1............155 K5
Courtenay Square SE11............154 F7
Courtenay Street SE11............154 F6
Courtfield Gardens SW5............152 B5
Courtfield Road SW7............152 C5
Court Street E1............156 E1
Cousin Lane SE1............151 K8
Covent Garden ⊖ WC2E............150 D7
Covent Garden WC2E............150 D7
Coventry Street W1D............150 B8
Cowcross Street EC1M............151 H4
Cowper Street EC2A............151 L3
Crail Row SE17............155 L5
Cramer Street W1U............149 J5
Crampton Street SE17............155 J6
Cranbourn Street WC2H............150 C7
Cranbury Road SW6............152 A8
Cranleigh Street NW1............150 A1
Cranley Gardens SW7............152 D6
Cranley Mews SW7............152 D6
Cranley Place SW7............152 E6
Cranston Estate N1............151 L1
Cranwood Street EC1V............151 L2
Craven Hill W2............148 C7
Craven Hill W2............148 D7
Craven Hill Gardens W2............148 C7
Craven Road W2............148 D7
Craven Street WC2N............154 D1
Craven Terrace W2............148 D7
Crawford Passage EC1R............151 G3
Crawford Place W1H............149 G5
Crawford Street W1H............149 G5
Creechurch Lane EC3A............156 A3
Creed Lane EC4V............151 H7
Cresswell Place SW10............152 D6
Cressy Place E1............157 G1
Crestfield Street WC1H............150 D2
Crimscott Street SE1............156 A8
Crispin Street E1............156 B1
Cromer Street WC1H............150 D2
Crompton Street W2............148 D4
Cromwell Place SW7............152 E5
Cromwell Road SW7............152 B5
Cromwell Road SW5............152 B5
Crondall Court N1............151 M1
Crondall Street N1............151 L1
Cropley Street N1............151 K1
Crosby Row SE1............155 L3
Cross Lane EC3R............155 A4
Crosswall EC3N............156 B3
Crowder Street E1............156 A6
Crucifix Lane SE1............156 A6
Cruikshank Street WC1X............150 F1
Crutched Friars EC3N............156 A3
Cuba Street E14............157 M6
Cubitt Street WC1X............150 E2
Culford Gardens SW3............153 H6
Culling Road SE16............156 F7
Cullum Street EC3M............151 M7
Culross Street W1K............149 J8
Culworth Street NW8............148 F1
Cumberland Gardens WC1X............150 F2
Cumberland Gate W2............149 H7
Cumberland Market NW1............149 L2
Cumberland Street SW1V............153 L6
Cumberland Terrace NW1............149 K1
Cumberland Terrace
 Mews NW1............149 L1
Cumberland Wharf SE16............157 G6
Cumming Street N1............150 E1
Cundy Street SW1W............153 K6
Cunningham Place NW8............148 E3
Cureton Street SW1P............154 C6
Curlew Street SE1............156 B6
Cursitor Street EC4A............150 F6
Curtain Road EC2A............151 M3
Curtain Road EC2A............151 M4
Curzon Gate W2............153 K2
Curzon Street W1J............153 K1
Cuthbert Street W2............148 E4
Cynthia Street N1............150 E1
Cypress Place W1T............150 A4
Cyrus Street EC1V............151 H3

Dacre Street SW1H............154 B3
Dakin Place E1............157 J1
Dallington Street EC1V............151 H3
Damien Street E1............156 F2
Damien Street WC1R............150 E5
Dansey Place W1D............150 B7
Dante Road SE11............155 H5
Danvers Street SW3............152 F8
D'Arblay Street W1F............150 A6
Dartford Street SE17............155 K8
Dartmouth Street SW1H............154 B3
Darwin Street SE17............155 L5
Davenant Street E1............156 D1
Daventry Street NW1............148 F4
Davidge Street SE1............155 H3
Davies Mews W1K............149 K7
Davies Street W1K............149 K7
Dawes Street SE17............155 L6
Dawson Place W2............148 A7

Deacon Way SE17............155 J5
Deal Porters Way SE16............157 G8
Deal Street E1............156 D1
Dean Bradley Street SW1P............154 C5
Dean Close SE16............157 H6
Deancross Street E1............156 F3
Deanery Street W1K............153 K1
Dean Farrar Street SW1H............154 B3
Dean Ryle Street SW1P............154 C5
Dean Stanley Street SW1P............154 C4
Dean Street W1D............150 B6
Dean's Buildings SE17............155 L6
Dean's Yard SW1P............154 C4
Decima Street SE1............155 M4
Deck Close SE16............157 J6
Defoe Close SE16............157 K7
Delamere Terrace W2............148 B4
De Laune Street SE17............155 H7
Delaware Road W9............148 B3
Dellow Street E1............156 F3
Delverton Road SE17............155 H7
Denbigh Place SW1V............153 M6
Denman Street W1D............150 B7
Denmark Street WC2H............150 C6
Denny Close SE11............155 G6
Denyer Street SW3............153 G5
Derby Gate SW1A............154 D3
Derby Street W1J............153 K1
Dering Street W1S............149 L6
Derry Street W8............152 B3
De Vere Gardens W8............152 C3
Deverell Street SE1............155 L4
Devonport Street E1............157 G3
Devonshire Close W1G............149 K4
Devonshire Mews
 South W1G............149 K4
Devonshire Mews
 West W1G............149 K4
Devonshire Place W1G............149 K4
Devonshire Place
 Mews W1G............149 K4
Devonshire Row EC2M............156 A2
Devonshire Square EC2M............156 A2
Devonshire Street W1G............149 K4
Devonshire Terrace W2............148 D7
De Walden Street W1G............149 K5
Dickens Estate SE16............156 D7
Dickens Square SE1............155 K4
Dilke Street SW3............153 H8
Dingley Place EC1V............151 K2
Dingley Road EC1V............151 J2
Discovery Walk E1W............156 E5
Disney Place SE1............155 K2
Distaff Lane EC4V............151 J7
Distin Street SE11............154 F6
Dockhead SE1............156 C7
Dockley Road SE16............156 D8
Dock Street E1............156 D4
Doddington Grove SE17............155 H7
Doddington Place SE17............155 H8
Dodson Street SE1............155 G3
Dod Street E14............157 M2
Dolben Street SE1............155 H2
Dolland Street SE11............154 E7
Dolphin Square SW1V............154 A7
Dolphin Square SW1V............154 B7
Dombey Street WC1N............150 E4
Dominion Street EC2A............151 L5
Donegal Street N1............150 F1
Dongola Road E1............157 J1
Donne Place SW3............153 G5
Doon Street SE1............154 F1
Dora Street E14............157 L2
Doric Way NW1............150 B2
Dorset Rise EC4Y............151 G7
Dorset Square NW1............149 H4
Dorset Street W1U............149 H5
Doughty Mews WC1N............150 E3
Doughty Street WC1N............150 E3
Douglas Street SW1P............154 B6
Douro Place W8............152 C3
Douthwaite Square * E1W............156 D5
Dovehouse Street SW3............152 E6
Dover Street W1J............153 L1
Dover Street W1S............149 L8
Dowgate Hill EC4R............151 K7
Downfield Close W9............148 B4
Downing Street SW1A............154 C2
Down Street W1J............153 K2
Downtown Road SE16............157 K6
D'Oyley Street SW1X............153 J5
Draco Street SE17............155 J8
Drake Close SE16............157 H6
Draycott Avenue SW3............153 G5
Draycott Place SW3............153 H6
Draycott Terrace SW3............153 H5
Drayson Mews W8............152 A3
Drayton Gardens SW10............152 D6
Druid Street SE1............156 A6
Druid Street SE1............156 B6
Drummond Crescent NW1............150 B2
Drummond Road SE16............156 E8
Drummond Street NW1............150 A3
Drury Lane WC2B............150 D6
Dryden Court SE11............155 G5
Dryden Street WC2B............150 D6
Duchess Mews W1G............149 L5
Duchess Street W1B............149 L5
Duchy Street SE1............155 G1
Duckett Street E1............157 J1
Duck Lane W1F............150 B6
Dufferin Street EC1Y............151 K4
Duke of Wellington
 Place SW1W............153 K3
Duke of York Square SW3............153 H6
Duke of York Street SW1Y............154 A8
Duke Shore Wharf E14............157 K4
Duke's Lane W8............152 A2
Duke's Place EC3A............156 B2
Duke's Road WC1H............150 C2
Duke Street W1K............149 K7
Duke Street W1U............149 J6
Duke Street Hill SE1............155 L1
Duke Street
 St James's SW1Y............154 A1
Dunbar Wharf E14............157 L4
Duncannon Street WC2N............154 C1
Duncan Terrace N1............151 H1
Dundee Street E1W............156 E5
Dundee Wharf E14............157 L4
Dunelm Street E1............157 H2
Dunlop Place SE16............156 C8
Dunraven Street W1K............149 H7
Dunster Court EC3R............156 A3
Duplex Ride SW1X............153 H3
Durand's Wharf SE16............157 L6
Durham Row E1............157 J1
Durham Street SE11............154 E7
Durham Terrace W2............148 A6
Dyott Street WC1A............150 C6
Dysart Street EC2A............151 M4

Eagle Close EC1M............151 H4
Eagle Street WC1R............150 E5
Eardley Crescent SW5............152 A7
Earlham Street WC2H............150 C7
Earl's Court ⇌ ⊖ SW5............152 A6
Earl's Court Gardens SW5............152 B6
Earl's Court Road SW5............152 A6
Earl's Court Square SW5............152 A6
Earlstoke Street EC1V............151 H2
Earl Street EC2A............151 M4
Earnshaw Street WC2H............150 C6
East Arbour Street E1............157 H2
Eastbourne Mews W2............148 D6
Eastbourne Terrace W2............148 D6
Eastcastle Street W1W............150 A6
Eastcheap EC3M............151 M7
Eastfield Street E14............157 K1
East India Dock Road E14............157 M3
East Lane SE16............156 D6
Easton Street WC1X............150 F3
East Poultry Avenue EC1A............151 H5
East Road N1............151 L2
East Smithfield E1W............156 C4
East Street SE17............155 L6
Eaton Close SW1W............153 J5
Eaton Gate SW1W............153 J5
Eaton Lane SW1W............153 L4
Eaton Mews North SW1W............153 J5
Eaton Mews South SW1W............153 K5
Eaton Mews West SW1W............153 K5
Eaton Place SW1X............153 J4
Eaton Row SW1W............153 K4
Eaton Square SW1W............153 J5
Eaton Terrace SW1W............153 J5
Ebbisham Drive SW8............154 E8
Ebury Bridge SW1W............153 K6
Ebury Bridge Road SW1W............153 K7
Ebury Mews SW1W............153 K5
Ebury Square SW1W............153 K6
Ebury Street SW1W............153 K5
Eccleston Bridge SW1W............153 L5
Eccleston Mews SW1X............153 K4
Eccleston Place SW1W............153 L5
Eccleston Square SW1V............153 L6
Eccleston Street SW1X............153 K4
Edbrooke Road W9............148 A3
Edge Street W8............152 A1
Edgware Road W2............148 F5
Edgware Road ⊖ NW1............148 F5
Edinburgh Gate SW1X............153 H3
Edith Grove SW10............152 C8
Edwards Mews W1H............149 J6
Egerton Crescent SW3............152 F5
Egerton Gardens SW3............152 F5
Egerton Terrace SW3............153 G4
Eglington Court SE17............155 J7
Elba Place SE17............155 K5
Eldon Place EC2M............151 L5
Eldon Road W8............152 B4
Eleanor Close SE16............157 H6
Elephant & Castle SE1............155 J4
Elephant & Castle ⇌ ⊖ SE1............155 J5
Elephant Lane SE16............156 F6
Elephant Road SE17............155 J5
Elf Row E1W............157 G3
Elgar Street SE16............157 K7
Elgin Avenue W9............148 B2
Elgin Mews North W9............148 C2
Elgin Mews South W9............148 C2
Elia Mews N1............151 H1
Elia Street N1............151 H1
Elim Estate SE1............155 M3
Elim Street SE1............155 M3
Elizabeth Street SW1W............153 K5
Ellen Street E1............156 D3
Elliott's Row SE11............155 H5
Ellis Street SW1X............153 J5
Elmfield Way W9............148 A4
Elm Park Gardens SW10............152 E7
Elm Park Lane SW3............152 E7
Elm Park Road SW3............152 E7
Elm Place SW7............152 E7
Elms Mews W2............148 D7
Elm Street WC1X............150 F4
Elm Tree Road NW8............148 E2
Elnathan Mews W9............148 B4
Elsa Street E1............157 J1
Elsted Street SE17............155 L6
Elvaston Mews SW7............152 D4
Elvaston Place SW7............152 D4
Elverton Street SW1P............154 B5
Ely Place EC1N............151 G5
Elystan Place SW3............153 G6
Elystan Street SW3............152 F6
Embankment ⊖ WC2N............154 D1
Embankment Gardens SW3............153 H8
Embankment Place WC2N............154 D1
Emba Street SE16............156 D7
Emerald Street WC1N............150 E4
Emerson Street SE1............155 J1
Emery Hill Street SW1P............154 A5
Emery Street SE1............155 G3
Emperor's Gate SW7............152 C5
Empire Square SE1............155 L3
Empress Place SW6............152 A7
Endell Street WC2H............150 C6
Endsleigh Gardens WC1H............150 B3
Endsleigh Place WC1H............150 B3
Endsleigh Street WC1H............150 B3
Enford Street W1H............149 G5
English Grounds SE1............155 M1
Enid Street SE16............156 C8
Ennismore Gardens SW7............152 F3
Ennismore Gardens
 Mews SW7............152 F3
Ennismore Mews SW7............152 F3
Ennismore Street SW7............152 F4
Enny Street SE11............155 G6
Ensign Street E1............156 D3
Epworth Street EC2A............151 L3
Erasmus Street SW1P............154 C6
Errol Street EC1Y............151 K4
Essendine Road W9............148 A3
Essex Street WC2R............150 F7
Essex Villas W8............152 A3
Europa Place EC1V............151 J2
Euston ⇌ ⊖ NW1............150 B2
Euston Road NW1............150 B2
Euston Square NW1............150 B3
Euston Square ⊖ NW1............150 A3
Euston Street NW1............150 A3
Evelyn Gardens SW7............152 D7
Evelyn Way N1............151 L1
Eversholt Street NW1............150 A1
Everton Buildings NW1............149 M2
Ewer Street SE1............155 J2
Ewhurst Close E1............157 G1
Exchange Square EC2A............151 M4

Exeter Street WC2E............ 150 D7
Exhibition Road SW7............ 152 E3
Exmouth Market EC1R............ 151 G3
Exon Street SE17............ 155 M6
Exton Street SE1............ 154 F2
Eyre Street Hill EC1R............ 150 F4

F

Fairclough Street E1............ 156 D3
Fair Street SE1............ 156 B6
Falmouth Road SE1............ 155 K4
Fann Street EC1M............ 151 J4
Fanshaw Street N1............ 151 M1
Fareham Street W1D............ 150 B6
Farmer Street W8............ 152 A1
Farm Lane SW6............ 152 A8
Farm Street W1K............ 149 K8
Farnham Place SE1............ 155 J1
Farrance Street E14............ 157 M3
Farringdon ⊖ EC1M............ 151 G4
Farringdon Lane EC1R............ 151 G4
Farringdon Road EC1R............ 150 F3
Farringdon Street EC1M............ 151 H5
Farrins Rents SE16............ 157 J5
Farrow Place SE16............ 157 K7
Farthing Fields * E1W............ 156 F5
Fashion Street E1............ 156 B1
Faunce Street SE17............ 155 H7
Fawcett Street SW10............ 152 C8
Featherstone Street EC1Y............ 151 L3
Fenchurch Avenue EC3M............ 156 A3
Fenchurch Buildings EC3M............ 156 A3
Fenchurch Place EC3M............ 156 A3
Fenchurch Street EC3M............ 156 A3
Fenchurch Street ⊖ EC3M............ 156 A3
Fendall Street SE1............ 156 B8
Fenning Street SE1............ 155 M2
Fentiman Road SW8............ 154 D8
Fernsbury Street WC1X............ 150 F2
Fetter Lane EC4A............ 151 G6
Fieldgate Street E1............ 156 D2
Fielding Street SE17............ 155 J7
Field Street WC1X............ 150 E1
Finborough Road SW10............ 152 B8
Finch Lane EC3V............ 151 L6
Finland Street SE16............ 157 K8
Finsbury Circus EC2M............ 151 L5
Finsbury Estate EC1R............ 151 G3
Finsbury Market EC2A............ 151 M4
Finsbury Square EC2Y............ 151 L4
Finsbury Street EC2Y............ 151 L4
First Street SW3............ 153 G5
Fishermans Drive SE16............ 157 J5
Fisher Street WC1R............ 150 D5
Fisherton Street NW8............ 148 E3
Fish Street Hill EC3R............ 151 L7
Fitzalan Street SE11............ 154 F5
Fitzhardinge Street W1H............ 149 J6
Fitzroy Square W1T............ 149 M4
Fitzroy Street W1T............ 149 M4
Flamborough Street E14............ 157 J3
Flank Street E1............ 156 C4
Flaxman Terrace WC1H............ 150 C3
Fleet Street EC4A............ 151 G6
Fleming Road SE17............ 155 H8
Fletcher Street E1............ 156 D3
Flint Street SE17............ 155 L6
Flitcroft Street WC2H............ 150 C6
Flockton Street SE16............ 156 D7
Flood Street SW3............ 153 G7
Flood Walk SW3............ 153 G7
Floral Street WC2E............ 150 D7
Foley Street W1W............ 149 M5
Forbes Street E1............ 156 D3
Fordham Street E1............ 156 D2
Ford Square E1............ 156 F2
Fore Street EC2Y............ 151 K5
Formosa Street W9............ 148 C4
Forset Street W1H............ 149 G6
Forsyth Gardens SE17............ 155 H8
Fort Street E1............ 156 B1
Fortune Street EC1Y............ 151 K4
Foster Lane EC2V............ 151 J6
Foulis Terrace SW7............ 152 E6
Foundry Close SE16............ 157 J5
Fournier Street E1............ 156 B1
Fowey Close E1W............ 156 E5
Frampton Street NW8............ 148 E4
Francis Street SW1P............ 154 A5
Frankland Close SE16............ 156 F8
Franklin's Row SW3............ 153 H6
Frazier Street SE1............ 155 G3
Frean Street SE16............ 156 C8
Frederick Close W2............ 149 G7
Frederick Street WC1X............ 150 E2
Frederic Mews * SW1X............ 153 J3
Freemantle Street SE17............ 155 M6
Friend Street EC1V............ 151 H2
Frith Street W1D............ 150 B6
Fulbourne Street E1............ 156 E1
Fulford Street SE16............ 156 F7
Fulham Road SW10............ 152 D8
Fulham Road SW3............ 152 C6
Furnival Street EC4A............ 150 F5
Fynes Street SW1P............ 154 B5

G

Gabriel's Wharf SE1............ 155 G1
Gainsford Street SE1............ 156 B6
Galleon Close SE16............ 157 G6
Galsworthy Avenue E14............ 157 K2
Galway Street EC1V............ 151 K2
Gambia Street SE1............ 155 H2
Garden Road NW8............ 148 D1
Garden Row SE1............ 155 H4
Garden Street E1............ 157 H1
Garden Walk EC2A............ 151 M3
Gard Street EC1V............ 151 J2
Garford Street E14............ 157 M4
Garnault Place EC1R............ 151 G3
Garnet Street E1W............ 156 F4
Garrett Street EC1Y............ 151 K3
Garrick Street WC2E............ 150 C7
Garterway SE16............ 157 H7
Garway Road W2............ 148 B6
Gataker Street * SE16............ 156 E8
Gate Mews SW7............ 152 F3
Gateforth Street NW8............ 148 F3
Gate Mews NW1............ 149 F3
Gatesborough Street * EC2A............ 151 M3
Gate Street WC2A............ 150 E5
Gatliff Road SW1W............ 153 K7
Gaunt Street SE1............ 155 J4
Gayfere Street SW1P............ 154 C4
Gaywood Street SE1............ 155 H4

Gaza Street SE17............ 155 H7
Gedling Place SE1............ 156 C7
Gee Street EC1V............ 151 J3
George Mathers Road SE11............ 155 H5
George Row SE16............ 156 C7
George Street W1H............ 149 H6
George Yard W1K............ 149 K7
Geraldine Street SE1............ 155 H4
Gerald Road SW1W............ 153 K5
Gerridge Street SE1............ 155 G3
Gertrude Street SW10............ 152 D8
Gibson Road SE11............ 154 F6
Gilbert Place WC1A............ 150 C5
Gilbert Road SE11............ 155 G5
Gilbert Street W1K............ 149 K7
Gilston Road SW10............ 152 D7
Giltspur Street EC1A............ 151 H5
Gladstone Street SE1............ 155 H4
Glamis Place E1W............ 157 G4
Glamis Road E1W............ 157 G4
Glasgow Terrace SW1V............ 153 M7
Glasshill Street SE1............ 155 J3
Glasshouse Street W1B............ 150 A8
Glasshouse Walk SE11............ 154 D7
Glebe Place SW3............ 152 F7
Gledhow Gardens SW5............ 152 C6
Glentworth Street NW1............ 149 H4
Globe Pond Road SE16............ 157 J5
Globe Street SE1............ 155 K3
Gloucester Court * EC3R............ 156 A4
Gloucester Gardens W2............ 148 C6
Gloucester Mews W2............ 148 D6
Gloucester Mews West W2............ 148 C6
Gloucester Place NW1............ 149 H3
Gloucester Place W1U............ 149 H5
Gloucester Place Mews W1U............ 149 H5
Gloucester Road SW7............ 152 C6
Gloucester Road SW7............ 152 D6
Gloucester Road ⊖ SW7............ 152 C5
Gloucester Square W2............ 148 F6
Gloucester Street SW1V............ 153 M7
Gloucester Terrace W2............ 148 B5
Gloucester Terrace W2............ 148 D6
Gloucester Walk W8............ 152 A3
Gloucester Way EC1R............ 151 G2
Glyn Street SE11............ 154 E7
Godfrey Street SW3............ 153 G6
Goding Street SE11............ 154 D7
Godliman Street EC4V............ 151 J7
Godwin Close N1............ 151 K1
Golden Hinde II SE1............ 155 L1
Golden Jubilee Bridge WC2N............ 154 D1
Golden Lane EC1Y............ 151 J4
Golden Square W1F............ 150 A7
Golding Street E1............ 156 E3
Goldney Road W9............ 148 A4
Goldsmith Street EC2V............ 151 K6
Gomm Road SE16............ 157 G8
Goodge Place W1T............ 150 A5
Goodge Street W1T............ 150 A5
Goodge Street ⊖ W1T............ 150 B5
Goodwin Close SE16............ 156 C8
Gordon Place W8............ 152 A2
Gordon Square WC1H............ 150 B3
Gordon Street WC1H............ 150 B3
Gore Street SW7............ 152 D4
Goring Street * EC3A............ 156 A2
Gosfield Street W1W............ 149 L5
Goslett Yard WC2H............ 150 B6
Goswell Road EC1V............ 151 H1
Gough Street WC1X............ 150 F3
Goulston Street E1............ 156 B2
Gower Mews WC1E............ 150 B5
Gower Place NW1............ 150 A3
Gower Street WC1E............ 150 B3
Gower's Walk E1............ 156 D2
Gracechurch Street EC3V............ 151 M7
Grafton Place NW1............ 150 B2
Grafton Street W1S............ 149 L8
Grafton Way W1T............ 150 A4
Graham Street N1............ 151 J1
Graham Terrace SW1W............ 153 J6
Granby Terrace NW1............ 149 M1
Grand Avenue EC1A............ 151 H5
Grange Road SE1............ 156 B8
Grange Walk SE1............ 156 A8
Grange Yard SE1............ 156 B8
Grantully Road W9............ 148 B2
Granville Place W1H............ 149 J6
Granville Road NW6............ 148 A1
Granville Square WC1X............ 150 F2
Grape Street WC2H............ 150 C6
Gravel Lane E1............ 156 B2
Gray's Inn Road WC1X............ 150 D2
Gray's Inn Square WC1R............ 150 F5
Gray Street SE1............ 155 G3
Great Castle Street W1G............ 149 L6
Great Central Street NW1............ 149 G4
Great Chapel Street W1D............ 150 B6
Great College Street SW1P............ 154 C4
Great Cumberland
  Place W1H............ 149 H6
Great Dover Street SE1............ 155 K3
Great Eastern Street EC2A............ 151 M3
Great George Street SW1P............ 154 C3
Great Guildford Street SE1............ 155 J1
Great James Street WC1N............ 150 E4
Great Marlborough
  Street W1F............ 149 M7
Great Maze Pond SE1............ 155 L2
Great New Portland
  Street WC2H............ 150 C7
Greatorex Street E1............ 156 D1
Great Ormond Street WC1N............ 150 D4
Great Percy Street WC1X............ 150 F2
Great Peter Street SW1P............ 154 B4
Great Portland Street W1W............ 149 L4
Great Portland
  Street ⊖ W1W............ 149 L4
Great Pulteney Street W1F............ 150 A7
Great Queen Street WC2B............ 150 D6
Great Russell Street WC1B............ 150 C5
Great Scotland Yard SW1A............ 154 C1
Great Smith Street SW1P............ 154 C4
Great Suffolk Street SE1............ 155 H2
Great Sutton Street EC1V............ 151 H4
Great Swan Alley EC2R............ 151 L6
Great Titchfield Street W1W............ 149 M4
Great Tower Street EC3M............ 156 A3
Great Tower Street EC3R............ 156 A4
Great Winchester
  Street EC2N............ 151 L6
Great Windmill Street W1D............ 150 B7
Greek Street W1D............ 150 B6
Greenacre Square SE16............ 157 J6
Green Bank E1W............ 156 F4
Greenberry Street NW8............ 148 F1

Greencoat Place SW1P............ 154 A5
Green Coat Row SW1P............ 154 A4
Greenfield Road E1............ 156 D2
Greenham Close SE1............ 154 F3
Green Park ⊖ W1J............ 153 M1
Green Street W1K............ 149 J7
Greenwell Street W1W............ 149 L4
Greet Street SE1............ 155 G2
Grenade Street E14............ 157 L4
Grendon Street NW8............ 148 F3
Grenville Place SW7............ 152 C5
Gresham Street EC2V............ 151 J6
Gresse Street W1T............ 150 B5
Greville Street EC1N............ 151 G5
Greycoat Place SW1P............ 154 B4
Greycoat Street SW1P............ 154 B4
Grigg's Place SE1............ 156 A8
Grosvenor Bridge SW8............ 153 L8
Grosvenor Crescent SW1X............ 153 J3
Grosvenor Crescent
  Mews SW1X............ 153 J3
Grosvenor Gardens SW1W............ 153 L4
Grosvenor Gardens Mews
  East SW1W............ 153 L4
Grosvenor Gardens Mews
  North SW1W............ 153 L4
Grosvenor Gardens Mews
  South * SW1W............ 153 L4
Grosvenor Gate W2............ 149 H8
Grosvenor Hill W1K............ 149 L7
Grosvenor Place SW1X............ 153 K3
Grosvenor Road SW1V............ 153 L8
Grosvenor Square W1K............ 149 J7
Grosvenor Street W1K............ 149 K7
Grosvenor Terrace SE5............ 155 J8
Grove End Road NW8............ 148 D2
Guildhouse Street SW1V............ 153 M5
Guilford Street WC1N............ 150 D4
Guinness Square SE1............ 155 M5
Gulliver Street SE16............ 157 K8
Gunpowder Square EC4A............ 151 G6
Gun Street E1............ 156 B1
Gunthorpe Street E1............ 156 C2
Gutter Lane EC2V............ 151 J6
Guy Street SE1............ 155 L3

H

Haberdasher Street N1............ 151 L2
Haddonhall Estate SE1............ 155 M4
Hainton Close E1............ 156 F3
Halcrow Street * E1............ 156 F2
Half Moon Street W1J............ 153 L1
Halford Road SW6............ 152 A8
Halkin Place SW1X............ 153 J4
Halkin Street SW1X............ 153 K3
Hallam Street W1W............ 149 L5
Halley Street E14............ 157 K1
Hallfield Estate W2............ 148 C6
Hall Place W2............ 148 E4
Hall Road NW8............ 148 D2
Hall Street EC1V............ 151 H2
Halpin Place SE17............ 155 M6
Halsey Street SW3............ 153 G5
Hamilton Close NW8............ 148 D2
Hamilton Close SE16............ 157 K7
Hamilton Gardens NW8............ 148 D2
Hamilton Place W1J............ 153 K2
Hamilton Terrace NW8............ 148 C1
Hamlet Way SE1............ 155 L3
Hammett Street EC3N............ 156 B4
Hampden Close NW1............ 150 B1
Hampden Gurney Street W2............ 149 H6
Hampstead Road NW1............ 149 M2
Hampton Street SE17............ 155 J6
Hanbury Street E1............ 156 C1
Hand Court WC1V............ 150 E5
Handel Street WC1N............ 150 D3
Hankey Place SE1............ 155 L3
Hannibal Road E1............ 157 G1
Hanover Square W1S............ 149 L6
Hanover Street W1S............ 149 L7
Hans Crescent SW3............ 153 H3
Hanson Street W1W............ 149 M4
Hans Place SW1X............ 153 H4
Hans Road SW3............ 153 G4
Hans Street SW1X............ 153 H4
Hanway Place W1T............ 150 B6
Hanway Street W1T............ 150 B6
Harbet Road W2............ 148 F5
Harbour Street WC1N............ 150 E4
Harcourt Street W1H............ 149 G5
Harcourt Terrace SW10............ 152 C7
Hardinge Street E1W............ 157 G2
Hardwick Street EC1R............ 151 G2
Hardwidge Street SE1............ 155 M2
Hardy Close SE16............ 157 H6
Harewood Place W1G............ 149 L6
Harewood Row NW1............ 149 G4
Harewood Avenue NW1............ 149 G4
Harford Street E1............ 157 J1
Harleyford Road SE11............ 154 E8
Harley Gardens SW10............ 152 D7
Harley Street W1G............ 149 K4
Harmsworth Street SE17............ 155 G7
Harold Estate SE1............ 156 A8
Harper Road SE1............ 155 K4
Harriet Street SW1X............ 153 H3
Harriet Walk SW1X............ 153 H3
Harrington Gardens SW7............ 152 C6
Harrington Road SW7............ 152 E5
Harrington Square NW1............ 149 M1
Harrington Street NW1............ 149 M2
Harrison Street WC1H............ 150 D2
Harrods SW1X............ 153 G3
Harrowby Street W1H............ 149 G6
Harrow Place E1............ 156 B2
Harrow Road W2............ 148 A4
Hart Street EC3R............ 156 A3
Hasker Street SW3............ 153 G5
Hastings Street WC1H............ 150 C2
Hatfields SE1............ 155 G1
Hatherley Grove W2............ 148 B6
Hatteraick Road SE16............ 157 G6
Hatton Garden EC1N............ 151 G4
Hatton Street W2............ 148 E4
Hatton Wall EC1N............ 151 G4
Havering Street E1............ 157 H3
Haverstock Street N1............ 151 J1
Hawke Place * SE16............ 157 H6
Haydon Street EC3N............ 156 B3
Hayes Place NW1............ 149 G4
Hay Hill W1J............ 149 L8
Hayles Street SE11............ 155 H5
Haymarket SW1Y............ 150 B8
Hay's Lane SE1............ 155 M1
Hay's Mews W1J............ 149 L8
Haywood Place EC1R............ 151 H3

Headfort Place SW1X............ 153 K3
Head Street E1............ 157 H2
Hearnshaw Street E14............ 157 M4
Hearn Street EC2A............ 151 M4
Heathcote Street WC1N............ 150 E3
Heddon Street W1B............ 149 M7
Heddon Street W1S............ 150 A7
Hedger Street SE11............ 155 H5
Heiron Street SE17............ 155 J8
Hellings Street E1W............ 156 D5
Helmet Row EC1V............ 151 K3
Helsinki Square SE16............ 157 K7
Henderson Drive NW8............ 148 E3
Heneage Lane EC3A............ 156 A3
Heneage Street E1............ 156 C1
Henrietta Place W1G............ 149 L6
Henrietta Street WC2E............ 150 D7
Henriques Street E1............ 156 D2
Henshaw Street SE17............ 155 L5
Herbal Hill EC1R............ 151 G4
Herbert Crescent SW1X............ 153 H4
Herbrand Street WC1H............ 150 C3
Hercules Road SE1............ 154 F4
Hereford Road W2............ 148 A6
Hereford Square SW7............ 152 D6
Hermitage Street W2............ 148 E5
Hermitage Wall E1W............ 156 D5
Hermit Street EC1V............ 151 H2
Heron Place SE16............ 157 K5
Heron Quay E14............ 157 M5
Herrick Street SW1P............ 154 C6
Hertford Street W1J............ 153 K2
Hertsmere Road E14............ 157 M4
Hesper Mews SW5............ 152 B6
Hessel Street E1............ 156 E3
Hewett Street EC2A............ 151 M3
Heygate Estate SE17............ 155 J5
Heygate Street SE17............ 155 J5
Hide Place SW1P............ 154 B6
High Holborn WC1V............ 150 E5
High Street
  Kensington ⊖ W8............ 152 A3
Hildyard Road SW6............ 152 A8
Hilliards Court E1W............ 156 F5
Hillingdon Street SE17............ 155 J8
Hill Road NW8............ 148 D1
Hills Place W1F............ 149 M6
Hill Street W1J............ 149 K8
Hinde Street W1U............ 149 K6
Hind Grove E14............ 157 M3
Hindgrove Area E14............ 157 M3
Hithe Grove SE16............ 157 G8
HMS Belfast SE1............ 156 A5
Hobart Place SW1W............ 153 K4
Hobury Street SW10............ 152 D8
Hogarth Road SW5............ 152 B6
Holbein Mews SW1W............ 153 J6
Holbein Place SW1W............ 153 J6
Holborn ⊖ EC1N............ 151 G5
Holborn EC1N............ 150 E5
Holborn Circus EC1N............ 151 G5
Holborn Viaduct EC1A............ 151 G5
Holford Street WC1X............ 150 F2
Holland Street SE1............ 155 H1
Holland Street W8............ 152 A3
Hollen Street W1F............ 150 A6
Holles Street W1C............ 149 L6
Hollywood Road SW10............ 152 C8
Holyoak Road SE11............ 155 H5
Holyrood Street SE1............ 155 M2
Holyrood Street SE1............ 156 A6
Holywell Row EC2A............ 151 M4
Homefield Street * N1............ 151 M1
Homer Row W1H............ 149 G5
Homer Street W1H............ 149 G5
Hooper Street E1............ 156 D3
Hopetown Street E1............ 156 C1
Hopkins Street W1F............ 150 A7
Hopton Street SE1............ 155 H1
Hopwood Road SE17............ 155 L8
Hornton Place W8............ 152 A3
Hornton Street W8............ 152 A2
Horse & Dolphin Yard W1D............ 150 B7
Horseferry Road E14............ 157 J3
Horseferry Road SW1P............ 154 B4
Horse Guards Avenue SW1A............ 154 C2
Horse Guards Parade SW1A............ 154 C2
Horse Guards Road SW1A............ 154 C2
Horselydown Lane SE1............ 156 B6
Horsley Street SE17............ 155 K8
Hosier Lane EC1A............ 151 H5
Hothfield Place SE16............ 157 G8
Hotspur Street SE11............ 154 F6
Houghton Street WC2A............ 150 E6
Houndsditch EC3A............ 156 A2
Houses of Parliament SW1A............ 154 D3
Howick Place SW1E............ 154 A4
Howland Street W1T............ 150 A4
Howland Way SE16............ 157 K7
Howley Place W2............ 148 D4
Hoxton Square N1............ 151 M1
Hoxton Street N1............ 151 M1
Hugh Mews SW1V............ 153 L6
Hugh Street SW1V............ 153 L6
Hugh Street SW1V............ 153 L6
Hull Close SE16............ 157 J6
Hull Street EC1V............ 151 J2
Hungerford Bridge SE1............ 154 E1
Hunter Close SE1............ 155 M4
Hunter Street WC1N............ 150 D3
Huntley Street WC1E............ 150 A4
Huntsman Street SE17............ 155 M6
Huntsworth Mews NW1............ 149 H3
Hurley Crescent SE16............ 157 H6
Hutching's Street E14............ 157 M7
Hutton Street EC4Y............ 151 G7
Hyde Park W2............ 153 G1
Hyde Park Corner W1J............ 153 K2
Hyde Park Corner ⊖ W1J............ 153 K2
Hyde Park Court SW7............ 152 D3
Hyde Park Crescent W2............ 148 F6
Hyde Park Garden Mews W2............ 148 F7
Hyde Park Gardens W2............ 148 F7
Hyde Park Gate W2............ 152 C3
Hyde Park Gate SW7............ 152 D3
Hyde Park Square W2............ 148 F7
Hyde Park Street W2............ 148 F7

I

Idol Lane EC3R............ 151 M7
Ifield Road SW10............ 152 B8
Iliffe Street SE17............ 155 J6
Iliffe Yard SE17............ 155 J6
Imperial College Road SW7............ 152 D4
Imperial War Museum SE1............ 155 G4
India Street EC3N............ 156 B3
Ingestre Place W1F............ 150 A7
Inglebert Street EC1R............ 151 G2

Ingram Close SE11............ 154 E5
Inner Circle NW1............ 149 J2
Inverness Terrace W2............ 148 B6
Inverness Terrace Gate W2............ 148 C8
Invicta Plaza SE1............ 155 H1
Inville Road SE17............ 155 L7
Ironmonger Lane EC2V............ 151 K6
Ironmonger Row EC1V............ 151 K2
Irving Street WC2N............ 150 C8
Isambard Place SE16............ 157 G6
Island Row E14............ 157 K3
Iverna Court W8............ 152 A4
Iverna Gardens W8............ 152 A4
Ives Street SW3............ 153 G5
Ivor Place NW1............ 149 G4
Ixworth Place SW3............ 152 F6

J

Jacob Street SE1............ 156 C6
Jamaica Gate SE16............ 156 F8
Jamaica Road SE1............ 156 C7
Jamaica Road SE16............ 156 E7
Jamaica Street E1............ 157 G2
Jamaica Wharf SE1............ 156 C6
James Street W1U............ 149 K6
James Street WC2E............ 150 D7
Jameson Street W8............ 152 A1
Jamuna Close E14............ 157 K1
Janeway Street SE16............ 156 D7
Jardine Road E1W............ 157 J4
Java Wharf SE1............ 156 C6
Jay Mews SW7............ 152 D3
Jermyn Street SW1Y............ 150 A8
Jerome Crescent NW8............ 148 F3
Jewery Street EC3N............ 156 B3
Joan Street SE1............ 155 G2
Jockey's Fields WC1R............ 150 E4
Johanna Street SE1............ 154 F3
John Adam Street WC2N............ 150 D8
John Carpenter Street EC4Y............ 151 G7
John Felton Road SE16............ 156 D7
John Fisher Street E1............ 156 C4
John Islip Street SW1P............ 154 C5
John Prince's Street W1G............ 149 L6
John Roll Way SE16............ 156 D7
John Ruskin Street SE5............ 155 J8
John Slip Street SW1P............ 154 C6
John's Mews WC1N............ 150 E4
Johnson's Place SW1V............ 154 A7
Johnson Street E1............ 157 G3
John Street WC1N............ 150 E4
Joiner Street SE1............ 155 L1
Jonathan Street SE11............ 154 E6
Jubilee Place SW3............ 153 G6
Jubilee Street E1............ 157 G2
Jubilee Walk W8............ 152 B1
Judd Street WC1H............ 150 C2
Junction Mews W2............ 148 F5
Juxon Street SE11............ 154 E5

K

Katherine Close SE16............ 157 H5
Kean Street WC2B............ 150 E6
Keel Close SE16............ 157 J6
Keeley Street WC2B............ 150 E6
Keeton's Road SE16............ 156 E7
Kell Street SE1............ 155 H3
Kelso Place W8............ 152 B4
Kemble Street WC2B............ 150 E6
Kempsford Gardens SW5............ 152 A7
Kempsford Road SE11............ 155 G6
Kendall Place W1U............ 149 J5
Kendal Street W2............ 149 G6
Kennet Street E1W............ 156 D5
Kenning Street SE16............ 157 G6
Kennings Way SE11............ 155 G7
Kennington ⊖ SE11............ 155 H7
Kennington Lane SE11............ 154 E7
Kennington Oval SE11............ 154 E8
Kennington Park
  Gardens SE11............ 155 G8
Kennington Park Place SE11............ 155 G7
Kennington Park Road SE11............ 155 G7
Kennington Road SE1............ 154 F4
Kennington Road SE11............ 155 G5
Kennnington Oval SE11............ 154 F8
Kenrick Place W1U............ 149 J5
Kensington Church Street W8............ 152 A1
Kensington Court W8............ 152 B3
Kensington Gardens W2............ 152 C1
Kensington Gardens
  Square W2............ 148 B6
Kensington Gate W8............ 152 C4
Kensington Gore SW7............ 152 D3
Kensington High Street W8............ 152 A4
Kensington Palace W8............ 152 B2
Kensington Palace
  Gardens W8............ 152 B1
Kensington Palace
  Gardens W8............ 152 B2
Kensington Place W8............ 152 A1
Kensington Road SW7............ 153 G3
Kensington Road W8............ 152 B3
Kensington Square W8............ 152 B3
Kenton Street WC1H............ 150 C3
Kenway Road SW5............ 152 A6
Keystone Close N1............ 150 D1
Keyworth Street SE1............ 155 H4
Kilburn Park Road NW6............ 148 A2
Kildare Terrace W2............ 148 A6
Killick Street N1............ 150 E1
Kinburn Street SE16............ 157 H6
Kinder Street E1............ 156 E2
King & Queen Wharf SE16............ 157 H5
King and Queen Street SE17............ 155 K6
King Charles Street SW1A............ 154 C3
Kingdom Street W2............ 148 C5
King Edward Street EC1A............ 151 J6
King Edward Walk SE1............ 155 G4
King James Street SE1............ 155 H3
Kingly Street W1F............ 149 M7
King's Arms Yard EC2R............ 151 L6
King's Bench Street SE1............ 155 H2
Kingscote Street EC4V............ 151 H7
King's Cross ⊖ N1C............ 150 D1
King's Cross Road WC1X............ 150 E2
King's Cross St
  Pancras ⊖ N1C............ 150 D1
King's Head Yard SE1............ 155 L1
King's Mews WC1N............ 150 F4
Kingsmill Terrace NW8............ 148 E1
King Square EC1V............ 151 J2
King's Road SW3............ 152 E8
King's Scholars
  Passage SW1P............ 153 M5

King's Stairs Close - Paddington Street 16

King's Stairs Close SE16 156 F6
King Street WC2E 150 D7
King Street SW1Y 154 A1
King Street EC2V 151 K6
Kingsway WC2B 150 E6
King William Street EC4N 151 L7
Kinnerton Place North * SW1X 153 J3
Kinnerton Place South * SW1X 153 J3
Kinnerton Street SW1X 153 J3
Kinnerton Yard * SW1X 153 J3
Kipling Estate SE1 155 L3
Kipling Street SE1 155 L3
Kirby Estate SE16 156 D7
Kirby Grove SE1 155 M3
Kirby Street EC1N 151 G4
Knaresborough Place SW5 152 B5
Knightrider Street EC4V 151 H7
Knightsbridge SW1X 153 H3
Knightsbridge ⊖ SW3 153 H3
Knox Street W1H 149 H4
Kynance Mews SW7 152 C4
Kynance Place SW7 152 C4

L

Lackington Street EC2A 151 L4
Lafone Street SE1 156 B6
Lagado Mews SE16 157 H5
Lambeth Bridge SW1P 154 D5
Lambeth High Street SE1 154 E5
Lambeth Hill EC4V 151 J7
Lambeth North ⊖ SE1 154 F3
Lambeth Palace Road SE1 154 E4
Lambeth Road SE1 154 F4
Lambeth Walk SE11 154 F5
Lamb's Conduit Street WC1N 150 E4
Lamb's Passage EC1Y 151 K4
Lamb Street E1 156 B1
Lamb Way SE1 156 A7
Lamlash Street SE11 155 H5
Lanark Place W9 148 D3
Lanark Road W9 148 B1
Lancaster Gate W2 148 D7
Lancaster Gate W2 148 D8
Lancaster Gate ⊖ W2 148 E7
Lancaster Mews W2 148 D7
Lancaster Place WC2E 150 E7
Lancaster Street SE1 155 H3
Lancaster Terrace W2 148 E7
Lancaster Walk W2 148 D8
Lancelot Place SW7 153 G3
Lancing Street NW1 150 B2
Lanesborough Place * SW1X 153 J3
Langdale Street E1 156 E3
Langford Place NW8 148 D1
Langham Place W1B 149 L5
Langham Street W1W 149 L5
Langham Street W1W 149 M5
Langley Lane SW8 154 D8
Langley Street WC2H 150 C7
Langton Close WC1X 150 E3
Lanhill Road W9 148 A3
Lansdowne Place SE1 155 L4
Lant Street SE1 155 J3
Larcom Street SE17 155 K6
Lauderdale Road W9 148 B3
Laud Street SE11 154 E7
Launcelot Street SE1 154 F3
Launceston Place W8 152 C4
Laurence Pountney Lane EC4V 151 L7
Lavender Road SE16 157 K5
Lavender Wharf SE16 157 K4
Lavington Street SE1 155 J1
Lawn Lane SW8 154 D8
Lawrence Street SW3 152 F8
Lawrence Wharf SE16 157 L6
Law Street SE1 155 L4
Laxton Place NW1 149 L3
Laystall Street EC1R 150 F4
Leadenhall Street EC3A 156 A3
Leadenhall Street EC3V 151 M6
Leake Street SE1 154 E2
Leather Lane EC1N 151 G4
Leathermarket Street SE1 155 M3
Leeke Street WC1X 150 E2
Lees Place W1K 149 J7
Leicester Square ⊖ WC2H 150 C7
Leicester Square WC2H 150 C7
Leicester Street WC2H 150 B7
Leigh Street WC1H 150 C3
Leinster Gardens W2 148 C6
Leinster Mews W2 148 C7
Leinster Place W2 148 C7
Leinster Square W2 148 A7
Leinster Terrace W2 148 C7
Leman Street E1 156 C3
Lennox Gardens SW1X 153 G4
Lennox Gardens Mews SW1X 153 G5
Leonard Street EC2A 151 L3
Leopold Estate E3 157 M1
Leopold Street E3 157 L1
Leroy Street SE1 155 M5
Lever Street EC1V 151 J2
Lewisham Street SW1H 154 B3
Lexham Gardens W8 152 A5
Lexham Mews W8 152 A5
Lexington Street W1F 150 A7
Leyden Street E1 156 B2
Leydon Close SE16 157 H5
Library Street SE1 155 H3
Lidlington Place NW1 150 A1
Lilestone Street NW8 148 F3
Lilley Close E1W 156 D5
Lillie Road SW6 152 A7
Lillie Yard SW6 152 A7
Limeburner Lane EC4M 151 H6
Lime Close E1W 156 D5
Limehouse Causeway E14 157 L4
Limehouse Link E14 157 L3
Limehouse ⇌ ⊖ E14 157 J3
Limerston Street SW10 152 D8
Lime Street EC3M 151 M7
Lincoln's Inn Fields WC2A 150 E6
Linden Gardens W2 148 A8
Lindley Street E1 156 F1
Lindsay Square SW1V 154 B7
Lindsey Street EC1A 151 H4
Linhope Street NW1 149 G3
Linsey Street SE16 156 D8
Lisle Street WC2H 150 B7
Lisson Green Estate NW8 148 F3
Lisson Grove NW1 149 G4
Lisson Grove NW8 148 F3
Lisson Street NW1 148 F4
Litchfield Street WC2H 150 C7
Little Argyll Street W1F 149 M6
Little Britain EC1A 151 J5
Little Chester Street SW1X 153 K4
Little George Street SW1P 154 C3
Little Marlborough Street W1F 150 A7
Little New Street EC4A 151 G6
Little Portland Street W1G 149 L6
Little Russell Street WC1A 150 C5
Little St James's Street SW1A 153 M2
Little Sanctuary SW1A 154 C3
Little Somerset Street E1 156 B3
Little Titchfield Street W1W 149 M5
Liverpool Grove SE17 155 K7
Liverpool Street EC2M 151 M5
Liverpool Street ⇌ ⊖ EC2M 151 M5
Lizard Street EC1V 151 K3
Llewellyn Street SE16 156 D7
Lloyd Baker Street WC1X 150 F2
Lloyd's Avenue EC3N 156 B3
Lloyd Square WC1X 150 F2
Lloyds Row EC1R 151 G2
Lloyd's Street WC1X 150 F2
Locksley Estate E14 157 L2
Locksley Street E14 157 L1
Lockyer Street SE1 155 L3
Lodge Road NW8 148 F3
Loftie Street SE16 156 D7
Logan Place W8 152 A5
Lolesworth Close E1 156 B1
Lollard Street SE11 154 F5
Lollard Street SE11 154 F6
Loman Street SE1 155 J2
Lomas Street E1 156 D1
Lombard Lane EC4Y 151 G6
Lombard Street EC3V 151 L7
London Bridge EC4R 151 L8
London Bridge ⇌ ⊖ SE1 155 L1
London Bridge Street SE1 155 L1
London Dungeon SE1 154 E2
London Eye SE1 154 E2
London Mews W2 148 E6
London Road SE1 155 H4
London Street EC3R 156 A3
London Street W2 148 E6
London Transport Museum WC2E 150 D7
London Wall EC2M 151 K5
London Zoo ZSL NW1 149 J1
Long Acre WC2E 150 D7
Longford Street NW1 149 L3
Long Lane EC1A 151 J5
Long Lane SE1 155 L3
Longmoore Street SW1V 153 M5
Longridge Road SW5 152 A5
Longville Road SE11 155 H5
Long Walk SE1 156 A8
Long Yard WC1N 150 E4
Lord North Street SW1P 154 C4
Lord's Cricket Ground NW8 148 E2
Lorenzo Street WC1X 150 E1
Lorrimore Road SE17 155 J8
Lorrimore Square SE17 155 H8
Lothbury EC2R 151 L6
Loughborough Street SE11 154 F7
Lovat Lane EC3R 151 M7
Love Lane EC2V 151 K6
Lovell Place SE16 157 K7
Lowell Street E14 157 K2
Lower Belgrave Street SW1W 153 K4
Lower Grosvenor Place SW1W 153 L4
Lower James Street W1F 150 A7
Lower John Street W1F 150 A7
Lower Marsh SE1 154 F3
Lower Road SE16 157 G7
Lower Sloane Street SW1W 153 J6
Lower Thames Street EC3R 156 A4
Lowndes Close * SW1X 153 J4
Lowndes Place SW1X 153 J4
Lowndes Square SW1X 153 H3
Lowndes Street SW1X 153 J4
Lucan Place SW3 152 F5
Lucey Road SE16 156 C8
Ludgate Circus EC4M 151 H6
Ludgate Hill EC4M 151 H6
Luke Street EC2A 151 M3
Lukin Street E1 157 G3
Lumley Street W1K 149 K7
Lupus Street SW1V 153 L7
Lupus Street SW1V 154 B7
Luton Street NW8 148 E4
Luxborough Street W1U 149 J4
Lyall Mews SW1X 153 J4
Lyall Street SW1X 153 J4
Lyons Place NW8 148 E3
Lytham Street SE17 155 K7

M

Macclesfield Road EC1V 151 J2
Macclesfield Street * W1D 150 B7
Mace Close E1W 156 E5
Macklin Street WC2B 150 D6
Mackworth Street NW1 149 M2
Macleod Street SE17 155 K7
Madame Tussauds NW1 149 J4
Maddox Street W1S 149 M7
Magdalen Street SE1 155 M2
Magee Street SE11 154 F8
Maguire Street SE1 156 C6
Maida Avenue W9 148 D4
Maida Vale W9 148 C2
Maida Vale ⊖ W9 148 C2
Maiden Lane SE1 155 K1
Maiden Lane WC2E 150 D7
Major Road SE16 156 D7
Makins Street SW3 153 G6
Malet Street WC1E 150 B4
Mallord Street SW3 152 E8
Mallory Street NW8 148 F3
Mallow Street EC1Y 151 L3
Malta Street EC1V 151 H3
Maltby Street SE1 156 B7
Manchester Square W1U 149 J6
Manchester Street W1U 149 J5
Manciple Street SE1 155 L3
Mandeville Place W1U 149 K6
Manette Street W1D 150 B6
Manilla Street E14 157 M6
Manningford Close EC1V 151 H2
Manor Place SE17 155 J7
Manresa Road SW3 152 F7
Mansell Street E1 156 C3
Mansfield Mews W1G 149 K5
Mansfield Street W1G 149 L5
Mansion House ⊖ EC4V 151 K7
Manson Mews SW7 152 D5
Manson Place SW7 152 D6
Mapleleaf Square SE16 157 J6
Maples Place E1 156 F1
Maple Street W1T 149 M4
Marble Arch ⊖ W1C 149 H7
Marchmont Street WC1H 150 C3
Margaret Street W1W 149 L6
Margaretta Terrace SW3 152 F7
Margery Street WC1X 150 F3
Marigold Street SE16 156 E7
Marine Street SE16 156 C7
Market Mews W1J 153 K1
Market Place W1W 149 M6
Markham Square SW3 153 G6
Markham Street SW3 153 G6
Mark Lane EC3R 156 A4
Marlborough Gate W2 148 E7
Marlborough Place NW8 148 C1
Marlborough Road SW1A 154 A2
Marlborough Street SW3 152 F6
Marloes Road W8 152 B4
Marlow Way SE16 157 H6
Maroon Street E14 157 K2
Marshall Street W1F 150 A7
Marshalsea Road SE1 155 J2
Marsham Street SW1P 154 C5
Marsh Wall E14 157 M5
Martha's Buildings EC1V 151 K3
Martha Street E1 156 F3
Martin Lane EC4V 151 L7
Maryland Road W9 148 A4
Marylands Road W9 148 A4
Marylebone ⇌ ⊖ NW1 149 G4
Marylebone Flyover W2 148 E5
Marylebone High Street W1U 149 K5
Marylebone Lane W1U 149 K6
Marylebone Road NW1 149 G4
Marylebone Street W1G 149 K5
Marylee Way SE11 154 F6
Masjid Lane E14 157 M2
Mason Street SE17 155 M5
Massinger Street SE17 155 M6
Masters Street E1 157 J1
Matlock Street E14 157 J2
Matthew Parker Street SW1H 154 C3
Maunsel Street SW1P 154 B5
Mayfair Place W1J 153 L1
Mayflower Street SE16 156 F7
Mayford Estate NW1 150 A1
Maynards Quay E1W 156 F4
May's Street WC2N 150 C8
McAuley Close SE1 154 F4
McLeod's Mews SW7 152 C5
Meadcroft Road SE11 155 G8
Meadcroft Road SE11 155 H8
Meadow Road SW8 154 E8
Meadow Row SE1 155 J5
Mead Row SE1 154 F4
Meakin Estate SE1 155 M4
Mecklenburgh Square WC1N 150 E3
Medway Street SW1P 154 B5
Meeting House Alley E1W 156 E5
Melcombe Place NW1 149 G4
Melcombe Street W1U 149 H4
Melina Place NW8 148 D2
Melior Street SE1 155 M2
Melton Street NW1 150 A2
Memorial Gates SW1W 153 K3
Mepham Street SE1 154 F2
Mercer Street WC2H 150 C7
Merchant Square W2 148 E5
Merlin Street EC1R 150 F2
Mermaid Court SE1 155 K2
Merrick Square SE1 155 K4
Merrington Road SW6 152 A8
Merrow Street SE17 155 L7
Methley Street SE11 155 G7
Meymott Street SE1 155 G2
Micawber Street N1 151 K1
Micklethwaite Lane SW6 152 A8
Middlesex Street E1 156 A1
Middlesex Street E1 156 B2
Middle Street EC1A 151 J5
Middle Temple WC2R 150 F7
Middle Temple Lane EC4Y 150 F7
Middleton Drive SE16 157 H6
Midland Road NW1 150 C1
Midship Close SE16 157 H6
Milborne Grove SW10 152 D7
Milcote Street SE1 155 H3
Miles Street SW8 154 D8
Milford Lane WC2R 150 F7
Milk Street EC2V 151 K6
Milk Yard E1W 157 G4
Millbank SW1P 154 D4
Millennium Bridge SE1 151 J8
Millennium Harbour E14 157 M6
Milligan Street E14 157 L4
Millman Mews WC1N 150 E4
Millman Street WC1N 150 E4
Mill Place E14 157 K3
Millstream Road SE1 156 B7
Mill Street SE1 156 C6
Mill Street W1S 149 L7
Milner Street SW3 153 G5
Milton Street EC2Y 151 K4
Milverton Street SE11 155 G7
Mincing Lane EC3M 156 A4
Minera Mews SW1W 153 J5
Minories EC3N 156 B3
Mitchell Street EC1V 151 J3
Mitre Road SE1 155 G2
Mitre Street EC3A 156 A3
Molyneux Street W1H 149 G5
Monck Street SW1P 154 C4
Monkton Street SE11 155 G5
Monkwell Square EC2Y 151 K5
Monmouth Place W2 148 A6
Monmouth Road W2 148 A6
Monmouth Street WC2H 150 C6
Montague Close SE1 155 L1
Montague Place EC3R 150 C5
Montague Street WC1B 150 C5
Montagu Mansions W1U 149 H5
Montagu Mews North W1H 149 H5
Montagu Mews West W1H 149 H6
Montagu Place W1H 149 H5
Montagu Row W1U 149 H5
Montagu Square W1H 149 H5
Montagu Street W1H 149 H6
Montford Place SE11 154 F7
Monthorpe Road E1 156 C1
Montpelier Square SW7 153 G3
Montpelier Street SW7 153 G3
Montpelier Walk SW7 152 G3
Montrose Place SW1X 153 K3
Monument ⊖ EC4R 151 L7
Monument Street EC3R 151 L7
Monument Street EC3R 151 M7
Monza Street E1W 157 G4
Moodkee Street SE16 157 G7
Moore Street SW3 153 H5
Moorfields EC2Y 151 L5
Moorgate EC2R 151 L6
Moorgate ⇌ ⊖ EC2Y 151 L5
Moor Lane EC2Y 151 K5
Moor Street W1D 150 C7
Mora Street EC1V 151 K2
Morecambe Street SE17 155 K6
Moreland Street EC1V 151 H2
More London SE1 156 A5
Moreton Place SW1V 154 A6
Moreton Street SW1V 154 B6
Moreton Terrace SW1V 154 A6
Morgan's Lane SE1 155 M2
Morgan's Lane SE1 156 A5
Morley Street SE1 155 G3
Mornington Crescent NW1 149 M1
Mornington Place NW1 149 L1
Mornington Terrace NW1 149 L1
Morocco Street SE1 156 A7
Morpeth Terrace SW1P 153 M5
Morris Street E1 156 F3
Morshead Road W9 148 A2
Mortimer Market WC1E 150 A4
Mortimer Street W1T 150 A5
Mortimer Street W1W 149 M5
Morton Place SE1 154 F4
Morwell Street WC1B 150 B5
Moscow Place W2 148 B7
Moscow Road W2 148 B7
Mossop Street SW3 153 G5
Motcomb Street SW1X 153 J4
Mount Gate W2 152 E2
Mount Mills EC1V 151 J3
Mount Pleasant WC1X 150 F4
Mount Row W1K 149 K8
Mount Street W1K 149 K8
Mount Street Mews W1K 149 K8
Mount Terrace E1 156 E1
Moxon Street W1U 149 J5
Mulberry Street E1 156 D2
Mulberry Walk SW3 152 E8
Mulready Street NW8 148 F4
Mundy Street N1 151 M2
Munster Square NW1 149 L3
Munton Road SE17 155 K5
Murphy Street SE1 154 F3
Murray Grove N1 151 K1
Musbury Street E1 157 G2
Muscovy Street EC3N 156 A4
Museum of London EC2Y 151 J5
Museum Street WC1A 150 C5
Myddelton Passage EC1R 151 G2
Myddelton Square EC1R 151 G1
Myddelton Street EC1R 151 G3
Myrdle Street E1 156 D2

N

Naoroji Street WC1X 150 F2
Napier Grove N1 151 K1
Narrow Street E14 157 K4
Nash Street NW1 149 L2
Nassau Street W1W 149 M5
Nathaniel Close * E1 156 C2
National Portrait Gallery WC2H 150 C8
Natural History Museum SW7 152 E4
Neal Street WC2H 150 C6
Neckinger SE1 156 C8
Needleman Street SE16 157 H7
Nelson Close NW6 148 A1
Nelson Place N1 151 H1
Nelson's Column WC2N 150 C8
Nelson Square SE1 155 H2
Nelson Street E1 156 E2
Nelson Terrace N1 151 H1
Neptune Street SE16 157 G7
Nesham Street E1W 156 D4
Netherton Grove SW10 152 D8
Netley Street NW1 149 M2
Nevern Place SW5 152 A6
Nevern Square SW5 152 A6
Neville Street SW7 152 E6
Newark Street E1 156 E2
New Atlas Wharf E14 157 M8
New Bond Street W1S 149 L7
New Bond Street W1S 149 L8
New Bridge Street EC4V 151 H6
New Broad Street EC2M 151 M5
New Burlington Street W1S 149 M7
Newburn Street SE11 154 F7
Newbury Street EC1A 151 J5
Newcastle Place W2 148 E5
New Cavendish Street W1G 149 K5
New Change EC4M 151 J6
New Church Road SE5 155 L8
Newcomen Street SE1 155 K2
Newcourt Street NW8 148 F1
Newell Street E14 157 L3
New Fetter Lane EC4A 151 G6
Newgate Street WC1A 151 H6
New Goulston Street E1 156 B2
Newham's Row SE1 156 A7
Newington Butts SE1 155 H6
Newington Causeway SE1 155 J4
New Kent Road SE1 155 K5
Newlands Quay E1W 156 F4
Newman Street W1T 150 A5
New North Place EC2A 151 M3
New North Road N1 151 L1
New North Street WC1N 150 D4
New Oxford Street WC1A 150 C6
Newport Street SE11 154 E5
New Quebec Street W1H 149 H6
New Ride SW7 152 E3
New Road E1 156 E2
New Row WC2N 150 C7
New Spring Gardens Walk SE1 154 D7
New Square WC2A 150 F6
New Street EC2M 156 A2
New Street Square EC4A 151 G6
Newton Road W2 148 A6
Newton Street WC2B 150 D5
New Union Street EC2Y 151 K5
Nicholas Lane EC3V 151 L7
Nicholson Street SE1 155 H1
Nightingale Place SW10 152 D8
Nile Street N1 151 K2
Nine Elms Lane SW8 154 C8
Noble Street EC2V 151 J6
Noel Road N1 151 J1
Noel Street W1F 150 A6
Norbiton Road E14 157 L2
Norfolk Crescent W2 149 G6
Norfolk Place W2 148 E6
Norfolk Square W2 148 E6
Norman Street EC1V 151 J3
Norris Street SW1Y 150 B8
Northampton Road EC1R 151 G3
Northampton Square EC1V 151 H2
North Audley Street W1K 149 J7
North Bank NW8 148 F2
Northburgh Street EC1V 151 H3
North Carriage Drive W2 148 F7
Northdown Street N1 150 D1
Northey Street E14 157 K4
North Gower Street NW1 150 A2
Northington Street WC1N 150 E4
North Mews WC1N 150 E4
North Ride W2 149 G7
North Row W1K 149 J7
North Tenter Street E1 156 C3
North Terrace SW3 152 F5
Northumberland Alley EC3N 156 B3
Northumberland Avenue WC2N 154 C1
Northumberland Place W2 148 A6
Northumberland Street WC2N 154 C1
North Wharf Road W2 148 E5
Northwick Terrace NW8 148 D3
Norway Gate SE16 157 K7
Norway Place E14 157 L3
Norwich Street EC4A 150 F5
Nottingham Place W1U 149 J4
Nottingham Street W1U 149 J4
Notting Hill Gate W11 148 A8
Notting Hill Gate ⊖ W11 152 A1
Nugent Terrace NW8 148 D1
Nutford Place W1H 149 G6

O

Oakden Street SE11 155 G5
Oakington Road W9 148 A3
Oak Lane E14 157 L3
Oakley Close EC1V 151 H1
Oakley Gardens SW3 153 G8
Oakley Square NW1 150 A1
Oakley Street SW3 152 F8
Oak Tree Road NW8 148 F2
Oat Lane EC2V 151 J5
Occupation Road SE17 155 J6
Ocean Square E1 157 J1
Odessa Street SE16 157 L7
Ogle Street W1W 149 M5
Old Bailey EC4M 151 H6
Old Barrack Yard SW1X 153 J3
Old Bond Street W1S 149 M8
Old Broad Street EC2N 151 M6
Old Brompton Road SW5 152 B6
Old Brompton Road SW7 152 D6
Old Burlington Street W1S 149 M7
Oldbury Place W1U 149 J4
Old Castle Street E1 156 B2
Old Cavendish Street W1G 149 L6
Old Church Road E1 157 H2
Old Church Street SW3 152 E7
Old Compton Street W1D 150 B7
Old Court Place W8 152 B3
Old Gloucester Street WC1N 150 D4
Old Jamaica Road SE16 156 C7
Old Jewry EC2R 151 K6
Old Kent Road SE1 155 M5
Old Marylebone Road NW1 149 G5
Old Montague Street E1 156 C1
Old North Street WC1X 150 E5
Old Paradise Street SE11 154 E5
Old Park Lane W1J 153 K2
Old Pye Street SW1P 154 B4
Old Queen Street SW1H 154 B3
Old Square WC2A 150 F6
Old Street EC1V 151 J3
Old Street ⇌ ⊖ EC1Y 151 L3
Old Street Junction EC1Y 151 L3
Oliver's Yard EC1Y 151 L3
Olney Road SE17 155 J8
O'Meara Street SE1 155 K2
Omega Place N1 150 D1
Onega Gate SE16 157 J8
Ongar Road SW6 152 A8
Onslow Gardens SW7 152 D6
Onslow Square SW7 152 E5
Onslow Square SW7 152 E6
Ontario Street SE1 155 J4
Ontario Way E14 157 M4
Opal Street SE1 155 H6
Orange Place SE16 157 G8
Orange Square SW1W 153 K6
Orange Street E1W 156 D5
Orange Street WC2H 150 B8
Orb Street SE17 155 L6
Orchardson Street NW8 148 E4
Orchard Street W1H 149 J6
Ordehall Street WC1N 150 E4
Orient Street SE11 155 H5
Orme Court W2 148 B8
Orme Lane W2 148 B8
Orme Square Gate W2 148 B8
Ormond Close WC1N 150 D4
Ormonde Gate SW3 153 H7
Ormond Yard SW1Y 150 A8
Orsett Street SE11 154 E6
Orsett Terrace W2 148 C6
Orton Street E1W 156 D5
Osbert Street SW1V 154 B6
Osborn Street E1 156 C2
Oslo Square SE16 157 K7
Osnaburgh Street NW1 149 L3
Osnaburgh Terrace NW1 149 L3
Ossington Buildings W1U 149 J5
Ossington Street W2 148 A7
Ossulston Street NW1 150 B1
Oswin Street SE11 155 H5
Othello Close SE1 155 H6
Otto Street SE17 155 H8
Outer Circle NW1 149 H3
Outer Circle NW1 149 K1
Oval ⊖ SE11 154 F8
Oval Way SE11 154 E7
Ovington Square SW3 153 G4
Ovington Street SW3 153 G5
Owen Street EC1V 151 G1
Oxendon Street SW1Y 150 B8
Oxford Circus ⊖ W1B 149 M6
Oxford Road NW6 148 A1
Oxford Square W2 148 F6
Oxford Street W1C 149 L6
Oxford Street WC1A 150 A6

P

Pace Place E1 156 E3
Pacific Wharf SE16 157 H5
Paddington ⇌ ⊖ W2 148 D6
Paddington Green W2 148 E5
Paddington Street W1U 149 J5

Pageant Crescent SE16 ... 157 K5
Page Street SW1P ... 154 B5
Paget Street EC1V ... 151 H2
Pakenham Street WC1X ... 150 E3
Palace Avenue W8 ... 152 B2
Palace Court W2 ... 148 A7
Palace Gardens
Terrace W8 ... 152 A1
Palace Gate W8 ... 152 C3
Palace Green W8 ... 152 B2
Palace Place SW1E ... 153 M4
Palace Street SW1E ... 153 M4
Pall Mall SW1Y ... 154 A1
Pall Mall East SW1Y ... 154 B1
Palmer Street SW1H ... 154 B3
Pancras Lane EC4N ... 151 K6
Pancras Road N1C ... 150 C1
Panton Street SW1Y ... 150 B8
Paradise Street SE16 ... 156 E7
Paradise Walk SW3 ... 153 H8
Pardoner Street SE1 ... 155 L4
Pardon Street EC1V ... 151 H3
Parfett Street E1 ... 156 D2
Paris Garden SE1 ... 155 G1
Park Crescent W1B ... 149 K4
Parker's Row SE1 ... 156 C7
Parker Street WC2B ... 150 D6
Park Lane W1K ... 149 H7
Park Lane W2 ... 153 J1
Park Place SW1A ... 153 M1
Park Road NW1 ... 149 H3
Park Square East NW1 ... 149 L3
Park Square Mews NW1 ... 149 K3
Park Square West NW1 ... 149 K3
Park Street SE1 ... 155 K1
Park Street W1K ... 149 J7
Park Village East NW1 ... 149 L1
Park Walk SW10 ... 152 D8
Park West Place W2 ... 149 G6
Parliament Street SW1A ... 154 C2
Parry Street SW8 ... 154 D8
Passmore Street SW1W ... 153 J6
Paternoster Square ... 151 J6
Pater Street W8 ... 152 A4
Pattina Walk SE16 ... 157 K5
Paul Street EC2A ... 151 M3
Paultons Square SW3 ... 152 E8
Paveley Street NW1 ... 149 G3
Pavilion Road SW1X ... 153 H3
Pavilion Street SW1X ... 153 H4
Paxton Terrace SW1 ... 153 L7
Peabody Avenue SW1V ... 153 L7
Peabody Estate SE1 ... 155 J1
Peacock Street SE17 ... 155 J6
Pearl Street E1W ... 156 F5
Pearman Street SE1 ... 155 G3
Pear Tree Court EC1R ... 151 G3
Peartree Lane E1W ... 157 G4
Pear Tree Street EC1V ... 151 J3
Peel Street W8 ... 152 A1
Peerless Street EC1V ... 151 K2
Pelham Crescent SW7 ... 152 F6
Pelham Place SW7 ... 152 F5
Pelham Street SW7 ... 152 F5
Pelier Street SE17 ... 155 K8
Pemberton Row EC4A ... 151 G6
Pembridge Gardens W2 ... 148 A8
Pembridge Place W2 ... 148 A7
Pembridge Square W2 ... 148 A7
Pembridge Villas W11 ... 148 A7
Pembroke Close SW1X ... 153 J3
Penang Street E1W ... 156 F5
Penfold Place NW8 ... 148 F5
Penfold Street NW8 ... 148 E4
Pennant Mews W8 ... 152 B5
Pennington Street E1W ... 156 D4
Pennyfields E14 ... 157 M4
Penrose Grove SE17 ... 155 J7
Penrose Street SE17 ... 155 J7
Penryn Road SE16 ... 156 E7
Penton Place SE17 ... 155 H6
Penton Rise WC1X ... 150 E2
Penton Street N1 ... 150 F1
Pentonville Road N1 ... 150 C1
Penywern Road SW5 ... 152 A6
Pepper Street SE1 ... 155 J2
Pepys Street EC3N ... 156 A4
Percival Street EC1V ... 151 H3
Percy Circus WC1X ... 150 F2
Percy Street W1T ... 150 B5
Perkin's Rent SE1 ... 154 B4
Petersham Mews SW7 ... 152 D4
Petersham Place SW7 ... 152 C4
Peter Street W1F ... 150 B7
Peto Place NW1 ... 149 L3
Petticoat Lane E1 ... 156 B2
Petty France SW1H ... 154 A3
Petty Wales EC3R ... 156 A4
Petyward SW3 ... 153 G6
Phelp Street SE17 ... 155 L7
Phene Street SW3 ... 153 G8
Phillimore Walk W8 ... 152 A3
Philpot Lane EC3M ... 151 M7
Philpot Street E1 ... 156 E2
Phipp's Mews SW1 ... 153 L5
Phipp Street EC2A ... 151 M3
Phoenix Place WC1X ... 150 F3
Phoenix Road NW1 ... 150 B2
Phoenix Street WC2H ... 150 C6
Piccadilly W1J ... 153 L2
Piccadilly Arcade SW1Y ... 153 M1
Piccadilly Circus W1J ... 150 A8
Piccadilly Circus ⊖ W1J ... 150 B8
Pickard Street EC1V ... 151 J2
Picton Place W1U ... 149 K6
Pier Head E1W ... 156 E6
Pigott Street E14 ... 157 M3
Pilgrimage Street SE1 ... 155 L3
Pimlico ⊖ SW1V ... 154 B6
Pimlico Road SW1W ... 153 J6
Pinchin Street E1 ... 156 D3
Pindar Street EC2A ... 151 M4
Pindock Mews W9 ... 148 B3
Pine Street EC1R ... 150 F3
Pitfield Street N1 ... 151 M1
Pitsea Street E1 ... 157 H3
Pitt's Head Mews W1J ... 153 K2
Pitt Street W8 ... 152 A2
Pixley Street E14 ... 157 L2
Platina Street * EC2A ... 151 L3
Plover Way SE16 ... 157 K8
Plumbers Row E1 ... 156 D2
Plumtree Court EC4A ... 151 G5
Plympton Street NW8 ... 148 F4
Pocock Street SE1 ... 155 H2
Poland Street W1F ... 150 A6
Pollen Street W1S ... 149 L7
Pollitt Drive NW8 ... 148 E3
Polperro Mews SE11 ... 155 G5
Polygon Road NW1 ... 150 B1
Pond Place SW3 ... 152 F6

Ponler Street E1 ... 156 E3
Ponsonby Place SW1P ... 154 C6
Ponsonby Terrace SW1P ... 154 C6
Ponton Road SW1V ... 154 B8
Pont Street SW1X ... 153 H4
Poolmans Street SE16 ... 157 H6
Pope Street SE1 ... 156 B7
Poplar Place W2 ... 148 B7
Poppin's Court EC4A ... 151 H6
Porchester Gardens W2 ... 148 B7
Porchester Gate W2 ... 148 C8
Porchester Place W2 ... 149 G6
Porchester Road W2 ... 148 B5
Porchester Square W2 ... 148 B6
Porchester Terrace W2 ... 148 C7
Porchester Terrace
North W2 ... 148 C6
Porlock Street SE1 ... 155 L3
Porter Street NW1 ... 149 H4
Porteus Road W2 ... 148 D5
Portland Place W1B ... 149 L4
Portland Place W1B ... 149 L5
Portland Square E1W ... 156 E5
Portland Street SE17 ... 155 L7
Portman Close W1H ... 149 J6
Portman Mews South W1H ... 149 J6
Portman Square W1H ... 149 J6
Portman Street W1H ... 149 J6
Portpool Lane EC1N ... 150 F4
Portsea Place W1H ... 149 G6
Portsmouth Street WC2A ... 150 E6
Portsoken Street E1 ... 156 B3
Portugal Street WC2A ... 150 E6
Potier Street SE1 ... 155 L4
Potters Fields SE1 ... 156 B6
Pottery Street SE16 ... 156 E7
Poultry EC2V ... 151 K6
Powis Place WC1N ... 150 D4
Praed Mews W2 ... 148 E6
Praed Street W2 ... 148 E6
Pratt Walk SE1 ... 154 E5
Premier Place E14 ... 157 M4
Prescot Street E1 ... 156 C3
Preston Close SE1 ... 155 M5
Price's Street SE1 ... 155 H1
Prideaux Place WC1X ... 150 F2
Primrose Street EC2A ... 156 A1
Prince Albert Road NW8 ... 148 F1
Prince Consort Road SW7 ... 152 D3
Princelet Street E1 ... 156 C1
Prince of Wales Gate SW7 ... 152 F3
Prince's Arcade SW1Y ... 150 A8
Prince's Gardens SW7 ... 152 E3
Prince's Gate Mews SW7 ... 152 E4
Princes Riverside
Road SE16 ... 157 H5
Prince's Square W2 ... 148 A7
Princess Road NW6 ... 148 A1
Princess Street SE1 ... 155 H4
Princes Street W1B ... 149 L6
Prince's Street EC2R ... 151 L6
Princeton Street WC1R ... 150 E5
Prioress Street SE1 ... 155 L4
Priory Green Estate N1 ... 150 E1
Priory Walk SW10 ... 152 D7
Proctor Street WC1V ... 150 E5
Prospect Place E1W ... 157 G5
Prospect Street SE16 ... 156 E7
Provident Court W1K ... 149 J7
Provost Street N1 ... 151 L1
Prusom Street E1W ... 156 F5
Pudding Lane EC3R ... 151 M7
Pumphouse Mews E1 ... 156 D3
Purbrook Street SE1 ... 156 A7
Purcell Street N1 ... 151 M1
Purchese Street NW1 ... 150 B1

Q

Quebec Way SE16 ... 157 J7
Queen Anne's Gate SW1H ... 154 B3
Queen Anne Street W1G ... 149 K5
Queen Elizabeth Street SE1 ... 156 B6
Queen Mother Gate W2 ... 153 J2
Queensborough
Terrace W2 ... 148 C7
Queensburry Place SW7 ... 152 E5
Queen's Gardens W2 ... 148 C7
Queen's Gate SW7 ... 152 D3
Queen's Gate SW7 ... 152 D4
Queen's Gate
Gardens SW7 ... 152 D5
Queen's Gate Mews SW7 ... 152 D4
Queen's Gate Place SW7 ... 152 D4
Queen's Gate Place
Mews SW7 ... 152 D4
Queen's Gate Terrace SW7 ... 152 C4
Queen's Head Yard SE1 ... 155 L2
Queen's Mews W2 ... 148 B7
Queen Square WC1N ... 150 D4
Queen's Row SE17 ... 155 K7
Queen Street EC4N ... 151 K7
Queen Street W1J ... 153 L1
Queen Street Place EC4R ... 151 K7
Queen's Walk SE1 ... 156 A5
Queen's Walk SW1A ... 153 M2
Queensway W2 ... 148 B6
Queensway ⊖ W2 ... 148 B8
Queen Victoria Street EC4V ... 151 J7
Quick Street N1 ... 151 H1

R

Raby Street E14 ... 157 K2
Radcliffe Road SE1 ... 156 B8
Radcot Street SE11 ... 155 G7
Radnor Mews W2 ... 148 E6
Radnor Place W2 ... 148 F6
Radnor Street EC1V ... 151 K3
Radnor Walk SW3 ... 153 G7
Railway Approach SE1 ... 155 L1
Railway Avenue SE16 ... 157 G6
Railway Street N1 ... 150 D1
Raine Street E1W ... 156 F5
Ralston Street SW3 ... 153 H7
Ramillies Place W1F ... 149 M6
Ramillies Street W1F ... 149 M6
Rampart Street E1 ... 156 E2
Rampayne Street SW1V ... 154 B6
Randall Road SE11 ... 154 D6
Randall Row SE11 ... 154 E6
Randolph Avenue W9 ... 148 C3
Randolph Crescent W9 ... 148 C4
Randolph Gardens NW6 ... 148 B1
Randolph Mews W9 ... 148 D4
Randolph Road W9 ... 148 C4
Ranelagh Grove SW1W ... 153 K6

Ranelagh Road SW1V ... 154 A7
Rangoon Street * EC3N ... 156 B3
Ranston Street NW8 ... 148 F4
Raphael Street SW7 ... 153 G3
Ratcliffe Cross Street E1W ... 157 J3
Ratcliffe Lane E14 ... 157 J3
Rathbone Place W1T ... 150 B5
Rathbone Street W1T ... 150 A5
Raven Row E1 ... 156 F1
Ravensdon Street SE11 ... 155 G7
Ravey Street EC2A ... 151 M3
Rawlings Street SW3 ... 153 G5
Rawstone Street EC1V ... 151 H2
Ray Street EC1R ... 151 G3
Reardon Place E1W ... 156 E5
Reardon Street E1W ... 156 E5
Rectory Square E1 ... 157 H1
Redan Place W2 ... 148 B6
Redburn Street SW3 ... 153 G7
Redcastle Close E1 ... 157 G4
Redcliffe Gardens SW10 ... 152 C7
Redcliffe Mews SW10 ... 152 C7
Redcliffe Place SW10 ... 152 C8
Redcliffe Road SW10 ... 152 D7
Redcliffe Square SW10 ... 152 B7
Redcliffe Street SW10 ... 152 B8
Redcross Way SE1 ... 155 K2
Redesdale Street SW3 ... 153 G7
Redfield Lane SW5 ... 152 A5
Redhill Street NW1 ... 149 L1
Red Lion Row SE5 ... 155 K8
Red Lion Square WC1R ... 150 E5
Red Lion Street WC2B ... 150 E5
Redman's Road E1 ... 157 G1
Red Place W1K ... 149 J7
Redriff Road SE16 ... 157 J8
Reedworth Street SE11 ... 155 G6
Reeves Mews W1K ... 149 J8
Regal Close E1 ... 156 D1
Regan Way N1 ... 151 M1
Regency Street SW1P ... 154 B5
Regent Place W1B ... 150 A7
Regent Square WC1H ... 150 D2
Regent Street SW1Y ... 150 B8
Regent Street W1S ... 149 M7
Regent's Park ⊖ W1B ... 149 L4
Regent's Park NW1 ... 149 J1
Regent's Park
Estate NW1 ... 149 L2
Relton Mews SW7 ... 153 G4
Remington Street N1 ... 151 H1
Remnant Street WC2A ... 150 E6
Renforth Street SE16 ... 157 G7
Renfrew Road SE11 ... 155 H5
Rennie Street SE1 ... 155 H1
Rephidim Street SE1 ... 155 M4
Repton Street E14 ... 157 K2
Reveley Square SE16 ... 157 K7
Rex Place W1K ... 149 J8
Rhodeswell Road E14 ... 157 L2
Rich Street E14 ... 157 M3
Rickett Street SW6 ... 152 A8
Ridgemount
Street WC1E ... 150 B4
Ridgemount
Gardens WC1E ... 150 B4
Riding House Street W1W ... 149 M5
Riley Road SE1 ... 156 B7
Ripley's Believe it or
Not! W1J ... 150 B8
Risborough Street SE1 ... 155 J2
Risdon Street SE16 ... 157 G7
Rissinghill Street N1 ... 150 F1
River Street EC1R ... 150 F2
Rivington Street EC2A ... 151 M3
Robert Adam Street W1U ... 149 J6
Roberts Close SE16 ... 157 J7
Robert Street NW1 ... 149 L2
Rochester Row SW1P ... 154 A5
Rochester Street SW1P ... 154 B5
Rockingham Street SE1 ... 155 J4
Rocliffe Street N1 ... 151 H1
Roding Mews E1W ... 156 D5
Rodmarton Street W1U ... 149 H5
Rodney Place SE17 ... 155 K5
Rodney Road SE17 ... 155 K5
Rodney Street N1 ... 150 E1
Roger Street WC1N ... 150 E4
Roland Gardens SW7 ... 152 D6
Roland Way SE17 ... 155 L7
Romford Street E1 ... 156 E2
Romilly Street W1D ... 150 B7
Romney Street SW1P ... 154 C4
Rood Lane EC3M ... 151 M7
Ropemaker Road SE16 ... 157 K7
Ropemaker Street EC2Y ... 151 L4
Roper Lane SE1 ... 156 B7
Rope Street SE16 ... 157 K8
Rope Walk Gardens E1 ... 156 E2
Rosary Gardens SW7 ... 152 D6
Roscoe Street EC1Y ... 151 K3
Rose Alley SE1 ... 151 K8
Rosebery Avenue EC1R ... 151 G3
Rosemoor Street SW3 ... 153 G6
Rose Street WC2E ... 150 C7
Rossmore Road NW1 ... 149 G3
Rotary Street SE1 ... 155 H3
Rotherhithe ⊖ SE16 ... 157 G5
Rotherhithe Street SE16 ... 157 G6
Rotherhithe Street SE16 ... 157 J4
Rotherhithe Tunnel SE16 ... 157 H5
Rothsay Street SE1 ... 155 M4
Rotten Row W2 ... 152 F2
Rouel Road SE16 ... 156 C8
Roupell Street SE1 ... 155 G2
Royal Albert Hall SW7 ... 152 E3
Royal Avenue SW3 ... 153 H6
Royal Hospital Road SW3 ... 153 H7
Royal Mint Street E1 ... 156 C4
Royal Oak ⊖ W2 ... 148 B5
Royal Oak Yard SE1 ... 156 A7
Royal Opera House WC2E ... 150 D7
Royal Road SE17 ... 155 H8
Royal Street SE1 ... 154 E3
Rudolph Road NW6 ... 148 A3
Rugby Street WC1N ... 150 E4
Rum Close E1W ... 156 F4
Rupert Street W1D ... 150 B7
Rushworth Street SE1 ... 155 H2
Russell Court SW1A ... 154 A2
Russell Square WC1B ... 150 C4
Russell Square ⊖ WC1B ... 150 D4
Russell Street WC2B ... 150 D7
Russia Dock Road SE16 ... 157 K6
Rutherford Street SW1P ... 154 B5
Rutland Gardens SW7 ... 153 G3
Rutland Gate SW7 ... 152 F3
Rutland Mews SW7 ... 152 F4
Rutland Street SW7 ... 152 F4
Ryder Street SW1Y ... 154 A1

S

Sackville Street W1S ... 150 A8
Saffron Hill EC1N ... 151 G4
Saffron Street EC1N ... 151 G4
Sail Street SE11 ... 154 F5
St Agnes Place SE11 ... 155 G8
St Alban's Grove W8 ... 152 B4
St Alban's Street SW1Y ... 150 B8
St Alphage Garden EC2Y ... 151 K5
St Andrews Hill EC4V ... 151 H7
St Andrew's Place NW1 ... 149 L4
St Andrew Street EC4A ... 151 G5
St Anne's Court W1F ... 150 B6
St Ann's Street SW1P ... 154 C4
St Anselm's Place W1K ... 149 K7
St Barnabas Street SW1W ... 153 K6
St Botolph Street EC3N ... 156 B2
St Bride Street EC4A ... 151 G6
St Chad's Street WC1H ... 150 D2
St Clare Street EC3N ... 156 B3
St Clements Lane WC2A ... 150 E6
St Cross Street EC1N ... 151 G4
St Dunstan's Hill EC3R ... 151 M7
St Dunstan's Lane EC3R ... 151 M7
St Elmos Road SE16 ... 157 J7
St Ermin's Hill SW1H ... 154 B4
St George's Circus SE1 ... 155 H3
St George's Drive SW1V ... 153 M6
St George's Estate E1 ... 156 D3
St George's Lane * EC3R ... 151 M7
St George's Road SE1 ... 155 G4
St George's Square SW1V ... 154 B7
St George Street W1S ... 149 L7
St Giles High Street WC2H ... 150 C5
St Helen's Place EC3A ... 151 M6
St James Market * SW1Y ... 150 B8
St James's Park SW1H ... 154 B3
St James's Park ⊖ SW1H ... 154 B3
St James's Place SW1A ... 153 M2
St James's Road SE16 ... 156 D8
St James's Square SW1Y ... 154 A1
St James's Street SW1A ... 153 M1
St James Walk EC1R ... 151 G3
St John's Lane EC1M ... 151 H4
St John's Place EC1M ... 151 H4
St John's Square EC1V ... 151 H4
St John's Street EC1V ... 151 H2
St John's Wood High
Street NW8 ... 148 F1
St John's Wood Road NW8 ... 148 E3
St Katharine's Way E1W ... 156 C5
St Leonard's Terrace SW3 ... 153 H7
St Loo Avenue SW3 ... 153 G8
St Luke's Close EC1V ... 151 K3
St Luke's Street SW3 ... 152 F6
St Manningtree E1 ... 156 C2
St Mark Street E1 ... 156 C3
St Martin's Lane WC2N ... 150 C7
St Martin's le Grand EC1A ... 151 J6
St Mary at Hill EC3R ... 151 M8
St Mary Axe EC3A ... 156 A3
St Mary Church Street SE16 ... 156 F7
St Mary's Gardens SE11 ... 155 G5
St Mary's Terrace W2 ... 148 D4
St Mary's Walk SE11 ... 155 G5
St Matthew Street SW1P ... 154 B4
St Michael's Street W2 ... 148 F6
St Olav's Square SE16 ... 156 F7
St Oswald's Place SE11 ... 154 E7
St Pancras
International ≷ N1C ... 150 C1
St Paul's ⊖ EC1A ... 151 J6
St Paul's Avenue SE16 ... 157 J6
St Paul's Cathedral EC4M ... 151 J6
St Paul's Churchyard EC4M ... 151 J6
St Paul's Way SE1 ... 151 L1
St Petersburgh Mews W2 ... 148 B7
St Petersburgh Place W2 ... 148 B7
St Saviours Wharf SE1 ... 156 C6
St Stephen's Gardens W2 ... 148 A5
St Swithin's Lane EC4N ... 151 L7
St Thomas Street SE1 ... 155 L2
St Vincent Street W1U ... 149 J5
Salamanca Street SE1 ... 154 D6
Sale Place W2 ... 148 F5
Salisbury Court EC4Y ... 151 G6
Salisbury Place W1H ... 149 H4
Salisbury Street NW8 ... 148 F4
Salmon Lane E14 ... 157 J2
Salter Road SE16 ... 157 J5
Salter Street E14 ... 157 M4
Samford Street NW8 ... 148 F4
Sampson Street E1W ... 156 D5
Sancroft Street SE11 ... 154 F6
Sandford Row SE17 ... 155 L6
Sandland Street WC1R ... 150 E5
Sandpiper Close SE16 ... 157 L6
Sandwich Street WC1H ... 150 C2
Sandy's Row E1 ... 156 B1
Sans Walk EC1R ... 151 G3
Sardinia Street WC2A ... 150 E6
Savage Gardens EC3N ... 156 B3
Savile Row W1S ... 149 M7
Savoy Hill WC2R ... 150 E8
Savoy Place WC2R ... 150 D8
Savoy Street WC2E ... 150 E7
Sawyer Street SE1 ... 155 J2
Scala Street W1T ... 150 A5
Scandrett Street E1W ... 156 E5
Scarborough Street E1 ... 156 C3
Scarsdale Villas W8 ... 152 A4
Schooner Close * SE16 ... 157 H6
Science Museum SW7 ... 152 E4
Scoresby Street SE1 ... 155 H2
Scotch House Junction SW1X ... 153 H3
Scotland Place SW1A ... 154 C1
Scott Ellis Grove NW8 ... 148 E2
Scott Lidgett Crescent SE16 ... 156 D7
Scrutton Street EC2A ... 151 M3
Seaford Street WC1H ... 150 D2
Searles Road SE1 ... 155 L5
Sea Life London
Aquarium SE1 ... 154 E3
Sebastian Street EC1V ... 151 H2
Secker Street SE1 ... 155 G2
Sedan Way SE17 ... 155 M6
Sedding Street SW1X ... 153 J5
Seddon Street WC1X ... 150 E2
Seething Lane EC3N ... 156 A4
Sekforde Street EC1R ... 151 H3
Selfridges W1A ... 149 J6
Selsey Street E14 ... 157 M1
Selwood Place SW7 ... 152 E6
Semley Place SW1W ... 153 K6
Senior Street W2 ... 148 B4
Senrab Street E1 ... 157 H2
Serle Street WC2A ... 150 F6

Serpentine Bridge W2 ... 152 E1
Serpentine Road W2 ... 152 F2
Seth Street SE16 ... 157 G7
Settles Street E1 ... 156 D2
Seven Dials WC2H ... 150 C6
Seville Street SW1X ... 153 H3
Sevington Street W9 ... 148 A3
Seward Street EC1V ... 151 J3
Seymour Mews W1H ... 149 J6
Seymour Place W1H ... 149 G5
Seymour Street W1H ... 149 H6
Seymour Street W2 ... 149 G7
Seymour Walk SW10 ... 152 C7
Shad Thames SE1 ... 156 B6
Shad Thames SE1 ... 156 C6
Shadwell ⊖ ⊖ E1 ... 156 F3
Shadwell Gardens E1 ... 156 F3
Shaftesbury Avenue W1D ... 150 B7
Shaftesbury Avenue WC2H ... 150 C6
Shaftesbury Street N1 ... 151 K1
Shakespeare's Globe SE1 ... 151 J8
Shand Street SE1 ... 156 A6
Sharsted Street SE17 ... 155 H7
Shaw Crescent E14 ... 157 K2
Shawfield Street SW3 ... 153 G7
Sheffield Terrace W8 ... 152 A2
Sheldon Square W2 ... 148 D5
Shelmerdine Close E3 ... 157 M1
Shelton Street WC2H ... 150 D6
Shepherdess Walk N1 ... 151 K1
Shepherd Street W1J ... 153 K1
Sheraton Street W1F ... 150 B6
Sherborne Lane EC4N ... 151 L7
Ship and Mermaid Row SE1 ... 155 M2
Shipwright Road SE16 ... 157 K7
Shirland Road W9 ... 148 A3
Shoe Lane EC4A ... 151 G5
Shorter Street EC3N ... 156 B4
Shorts Gardens WC2H ... 150 C6
Short Street SE1 ... 155 G2
Shoulder of Mutton
Alley E14 ... 157 K4
Shouldham Street W1H ... 149 G5
Shroton Street NW1 ... 148 F4
Siddons Lane W1H ... 149 H4
Sidmouth Street WC1N ... 150 D3
Sidney Square E1 ... 156 F2
Sidney Street E1 ... 156 F1
Silex Street SE1 ... 155 H3
Silk Street EC2Y ... 151 K4
Silver Walk SE16 ... 157 K5
Silvester Street SE1 ... 155 K3
Singer Street EC2A ... 151 L3
Sir John Soane's
Museum WC2A ... 150 E5
Skinner Place * SW1W ... 153 J6
Skinners Lane EC4V ... 151 K7
Skinner Street EC1R ... 151 G3
Slippers Place SE16 ... 156 F8
Sloane Avenue SW3 ... 153 G6
Sloane Court SW3 ... 153 J6
Sloane Court East SW3 ... 153 J6
Sloane Gardens SW1W ... 153 J6
Sloane Square SW1W ... 153 J5
Sloane Square ⊖ SW1W ... 153 J5
Sloane Street SW1X ... 153 H3
Sloane Terrace SW1X ... 153 J5
Smeaton Street E1W ... 156 E5
Smithfield Street EC1A ... 151 H5
Smith Square SW1P ... 154 C4
Smith Street SW3 ... 153 G7
Smith Terrace SW3 ... 153 G7
Smithy Street E1 ... 157 G1
Snowden Street EC2A ... 151 M4
Snow Hill EC1A ... 151 H5
Snowsfields SE1 ... 155 L2
Soho Square W1D ... 150 B6
Somerford Way SE16 ... 157 K7
Somers Crescent W2 ... 148 F6
Somerset House WC2R ... 150 E7
Somerstown Estate NW1 ... 150 A1
Sondes Street SE17 ... 155 L7
South & West Africa
Gate SW1A ... 154 A3
Southall Place SE1 ... 155 L3
Southampton
Buildings WC2A ... 150 F5
Southampton Place WC1A ... 150 D5
Southampton Row WC1B ... 150 D4
Southampton Street WC2E ... 150 D7
South Audley Street W1K ... 149 J8
South Carriage Drive SW1X ... 153 H3
South Carriage Drive SW7 ... 152 F3
South Eaton Place SW1W ... 153 J5
Southern Street N1 ... 150 E1
South Kensington ⊖ SW7 ... 152 E5
South Kensington ⊖ SW7 ... 152 E5
South Lambeth Road SW8 ... 154 D8
South Molton Lane W1K ... 149 K7
South Molton Street W1K ... 149 K7
South Parade SW3 ... 152 E7
South Place EC2M ... 151 L5
South Sea Street SE16 ... 157 L8
South Square WC1R ... 150 F5
South Street W1K ... 153 J1
South Tenter Street E1 ... 156 C3
South Terrace SW7 ... 152 F5
Southwark ⊖ SE1 ... 155 H2
Southwark Bridge SE1 ... 151 K8
Southwark Bridge Road SE1 ... 155 J3
Southwark Park Road SE16 ... 156 E8
Southwark Street SE1 ... 155 H1
Southwell Gardens SW7 ... 152 C5
South Wharf Road W2 ... 148 E6
Southwick Mews W2 ... 148 F6
Southwick Place W2 ... 148 F6
Southwick Street W2 ... 148 F6
Sovereign Close E1W ... 156 F4
Sovereign Crescent SE16 ... 157 J4
Spanish Place W1U ... 149 J5
Spa Road SE16 ... 156 C8
Spear Mews SW5 ... 152 A6
Spelman Street E1 ... 156 C1
Spence Close SE16 ... 157 K7
Spencer Street EC1V ... 151 H2
Spenser Street SW1E ... 154 A4
Spert Street E14 ... 157 J4
Spital Square E1 ... 156 A1
Spring Gardens SW1A ... 154 C1
Spring Street W2 ... 148 E6
Spurgeon Street SE1 ... 155 L4
Spur Road SE1 ... 154 F3
Stables Way SE11 ... 154 F7
Stable Yard Road SW1A ... 154 A2
Stacey Street WC2H ... 150 C6
Stafford Place SW1E ... 153 M3
Stafford Road NW6 ... 148 A2
Stafford Street W1S ... 149 M8
Stafford Terrace W8 ... 152 A3
Stainer Street SE1 ... 155 L2

Stainsby Road E14 157 M2
Stalham Street SE16 156 F8
Stamford Street SE1 155 G1
Stanford Place SE1 155 M6
Stanford Road W8 152 B4
Stanhope Close * SE16 157 H6
Stanhope Gardens SW7 152 D5
Stanhope Gate W1K 153 J1
Stanhope Mews SW7 152 D5
Stanhope Mews East SW7 152 D5
Stanhope Mews West SW7 152 D5
Stanhope Place W2 149 G7
Stanhope Place Gate W2 149 G7
Stanhope Row W1J 153 K1
Stanhope Street NW1 149 M1
Stanhope Terrace W2 148 E7
Stannary Street SE11 155 G7
Staples Close SE16 157 J5
Staple Street SE1 155 L3
Starcross Street NW1 150 A2
Star Street W2 148 F6
Station Approach Road SE1 155 J7
Stave Yard Road SE16 157 J5
Stead Street SE17 155 K6
Steedman Street SE17 155 J5
Steel's Lane E1 157 G3
Steeres Way SE16 157 K7
Stephenson Way NW1 150 A3
Stephen Street W1T 150 B5
Stepney Green E1 157 H1
Stepney High Street E1 157 J1
Stepney Way E1 156 E1
Sterling Street SW7 153 G3
Stevedore Street E1W 156 E5
Stevens Street SE1 156 A7
Steward Street * E1 156 B1
Stewart's Grove SW3 152 F6
Stew Lane EC4V 151 J7
Stillington Street SW1P 154 A5
Stockholm Way E1W 156 D5
Stocks Place E14 157 M3
Stone Buildings WC2A 150 F5
Stonecutter Street EC4A 151 G6
Stoney Lane E1 156 B2
Stoney Street SE1 155 K1
Stopford Road SE17 155 J7
Store Street WC1E 150 B5
Storey's Gate SW1H 154 C3
Storks Road SE16 156 D8
Stoughton Close SE11 154 E6
Stourcliffe Street W1H 149 G6
Strafford Street E14 157 M6
Strand WC2R 150 D8
Stratford Place W1C 149 K6
Stratford Road W8 152 A5
Strathearn Place W2 148 F7
Stratton Street W1J 153 L1
Strype Street E1 156 B2
Stuart Road NW6 148 A2
Stukeley Street WC2B 150 D6
Sturgeon Road SE17 155 J7
Sturge Street SE1 155 J3
Sturt Street N1 151 K1
Stutfield Street E1 156 D3
Sudley Street N1 151 H1
Sudrey Street SE1 155 J3
Suffolk Lane EC4V 151 L7
Suffolk Street SW1Y 150 B8
Sugar Quay Walk EC3R 156 A4
Sullivan Road SE11 155 G5
Summercourt Road E1 157 G2
Summer Place SW7 152 E6
Summers Street EC1R 150 F4
Sumner Street SE1 155 J1
Sunderland Terrace W2 148 A6
Sun Passage SE16 156 D8
Sun Street EC2M 151 M4
Surrendale Place W9 148 A4
Surrey Quays Road SE16 157 H7
Surrey Row SE1 155 H2
Surrey Square SE17 155 M6
Surrey Street WC2E 150 E7
Surrey Water Road SE16 157 H6
Sussex Gardens W2 148 E6
Sussex Mews East W2 148 E7
Sussex Place NW1 149 H3
Sussex Place W2 148 E6
Sussex Square W2 148 E7
Sussex Street SW1V 153 L7
Sutherland Avenue W9 148 A4
Sutherland Row SW1V 153 L6
Sutherland Square SE17 155 J7
Sutherland Street SW1V 153 L7
Sutton Row W1D 150 B6
Sutton Street E1 157 G3
Suttons Way EC1Y 151 K4
Swain Street NW8 148 F3
Swallow Place W1B 149 L6
Swallow Street W1B 150 A8
Swan Lane EC4R 151 L8
Swan Mead SE1 155 M4
Swan Road SE16 157 G6
Swan Street SE1 155 K3
Swan Walk SW3 153 H8
Swedenborg Gardens E1 156 E4
Sweeney Crescent SE1 156 C7
Swinton Street WC1X 150 E2
Sydney Street SW3 152 F6
Symons Street SW3 153 H6

T

Tabard Gardens Estate SE1 155 L3
Tabard Street SE1 155 L3
Tabernacle Street EC2A 151 L3
Tachbrook Street SW1V 154 A6
Talbot Road W2 148 A6
Talbot Square W2 148 E6
Tallis Street EC4Y 151 G7
Tamworth Street SW6 152 A8
Tanner Street SE1 156 A7
Taplow Street N1 151 K1
Tarling Street E1 156 F3
Tarver Road SE17 155 H7
Tate Britain SW1P 154 C6
Tate Modern SE1 151 J8
Tatum Street SE17 155 M6
Taunton Place NW1 149 G3
Tavistock Place WC1H 150 C3
Tavistock Square WC1H 150 C3
Tavistock Street WC2E 150 D7
Taviton Street WC1H 150 B3
Teak Close SE16 157 K6
Tedworth Square SW3 153 G7
Telford Terrace SW1V 153 M7
Temeraire Street SE16 157 G6
Temple ⊖ WC2R 150 F7
Temple Avenue EC4Y 151 G7
Temple Lane EC4Y 151 G7

Temple Place WC2R 150 F7
Templeton Place SW5 152 A5
Tench Street E1W 156 E5
Tenniel Close W2 148 C7
Tennis Street SE1 155 L2
Tenterden Street W1S 149 L6
Tenterground E1 156 B1
Teredo Street SE16 157 J8
Terminus Place SW1V 153 L4
Thame Road SE16 157 H6
Thanet Street WC1H 150 C2
Thavies Inn EC4A 151 G6
Thayer Street W1U 149 K5
The Arches WC2N 150 D8
The Boltons SW10 152 C7
The British Library NW1 150 C2
The Broad Walk W2 148 B8
The Broad Walk W8 152 C2
The Cut SE1 155 G2
Theed Street SE1 155 G2
The Flower Walk W2 152 D3
The Grange SE1 156 B8
The Highway E1W 156 F4
The Little Boltons SW10 152 C7
The Mall SW1A 154 B2
The Mitre E14 157 L3
The Monument EC3R 151 L7
The National Gallery WC2N 150 C8
Theobald's Road WC1X 150 E4
Theobald Street SE1 155 L5
The Oval (Surrey County
Cricket Ground) SE11 154 F8
The Shard SE1 155 L2
The Vale SW3 152 E8
Thirleby Road SW1P 154 A4
Thomas More Street E1W 156 D4
Thomas Road E14 157 M2
Thoresby Street N1 151 K1
Thorney Street SW1P 154 C5
Thornton Place W1H 149 H4
Thrale Street SE1 155 K1
Thrawl Street E1 156 C1
Threadneedle Street EC2R 151 L6
Three Colt Street E14 157 L3
Three Oak Lane SE1 156 B7
Throgmorton Avenue EC2N 151 L6
Throgmorton Street EC2N 151 L6
Thurland Road SE16 156 D8
Thurloe Place SW7 152 F5
Thurloe Square SW7 152 F5
Thurloe Street SW7 152 E5
Thurlow Street SE17 155 M7
Tichbourne Row W2 148 F6
Tiller Road E14 157 M8
Tillman Street E1 156 E3
Tilney Street W1J 153 K1
Timber Pond Road SE16 157 J6
Tinsley Road E1 157 G1
Tinworth Street SE11 154 D6
Tisdall Place SE17 155 L6
Tite Street SW3 153 H8
Tiverton Street SE1 155 J4
Token House Yard EC2R 151 L6
Tolmer's Square NW1 150 A3
Tomlin's Terrace E14 157 K2
Tonbridge Street WC1H 150 D2
Tooley Street SE1 155 L1
Tooley Street SE1 156 B6
Tor Gardens W8 152 A2
Torquay Street W2 148 A5
Torrens Street EC1V 151 G1
Torrington Place SE16 156 D5
Torrington Place WC1E 150 B4
Torrington Square WC1E 150 B4
Tothill Street SW1H 154 B3
Tottenham Court Road W1T 150 A4
Tottenham Court
Road ⊖ W1D 150 B6
Tottenham Street W1T 150 A5
Toulmin Street SE1 155 J3
Tower Bridge EC3N 156 B5
Tower Bridge
Approach EC3N 156 B5
Tower Bridge Road SE1 156 A7
Tower Bridge Wharf E1W 156 C5
Tower Gateway ⊖ EC3N 156 B4
Tower Hill EC3N 156 B4
Tower Hill ⊖ EC3N 156 B4
Tower of London EC3N 156 B4
Tower Place SE16 156 A4
Tower Street WC2H 150 C7
Townsend Street SE17 155 M5
Toynbee Street E1 156 B1
Trafalgar Gardens E1 157 H1
Trafalgar Square WC2N 150 C8
Trafalgar Street SE17 155 L7
Transept Street NW1 148 F5
Trebeck Street W1J 153 L1
Trebovir Road SW5 152 A6
Tregunter Road SW10 152 C7
Trenton Road SE16 156 E8
Tresham Crescent NW8 148 F3
Trevor Place SW7 153 G3
Trevor Square SW7 153 G3
Trevor Street SW7 153 G3
Trinidad Street E14 157 M4
Trinity Church Square SE1 155 K3
Trinity Square EC3N 156 B4
Trinity Street SE1 155 K3
Trump Street EC2V 151 K6
Tudor Street EC4Y 151 G7
Tufton Street SW1P 154 C4
Tunnel Road SE16 157 G6
Turks Row SW3 153 J6
Turner's Road E3 157 L2
Turner Street E1 156 E2
Turnmill Street EC1N 151 G4
Turpentine Lane SW1V 153 L7
Turquand Street SE17 155 K6
Tyers Gate SE1 155 M3
Tyers Street SE11 154 E7
Tyers Terrace SE11 154 E7
Tyron Street SW3 153 H6
Tysoe Street EC1R 151 G3

U

Udall Street SW1P 154 A5
Ufford Street SE1 155 G3
Ulster Place NW1 149 K4
Umberston Street E1 156 E2
Undershaft EC3A 156 A2
Underwood Road E1 156 D1
Underwood Street N1 151 K2
Union Street SE1 155 H2
University Street WC1E 150 A4
Upbrook Mews W2 148 D6
Upper Belgrave Street SW1X 153 J4
Upper Berkeley Street W1H 149 H6

Upper Brook Street W1K 149 J7
Upper Cheyne Row SW3 152 F8
Upper Grosvenor Street W1K 149 J8
Upper Ground SE1 155 F1
Upper Harley Street NW1 149 K3
Upper James Street W1F 150 A7
Upper John Street W1F 150 A7
Upper Marsh SE1 154 E3
Upper Montagu Street W1H 149 H5
Upper St Martin's WC2H 150 C7
Upper Tachbrook
Street SW1V 154 A5
Upper Thames Street EC4V 151 J7
Upper Wimpole Street W1G 149 K4
Upper Woburn Place WC1H 150 B2
Urlwin Street SE5 155 J8
Uxbridge Street W8 152 A1

V

Valentine Place SE1 155 G3
Vandon Passage SW1H 154 A3
Vandon Street SW1H 154 A4
Vandy Street EC2A 151 M4
Varden Street E1 156 E2
Varndell Street NW1 149 M2
Vauban Street SE16 156 C8
Vaughan Street SE16 157 L7
Vaughan Way E1W 156 D5
Vauxhall ⊖ ≷ SW8 154 D7
Vauxhall Bridge SW1V 154 C7
Vauxhall Bridgefoot SE1 154 D7
Vauxhall Bridge Road SW1V 153 M5
Vauxhall Cross SW8 154 D7
Vauxhall Grove SW8 154 D8
Vauxhall Street SE11 154 E6
Vauxhall Walk SE11 154 E6
Venables Street W2 148 E4
Vere Street W1G 149 K6
Vernon Place WC1A 150 D5
Vernon Rise WC1X 150 E2
Verulam Street WC1X 150 F4
Vestry Street N1 151 L2
Victoria ≷ ⊖ SW1V 153 L5
Victoria & Albert
Museum SW7 152 F4
Victoria Embankment SW1A 154 D2
Victoria Embankment WC2R 150 F7
Victoria Gate W2 148 F7
Victoria Road W8 152 C4
Victoria Square SW1W 153 L4
Victoria Street SW1E 153 L4
Victoria Place SE17 155 K5
Victory Way SE16 157 K7
Vigo Street W1S 149 M8
Villa Street SE17 155 L7
Villiers Street WC2N 150 D8
Vincent Close SE16 157 K7
Vincent Square SW1P 154 B5
Vincent Street SW1P 154 B5
Vincent Terrace N1 151 H1
Vince Street EC1V 151 L2
Vine Court E1 156 D1
Vinegar Street E1W 156 E5
Vine Hill EC1R 150 F4
Vine Lane SE1 156 A6
Vine Street EC3N 156 B3
Violet Hill NW8 148 C1
Virgil Street SE1 154 F4
Virginia Street E1W 156 D4
Viscount Street EC2Y 151 J4

W

Wadding Street SE17 155 K6
Wakefield Street WC1H 150 D3
Wakeling Street E14 157 J3
Wakley Street EC1V 151 H2
Walbrook EC4N 151 L7
Walcorde Avenue SE17 155 K6
Walcot Square SE11 155 G5
Walden Street E1 156 E2
Wallwood Street E14 157 M1
Walpole Street SW3 153 H6
Walter Terrace E1 157 H2
Walton Place SW3 153 H4
Walton Street SW3 153 G4
Walworth Place SE17 155 K7
Walworth Road SE17 155 J5
Wandsworth Road SW8 154 C8
Wansey Street SE17 155 J6
Wapping ⊖ E1W 156 F5
Wapping High Street E1W 156 E6
Wapping Lane E1W 156 F4
Wapping Wall E1W 157 G5
Warden's Grove SE1 155 J2
Wardour Street W1F 150 B6
Warner Street EC1R 150 F4
Warren Street E1 149 M4
Warren Street ⊖ NW1 149 M3
Warrington Crescent W9 148 C3
Warrington Gardens W9 148 C4
Warwick Avenue W9 148 C4
Warwick Avenue ⊖ W9 148 C4
Warwick Crescent W2 148 C5
Warwick House Street SW1Y 154 B1
Warwick Lane EC4M 151 H6
Warwick Place W9 148 C4
Warwick Road SW5 152 A6
Warwick Row SW1E 153 L4
Warwick Square SW1V 153 M6
Warwick Street W1B 150 A7
Warwick Way SW1V 153 L6
Waterhouse Square EC1N 151 G5
Waterloo ≷ ⊖ SE1 154 F2
Waterloo Bridge SE1 154 E1
Waterloo Bridge WC2R 150 E8
Waterloo East ≷ SE1 155 G2
Waterloo Place SW1Y 154 B1
Waterloo Road SE1 154 F1
Waterloo Road SE1 155 G2
Waterman Way E1W 156 E5
Waterside Close SE16 156 D7
Watling Street EC4N 151 K7
Watney Street E1 156 F3
Watts Street E1W 156 E5
Waveney Close E1W 156 D5
Weavers Lane SE1 156 A6
Webber Row SE1 155 G3
Webber Street SE1 155 H3
Webb Street SE1 156 A8
Webster Road SE16 156 D8
Weigh House Street W1K 149 K7
Welbeck Street W1G 149 K5
Welbeck Way W1G 149 K6

Welland Mews E1W 156 E5
Wellclose Square E1 156 D4
Wellesley Street E1 157 H2
Wellesley Terrace N1 151 K2
Wellington Arch W1J 153 K2
Wellington Square SW3 153 H6
Wellington Place NW8 148 E2
Wellington Road NW8 148 E1
Wellington Street WC2E 150 D7
Wells Mews W1T 150 A5
Wells Street W1T 150 A5
Wells Way SE5 155 M8
Wenlock Road N1 151 K1
Wenlock Street N1 151 K1
Wentworth Street E1 156 B2
Werrington Street NW1 150 A1
Wesley Street W1G 149 K5
West Arbour Street E1 157 G2
Westbourne Crescent W2 148 D7
Westbourne Gardens W2 148 B6
Westbourne Gate W2 148 E7
Westbourne Grove W2 148 A6
Westbourne Grove
Terrace W2 148 B6
Westbourne Park Road W2 148 A5
Westbourne Park Villas W2 148 A5
Westbourne Terrace W2 148 D6
Westbourne Terrace
Mews W2 148 C6
Westbourne Terrace
Road W2 148 C5
West Brompton ⊖ ≷ SW5 152 A7
West Carriage Drive W2 152 E2
Westcott Road SE17 155 H8
West Cromwell Road SW5 152 A5
Western Place SE16 157 G6
Westferry ⊖ E14 157 M4
Westferry Circus E14 157 M5
Westferry Road E14 157 M5
Westgate Terrace SW10 152 B7
West Halkin Street SW1X 153 J4
West India Avenue E14 157 M5
West India Dock Road E14 157 M4
Westland Place N1 151 K2
West Lane SE16 156 E7
Westminster ⊖ SW1A 154 D3
Westminster Abbey SW1P 154 C3
Westminster Bridge
Road SE1 154 F3
Westmoreland Place SW1V 153 L7
Westmoreland Road SE17 155 K8
Westmoreland Street W1G 149 K5
Westmoreland Terrace SW1V 153 L7
Weston Rise WC1X 150 E1
Weston Street SE1 155 M2
Weston Street SE1 155 M3
Westport Street E1 157 H2
West Poultry Avenue EC1A 151 H5
West Road SW3 153 H7
West Smithfield EC1A 151 H5
West Square SE11 155 H4
West Tenter Street E1 156 C3
West Street WC2H 150 C7
West Warwick Place SW1V 153 M6
Westway W2 148 B5
Wetherby Gardens SW5 152 C6
Weyhill Road E1 156 D2
Weymouth Mews W1G 149 L5
Weymouth Street W1G 149 K5
Wharfdale Road N1 150 D1
Wharfedale Street SW10 152 B7
Wharf Road N1 151 J1
Wharton Street WC1X 150 F2
Wheatley Street W1G 149 K5
Whetstone Park WC2A 150 E5
Whidborne Street WC1H 150 D2
Whiskin Street EC1R 151 G2
Whitcomb Street WC2H 150 B8
Whitechapel ≷ ⊖ E1 156 E1
Whitechapel Estate E1 156 C4
Whitechapel High Street E1 156 C2
Whitechapel Road E1 156 D1
Whitecross Street EC1Y 151 K3
Whitefriars Street EC4Y 151 G6
Whitehall SW1A 154 C2
Whitehall Court SW1A 154 D2
Whitehall Place SW1A 154 D1
White Hart Street SE11 155 G6
White Hart Yard SE1 155 L2
Whitehaven Street NW8 148 F4
White Horse Lane E1 157 H1
Whitehorse Road E1 157 J1
Whitehorse Road E1 157 J3
White Horse Street W1J 153 L1
White Kennett Street E1 156 B2
White Lion Hill EC4V 151 H7
White Lion Street N1 150 F1
White's Grounds SE1 156 A7
White's Row E1 156 B1
White Tower Way E1 157 J1
Whitfield Place W1T 150 A4
Whitfield Street W1T 150 A4
Whitgift Street SE11 154 E5
Whittaker Street SW1W 153 J6
Whittlesey Street SE1 155 G2
Wicker Street E1 156 E3
Wickham Close E1 157 G1
Wickham Street SE11 154 E7
Wicklow Street WC1X 150 E2
Widegate Street E1 156 A1
Widley Road W9 148 A3
Wigmore Place W1G 149 K5
Wigmore Street W1U 149 K6
Wigton Place SE11 155 G7
Wilbraham Place SW1X 153 J5
Wild Court WC2B 150 E6
Wild's Rents SE1 155 M4
Wild Street WC2B 150 D6
Wilfred Street SW1E 153 M4
Wilkes Street E1 156 B1
William IV Street WC2N 150 C8
William Mews SW1X 153 H3
William Road NW1 149 M3
Willow Place SW1P 154 A5
Willow Street EC2A 151 M3
Wilmington Square WC1X 150 F3
Wilmington Street WC1X 150 F2
Wilson Grove SE16 156 E7
Wilson Street EC2A 151 L4
Wilton Crescent SW1X 153 J3
Wilton Mews SW1X 153 K4
Wilton Place SW1X 153 J3
Wilton Road SW1V 153 L4
Wilton Row SW1X 153 J3
Wimpole Mews W1G 149 K5
Wimpole Street W1G 149 K5

Winchester Street SW1V 153 L6
Winchester Walk SE1 155 K1
Wincott Street SE11 155 G5
Windmill Road SE11 154 F7
Windmill Street W1T 150 B5
Windrose Close SE16 157 H6
Windsor Terrace N1 151 K1
Wine Close E1W 156 F5
Winnett Street W1D 150 B7
Winsland Mews W2 148 E6
Winsland Street W2 148 E6
Winsley Street W1W 150 A6
Winthrop Street E1 156 E1
Woburn Place WC1H 150 C3
Woburn Square WC1H 150 C4
Wodeham Gardens E1 156 E1
Wolfe Crescent SE16 157 H7
Wolseley Street SE1 156 C6
Woodbridge Street EC1R 151 G3
Woodchester Square W9 148 A4
Woodfall Street SW3 153 H7
Woodland Crescent SE16 157 H7
Woodseer Street E1 156 C1
Woods Mews W1K 149 J7
Woods Place SE1 156 A8
Woodstock Street W1C 149 K6
Wood Street EC2V 151 K6
Woolaston Close SE1 155 J5
Wooler Street SE17 155 L7
Wooton Street SE1 155 G2
Worgan Street SE11 154 E6
Worgan Street SE16 157 H8
Wormwood Street EC2M 151 M5
Worship Street EC2A 151 M4
Wren Street WC1X 150 E3
Wright's Lane W8 152 A3
Wyatt Close SE16 157 L7
Wyclif Street EC1V 151 H2
Wymering Road W9 148 A2
Wynard Terrace SE11 154 F7
Wyndham Place W1H 149 H5
Wyndham Street W1H 149 G4
Wynnstay Gardens W8 152 A4
Wynyat Street EC1V 151 H2
Wythburn Place W1H 149 H6

Y

Yalding Road SE16 156 C8
Yardley Street WC1X 150 F2
Yeomans Row SW3 153 G4
York Boulevard WC2N 150 D8
York Bridge NW1 149 J3
York Gate NW1 149 J4
York Road SE1 154 E2
Yorkshire Road E14 157 K3
York Square E14 157 J2
York Street W1H 149 G5
York Terrace East NW1 149 J4
York Terrace West NW1 149 J4
York Way N1 150 D1

Z

Zoar Street SE1 155 J1
ZSL London Zoo NW1 149 J1

Index to place names

This index lists places appearing in the main-map section of the atlas in alphabetical order. The reference following each name gives the atlas page number and gri reference of the square in which the place appears. The map shows counties, unitary authorities and administrative areas, together with a list of the abbreviated name forms used in the index. The top 100 places of tourist interest are indexed in **red**, World Heritage sites in **green**, motorway service areas in **blue**, airports in blue *italic* and National Parks in green *italic*.

Scotland

Abers	**Aberdeenshire**
Ag & B	**Argyll and Bute**
Angus	**Angus**
Border	**Scottish Borders**
C Aber	**City of Aberdeen**
C Dund	**City of Dundee**
C Edin	**City of Edinburgh**
C Glas	**City of Glasgow**
Clacks	**Clackmannanshire (1)**
D & G	**Dumfries & Galloway**
E Ayrs	**East Ayrshire**
E Duns	**East Dunbartonshire (2)**
E Loth	**East Lothian**
E Rens	**East Renfrewshire (3)**
Falk	**Falkirk**
Fife	**Fife**
Highld	**Highland**
Inver	**Inverclyde (4)**
Mdloth	**Midlothian (5)**
Moray	**Moray**
N Ayrs	**North Ayrshire**
N Lans	**North Lanarkshire (6)**
Ork	**Orkney Islands**
P & K	**Perth & Kinross**
Rens	**Renfrewshire (7)**
S Ayrs	**South Ayrshire**
Shet	**Shetland Islands**
S Lans	**South Lanarkshire**
Stirlg	**Stirling**
W Duns	**West Dunbartonshire (8)**
W Isls	**Western Isles (Na h-Eileanan an Iar)**
W Loth	**West Lothian**

Wales

Blae G	**Blaenau Gwent (9)**
Brdgnd	**Bridgend (10)**
Caerph	**Caerphilly (11)**
Cardif	**Cardiff**
Carmth	**Carmarthenshire**
Cerdgn	**Ceredigion**
Conwy	**Conwy**
Denbgs	**Denbighshire**
Flints	**Flintshire**
Gwynd	**Gwynedd**
IoA	**Isle of Anglesey**
Mons	**Monmouthshire**
Myr Td	**Merthyr Tydfil (12)**
Neath	**Neath Port Talbot (13)**
Newpt	**Newport (14)**
Pembks	**Pembrokeshire**
Powys	**Powys**
Rhondd	**Rhondda Cynon Taff (15)**
Swans	**Swansea**
Torfn	**Torfaen (16)**
V Glam	**Vale of Glamorgan (17)**
Wrexhm	**Wrexham**

Channel Islands & Isle of Man

Guern	**Guernsey**
Jersey	**Jersey**
IoM	**Isle of Man**

England

BaNES	**Bath & N E Somerset (18)**
Barns	**Barnsley (19)**
Bed	**Bedford**
Birm	**Birmingham**
Bl w D	**Blackburn with Darwen (20)**
Bmouth	**Bournemouth**
Bolton	**Bolton (21)**
Bpool	**Blackpool**
Br & H	**Brighton & Hove (22)**
Br For	**Bracknell Forest (23)**
Bristl	**City of Bristol**
Bucks	**Buckinghamshire**
Bury	**Bury (24)**
C Beds	**Central Bedfordshire**
C Brad	**City of Bradford**
C Derb	**City of Derby**
C KuH	**City of Kingston upon Hull**
C Leic	**City of Leicester**
C Nott	**City of Nottingham**
C Pete	**City of Peterborough**
C Plym	**City of Plymouth**
C Port	**City of Portsmouth**
C Sotn	**City of Southampton**
C Stke	**City of Stoke-on-Trent**
C York	**City of York**
Calder	**Calderdale (25)**
Cambs	**Cambridgeshire**
Ches E	**Cheshire East**
Ches W	**Cheshire West and Chester**
Cnwll	**Cornwall**
Covtry	**Coventry**
Cumb	**Cumbria**
Darltn	**Darlington (26)**
Derbys	**Derbyshire**
Devon	**Devon**
Donc	**Doncaster (27)**
Dorset	**Dorset**
Dudley	**Dudley (28)**
Dur	**Durham**
E R Yk	**East Riding of Yorkshire**
E Susx	**East Sussex**
Essex	**Essex**
Gatesd	**Gateshead (29)**
Gloucs	**Gloucestershire**
Gt Lon	**Greater London**
Halton	**Halton (30)**
Hants	**Hampshire**
Hartpl	**Hartlepool (31)**
Herefs	**Herefordshire**
Herts	**Hertfordshire**
IoS	**Isles of Scilly**
IoW	**Isle of Wight**
Kent	**Kent**
Kirk	**Kirklees (32)**
Knows	**Knowsley (33)**
Lancs	**Lancashire**
Leeds	**Leeds**
Leics	**Leicestershire**
Lincs	**Lincolnshire**
Lpool	**Liverpool**
Luton	**Luton**
M Keyn	**Milton Keynes**
Manch	**Manchester**
Medway	**Medway**
Middsb	**Middlesbrough**
NE Lin	**North East Lincolnshire**
N Linc	**North Lincolnshire**
N Som	**North Somerset (34)**
N Tyne	**North Tyneside (35)**
N u Ty	**Newcastle upon Tyne**
N York	**North Yorkshire**
Nhants	**Northamptonshire**
Norfk	**Norfolk**
Notts	**Nottinghamshire**
Nthumb	**Northumberland**
Oldham	**Oldham (36)**
Oxon	**Oxfordshire**
Poole	**Poole**
R & Cl	**Redcar & Cleveland**
Readg	**Reading**
Rochdl	**Rochdale (37)**
Rothm	**Rotherham (38)**
Rutlnd	**Rutland**
S Glos	**South Gloucestershire (39)**
S on T	**Stockton-on-Tees (40)**
S Tyne	**South Tyneside (41)**
Salfd	**Salford (42)**
Sandw	**Sandwell (43)**
Sefton	**Sefton (44)**
Sheff	**Sheffield**
Shrops	**Shropshire**
Slough	**Slough (45)**
Solhll	**Solihull (46)**
Somset	**Somerset**
St Hel	**St Helens (47)**
Staffs	**Staffordshire**
Sthend	**Southend-on-Sea**
Stockp	**Stockport (48)**
Suffk	**Suffolk**
Sundld	**Sunderland**
Surrey	**Surrey**
Swindn	**Swindon**
Tamesd	**Tameside (49)**
Thurr	**Thurrock (50)**
Torbay	**Torbay**
Traffd	**Trafford (51)**
W & M	**Windsor and Maidenhead (52)**
W Berk	**West Berkshire**
W Susx	**West Sussex**
Wakefd	**Wakefield (53)**
Warrtn	**Warrington (54)**
Warwks	**Warwickshire**
Wigan	**Wigan (55)**
Wilts	**Wiltshire**
Wirral	**Wirral (56)**
Wokham	**Wokingham (57)**
Wolves	**Wolverhampton (58)**
Worcs	**Worcestershire**
Wrekin	**Telford & Wrekin (59)**
Wsall	**Walsall (60)**

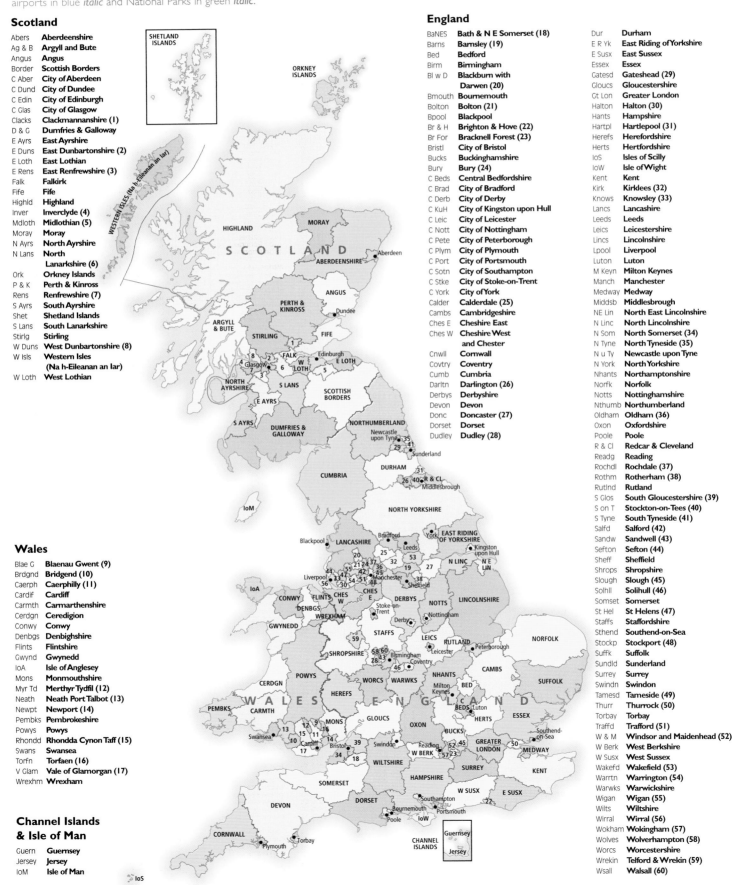

A

Abbas Combe Somset 17 Q10
Abberley Worcs 39 N8
Abberley Common Worcs ..39 N8
Abberton Essex 34 G11
Abberton Worcs 30 C9
Abbess Roding Essex 22 C2
Abbeydale Sheff 50 H4
Abbey Green Staffs 50 C8
Abbey St Bathans Border 87 P9
Abbeystead Lancs 63 K10
Abbey Town Cumb 71 J5
Abbey Village Lancs 57 M4
Abbey Wood Gt Lon 21 P7
Abbotrule Border 80 E10
Abbots Bickington
  Devon 14 G9
Abbots Bromley Staffs 40 E3
Abbotsbury Dorset 7 N6
Abbots Deuglie P & K 92 G12
Abbotsham Devon 14 H6
Abbotskerswell Devon 6 B8
Abbots Langley Herts 20 H3
Abbots Leigh N Som 17 M2
Abbotsley Cambs 32 H5
Abbots Morton Worcs 30 D3
Abbots Ripton Cambs 32 H2
Abbot's Salford Warwks 30 E4
Abbots Worthy Hants 9 N2
Abbotts Ann Hants 19 K11
Abbott Street Dorset 8 E7
Abdon Shrops 39 L5
Aberaeron Cerdgn 36 G7
Aberaman Rhondd 27 L8
Aberangell Gwynd 47 N8
Aberarder Highld 99 J4
Aberargie P & K 92 H11
Aberarth Cerdgn 36 G6
Aberavon Neath 26 G10
Abercanaid Myr Td 27 M7
Abercarn Caerph 27 P9
Abercastle Pembks 24 F3
Abercegir Powys 47 N10
Aberchalder Lodge Highld ..98 D8
Aberchirder Abers 102 E5
Abercraf Powys 26 H6
Abercregan Neath 26 H9
Abercwmboi Rhondd 27 L8
Abercych Pembks 36 D11
Abercynon Rhondd 27 M9
Aberdalgie P & K 92 G10
Aberdare Rhondd 27 L8
Aberdaron Gwynd 46 C6
Aberdeen C Aber 95 Q1
Aberdeen Airport C Aber ..103 J11
Aberdeen Crematorium
  C Aber 95 P2
Aberdour Fife 86 E5
Aberdulais Neath 26 G8
Aberdyfi Gwynd 47 K11
Aberedw Powys 38 C11
Abereiddy Pembks 24 E3
Abererch Gwynd 46 G4
Aberfan Myr Td 27 M8
Aberfeldy P & K 92 C6
Aberffraw IoA 54 E7
Aberford Leeds 59 K6
Aberfoyle Stirlg 85 J3
Abergavenny Mons 28 C6
Abergele Conwy 55 P6
Abergorlech Carmth 26 D3
Abergwesyn Powys 37 P9
Abergwili Carmth 25 Q5
Abergwynfi Neath 27 J3
Abergwyngregyn Gwynd ..55 J7
Abergynolwyn Gwynd 47 L9
Aberkenfig Brdgnd 27 J11
Aberlady E Loth 87 J6
Aberlemno Angus 93 N5
Aberllefenni Gwynd 47 M8
Aberllynfi Powys 27 N2
Aberlour Moray 101 K6
Abermule Powys 38 D4
Abernant Carmth 25 N4
Aber-nant Rhondd 27 L7
Abernethy P & K 92 H11
Abernyte P & K 93 J8
Aberporth Cerdgn 36 D9
Abersoch Gwynd 46 E6
Abersychan Torfn 28 B7
Aberthin V Glam 16 D2
Abertillery Blae G 27 P7
Abertridwr Caerph 27 N10
Abertridwr Powys 48 B10
Aberuthven P & K 92 E11
Aberystwyth Cerdgn 37 J4
Aberystwyth
  Crematorium Cerdgn ..37 K4
Abingdon-on-Thames
  Oxon 19 M2
Abinger Common Surrey ..10 H2
Abinger Hammer Surrey ..10 H1
Abington Nhants 32 A5
Abington S Lans 78 F4
Abington Pigotts Cambs ..33 K7
Abingworth W Susx 10 H6
Ab Kettleby Leics 41 Q3
Ablington Gloucs 30 E11
Abney Derbys 50 G5
Aboyne Abers 95 J3
Abram Wigan 57 L8
Abriachan Highld 98 H2
Abridge Essex 21 P4
Abronhill N Lans 85 N7
Abson S Glos 17 Q2
Abthorpe Nhants 31 N5
Aby Lincs 53 L7
Acaster Malbis C York 59 N5
Acaster Selby N York 59 N6
Accrington Lancs 57 N3
Accrington
  Crematorium Lancs ..57 N3
Acha Ag & B 88 F5
Achahoish Ag & B 83 L7
Achaladur P & K 92 C6
Achaleven Ag & B 90 C9
Acha Mor W Isls 111 d2
Achanalt Highld 106 D9
Achandunie Highld 107 K7
Achany Highld 107 J3
Acharacle Highld 89 N3
Acharn Highld 89 P6
Acharn P & K 92 B6

Achavanich Highld 110 E7
Achduart Highld 105 Q2
Achfary Highld 108 F7
A'Chill Highld 96 C8
Achiltibuie Highld 105 Q1
Achina Highld 109 M4
Achinhoan Ag & B 75 L8
Achintee Highld 97 N2
Achintraid Highld 97 L2
Achlyness Highld 108 B10
Achmore Highld 97 M3
Achmore W Isls 111 d2
Achnacarnin Highld 108 B8
Achnacarry Highld 98 B10
Achnacloich Highld 96 H7
Achnaconeran Highld 98 F5
Achnacroish Ag & B 90 B7
Achnadrish House Ag & B ..89 K6
Achnafauld P & K 92 D8
Achnagarron Highld 107 L8
Achnaha Highld 89 K3
Achnahaird Highld 108 A11
Achnairn Highld 109 K12
Achnalea Highld 90 B4
Achnamara Ag & B 83 L5
Achnasheen Highld 106 C10
Achnashellach Lodge
  Highld 105 Q11
Achnastank Moray 101 K8
Achosnich Highld 89 K3
Achranich Highld 89 P6
Achreamie Highld 110 B3
Achriabhach Highld 90 F3
Achriesgill Highld 108 E5
Achtoty Highld 109 M3
Achurch Nhants 42 E12
Achvaich Highld 107 L4
Achvarasdal Highld 110 B3
Ackergill Highld 110 G5
Acklam Middsb 66 C4
Acklam N York 60 D2
Ackleton Shrops 39 P3
Acklington Nthumb 73 M1
Ackton Wakefd 59 K9
Ackworth Moor Top
  Wakefd 59 K10
Acle Norfk 45 N7
Acock's Green Birm 40 E10
Acol Kent 23 P9
Acomb C York 59 M4
Acomb Nthumb 72 G7
Aconbury Herefs 28 F3
Acton Ches E 49 L5
Acton Gt Lon 21 K7
Acton Staffs 49 P7
Acton Suffk 34 E7
Acton Beauchamp Herefs ..39 M11
Acton Bridge Ches W 49 L1
Acton Burnell Shrops 39 K2
Acton Green Herefs 39 M11
Acton Park Wrexhm 48 G5
Acton Round Shrops 39 L3
Acton Scott Shrops 39 J4
Acton Trussell Staffs 40 C4
Acton Turville S Glos 18 B5
Adbaston Staffs 49 N9
Adber Dorset 17 N11
Adbolton Notts 51 N12
Adderbury Oxon 31 L7
Adderley Shrops 49 M7
Addewell W Loth 86 B9
Addingham C Brad 58 E4
Addington Bucks 31 Q8
Addington Gt Lon 21 M9
Addington Kent 22 D10
Addiscombe Gt Lon 21 M9
Addlestone Surrey 20 G9
Addlethorpe Lincs 53 N9
Adeyfield Herts 20 H2
Adfa Powys 38 C2
Adforton Herefs 38 H7
Adisham Kent 23 N11
Adlestrop Gloucs 30 G8
Adlingfleet E R Yk 60 E9
Adlington Lancs 57 L6
Admaston Staffs 40 D3
Admaston Wrekin 49 L11
Adpar Cerdgn 36 E11
Adsborough Somset 16 H9
Adscombe Somset 16 G8
Adstock Bucks 31 Q6
Adstone Nhants 31 N4
Adversane W Susx 10 H5
Advie Highld 100 H8
Adwick Le Street Donc ..59 M11
Adwick upon Dearne
  Donc 51 L1
Ae D & G 78 G10
Ae Bridgend D & G 78 G10
Afan Forest Park Neath ..26 H8
Affleck Abers 102 D7
Affpuddle Dorset 8 C9
Affric Lodge Highld 98 B5
Afon-wen Flints 48 D2
Afton IoW 9 L9
Agecroft Crematorium
  Salfd 57 P8
Agglethorpe N York 65 J9
Aigburth Lpool 56 H10
Aike E R Yk 60 H5
Aiketgate Cumb 71 P6
Aikton Cumb 71 L5
Ailsworth C Pete 42 G9
Ainderby Quernhow
  N York 65 N10
Ainderby Steeple N York ..65 N8
Aingers Green Essex 35 J11
Ainsdale Sefton 56 F6
Ainstable Cumb 71 Q6
Ainsworth Bury 57 N6
Ainthorpe N York 66 G6
Ainville W Loth 86 D9
Aird Ag & B 83 L3
Aird D & G 68 E7
Aird W Isls 111 e2
Aird a Mhulaidh W Isls ..111 c3
Aird Asaig W Isls 111 c3
Aird Dhubh Highld 97 J3
Airdeny Ag & B 90 D9
Aird of Kinloch Ag & B ..89 L9
Aird of Sleat Highld 96 H9
Airdrie N Lans 85 N9
Airdriehill N Lans 85 N9
Airds of Kells D & G 69 N5
Aird Uig W Isls 111 c2
Airidh a bhruaich W Isls ..111 c3
Airieland D & G 70 C4

Airlie Angus 93 K5
Airmyn E R Yk 60 C8
Airntully P & K 92 G8
Airor Highld 97 J8
Airth Falk 85 Q5
Airton N York 58 B3
Aisby Lincs 42 E3
Aisby Lincs 52 C5
Aish Devon 5 N7
Aish Devon 6 A10
Aisholt Somset 16 G8
Aiskew N York 65 M9
Aislaby N York 66 H9
Aislaby N York 67 J6
Aislaby S on T 65 P5
Aisthorpe Lincs 52 D7
Aith Shet 111 k4
Akeld Nthumb 81 K8
Akeley Bucks 31 P6
Albaston Cnwll 5 J6
Alberbury Shrops 48 G11
Albourne W Susx 11 K6
Albrighton Shrops 39 P2
Albrighton Shrops 49 J10
Alburgh Norfk 45 L11
Albury Herts 33 M10
Albury Surrey 10 G1
Albury Heath Surrey 10 G2
Alcaig Highld 107 J10
Alcaston Shrops 39 J5
Alcester Warwks 30 E3
Alciston E Susx 11 P8
Alcombe Somset 16 C7
Alconbury Cambs 32 H2
Alconbury Weston Cambs ..32 H2
Aldborough N York 59 K2
Aldborough Norfk 45 K4
Aldbourne Wilts 19 J5
Aldbrough E R Yk 61 L6
Aldbrough St John N York ..65 L5
Aldbury Herts 20 F2
Aldcliffe Lancs 63 J9
Aldclune P & K 92 D3
Aldeburgh Suffk 35 P5
Aldeby Norfk 45 P10
Aldenham Herts 21 J4
Alderbury Wilts 8 H2
Alderford Norfk 45 J6
Alderholt Dorset 8 G5
Alderley Gloucs 29 K10
Alderley Edge Ches E 57 Q12
Aldermans Green Covtry ..41 J10
Aldermaston W Berk 19 P7
Alderminster Warwks 30 G4
Aldershot Hants 20 D12
Alderton Gloucs 30 D7
Alderton Nhants 31 Q5
Alderton Suffk 35 M8
Alderton Wilts 18 C4
Alderwasley Derbys 51 J9
Aldfield N York 58 H1
Aldford Ches W 48 H4
Aldgate Rutlnd 42 E9
Aldham Essex 34 F10
Aldham Suffk 34 H7
Aldingbourne W Susx 10 E8
Aldingham Cumb 62 F7
Aldington Kent 13 K3
Aldington Worcs 30 E5
Aldington Corner Kent 13 K3
Aldivalloch Moray 101 M9
Aldochlay Ag & B 84 F5
Aldreth Cambs 33 M3
Aldridge Wsall 40 D7
Aldringham Suffk 35 P5
Aldsworth Gloucs 30 F11
Aldunie Moray 101 M9
Aldwark Derbys 50 G8
Aldwark N York 59 L2
Aldwick W Susx 10 E9
Aldwincle Nhants 32 E1
Aldworth W Berk 19 P5
Alexandria W Duns 84 G7
Aley Somset 16 G8
Alfington Devon 6 F4
Alfold Surrey 10 G4
Alfold Crossways Surrey ..10 G3
Alford Abers 102 D11
Alford Lincs 53 M8
Alford Somset 17 N9
Alford Crematorium
  Lincs 53 M8
Alfreton Derbys 51 K9
Alfrick Worcs 39 N10
Alfrick Pound Worcs 39 N10
Alfriston E Susx 11 P9
Algarkirk Lincs 43 J3
Alhampton Somset 17 P8
Alkborough N Linc 60 F9
Alkham Kent 13 N2
Alkmonton Derbys 50 F12
Allaleigh Devon 5 Q9
Allanaquoich Abers 94 B4
Allanbank N Lans 85 P10
Allanton Border 81 J4
Allanton N Lans 85 P10
Allanton S Lans 85 M11
Allaston Gloucs 28 H7
Allbrook Hants 9 M4
All Cannings Wilts 18 F8
Allendale Nthumb 72 F9
Allen End Warwks 40 F9
Allenheads Nthumb 72 F10
Allen's Green Herts 33 M12
Allensmore Herefs 28 F2
Allenton C Derb 41 J2
Aller Devon 5 N7
Aller Somset 17 K9
Allerby Cumb 70 H7
Allercombe Devon 6 E4
Allerford Somset 16 B6
Allerston N York 67 J10
Allerthorpe E R Yk 60 D5
Allerton C Brad 58 E7
Allerton Highld 107 M8
Allerton Lpool 56 H10
Allerton Bywater Leeds ..59 K8
Allerton Mauleverer
  N York 59 K3

Allington Wilts 18 F8
Allington Wilts 18 H11
Allithwaite Cumb 62 H6
Allonby Cumb 70 H7
Alloway S Ayrs 76 F7
Allowenshay Somset 17 K12
All Stretton Shrops 39 J3
Alltchaorunn Highld 90 G6
Alltwalis Carmth 25 Q3
Alltwen Neath 26 G7
Allweston Dorset 17 P12
Almeley Herefs 38 G11
Almington Staffs 49 N8
Almodington W Susx 10 D9
Almondbank P & K 92 G9
Almondbury Kirk 58 F10
Almondsbury S Glos 28 H11
Alne N York 59 L2
Alness Highld 107 L8
Alnham Nthumb 81 L11
Alnmouth Nthumb 81 P11
Alnwick Nthumb 81 P10
Alperton Gt Lon 21 J6
Alphamstone Essex 34 E9
Alpheton Suffk 34 E6
Alphington Devon 6 C5
Alport Derbys 50 G7
Alpraham Ches E 49 L4
Alresford Essex 34 H11
Alrewas Staffs 40 F5
Alsager Ches E 49 P4
Alsop en le Dale Derbys ..50 F9
Alston Cumb 72 D10
Alston Devon 7 J3
Alstone Gloucs 29 N3
Alstonefield Staffs 50 F9
Alston Sutton Somset 17 K6
Alswear Devon 15 M7
Altandhu Highld 108 A12
Altarnun Cnwll 4 F4
Altass Highld 106 H3
Altcreich Ag & B 89 N8
Altgaltraig Ag & B 83 Q8
Althorne Essex 22 H4
Althorpe N Linc 60 E11
Altnabreac Station
  Highld 110 B6
Altnaharra Highld 109 K8
Alton Derbys 51 J7
Alton Hants 10 B3
Alton Staffs 50 E11
Alton Barnes Wilts 18 G8
Alton Pancras Dorset 7 Q3
Alton Priors Wilts 18 G8
Alton Towers Staffs 50 E11
Altrincham Traffd 57 P10
Altrincham
  Crematorium Traffd ..57 N10
Altskeith Hotel Stirlg 84 H3
Alva Clacks 85 P4
Alvanley Ches W 49 J1
Alvaston C Derb 41 K2
Alvechurch Worcs 40 D11
Alvecote Warwks 40 G6
Alvediston Wilts 8 E3
Alveley Shrops 39 N5
Alverdiscott Devon 15 J7
Alverstoke Hants 9 P7
Alverstone IoW 9 P9
Alverthorpe Wakefd 58 H9
Alverton Notts 42 B2
Alves Moray 100 H3
Alvescot Oxon 30 H12
Alveston S Glos 28 H10
Alveston Warwks 30 G3
Alvingham Lincs 53 K5
Alvington Gloucs 28 H8
Alwalton C Pete 42 G10
Alwinton Nthumb 81 J11
Alwoodley Leeds 58 H6
Alyth P & K 93 J6
Ambergate Derbys 51 J9
Amberley Gloucs 29 L8
Amberley W Susx 10 G6
Amble Nthumb 81 Q12
Amblecote Dudley 40 B9
Ambler Thorn C Brad 58 E8
Ambleside Cumb 62 G2
Ambleston Pembks 24 H4
Ambrosden Oxon 31 N9
Amcotts N Linc 60 E10
Amersham Bucks 20 F4
Amersham Common
  Bucks 20 F4
Amersham Old Town
  Bucks 20 F4
Amersham on the Hill
  Bucks 20 F4
Amerton Railway &
  Farm Staffs 40 C2
Amesbury Wilts 18 H11
Amhuinnsuidhe W Isls ..111 c3
Amington Staffs 40 G6
Amisfield Town D & G 78 G11
Amlwch IoA 54 F3
Ammanford Carmth 26 E6
Amotherby N York 66 G11
Ampfield Hants 9 L3
Ampleforth N York 66 E10
Ampney Crucis Gloucs 18 F1
Ampney St Mary Gloucs ..18 G1
Ampney St Peter Gloucs ..18 F1
Amport Hants 19 K11
Ampthill C Beds 32 E8
Ampton Suffk 34 E3
Amroth Pembks 25 K7
Amulree P & K 92 D8
Amwell Herts 21 J2
Anaheilt Highld 89 Q4
Ancaster Lincs 42 E2
Ancroft Nthumb 81 N5
Ancrum Border 80 E8
Anderby Lincs 53 N8
Anderby Creek Lincs 53 N8
Andover Hants 19 L10
Andoversford Gloucs 30 D9
Andreas IoM 56 d2
Anerley Gt Lon 21 M9
Anfield Lpool 56 G9
Anfield Crematorium
  Lpool 56 G9
Angarrack Cnwll 2 E7
Angarrick Cnwll 3 J6
Angelbank Shrops 39 L7
Angle Pembks 24 F8
Anglesey IoA 54 F4
Anglesey Abbey Cambs ..33 N4
Angmering W Susx 10 G8

Angram N York 59 M5
Ankerville Highld 107 N7
Anlaby E R Yk 60 H8
Anmer Norfk 44 C4
Anmore Hants 9 Q5
Annan D & G 71 K3
Annandale Water
  Services D & G 78 H9
Annat Highld 105 N10
Annathill N Lans 85 M8
Anna Valley Hants 19 L11
Annbank S Ayrs 76 G6
Anne Hathaway's
  Cottage Warwks 30 F3
Annfield Plain Dur 73 L9
Anniesland C Glas 85 J8
Ansdell Lancs 56 G3
Ansford Somset 17 P9
Ansley Warwks 40 H8
Anslow Staffs 40 G3
Anslow Gate Staffs 40 G3
Anstey Herts 33 L9
Anstey Leics 41 M6
Anstruther Fife 87 L2
Ansty W Susx 11 L5
Ansty Warwks 41 K10
Ansty Wilts 8 E3
Anthorn Cumb 71 K4
Antingham Norfk 45 L4
An t-Ob W Isls 111 c4
Antonine Wall Falk 85 P7
Anton's Gowt Lincs 43 J2
Antony Cnwll 5 J8
Antrobus Ches W 57 M11
Anwick Lincs 52 G12
Anwoth D & G 69 N7
Aperfield Gt Lon 21 N10
Apethorpe Nhants 42 E10
Apley Lincs 52 G8
Apperknowle Derbys 51 J5
Apperley Gloucs 29 M3
Appin Ag & B 90 C7
Appleby N Linc 60 G10
Appleby-in-
  Westmorland Cumb ..64 C4
Appleby Magna Leics 40 H5
Appleby Parva Leics 40 H6
Applecross Highld 97 J2
Appledore Devon 14 H6
Appledore Devon 16 E12
Appledore Kent 13 J4
Appleford Oxon 19 N3
Apple015garth Town D & G ..78 H11
Appleshaw Hants 19 K10
Appleton Halton 57 K10
Appleton Oxon 19 M1
Appleton Warrtn 57 L11
Appleton-le-Moors N York ..66 G9
Appleton-le-Street N York ..66 G11
Appleton Roebuck N York ..59 M6
Appleton Thorn Warrtn ..57 M11
Appleton Wiske N York ..65 P6
Appletreehall Border 80 C10
Appletreewick N York 58 D3
Appley Somset 16 E10
Appley Bridge Lancs 57 K7
Apse Heath IoW 9 P10
Apsley End C Beds 32 G9
Apuldram W Susx 10 D9
Arabella Highld 107 N7
Arbirlot Angus 93 Q7
Arboll Highld 107 P6
Arborfield Wokham 20 C9
Arborfield Cross Wokham ..20 C9
Arbroath Angus 93 Q7
Arbuthnott Abers 95 N6
Archdale Carmth 25 Q7
Archdeacon Newton
  Darltn 65 M4
Archencarroch W Duns ..84 G6
Archiestown Moray 101 J6
Arclid Green Ches E 49 P3
Ardallie Abers 103 L7
Ardanaiseig Hotel Ag & B ..90 E11
Ardaneaskan Highld 97 L3
Ardarroch Highld 97 L2
Ardbeg Ag & B 74 F4
Ardbeg Ag & B 83 B9
Ardbeg Ag & B 84 C6
Ardcharnich Highld 106 C5
Ardchiavaig Ag & B 89 J11
Ardchonnel Ag & B 83 P1
Ardchullarie More Stirlg ..85 K1
Arddarroch Ag & B 84 D4
Arddleen Powys 48 F11
Ardechive Highld 98 A10
Ardeer N Ayrs 76 E4
Ardeley Herts 33 K10
Ardelve Highld 97 M4
Arden Ag & B 84 F6
Ardens Grafton Warwks ..30 E4
Ardentallen Ag & B 90 B10
Ardentinny Ag & B 84 D5
Ardentraive Ag & B 83 Q7
Ardeonaig Stirlg 91 P8
Ardersier Highld 107 N10
Ardessie Highld 105 Q5
Ardfern Ag & B 83 M3
Ardfernal Ag & B 82 H8
Ardgay Highld 107 K4
Ardgour Highld 90 D4
Ardgowan Inver 84 D8
Ardhallow Ag & B 84 C7
Ardhasig W Isls 111 c3
Ardheslaig Highld 105 L10
Ardindrean Highld 106 C5
Ardingly W Susx 11 M4
Ardington Oxon 19 M3
Ardlamont Ag & B 83 P9
Ardleigh Essex 34 H10
Ardleigh Heath Essex 34 H10
Ardler P & K 93 J7
Ardley Oxon 31 M8
Ardlui Ag & B 91 J12
Ardlussa Ag & B 83 J5
Ardmair Highld 106 B3
Ardmaleish Ag & B 84 B8
Ardminish Ag & B 75 J3
Ardmolich Highld 89 P2
Ardmore Ag & B 84 F7
Ardmore Highld 107 L5
Ardnadam Ag & B 84 C7
Ardnagrask Highld 106 H11
Ardnarff Highld 97 M3
Ardnastang Highld 89 Q4
Ardpatrick Ag & B 83 L10
Ardrishaig Ag & B 83 M6

166 Ardross - Barcombe Cross

Ardross Highld 107 K7
Ardrossan N Ayrs 76 D3
Ardsley East Leeds 58 H8
Ardslignish Highld 89 L4
Ardtalla Ag & B 82 G11
Ardtoe Highld 89 M3
Arduaine Ag & B 83 M2
Ardullie Highld 107 J9
Ardvasar Highld 96 H8
Ardvorlich P & K 91 P10
Ardvourlie W Isls 111 c3
Ardwell D & G 68 F9
Ardwick Manch 57 Q9
Areley Kings Worcs 39 P7
Arevegaig Highld 89 N3
Arford Hants 10 D3
Argoed Caerph 27 N8
Argyll Forest Park Ag & B 84 D3
Aribruach W Isls 111 c3
Aridhglas Ag & B 88 H10
Arileod Ag & B 88 E5
Arinagour Ag & B 88 F5
Ariogan Ag & B 90 B10
Arisaig Highld 97 J11
Arisaig House Highld 97 J11
Arkendale N York 59 K2
Arkesden Essex 33 M9
Arkholme Lancs 63 L7
Arkleton D & G 79 N10
Arkley Gt Lon 21 K4
Arksey Donc 59 M11
Arkwright Town Derbys 51 K6
Arle Gloucs 29 N4
Arlecdon Cumb 70 G10
Arlesey C Beds 32 H9
Arleston Wrekin 49 M12
Arley Ches E 57 M11
Arley Warwks 40 H8
Arlingham Gloucs 29 J6
Arlington Devon 15 K4
Arlington E Susx 12 B8
Armadale Highld 96 H8
Armadale Highld 109 N3
Armadale W Loth 85 Q8
Armathwaite Cumb 71 Q6
Arminghall Norfk 45 L8
Armitage Staffs 40 E4
Armley Leeds 58 H7
Armscote Warwks 30 G5
Armthorpe Donc 59 N12
Arnabost Ag & B 88 F4
Arncliffe N York 64 G12
Arncroach Fife 87 K2
Arndilly House Moray 101 K6
Arne Dorset 8 E9
Arnesby Leics 41 N8
Arngask P & K 92 H12
Arnisdale Highld 97 L7
Arnish Highld 104 H11
Arniston Mdloth 86 G9
Arnol W Isls 111 d1
Arnold E R Yk 61 J6
Arnold Notts 51 N10
Arnprior Stirlg 85 K4
Arnside Cumb 63 J6
Aros Ag & B 89 L7
Arrad Foot Cumb 62 F6
Arram E R Yk 60 H5
Arran N Ayrs 75 P5
Arrathorne N York 65 L8
Arreton IoW 9 N9
Arrina Highld 105 L10
Arrington Cambs 33 K6
Arrochar Ag & B 84 E3
Arrow Warwks 30 E3
Arscott Shrops 38 H1
Artafallie Highld 107 K11
Arthington Leeds 58 H5
Arthingworth Nhants 41 Q10
Arthrath Abers 103 K7
Artrochie Abers 103 L8
Arundel W Susx 10 G8
Asby Cumb 70 H10
Ascog Ag & B 84 B9
Ascot W & M 20 E9
Ascott-under-Wychwood Oxon 30 H9
Asenby N York 65 P11
Asfordby Leics 41 P4
Asfordby Hill Leics 41 Q4
Asgarby Lincs 42 G2
Ash Kent 22 C9
Ash Kent 23 P10
Ash Somset 17 L11
Ash Surrey 20 E12
Ashampstead W Berk 19 P5
Ashbocking Suffk 35 K6
Ashbourne Derbys 50 F10
Ashbrittle Somset 16 E11
Ashburton Devon 5 P6
Ashbury Devon 15 J11
Ashbury Oxon 19 J4
Ashby N Linc 52 C2
Ashby by Partney Lincs 53 L9
Ashby cum Fenby NE Lin 53 J4
Ashby de la Launde Lincs 52 F11
Ashby-de-la-Zouch Leics 41 J4
Ashby Folville Leics 41 P5
Ashby Magna Leics 41 M9
Ashby Parva Leics 41 M9
Ashby Puerorum Lincs 53 K8
Ashby St Ledgers Nhants 31 M1
Ashby St Mary Norfk 45 M9
Ashchurch Gloucs 29 N3
Ashcombe Devon 6 C6
Ashcombe N Som 17 J4
Ashcott Somset 17 L8
Ashdon Essex 33 P8
Ashe Hants 19 N10
Asheldham Essex 23 J3
Ashen Essex 34 C8
Ashendon Bucks 31 P10
Asheridge Bucks 20 F3
Ashfield Stirlg 85 N3
Ashfield cum Thorpe Suffk 35 K4
Ashfield Green Suffk 35 L3
Ashford Devon 5 N9
Ashford Devon 15 J5
Ashford Kent 13 J2
Ashford Surrey 20 H8
Ashford Bowdler Shrops 39 K7
Ashford Carbonell Shrops 39 K7
Ashford Hill Hants 19 P8
Ashford in the Water Derbys 50 G6
Ashgill S Lans 77 N2
Ash Green Surrey 20 E12
Ash Green Warwks 41 J9
Ashill Devon 6 E1
Ashill Norfk 44 E8
Ashill Somset 17 J11
Ashingdon Essex 22 G5
Ashington Nthumb 73 M4
Ashington Somset 17 N11
Ashington W Susx 11 J7
Ashkirk Border 79 P4
Ashleworth Gloucs 29 L4
Ashleworth Quay Gloucs 29 L4
Ashley Cambs 34 B5
Ashley Ches E 57 P11
Ashley Devon 15 L9
Ashley Gloucs 29 N9
Ashley Hants 9 J8
Ashley Hants 9 L2
Ashley Kent 13 P1
Ashley Nhants 42 B11
Ashley Staffs 49 N7
Ashley Wilts 18 B7
Ashley Green Bucks 20 F3
Ash Magna Shrops 49 K7
Ashmansworth Hants 19 M8
Ashmansworthy Devon 14 F8
Ash Mill Devon 15 N7
Ashmore Dorset 8 D4
Ashmore Green W Berk 19 N6
Ashorne Warwks 30 H3
Ashover Derbys 51 J8
Ashow Warwks 40 H12
Ashperton Herefs 28 H1
Ashprington Devon 5 Q8
Ash Priors Somset 16 F9
Ashreigney Devon 15 L9
Ash Street Suffk 34 G7
Ashtead Surrey 21 J10
Ash Thomas Devon 6 D1
Ashton Ches W 49 J2
Ashton Cnwll 2 F9
Ashton Devon 6 B6
Ashton Herefs 39 K8
Ashton Inver 84 D7
Ashton Nhants 31 Q4
Ashton Nhants 42 F11
Ashton Common Wilts 18 D8
Ashton-in-Makerfield Wigan 57 L8
Ashton Keynes Wilts 18 F2
Ashton under Hill Worcs 30 C6
Ashton-under-Lyne Tamesd 50 C2
Ashurst Hants 9 K5
Ashurst Kent 11 P3
Ashurst Lancs 57 J7
Ashurst W Susx 11 J6
Ashurstwood W Susx 11 N3
Ash Vale Surrey 20 E11
Ashwater Devon 5 J2
Ashwell Herts 33 J8
Ashwell Rutlnd 42 C7
Ashwell End Herts 33 J8
Ashwellthorpe Norfk 45 J9
Ashwick Somset 17 P6
Ashwicken Norfk 44 B6
Askam in Furness Cumb 62 E6
Askern Donc 59 M10
Askerswell Dorset 7 M4
Askett Bucks 20 D3
Askham Cumb 71 Q10
Askham Notts 51 Q6
Askham Bryan C York 59 M5
Askham Richard C York 59 M5
Asknish Ag & B 83 P5
Askrigg N York 64 G8
Askwith N York 58 F5
Aslackby Lincs 42 F4
Aslacton Norfk 45 J11
Aslockton Notts 51 Q11
Aspatria Cumb 71 J7
Aspenden Herts 33 K10
Aspley Guise C Beds 32 D9
Aspley Heath C Beds 32 D9
Aspull Wigan 57 L7
Asselby E R Yk 60 C8
Assington Suffk 34 F8
Assington Green Suffk 34 C6
Astbury Ches E 49 Q3
Astcote Nhants 31 P4
Asterby Lincs 53 J7
Asterley Shrops 38 G1
Asterton Shrops 38 H4
Asthall Oxon 30 H10
Asthall Leigh Oxon 30 H10
Astle Highld 107 M4
Astley Shrops 49 K10
Astley Warwks 40 H9
Astley Wigan 57 M8
Astley Worcs 39 P8
Astley Abbots Shrops 39 N3
Astley Bridge Bolton 57 N6
Astley Cross Worcs 39 P8
Aston Ches E 49 L6
Aston Ches W 57 K12
Aston Derbys 50 F4
Aston Flints 48 F3
Aston Herts 33 J11
Aston Oxon 31 J12
Aston Rothm 51 L4
Aston Shrops 39 P4
Aston Shrops 49 K9
Aston Staffs 40 B3
Aston Staffs 49 N7
Aston Wokham 20 C6
Aston Wrekin 49 L12
Aston Abbotts Bucks 32 C11
Aston Botterell Shrops 39 L5
Aston-by-Stone Staffs 40 B2
Aston Cantlow Warwks 30 F3
Aston Clinton Bucks 20 E2
Aston Crews Herefs 29 J4
Aston End Herts 33 J11
Aston Fields Worcs 40 C12
Aston Flamville Leics 41 L8
Aston Ingham Herefs 29 J4
Aston le Walls Nhants 31 L4
Aston Magna Gloucs 30 G7
Aston Munslow Shrops 39 K5
Aston on Clun Shrops 38 H6
Aston Pigott Shrops 38 G2
Aston Rogers Shrops 38 G2
Aston Rowant Oxon 20 B4
Aston Somerville Worcs 30 D6
Aston-sub-Edge Gloucs 30 F6
Aston Tirrold Oxon 19 P4
Aston-upon-Trent Derbys 41 K2
Aston Upthorpe Oxon 19 P4
Astwick C Beds 32 H8
Astwood M Keyn 32 D7
Astwood Worcs 30 C2
Astwood Bank Worcs 30 D2
Aswarby Lincs 42 F3
Aswardby Lincs 53 L9
Atcham Shrops 39 K1
Athelhampton Dorset 8 B8
Athelington Suffk 35 K3
Athelney Somset 17 J9
Athelstaneford E Loth 87 K6
Atherington Devon 15 K7
Atherstone Warwks 40 H7
Atherstone on Stour Warwks 30 G4
Atherton Wigan 57 M8
Atlow Derbys 50 G10
Attadale Highld 97 N3
Atterby Lincs 52 E5
Attercliffe Sheff 51 J3
Atterton Leics 41 J7
Attingham Park Shrops 49 K12
Attleborough Norfk 44 H10
Attleborough Warwks 41 J8
Attlebridge Norfk 45 J6
Attleton Green Suffk 34 C6
Atwick E R Yk 61 K4
Atworth Wilts 18 C7
Aubourn Lincs 52 D10
Auchbreck Moray 101 J9
Auchedly Abers 103 J8
Auchenblae Abers 95 M6
Auchenbowie Stirlg 85 N5
Auchencairn D & G 70 D5
Auchencairn D & G 78 F11
Auchencairn N Ayrs 75 Q6
Auchencrow Border 87 Q9
Auchendinny Mdloth 86 F9
Auchengray S Lans 86 B10
Auchenhalrig Moray 101 M3
Auchenheath S Lans 77 N3
Auchenhessnane D & G 77 N11
Auchenlochan Ag & B 83 P8
Auchenmade N Ayrs 76 F2
Auchenmalg D & G 68 G8
Auchentiber N Ayrs 76 F2
Auchindrain Ag & B 83 Q3
Auchindrean Highld 106 C6
Auchininna Abers 102 E6
Auchinleck E Ayrs 77 J7
Auchinloch N Lans 85 L8
Auchinstarry N Lans 85 M7
Auchintore Highld 90 F2
Auchiries Abers 103 M7
Auchlean Highld 99 M9
Auchlee Abers 95 P3
Auchleven Abers 102 E9
Auchlochan S Lans 77 N4
Auchlossan Abers 95 J2
Auchlyne Stirlg 91 M9
Auchmillan E Ayrs 77 J5
Auchmithie Angus 93 R6
Auchmuirbridge Fife 86 E3
Auchnacree Angus 94 H8
Auchnagatt Abers 103 J7
Auchnarrow Moray 101 J9
Auchnotteroch D & G 68 D7
Auchroisk Moray 101 L5
Auchterarder P & K 92 E12
Auchteraw Highld 98 E7
Auchterblair Highld 99 N5
Auchtercairn Highld 105 M7
Auchterderran Fife 86 E3
Auchterhouse Angus 93 L8
Auchterless Abers 102 F7
Auchtermuchty Fife 93 J12
Auchterneed Highld 106 H9
Auchtertool Fife 86 E4
Auchtertyre Highld 97 L4
Auchtubh Stirlg 91 N11
Auckengill Highld 110 G3
Auckley Donc 51 P1
Audenshaw Tamesd 50 B2
Audlem Ches E 49 M6
Audley Staffs 49 P5
Audley End Essex 33 N8
Audley End House & Gardens Essex 33 N8
Aughton E R Yk 60 C6
Aughton Lancs 56 H7
Aughton Lancs 63 K8
Aughton Rothm 51 L4
Aughton Wilts 19 J9
Aughton Park Lancs 56 H7
Auldearn Highld 100 E4
Aulden Herefs 39 J10
Auldgirth D & G 78 E10
Auldhouse S Lans 77 K2
Ault a' chruinn Highld 97 N5
Aultbea Highld 105 N5
Aultgrishin Highld 105 L5
Aultguish Inn Highld 106 F8
Ault Hucknall Derbys 51 L7
Aultmore Moray 101 M5
Aultnagoire Highld 98 H4
Aultnamain Inn Highld 107 L6
Aunsby Lincs 42 F3
Aust S Glos 28 G10
Austerfield Donc 51 P2
Austrey Warwks 40 H6
Austwick N York 63 N8
Authorpe Lincs 53 L7
Avebury Wilts 18 G6
Avebury Wilts 18 G6
Aveley Thurr 22 C7
Avening Gloucs 29 M8
Averham Notts 51 Q9
Aveton Gifford Devon 5 N10
Aviemore Highld 99 N6
Avington W Berk 19 L7
Avoch Highld 107 L10
Avon Hants 8 G7
Avonbridge Falk 85 Q8
Avon Dassett Warwks 31 K4
Avonmouth Bristl 28 F12
Avonwick Devon 5 P8
Awbridge Hants 9 K3
Awliscombe Devon 6 F3
Awre Gloucs 29 J7
Awsworth Notts 51 L11
Axbridge Somset 17 L5
Axford Hants 19 Q11
Axford Wilts 19 J6
Axminster Devon 6 H3
Axmouth Devon 6 H5
Aycliffe Dur 65 M3
Aydon Nthumb 72 H7
Aylburton Gloucs 28 H8
Aylesbeare Devon 6 D4
Aylesbury Bucks 20 D1
Aylesby NE Lin 52 H3
Aylesford Kent 22 E10
Aylesham Kent 23 N11
Aylestone C Leic 41 M7
Aylmerton Norfk 45 K3
Aylsham Norfk 45 K5
Aylton Herefs 28 H2
Aylworth Gloucs 30 E9
Aymestrey Herefs 38 H8
Aynho Nhants 31 L7
Ayot St Lawrence Herts 32 H12
Ayr S Ayrs 76 F7
Aysgarth N York 64 H9
Ayshford Devon 16 E11
Ayside Cumb 62 H5
Ayston Rutlnd 42 C9
Ayton Border 81 J3
Azerley N York 65 M11

B

Babbacombe Torbay 6 C9
Babbs Green Herts 33 L12
Babcary Somset 17 N9
Babraham Cambs 33 N6
Babworth Notts 51 P5
Backaland Ork 111 h1
Backfolds Abers 103 L5
Backford Ches W 48 H2
Backies Highld 107 N3
Back of Keppoch Highld 97 J11
Backwell N Som 17 L3
Baconsthorpe Norfk 45 J3
Bacton Herefs 28 D3
Bacton Norfk 45 M4
Bacton Suffk 34 H4
Bacup Lancs 57 Q4
Badachro Highld 105 L7
Badbury Swindn 18 H5
Badby Nhants 31 M3
Badcall Highld 108 D7
Badcall Highld 108 E5
Badcaul Highld 105 Q4
Baddesley Clinton Warwks 40 G11
Baddesley Ensor Warwks 40 H7
Baddidarrach Highld 108 C10
Baddinsgill Border 86 D10
Badenscoth Abers 102 F7
Badentarbet Highld 105 Q1
Badenyon Abers 101 L10
Badger Shrops 39 N3
Badgeworth Gloucs 29 M5
Badgworth Somset 17 K5
Badicaul Highld 97 K4
Badingham Suffk 35 M3
Badlesmere Kent 23 J11
Badlieu Border 78 H5
Badlipster Highld 110 F6
Badluarach Highld 105 P4
Badninish Highld 107 M4
Badrallach Highld 105 Q4
Badsey Worcs 30 E5
Badshot Lea Surrey 10 D1
Badsworth Wakefd 59 L10
Badwell Ash Suffk 34 G3
Bagber Dorset 17 Q12
Bagby N York 66 C10
Bag Enderby Lincs 53 K8
Bagendon Gloucs 30 D11
Bagh a Chaisteil W Isls 111 a7
Bagh a Tuath W Isls 111 a7
Bagillt Flints 48 E1
Baginton Warwks 41 J11
Baglan Neath 26 G9
Bagley Shrops 48 H9
Bagley Somset 17 L7
Bagnall Staffs 50 B10
Bagshot Surrey 20 E10
Bagstone S Glos 29 J10
Bagworth Leics 41 K6
Bagwy Llydiart Herefs 28 E4
Baildon C Brad 58 F6
Baildon Green C Brad 58 F6
Baile Ailein W Isls 111 d2
Baile a Mhanaich W Isls 111 b5
Baile Mor Ag & B 88 G10
Baillieston C Glas 85 L9
Bainbridge N York 64 G9
Bainshole Abers 102 D8
Bainton C Pete 42 F8
Bainton E R Yk 60 G4
Baintown Fife 86 G2
Bairnkine Border 80 E10
Bakewell Derbys 50 G7
Bala Gwynd 47 Q4
Balallan W Isls 111 d2
Balbeg Highld 98 F3
Balbeggie P & K 92 H9
Balblair Highld 106 H12
Balblair Highld 107 L8
Balby Donc 51 M1
Balcary D & G 70 D5
Balchraggan Highld 98 G1
Balchreick Highld 108 D4
Balcombe W Susx 11 L4
Balcomie Links Fife 87 M1
Baldersby N York 65 N10
Baldersby St James N York 65 P11
Balderstone Lancs 57 L3
Balderton Notts 52 B12
Baldinnie Fife 93 M12
Baldinnies P & K 92 F11
Baldock Herts 33 J9
Baldock Services Herts 32 H9
Baldovie C Dund 93 M8
Baldrine IoM 56 d5
Baldslow E Susx 12 F7
Bale Norfk 44 G3
Baledgarno P & K 93 K9
Balemartine Ag & B 88 C7
Balerno C Edin 86 D8
Balfarg Fife 86 F2
Balfield Angus 95 J8
Balfour Ork 111 h2
Balfron Stirlg 85 J5
Balgaveny Abers 102 E7
Balgonar Fife 86 B4
Balgowan D & G 68 F9
Balgowan Highld 99 J9
Balgown Highld 104 E8
Balgracie D & G 68 D7
Balgray S Lans 78 E4
Balham Gt Lon 21 L8
Balhary P & K 93 J6
Balholmie P & K 92 H8
Baligill Highld 109 P3
Balintore Angus 93 K4
Balintore Highld 107 P7
Balintraid Highld 107 M8
Balivanich W Isls 111 b5
Balkeerie Angus 93 K6
Balkholme E R Yk 60 D8
Ballachulish Highld 90 E5
Ballajora IoM 56 e4
Ballanlay Ag & B 83 Q9
Ballantrae S Ayrs 68 E3
Ballasalla IoM 56 b6
Ballater Abers 94 F3
Ballaugh IoM 56 c3
Ballchraggan Highld 107 M7
Ballencrieff E Loth 87 J6
Ballevullin Ag & B 88 B7
Ballidon Derbys 50 G9
Balliekine N Ayrs 75 N5
Balliemore Ag & B 84 B3
Balligmorrie S Ayrs 68 G2
Ballimore Stirlg 91 M11
Ballindalloch Moray 101 J7
Ballindean P & K 93 J9
Ballinger Common Bucks 20 E3
Ballingham Herefs 28 G3
Ballingry Fife 86 E3
Ballinluig P & K 92 E5
Ballinshoe Angus 93 M5
Ballintuim P & K 92 G5
Balloch Highld 107 M11
Balloch N Lans 85 M7
Balloch P & K 92 C10
Balloch S Ayrs 76 F11
Balloch W Duns 84 G6
Balls Cross W Susx 10 F5
Balls Green E Susx 11 P3
Ballygown Ag & B 89 J7
Ballygrant Ag & B 82 E9
Ballyhaugh Ag & B 88 E5
Balmaclellan D & G 69 P4
Balmae D & G 69 P9
Balmaha Stirlg 84 G5
Balmalcolm Fife 86 G1
Balmangan D & G 69 P9
Balmedie Abers 103 K10
Balmerino Fife 93 L10
Balmichael N Ayrs 75 P6
Balmore E Duns 85 K8
Balmuchy Highld 107 P6
Balmule Fife 86 E5
Balmullo Fife 93 M10
Balnacoil Lodge Highld 109 P12
Balnacra Highld 105 P12
Balnacroft Abers 94 E3
Balnafoich Highld 99 K2
Balnaguard P & K 92 E5
Balnahard Ag & B 82 F3
Balnahard Ag & B 89 K9
Balnain Highld 98 F3
Balnakeil Highld 108 G3
Balne N York 59 N9
Balquharn P & K 92 F8
Balquhidder Stirlg 91 M11
Balsall Common Solhll 40 G11
Balsall Heath Birm 40 E9
Balscote Oxon 31 K6
Balsham Cambs 33 P6
Baltasound Shet 111 m2
Baltersan D & G 69 K6
Baltonsborough Somset 17 M8
Balvicar Ag & B 89 Q11
Balvraid Highld 97 M6
Balvraid Highld 99 M3
Bamber Bridge Lancs 57 K4
Bamber's Green Essex 33 P11
Bamburgh Nthumb 81 N7
Bamburgh Castle Nthumb 81 N7
Bamford Derbys 50 G4
Bampton Cumb 71 Q11
Bampton Devon 16 C10
Bampton Oxon 30 H12
Bampton Grange Cumb 71 Q11
Banavie Highld 90 F2
Banbury Oxon 31 L6
Banbury Crematorium Oxon 31 L5
Bancffosfelen Carmth 26 C6
Banchory Abers 95 L3
Banchory-Devenick Abers 95 P2
Bancycapel Carmth 25 P6
Bancyfelin Carmth 25 N5
Bandirran P & K 93 J9
Banff Abers 102 F3
Bangor Gwynd 54 H7
Bangor Crematorium Gwynd 54 H7
Bangor-on-Dee Wrexhm 48 H6
Bangors Cnwll 14 D11
Banham Norfk 44 H11
Bank Hants 9 K6
Bankend D & G 70 G2
Bankfoot P & K 92 F8
Bankglen E Ayrs 77 K8
Bankhead C Aber 103 J12
Bankhead S Lans 86 B12
Banknock Falk 85 N7
Banks Lancs 56 H5
Bankshill D & G 79 K11
Banningham Norfk 45 K4
Bannister Green Essex 34 B11
Bannockburn Stirlg 85 N5
Banstead Surrey 21 K10
Bantham Devon 5 N10
Banton N Lans 85 M7
Banwell N Som 17 K4
Bapchild Kent 22 H10
Bapton Wilts 18 E12
Barabhas W Isls 111 d1
Barassie S Ayrs 76 F5
Barbaraville Highld 107 M7
Barbieston S Ayrs 76 G7
Barbon Cumb 63 L6
Barbrook Devon 15 M3
Barby Nhants 41 M12
Barcaldine Ag & B 90 D7
Barcombe E Susx 11 N7
Barcombe Cross E Susx 11 N6

Barden Park Kent 12 C2
Bardfield End Green Essex 33 Q9
Bardfield Saling Essex 34 B10
Bardney Lincs 52 G9
Bardon Leics 41 K5
Bardon Mill Nthumb 72 E7
Bardowie E Duns 85 K8
Bardrainney Inver 84 F8
Bardsea Cumb 62 F7
Bardsey Leeds 59 J5
Bardsey Island Gwynd 46 B7
Bardwell Suffk 34 F3
Bare Lancs 63 J8
Barfad D & G 69 J6
Barford Norfk 45 J8
Barford Warwks 30 H2
Barford St John Oxon 31 K7
Barford St Martin Wilts 8 F2
Barford St Michael Oxon 31 K7
Barfrestone Kent 23 N12
Bargeddie N Lans 85 L9
Bargoed Caerph 27 N8
Bargrennan D & G 69 J4
Barham Cambs 32 G2
Barham Kent 23 N12
Barham Suffk 35 J6
Barham Crematorium Kent 13 N1
Bar Hill Cambs 33 L4
Barholm Lincs 42 F7
Barkby Leics 41 N5
Barkby Thorpe Leics 41 N5
Barkestone-le-Vale Leics 41 R1
Barkham Wokham 20 C9
Barking Gt Lon 21 N6
Barking Suffk 34 H6
Barkingside Gt Lon 21 N5
Barking Tye Suffk 34 H6
Barkisland Calder 58 D9
Barkla Shop Cnwll 2 H5
Barkston Lincs 42 D2
Barkston Ash N York 59 L7
Barkway Herts 33 L9
Barlanark C Glas 85 L9
Barlaston Staffs 50 B11
Barlavington W Susx 10 F6
Barlborough Derbys 51 L5
Barlby N York 59 N7
Barlestone Leics 41 K6
Barley Herts 33 L8
Barley Lancs 57 P1
Barleythorpe Rutlnd 42 C8
Barling Essex 22 H5
Barlings Lincs 52 F8
Barlochan D & G 70 D4
Barlow Derbys 51 J6
Barlow Gatesd 73 K8
Barlow N York 59 N8
Barmby Moor E R Yk 60 D4
Barmby on the Marsh E R Yk 59 P8
Barmollack Ag & B 75 M4
Barmouth Gwynd 47 K7
Barmpton Darltn 65 N4
Barmston E R Yk 61 K3
Barnacarry Ag & B 83 Q4
Barnack C Pete 42 F8
Barnard Castle Dur 65 J4
Barnard Gate Oxon 31 K11
Barnardiston Suffk 34 B7
Barnbarroch D & G 70 D4
Barnburgh Donc 59 L12
Barnby Suffk 45 P11
Barnby Dun Donc 59 N11
Barnby in the Willows Notts 52 C11
Barnby Moor Notts 51 P4
Barncorkrie D & G 68 E11
Barnes Gt Lon 21 K7
Barnes Street Kent 12 D1
Barnet Gt Lon 21 K4
Barnetby le Wold N Linc 52 F2
Barney Norfk 44 G4
Barnham Suffk 34 E2
Barnham W Susx 10 F8
Barnham Broom Norfk 44 H8
Barnhead Angus 93 R4
Barnhill C Dund 93 N8
Barnhill Moray 100 H4
Barnhills D & G 68 D5
Barningham Dur 65 J5
Barningham Suffk 34 F2
Barnoldby le Beck NE Lin 52 H3
Barnoldswick Lancs 63 Q11
Barns Green W Susx 10 H5
Barnsley Barns 59 J11
Barnsley Gloucs 30 E12
Barnsley Crematorium Barns 59 J12
Barnstaple Devon 15 K5
Barnston Essex 33 Q11
Barnston Wirral 56 F11
Barnstone Notts 41 Q1
Barnt Green Worcs 40 D11
Barnton C Edin 86 E7
Barnton Ches W 49 L1
Barnwell All Saints Nhants 42 F12
Barnwell St Andrew Nhants 42 F12
Barnwood Gloucs 29 M5
Barr S Ayrs 76 E11
Barra W Isls 111 a7
Barra Airport W Isls 111 a6
Barrachan D & G 69 J8
Barraigh W Isls 111 a7
Barrapoll Ag & B 88 B7
Barrasford Nthumb 72 G6
Barrhead E Rens 84 H10
Barrhill S Ayrs 68 H3
Barrington Cambs 33 L6
Barrington Somset 17 K11
Barripper Cnwll 2 F7
Barrmill N Ayrs 84 F11
Barrock Highld 110 F2
Barrow Gloucs 29 M4
Barrow Lancs 57 N2
Barrow Rutlnd 42 C7
Barrow Somset 17 Q9
Barrow Suffk 34 C4
Barrowby Lincs 42 C3
Barrowden Rutlnd 42 D9
Barrowford Lancs 57 Q2
Barrow Gurney N Som 17 M3
Barrow Haven N Linc 60 H9
Barrow-in-Furness Cumb 62 E8
Barrow Island Cumb 62 E8
Barrow-upon-Humber N Linc 60 H9
Barrow upon Soar Leics 41 M4
Barrow upon Trent Derbys 41 J2
Barry Angus 93 P8
Barry V Glam 16 F3
Barry Island V Glam 16 F3
Barsby Leics 41 P5
Barsham Suffk 45 N11
Barston Solhll 40 G10
Bartestree Herefs 28 G1
Barthol Chapel Abers 102 H8
Bartholomew Green Essex 34 C11
Barthomley Ches E 49 N5
Bartley Hants 9 K5
Bartley Green Birm 40 D10
Bartlow Cambs 33 P7
Barton Cambs 33 L5
Barton Ches W 49 J5
Barton Gloucs 30 E8
Barton Lancs 56 G7
Barton Lancs 57 K2
Barton N York 65 M6
Barton Oxon 31 M11
Barton Torbay 6 C8
Barton Bendish Norfk 44 B8
Barton End Gloucs 29 L8
Barton Hartshorn Bucks 31 N7
Barton in Fabis Notts 41 M2
Barton in the Beans Leics 41 K6
Barton-le-Clay C Beds 32 F9
Barton-le-Street N York 66 G11
Barton-le-Willows N York 60 C2
Barton Mills Suffk 34 C3
Barton-on-Sea Hants 9 J8
Barton-on-the-Heath Warwks 30 G7
Barton St David Somset 17 M9
Barton Seagrave Nhants 32 C2
Barton Stacey Hants 19 M11
Barton Town Devon 15 L4
Barton Turf Norfk 45 M5
Barton-under-Needwood Staffs 40 F4
Barton-upon-Humber N Linc 60 H9
Barton Waterside N Linc 60 H9
Barvas W Isls 111 d1
Barway Cambs 33 N2
Barwell Leics 41 K8
Barwick Devon 15 K10
Barwick Somset 17 M12
Barwick in Elmet Leeds 59 K6
Baschurch Shrops 48 H10
Bascote Warwks 31 K2
Bashall Eaves Lancs 63 M12
Basildon Essex 22 E5
Basildon & District Crematorium Essex 22 E6
Basingstoke Hants 19 Q9
Basingstoke Crematorium Hants 19 P10
Baslow Derbys 50 G6
Bason Bridge Somset 17 J7
Bassaleg Newpt 28 C10
Bassendean Border 80 E5
Bassenthwaite Cumb 71 K8
Bassett C Sotn 9 M4
Bassingbourn Cambs 33 K7
Bassingham Lincs 52 C10
Bassingthorpe Lincs 42 D5
Bassus Green Herts 33 K10
Baston Lincs 42 G7
Bastwick Norfk 45 N6
Batchworth Herts 20 G5
Batcombe Dorset 7 N3
Batcombe Somset 17 Q8
Batford Herts 21 J1
Bath BaNES 17 Q4
Bathampton BaNES 18 B7
Bath, City of BaNES 17 Q3
Bathealton Somset 16 E10
Batheaston BaNES 18 B7
Bathford BaNES 18 B7
Bathgate W Loth 86 B8
Bathley Notts 51 Q8
Bathpool Cnwll 4 G5
Bathpool Somset 16 H10
Bath Side Essex 35 L9
Bathville W Loth 85 Q9
Bathway Somset 17 N6
Batley Kirk 58 G8
Batsford Gloucs 30 F7
Battersby N York 66 E6
Battersea Gt Lon 21 L7
Battisford Tye Suffk 34 G6
Battle E Susx 12 E7
Battle Powys 27 L3
Battledykes Angus 93 M5
Battlesbridge Essex 22 F5
Battleton Somset 16 C10
Baughton Worcs 29 M1
Baughurst Hants 19 P8
Baulds Abers 95 K4
Baulking Oxon 19 K3
Baumber Lincs 52 H8
Baunton Gloucs 30 D12
Baverstock Wilts 8 F2
Bawburgh Norfk 45 J8
Bawdeswell Norfk 44 H6
Bawdrip Somset 17 J8
Bawdsey Suffk 35 M8
Bawtry Donc 51 P3
Baxenden Lancs 57 P4
Baxterley Warwks 40 H7
Bay Highld 104 C10
Bayble W Isls 111 e2
Baybridge Hants 9 N3
Baycliff Cumb 62 F7
Baydon Wilts 19 K5
Bayford Herts 21 L2
Bayford Somset 17 Q9
Bayhead W Isls 111 a4
Baylham Suffk 34 H6
Baysham Herefs 28 G4
Bayston Hill Shrops 39 J1
Baythorne End Essex 34 C8
Bayton Worcs 39 M7
Bayworth Oxon 19 N1
Beachampton Bucks 31 Q6
Beachamwell Norfk 44 C8
Beachy Head E Susx 12 C10
Beacon Devon 6 G2
Beacon End Essex 34 F10
Beacon Hill Surrey 10 E3
Beacon's Bottom Bucks 20 C4
Beaconsfield Bucks 20 F5
Beaconsfield Services Bucks 20 F5
Beadlam N York 66 F9
Beadlow C Beds 32 F8
Beadnell Nthumb 81 P8
Beaford Devon 15 K8
Beal N York 59 M8
Beal Nthumb 81 M6
Bealsmill Cnwll 4 H5
Beaminster Dorset 7 L3
Beamish Dur 73 L9
Beamish Museum Dur 73 L9
Beamsley N York 58 E4
Beanacre Wilts 18 D7
Beanley Nthumb 81 M9
Beardon Devon 5 L4
Beare Green Surrey 11 J2
Bearley Warwks 30 F3
Bearpark Dur 73 M11
Bearsden E Duns 85 J8
Bearsted Kent 22 F11
Bearstone Shrops 49 N7
Bearwood Birm 40 D9
Bearwood Herefs 38 H10
Bearwood Poole 8 F7
Beattock D & G 78 H8
Beauchamp Roding Essex 22 C2
Beaufort Blae G 27 N6
Beaulieu Hants 9 L7
Beauly Highld 107 J11
Beaumaris IoA 54 H6
Beaumaris Castle IoA 54 H6
Beaumont Cumb 71 M4
Beaumont Essex 35 J10
Beaumont Jersey 7 b2
Beausale Warwks 40 G12
Beauworth Hants 9 P3
Beaworthy Devon 14 H11
Beazley End Essex 34 C10
Bebington Wirral 56 G11
Beccles Suffk 45 N11
Becconsall Lancs 57 J4
Beckbury Shrops 39 N2
Beckenham Gt Lon 21 M9
Beckenham Crematorium Gt Lon 21 M9
Beckermet Cumb 62 B2
Beckfoot Cumb 70 H5
Beckford Worcs 29 N2
Beckhampton Wilts 18 G7
Beckingham Lincs 52 C11
Beckingham Notts 51 R3
Beckington Somset 18 B9
Beckjay Shrops 38 H6
Beckley E Susx 12 G5
Beckley Oxon 31 M10
Beck Row Suffk 34 B2
Beck Side Cumb 62 E6
Beckton Gt Lon 21 N7
Beckwithshaw N York 58 H4
Becontree Gt Lon 21 P6
Bedale N York 65 M9
Bedchester Dorset 8 C4
Beddau Rhondd 27 M10
Beddgelert Gwynd 54 H11
Beddingham E Susx 11 N8
Beddington Gt Lon 21 L9
Beddington Corner Gt Lon 21 L9
Bedfield Suffk 35 K4
Bedford Bed 32 F6
Bedford Crematorium Bed 32 F6
Bedhampton Hants 10 B8
Bedingfield Suffk 35 K3
Bedlam N York 58 H2
Bedlington Nthumb 73 M5
Bedlinog Myr Td 27 M8
Bedminster Bristl 17 N2
Bedminster Down Bristl 17 N3
Bedmond Herts 20 H3
Bednall Staffs 40 C4
Bedrule Border 80 E10
Bedstone Shrops 38 G7
Bedwas Caerph 27 N10
Bedwellty Caerph 27 N8
Bedworth Warwks 41 J9
Beeby Leics 41 P6
Beech Hants 10 B3
Beech Staffs 49 Q7
Beech Hill W Berk 20 B9
Beechingstoke Wilts 18 G8
Beedon W Berk 19 N5
Beeford E R Yk 61 J4
Beeley Derbys 50 H7
Beelsby NE Lin 52 H3
Beenham W Berk 19 P7
Beer Devon 6 G5
Beer Somset 17 K9
Beercrocombe Somset 17 J11
Beer Hackett Dorset 7 N1
Beesands Devon 5 Q11
Beesby Lincs 53 M7
Beeson Devon 5 Q11
Beeston C Beds 32 G7
Beeston Ches W 49 K4
Beeston Leeds 58 H7
Beeston Norfk 44 E7
Beeston Notts 51 M12
Beeston Regis Norfk 45 J2
Beeswing D & G 70 E2
Beetham Cumb 63 J6
Beetham Somset 6 H1
Beetley Norfk 44 F6
Begbroke Oxon 31 L10
Begelly Pembks 25 K7
Beguildy Powys 38 E6
Beighton Norfk 45 N8
Beighton Sheff 51 K4
Beinn Na Faoghla W Isls 111 b5
Beith N Ayrs 84 F11
Bekesbourne Kent 23 M11
Belaugh Norfk 45 L6
Belbroughton Worcs 40 B11
Belchalwell Dorset 8 B5
Belchamp Otten Essex 34 D8
Belchamp St Paul Essex 34 D8
Belchamp Walter Essex 34 D8
Belchford Lincs 53 J8
Belford Nthumb 81 M7
Belgrave C Leic 41 N6
Belhaven E Loth 87 M6
Belhelvie Abers 103 K10
Belhinnie Abers 101 N9
Bellabeg Abers 101 L11
Bellanoch Ag & B 83 M5
Bellaty Angus 93 J4
Bell Busk N York 58 B3
Belleau Lincs 53 L7
Bell End Worcs 40 C11
Bellerby N York 65 K8
Belle Vue Cumb 71 M4
Belle Vue Wakefd 59 J9
Bellfield S Lans 78 D2
Bellfield S Lans 78 F5
Bellingdon Bucks 20 F3
Bellingham Nthumb 72 F4
Belloch Ag & B 75 K5
Bellochantuy Ag & B 75 K6
Bell o' th' Hill Ches W 49 K6
Bellshill N Lans 85 M10
Bellside N Lans 85 N10
Bellsquarry W Loth 86 C8
Bells Yew Green E Susx 12 C3
Belluton BaNES 17 N4
Belmaduthy Highld 107 K10
Belmont Bl w D 57 M6
Belmont Gt Lon 21 K10
Belmont S Ayrs 76 F7
Belmont Shet 111 m2
Belnacraig Abers 101 M11
Belper Derbys 51 J10
Belsay Nthumb 73 K5
Belses Border 80 D8
Belsford Devon 5 P8
Belsize Herts 20 G4
Belstead Suffk 35 J8
Belstone Devon 5 M2
Belthorn Lancs 57 N4
Beltinge Kent 23 M9
Beltingham Nthumb 72 E7
Beltoft N Linc 52 B3
Belton Leics 41 K4
Belton Lincs 42 D3
Belton N Linc 52 B3
Belton Norfk 45 P9
Belton Rutlnd 42 B9
Belton House Lincs 42 D3
Belvedere Gt Lon 21 P7
Belvoir Leics 42 B4
Bembridge IoW 9 Q9
Bemerton Wilts 8 G2
Bempton E R Yk 67 P12
Benacre Suffk 45 Q12
Benbecula W Isls 111 b5
Benbecula Airport W Isls 111 b5
Benbuie D & G 77 M11
Benderloch Ag & B 90 C8
Benenden Kent 12 F4
Benfieldside Dur 73 J9
Bengeo Herts 21 L1
Bengeworth Worcs 30 D5
Benhall Green Suffk 35 N5
Benhall Street Suffk 35 M5
Benholm Abers 95 N7
Beningbrough N York 59 M3
Benington Herts 33 J11
Benington Lincs 43 L2
Benllech IoA 54 G5
Benmore Ag & B 84 C6
Bennan N Ayrs 75 Q8
Ben Nevis Highld 90 G3
Benniworth Lincs 52 H7
Benover Kent 12 E1
Ben Rhydding C Brad 58 F5
Benslie N Ayrs 76 F3
Benson Oxon 19 Q3
Benthoul C Aber 95 N2
Bentley Donc 59 M11
Bentley E R Yk 60 H7
Bentley Hants 10 C2
Bentley Suffk 35 J8
Bentley Warwks 40 H8
Bentley Crematorium Essex 22 C4
Bentpath D & G 79 M10
Bentwichen Devon 15 M5
Bentworth Hants 19 Q11
Benvie Angus 93 K8
Benville Dorset 7 M3
Benwick Cambs 43 K11
Beoley Worcs 40 E12
Beoraidbeg Highld 97 J10
Bepton W Susx 10 D6
Berden Essex 33 M10
Berea Pembks 24 E3
Bere Alston Devon 5 J6
Bere Ferrers Devon 5 K7
Bere Regis Dorset 8 C8
Bergh Apton Norfk 45 M9
Berinsfield Oxon 19 P2
Berkeley Gloucs 29 J8
Berkhamsted Herts 20 F2
Berkley Somset 18 B10
Berkswell Solhll 40 G10
Bermondsey Gt Lon 21 M7
Bernera Highld 97 L5
Bernisdale Highld 104 E11
Berrick Prior Oxon 19 Q2
Berrick Salome Oxon 19 Q3
Berriedale Highld 110 D10
Berrier Cumb 71 N9
Berriew Powys 38 E2
Berrington Shrops 39 K2
Berrington Worcs 39 L8
Berrington Green Worcs 39 L8
Berrow Somset 16 H6
Berrow Green Worcs 39 N9
Berryhillock Moray 101 P3
Berryhillock Moray 101 P5
Berrynarbor Devon 15 K3
Berry Pomeroy Devon 5 Q7
Bersham Wrexhm 48 F6
Berwick E Susx 11 P8
Berwick Bassett Wilts 18 G6
Berwick Hill Nthumb 73 L6
Berwick St James Wilts 18 F11
Berwick St John Wilts 8 D3
Berwick St Leonard Wilts 8 D2
Berwick-upon-Tweed Nthumb 81 L4
Bescar Lancs 56 H6
Besford Worcs 30 B5
Bessacarr Donc 51 N1
Bessingby E R Yk 61 K2
Bessingham Norfk 45 J3
Besthorpe Norfk 44 H10
Besthorpe Notts 52 B9
Bestwood Village Notts 51 M10
Beswick E R Yk 60 H5
Betchworth Surrey 21 K12
Bethel Gwynd 54 G8
Bethel IoA 54 E7
Bethersden Kent 12 H3
Bethesda Gwynd 55 J8
Bethesda Pembks 25 J5
Bethlehem Carmth 26 F4
Bethnal Green Gt Lon 21 M6
Betley Staffs 49 N6
Betsham Kent 22 C8
Betteshanger Kent 23 P11
Bettiscombe Dorset 7 K3
Bettisfield Wrexhm 49 J8
Bettws Newpt 28 C10
Bettws Bledrws Cerdgn 37 K9
Bettws Cedewain Powys 38 D3
Bettws Evan Cerdgn 36 E10
Bettws-Newydd Mons 28 D7
Bettyhill Highld 109 M4
Betws Brdgnd 27 J10
Betws Gwerfil Goch Denbgs 48 B6
Betws-y-Coed Conwy 55 L9
Betws-yn-Rhos Conwy 55 N6
Beulah Cerdgn 36 E10
Beulah Powys 37 Q9
Bevercotes Notts 51 P6
Beverley E R Yk 60 H6
Beverston Gloucs 29 M9
Bewcastle Cumb 71 Q1
Bewdley Worcs 39 P7
Bewerley N York 58 F2
Bewholme E R Yk 61 K4
Bexhill E Susx 12 E8
Bexley Gt Lon 21 P8
Bexleyheath Gt Lon 21 P8
Bexwell Norfk 43 Q9
Beyton Suffk 34 F4
Beyton Green Suffk 34 F4
Bhaltos W Isls 111 c2
Bhatarsaigh W Isls 111 a7
Bibury Gloucs 30 E11
Bicester Oxon 31 N9
Bickenhill Solhll 40 F10
Bicker Lincs 42 H3
Bickerstaffe Lancs 57 J7
Bickerton N York 59 K4
Bickford Staffs 40 B5
Bickington Devon 5 Q6
Bickington Devon 15 J6
Bickleigh Devon 5 L7
Bickleigh Devon 6 C2
Bickley Ches W 49 K6
Bickley Gt Lon 21 N9
Bickley N York 67 K8
Bicknacre Essex 22 F3
Bicknoller Somset 16 F8
Bicknor Kent 22 G10
Bicton Shrops 38 F5
Bicton Shrops 49 J11
Bidborough Kent 12 C2
Biddenden Kent 12 G3
Biddenham Bed 32 E6
Biddestone Wilts 18 C6
Biddisham Somset 17 K5
Biddlesden Bucks 31 N6
Biddulph Staffs 50 B8
Biddulph Moor Staffs 50 B8
Bideford Devon 14 H6
Bidford-on-Avon Warwks 30 E4
Bielby E R Yk 60 D5
Bieldside C Aber 95 P2
Bierley IoW 9 N10
Bierton Bucks 20 D1
Big Balcraig D & G 69 K9
Bigbury Devon 5 N10
Bigbury-on-Sea Devon 5 N10
Bigby Lincs 52 F3
Big Carlae D & G 77 L10
Biggar S Lans 78 G2
Biggin Derbys 50 F8
Biggin Hill Gt Lon 21 N10
Biggin Hill Airport Gt Lon 21 N10
Biggleswade C Beds 32 H7
Bigholms D & G 79 M11
Bighouse Highld 109 Q3
Bighton Hants 9 Q1
Biglands Cumb 71 L5
Bignor W Susx 10 F7
Bigrigg Cumb 70 G11
Big Sand Highld 105 L6
Bigton Shet 111 k5
Bilborough C Nott 51 M11
Bilbrook Somset 16 D7
Bilbrough N York 59 M5
Bilbster Highld 110 F5
Bildershaw Dur 65 L3
Bildeston Suffk 34 G6
Billericay Essex 22 D5
Billesdon Leics 41 Q7
Billesley Warwks 30 F3
Billingborough Lincs 42 G4
Billinge St Hel 57 K8
Billingford Norfk 35 J2
Billingford Norfk 44 G6
Billingham S on T 66 C3
Billinghay Lincs 52 G11
Billingley Barns 59 K12
Billingshurst W Susx 10 H5
Billingsley Shrops 39 N5
Billington C Beds 32 D11
Billington Lancs 57 N2
Billockby Norfk 45 N7
Billy Row Dur 73 L12
Bilsborrow Lancs 57 K2
Bilsby Lincs 53 M8
Bilsham W Susx 10 F9
Bilsington Kent 13 K3
Bilsthorpe Notts 51 N8
Bilston Mdloth 86 F8
Bilston Wolves 40 C8
Bilstone Leics 41 J6
Bilton E R Yk 61 K7
Bilton N York 58 H3
Bilton N York 59 L4
Bilton Warwks 41 L11
Binbrook Lincs 52 H5
Bincombe Dorset 7 P6
Binegar Somset 17 N6
Binfield Br For 20 D8
Binfield Heath Oxon 20 C7
Bingfield Nthumb 72 H6
Bingham Notts 51 P11
Bingley C Brad 58 E6
Binham Norfk 44 G3
Binley Covtry 41 J10
Binley Hants 19 M9
Binley Woods Warwks 41 K11

Binnegar Dorset 8 C9
Binniehill Falk 85 P8
Binscombe Surrey 10 F2
Binstead IoW 9 P8
Binsted Hants 10 C2
Binsted W Susx 10 F8
Binton Warwks 30 F4
Bintree Norfk 44 G5
Birch Essex 34 F11
Bircham Newton Norfk 44 C4
Bircham Tofts Norfk 44 C4
Birchanger Essex 33 N11
Birchanger Green Services Essex 33 N11
Birch Cross Staffs 40 E2
Bircher Herefs 39 J8
Birch Green Essex 34 F11
Birchgrove Cardif 27 N11
Birchgrove Swans 26 F8
Birchgrove W Susx 11 N4
Birchington Kent 23 P9
Birchley Heath Warwks 40 H8
Birchover Derbys 50 G8
Birch Services Rochdl 57 Q7
Birch Vale Derbys 50 D4
Birchwood Lincs 52 D9
Birch Wood Somset 16 H12
Birchwood Warrtn 57 M9
Bircotes Notts 51 N3
Birdbrook Essex 34 C8
Birdforth N York 66 C11
Birdham W Susx 10 D9
Birdingbury Warwks 31 K1
Birdlip Gloucs 29 N6
Birdsall N York 60 E2
Birds Edge Kirk 58 G11
Birds Green Essex 22 C2
Birdsgreen Shrops 39 P5
Birdsmoorgate Dorset 7 K3
Birdwell Barns 51 J1
Birgham Border 80 G6
Birichin Highld 107 M4
Birkby N York 65 N7
Birkdale Sefton 56 G6
Birkenbog Abers 102 C3
Birkenhead Wirral 56 G10
Birkenhills Abers 102 H6
Birkenshaw Kirk 58 G8
Birkhall Abers 94 F4
Birkhill Angus 93 L8
Birkhill D & G 79 K6
Birkin N York 59 M8
Birley Herefs 39 J10
Birley Carr Sheff 51 J3
Birling Kent 22 D10
Birlingham Worcs 30 C5
Birmingham Birm 40 E9
Birmingham Airport Solhll 40 F10
Birnam P & K 92 F7
Birness Abers 103 K8
Birse Abers 95 J3
Birsemore Abers 95 J3
Birstall Kirk 58 G8
Birstall Leics 41 N5
Birstwith N York 58 G3
Birtley Gatesd 73 M9
Birtley Herefs 38 G8
Birtley Nthumb 72 F5
Birtley Crematorium Gatesd 73 M9
Birts Street Worcs 29 K2
Bisbrooke Rutlnd 42 C9
Biscathorpe Lincs 52 H6
Bisham W & M 20 D6
Bishampton Worcs 30 C4
Bish Mill Devon 15 M7
Bishop Auckland Dur 65 L2
Bishopbridge Lincs 52 E5
Bishopbriggs E Duns 85 K8
Bishop Burton E R Yk 60 G6
Bishopmill Moray 101 J3
Bishop Middleham Dur 65 N2
Bishop Monkton N York 59 J2
Bishop Norton Lincs 52 E5
Bishopsbourne Kent 23 M11
Bishops Cannings Wilts 18 F7
Bishop's Castle Shrops 38 G4
Bishop's Caundle Dorset 17 Q12
Bishop's Cleeve Gloucs 29 N4
Bishop's Frome Herefs 39 M11
Bishop's Green Essex 33 Q12
Bishops Hull Somset 16 G10
Bishop's Itchington Warwks 31 K3
Bishops Lydeard Somset 16 G9
Bishop's Norton Gloucs 29 L4
Bishop's Nympton Devon 15 N7
Bishop's Offley Staffs 49 P9
Bishop's Stortford Herts 33 M11
Bishop's Sutton Hants 9 Q2
Bishop's Tachbrook Warwks 30 H2
Bishop's Tawton Devon 15 K6
Bishopsteignton Devon 6 B7
Bishopstoke Hants 9 M4
Bishopston Swans 26 D10
Bishopstone Bucks 20 C2
Bishopstone E Susx 11 P9
Bishopstone Herefs 38 H12
Bishopstone Kent 23 N9
Bishopstone Swindn 19 J4
Bishopstone Wilts 8 F3
Bishopstrow Wilts 18 D11
Bishop Sutton BaNES 17 N4
Bishop's Waltham Hants 9 P4
Bishopswood Somset 6 H1
Bishop's Wood Staffs 49 Q12
Bishopsworth Bristl 17 N3
Bishop Thornton N York 58 H2
Bishopthorpe C York 59 N5
Bishopton Darltn 65 P4
Bishopton Rens 84 G8
Bishop Wilton E R Yk 60 D4
Bishton Newpt 28 D10
Bishton Staffs 40 D4
Bisley Gloucs 29 M7
Bisley Surrey 20 F10
Bissoe Cnwll 2 H7
Bisterne Hants 8 G7
Bitchfield Lincs 42 E4
Bittadon Devon 15 J4
Bittaford Devon 5 N8
Bitterley Shrops 39 K6
Bitterne C Sotn 9 M5
Bitteswell Leics 41 M9
Bitton S Glos 17 P3
Bix Oxon 20 B6

Bixter Shet 111 k4
Blaby Leics 41 M7
Blackadder Border 80 H4
Blackawton Devon 5 N9
Blackborough Devon 6 E2
Blackborough End Norfk 43 Q7
Black Bourton Oxon 30 H12
Blackboys E Susx 11 Q6
Blackbrook Derbys 51 J10
Blackbrook St Hel 57 N9
Blackbrook Staffs 49 N7
Blackburn Abers 102 H11
Blackburn Bl w D 57 M4
Blackburn W Loth 86 B8
Blackburn with Darwen Services Bl w D 57 M4
Black Callerton N u Ty 73 L7
Blackcraig E Ayrs 77 K9
Black Crofts Ag & B 90 C6
Blackdog Abers 103 K11
Black Dog Devon 15 N9
Blackdown Dorset 7 K3
Blacker Hill Barns 51 J1
Blackfen Gt Lon 21 P8
Blackfield Hants 9 M7
Blackford P & K 85 P2
Blackford Somset 17 M5
Blackford Somset 17 P10
Blackfordby Leics 41 J4
Blackhall C Edin 86 E7
Blackhall Colliery Dur 73 Q11
Blackhall Mill Gatesd 73 K9
Blackhaugh Border 79 N2
Blackheath Gt Lon 21 M7
Blackheath Sandw 40 C9
Blackheath Suffk 35 N2
Blackheath Surrey 10 G2
Blackhill Abers 103 M4
Blackhill Abers 103 M6
Blackhill Dur 73 J9
Blackhill of Clackriach Abers 103 J6
Blackhorse Devon 6 D4
Blacklaw D & G 78 G7
Blackley Manch 57 Q8
Blackley Crematorium Manch 57 Q7
Blacklunans P & K 94 C9
Blackmarstone Herefs 28 F2
Blackmill Brdgnd 27 K10
Blackmoor Hants 10 C4
Blackmoor N Som 17 L4
Blackmoorfoot Kirk 58 E10
Blackmore Essex 22 C3
Blackmore End Essex 34 C9
Blackness Falk 86 C6
Blacknest Hants 10 C2
Black Notley Essex 34 C11
Blacko Lancs 57 Q1
Black Pill Swans 26 E10
Blackpool Bpool 56 F2
Blackpool Devon 6 B12
Blackridge W Loth 85 P9
Blackrod Bolton 57 L6
Blacksboat Moray 101 J7
Blackshaw D & G 70 G3
Blackshaw Head Calder 58 C8
Blackstone W Susx 11 K6
Black Street Suffk 45 Q11
Blackthorn Oxon 31 N9
Blackthorpe Suffk 34 E4
Blacktoft E R Yk 60 E8
Blacktop C Aber 95 P2
Black Torrington Devon 14 H10
Blackwall Derbys 50 G10
Blackwater Cnwll 2 H6
Blackwater Hants 20 D10
Blackwater IoW 9 N9
Blackwater Somset 16 H11
Blackwaterfoot N Ayrs 75 N6
Blackwell Cumb 71 N5
Blackwell Derbys 50 E8
Blackwell Derbys 51 K8
Blackwell Warwks 30 G5
Blackwell Worcs 40 C11
Blackwood Caerph 27 N8
Blackwood D & G 78 E10
Blackwood S Lans 77 N3
Blacon Ches W 48 H2
Bladnoch D & G 69 K8
Bladon Oxon 31 K10
Blaenannerch Cerdgn 36 D10
Blaenau Ffestiniog Gwynd 47 L3
Blaenavon Torfn 27 Q7
Blaenavon Industrial Landscape Torfn 27 P7
Blaenffos Pembks 25 L2
Blaengarw Brdgnd 27 J9
Blaengwrach Neath 27 J7
Blaengwynfi Neath 27 J9
Blaenpennal Cerdgn 37 K7
Blaenplwyf Cerdgn 37 J5
Blaenporth Cerdgn 36 D10
Blaenrhondda Rhondd 27 K8
Blaenwaun Carmth 25 N4
Blaen-y-Coed Carmth 25 N4
Blaen-y-cwm Rhondd 27 K8
Blagdon N Som 17 M4
Blagdon Somset 16 G11
Blagdon Torbay 6 B9
Blagdon Hill Somset 16 G11
Blaich Highld 90 E2
Blain Highld 89 N3
Blaina Blae G 27 P7
Blair Atholl P & K 92 C3
Blair Drummond Stirlg 85 M3
Blairgowrie P & K 92 H6
Blairhall Fife 86 B5
Blairingone P & K 85 Q4
Blairlogie Stirlg 85 N4
Blairmore Ag & B 84 D6
Blairmore Highld 108 D4
Blair's Ferry Ag & B 83 P7
Blaisdon Gloucs 29 J5
Blakebrook Worcs 39 Q6
Blakedown Worcs 39 Q6
Blake End Essex 34 B11
Blakemere Ches W 49 K2
Blakemere Herefs 28 E1
Blakenall Heath Wsall 40 D7
Blakeney Gloucs 29 J6
Blakeney Norfk 44 G2
Blakenhall Ches E 49 N6
Blakenhall Wolves 40 B7
Blakeshall Worcs 39 Q5
Blakesley Nhants 31 N4
Blanchland Nthumb 72 H10

Blandford Forum Dorset 8 C6
Blandford St Mary Dorset 8 C6
Blanefield Stirlg 85 J7
Blankney Lincs 52 F10
Blantyre S Lans 85 L10
Blar a' Chaorainn Highld 90 F4
Blargie Highld 98 H9
Blarmachfoldach Highld 90 F3
Blaston Leics 42 B10
Blatherwycke Nhants 42 D10
Blawith Cumb 62 F5
Blawquhairn D & G 69 P3
Blaxhall Suffk 35 M5
Blaxton Donc 51 P2
Blaydon Gatesd 73 L8
Bleadney Somset 17 L7
Bleadon N Som 17 J5
Blean Kent 23 L10
Bleasby Lincs 52 G7
Bleasby Notts 51 Q10
Blebocraigs Fife 93 M11
Bleddfa Powys 38 E8
Bledington Gloucs 30 G9
Bledlow Bucks 20 C3
Bledlow Ridge Bucks 20 C4
Blegbie E Loth 87 J9
Blencarn Cumb 64 B2
Blencogo Cumb 71 K6
Blendworth Hants 10 B7
Blenheim Palace Oxon 31 K10
Blennerhasset Cumb 71 J7
Bletchingdon Oxon 31 L9
Bletchingley Surrey 21 M12
Bletchley M Keyn 32 C9
Bletchley Shrops 49 L8
Bletherston Pembks 25 J5
Bletsoe Bed 32 E5
Blewbury Oxon 19 N4
Blickling Norfk 45 K4
Blidworth Notts 51 N9
Blidworth Bottoms Notts 51 N9
Blindcrake Cumb 71 J8
Blindley Heath Surrey 11 M2
Blisland Cnwll 4 D5
Blissford Hants 8 H5
Bliss Gate Worcs 39 N7
Blisworth Nhants 31 Q4
Blithbury Staffs 40 E4
Blockley Gloucs 30 F7
Blofield Norfk 45 M8
Blofield Heath Norfk 45 M7
Blo Norton Norfk 34 G2
Bloomfield Border 80 D8
Blore Staffs 50 F10
Blounce Hants 20 B12
Blounts Green Staffs 40 E2
Bloxham Oxon 31 K7
Bloxholm Lincs 52 F11
Bloxwich Wsall 40 D7
Bloxworth Dorset 8 C8
Blubberhouses N York 58 F3
Blue Anchor Somset 16 D7
Blue Bell Hill Kent 22 E10
Blue John Cavern Derbys 50 F4
Blundellsands Sefton 56 F8
Blundeston Suffk 45 Q10
Blunham C Beds 32 G6
Blunsdon St Andrew Swindn 18 G3
Bluntington Worcs 40 B11
Bluntisham Cambs 33 K2
Blyborough Lincs 52 D5
Blyford Suffk 35 N2
Blymhill Staffs 49 P11
Blyth Notts 51 N4
Blyth Nthumb 73 N5
Blyth Bridge Border 86 D12
Blythburgh Suffk 35 P2
Blyth Crematorium Nthumb 73 N5
Blythe Border 80 D4
Blyton Lincs 52 C5
Boarhills Fife 93 P11
Boarhunt Hants 9 P6
Boarstall Bucks 31 N10
Boath Highld 107 J7
Boat of Garten Highld 99 P5
Bobbing Kent 22 H9
Bobbington Staffs 39 P4
Bocking Essex 34 C11
Bocking Churchstreet Essex 34 C10
Boddam Abers 103 M6
Boddam Shet 111 k5
Boddington Gloucs 29 M4
Bodedern IoA 54 D5
Bodelwyddan Denbgs 55 Q6
Bodenham Herefs 39 K11
Bodenham Wilts 8 H3
Bodenham Moor Herefs 39 K11
Bodewryd IoA 54 E4
Bodfari Denbgs 48 C2
Bodffordd IoA 54 F6
Bodfuan Gwynd 46 E4
Bodham Norfk 45 J3
Bodiam E Susx 12 F5
Bodicote Oxon 31 L6
Bodinnick Cnwll 4 E9
Bodle Street Green E Susx 12 D7
Bodmin Cnwll 4 N3
Bodmin Moor Cnwll 4 F5
Bodsham Kent 13 L2
Bodwen Cnwll 3 M4
Bogallan Highld 107 K11
Bogbrae Abers 103 L8
Bogend S Ayrs 76 G5
Boggs Holdings E Loth 87 J7
Boghall Mdloth 86 F8
Boghall W Loth 86 B8
Boghead S Lans 77 N3
Bogmoor Moray 101 L3
Bogmuir Abers 95 K7
Bogniebrae Abers 102 D6
Bognor Regis W Susx 10 E9
Bogroy Highld 99 N4
Bogue D & G 69 N3
Bohortha Cnwll 3 J8
Bohuntine Highld 98 D11
Bolam Dur 65 L3
Bolberry Devon 5 N11
Boldmere Birm 40 E8
Boldre Hants 9 K7
Boldron Dur 65 J4
Bole Notts 52 B6
Bolehill Derbys 50 H9
Bolham Devon 16 C12
Bolham Water Devon 6 F1
Bolingey Cnwll 2 H5
Bollington Ches E 50 C5
Bolney W Susx 11 L5

Bolnhurst Bed 32 F5
Bolshan Angus 93 Q5
Bolsover Derbys 51 L6
Bolsterstone Sheff 50 H2
Boltby N York 66 C9
Boltenstone Abers 101 M12
Bolton Bolton 57 N7
Bolton Cumb 64 B3
Bolton E Loth 87 K8
Bolton E R Yk 60 D4
Bolton Nthumb 81 M10
Bolton Abbey N York 58 E4
Bolton-by-Bowland Lancs 63 P11
Boltonfellend Cumb 71 Q2
Boltongate Cumb 71 K7
Bolton le Sands Lancs 63 J8
Bolton Low Houses Cumb 71 K6
Bolton-on-Swale N York 65 M7
Bolton Percy N York 59 M6
Bolton Upon Dearne Barns 51 L1
Bolventor Cnwll 4 E5
Bomere Heath Shrops 49 J10
Bonar Bridge Highld 107 K4
Bonawe Ag & B 90 D9
Bonby N Linc 60 G10
Boncath Pembks 25 L2
Bonchester Bridge Border 80 D10
Bondleigh Devon 15 L10
Bonds Lancs 63 J12
Bo'ness Falk 86 B6
Boney Hay Staffs 40 D5
Bonhill W Duns 84 G7
Boningale Shrops 39 P2
Bonjedward Border 80 E9
Bonkle N Lans 85 P10
Bonnington Kent 13 J3
Bonnybank Fife 86 G2
Bonnybridge Falk 85 N7
Bonnykelly Abers 102 H5
Bonnyrigg Mdloth 86 G8
Bonnyton Angus 93 L7
Bonsall Derbys 50 H8
Bonshaw Tower D & G 71 K2
Bont-Dolgadfan Powys 47 P10
Bont-goch or Elerch Cerdgn 37 L4
Bontnewydd Cerdgn 37 K7
Bontnewydd Gwynd 54 G9
Bontuchel Denbgs 48 C4
Bonvilston V Glam 16 E2
Boode Devon 15 J5
Booker Bucks 20 D5
Boon Border 80 D5
Boosbeck R & Cl 66 F4
Boose's Green Essex 34 E9
Boot Cumb 62 D3
Booth Calder 58 D8
Boothby Graffoe Lincs 52 E10
Boothby Pagnell Lincs 42 D4
Boothferry E R Yk 60 C8
Boothstown Salfd 57 N8
Boothtown Calder 58 E8
Bootle Cumb 62 C5
Bootle Sefton 56 G9
Boraston Shrops 39 L8
Bordeaux Guern 6 c1
Borden Kent 22 G10
Border Forest Park 72 B4
Borders Crematorium Border 80 D7
Boreham Essex 22 F2
Boreham Wilts 18 D11
Boreham Street E Susx 12 D7
Borehamwood Herts 21 J4
Boreland D & G 79 J10
Boreraig Highld 104 B10
Borgh W Isls 111 a7
Borgh W Isls 111 d1
Borgie Highld 109 M4
Borgue D & G 69 P9
Borgue Highld 110 D9
Borley Essex 34 E7
Borneskitaig Highld 104 E7
Borness D & G 69 N9
Boroughbridge N York 59 K2
Borough Green Kent 22 C11
Borrowash Derbys 41 K1
Borrowby N York 65 Q9
Borrowstoun Falk 86 B6
Borstal Medway 22 E9
Borth Cerdgn 37 K3
Borthwickbrae Border 79 N6
Borthwickshiels Border 79 N6
Borth-y-Gest Gwynd 47 J4
Borwick Lancs 63 K7
Bosbury Herefs 39 M12
Boscastle Cnwll 4 D3
Boscombe Bmouth 8 G8
Boscombe Wilts 8 H11
Bosham W Susx 10 D8
Bosherston Pembks 24 G9
Bosley Ches E 50 B7
Bossall N York 60 C3
Bossiney Cnwll 4 D3
Bossingham Kent 13 M1
Bossington Somset 16 B6
Bostock Green Ches W 49 M2
Boston Lincs 43 K2
Boston Crematorium Lincs 43 J2
Boston Spa Leeds 59 K5
Boswinger Cnwll 3 L7
Botallack Cnwll 2 B8
Botany Bay Gt Lon 21 L4
Botesdale Suffk 34 H2
Bothal Nthumb 73 M4
Bothamsall Notts 51 P6
Bothel Cumb 71 J7
Bothenhampton Dorset 7 L5
Bothwell S Lans 85 L10
Bothwell Services S Lans 85 M10
Botley Bucks 20 F3
Botley Hants 9 N5
Botley Oxon 31 L11
Botolph Claydon Bucks 31 Q8
Botolphs W Susx 11 J8
Bottesford Leics 42 B3
Bottesford N Linc 52 C3
Bottisham Cambs 33 N5
Bottomcraig Fife 93 L10
Bottoms Calder 58 B9

Botusfleming Cnwll 5 J7
Botwnnog Gwynd 46 D5
Bough Beech Kent 11 P1
Boughrood Powys 27 N2
Boughton Nhants 31 Q2
Boughton Norfk 44 B9
Boughton Notts 51 P7
Boughton Aluph Kent 13 K1
Boughton Green Kent 22 F12
Boughton Monchelsea Kent 22 F12
Boughton Street Kent 23 K10
Bouldon Shrops 39 K5
Boulmer Nthumb 81 Q10
Boultham Lincs 52 D9
Bourn Cambs 33 K5
Bourne Lincs 42 F5
Bournebridge Essex 21 P5
Bournebrook Birm 40 D10
Bourne End Bucks 20 E6
Bourne End C Beds 32 D7
Bourne End Herts 20 G3
Bournemouth Bmouth 8 G8
Bournemouth Airport Dorset 8 G7
Bournemouth Crematorium Bmouth 8 G8
Bournes Green Sthend 22 H6
Bournheath Worcs 40 C11
Bournmoor Dur 73 N9
Bournville Birm 40 D10
Bourton Dorset 8 B2
Bourton Oxon 19 J4
Bourton Shrops 39 L3
Bourton Wilts 18 F7
Bourton on Dunsmore Warwks 41 K12
Bourton-on-the-Hill Gloucs 30 F7
Bourton-on-the-Water Gloucs 30 F9
Bousd Ag & B 88 G4
Bouth Cumb 62 G5
Bouthwaite N York 65 K12
Boveridge Dorset 8 F4
Bovey Tracey Devon 5 Q5
Bovingdon Herts 20 G3
Bow Devon 15 M10
Bow Gt Lon 21 M6
Bow Ork 111 h3
Bow Brickhill M Keyn 32 C9
Bowbridge Gloucs 29 M7
Bowburn Dur 73 N12
Bowcombe IoW 9 M9
Bowd Devon 6 F5
Bowden Border 80 D7
Bowden Hill Wilts 18 D7
Bowdon Traffd 57 N10
Bower Highld 110 E3
Bowerchalke Wilts 8 F3
Bowermadden Highld 110 E3
Bowers Staffs 49 P8
Bowers Gifford Essex 22 F4
Bowershall Fife 86 C4
Bower's Row Leeds 59 K8
Bowes Dur 64 H5
Bowgreave Lancs 63 J12
Bowhouse D & G 70 G3
Bowland Border 79 P2
Bowley Herefs 39 K10
Bowlhead Green Surrey 10 E3
Bowling C Brad 58 F7
Bowling W Duns 84 G8
Bowmanstead Cumb 62 F3
Bowmore Ag & B 82 D10
Bowness-on-Solway Cumb 71 K3
Bowness-on-Windermere Cumb 62 H3
Bow of Fife Fife 93 K12
Bowriefauld Angus 93 N6
Bowsden Nthumb 81 L6
Bow Street Cerdgn 37 K4
Box Gloucs 29 M8
Box Wilts 18 C7
Boxford Suffk 34 F8
Boxford W Berk 19 M6
Boxgrove W Susx 10 E8
Boxley Kent 22 F10
Boxmoor Herts 20 G3
Boxted Essex 34 G9
Boxted Suffk 34 D6
Boxted Cross Essex 34 G9
Boxworth Cambs 33 K4
Boyden Gate Kent 23 N9
Boylestone Derbys 40 F1
Boyndie Abers 102 E3
Boyndlie Abers 103 J3
Boynton E R Yk 61 K1
Boysack Angus 93 Q6
Boyton Cnwll 4 H2
Boyton Suffk 35 N7
Boyton Wilts 18 D11
Boyton Cross Essex 34 D2
Boyton End Suffk 34 C7
Bozeat Nhants 32 C5
Brabourne Kent 13 L2
Brabourne Lees Kent 13 L3
Brabstermire Highld 110 G2
Bracadale Highld 96 D2
Braceborough Lincs 42 F7
Bracebridge Heath Lincs 52 E9
Bracebridge Low Fields Lincs 52 D9
Braceby Lincs 42 E3
Bracewell Lancs 63 Q11
Brackenfield Derbys 51 J8
Brackenhirst N Lans 85 M8
Bracklesham W Susx 10 D10
Brackletter Highld 98 B11
Brackley Nhants 31 N6
Braco P & K 85 N2
Bracobrae Moray 101 P5
Bracon Ash Norfk 45 K9
Bracora Highld 97 K10
Bracorina Highld 97 K10
Bradbourne Derbys 50 G9
Bradbury Dur 65 N2
Bradden Nhants 31 N5
Bradenham Bucks 20 D4
Bradenstoke Wilts 18 E5
Bradfield Devon 6 E2
Bradfield Essex 35 J9
Bradfield Norfk 45 L4
Bradfield Sheff 50 H3

Bradfield - Buckland in the Moor 169

Bradfield W Berk 19 P6
Bradfield Combust Suffk 34 E5
Bradfield Green Ches E 49 M4
Bradfield Heath Essex 35 J10
Bradfield St Clare Suffk 34 E5
Bradfield St George Suffk 34 E5
Bradford C Brad 58 F7
Bradford Devon 14 G10
Bradford Abbas Dorset 17 N12
Bradford Leigh Wilts 18 C8
Bradford-on-Avon Wilts 18 C8
Bradford-on-Tone Somset 16 G10
Bradford Peverell Dorset 7 P4
Bradiford Devon 15 K5
Brading IoW 9 Q9
Bradley Derbys 50 G10
Bradley Hants 19 Q11
Bradley NE Lin 53 J3
Bradley Staffs 49 Q11
Bradley Wolves 40 C8
Bradley Worcs 30 C2
Bradley Green Worcs 30 C2
Bradley in the Moors Staffs 50 D11
Bradley Stoke S Glos 28 H11
Bradmore Notts 41 N2
Bradninch Devon 6 D3
Bradnop Staffs 50 D9
Bradpole Dorset 7 L4
Bradshaw Calder 58 E8
Bradstone Devon 4 H4
Bradwall Green Ches E 49 N3
Bradwell Derbys 50 F5
Bradwell Essex 34 D11
Bradwell M Keyn 32 B8
Bradwell Norfk 45 Q8
Bradwell Crematorium Staffs 49 Q5
Bradwell-on-Sea Essex 23 J3
Bradwell Waterside Essex 23 J2
Bradworthy Devon 14 F8
Brae Highld 107 L9
Brae Shet 111 k3
Braeface Falk 85 N7
Braehead Angus 95 L10
Braehead D & G 69 K8
Braehead S Lans 77 Q2
Braemar Abers 94 C4
Braemore Highld 106 C6
Braemore Highld 110 C9
Brae Roy Lodge Highld 98 D10
Braeside Inver 84 D7
Braes of Coul Angus 93 K4
Braes of Enzie Moray 101 M4
Braeswick Ork 111 i1
Braevallich Ag & B 83 P2
Brafferton Darltn 65 N4
Brafferton N York 66 B12
Brafield-on-the-Green Nhants 32 B5
Bragar W Isls 111 d1
Bragbury End Herts 33 J11
Braidwood S Lans 77 P2
Brailsford Derbys 50 G11
Braintree Essex 34 C11
Braiseworth Suffk 35 J3
Braishfield Hants 9 L3
Braithwaite Cumb 71 K10
Braithwell Donc 51 M2
Bramber W Susx 11 J7
Bramcote Warwks 41 K9
Bramcote Crematorium Notts 51 L11
Bramdean Hants 9 Q2
Bramerton Norfk 45 L8
Bramfield Herts 33 J12
Bramfield Suffk 35 N3
Bramford Suffk 35 J7
Bramhall Stockp 50 B4
Bramham Leeds 59 K5
Bramhope Leeds 58 G5
Bramley Hants 19 Q8
Bramley Leeds 58 G7
Bramley Rothm 51 L3
Bramley Surrey 10 G2
Bramley Corner Hants 19 Q8
Bramling Kent 23 N11
Brampford Speke Devon 6 C3
Brampton Cambs 32 H3
Brampton Cumb 64 C3
Brampton Cumb 71 Q4
Brampton Lincs 52 B7
Brampton Norfk 45 K5
Brampton Rothm 51 K1
Brampton Suffk 35 P1
Brampton Abbotts Herefs 28 H4
Brampton Ash Nhants 42 B11
Brampton Bryan Herefs 38 G7
Brampton-en-le-Morthen Rothm 51 L4
Bramshall Staffs 40 D2
Bramshaw Hants 9 J4
Bramshott Hants 10 D4
Bramwell Somset 17 L9
Branault Highld 89 L3
Brancaster Norfk 44 C2
Brancaster Staithe Norfk 44 D2
Brancepeth Dur 73 L12
Branchill Moray 100 G5
Branderburgh Moray 101 K2
Brandesburton E R Yk 61 J5
Brandeston Suffk 35 L5
Brandiston Norfk 45 J6
Brandon Dur 73 M11
Brandon Lincs 42 C1
Brandon Suffk 44 D11
Brandon Warwks 41 K11
Brandon Parva Norfk 44 H8
Brandsby N York 66 E11
Brandy Wharf Lincs 52 E4
Bran End Essex 33 Q10
Branksome Poole 8 F8
Branksome Park Poole 8 F8
Bransbury Hants 19 M11
Bransby Lincs 52 C7
Branscombe Devon 6 G5
Bransford Worcs 39 P10
Bransgore Hants 8 H7
Bransholme C KuH 61 J7
Bransley Shrops 39 M7
Branston Leics 42 B4
Branston Lincs 52 E9
Branston Staffs 40 G4
Branston Booths Lincs 52 F9
Branstone IoW 9 P10
Brant Broughton Lincs 52 D11
Brantham Suffk 35 J9
Branthwaite Cumb 70 H9
Branthwaite Cumb 71 L7
Brantingham E R Yk 60 G8
Branton Donc 51 N1
Branton Nthumb 81 L10
Branton Green N York 59 K2
Branxton Nthumb 81 J6
Brassington Derbys 50 G9
Brasted Kent 21 P11
Brasted Chart Kent 21 P11
Brathens Abers 95 L3
Bratoft Lincs 53 M9
Brattleby Lincs 52 D7
Bratton Wilts 18 D9
Bratton Wrekin 49 L11
Bratton Clovelly Devon 5 K2
Bratton Fleming Devon 15 L5
Bratton Seymour Somset 17 P9
Braughing Herts 33 L10
Braunston Nhants 31 M2
Braunston Rutlnd 42 B8
Braunstone Leics 41 M7
Braunton Devon 14 H5
Brawby N York 66 G11
Brawl Highld 109 P3
Bray W & M 20 E7
Braybrooke Nhants 41 Q9
Brayford Devon 15 M5
Bray Shop Cnwll 4 H5
Brayton N York 59 N7
Braywick W & M 20 E7
Breachwood Green Herts 32 G11
Breadsall Derbys 51 J11
Breadstone Gloucs 29 J8
Breage Cnwll 2 F9
Breakachy Highld 106 H12
Breakspear Crematorium Gt Lon 20 H5
Brealangwell Lodge Highld 106 H4
Bream Gloucs 28 H7
Breamore Hants 8 H4
Brean Somset 16 H5
Breanais W Isls 111 b2
Brearton N York 58 H3
Breascleit W Isls 111 c2
Breasclete W Isls 111 c2
Breaston Derbys 41 L2
Brechfa Carmth 26 C3
Brechin Angus 95 K9
Breckles Norfk 44 F10
Brecon Powys 27 L3
Brecon Beacons National Park 27 L4
Bredbury Stockp 50 B3
Brede E Susx 12 G6
Bredenbury Herefs 39 L10
Bredfield Suffk 35 L6
Bredgar Kent 22 G10
Bredhurst Kent 22 F10
Bredon Worcs 29 N2
Bredon's Hardwick Worcs 29 M2
Bredon's Norton Worcs 29 N2
Bredwardine Herefs 38 G12
Breedon on the Hill Leics 41 K3
Breich W Loth 85 Q10
Breightmet Bolton 57 N7
Breighton E R Yk 60 C7
Breinton Herefs 28 F2
Bremhill Wilts 18 E6
Brenchley Kent 12 D2
Brendon Devon 15 N3
Brenfield Ag & B 83 M6
Brenish W Isls 111 b2
Brent Cross Gt Lon 21 K6
Brent Eleigh Suffk 34 F7
Brentford Gt Lon 21 J7
Brentingby Leics 42 B6
Brent Knoll Somset 17 J6
Brent Mill Devon 5 N8
Brent Pelham Herts 33 M10
Brentwood Essex 22 C5
Brenzett Kent 13 J5
Brenzett Green Kent 13 J4
Brereton Staffs 40 D4
Brereton Green Ches E 49 P3
Bressay Shet 111 k4
Bressingham Norfk 34 H1
Bretby Derbys 40 H3
Bretby Crematorium Derbys 40 H3
Bretford Warwks 41 K11
Bretforton Worcs 30 E5
Bretherton Lancs 57 J5
Brettabister Shet 111 k4
Brettenham Norfk 44 F12
Brettenham Suffk 34 F6
Bretton Flints 48 G3
Brewood Staffs 40 B6
Briantspuddle Dorset 8 B8
Brickendon Herts 21 L2
Bricket Wood Herts 20 H3
Brick Houses Sheff 50 H5
Bricklehampton Worcs 29 N1
Bride IoM 56 e2
Bridekirk Cumb 71 J8
Bridestowe Devon 5 L3
Brideswell Abers 102 D7
Bridford Devon 5 Q3
Bridge Kent 23 M11
Bridgehampton Somset 17 N10
Bridge Hewick N York 65 N12
Bridgehill Dur 73 K9
Bridgemary Hants 9 P6
Bridgend Abers 101 P7
Bridgend Ag & B 75 M5
Bridgend Ag & B 82 E9
Bridgend Angus 95 J8
Bridgend Brdgnd 27 J11
Bridgend D & G 78 H7
Bridgend Devon 5 L9
Bridgend Fife 93 L12
Bridgend Moray 101 M8
Bridgend P & K 92 G10
Bridgend W Loth 86 C7
Bridgend of Lintrathen Angus 93 K5
Bridge of Alford Abers 102 D10
Bridge of Allan Stirlg 85 N4
Bridge of Avon Moray 100 H10
Bridge of Avon Moray 101 J7
Bridge of Balgie P & K 91 N7
Bridge of Brewlands Angus 94 C9
Bridge of Brown Highld 100 H10
Bridge of Cally P & K 92 H5
Bridge of Canny Abers 95 K3
Bridge of Craigisla Angus 93 J5
Bridge of Dee D & G 70 C4
Bridge of Don C Aber 103 K12
Bridge of Dulsie Highld 100 E7
Bridge of Dye Abers 95 K5
Bridge of Earn P & K 92 G11
Bridge of Ericht P & K 91 M5
Bridge of Feugh Abers 95 L3
Bridge of Forss Highld 110 B3
Bridge of Gairn Abers 94 F3
Bridge of Gaur P & K 91 M5
Bridge of Marnoch Abers 102 D5
Bridge of Orchy Ag & B 91 J8
Bridge of Tilt P & K 92 D3
Bridge of Tynet Moray 101 M3
Bridge of Walls Shet 111 j4
Bridge of Weir Rens 84 G9
Bridgerule Devon 14 E10
Bridge Sollers Herefs 28 E1
Bridge Street Suffk 34 E6
Bridgetown Somset 16 C9
Bridge Trafford Ches W 49 J2
Bridgham Norfk 44 F11
Bridgnorth Shrops 39 N4
Bridgwater Somset 16 H8
Bridgwater Services Somset 17 J8
Bridlington E R Yk 61 K2
Bridport Dorset 7 L4
Bridstow Herefs 28 G4
Brierfield Lancs 57 Q2
Brierley Barns 59 K11
Brierley Gloucs 28 H6
Brierley Hill Dudley 40 B9
Brigg N Linc 52 E3
Briggate Norfk 45 M5
Briggswath N York 67 J6
Brigham Cumb 70 H9
Brigham E R Yk 61 J4
Brighouse Calder 58 F9
Brighstone IoW 9 M10
Brighthampton Oxon 31 K12
Brightley Devon 15 K11
Brightling E Susx 12 D6
Brightlingsea Essex 34 H12
Brighton Br & H 11 L8
Brighton le Sands Sefton 56 F8
Brightons Falk 85 Q7
Brightwalton W Berk 19 M5
Brightwell Suffk 35 L7
Brightwell Baldwin Oxon 19 Q2
Brightwell-cum-Sotwell Oxon 19 P3
Brightwell Upperton Oxon 19 Q2
Brignall Dur 65 J5
Brig o'Turk Stirlg 85 J2
Brigsley NE Lin 53 J3
Brigsteer Cumb 63 J4
Brigstock Nhants 42 D11
Brill Bucks 31 P10
Brill Cnwll 2 G9
Brilley Herefs 38 F11
Brimfield Herefs 39 K8
Brimfield Cross Herefs 39 K8
Brimington Derbys 51 K6
Brimley Devon 5 Q5
Brimpsfield Gloucs 29 N6
Brimpton W Berk 19 P7
Brimscombe Gloucs 29 M8
Brimstage Wirral 56 F11
Brincliffe Sheff 51 J4
Brind E R Yk 60 C7
Brindister Shet 111 j4
Brindle Lancs 57 L4
Brineton Staffs 49 P11
Bringhurst Leics 42 B10
Bringsty Common Herefs 39 M10
Brington Cambs 32 F2
Briningham Norfk 44 G4
Brinkhill Lincs 53 L8
Brinkley Cambs 33 Q6
Brinklow Warwks 41 K10
Brinkworth Wilts 18 E4
Brinscall Lancs 57 L5
Brinsley Notts 51 L10
Brinsworth Rothm 51 K3
Brinton Norfk 44 G3
Brinyan Ork 111 h2
Brisley Norfk 44 F6
Brislington Bristl 17 N3
Brissenden Green Kent 12 H3
Bristol Bristl 17 N2
Bristol Airport N Som 17 M3
Bristol Zoo Gardens Bristl 17 N2
Briston Norfk 44 H4
Britford Wilts 8 H2
Brithdir Caerph 27 N8
Brithdir Gwynd 47 M7
British Legion Village Kent 22 E11
Briton Ferry Neath 26 G9
Britwell Salome Oxon 19 R3
Brixham Torbay 6 C10
Brixton Devon 5 L9
Brixton Gt Lon 21 L8
Brixton Deverill Wilts 18 C11
Brixworth Nhants 41 Q12
Brize Norton Oxon 30 H11
Brize Norton Airport Oxon 30 H11
Broad Alley Worcs 30 B1
Broad Blunsdon Swindn 18 G3
Broadbottom Tamesd 50 C3
Broadbridge W Susx 10 D8
Broadbridge Heath W Susx 11 J4
Broad Campden Gloucs 30 F6
Broad Carr Calder 58 E9
Broad Chalke Wilts 8 F3
Broadclyst Devon 6 D4
Broadfield Inver 84 F8
Broadford Highld 96 H5
Broadford Bridge W Susx 10 H6
Broadgairhill Border 79 K6
Broad Green Worcs 39 P10
Broadhaugh Border 81 J4
Broad Haven Pembks 24 F6
Broadheath Traffd 57 N10
Broadhembury Devon 6 E2
Broadhempston Devon 5 Q7
Broad Hinton Wilts 18 G5
Broadland Row E Susx 12 G6
Broad Layings Hants 19 M8
Broadley Moray 101 M3
Broad Marston Worcs 30 F5
Broadmayne Dorset 7 Q5
Broadmoor Pembks 25 J7
Broadoak Dorset 7 L4
Broad Oak E Susx 12 C5
Broad Oak E Susx 12 G6
Broad Oak Herefs 28 F5
Broad Oak Kent 23 M10
Broad Oak St Hel 57 K9
Broad's Green Essex 22 E2
Broadstairs Kent 23 Q9
Broadstone Poole 8 E8
Broadstone Shrops 39 K4
Broad Street E Susx 12 G6
Broad Street Kent 22 G11
Broad Town Wilts 18 G5
Broadwas Worcs 39 N10
Broadwater Herts 33 J11
Broadwater W Susx 11 J8
Broadwaters Worcs 39 Q6
Broadway Pembks 24 F6
Broadway Somset 17 J11
Broadway Worcs 30 E6
Broadwell Gloucs 28 G6
Broadwell Gloucs 30 G8
Broadwell Oxon 30 G12
Broadwell Warwks 31 L2
Broadwindsor Dorset 7 L3
Broadwood Kelly Devon 15 K10
Broadwoodwidger Devon 5 J3
Brochel Highld 104 H12
Brochroy Ag & B 90 D9
Brockamin Worcs 39 P10
Brockbridge Hants 9 Q4
Brockdish Norfk 35 K2
Brockenhurst Hants 9 K7
Brocketsbrae S Lans 78 D2
Brockford Street Suffk 35 J4
Brockhall Nhants 31 N2
Brockham Surrey 21 K12
Brockhampton Gloucs 30 D9
Brockhampton Hants 10 B8
Brockhampton Herefs 28 H3
Brockholes Kirk 58 F11
Brocklesby Lincs 61 K11
Brockley N Som 17 L3
Brockley Suffk 34 D3
Brockley Green Suffk 34 C7
Brockley Green Suffk 34 D6
Brockton Shrops 38 G2
Brockton Shrops 38 G5
Brockton Shrops 39 L4
Brockweir Gloucs 28 G8
Brockworth Gloucs 29 M5
Brocton Staffs 40 C4
Brodick N Ayrs 75 Q5
Brodie Moray 100 F4
Brodsworth Donc 59 L11
Brogaig Highld 104 F8
Brokenborough Wilts 18 D3
Broken Cross Ches E 50 B6
Brokerswood Wilts 18 C9
Bromborough Wirral 56 G11
Brome Suffk 35 J2
Brome Street Suffk 35 J2
Bromeswell Suffk 35 M6
Bromfield Cumb 71 J6
Bromfield Shrops 39 J6
Bromham Bed 32 E6
Bromham Wilts 18 E7
Bromley Gt Lon 21 N9
Bromley Shrops 39 N3
Bromley Cross Bolton 57 N6
Brompton Medway 22 F9
Brompton N York 65 P8
Brompton-by-Sawdon N York 67 K10
Brompton-on-Swale N York 65 L7
Brompton Ralph Somset 16 E9
Brompton Regis Somset 16 C9
Bromsberrow Gloucs 29 K3
Bromsberrow Heath Gloucs 29 K3
Bromsgrove Worcs 40 C12
Bromyard Herefs 39 M10
Bronant Cerdgn 37 K7
Brongest Cerdgn 36 E10
Bronington Wrexhm 49 J7
Bronllys Powys 27 N2
Bronwydd Carmth 25 P4
Bronygarth Shrops 48 F7
Bron-y-Nant Crematorium Conwy 55 M6
Brook Hants 9 J5
Brook IoW 9 L9
Brook Kent 13 K2
Brook Surrey 10 E3
Brooke Norfk 45 L9
Brooke Rutlnd 42 C8
Brookenby Lincs 52 H4
Brookfield Rens 84 G9
Brookhampton Somset 17 P9
Brook Hill Hants 9 J5
Brookhouse Lancs 63 K8
Brookhouse Rothm 51 L3
Brookhouse Green Ches E 49 P4
Brookhouses Derbys 50 D3
Brookland Kent 13 J5
Brooklands Traffd 57 P10
Brookmans Park Herts 21 K3
Brook Street Essex 22 C5
Brook Street Kent 12 H4
Brookthorpe Gloucs 29 L6
Brookwood Surrey 20 F11
Broom C Beds 32 G8
Broom Rothm 51 K3
Broom Warwks 30 E4
Broome Norfk 45 M10
Broome Shrops 38 H6
Broome Worcs 40 B10
Broomedge Warrtn 57 N10
Broomfield Essex 22 E2
Broomfield Kent 22 G11
Broomfield Kent 23 M9
Broomfield Somset 16 G9
Broomfleet E R Yk 60 F8
Broomhaugh Nthumb 72 H8
Broom Hill Barns 59 K12
Broom Hill Notts 51 M10
Broomhill Nthumb 73 M1
Broompark Dur 73 M11
Brora Highld 107 P2
Broseley Shrops 39 M2
Brotherlee Dur 72 G12
Brotherton N York 59 L8
Brotton R & Cl 66 F4
Broubster Highld 110 B4
Brough Cumb 64 E5
Brough E R Yk 60 F8
Brough Highld 110 E2
Brough Notts 52 B10
Brough Shet 111 m3
Broughall Shrops 49 K7
Brough Lodge Shet 111 m2
Brough Sowerby Cumb 64 E5
Broughton Border 78 H2
Broughton Cambs 33 J2
Broughton Flints 48 G3
Broughton Hants 9 K2
Broughton Lancs 57 K2
Broughton M Keyn 32 C8
Broughton N Linc 52 D2
Broughton N York 58 C4
Broughton N York 66 H11
Broughton Nhants 32 B2
Broughton Oxon 31 K6
Broughton Salfd 57 P8
Broughton V Glam 16 C3
Broughton Astley Leics 41 M8
Broughton Gifford Wilts 18 C7
Broughton Green Worcs 30 C2
Broughton Hackett Worcs 30 B3
Broughton-in-Furness Cumb 62 E5
Broughton Mains D & G 69 L9
Broughton Mills Cumb 62 E4
Broughton Moor Cumb 70 H8
Broughton Poggs Oxon 30 G12
Broughty Ferry C Dund 93 N9
Brown Candover Hants 19 P11
Brown Edge Staffs 50 B9
Brownhill Abers 102 H7
Brownhills Fife 93 P11
Brownhills Wsall 40 D6
Browninghill Green Hants 19 P8
Brown Lees Staffs 49 Q4
Brownsea Island Dorset 8 F9
Browns Hill Gloucs 29 M8
Brownston Devon 5 N9
Broxa N York 67 K8
Broxbourne Herts 21 M3
Broxburn E Loth 87 N6
Broxburn W Loth 86 C7
Broxted Essex 33 P10
Bruan Highld 110 G7
Bruar P & K 92 C3
Brucefield Highld 107 Q5
Bruchag Ag & B 84 B10
Bruichladdich Ag & B 82 C10
Bruisyard Suffk 35 M4
Bruisyard Street Suffk 35 M4
Brumby N Linc 52 C2
Brund Staffs 50 E8
Brundall Norfk 45 M8
Brundish Suffk 35 L3
Brundish Street Suffk 35 L3
Brunery Highld 89 P2
Brunswick Village N u Ty 73 M6
Brunthwaite C Brad 58 D5
Bruntingthorpe Leics 41 N9
Brunton Fife 93 K10
Brunton Wilts 19 J9
Brushford Devon 15 L9
Brushford Somset 16 C10
Bruton Somset 17 P8
Bryan's Green Worcs 30 B1
Bryanston Dorset 8 C6
Brydekirk D & G 71 K2
Bryher IoS 2 b2
Brympton Somset 17 M11
Bryn Carmth 26 D8
Bryn Neath 26 H9
Brynamman Carmth 26 F6
Brynberian Pembks 25 J2
Bryncir Gwynd 46 H3
Bryn-coch Neath 26 G8
Bryncroes Gwynd 46 D5
Bryncrug Gwynd 47 K9
Bryneglwys Denbgs 48 D6
Brynford Flints 48 D1
Bryn Gates Wigan 57 L8
Bryngwran IoA 54 D6
Bryngwyn Mons 28 D7
Bryngwyn Powys 38 E11
Bryn-Henllan Pembks 24 H2
Brynhoffnant Cerdgn 36 E9
Brynmawr Blae G 27 P6
Bryn-mawr Gwynd 46 D5
Brynmenyn Brdgnd 27 J10
Brynmill Swans 26 E9
Brynna Rhondd 27 L11
Brynrefail Gwynd 54 H8
Brynsadler Rhondd 27 L11
Bryn Saith Marchog Denbgs 48 C5
Brynsiencyn IoA 54 F7
Brynteg IoA 54 G5
Bryn-y-Maen Conwy 55 M6
Bualintur Highld 96 E5
Bubbenhall Warwks 41 J11
Bubwith E R Yk 60 C7
Buccleuch Border 79 M6
Buchanan Smithy Stirlg 84 H5
Buchanhaven Abers 103 M6
Buchanty P & K 92 D9
Buchany Stirlg 85 M3
Buchlyvie Stirlg 85 J4
Buckabank Cumb 71 M6
Buckden Cambs 32 H4
Buckden N York 64 G11
Buckenham Norfk 45 M8
Buckerell Devon 6 F3
Buckfast Devon 5 P6
Buckfastleigh Devon 5 P7
Buckhaven Fife 86 G3
Buckholt Mons 28 F5
Buckhorn Weston Dorset 17 R10
Buckhurst Hill Essex 21 N5
Buckie Moray 101 M3
Buckingham Bucks 31 P7
Buckland Bucks 20 E2
Buckland Devon 5 N10
Buckland Gloucs 30 E7
Buckland Herts 33 K9
Buckland Kent 13 P2
Buckland Oxon 19 K2
Buckland Surrey 21 K12
Buckland Brewer Devon 14 G7
Buckland Common Bucks 20 E3
Buckland Dinham Somset 17 R6
Buckland Filleigh Devon 14 H9
Buckland in the Moor Devon 5 P5

Buckland Monachorum
Devon 5 K6
Buckland Newton Dorset 7 P2
Buckland Ripers Dorset 7 P6
Buckland St Mary Somset 16 H12
Buckland-Tout-Saints
Devon 5 P10
Bucklebury W Berk 19 P6
Bucklers Hard Hants 9 L7
Bucklesham Suffk 35 L8
Buckley Flints 48 F3
Bucklow Hill Ches E 57 N11
Buckminster Leics 42 C5
Bucknall C Stke 50 B10
Bucknall Lincs 52 G9
Bucknell Oxon 31 M8
Bucknell Shrops 38 G7
Buckpool Moray 101 M3
Bucksburn C Aber 103 J12
Buck's Cross Devon 14 F7
Bucks Green W Susx 10 H4
Buckshaw Village Lancs 57 K5
Bucks Horn Oak Hants 10 D2
Buck's Mills Devon 14 F7
Buckton E R Yk 67 P11
Buckton Nthumb 81 N6
Buckworth Cambs 32 G2
Budby Notts 51 N6
Bude Cnwll 14 D10
Budge's Shop Cnwll 4 H8
Budleigh Salterton Devon 6 E6
Budock Water Cnwll 2 H9
Buerton Ches E 49 M6
Bugbrooke Nhants 31 P3
Bugle Cnwll 3 M4
Bugley Dorset 8 B3
Bugthorpe E R Yk 60 D3
Buildwas Shrops 39 L2
Builth Wells Powys 38 B11
Bulbridge Wilts 8 G2
Bulford Wilts 18 H11
Bulkeley Ches E 49 K5
Bulkington Warwks 41 K9
Bulkington Wilts 18 D8
Bulkworthy Devon 14 G8
Bullbrook Br For 20 E9
Bullington Hants 19 M11
Bullington Lincs 52 F7
Bullinghope Herefs 28 C2
Bull's Green Essex 21 N3
Bulmer Essex 34 D8
Bulmer N York 60 C1
Bulmer Tye Essex 34 D8
Bulphan Thurr 22 D6
Bulwark Abers 103 J6
Bulwell C Nott 51 M11
Bulwick Nhants 42 D10
Bumble's Green Essex 21 N3
Bunacaimb Highld 97 J11
Bunarkaig Highld 98 B10
Bunbury Ches E 49 K4
Bunchrew Highld 107 K12
Bundalloch Highld 97 M4
Bunessan Ag & B 89 J11
Bungay Suffk 45 M11
Bunnahabhain Ag & B 82 F8
Bunny Notts 41 N2
Buntait Highld 98 E3
Buntingford Herts 33 K10
Bunwell Norfk 45 J10
Burbage Leics 41 K8
Burbage Wilts 19 J8
Burchett's Green W & M 20 D7
Burcombe Wilts 8 F2
Burcott Bucks 32 C11
Bures Essex 34 E9
Burford Oxon 30 G10
Burford Shrops 39 L8
Burg Ag & B 89 J7
Burgates Hants 10 C4
Burgess Hill W Susx 11 L6
Burgh Suffk 35 K6
Burgh by Sands Cumb 71 M4
Burgh Castle Norfk 45 P8
Burghclere Hants 19 M8
Burghead Moray 100 H2
Burghfield W Berk 19 Q7
Burghfield Common
W Berk 19 Q7
Burgh Heath Surrey 21 K10
Burghill Herefs 39 J12
Burgh Island Devon 5 M10
Burgh le Marsh Lincs 53 N9
Burgh next Aylsham
Norfk 45 K5
Burgh on Bain Lincs 52 H6
Burgh St Margaret Norfk 45 P7
Burgh St Peter Norfk 45 P10
Burghwallis Donc 59 M10
Burham Kent 22 E10
Buriton Hants 10 C6
Burland Ches E 49 L5
Burlawn Cnwll 3 M2
Burleigh Gloucs 29 M8
Burlescombe Devon 16 E11
Burleston Dorset 8 B8
Burley Hants 8 H6
Burley Rutlnd 42 C7
Burleydam Ches E 49 L7
Burley Gate Herefs 39 L11
Burley in Wharfedale
C Brad 58 F5
Burley Street Hants 8 H6
Burley Wood Head C Brad 58 F5
Burlton Shrops 49 J9
Burmarsh Kent 13 L4
Burmington Warwks 30 H6
Burn N York 59 N8
Burnage Manch 57 Q9
Burnaston Derbys 40 H2
Burnbrae N Lans 85 P10
Burnby E R Yk 60 E5
Burneside Cumb 63 J3
Burneston N York 65 N3
Burnett BaNES 17 P3
Burnfoot Border 79 N6
Burnfoot Border 80 C10
Burnfoot D & G 78 F9
Burnfoot D & G 79 M10
Burnfoot D & G 79 N9
Burnfoot P & K 86 B2
Burnham Bucks 20 E7
Burnham Deepdale Norfk 44 D2
Burnham Market Norfk 44 D2
Burnham Norton Norfk 44 D2
Burnham-on-Crouch
Essex 23 J4
Burnham-on-Sea Somset 17 J6
Burnham Overy Norfk 44 D2

Burnham Overy Staithe
Norfk 44 D2
Burnham Thorpe Norfk 44 E2
Burnhaven Abers 103 M6
Burnhead D & G 78 E9
Burnhervie Abers 102 F10
Burnhill Green Staffs 39 P3
Burnhope Dur 73 L10
Burnhouse N Ayrs 76 G2
Burniston N York 67 L8
Burnley Lancs 57 Q3
Burnley Crematorium
Lancs 57 P3
Burnmouth Border 81 K3
Burn of Cambus Stirlg 85 M3
Burnopfield Dur 73 L9
Burnsall N York 58 D2
Burnside Angus 93 M4
Burnside Angus 93 N5
Burnside Fife 86 D1
Burnside Moray 101 J2
Burnside W Loth 86 C7
Burnside of Duntrune
Angus 93 M8
Burntisland Fife 86 F5
Burntwood Staffs 40 D5
Burntwood Green Staffs 40 E6
Burnt Yates N York 58 G2
Burnworthy Somset 16 G11
Burpham Surrey 20 G11
Burpham W Susx 10 G8
Burradon Nthumb 81 K11
Burrafirth Shet 111 m2
Burravoe Shet 111 k3
Burrells Cumb 64 C4
Burrelton P & K 92 H8
Burridge Devon 7 J2
Burridge Hants 9 N5
Burrill N York 65 M9
Burringham N Linc 52 B2
Burrington Devon 15 L8
Burrington Herefs 38 H7
Burrington N Som 17 L4
Burrough Green Cambs 33 Q6
Burrough on the Hill Leics 41 Q5
Burrow Lancs 63 L7
Burrow Somset 16 C7
Burrow Bridge Somset 17 J9
Burrowhill Surrey 20 F10
Burry Green Swans 25 P9
Burry Port Carmth 25 Q8
Burscough Lancs 56 H6
Burscough Bridge Lancs 57 J6
Bursea E R Yk 60 D7
Bursledon Hants 9 N5
Burslem C Stke 49 Q5
Burstall Suffk 34 H7
Burstock Dorset 7 K3
Burston Norfk 45 J12
Burstow Surrey 11 L2
Burstwick E R Yk 61 L8
Burtersett N York 64 F9
Burtholme Cumb 71 Q3
Burthorpe Green Suffk 34 C4
Burtoft Lincs 43 J3
Burton Ches W 48 G1
Burton Ches W 49 K3
Burton Dorset 8 H8
Burton Lincs 52 D8
Burton Pembks 24 H7
Burton Somset 16 G7
Burton Wilts 18 B5
Burton Agnes E R Yk 61 J2
Burton Bradstock Dorset 7 L5
Burton Coggles Lincs 42 E5
Burton End Essex 33 N11
Burton Fleming E R Yk 67 M12
Burton Hastings Warwks 41 K9
Burton-in-Kendal Cumb 63 K7
Burton-in-Kendal
Services Cumb 63 K7
Burton in Lonsdale N York 63 M7
Burton Joyce Notts 51 N11
Burton Latimer Nhants 32 C2
Burton Lazars Leics 41 Q4
Burton Leonard N York 59 J2
Burton on the Wolds
Leics 41 N4
Burton Overy Leics 41 P7
Burton Pedwardine Lincs 42 G2
Burton Pidsea E R Yk 61 L7
Burton Salmon N York 59 L8
Burton's Green Essex 34 D10
Burton upon Stather
N Linc 60 E9
Burton upon Trent Staffs 40 G3
Burton Waters Lincs 52 D8
Burtonwood Warrtn 57 K9
Burtonwood Services
Warrtn 57 L9
Burwardsley Ches W 49 K4
Burwarton Shrops 39 L5
Burwash E Susx 12 D5
Burwash Common E Susx 12 D5
Burwash Weald E Susx 12 D5
Burwell Cambs 33 P4
Burwell Lincs 53 K7
Burwen IoA 54 F3
Burwick Ork 111 h3
Bury Bury 57 P6
Bury Cambs 43 J12
Bury Somset 16 C10
Bury W Susx 10 G7
Bury Green Herts 33 M11
Bury St Edmunds Suffk 34 E4
Burythorpe N York 60 D2
Busby E Rens 85 K10
Buscot Oxon 19 J2
Bush Abers 95 M8
Bush Bank Herefs 39 J10
Bushbury Wolves 40 B7
Bushbury Crematorium
Wolves 40 B6
Bushey Herts 21 J4
Bushey Heath Herts 21 J5
Bush Hill Park Gt Lon 21 M4
Bushley Worcs 29 M2
Bushmoor Shrops 38 H5
Bushton Wilts 18 F5
Bussage Gloucs 29 M7
Bussex Somset 17 J9
Butcombe N Som 17 M4
Bute Ag & B 83 Q8
Butleigh Somset 17 M9
Butleigh Wootton Somset 17 M8
Butlers Marston Warwks 30 H4
Butley Suffk 35 N6

Buttercrambe N York 60 C3
Butterdean Border 87 M8
Butterknowle Dur 65 K3
Butterleigh Devon 6 C2
Buttermere Cumb 71 J11
Buttershaw C Brad 58 F8
Butterstone P & K 92 F6
Butterton Staffs 49 P7
Butterton Staffs 50 E7
Butterwick Lincs 43 L2
Butterwick N York 66 G11
Butterwick N York 67 L12
Buttington Powys 38 F1
Buttonoak Shrops 39 N6
Buxhall Suffk 34 G5
Buxted E Susx 11 P5
Buxton Derbys 50 D6
Buxton Norfk 45 K5
Buxton Heath Norfk 45 K6
Bwlch Powys 27 N4
Bwlchgwyn Wrexhm 48 F5
Bwlchllan Cerdgn 37 J8
Bwlchtocyn Gwynd 46 E6
Bwlch-y-cibau Powys 48 D11
Bwlch-y-ffridd Powys 38 C3
Bwlch-y-groes Pembks 25 M2
Bwlch-y-sarnau Powys 38 B7
Byers Green Dur 65 L2
Byfield Nhants 31 M4
Byfleet Surrey 20 G10
Byford Herefs 38 H12
Byker N u Ty 73 M7
Bylchau Conwy 55 P8
Byley Ches W 49 N2
Bynea Carmth 26 D6
Bythorn Cambs 32 F2
Byton Herefs 38 G8
Bywell Nthumb 73 J8
Byworth W Susx 10 F6

C

Cabourne Lincs 52 G3
Cabrach Ag & B 82 G9
Cabrach Moray 101 M9
Cabus Lancs 63 J11
Cadbury Devon 6 C2
Cadbury World Birm 40 D10
Cadder E Duns 85 K8
Caddington C Beds 32 F11
Caddonfoot Border 79 P2
Cadeby Donc 51 L1
Cadeby Leics 41 K7
Cadeleigh Devon 6 C2
Cade Street E Susx 12 C6
Cadgwith Cnwll 2 G11
Cadham Fife 86 F2
Cadishead Salfd 57 N9
Cadle Swans 26 E9
Cadley Lancs 57 K3
Cadley Wilts 18 H7
Cadley Wilts 19 J9
Cadmore End Bucks 20 C5
Cadnam Hants 9 K5
Cadney N Linc 52 E3
Cadoxton V Glam 16 F3
Cadoxton Juxta-Neath
Neath 26 G8
Caeathro Gwynd 54 G8
Caenby Lincs 52 E5
Caeo Carmth 37 L11
Caerau Brdgnd 27 J9
Caerau Cardif 16 F2
Caer Farchell Pembks 24 E4
Caergeiliog IoA 54 D6
Caergwrle Flints 48 F4
Caerlanrig Border 79 N7
Caerleon Newpt 28 D10
Caernarfon Gwynd 54 F8
Caernarfon Castle Gwynd 54 F8
Caerphilly Caerph 27 N10
Caersws Powys 38 B4
Caerwedros Cerdgn 36 F9
Caerwent Mons 28 F10
Caerwys Flints 48 D2
Cairinis W Isls 111 b5
Cairnbaan Ag & B 83 M5
Cairnbulg Abers 103 L3
Cairncross Border 81 J2
Cairncurran Inver 84 F8
Cairndow Ag & B 84 C2
Cairneyhill Fife 86 C5
Cairngarroch D & G 68 E8
Cairngorms National Park 99 N8
Cairnie Abers 101 N6
Cairnorrie Abers 102 H7
Cairnryan D & G 68 E5
Cairnty Moray 101 L5
Caister-on-Sea Norfk 45 Q7
Caistor Lincs 52 G3
Caistor St Edmund Norfk 45 K8
Calanais W Isls 111 c2
Calbourne IoW 9 M9
Calcot Flints 48 D1
Calcot Gloucs 30 E11
Calcot Row W Berk 19 R6
Calcots Moray 101 K3
Caldbeck Cumb 71 M7
Caldecote Cambs 33 K5
Caldecote Cambs 42 G11
Caldecote Highfields
Cambs 33 K5
Caldecott Nhants 32 E3
Caldecott Oxon 19 N2
Caldecott Rutlnd 42 C10
Calder Bridge Cumb 62 B2
Caldercruix N Lans 85 N10
Calder Grove Wakefd 58 H10
Calderwood S Lans 77 L3
Calder Vale Lancs 63 K11
Calderwood S Lans 85 L11
Caldey Island Pembks 25 K9
Caldicot Mons 28 F10
Caldmore Wsall 40 D7
Caldwell N York 65 L5
Calf of Man IoM 56 a7
Calfsound Ork 111 h1
Calgary Ag & B 89 J6
Califer Moray 100 G4
California Falk 85 Q8
California Norfk 45 Q7
Calke Derbys 41 J3
Calke Abbey Derbys 41 J3

Callakille Highld 105 K10
Callander Stirlg 85 K2
Callanish W Isls 111 c2
Callestick Cnwll 2 H6
Calligarry Highld 96 H8
Callington Cnwll 4 H6
Callow Herefs 28 F2
Callow End Worcs 39 Q11
Callow Hill Wilts 18 F4
Calmore Hants 9 K5
Calmsden Gloucs 30 D11
Calne Wilts 18 E6
Calshot Hants 9 N7
Calstock Cnwll 5 J6
Calstone Wellington Wilts 18 F7
Calthorpe Norfk 45 K4
Calthorpe Street Norfk 45 N5
Calthwaite Cumb 71 P7
Calton Staffs 50 E9
Calveley Ches E 49 L4
Calver Derbys 50 G6
Calverhall Shrops 49 L7
Calverleigh Devon 16 C12
Calverton M Keyn 32 B8
Calverton Notts 51 N10
Calvine P & K 92 B3
Calzeat Border 78 H2
Cam Gloucs 29 K8
Camasachoirce Highld 89 Q4
Camasine Highld 89 P4
Camas Luinie Highld 97 N4
Camastianavaig Highld 96 F2
Camault Muir Highld 98 G2
Camber E Susx 13 J6
Camberley Surrey 20 E10
Camberwell Gt Lon 21 L7
Camblesforth N York 59 N8
Cambo Nthumb 72 H4
Camborne Cnwll 2 F7
Camborne and Redruth
Mining District Cnwll 2 F7
Cambourne Cambs 33 K5
Cambridge Cambs 33 M5
Cambridge Gloucs 29 K7
Cambridge Airport Cambs 33 M5
Cambridge City
Crematorium Cambs 33 L4
Cambrose Cnwll 2 G6
Cambus Clacks 85 P4
Cambusavie Platform
Highld 107 M3
Cambusbarron Stirlg 85 N5
Cambuskenneth Stirlg 85 N4
Cambuslang S Lans 85 L10
Cambus o' May Abers 94 G3
Cambuswallace S Lans 78 G2
Camden Town Gt Lon 21 L6
Cameley BaNES 17 N5
Camelford Cnwll 4 D4
Camelon Falk 85 P6
Camerory Highld 100 F8
Camerton BaNES 17 P5
Camerton Cumb 70 G8
Camghouran P & K 91 N5
Camieston Border 80 D8
Cammachmore Abers 95 P3
Cammeringham Lincs 52 D7
Camore Highld 107 N4
Campbeltown Ag & B 75 K8
Campbeltown Airport
Ag & B 75 K7
Cample D & G 78 E9
Campmuir P & K 93 J7
Camps W Loth 86 C8
Campsall Donc 59 M10
Campsea Ash Suffk 35 M5
Campton C Beds 32 G8
Camptown Border 80 F10
Camrose Pembks 24 G5
Camserney P & K 92 C6
Camusnagaul Highld 90 E2
Camusnagaul Highld 105 Q5
Camusteel Highld 97 J2
Camusterrach Highld 97 J2
Canada Hants 9 K4
Candacraig Abers 94 F3
Candlesby Lincs 53 M9
Candy Mill Border 78 H1
Cane End Oxon 20 B7
Canewdon Essex 22 H5
Canford Cliffs Poole 8 F9
Canford Crematorium
Bristl 28 G12
Canford Heath Poole 8 F8
Canisbay Highld 110 G2
Canley Covtry 40 H11
Canley Crematorium
Covtry 40 H11
Cann Dorset 8 C3
Canna Highld 96 B8
Cannich Highld 98 D3
Cannington Somset 16 H8
Canning Town Gt Lon 21 N7
Cannock Staffs 40 C5
Cannock Chase Staffs 40 C4
Cannon Bridge Herefs 28 E1
Canonbie D & G 71 N1
Canon Frome Herefs 39 M12
Canon Pyon Herefs 39 J11
Canons Ashby Nhants 31 M4
Canonstown Cnwll 2 D8
Canterbury Kent 23 M10
Canterbury Cathedral
Kent 23 M10
Cantley Norfk 45 N8
Canton Cardif 16 F2
Cantraywood Highld 107 N11
Cantsfield Lancs 63 L7
Canvey Island Essex 22 F6
Canwick Lincs 52 D9
Canworthy Water Cnwll 4 F2
Caol Highld 90 F2
Caolas Scalpaigh W Isls 111 c3
Caoles Ag & B 88 D6
Caonich Highld 97 Q10
Capel Kent 12 D2
Capel Surrey 11 J2
Capel Bangor Cerdgn 37 K5
Capel Coch IoA 54 F5
Capel Curig Conwy 55 K9
Capel Dewi Carmth 26 C5
Capel Dewi Cerdgn 37 G11
Capel-Dewi Cerdgn 37 K4
Capel Garmon Conwy 55 M9
Capel Hendre Carmth 26 D6
Capel Iwan Carmth 25 M2
Capel le Ferne Kent 13 N3

Capel Parc IoA 54 F4
Capel St Andrew Suffk 35 N7
Capel St Mary Suffk 34 H8
Capel Seion Cerdgn 37 K5
Capelulo Conwy 55 L6
Capenhurst Ches W 48 G3
Capheaton Nthumb 73 J5
Caplaw E Rens 84 G10
Capton Devon 5 Q9
Caputh P & K 92 G7
Caradon Mining District
Cnwll 4 F6
Carbeth Inn Stirlg 85 J7
Carbis Bay Cnwll 2 D7
Carbost Highld 96 D4
Carbost Highld 104 F11
Carbrook Sheff 51 J3
Carbrooke Norfk 44 F9
Car Colston Notts 51 Q11
Carcroft Donc 59 M11
Cardenden Fife 86 E4
Cardeston Shrops 48 G11
Cardhu Moray 101 J6
Cardiff Cardif 16 G2
Cardiff Airport V Glam 16 E3
Cardiff Gate Services
Cardif 27 P11
Cardiff West Services
Cardif 27 M11
Cardigan Cerdgn 36 C10
Cardington Bed 32 F7
Cardington Shrops 39 J3
Cardinham Cnwll 4 D6
Cardrain D & G 68 F11
Cardrona Border 79 L2
Cardross Ag & B 84 F7
Cardross Crematorium
Ag & B 84 F7
Cardryne D & G 68 F11
Cardurnock Cumb 71 J4
Careby Lincs 42 E6
Careston Angus 95 J9
Carew Pembks 24 H7
Carew Cheriton Pembks 24 H8
Carew Newton Pembks 24 H7
Carey Herefs 28 G3
Carfin N Lans 85 N10
Carfraemill Border 80 C4
Cargate Green Norfk 45 N7
Cargenbridge D & G 70 F1
Cargill P & K 92 H8
Cargo Cumb 71 M4
Cargreen Cnwll 5 J7
Carham Nthumb 80 H6
Carhampton Somset 16 D7
Carharrack Cnwll 2 G7
Carie P & K 91 P5
Carinish W Isls 111 b5
Carisbrooke IoW 9 N9
Cark Cumb 62 G6
Carkeel Cnwll 5 J7
Carlabhagh W Isls 111 c2
Carlbury Darltn 65 L4
Carlby Lincs 42 F7
Carleen Cnwll 2 F9
Carleton N York 58 C4
Carleton Crematorium
Bpool 56 G2
Carleton Forehoe Norfk 44 H8
Carleton Rode Norfk 44 H10
Carleton St Peter Norfk 45 M9
Carlincraig Abers 102 E6
Carlingcott BaNES 17 Q5
Carlisle Cumb 71 N4
Carlisle Airport Cumb 71 P4
Carlisle Crematorium
Cumb 71 N5
Carlops Border 86 D10
Carloway W Isls 111 c2
Carlton Barns 59 J11
Carlton Bed 32 D6
Carlton Cambs 33 Q6
Carlton Leeds 59 J8
Carlton Leics 41 K6
Carlton N York 59 N9
Carlton N York 65 J9
Carlton N York 66 E9
Carlton Notts 51 N11
Carlton S on T 65 P3
Carlton Suffk 35 N4
Carlton Colville Suffk 45 Q11
Carlton Curlieu Leics 41 P7
Carlton Green Cambs 33 Q6
Carlton Husthwaite
N York 66 C11
Carlton-in-Cleveland
N York 66 C6
Carlton in Lindrick Notts 51 N4
Carlton-le-Moorland Lincs 52 C10
Carlton Miniott N York 65 P10
Carlton-on-Trent Notts 52 B10
Carlton Scroop Lincs 42 D2
Carluke S Lans 77 P2
Carmacoup S Lans 77 N6
Carmarthen Carmth 25 P5
Carmel Carmth 26 D6
Carmel Flints 56 D12
Carmel Gwynd 54 G9
Carmichael S Lans 78 F2
Carmountside
Crematorium C Stke 50 B10
Carmunnock C Glas 85 K10
Carmyle C Glas 85 L9
Carmyllie Angus 93 P7
Carnaby E R Yk 61 K2
Carnbee Fife 87 K2
Carnbo P & K 86 C2
Carn Brea Cnwll 2 G7
Carnbrogie Abers 102 H9
Carndu Highld 97 M4
Carnduff S Lans 77 L3
Carnell E Ayrs 76 H5
Carnforth Lancs 63 J7
Carn-gorm Highld 97 N5
Carnhell Green Cnwll 2 F8
Carnie Abers 95 N2
Carnkie Cnwll 2 G7
Carnkie Cnwll 2 G8
Carno Powys 47 Q11
Carnock Fife 86 C4
Carnon Downs Cnwll 3 J7
Carnousie Abers 102 E5
Carnoustie Angus 93 P8
Carnwath S Lans 86 B11
Carol Green Solhll 40 H11
Carperby N York 64 H9
Carradale Ag & B 75 M5

Carrbridge Highld 99 N4
Carrefour Jersey 7 b1
Carreglefn IoA 54 E4
Carr Gate Wakefd 58 H8
Carrhouse N Linc 60 D11
Carrick Ag & B 83 N5
Carrick Castle Ag & B 84 D4
Carriden Falk 86 B6
Carrington Mdloth 86 G9
Carrington Traffd 57 N9
Carron Falk 85 P6
Carron Moray 101 J7
Carronbridge D & G 78 E8
Carron Bridge Stirlg 85 M6
Carronshore Falk 85 P6
Carr Shield Nthumb 72 E10
Carruth House Inver 84 F9
Carrutherstown D & G 70 H2
Carrville Dur 73 N11
Carsaig Ag & B 89 L11
Carscreugh D & G 69 J5
Carsethorn D & G 70 G4
Carsington Derbys 50 G9
Carskey Ag & B 75 J10
Carsluith D & G 69 L8
Carsphairn D & G 77 J11
Carstairs S Lans 77 Q3
Carstairs Junction S Lans 77 Q3
Carterton Oxon 30 H11
Cartland S Lans 77 P3
Cartmel Cumb 62 H6
Carway Carmth 26 C7
Cashe's Green Gloucs 29 N6
Cassington Oxon 31 L11
Cassop Colliery Dur 73 N12
Castel Guern 6 b2
Casterton Cumb 63 L6
Castle Acre Norfk 44 D7
Castle Ashby Nhants 32 C5
Castlebay W Isls 111 a7
Castlebythe Pembks 24 H3
Castle Bolton N York 65 J8
Castle Bromwich Solhll 40 F9
Castle Bytham Lincs 42 E6
Castlebythe Pembks 24 H3
Castle Caereinion Powys 38 D2
Castle Camps Cambs 33 P8
Castle Carrock Cumb 71 Q5
Castlecary Falk 85 N7
Castle Cary Somset 17 P9
Castle Combe Wilts 18 C5
Castle Donington Leics 41 K3
Castle Douglas D & G 70 C3
Castle Eaton Swindn 18 G2
Castle Eden Dur 73 Q12
Castleford Wakefd 59 K8
Castle Frome Herefs 39 M11
Castle Gresley Derbys 40 H4
Castle Hedingham Essex 34 D9
Castlehill Border 79 K2
Castlehill Highld 110 E3
Castle Hill Suffk 35 J7
Castlehill W Duns 84 G7
Castle Howard N York 66 G12
Castle Kennedy D & G 68 F7
Castle Lachlan Ag & B 83 Q4
Castlemartin Pembks 24 F8
Castlemilk C Glas 85 K10
Castlemorton Worcs 29 L2
Castlemorton Common Worcs 29 K2
Castle O'er D & G 79 L9
Castle Pulverbatch Shrops 38 H2
Castle Rising Norfk 43 Q5
Castleside Dur 73 J10
Castle Stuart Highld 107 M11
Castlethorpe M Keyn 32 B7
Castleton Border 79 Q10
Castleton Derbys 50 F4
Castleton N York 66 F6
Castleton Newpt 27 Q11
Castleton Rochdl 58 B11
Castletown Highld 110 E3
Castletown IoM 56 b7
Castletown Sundld 73 P8
Castley N York 58 H5
Caston Norfk 44 F9
Castor C Pete 42 G9
Catacol N Ayrs 75 N3
Catcliffe Rothm 51 K3
Catcomb Wilts 18 E5
Catcott Somset 17 K8
Catcott Burtle Somset 17 K7
Caterham Surrey 21 M11
Catfield Norfk 45 N6
Catford Gt Lon 21 M8
Catforth Lancs 57 J2
Cathcart C Glas 85 K10
Cathedine Powys 27 N4
Catherington Hants 10 B7
Catherston Leweston Dorset 7 K4
Catisfield Hants 9 P6
Catlodge Highld 99 J9
Catmere End Essex 33 M8
Catmore W Berk 19 M5
Caton Lancs 63 K8
Caton Green Lancs 63 K8
Catrine E Ayrs 77 J6
Catsfield E Susx 12 E7
Catsgore Somset 17 M10
Catshill Worcs 40 C11
Cattadale Ag & B 75 K9
Cattal N York 59 K4
Cattawade Suffk 34 H9
Catterall Lancs 57 J1
Catterick N York 65 M7
Catterick Bridge N York 65 M7
Catterlen Cumb 71 P8
Catterline Abers 95 P6
Catterton N York 59 L5
Catteshall Surrey 10 F2
Catthorpe Leics 41 M10
Cattistock Dorset 7 N3
Catton N York 65 P11
Catton Nthumb 72 E8
Catwick E R Yk 61 J5
Catworth Cambs 32 F3
Caudle Green Gloucs 29 N6
Caulcott Oxon 31 L8
Cauldcots Angus 93 Q6
Cauldhame Stirlg 85 L4
Cauldmill Border 80 C10

Cauldon Staffs 50 E10
Cauldwell Derbys 40 G4
Caulkerbush D & G 70 F4
Caulside D & G 79 P11
Caunton Notts 51 Q8
Causeway End D & G 69 K7
Causeway End Essex 34 B11
Causewayend S Lans 78 G2
Causewayhead Stirlg 85 N4
Causeyend Abers 103 K10
Causey Park Bridge Nthumb 73 L2
Cavendish Suffk 34 D7
Cavenham Suffk 34 C3
Caversfield Oxon 31 M8
Caversham Readg 20 B8
Caverswall Staffs 50 C11
Caverton Mill Border 80 G8
Cawdor Highld 100 D5
Cawood N York 59 M6
Cawsand Cnwll 5 J9
Cawston Norfk 45 J5
Cawthorne Barns 58 H11
Cawthorpe Lincs 42 D1
Cawton N York 67 M10
Caxton Cambs 33 K5
Caynham Shrops 39 K7
Caythorpe Lincs 42 D1
Caythorpe Notts 51 P10
Cayton N York 67 M10
Ceann a Bhaigh W Isls 111 a4
Ceannacroc Lodge Highld 98 C6
Cearsiadar W Isls 111 d2
Cefn Newpt 28 C10
Cefn-brith Conwy 55 N10
Cefn-bryn-brain Carmth 26 G6
Cefn Cribwr Brdgnd 27 J11
Cefneithin Carmth 26 D6
Cefngorwydd Powys 37 P10
Cefn-mawr Wrexhm 48 F7
Cefn-y-pant Carmth 25 L4
Cellardyke Fife 87 L2
Cellarhead Staffs 50 C10
Cemaes IoA 54 E3
Cemmaes Powys 47 N9
Cemmaes Road Powys 47 N9
Cenarth Cerdgn 36 E11
Ceres Fife 93 M12
Cerne Abbas Dorset 7 P3
Cerney Wick Gloucs 18 F2
Cerrigydrudion Conwy 55 P11
Ceunant Gwynd 54 G8
Chaceley Gloucs 29 M3
Chacewater Cnwll 2 H6
Chackmore Bucks 31 P7
Chacombe Nhants 31 L5
Chadbury Worcs 30 D5
Chadderton Oldham 58 B12
Chaddesden C Derb 51 J12
Chaddesley Corbett Worcs 40 B11
Chaddlehanger Devon 5 K5
Chaddleworth W Berk 19 M5
Chadlington Oxon 31 J9
Chadshunt Warwks 31 J4
Chadwell Leics 42 B5
Chadwell Heath Gt Lon 21 P6
Chadwell St Mary Thurr 22 D7
Chadwick Worcs 39 Q8
Chadwick End Solhll 40 G11
Chaffcombe Somset 7 J2
Chagford Devon 5 N3
Chailey E Susx 11 N6
Chainhurst Kent 12 E1
Chaldon Surrey 21 L11
Chaldon Herring or East Chaldon Dorset 7 P6
Chale IoW 9 N11
Chale Green IoW 9 N10
Chalfont Common Bucks 20 G5
Chalfont St Giles Bucks 20 F5
Chalfont St Peter Bucks 20 G5
Chalford Gloucs 29 M8
Chalford Wilts 18 C10
Chalgrove Oxon 19 Q2
Chalk Kent 22 D8
Chalkwell Kent 22 H10
Challaborough Devon 5 M4
Challacombe Devon 15 M4
Challoch D & G 69 K5
Challock Kent 23 J12
Chalton C Beds 32 E10
Chalton Hants 10 B6
Chalvey Slough 20 F7
Chalvington E Susx 11 P8
Chandler's Cross Herts 20 H4
Chandler's Ford Hants 9 M4
Chanterlands Crematorium C KuH 61 J7
Chantry Somset 17 Q6
Chantry Suffk 35 J7
Chapel Fife 86 F4
Chapel Allerton Leeds 58 H6
Chapel Allerton Somset 17 K6
Chapel Amble Cnwll 3 M1
Chapel Brampton Nhants 31 Q2
Chapel Chorlton Staffs 49 P7
Chapelend Way Essex 34 B8
Chapel-en-le-Frith Derbys 50 D5
Chapel Green Warwks 31 L3
Chapel Haddlesey N York 59 N8
Chapelhall N Lans 85 N9
Chapel Hill Abers 103 K8
Chapel Hill Lincs 52 H11
Chapel Hill Mons 28 G8
Chapel Hill N York 59 J5
Chapelhope Border 79 K5
Chapelknowe D & G 71 M2
Chapel Lawn Shrops 38 G6
Chapel-le-Dale N York 64 D11
Chapel Leigh Somset 16 F9
Chapel of Garioch Abers 102 F9
Chapel Rossan D & G 68 F9
Chapel Row W Berk 19 P6
Chapel St Leonards Lincs 53 N8
Chapel Stile Cumb 62 G2
Chapelton Angus 93 Q6
Chapelton Devon 15 K6
Chapelton S Lans 77 L3
Chapeltown Bl w D 57 N7
Chapeltown Moray 101 K10
Chapeltown Sheff 51 J2
Chapmanslade Wilts 18 C10
Chapmans Well Devon 4 H3
Chapmore End Herts 33 K12
Chappel Essex 34 E10
Chard Somset 7 J2
Chard Junction Somset 7 J2
Chardleigh Green Somset 7 J1
Chardstock Devon 7 J2

Charfield S Glos 29 J9
Charing Kent 23 J12
Charing Crematorium Kent 13 J1
Charingworth Gloucs 30 G6
Charlbury Oxon 31 J9
Charlcombe BaNES 17 Q3
Charlcutt Wilts 18 E5
Charlecote Warwks 30 H3
Charlemont Sandw 40 D8
Charles Devon 15 M5
Charleston Angus 93 L6
Charlestown C Aber 95 Q2
Charlestown C Brad 58 F6
Charlestown Calder 58 C8
Charlestown Cnwll 3 M5
Charlestown Cnwll 3 M5
Charlestown Fife 86 C5
Charlestown Highld 105 M7
Charlestown Highld 107 K11
Charlestown Salfd 57 P8
Charles Tye Suffk 34 G6
Charlesworth Derbys 50 D3
Charlinch Somset 16 H8
Charlottetown Fife 93 K12
Charlton Gt Lon 21 N7
Charlton Nhants 31 M7
Charlton Nthumb 72 E4
Charlton Oxon 19 L3
Charlton Somset 16 H10
Charlton Somset 17 P6
Charlton W Susx 10 E7
Charlton Wilts 8 D3
Charlton Wilts 18 E3
Charlton Worcs 30 D5
Charlton Wrekin 49 L12
Charlton Abbots Gloucs 30 D8
Charlton Adam Somset 17 M9
Charlton All Saints Wilts 8 H3
Charlton Down Dorset 7 P4
Charlton Horethorne Somset 17 P10
Charlton Kings Gloucs 29 N5
Charlton Mackrell Somset 17 M9
Charlton Marshall Dorset 8 D6
Charlton Musgrove Somset 17 Q9
Charlton-on-Otmoor Oxon 31 M10
Charlton on the Hill Dorset 8 D6
Charlton St Peter Wilts 18 G9
Charlwood Hants 10 A4
Charlwood Surrey 11 K2
Charminster Dorset 7 P4
Charmouth Dorset 7 J4
Charndon Bucks 31 P8
Charney Bassett Oxon 19 L2
Charnock Richard Lancs 57 K6
Charnock Richard Crematorium Lancs 57 K5
Charnock Richard Services Lancs 57 K6
Charsfield Suffk 35 L5
Charter Alley Hants 19 P8
Charterhouse Border 80 G5
Charterhouse Somset 17 M5
Chartershall Stirlg 85 N5
Chartham Kent 23 L11
Chartham Hatch Kent 23 L11
Chartridge Bucks 20 E3
Chart Sutton Kent 22 F12
Charvil Wokham 20 C8
Charwelton Nhants 31 M3
Chase Terrace Staffs 40 D5
Chasetown Staffs 40 D5
Chastleton Oxon 30 G8
Chasty Devon 14 F10
Chatburn Lancs 63 P12
Chatcull Staffs 49 P8
Chatham Medway 22 F9
Chatham Green Essex 22 E1
Chathill Nthumb 81 P8
Chatsworth House Derbys 50 H6
Chattenden Medway 22 F8
Chatteris Cambs 43 L11
Chatterton Lancs 57 P5
Chattisham Suffk 34 H8
Chatto Border 80 G10
Chatton Nthumb 81 M9
Chawleigh Devon 15 M9
Chawton Hants 10 B3
Cheadle Staffs 50 D11
Cheadle Stockp 57 Q10
Cheadle Hulme Stockp 57 Q10
Cheam Gt Lon 21 K10
Chearsley Bucks 31 Q11
Chebsey Staffs 49 Q9
Checkendon Oxon 19 Q4
Checkley Ches E 49 N6
Checkley Staffs 50 D12
Chedburgh Suffk 34 D5
Cheddar Somset 17 L6
Cheddington Bucks 32 D12
Cheddleton Staffs 50 C9
Cheddon Fitzpaine Somset 16 H10
Chedgrave Norfk 45 M9
Chedington Dorset 7 L2
Chediston Suffk 35 M2
Chedworth Gloucs 30 D10
Chedzoy Somset 17 J8
Cheetham Hill Manch 57 Q8
Cheldon Devon 15 M9
Chelford Ches E 49 P1
Chellaston C Derb 41 J2
Chellington Bed 32 D5
Chelmarsh Shrops 39 N5
Chelmondiston Suffk 35 K8
Chelmorton Derbys 50 F6
Chelmsford Essex 22 E3
Chelmsford Crematorium Essex 22 E3
Chelmsley Wood Solhll 40 F9
Chelsea Gt Lon 21 L7
Chelsfield Gt Lon 21 P9
Chelsworth Suffk 34 G7
Cheltenham Gloucs 29 N4
Cheltenham Crematorium Gloucs 29 N4
Chelveston Nhants 32 D3
Chelvey N Som 17 L3
Chelwood BaNES 17 P4
Chelwood Gate E Susx 11 N4
Cheney Longville Shrops 38 H5
Chenies Bucks 20 G4

Chepstow Mons 28 G9
Cherhill Wilts 18 F6
Cherington Gloucs 29 M8
Cherington Warwks 30 H6
Cheriton Hants 9 P2
Cheriton Kent 13 M3
Cheriton Swans 26 B9
Cheriton Bishop Devon 5 P2
Cheriton Fitzpaine Devon 15 P10
Cheriton or Stackpole Elidor Pembks 24 H8
Cherrington Wrekin 49 M10
Cherry Burton E R Yk 60 G6
Cherry Hinton Cambs 33 M5
Cherry Orchard Worcs 39 Q10
Cherry Willingham Lincs 52 E8
Chertsey Surrey 20 G9
Cherwell Valley Services Oxon 31 M8
Cheselbourne Dorset 8 B7
Chesham Bucks 20 F3
Chesham Bury 57 P6
Chesham Bois Bucks 20 F4
Cheshire Farm Ice Cream Ches W 49 J4
Cheshunt Herts 21 M3
Chesil Beach Dorset 7 N6
Cheslyn Hay Staffs 40 C6
Chessetts Wood Warwks 40 F11
Chessington Gt Lon 21 J10
Chessington World of Adventures Gt Lon 21 J10
Chester Ches W 48 H3
Chesterblade Somset 17 P7
Chester Crematorium Ches W 48 H2
Chesterfield Derbys 51 K6
Chesterfield Crematorium Derbys 51 K6
Chesterhill Mdloth 86 H8
Chester-le-Street Dur 73 M9
Chester Moor Dur 73 M10
Chesters Border 80 E11
Chesters Border 80 E9
Chester Services Ches W 49 J1
Chesterton Cambs 33 M5
Chesterton Cambs 42 G10
Chesterton Gloucs 18 E1
Chesterton Oxon 31 M9
Chesterton Shrops 39 P3
Chesterton Green Warwks 31 J3
Chesterwood Nthumb 72 E7
Chester Zoo Ches W 48 H2
Chestfield Kent 23 L9
Cheston Devon 5 N8
Cheswardine Shrops 49 N9
Cheswick Nthumb 81 L5
Chetnole Dorset 7 N2
Chettisham Cambs 43 N12
Chettle Dorset 8 D5
Chetton Shrops 39 M4
Chetwynd Wrekin 49 N10
Chetwynd Aston Wrekin 49 N11
Cheveley Cambs 34 B5
Chevening Kent 21 P11
Chevington Suffk 34 D5
Cheviot Hills 80 G11
Chevithorne Devon 16 D11
Chew Magna BaNES 17 N4
Chew Stoke BaNES 17 M4
Chewton Keynsham BaNES 17 P3
Chewton Mendip Somset 17 N5
Chicheley M Keyn 32 C7
Chichester W Susx 10 D8
Chichester Crematorium W Susx 10 E8
Chickerell Dorset 7 P6
Chicklade Wilts 8 D1
Chidden Hants 9 Q4
Chiddingfold Surrey 10 F3
Chiddingly E Susx 12 B7
Chiddingstone Kent 11 P2
Chiddingstone Causeway Kent 11 Q1
Chideock Dorset 7 K4
Chidham W Susx 10 C8
Chidswell Kirk 58 H9
Chieveley W Berk 19 M6
Chieveley Services W Berk 19 N6
Chignall St James Essex 22 D2
Chignall Smealy Essex 22 D2
Chigwell Essex 21 N5
Chigwell Row Essex 21 P5
Chilbolton Hants 19 L11
Chilcomb Hants 9 N2
Chilcombe Dorset 7 M5
Chilcompton Somset 17 P6
Chilcote Leics 40 H5
Childer Thornton Ches W 56 G12
Child Okeford Dorset 8 C5
Childrey Oxon 19 L3
Child's Ercall Shrops 49 M9
Childswickham Worcs 30 E6
Childwall Lpool 56 H10
Chilfrome Dorset 7 N3
Chilgrove W Susx 10 D7
Chilham Kent 23 K11
Chillaton Devon 5 J4
Chillenden Kent 23 N11
Chillerton IoW 9 N10
Chillesford Suffk 35 N6
Chillington Devon 5 Q10
Chillington Somset 7 K1
Chilmark Wilts 8 E2
Chilmington Green Kent 13 J3
Chilson Oxon 30 H9
Chilsworthy Cnwll 5 J6
Chilsworthy Devon 14 F10
Chiltern Hills 20 C4
Chilterns Crematorium Bucks 20 F4
Chilthorne Domer Somset 17 M11
Chilton Bucks 31 P10
Chilton Dur 65 M2
Chilton Oxon 19 N4
Chilton Candover Hants 19 P11
Chilton Cantelo Somset 17 N10
Chilton Foliat Wilts 19 K6
Chilton Polden Somset 17 K7
Chilton Street Suffk 34 C7
Chilton Trinity Somset 16 H8
Chilwell Notts 41 L2
Chilworth Hants 9 L4
Chilworth Surrey 10 H2
Chimney Oxon 19 L1
Chineham Hants 19 Q9

Chingford Gt Lon 21 M5
Chinley Derbys 50 D4
Chinnor Oxon 20 C3
Chipnall Shrops 49 N8
Chippenham Cambs 33 Q3
Chippenham Wilts 18 D6
Chipperfield Herts 20 G3
Chipping Herts 33 K9
Chipping Lancs 63 L12
Chipping Campden Gloucs 30 F6
Chipping Norton Oxon 30 H8
Chipping Ongar Essex 22 B3
Chipping Sodbury S Glos 29 K11
Chipping Warden Nhants 31 L5
Chipstable Somset 16 E10
Chipstead Kent 21 P11
Chipstead Surrey 21 L11
Chirbury Shrops 38 F3
Chirk Wrexhm 48 F7
Chirnside Border 81 J3
Chirnsidebridge Border 80 H3
Chirton Wilts 18 F8
Chisbury Wilts 19 J7
Chiselborough Somset 17 L12
Chiseldon Swindn 18 H5
Chiselhampton Oxon 19 P2
Chisholme Border 79 N6
Chislehurst Gt Lon 21 N9
Chislet Kent 23 N9
Chisley Calder 58 D8
Chiswell Green Herts 21 J3
Chiswick Gt Lon 21 K7
Chisworth Derbys 50 C3
Chithurst W Susx 10 D5
Chittering Cambs 33 M3
Chitterne Wilts 18 E11
Chittlehamholt Devon 15 L7
Chittlehampton Devon 15 L7
Chittoe Wilts 18 E7
Chivelstone Devon 5 Q11
Chivenor Devon 15 J5
Chlenry D & G 68 F6
Chobham Surrey 20 F10
Cholderton Wilts 19 J11
Cholesbury Bucks 20 E3
Chollerton Nthumb 72 G6
Cholsey Oxon 19 P4
Cholstrey Herefs 39 J9
Chop Gate N York 66 D7
Choppington Nthumb 73 M4
Chopwell Gatesd 73 K8
Chorley Ches E 49 K5
Chorley Lancs 57 L5
Chorley Shrops 39 M5
Chorleywood Herts 20 G4
Chorleywood West Herts 20 G4
Chorlton Ches E 49 N5
Chorlton-cum-Hardy Manch 57 P9
Chorlton Lane Ches W 49 J6
Choulton Shrops 38 H5
Chrishall Essex 33 M8
Chrisswell Inver 84 D7
Christchurch Cambs 43 M10
Christchurch Dorset 8 H8
Christchurch Newpt 28 D10
Christian Malford Wilts 18 E5
Christleton Ches W 49 J3
Christon N Som 17 K5
Christon Bank Nthumb 81 P9
Christow Devon 5 Q4
Chudleigh Devon 6 B6
Chudleigh Knighton Devon 5 B7
Chulmleigh Devon 15 M8
Church Lancs 57 N3
Churcham Gloucs 29 K5
Church Aston Wrekin 49 N11
Church Brampton Nhants 31 Q2
Church Broughton Derbys 40 G2
Church Cove Cnwll 2 G12
Church Crookham Hants 20 D12
Churchdown Gloucs 29 M5
Church Eaton Staffs 49 Q11
Church End C Beds 32 H8
Churchend Essex 23 J5
Church End Essex 34 C10
Church End Gt Lon 21 K5
Church Enstone Oxon 31 J8
Church Fenton N York 59 L6
Churchfield Sandw 40 D8
Church Green Devon 6 G4
Church Hanborough Oxon 31 K10
Church Houses N York 66 F7
Churchill Devon 6 H3
Churchill N Som 17 L4
Churchill Oxon 30 H8
Churchill Worcs 39 B4
Churchill Worcs 39 Q6
Churchinford Somset 6 G1
Church Knowle Dorset 8 D10
Church Langton Leics 41 Q8
Church Lawford Warwks 41 L11
Church Leigh Staffs 40 D1
Church Lench Worcs 30 D4
Church Mayfield Staffs 50 F11
Church Minshull Ches E 49 M4
Church Norton W Susx 10 L10
Churchover Warwks 41 L10
Church Preen Shrops 39 K3
Church Pulverbatch Shrops 38 H2
Churchstanton Somset 16 G12
Churchstoke Powys 38 F4
Churchstow Devon 5 P10
Church Stowe Nhants 31 N3
Church Street Kent 22 E8
Church Stretton Shrops 39 J4
Churchtown Cnwll 4 D5
Churchtown Derbys 50 H8
Churchtown IoM 56 d3
Churchtown Lancs 63 J12
Church Village Rhondd 27 M10
Church Warsop Notts 51 M7
Churston Ferrers Torbay 6 B10
Churt Surrey 10 D3
Churton Ches W 48 H4
Churwell Leeds 58 H8
Chwilog Gwynd 46 G4
Chyandour Cnwll 2 D9
Cilcennin Cerdgn 36 H9
Cilcain Flints 48 D3
Cilfrew Neath 27 K7
Cilfynydd Rhondd 27 M9

Cilgerran Pembks...........36 C11
Cilmaengwyn Neath...........26 G7
Cilmery Powys...........38 B11
Cilsan Carmth...........26 L4
Ciltalgarth Gwynd...........47 P4
Cilycwm Carmth...........37 M11
Cimla Neath...........26 G9
Cinderford Gloucs...........28 H6
Cippenham Slough...........20 F7
Cirencester Gloucs...........18 J1
City Gt Lon...........21 M7
City Airport Gt Lon...........21 N7
City of London
  Crematorium Gt Lon...........21 N6
Clabhach Ag & B...........88 F5
Clachaig Ag & B...........84 B6
Clachan Ag & B...........83 L4
Clachan Ag & B...........89 Q11
Clachan Ag & B...........90 B7
Clachan Highld...........96 G3
Clachan-a-Luib W Isls...........111 b4
Clachan Mor Ag & B...........88 C6
Clachan na Luib W Isls...........111 b4
Clachan of Campsie
  E Duns...........85 K7
Clachan-Seil Ag & B...........89 Q10
Clachnaharry Highld...........107 K11
Clachtoll Highld...........108 B9
Clackavoid P & K...........94 C8
Clacket Lane Services
  Surrey...........21 N11
Clackmannan Clacks...........85 Q5
Clackmarras Moray...........101 K4
Clacton-on-Sea Essex...........23 M1
Cladich Ag & B...........90 F11
Cladswell Worcs...........30 D3
Claggan Highld...........89 P6
Claigan Highld...........104 C10
Clanfield Hants...........10 B6
Clanfield Oxon...........19 K1
Clanville Hants...........19 K10
Clanville Somset...........17 P9
Claonaig Ag & B...........83 N10
Clapgate Herts...........33 M10
Clapham Bed...........32 E6
Clapham Gt Lon...........21 L8
Clapham N York...........63 N4
Clapham W Susx...........10 H8
Clapton Somset...........7 K2
Clapton Somset...........17 P5
Clapton-in-Gordano
  N Som...........17 L2
Clapton-on-the-Hill
  Gloucs...........30 F9
Claravale Gatesd...........73 K7
Clarbeston Pembks...........25 J3
Clarbeston Road Pembks...........24 H5
Clarborough Notts...........51 Q4
Clare Suffk...........34 C7
Clarebrand D & G...........70 C3
Clarencefield D & G...........70 H2
Clarilaw Border...........80 C9
Clarkston E Rens...........85 J10
Clashmore Highld...........107 M5
Clashmore Highld...........108 B9
Clashnessie Highld...........108 B9
Clashnoir Moray...........101 J10
Clathy P & K...........92 E10
Clathymore P & K...........92 F10
Clatt Abers...........102 C9
Clatter Powys...........38 B4
Clatworthy Somset...........16 E9
Claughton Lancs...........57 K1
Claughton Lancs...........63 K8
Claughton Wirral...........56 F10
Claverdon Warwks...........30 G2
Claverham N Som...........17 L3
Clavering Essex...........33 M9
Claverley Shrops...........39 P4
Claverton BaNES...........18 B7
Clawdd-coch V Glam...........27 M12
Clawdd-newydd Denbgs...........48 C5
Clawton Devon...........14 F11
Claxby Lincs...........52 G5
Claxton N York...........59 P4
Claxton Norfk...........45 M9
Claybrooke Magna Leics...........41 L9
Clay Coton Nhants...........41 N11
Clay Cross Derbys...........51 K8
Claydon Oxon...........31 L4
Claydon Suffk...........35 J6
Claygate D & G...........79 N11
Claygate Kent...........12 E2
Claygate Surrey...........21 J10
Clayhall Gt Lon...........21 N5
Clayhanger Devon...........16 D10
Clayhidon Devon...........16 F11
Clayhill E Susx...........12 F4
Clayock Highld...........110 D4
Claypits Gloucs...........29 K6
Claypole Lincs...........42 C1
Clayton C Brad...........58 E7
Clayton Donc...........59 L11
Clayton W Susx...........11 L7
Clayton-le-Moors Lancs...........57 N3
Clayton-le-Woods Lancs...........57 K4
Clayton West Kirk...........58 H11
Clayworth Notts...........51 Q4
Cleadale Highld...........96 F11
Cleadon S Tyne...........73 P8
Clearbrook Devon...........5 L7
Clearwell Gloucs...........28 G7
Cleasby N York...........65 M5
Cleat Ork...........111 h3
Cleatlam Dur...........65 K4
Cleator Cumb...........70 G11
Cleator Moor Cumb...........70 G11
Cleckheaton Kirk...........58 F8
Cleehill Shrops...........39 L7
Cleekhimin N Lans...........85 M10
Clee St Margaret Shrops...........39 K5
Cleethorpes NE Lin...........53 K4
Cleeton St Mary Shrops...........39 L6
Cleeve N Som...........17 L3
Cleeve Oxon...........19 Q5
Cleeve Hill Gloucs...........29 N4
Cleeve Prior Worcs...........30 E4
Cleghornie E Loth...........87 L5
Clehonger Herefs...........28 E2
Cleish P & K...........86 C3
Cleland N Lans...........85 N10
Clenamacrie Ag & B...........90 C9
Clenchwarton Norfk...........43 P6
Clenerty Abers...........102 G3
Clent Worcs...........40 B10
Cleobury Mortimer
  Shrops...........39 M7

Cleobury North Shrops...........39 L5
Cleongart Ag & B...........75 K5
Clephanton Highld...........107 N11
Clerkhill D & G...........79 L8
Cleuch-head D & G...........78 D8
Clevancy Wilts...........18 F6
Clevedon N Som...........17 K2
Cleveleys Lancs...........62 G12
Cleverton Wilts...........18 E4
Clewer Somset...........17 L6
Cley next the Sea Norfk...........44 H2
Cliburn Cumb...........64 B3
Cliddesden Hants...........19 Q10
Cliffe Medway...........22 E7
Cliffe N York...........59 P7
Cliff End E Susx...........12 H7
Cliffe Woods Medway...........22 E8
Clifford Herefs...........38 E11
Clifford Leeds...........59 K5
Clifford Chambers
  Warwks...........30 G4
Clifford's Mesne Gloucs...........29 J4
Clifton Bristl...........17 N2
Clifton C Beds...........32 G8
Clifton C Nott...........41 M1
Clifton C York...........59 N4
Clifton Calder...........58 F9
Clifton Cumb...........71 Q9
Clifton Derbys...........50 F11
Clifton Devon...........15 K4
Clifton Donc...........51 M2
Clifton Lancs...........57 J3
Clifton N York...........58 F5
Clifton Oxon...........31 L7
Clifton Worcs...........39 Q11
Clifton Campville Staffs...........40 G5
Clifton Hampden Oxon...........19 P2
Clifton Reynes M Keyn...........32 C6
Clifton upon Dunsmore
  Warwks...........41 M11
Clifton upon Teme Worcs...........39 N9
Cliftonville Kent...........23 Q8
Climping W Susx...........10 F9
Clink Somset...........18 B10
Clint N York...........58 H3
Clinterty C Aber...........102 H11
Clint Green Norfk...........44 G7
Clintmains Border...........80 E7
Clippesby Norfk...........45 N7
Clipsham Rutlnd...........42 D6
Clipston Nhants...........41 Q10
Clipston Notts...........41 N1
Clipstone C Beds...........32 D10
Clipstone Notts...........51 N8
Clitheroe Lancs...........57 N1
Clive Shrops...........49 K9
Clixby Lincs...........52 F3
Cloatley Wilts...........29 N10
Clocaenog Denbgs...........48 C5
Clochan Moray...........101 M3
Clodock Herefs...........28 C4
Clola Abers...........103 K6
Clophill C Beds...........32 F8
Clopton Nhants...........32 F1
Clopton Suffk...........35 K6
Clopton Corner Suffk...........35 K6
Clos du Valle Guern...........6 c1
Closeburn D & G...........78 E9
Closeburnmill D & G...........78 E9
Closworth Somset...........7 N2
Clothall Herts...........33 J9
Clotton Ches W...........49 K3
Clough Foot Calder...........58 B9
Clough Head Calder...........58 E9
Cloughton N York...........67 L8
Clousta Shet...........111 k4
Clova Angus...........94 F7
Clovelly Devon...........14 F7
Clovenfords Border...........79 P2
Clovulin Highld...........90 D4
Clows Top Worcs...........39 N7
Cluanie Inn Highld...........97 Q7
Cluanie Lodge Highld...........97 Q7
Clugston D & G...........69 J7
Clun Shrops...........38 F6
Clunas Highld...........100 D6
Clunbury Shrops...........38 G6
Clunderwen Carmth...........25 K5
Clune Highld...........99 L4
Clunes Highld...........98 B10
Clungunford Shrops...........38 H6
Clunie P & K...........92 G6
Clunton Shrops...........38 G6
Cluny Fife...........86 F3
Clutton BaNES...........17 N4
Clutton Ches W...........49 J5
Clutton Hill BaNES...........17 P4
Clydach Mons...........27 P6
Clydach Swans...........26 F8
Clydach Vale Rhondd...........27 K9
Clydebank W Duns...........84 H8
Clydebank
  Crematorium W Duns...........84 H8
Clyffe Pypard Wilts...........18 F5
Clynder Ag & B...........84 D6
Clyne Neath...........26 H8
Clynnog-fawr Gwynd...........54 E10
Clyro Powys...........38 E12
Clyst Honiton Devon...........6 D4
Clyst Hydon Devon...........6 D3
Clyst St George Devon...........6 D5
Clyst St Lawrence Devon...........6 D3
Clyst St Mary Devon...........6 C5
Cnoc W Isls...........111 d2
Cnwch Coch Cerdgn...........37 L5
Coad's Green Cnwll...........4 G5
Coal Aston Derbys...........51 J5
Coalbrookdale Wrekin...........39 M2
Coalburn S Lans...........77 N4
Coalburns Gatesd...........73 K8
Coaley Gloucs...........29 K8
Coalhill Essex...........22 F4
Coalpit Heath S Glos...........29 J11
Coalport Wrekin...........39 M2
Coalsnaughton Clacks...........85 Q4
Coaltown of Balgonie
  Fife...........86 G3
Coaltown of Wemyss Fife...........86 G3
Coalville Leics...........41 K5
Coanwood Nthumb...........72 D8
Coat Somset...........17 L11
Coatbridge N Lans...........85 M9
Coatdyke N Lans...........85 M9
Coate Swindn...........18 H4
Coate Wilts...........18 F8
Coates Cambs...........43 K9
Coates Gloucs...........29 N8

Coates Lincs...........52 C6
Coates W Susx...........10 F6
Cobbaton Devon...........15 K6
Coberley Gloucs...........29 N5
Cobham Kent...........22 D9
Cobham Surrey...........20 H10
Cobham Services Surrey...........20 H11
Cobnash Herefs...........39 J9
Cobo Guern...........6 b1
Coburby Abers...........103 J3
Cockayne Hatley C Beds...........33 J6
Cock Bridge Abers...........101 K12
Cockburnspath Border...........87 P7
Cock Clarks Essex...........22 F3
Cockenzie and Port
  Seton E Loth...........86 H7
Cockerham Lancs...........63 J10
Cockermouth Cumb...........71 J9
Cockernhoe Herts...........32 G11
Cockett Swans...........26 E9
Cockfield Dur...........65 K3
Cockfield Suffk...........34 E6
Cockfosters Gt Lon...........21 L4
Cock Green Essex...........34 B11
Cocking W Susx...........10 E6
Cocking Causeway
  W Susx...........10 E6
Cockington Torbay...........6 B9
Cocklake Somset...........17 L6
Cockley Cley Norfk...........44 D8
Cock Marling E Susx...........12 G6
Cockpole Green Wokham...........20 C7
Cockshutt Shrops...........48 H9
Cockthorpe Norfk...........44 G2
Cockwood Devon...........6 D6
Cockyard Derbys...........50 D5
Coddenham Suffk...........35 J6
Coddington Herefs...........29 J1
Coddington Notts...........52 B11
Codford St Mary Wilts...........18 E11
Codford St Peter Wilts...........18 E11
Codicote Herts...........32 H11
Codmore Hill W Susx...........10 G6
Codnor Derbys...........51 K10
Codrington S Glos...........29 K11
Codsall Staffs...........39 Q2
Codsall Wood Staffs...........39 Q2
Coed Talon Flints...........48 F4
Coed-y-paen Mons...........28 D8
Coffinswell Devon...........6 B8
Cofton Devon...........6 C6
Cofton Hackett Worcs...........40 D11
Cogan V Glam...........16 G2
Cogenhoe Nhants...........32 B5
Coggeshall Essex...........34 E11
Coignafearn Highld...........99 K5
Coilacriech Abers...........94 E3
Coilantogle Stirlg...........85 K2
Coillore Highld...........96 D3
Coity Brdgnd...........27 K11
Col W Isls...........111 d2
Colaboll Highld...........107 J1
Colan Cnwll...........3 K4
Colaton Raleigh Devon...........6 E5
Colbost Highld...........104 B11
Colburn N York...........65 L7
Colby Cumb...........64 C4
Colby IoM...........56 b6
Colby Norfk...........45 K3
Colchester Essex...........34 G10
Colchester
  Crematorium Essex...........34 G11
Colchester Zoo Essex...........34 F11
Cold Ash W Berk...........19 N6
Cold Ashby Nhants...........41 P11
Cold Ashton S Glos...........17 Q2
Cold Aston Gloucs...........30 F9
Coldbackie Highld...........109 L4
Cold Brayfield M Keyn...........32 D6
Coldean Br & H...........11 M8
Coldeast Devon...........5 Q5
Colden Calder...........58 C8
Colden Common Hants...........9 N3
Cold Hanworth Lincs...........52 E6
Coldharbour Surrey...........11 J2
Cold Higham Nhants...........31 P4
Coldingham Border...........81 J2
Cold Kirby N York...........66 D10
Coldmeece Staffs...........49 Q8
Cold Norton Essex...........22 G4
Cold Overton Leics...........42 B7
Coldred Kent...........13 N2
Coldridge Devon...........15 M10
Coldstream Border...........80 H6
Coldwaltham W Susx...........10 G6
Coldwell Herefs...........28 E3
Coldwells Abers...........103 K7
Cole Somset...........17 P9
Colebatch Shrops...........38 G5
Colebrook Devon...........6 D2
Colebrooke Devon...........15 N11
Coleby Lincs...........52 D10
Coleby N Linc...........52 D2
Coleford Devon...........15 N11
Coleford Gloucs...........28 G6
Coleford Somset...........17 P6
Colegate End Norfk...........45 K11
Colehill Dorset...........8 F7
Coleman's Hatch E Susx...........11 N4
Colemere Shrops...........48 H8
Colemore Hants...........10 B4
Colenden P & K...........92 G9
Colerne Wilts...........18 B6
Colesbourne Gloucs...........30 D10
Coleshill Bucks...........20 F4
Coleshill Oxon...........19 J3
Coleshill Warwks...........40 G9
Coley BaNES...........17 N5
Colgate W Susx...........11 K4
Colinsburgh Fife...........87 J2
Colinton C Edin...........86 E8
Colintraive Ag & B...........83 Q7
Colkirk Norfk...........44 F5
Coll Ag & B...........88 C5
Collace P & K...........93 J8
Collafirth Shet...........111 k3
Collaton Devon...........5 P11
Collaton St Mary Torbay...........6 B10
College of Roseisle Moray...........100 H3
College Town Br For...........20 D10
Collessie Fife...........93 K11
Collier Row Gt Lon...........21 P5
Collier's End Herts...........33 L11
Collier Street Kent...........12 E2
Collieston Abers...........103 L9
Collin D & G...........70 H2

Collingbourne Ducis Wilts...........19 J9
Collingbourne Kingston
  Wilts...........19 J9
Collingham Leeds...........59 K5
Collingham Notts...........52 B10
Collington Herefs...........39 M9
Collingtree Nhants...........31 Q3
Collins Green Warrtn...........57 K9
Colliston Angus...........93 Q6
Colliton Devon...........6 E2
Collyweston Nhants...........42 E9
Colmonell S Ayrs...........68 F2
Colmworth Bed...........32 F5
Colnabaichin Abers...........101 K12
Colnbrook Slough...........20 G7
Colne Cambs...........33 L2
Colne Lancs...........58 B6
Colne Engaine Essex...........34 E10
Colney Norfk...........45 K8
Colney Heath Herts...........21 K3
Coln Rogers Gloucs...........30 E11
Coln St Aldwyns Gloucs...........30 F12
Coln St Dennis Gloucs...........30 E11
Colonsay Ag & B...........82 E4
Colonsay Airport Ag & B...........82 E5
Colpy Abers...........102 E8
Colquhar Border...........79 M1
Colsterworth Lincs...........42 D5
Colston Bassett Notts...........41 P2
Coltfield Moray...........100 H3
Coltishall Norfk...........45 L6
Colton Cumb...........62 G5
Colton Leeds...........59 J7
Colton N York...........59 M5
Colton Norfk...........44 H7
Colton Staffs...........40 D4
Colt's Hill Kent...........12 D2
Colvend D & G...........70 E5
Colwall Herefs...........29 K1
Colwell Nthumb...........72 G6
Colwich Staffs...........40 D4
Colwinston V Glam...........16 C2
Colworth W Susx...........10 E9
Colwyn Bay Conwy...........55 M6
Colyford Devon...........6 H4
Colyton Devon...........6 H4
Combe Oxon...........31 K10
Combe W Berk...........19 L8
Combe Down BaNES...........18 B8
Combe Fishacre Devon...........6 A9
Combe Florey Somset...........16 F9
Combe Hay BaNES...........17 Q4
Combeinteignhead
  Devon...........6 B8
Combe Martin Devon...........15 K3
Combe Raleigh Devon...........6 F3
Comberbach Ches W...........57 M12
Comberford Staffs...........40 F6
Comberton Cambs...........33 L5
Comberton Herefs...........39 J8
Combe St Nicholas
  Somset...........7 J1
Combrook Warwks...........30 H4
Combs Derbys...........50 D5
Combs Suffk...........34 H5
Combs Ford Suffk...........34 H5
Combwich Somset...........16 H7
Comers Abers...........95 L1
Comhampton Worcs...........39 Q8
Commins Coch Powys...........47 N10
Commondale N York...........66 F5
Common End Cumb...........70 G10
Common Moor Cnwll...........4 F6
Compstall Stockp...........50 C3
Compstonend D & G...........69 P8
Compton Devon...........6 B9
Compton Hants...........9 M3
Compton Staffs...........39 P5
Compton Surrey...........10 F1
Compton W Berk...........19 N5
Compton W Susx...........10 C7
Compton Wilts...........18 G9
Compton Abbas Dorset...........8 C4
Compton Abdale Gloucs...........30 D10
Compton Bassett Wilts...........18 F6
Compton Beauchamp
  Oxon...........19 J4
Compton Bishop Somset...........17 K5
Compton
  Chamberlayne Wilts...........8 F2
Compton Dando BaNES...........17 P4
Compton Dundon Somset...........17 L9
Compton Durville Somset...........17 K11
Compton Greenfield
  S Glos...........28 G11
Compton Martin BaNES...........17 M5
Compton Pauncefoot
  Somset...........17 P10
Compton Valence Dorset...........7 N4
Comrie Fife...........86 B4
Comrie P & K...........92 B10
Conaglen House Highld...........90 E3
Conchra Highld...........97 M4
Concraigie P & K...........92 G6
Conderton Worcs...........30 N2
Condicote Gloucs...........30 F8
Condorrat N Lans...........85 M8
Condover Shrops...........39 J2
Coney Hill Gloucs...........29 L5
Coneyhurst Common
  W Susx...........10 H5
Coneysthorpe N York...........66 G12
Coney Weston Suffk...........34 F2
Congerstone Leics...........41 J6
Congham Norfk...........44 B5
Congleton Ches E...........49 Q3
Congresbury N Som...........17 L4
Conheath D & G...........70 G2
Conicavel Moray...........100 F5
Coningsby Lincs...........52 H11
Conington Cambs...........33 K4
Conington Cambs...........42 H11
Conisbrough Donc...........51 L2
Conisholme Lincs...........53 L4
Coniston Cumb...........62 F3
Coniston E R Yk...........61 K7
Coniston Cold N York...........58 B3
Conistone N York...........58 C1
Connah's Quay Flints...........48 F2
Connel Ag & B...........90 C9
Connel Park E Ayrs...........77 K6
Connor Downs Cnwll...........2 E7
Conon Bridge Highld...........107 J10
Cononley N York...........58 C5
Consall Staffs...........50 C10
Consett Dur...........73 K10
Constable Burton N York...........65 L8

Constable Lee Lancs...........57 P4
Constantine Cnwll...........2 G9
Constantine Bay Cnwll...........3 K2
Contin Highld...........106 G10
Conwy Conwy...........55 L6
Conwy Castle Conwy...........55 L6
Conyer's Green Suffk...........34 E3
Cooden E Susx...........12 E8
Cookbury Devon...........14 G10
Cookham W & M...........20 E6
Cookham Dean W & M...........20 D6
Cookham Rise W & M...........20 E6
Cookhill Worcs...........30 D3
Cookley Suffk...........35 M2
Cookley Worcs...........39 Q6
Cookley Green Oxon...........20 B5
Cookney Abers...........95 P4
Cook's Green Essex...........35 K11
Cooks Green Suffk...........34 G6
Cooksmill Green Essex...........22 D3
Coolham W Susx...........10 H5
Cooling Medway...........22 F8
Coombe Cnwll...........6 C7
Coombe Devon...........6 C7
Coombe Devon...........6 E2
Coombe Gloucs...........29 K9
Coombe Abbey Warwks...........41 K10
Coombe Bissett Wilts...........8 G3
Coombe Cellars Devon...........6 B8
Coombe Hill Gloucs...........29 M4
Coombe Keynes Dorset...........8 C9
Coombe Pafford Torbay...........6 C9
Coombes W Susx...........11 J8
Coombes-Moor Herefs...........38 G9
Coopersale Common
  Essex...........21 P3
Copdock Suffk...........35 J8
Copford Green Essex...........34 F11
Copgrove N York...........59 J2
Copister Shet...........111 k3
Cople Bed...........32 F7
Copley Dur...........65 J3
Copmanthorpe C York...........59 M5
Compere End Staffs...........49 P9
Copp Lancs...........56 H2
Coppenhall Staffs...........40 B4
Copperhouse Cnwll...........2 E8
Coppingford Cambs...........32 G2
Copplestone Devon...........15 N10
Coppull Lancs...........57 K6
Copsale W Susx...........11 J5
Copster Green Lancs...........57 M3
Copston Magna Warwks...........41 L9
Cop Street Kent...........23 P10
Copt Hewick N York...........65 N12
Copthorne W Susx...........11 L3
Copt Oak Leics...........41 L5
Copythorne Hants...........9 K5
Corbets Tey Gt Lon...........22 C6
Corbiere Jersey...........7 a2
Corbridge Nthumb...........72 H7
Corby Nhants...........42 C11
Corby Glen Lincs...........42 E5
Cordon N Ayrs...........75 Q6
Coreley Shrops...........39 L7
Corfe Somset...........16 G11
Corfe Castle Dorset...........8 E10
Corfe Mullen Dorset...........8 E8
Corfton Shrops...........39 J5
Corgarff Abers...........94 E1
Corhampton Hants...........9 Q4
Corley Warwks...........40 H9
Corley Services Warwks...........40 H9
Cormuir Angus...........94 E8
Cornard Tye Suffk...........34 E8
Cornforth Dur...........65 N1
Cornhill Abers...........102 D4
Cornhill-on-Tweed
  Nthumb...........81 J6
Cornholme Calder...........58 B8
Cornoigmore Ag & B...........88 C7
Cornsay Dur...........73 K11
Cornsay Colliery Dur...........73 L11
Corntown Highld...........107 J10
Corntown V Glam...........16 C2
Cornwell Oxon...........30 H8
Cornwood Devon...........5 M8
Cornworthy Devon...........6 B10
Corpach Highld...........90 F2
Corpusty Norfk...........45 J4
Corrachree Abers...........94 H2
Corran Highld...........90 D4
Corran Highld...........97 M7
Corrie D & G...........79 K10
Corrie N Ayrs...........75 Q4
Corriecravie N Ayrs...........75 P7
Corriegills N Ayrs...........75 Q5
Corriegour Lodge Hotel
  Highld...........98 C9
Corriemoille Highld...........106 F9
Corrimony Highld...........98 E3
Corringham Lincs...........52 C5
Corringham Thurr...........22 E6
Corris Gwynd...........47 M9
Corris Uchaf Gwynd...........47 M9
Corrow Ag & B...........84 D3
Corry Highld...........96 H5
Corscombe Devon...........15 L11
Corscombe Dorset...........7 M2
Corse Gloucs...........29 K3
Corse Lawn Gloucs...........29 L3
Corsham Wilts...........18 C6
Corsindae Abers...........102 F12
Corsley Wilts...........18 C10
Corsley Heath Wilts...........18 B10
Corsock D & G...........78 C12
Corston BaNES...........17 Q3
Corston Wilts...........18 D4
Corstorphine C Edin...........86 E7
Cortachy Angus...........94 F9
Corton Suffk...........45 Q10
Corton Wilts...........18 D11
Corton Denham Somset...........17 P10
Coruanan Highld...........90 E3
Corwen Denbgs...........48 C6
Coryton Devon...........5 K4
Coryton Thurr...........22 E6
Cosby Leics...........41 M8
Coscote Oxon...........19 P4
Coseley Dudley...........40 C8
Cosgrove Nhants...........32 B8
Cosham C Port...........9 Q6
Cosheston Pembks...........24 H7
Coshieville P & K...........91 Q7
Cossall Notts...........51 L11
Cossington Leics...........41 N5
Cossington Somset...........17 J7

Costessey Norfk.....45 K7
Costock Notts.....41 M3
Coston Leics.....42 B6
Coston Norfk.....44 H8
Cote Oxon.....19 L1
Cotebrook Ches W.....49 L3
Cotehill Cumb.....71 P5
Cotes Leics.....41 M4
Cotesbach Leics.....41 M10
Cotford St Luke Somset.....16 C9
Cotgrave Notts.....41 N1
Cothal Abers.....102 H11
Cotham Notts.....42 B1
Cotherstone Dur.....64 H4
Cothill Oxon.....19 M2
Cotleigh Devon.....6 G3
Cotmanhay Derbys.....51 L11
Coton Cambs.....33 L5
Coton Nhants.....41 P12
Coton Staffs.....49 P10
Coton Hill Shrops.....49 J11
Coton in the Elms Derbys.....40 G4
Cotswolds.....30 C11
Cotswold Wildlife Park & Gardens Oxon.....30 G11
Cott Devon.....5 Q7
Cottam Lancs.....57 J3
Cottam Notts.....52 B7
Cottenham Cambs.....33 M4
Cottered Herts.....33 K10
Cotterstock Nhants.....42 F11
Cottesbrooke Nhants.....41 P11
Cottesmore Rutlnd.....42 C7
Cottingham E R Yk.....60 H7
Cottingham Nhants.....42 B11
Cottingley C Brad.....58 E6
Cottingley Hall Crematorium Leeds.....58 H7
Cottisford Oxon.....31 N7
Cotton Suffk.....34 H4
Cottown Abers.....101 P9
Cottown Abers.....102 G11
Cottown of Gight Abers.....102 H7
Cotts Devon.....5 J7
Coughton Warwks.....30 E3
Coulaghailtro Ag & B.....83 K9
Coulags Highld.....97 N1
Coull Abers.....94 H2
Coulport Ag & B.....84 D5
Coulsdon Gt Lon.....21 L10
Coulston Wilts.....18 D9
Coulter S Lans.....78 G3
Coulton N York.....66 E11
Coultra Fife.....93 L13
Cound Shrops.....39 K2
Coundon Dur.....65 M2
Countersett N York.....64 G9
Countess Wear Devon.....6 C5
Countesthorpe Leics.....41 N8
Countisbury Devon.....15 M3
Coupar Angus P & K.....93 J7
Coupland Nthumb.....81 K7
Cour Ag & B.....75 M3
Courteachan Highld.....97 J9
Courteenhall Nhants.....31 Q4
Court Henry Carmth.....26 D4
Courtsend Essex.....23 K5
Courtway Somset.....16 G8
Cousland Mdloth.....86 H8
Cousley Wood E Susx.....12 D4
Cove Ag & B.....84 D6
Cove Border.....87 P7
Cove Devon.....16 C11
Cove Hants.....20 D11
Cove Highld.....105 M4
Cove Bay C Aber.....95 Q2
Covehithe Suffk.....35 Q1
Coven Staffs.....40 B6
Coveney Cambs.....33 M1
Covenham St Bartholomew Lincs.....53 K5
Covenham St Mary Lincs.....53 K5
Coventry Covtry.....41 J10
Coventry Airport Warwks.....41 J11
Coverack Cnwll.....2 H11
Coverack Bridges Cnwll.....2 G9
Coverham N York.....65 K9
Covington Cambs.....32 F3
Covington S Lans.....78 F2
Cowan Bridge Lancs.....63 L7
Cowbeech E Susx.....12 C7
Cowbit Lincs.....43 J6
Cowbridge V Glam.....16 D2
Cowden Kent.....11 P3
Cowdenbeath Fife.....86 D4
Cowers Lane Derbys.....50 H10
Cowes IoW.....9 N8
Cowesby N York.....66 C9
Cowfold W Susx.....11 K5
Cowhill S Glos.....28 H9
Cowie Stirlg.....85 P5
Cowley Devon.....6 B4
Cowley Gloucs.....29 N6
Cowley Gt Lon.....20 G7
Cowley Oxon.....31 M12
Cowling Lancs.....57 L5
Cowling N York.....58 C5
Cowling N York.....65 M9
Cowlinge Suffk.....34 B6
Cowpen Nthumb.....73 N5
Cowplain Hants.....10 B7
Cowshill Dur.....72 F11
Cowslip Green N Som.....17 L4
Cowthorpe N York.....59 K4
Coxbank Ches E.....49 M6
Coxbench Derbys.....51 J11
Coxford Cnwll.....14 C11
Coxford Norfk.....44 E4
Coxheath Kent.....22 E12
Coxhoe Dur.....65 N1
Coxley Somset.....17 M7
Coxley Wick Somset.....17 M7
Coxtie Green Essex.....22 C4
Coxwold N York.....66 D11
Coychurch Brdgnd.....27 K11
Coychurch Crematorium Brdgnd.....27 K11
Coylton S Ayrs.....76 G7
Coylumbridge Highld.....99 N6
Coytrahen Brdgnd.....27 J10
Crabbs Cross Worcs.....30 D2
Crabtree W Susx.....11 K5
Crackenthorpe Cumb.....64 C3
Crackington Haven Cnwll.....14 C11
Crackleybank Shrops.....49 N12
Cracoe N York.....58 C3

Craddock Devon.....6 E1
Cradley Dudley.....40 C9
Cradley Herefs.....39 N11
Cradley Heath Sandw.....40 C9
Cradoc Powys.....27 L3
Crafthole Cnwll.....4 H9
Craggan Highld.....100 F9
Craghead Dur.....73 L10
Cragside House & Garden Nthumb.....73
Crai Powys.....27 J4
Craibstone Moray.....101 P4
Craichie Angus.....93 N6
Craig Angus.....95 L10
Craig Highld.....105 Q11
Craigbank E Ayrs.....77 K8
Craigburn Border.....86 F10
Craigcleuch D & G.....79 M10
Craigdam Abers.....102 H8
Craigdhu Ag & B.....83 M2
Craigearn Abers.....102 F11
Craigellachie Moray.....101 K6
Craigend P & K.....92 G10
Craigend Rens.....84 H8
Craigendoran Ag & B.....84 E6
Craigends Rens.....84 G9
Craighlaw D & G.....69 J6
Craighouse Ag & B.....82 G9
Craigie P & K.....92 G7
Craigie S Ayrs.....76 G5
Craigiefold Abers.....103 J3
Craigley D & G.....70 C4
Craig Llangiwg Neath.....26 G7
Craiglockhart C Edin.....86 E7
Craigmillar C Edin.....86 G7
Craigneston D & G.....78 C10
Craigneuk N Lans.....85 N10
Craigneuk N Lans.....85 N9
Craignure Ag & B.....89 P8
Craigo Angus.....95 L8
Craigrothie Fife.....93 L12
Craigruie Stirlg.....91 M11
Craigton Angus.....93 N7
Craigton C Aber.....95 N2
Craigton E Rens.....84 H11
Craigton Crematorium C Glas.....85 J9
Craigton of Airlie Angus.....93 K5
Crail Fife.....87 L1
Crailing Border.....80 F8
Craiselound N Linc.....51 Q2
Crakehall N York.....65 M9
Crambe N York.....60 C2
Cramlington Nthumb.....73 M5
Cramond C Edin.....86 E7
Cramond Bridge C Edin.....86 E7
Cranage Ches E.....49 N2
Cranberry Staffs.....49 P8
Cranborne Dorset.....8 F5
Cranbourne Br For.....20 E8
Cranbrook Devon.....6 D4
Cranbrook Kent.....12 F3
Cranfield C Beds.....32 D8
Cranford Gt Lon.....20 H7
Cranford St Andrew Nhants.....32 D2
Cranford St John Nhants.....32 D2
Cranham Gloucs.....29 M6
Crank St Hel.....57 J8
Cranleigh Surrey.....10 G3
Cranmore Somset.....17 P7
Cranoe Leics.....41 Q8
Cransford Suffk.....35 M4
Cranshaws Border.....87 N9
Crantock Cnwll.....2 H4
Cranwell Lincs.....52 E12
Cranwich Norfk.....44 C10
Cranworth Norfk.....44 G8
Craobh Haven Ag & B.....83 M2
Crarae Ag & B.....83 Q4
Crask Inn Highld.....109 J10
Crask of Aigas Highld.....98 F1
Craster Nthumb.....81 Q9
Cratfield Suffk.....35 M2
Crathes Abers.....95 M3
Crathie Abers.....94 E3
Crathie Highld.....98 H9
Crathorne N York.....66 B6
Craven Arms Shrops.....38 H5
Crawcrook Gatesd.....73 K8
Crawford S Lans.....78 F5
Crawfordjohn S Lans.....78 E4
Crawley Hants.....9 M1
Crawley Oxon.....31 J10
Crawley W Susx.....11 L3
Crawley Down W Susx.....11 M3
Crawshawbooth Lancs.....57 P4
Crawton Abers.....95 P6
Cray N York.....64 G10
Crayford Gt Lon.....21 P8
Crayke N York.....66 D12
Crays Hill Essex.....22 E5
Creacombe Devon.....15 P9
Creagan Inn Ag & B.....90 D7
Creag Ghoraidh W Isls.....111 b5
Creagorry W Isls.....111 b5
Creaguaineach Lodge Highld.....91 J3
Creaton Nhants.....41 P12
Creca D & G.....71 K2
Credenhill Herefs.....39 J12
Crediton Devon.....15 P11
Creebank D & G.....69 J4
Creebridge D & G.....69 K6
Creech Heathfield Somset.....16 H10
Creech St Michael Somset.....16 H10
Creed Cnwll.....3 L6
Creekmouth Gt Lon.....21 P7
Creeting St Mary Suffk.....34 H5
Creeton Lincs.....42 E6
Creetown D & G.....69 L7
Cregneash IoM.....56 a7
Creich Fife.....93 L13
Creigiau Cardif.....27 M11
Cremyll Cnwll.....4 K9
Cressage Shrops.....39 L2
Cressbrook Derbys.....50 F6
Cresselly Pembks.....25 J7
Cressex Bucks.....20 D5
Cressing Essex.....34 D11
Cresswell Nthumb.....73 N3
Cresswell Pembks.....25 J7
Cresswell Staffs.....50 C11
Cretingham Suffk.....35 K5
Cretshengan Ag & B.....83 K9
Crewe Ches E.....49 N4

Crewe Ches W.....48 H5
Crewe Crematorium Ches E.....49 N4
Crewe Green Ches E.....49 N5
Crew Green Powys.....48 G11
Crewkerne Somset.....7 L2
Crewton C Derb.....51 J2
Crianlarich Stirlg.....91 K10
Cribyn Cerdgn.....36 H9
Criccieth Gwynd.....46 H4
Crich Derbys.....51 J9
Crichton Mdloth.....86 H9
Crick Nhants.....41 N11
Crickadarn Powys.....27 M1
Cricket St Thomas Somset.....7 J2
Crickhowell Powys.....27 P5
Cricklade Wilts.....18 G3
Cricklewood Gt Lon.....21 K6
Criggion Powys.....48 F11
Crigglestone Wakefd.....58 H10
Crimond Abers.....103 L4
Crimplesham Norfk.....43 Q8
Crimscote Warwks.....30 G5
Crinaglack Highld.....98 F12
Crinan Ag & B.....83 L4
Crindledyke N Lans.....85 N10
Cringleford Norfk.....45 K8
Crinow Pembks.....25 K6
Croachy Highld.....99 J4
Crockenhill Kent.....21 P9
Crocker End Oxon.....20 B6
Crockernwell Devon.....5 P2
Crockerton Wilts.....18 C11
Crocketford D & G.....70 D2
Crockham Hill Kent.....21 N12
Croeserw Neath.....27 J9
Croes-goch Pembks.....24 E3
Croes-lan Cerdgn.....36 F10
Croesor Gwynd.....47 K3
Croesyceiliog Carmth.....25 P5
Croesyceiliog Torfn.....28 C9
Croft Leics.....41 L8
Croft Lincs.....53 N10
Croft Warrtn.....57 L9
Croftamie Stirlg.....84 H6
Crofton Wakefd.....59 J9
Croft-on-Tees N York.....65 M5
Croftown Highld.....106 C5
Crofts Moray.....101 K5
Crofts of Dipple Moray.....101 L4
Crofts of Savoch Abers.....103 L4
Crofty Swans.....26 B9
Croggan Ag & B.....89 P10
Croglin Cumb.....71 R6
Croick Highld.....106 H4
Cromarty Highld.....107 N8
Crombie Fife.....86 C5
Cromdale Highld.....100 G9
Cromer Herts.....33 J10
Cromer Norfk.....45 K2
Cromford Derbys.....50 H9
Cromhall S Glos.....29 J10
Cromor W Isls.....111 d2
Cromwell Notts.....52 B10
Cronberry E Ayrs.....77 K6
Crondall Hants.....10 C1
Cronton Knows.....57 J10
Crook Cumb.....63 J3
Crook Dur.....65 L1
Crookedholm E Ayrs.....76 H4
Crookham Nthumb.....81 J6
Crookham W Berk.....19 P7
Crookham Village Hants.....20 C11
Crook Inn Border.....78 H4
Crooklands Cumb.....63 K5
Crook of Devon P & K.....86 C3
Cropredy Oxon.....31 L5
Cropston Leics.....41 M5
Cropthorne Worcs.....30 D5
Cropton N York.....66 G9
Cropwell Bishop Notts.....41 P1
Cropwell Butler Notts.....51 P12
Cros W Isls.....111 e1
Crosbost W Isls.....111 d2
Crosby Cumb.....70 H7
Crosby IoM.....56 c5
Crosby N Linc.....60 F10
Crosby Sefton.....56 G8
Crosby Garret Cumb.....63 N1
Crosby Ravensworth Cumb.....64 B5
Croscombe Somset.....17 N7
Cross Somset.....17 K5
Crossaig Ag & B.....75 M3
Crossapol Ag & B.....88 C7
Cross Ash Mons.....28 E5
Cross-at-Hand Kent.....12 F2
Crosscanonby Cumb.....70 H7
Crossdale Street Norfk.....45 K3
Cross Flatts C Brad.....58 E6
Crossford Fife.....86 C5
Crossford S Lans.....77 N3
Crossgatehall E Loth.....86 H8
Crossgates E Ayrs.....76 F3
Crossgates Fife.....86 D5
Cross Gates Leeds.....59 J7
Crossgates N York.....67 M10
Crossgill Lancs.....63 K9
Cross Green Leeds.....59 J7
Cross Green Suffk.....34 E5
Cross Green Suffk.....34 E5
Cross Hands Carmth.....26 D6
Crosshands E Ayrs.....76 H5
Crosshill Fife.....86 E3
Crosshill S Ayrs.....76 F9
Crosshouse E Ayrs.....76 G4
Cross Houses Shrops.....39 K1
Cross in Hand E Susx.....12 C6
Cross Inn Cerdgn.....36 F8
Cross Keys Caerph.....28 B9
Crosskeys Caerph.....27 P9
Crosskirk Highld.....110 B3
Cross Lane IoW.....9 N9
Cross Lane Head Shrops.....39 N3
Crosslee Rens.....84 G9
Crossmichael D & G.....70 C3
Cross of Jackston Abers.....102 H8
Cross o' th' hands Derbys.....50 H11
Crossroads Abers.....95 J1
Crossroads Abers.....95 M3
Cross Street Suffk.....35 K2
Crosston Angus.....93 N5
Cross Town Ches E.....57 N12
Crossway Green Worcs.....39 Q8
Crossways Dorset.....8 C9
Crosswell Pembks.....25 K2

Crosthwaite Cumb.....62 H4
Croston Lancs.....57 J5
Crostwick Norfk.....45 L7
Crouch End Gt Lon.....21 L6
Crouchers Wilts.....8 F3
Crouch Hill Dorset.....7 Q1
Croughton Nhants.....31 M7
Crovie Abers.....102 G3
Crowan Cnwll.....2 F8
Crowborough E Susx.....11 P4
Crowcombe Somset.....16 F8
Crowdecote Derbys.....50 E7
Crowden Derbys.....50 E2
Crow Edge Barns.....58 F12
Crowell Oxon.....20 C4
Crowfield Suffk.....35 J5
Crowhill E Loth.....87 N7
Crow Hill Herefs.....28 H4
Crowhurst E Susx.....12 F7
Crowhurst Surrey.....11 M1
Crowland Lincs.....43 J7
Crowland Lincs.....34 G3
Crowlas Cnwll.....2 D8
Crowle N Linc.....60 D10
Crowle Worcs.....30 B3
Crowle Green Worcs.....30 B3
Crowmarsh Gifford Oxon.....19 Q3
Crown Corner Suffk.....35 L3
Crownhill C Plym.....5 K8
Crownhill Crematorium M Keyn.....32 B8
Crownthorpe Norfk.....44 H9
Crowntown Cnwll.....2 F9
Crows-an-Wra Cnwll.....2 B9
Crowthorne Wokham.....20 D9
Crowton Ches W.....49 L1
Croxdale Dur.....73 M12
Croxden Staffs.....50 E11
Croxley Green Herts.....20 H4
Croxteth Lpool.....56 H9
Croxton Cambs.....33 J5
Croxton N Linc.....61 J10
Croxton Norfk.....44 E11
Croxton Norfk.....44 G4
Croxton Staffs.....49 P8
Croxton Kerrial Leics.....42 B4
Croy Highld.....107 M10
Croy N Lans.....85 M7
Croyde Devon.....14 H4
Croydon Cambs.....33 K6
Croydon Gt Lon.....21 L9
Croydon Crematorium Gt Lon.....21 L9
Crubenmore Highld.....99 K10
Cruckmeole Shrops.....38 H1
Cruckton Shrops.....48 H12
Cruden Bay Abers.....103 M7
Crudgington Wrekin.....49 L11
Crudwell Wilts.....29 N9
Crumlin Caerph.....27 P8
Crumplehorn Cnwll.....4 F9
Crumpsall Manch.....57 Q8
Crundale Kent.....13 K1
Crunwear Pembks.....25 L6
Crux Easton Hants.....19 M9
Crwbin Carmth.....26 C6
Cryers Hill Bucks.....20 E4
Crymych Pembks.....25 L3
Crynant Neath.....26 H7
Crystal Palace Gt Lon.....21 M8
Cuaig Highld.....105 K10
Cuan Ag & B.....89 P12
Cubbington Warwks.....31 J1
Cubert Cnwll.....2 H4
Cublington Bucks.....32 B11
Cublington Herefs.....28 E2
Cuckfield W Susx.....11 L5
Cucklington Somset.....17 R10
Cuckney Notts.....51 M6
Cuddesdon Oxon.....31 N12
Cuddington Bucks.....31 Q11
Cuddington Ches W.....49 L2
Cuddington Heath Ches W.....49 J6
Cudham Gt Lon.....21 N10
Cudliptown Devon.....5 L4
Cudnell Bmouth.....8 F7
Cudworth Barns.....59 K11
Cudworth Somset.....7 K1
Cuffley Herts.....21 L3
Cuil Highld.....90 D5
Culbokie Highld.....107 K9
Culburnie Highld.....98 G1
Culcabock Highld.....107 L12
Culcharry Highld.....100 D5
Culcheth Warrtn.....57 M9
Culdrain Abers.....101 P8
Culduie Highld.....97 K2
Culford Suffk.....34 D3
Culgaith Cumb.....64 B2
Culham Oxon.....19 N2
Culkein Highld.....108 B8
Culkein Drumbeg Highld.....108 C8
Culkerton Gloucs.....29 N9
Cullen Moray.....101 P2
Cullercoats N Tyne.....73 P6
Cullerlie Abers.....95 M2
Cullicudden Highld.....107 K9
Cullingworth C Brad.....58 E6
Cuillin Hills Highld.....96 F5
Cullipool Ag & B.....83 L1
Cullivoe Shet.....111 k3
Culloden Highld.....107 M12
Cullompton Devon.....6 E2
Cullompton Services Devon.....6 D2
Culm Davy Devon.....16 F12
Culmington Shrops.....39 J6
Culmstock Devon.....16 E12
Culnacraig Highld.....106 A2
Culnaightrie D & G.....70 C5
Culnaknock Highld.....104 G9
Culrain Highld.....107 J4
Culross Fife.....86 B5
Culroy S Ayrs.....76 F8
Culsalmond Abers.....102 E8
Culscadden D & G.....69 L8
Culshabbin D & G.....69 J8
Culswick Shet.....111 j4
Cultercullen Abers.....103 J9
Cults C Aber.....95 P2
Culverstone Green Kent.....22 D10
Culverthorpe Lincs.....42 F2
Culworth Nhants.....31 M5
Culzean Castle & Country Park S Ayrs.....76 D8

Crosthwaite Cumb.....62 H4
Cumbernauld N Lans.....85 M7
Cumbernauld Village N Lans.....85 M7
Cumberworth Lincs.....53 N8
Cuminestown Abers.....102 G5
Cumledge Border.....80 G3
Cummersdale Cumb.....71 N5
Cummertrees D & G.....71 J3
Cummingstown Moray.....100 H2
Cumnock E Ayrs.....77 J7
Cumnor Oxon.....31 L12
Cumrew Cumb.....71 Q5
Cumrue D & G.....78 H10
Cumwhinton Cumb.....71 P5
Cumwhitton Cumb.....71 Q5
Cundall N York.....65 Q11
Cunninghamhead N Ayrs.....76 F3
Cunningsburgh Shet.....111 k4
Cupar Fife.....93 L11
Cupar Muir Fife.....93 L11
Curbar Derbys.....50 G6
Curbridge Hants.....9 N5
Curbridge Oxon.....31 J11
Curdridge Hants.....9 N5
Curdworth Warwks.....40 F8
Curland Somset.....16 H11
Curridge W Berk.....19 N6
Currie C Edin.....86 E8
Curry Mallet Somset.....17 J10
Curry Rivel Somset.....17 K10
Curtisden Green Kent.....12 E2
Curtisknowle Devon.....5 P9
Cury Cnwll.....2 G10
Cushnie Abers.....102 C11
Cutcloy D & G.....69 L11
Cutcombe Somset.....16 C8
Cuthill Highld.....107 M5
Cutnall Green Worcs.....39 Q8
Cutsdean Gloucs.....30 E7
Cutthorpe Derbys.....51 J6
Cuxham Oxon.....19 Q2
Cuxton Medway.....22 E9
Cuxwold Lincs.....52 G4
Cwm Denbgs.....56 C12
Cwmafan Neath.....26 G9
Cwmaman Rhondd.....27 L8
Cwmbach Carmth.....25 M4
Cwmbach Powys.....27 N2
Cwmbach Powys.....27 L8
Cwmbach Llechrhyd Powys.....38 B10
Cwmbran Torfn.....28 C9
Cwmcarn Caerph.....27 P9
Cwmcarvan Mons.....28 F7
Cwm-cou Cerdgn.....36 E11
Cwm Crawnon Powys.....27 N5
Cwmdare Rhondd.....27 L7
Cwmdu Powys.....27 P4
Cwmdu Swans.....26 E9
Cwmduad Carmth.....25 P3
Cwmfelin Bridgend.....27 J10
Cwmfelin Myr Td.....27 M8
Cwmfelin Boeth Carmth.....25 L5
Cwmfelinfach Caerph.....27 P9
Cwmffrwd Carmth.....25 P5
Cwmgiedd Powys.....26 H6
Cwmgorse Carmth.....26 F6
Cwmgwili Carmth.....26 D6
Cwmhiraeth Carmth.....25 N2
Cwm Llinau Powys.....47 N9
Cwmllynfell Neath.....26 G6
Cwmmawr Carmth.....26 D6
Cwmparc Rhondd.....27 K9
Cwmpengraig Carmth.....25 N2
Cwmtillery Blae G.....27 P7
Cwm-twrch Isaf Powys.....26 G6
Cwm-twrch Uchaf Powys.....26 G6
Cwm-y-glo Gwynd.....54 H8
Cwmystwyth Cerdgn.....37 N6
Cwrt-newydd Cerdgn.....36 H10
Cyfarthfa Castle Museum Myr Td.....27 L7
Cylibebyll Neath.....26 G7
Cymer Neath.....27 J9
Cymmer Rhondd.....27 L10
Cynghordy Carmth.....37 N11
Cynonville Neath.....26 H9
Cynwyd Denbgs.....48 C7
Cynwyl Elfed Carmth.....25 P4

D

Daccombe Devon.....6 B8
Dacre Cumb.....71 P9
Dacre N York.....58 F3
Dacre Banks N York.....58 G2
Daddry Shield Dur.....72 F12
Dadford Bucks.....31 P6
Dadlington Leics.....41 K7
Dagenham Gt Lon.....21 P6
Daglingworth Gloucs.....30 C12
Dagnall Bucks.....32 E12
Dailly S Ayrs.....76 E10
Dairsie Fife.....93 M11
Dalabrog W Isls.....111 a6
Dalavich Ag & B.....83 P1
Dalbeattie D & G.....70 D4
Dalby IoM.....56 b5
Dalby N York.....66 F12
Dalcapon P & K.....92 E5
Dalchalm Highld.....107 Q2
Dalchreichart Highld.....98 D6
Dalchruin P & K.....91 Q11
Dalcrue P & K.....92 F9
Dalditch Devon.....6 E6
Daldowie Crematorium C Glas.....85 L9
Dale Derbys.....51 K12
Dale Pembks.....24 E7
Dalelia Highld.....89 P3
Dalgarven N Ayrs.....76 E3
Dalgety Bay Fife.....86 E5
Dalgig E Ayrs.....77 J8
Dalginross P & K.....92 B10
Dalguise P & K.....92 E6
Dalhalvaig Highld.....109 Q5
Dalham Suffk.....34 C4
Daliburgh W Isls.....111 a6
Dalkeith Mdloth.....86 G8
Dallas Moray.....100 H5
Dallinghoo Suffk.....35 L5
Dallington E Susx.....12 D6
Dallington Nhants.....31 Q3
Dalmally Ag & B.....90 G10

Place	Location	Page	Grid
Dalmary	Stirlg	85	J4
Dalmellington	E Ayrs	76	H9
Dalmeny	C Edin	86	D6
Dalmore	Highld	107	L8
Dalmuir	W Duns	84	H8
Dalnabreck	Highld	89	P3
Dalnacardoch	P & K	91	Q3
Dalnahaitnach	Highld	99	M5
Dalnaspidal	P & K	91	P2
Dalnawillan Lodge	Highld	110	B7
Daloist	P & K	92	B4
Dalqueich	P & K	86	C2
Dalquhairn	S Ayrs	76	F11
Dalreavoch Lodge	Highld	107	M1
Dalry	N Ayrs	76	E2
Dalrymple	E Ayrs	76	F8
Dalserf	S Lans	77	N2
Dalsmeran	Ag & B	75	J9
Dalston	Cumb	71	M5
Dalston	Gt Lon	21	M6
Dalswinton	D & G	78	F10
Dalton	D & G	70	H2
Dalton	N York	65	K6
Dalton	N York	66	B11
Dalton	Nthumb	73	K6
Dalton-in-Furness	Cumb	62	E7
Dalton-le-Dale	Dur	73	P10
Dalton-on-Tees	N York	65	N6
Dalton Piercy	Hartpl	66	C2
Dalveich	Stirlg	91	P10
Dalwhinnie	Highld	99	J11
Dalwood	Devon	6	H3
Damerham	Hants	8	G4
Damgate	Norfk	45	N8
Damnaglaur	D & G	68	F11
Danbury	Essex	22	F3
Danby	N York	66	G6
Danby Wiske	N York	65	N7
Dandaleith	Moray	101	K6
Danderhall	Mdloth	86	G8
Danebridge	Ches E	50	C7
Dane End	Herts	33	K11
Danehill	E Susx	11	N5
Dane Hills	C Leic	41	M6
Dane Street	Kent	23	K11
Danshillock	Abers	102	F4
Danskine	E Loth	87	L8
Darenth	Kent	22	C8
Daresbury	Halton	57	L11
Darfield	Barns	59	K12
Dargate	Kent	23	L10
Darite	Cnwll	4	G8
Darlaston	Wsall	40	C7
Darlaston Green	Wsall	40	C7
Darley	N York	58	G3
Darley Abbey	C Derb	51	J12
Darley Bridge	Derbys	50	H8
Darley Dale	Derbys	50	H8
Darley Green	Solhll	40	F11
Darleyhall	Herts	32	G11
Darley Head	N York	58	G3
Darlingscott	Warwks	30	G6
Darlington	Darltn	65	M5
Darlington Crematorium	Darltn	65	M5
Darlton	Notts	51	Q6
Darnick	Border	80	D7
Darowen	Powys	47	N10
Darra	Abers	102	F6
Darracott	Devon	14	E8
Darracott	Devon	14	H4
Darras Hall	Nthumb	73	K6
Darrington	Wakefd	59	L9
Darsham	Suffk	35	N3
Darshill	Somset	17	N7
Dartford	Kent	22	B8
Dartington	Devon	5	Q7
Dartmoor National Park	Devon	5	N4
Dartmouth	Devon	6	H10
Darton	Barns	58	H11
Darvel	E Ayrs	77	J4
Darwen	Bl w D	57	M4
Datchet	W & M	20	F7
Datchworth	Herts	33	J11
Daubhill	Bolton	57	M7
Daugh of Kinermony	Moray	101	K7
Dauntsey	Wilts	18	E4
Dava	Moray	100	F7
Davenham	Ches W	49	M2
Daventry	Nhants	31	M2
Davidson's Mains	C Edin	86	E7
Davidstow	Cnwll	4	E3
Davington	D & G	79	K8
Davington Hill	Kent	23	J10
Daviot	Abers	102	G9
Daviot	Highld	99	K2
Daviot House	Highld	99	K2
Davoch of Grange	Moray	101	N5
Dawesgreen	Surrey	11	K2
Dawley	Wrekin	39	M1
Dawlish	Devon	6	C7
Dawlish Warren	Devon	6	H7
Daybrook	Notts	51	M10
Daylesford	Gloucs	30	G8
Deal	Kent	23	Q11
Dean	Cumb	70	H9
Dean	Devon	5	N3
Dean	Devon	15	M3
Dean	Hants	9	P4
Dean	Oxon	31	J9
Dean	Somset	17	N7
Dean Bottom	Kent	22	C9
Deanburnhaugh	Border	79	N6
Deancombe	Devon	5	P7
Dean Court	Oxon	31	L11
Deane	Bolton	57	M7
Deane	Hants	19	P9
Deanhead	Kirk	58	D10
Deanland	Dorset	8	E4
Deanraw	Nthumb	72	E8
Deans	W Loth	86	B8
Deanscales	Cumb	70	H9
Deanshanger	Nhants	31	Q6
Deanshaugh	Moray	101	L5
Deanston	Stirlg	85	M3
Dearham	Cumb	70	H8
Debach	Suffk	35	L6
Debden	Essex	21	N4
Debden	Essex	33	N9
Debenham	Suffk	35	J4
Deblin's Green	Worcs	39	P11
Dechmont	W Loth	86	C7
Dechmont Road	W Loth	86	B8
Deddington	Oxon	31	L7
Dedham	Essex	34	H9
Dedworth	W & M	20	F8
Deene	Nhants	42	D10
Deenethorpe	Nhants	42	D10
Deepcar	Sheff	50	H2
Deeping Gate	C Pete	42	G8
Deeping St James	Lincs	42	G8
Deeping St Nicholas	Lincs	42	H7
Deerhurst	Gloucs	29	M3
Defford	Worcs	30	B5
Defynnog	Powys	27	K4
Deganwy	Conwy	55	L6
Degnish	Ag & B	83	L1
Deighton	C York	59	N5
Deighton	N York	65	P7
Deiniolen	Gwynd	54	H8
Delabole	Cnwll	4	D4
Delamere	Ches W	49	K2
Delfrigs	Abers	103	K10
Delliefure	Highld	100	G8
Dell Quay	W Susx	10	D8
Delnabo	Moray	100	H11
Delnashaugh Inn	Moray	101	J8
Delny	Highld	107	M7
Delph	Oldham	58	C11
Delves	Dur	73	K10
Dembleby	Lincs	42	E3
Denaby	Donc	51	L4
Denbigh	Denbgs	48	C3
Denbrae	Fife	93	L11
Denbury	Devon	5	Q6
Denby	Derbys	51	K10
Denby Dale	Kirk	58	G11
Denchworth	Oxon	19	L3
Dendron	Cumb	62	E7
Denfield	P & K	92	E11
Denford	Nhants	32	E2
Dengie	Essex	23	J3
Denham	Bucks	20	G6
Denham	Suffk	34	C5
Denham	Suffk	35	K2
Denham Green	Bucks	20	G6
Denhead	Abers	103	K5
Denhead	Fife	93	N11
Denhead of Gray	C Dund	93	L8
Denholm	Border	80	D9
Denholme	C Brad	58	E7
Denmead	Hants	9	Q5
Denmore	C Aber	103	K11
Dennington	Suffk	35	L4
Denny	Falk	85	N6
Dennyloanhead	Falk	85	N7
Den of Lindores	Fife	93	J11
Denshaw	Oldham	58	C11
Denside	Abers	95	N3
Densole	Kent	13	N2
Denston	Suffk	34	C6
Denstone	Staffs	50	E11
Denstroude	Kent	23	L10
Dent	Cumb	63	N5
Denton	Cambs	42	G11
Denton	Darltn	65	L4
Denton	E Susx	11	P9
Denton	Kent	13	N1
Denton	Lincs	42	C4
Denton	N York	58	F4
Denton	Nhants	32	B5
Denton	Norfk	45	L11
Denton	Tamesd	50	B2
Denver	Norfk	43	P9
Denwick	Nthumb	81	P10
Deopham	Norfk	44	H9
Deopham Green	Norfk	44	H9
Depden	Suffk	34	C5
Deptford	Gt Lon	21	M7
Deptford	Wilts	18	E12
Derby	C Derb	41	J1
Derby	Devon	15	K5
Derbyhaven	IoM	56	b7
Derculich	P & K	92	D5
Dereham	Norfk	44	G7
Deri	Caerph	27	N8
Derringstone	Kent	23	M12
Derrington	Staffs	40	B3
Derry Hill	Wilts	18	E6
Derrythorpe	N Linc	52	B2
Dersingham	Norfk	44	B4
Derwen	Denbgs	48	C5
Derwenlas	Powys	47	L10
Derwent Valley Mills	Derbys	50	H9
Derwent Water	Cumb	71	L10
Desborough	Nhants	42	B12
Desford	Leics	41	L6
Deskford	Moray	101	P3
Detling	Kent	22	F10
Devauden	Mons	28	F8
Devil's Bridge	Cerdgn	37	M5
Devizes	Wilts	18	F8
Devonport	C Plym	5	K8
Devonside	Clacks	85	Q4
Devoran	Cnwll	2	H7
Devoran & Perran	Cnwll	2	H7
Dewarton	Mdloth	86	H9
Dewlish	Dorset	8	B7
Dewsbury	Kirk	58	G9
Dewsbury Moor Crematorium	Kirk	58	G9
Deytheur	Powys	48	E11
Dial Post	W Susx	11	J6
Dibden	Hants	9	L6
Dibden Purlieu	Hants	9	M6
Dickleburgh	Norfk	35	J1
Didbrook	Gloucs	30	D7
Didcot	Oxon	19	N3
Diddington	Cambs	32	H4
Diddlebury	Shrops	39	K5
Didling	W Susx	10	D6
Didmarton	Gloucs	18	B4
Didsbury	Manch	57	Q9
Digby	Lincs	52	F11
Digg	Highld	104	H8
Diggle	Oldham	58	D11
Digmoor	Lancs	57	J7
Dihewyd	Cerdgn	36	H9
Dilham	Norfk	45	M5
Dilhorne	Staffs	50	C11
Dill Hall	Lancs	57	N3
Dillington	Cambs	32	G4
Dilston	Nthumb	72	H8
Dilton	Wilts	18	C10
Dilton Marsh	Wilts	18	C10
Dilwyn	Herefs	38	H10
Dinas	Gwynd	46	E4
Dinas	Pembks	24	H2
Dinas-Mawddwy	Gwynd	47	L7
Dinas Powys	V Glam	16	F2
Dinder	Somset	17	N7
Dinedor	Herefs	28	G2
Dingestow	Mons	28	G7
Dingle	Lpool	56	G10
Dingley	Nhants	41	Q9
Dingwall	Highld	107	J9
Dinnet	Abers	94	H3
Dinnington	N u Ty	73	L6
Dinnington	Rothm	51	M4
Dinnington	Somset	17	K12
Dinorwic	Gwynd	54	H8
Dinton	Bucks	31	Q11
Dinton	Wilts	8	E2
Dinwoodie	D & G	78	H10
Dinworthy	Devon	14	F8
Dipford	Somset	16	G10
Dippen	Ag & B	75	M5
Dippen	N Ayrs	75	Q7
Dippertown	Devon	5	J4
Dipple	Moray	101	L4
Dipple	S Ayrs	76	D10
Diptford	Devon	5	P8
Dipton	Dur	73	K9
Dirleton	E Loth	87	K5
Dirt Pot	Nthumb	72	F10
Diseworth	Leics	41	L3
Dishforth	N York	65	P11
Disley	Ches E	50	C4
Diss	Norfk	35	J1
Distington	Cumb	70	G10
Distington Hall Crematorium	Cumb	70	G10
Ditchampton	Wilts	8	G2
Ditcheat	Somset	17	P8
Ditchingham	Norfk	45	M11
Ditchling	E Susx	11	M7
Ditherington	Shrops	49	J11
Ditteridge	Wilts	18	B6
Dittisham	Devon	6	B10
Ditton	Kent	22	E10
Ditton Green	Cambs	33	Q5
Ditton Priors	Shrops	39	L4
Dixton	Mons	28	F6
Dobcross	Oldham	58	C11
Dobwalls	Cnwll	4	F7
Doccombe	Devon	5	Q3
Dochgarroch	Highld	99	J2
Docking	Norfk	44	C3
Docklow	Herefs	39	K10
Dockray	Cumb	71	N10
Doddinghurst	Essex	22	C4
Doddington	Cambs	43	L11
Doddington	Kent	22	H11
Doddington	Lincs	52	C9
Doddington	Nthumb	81	L7
Doddington	Shrops	39	L6
Doddiscombsleigh	Devon	6	B5
Dodd's Green	Ches E	49	L6
Dodford	Nhants	31	N3
Dodford	Worcs	40	C11
Dodington	S Glos	29	K11
Dodington	Somset	16	G7
Dodleston	Ches W	48	G4
Dodside	E Rens	84	H11
Dodworth	Barns	58	H12
Dogdyke	Lincs	52	H11
Dogmersfield	Hants	20	C11
Dolanog	Powys	48	C11
Dolbenmaen	Gwynd	46	H3
Dolfach	Powys	47	P10
Dolfor	Powys	38	C5
Dolgarrog	Conwy	55	L7
Dolgellau	Gwynd	47	M7
Doll	Highld	107	P2
Dollar	Clacks	85	Q4
Dollarfield	Clacks	85	Q4
Dolphin	Flints	48	E2
Dolphinholme	Lancs	63	K10
Dolphinton	S Lans	86	D11
Dolton	Devon	15	K9
Dolwen	Conwy	55	N6
Dolwyddelan	Conwy	55	K10
Domgay	Powys	48	F10
Doncaster	Donc	59	M12
Doncaster North Services	Donc	59	P11
Donhead St Andrew	Wilts	8	D3
Donhead St Mary	Wilts	8	D3
Donibristle	Fife	86	E5
Doniford	Somset	16	E7
Donington	Lincs	42	H3
Donington on Bain	Lincs	52	H7
Donington Park Services	Leics	41	L3
Donisthorpe	Leics	40	H5
Donnington	Gloucs	30	G8
Donnington	Shrops	39	L1
Donnington	W Berk	19	M7
Donnington	W Susx	10	D9
Donnington	Wrekin	49	N11
Donnington Wood	Wrekin	49	N11
Donyatt	Somset	17	J12
Doonfoot	S Ayrs	76	F7
Dorback Lodge	Highld	100	G11
Dorchester	Dorset	7	Q5
Dorchester	Oxon	19	P2
Dordon	Warwks	40	H7
Dore	Sheff	50	H5
Dores	Highld	98	H3
Dorking	Surrey	21	J12
Dormans Land	Surrey	11	N2
Dormington	Herefs	28	G2
Dormston	Worcs	30	C3
Dorney	Bucks	20	E7
Dornie	Highld	97	M5
Dornoch	Highld	107	N4
Dornock	D & G	71	K3
Dorrery	Highld	110	C4
Dorridge	Solhll	40	F11
Dorrington	Lincs	52	F11
Dorrington	Shrops	39	J2
Dorrington	Shrops	49	N7
Dorsington	Warwks	30	F4
Dorstone	Herefs	28	D2
Dorton	Bucks	31	P10
Dosthill	Staffs	40	G7
Dottery	Dorset	7	M4
Doublebois	Cnwll	4	F7
Dougarie	N Ayrs	75	N5
Douglas	IoM	56	d6
Douglas	S Lans	78	D3
Douglas and Angus	C Dund	93	M8
Douglas Borough Crematorium	IoM	56	d5
Douglas Pier	Ag & B	84	D3
Douglastown	Angus	93	M6
Douglas Water	S Lans	78	E2
Douglas West	S Lans	78	D3
Doulting	Somset	17	P7
Dounby	Ork	111	g2
Doune	Highld	106	G3
Doune	Highld	85	M3
Dounepark	S Ayrs	76	D11
Dounie	Highld	107	J4
Dousland	Devon	5	L6
Dove Holes	Derbys	50	E5
Dovenby	Cumb	70	H8
Dover	Kent	13	P2
Dover Castle	Kent	13	P2
Dovercourt	Essex	35	L9
Doverdale	Worcs	39	Q8
Doveridge	Derbys	40	F1
Doversgreen	Surrey	11	K1
Dowally	P & K	92	F5
Dowdeswell	Gloucs	30	D9
Dowlais	Myr Td	27	M7
Dowland	Devon	15	K9
Dowlish Wake	Somset	7	K1
Down Ampney	Gloucs	18	G2
Downderry	Cnwll	4	G9
Downe	Gt Lon	21	N10
Downend	Gloucs	29	L8
Downend	S Glos	28	H12
Downfield	C Dund	93	L8
Downgate	Cnwll	4	H5
Downham	Essex	22	E4
Downham	Gt Lon	21	M8
Downham	Lancs	63	P12
Downham Market	Norfk	43	P9
Down Hatherley	Gloucs	29	M4
Downhead	Somset	17	N10
Downhead	Somset	17	Q7
Downhill	P & K	92	G9
Downholme	N York	65	K7
Downies	Abers	95	Q3
Downley	Bucks	20	D4
Down St Mary	Devon	15	M10
Downs Crematorium	Br & H	11	M8
Downside	Surrey	20	H10
Down Thomas	Devon	5	K9
Downton	Wilts	8	H3
Dowsby	Lincs	42	G5
Doynton	S Glos	17	Q2
Draethen	Caerph	27	P10
Draffan	S Lans	77	N3
Drakeholes	Notts	51	P3
Drakemyre	N Ayrs	76	E2
Drakes Broughton	Worcs	30	B4
Draughton	N York	58	D4
Draughton	Nhants	41	Q11
Drax	N York	59	P8
Draycote	Warwks	41	K12
Draycott	Derbys	41	K2
Draycott	Gloucs	30	F7
Draycott	Somset	17	L6
Draycott in the Clay	Staffs	40	F2
Draycott in the Moors	Staffs	50	C11
Drayton	C Port	9	R6
Drayton	Leics	42	B10
Drayton	Norfk	45	K7
Drayton	Oxon	19	N2
Drayton	Oxon	31	K6
Drayton	Somset	17	K10
Drayton	Worcs	40	B11
Drayton Bassett	Staffs	40	G7
Drayton Beauchamp	Bucks	20	E2
Drayton Manor Park	Staffs	40	G7
Drayton Parslow	Bucks	32	B10
Drayton St Leonard	Oxon	19	P2
Dreen Hill	Pembks	24	G6
Drefach	Carmth	25	N2
Drefach	Carmth	26	D6
Drefach	Cerdgn	36	H10
Dreghorn	N Ayrs	76	F4
Drellingore	Kent	13	N2
Drem	E Loth	87	K6
Drewsteignton	Devon	5	P3
Driffield	E R Yk	60	H3
Driffield	Gloucs	18	F2
Drift	Cnwll	2	C9
Drigg	Cumb	62	C3
Drighlington	Leeds	58	G8
Drimnin	Highld	89	L5
Drimpton	Dorset	7	K2
Drimsallie	Highld	90	C1
Dringhouses	C York	59	N4
Drinkstone	Suffk	34	F5
Drinkstone Green	Suffk	34	F5
Drointon	Staffs	40	D3
Droitwich	Worcs	30	B2
Dron	P & K	92	H11
Dronfield	Derbys	51	J5
Drongan	E Ayrs	76	H7
Dronley	Angus	93	L8
Droop	Dorset	7	Q4
Droxford	Hants	9	Q4
Droylsden	Tamesd	50	B2
Druid	Denbgs	48	B6
Druidston	Pembks	24	F5
Druimarbin	Highld	90	D7
Druimavuic	Ag & B	90	D7
Druimdrishaig	Ag & B	83	L8
Druimindarroch	Highld	97	J11
Drum	Ag & B	83	P7
Drum	P & K	86	C3
Drumalbin	S Lans	78	D2
Drumbeg	Highld	108	C8
Drumblade	Abers	102	D7
Drumbreddon	D & G	68	E9
Drumbuie	Highld	97	K4
Drumburgh	Cumb	71	L4
Drumburn	D & G	70	E5
Drumchapel	C Glas	85	J8
Drumchastle	P & K	91	L4
Drumclog	S Lans	77	L4
Drumeldrie	Fife	87	J2
Drumelzier	Border	79	J2
Drumfearn	Highld	97	K6
Drumfrennie	Abers	95	M3
Drumgley	Angus	93	M5
Drumguish	Highld	99	L6
Drumin	Moray	101	J8
Drumjohn	D & G	77	J10
Drumlamford	S Ayrs	68	H4
Drumlasie	Abers	95	K2
Drumleaning	Cumb	71	L5
Drumlemble	Ag & B	75	K8
Drumlithie	Abers	95	N6
Drummoddie	D & G	69	K9
Drummore	D & G	68	F10
Drummuir	Moray	101	M6
Drumnadrochit	Highld	98	G3
Drumnagorrach	Moray	102	C5
Drumpark	D & G	78	E11
Drumrunie Lodge	Highld	106	C2
Drumshang	S Ayrs	76	E8
Drumuie	Highld	104	F11
Drumuillie	Highld	99	P5
Drumvaich	Stirlg	85	L3
Drunzie	P & K	86	D1
Drybeck	Cumb	64	C5
Drybridge	Moray	101	N3
Drybridge	N Ayrs	76	F5
Drybrook	Gloucs	28	H5
Dryburgh	Border	80	D7
Dry Doddington	Lincs	42	C2
Dry Drayton	Cambs	33	L4
Drymen	Stirlg	84	H5
Drymuir	Abers	103	J6
Drynoch	Highld	96	E3
Dubford	Abers	102	G3
Duchally	Highld	108	G11
Ducklington	Oxon	31	J11
Duddenhoe End	Essex	33	M9
Duddingston	C Edin	86	F7
Duddington	Nhants	42	E9
Duddlestone	Somset	16	H11
Duddo	Nthumb	81	M5
Duddon	Ches W	49	K3
Dudleston	Shrops	48	G8
Dudleston Heath	Shrops	48	G8
Dudley	Dudley	40	C8
Dudley	N Tyne	73	M6
Dudley Port	Sandw	40	C8
Dudsbury	Dorset	8	F7
Duffield	Derbys	51	J11
Duffryn	Neath	26	H9
Dufftown	Moray	101	L7
Duffus	Moray	101	J2
Dufton	Cumb	64	C3
Duggleby	N York	60	F1
Duirinish	Highld	97	L4
Duisdalemore	Highld	97	J7
Duisky	Highld	90	D2
Duke Street	Suffk	34	H8
Dukinfield	Tamesd	50	C2
Dukinfield Crematorium	Tamesd	50	C2
Dulcote	Somset	17	N7
Dulford	Devon	6	E2
Dull	P & K	92	B6
Dullatur	N Lans	85	M7
Dullingham	Cambs	33	Q5
Dulnain Bridge	Highld	99	P4
Duloe	Beds	32	G5
Duloe	Cnwll	4	F8
Dulverton	Somset	16	C9
Dulwich	Gt Lon	21	M8
Dumbarton	W Duns	84	G7
Dumbleton	Gloucs	30	D7
Dumfries	D & G	70	F1
Dumgoyne	Stirlg	85	J6
Dummer	Hants	19	P10
Dumpton	Kent	23	Q9
Dun	Angus	95	L9
Dunalastair	P & K	91	Q5
Dunan	Ag & B	84	C8
Dunan	Highld	96	G4
Dunan	P & K	91	L5
Dunaverty	Ag & B	75	K10
Dunball	Somset	17	J7
Dunbar	E Loth	87	M6
Dunbeath	Highld	110	D9
Dunbeg	Ag & B	90	B9
Dunblane	Stirlg	85	M4
Dunbog	Fife	93	K11
Duncanston	Highld	107	J10
Duncanstone	Abers	102	D9
Dunchideock	Devon	6	B5
Dunchurch	Warwks	41	L12
Duncow	D & G	78	F11
Duncrievie	P & K	86	D1
Duncton	W Susx	10	F6
Dundee	C Dund	93	M9
Dundee Airport	C Dund	93	L9
Dundee Crematorium	C Dund	93	L8
Dundon	Somset	17	L9
Dundonald	S Ayrs	76	F5
Dundonnell	Highld	106	B5
Dundraw	Cumb	71	K5
Dundreggan	Highld	98	D6
Dundrennan	D & G	70	C6
Dundry	N Som	17	N3
Dunecht	Abers	102	G12
Dunfermline	Fife	86	C5
Dunfermline Crematorium	Fife	86	D5
Dunfield	Gloucs	18	G2
Dungavel	S Lans	77	L4
Dungeness	Kent	13	L6
Dunham	Notts	52	B8
Dunham-on-the-Hill	Ches W	49	J2
Dunhampton	Worcs	39	Q8
Dunham Town	Traffd	57	N10
Dunham Woodhouses	Traffd	57	N10
Dunholme	Lincs	52	E7
Dunino	Fife	93	P12
Dunipace	Falk	85	N6
Dunkeld	P & K	92	F7
Dunkerton	BaNES	17	Q4
Dunkeswell	Devon	6	F2
Dunkeswick	N York	58	H5
Dunkirk	Kent	23	L10
Dunkirk	S Glos	18	B4
Dunk's Green	Kent	22	C11
Dunlappie	Angus	95	K8
Dunley	Worcs	39	P8
Dunlop	E Ayrs	76	G2
Dunmaglass	Highld	98	H5
Dunmore	Falk	85	P5
Dunnet	Highld	110	E2
Dunnichen	Angus	93	N5
Dunning	P & K	92	F11
Dunnington	C York	59	P4
Dunnington	E R Yk	61	K4
Dunnington	Warwks	30	E4
Dunoon	Ag & B	84	C7
Dunphail	Moray	100	F5
Dunragit	D & G	68	F7
Dunscore	D & G	78	E11
Dunscroft	Donc	59	P11
Dunsdale	R & Cl	66	H4

Dunsden Green Oxon......20 B7
Dunsdon Devon......14 F9
Dunsfold Surrey......10 G3
Dunsford Devon......5 Q3
Dunshalt Fife......93 J12
Dunshillock Abers......103 K5
Dunsill Notts......51 L8
Dunsley N York......67 J5
Dunsley Staffs......39 Q5
Dunsmore Bucks......20 D3
Dunsop Bridge Lancs......63 M11
Dunstable C Beds......32 E11
Dunstall Staffs......40 F4
Dunstan Nthumb......81 Q9
Dunster Somset......16 D7
Duns Tew Oxon......31 L8
Dunston Gatesd......73 M8
Dunston Lincs......52 F10
Dunston Norfk......45 K9
Dunston Staffs......40 B4
Dunstone Devon......5 M9
Dunstone Devon......5 P5
Dunsville Donc......59 N11
Dunswell E R Yk......61 J7
Dunsyre S Lans......86 C11
Dunterton Devon......4 H4
Duntisbourne Abbots
    Gloucs......29 N7
Duntisbourne Rouse
    Gloucs......29 P7
Duntish Dorset......7 Q2
Duntocher W Duns......84 H8
Dunton Bucks......32 B11
Dunton C Beds......33 J7
Dunton Norfk......44 E4
Dunton Bassett Leics......41 M8
Dunton Green Kent......21 P11
Duntulm Highld......104 F7
Dunure S Ayrs......76 E8
Dunvant Swans......26 D9
Dunvegan Highld......104 C11
Dunwich Suffk......35 P3
Durgan Cnwll......2 H9
Durham Dur......73 M11
Durham Cathedral Dur......73 M11
Durham Crematorium
    Dur......73 M11
Durham Services Dur......73 N12
Durham Tees Valley
    Airport S on T......65 P5
Durisdeer D & G......78 E8
Durisdeermill D & G......78 E7
Durleigh Somset......16 H8
Durley Hants......9 N4
Durley Wilts......19 J7
Durley Street Hants......9 N4
Durlock Kent......23 P10
Durlock Kent......23 P9
Durness Highld......108 G3
Durno Abers......102 F9
Duror Highld......90 D5
Durran Ag & B......83 P2
Durrington W Susx......10 H8
Durrington Wilts......18 H10
Durris Abers......95 M3
Dursley Gloucs......29 K8
Dursley Cross Gloucs......29 J5
Durston Somset......16 H9
Durweston Dorset......8 C6
Duston Nhants......31 Q2
Duthil Highld......99 P4
Dutton Ches W......57 L11
Duxford Cambs......33 M7
Duxford Oxon......19 L2
Duxford IWM Cambs......33 M7
Dwygyfylchi Conwy......55 K6
Dwyran IoA......54 F8
Dyce C Aber......103 J11
Dyffryn Ardudwy Gwynd......47 J6
Dyffryn Cellwen Neath......27 J6
Dyke Lincs......42 F5
Dyke Moray......100 F4
Dykehead Angus......93 J5
Dykehead Angus......94 F9
Dykehead N Lans......85 P10
Dykehead Stirlg......85 K4
Dykelands Abers......95 L8
Dykends Angus......93 J4
Dykeside Abers......102 F6
Dymchurch Kent......13 L4
Dymock Gloucs......29 J3
Dyrham S Glos......17 Q2
Dysart Fife......86 G4
Dyserth Denbgs......56 C11

E

Eagland Hill Lancs......62 H12
Eagle Lincs......52 C9
Eaglescliffe S on T......65 Q5
Eaglesfield Cumb......70 H9
Eaglesfield D & G......71 K1
Eaglesham E Rens......85 J11
Eagley Bolton......57 N6
Eakring Notts......51 P8
Ealand N Linc......60 D10
Ealing Gt Lon......21 J7
Eals Nthumb......72 C9
Eamont Bridge Cumb......71 Q9
Earby Lancs......58 B5
Eardington Shrops......39 N4
Eardisland Herefs......38 H9
Eardisley Herefs......38 F11
Eardiston Shrops......48 G9
Eardiston Worcs......39 M8
Earith Cambs......33 L2
Earlestown St Hel......57 L9
Earley Wokham......20 C8
Earlham Norfk......45 K8
Earlham Crematorium
    Norfk......45 K8
Earlish Highld......104 E9
Earls Barton Nhants......32 C4
Earls Colne Essex......34 E10
Earls Common Worcs......30 C3
Earl's Croome Worcs......29 M1
Earlsdon Covtry......40 H10
Earlsferry Fife......87 J3
Earlsfield Gt Lon......21 K8
Earlsford Abers......102 H8
Earlsheaton Kirk......58 H9
Earl Shilton Leics......41 L7
Earl Soham Suffk......35 K4
Earl Sterndale Derbys......50 E7
Earlston Border......80 D6

Earlston E Ayrs......76 G4
Earlswood Surrey......21 L12
Earlswood Warks......40 E11
Earnley W Susx......10 D10
Earsdon N Tyne......73 N6
Earsham Norfk......45 M11
Eartham W Susx......10 F8
Easby N York......66 E6
Easdale Ag & B......89 P11
Easebourne W Susx......10 E5
Easenhall Warks......41 L10
Eashing Surrey......10 F2
Easington Bucks......31 P11
Easington Dur......73 P11
Easington E R Yk......61 P9
Easington R & Cl......66 G4
Easington Colliery Dur......73 Q11
Easington Lane Sundld......73 P10
Easingwold N York......66 D12
Eassie and Nevay Angus......93 L6
East Aberthaw V Glam......16 D3
East Allington Devon......5 P9
East Anstey Devon......15 P6
East Ashey IoW......9 P9
East Ashling W Susx......10 D8
East Ayton N York......67 L9
East Barkwith Lincs......52 G7
East Barming Kent......22 E11
East Barnby N York......66 H5
East Barnet Gt Lon......21 L4
East Barns E Loth......87 N7
East Barsham Norfk......44 F4
East Beckham Norfk......45 J3
East Bedfont Gt Lon......20 H8
East Bergholt Suffk......34 H9
East Bilney Norfk......44 F6
East Blatchington E Susx......11 P9
East Boldon S Tyne......73 P8
East Boldre Hants......9 L7
Eastbourne Darltn......65 N5
Eastbourne E Susx......12 C9
Eastbourne
    Crematorium E Susx......12 D9
East Bradenham Norfk......44 F8
East Brent Somset......17 J6
Eastbridge Suffk......35 P4
East Bridgford Notts......51 P11
East Buckland Devon......15 L6
East Budleigh Devon......6 E6
Eastburn C Brad......58 D5
Eastbury Herts......20 H5
Eastbury W Berk......19 K5
East Butterwick N Linc......52 B3
Eastby N York......58 D4
East Calder W Loth......86 C8
East Carleton Norfk......45 K9
East Carlton Leeds......58 G5
East Carlton Nhants......42 B11
East Chaldon (Chaldon
    Herring) Dorset......8 B10
East Challow Oxon......19 L3
East Charleton Devon......5 P10
East Chelborough Dorset......7 M2
East Chiltington E Susx......11 M7
East Chinnock Somset......17 L12
East Chisenbury Wilts......18 G9
Eastchurch Kent......23 J8
East Clandon Surrey......20 G11
East Claydon Bucks......31 Q8
East Coker Somset......7 M1
Eastcombe Gloucs......29 M7
East Compton Somset......17 N7
East Cornworthy Devon......6 B10
Eastcote Gt Lon......20 H6
Eastcote Nhants......31 P4
Eastcote Solhll......40 G10
Eastcott Wilts......18 F9
East Cottingwith E R Yk......60 C6
Eastcourt Wilts......19 J8
East Cowes IoW......9 N8
East Cowick E R Yk......59 P9
East Cowton N York......65 N6
East Cranmore Somset......17 P7
East Dean E Susx......12 C9
East Dean Gloucs......28 H5
East Dean Hants......9 J3
East Dean W Susx......10 E7
East Devon
    Crematorium Devon......6 E4
East Drayton Notts......51 Q6
East Dulwich Gt Lon......21 M8
East Dundry N Som......17 N3
East Ella C KuH......60 H8
Eastend Essex......22 H5
East End Hants......9 L7
East End Hants......19 M8
East End Kent......12 G3
East End Oxon......31 K10
East End Somset......17 P6
Easter Balmoral Abers......94 E3
Easter Compton S Glos......28 G11
Easter Dalziel Highld......107 M11
Easterhouse C Glas......85 L9
Easter Howgate Mdloth......86 F9
Easter Kinkell Highld......107 J10
Easter Moniack Highld......98 H1
Eastern Green Covtry......40 H10
Easter Ord Abers......95 N2
Easter Pitkierie Fife......87 L2
Easter Skeld Shet......111 k4
Easter Softlaw Border......80 G7
Easterton Wilts......18 F9
Eastertown Somset......17 J4
East Everleigh Wilts......18 H9
East Farleigh Kent......22 E11
East Farndon Nhants......41 Q9
East Ferry Lincs......52 B4
Eastfield N Lans......85 P9
Eastfield N York......67 M10
East Firsby Lincs......52 E6
East Fortune E Loth......87 K6
Eastgate Dur......72 G12
Eastgate Norfk......45 J5
East Goscote Leics......41 N5
East Grafton Wilts......18 J8
East Grimstead Wilts......9 J2
East Grinstead W Susx......11 N3
East Guldeford E Susx......12 H6
East Haddon Nhants......31 P1
East Hagbourne Oxon......19 N3
East Halton N Linc......61 K9
East Ham Gt Lon......21 N6
Easthampstead Park
    Crematorium Br For......20 D9
Easthampton Herefs......38 H9
East Hanney Oxon......19 M3
East Hanningfield Essex......22 F3

East Hardwick Wakefd......59 L9
East Harling Norfk......44 G11
East Harlsey N York......65 Q7
East Harnham Wilts......8 G2
East Harptree BaNES......17 N5
East Hartburn S on T......65 Q4
East Harting W Susx......10 C6
East Hatch Wilts......8 D2
East Hatley Cambs......33 J6
East Hauxwell N York......65 L8
East Haven Angus......93 P8
East Heckington Lincs......42 H2
East Hedleyhope Dur......73 K11
East Helmsdale Highld......110 B10
East Hendred Oxon......19 M3
East Heslerton N York......67 K11
East Hoathly E Susx......11 Q6
East Holme Dorset......8 D9
Easthope Shrops......39 K3
Easthorpe Essex......34 F11
East Horrington Somset......17 N6
East Horsley Surrey......20 H11
East Howe Bmouth......8 F8
East Huntspill Somset......17 J7
East Ilsley W Berk......19 N5
Eastington Devon......15 M9
Eastington Gloucs......29 K7
Eastington Gloucs......30 F10
East Keal Lincs......53 L10
East Kennett Wilts......18 G7
East Keswick Leeds......59 J5
East Kilbride S Lans......85 K11
East Kirkby Lincs......53 K10
East Knighton Dorset......8 B9
East Knoyle Wilts......8 C2
East Lambrook Somset......17 L11
East Lancashire
    Crematorium Bury......57 P7
Eastlands D & G......70 D2
East Langdon Kent......13 P2
East Langton Leics......41 Q8
East Lavant W Susx......10 D8
East Lavington W Susx......10 F6
East Layton N York......65 L5
Eastleach Martin Gloucs......30 G12
Eastleach Turville
    Gloucs......30 G11
East Leake Notts......41 M3
Eastleigh Devon......15 H6
Eastleigh Hants......9 M4
East Lexham Norfk......44 E6
East Linton E Loth......87 L6
East Lockinge Oxon......19 M4
East London
    Crematorium Gt Lon......21 N6
East Lound N Linc......52 B4
East Lulworth Dorset......8 C10
East Lutton N York......60 G1
East Lydford Somset......17 N9
East Malling Kent......22 E11
East Marden W Susx......10 D7
East Markham Notts......51 Q6
East Martin Hants......8 F4
East Marton N York......58 B4
East Meon Hants......10 B5
East Mersea Essex......23 K1
East Midlands Airport
    Leics......41 K3
East Molesey Surrey......21 J9
East Morden Dorset......8 D8
East Morton C Brad......58 E6
East Morton D & G......78 E8
East Ness N York......66 F10
Eastney C Port......9 Q7
Eastnor Herefs......29 K2
East Norton Leics......42 B9
Eastoft N Linc......60 D10
East Ogwell Devon......5 Q6
Easton Cambs......32 G3
Easton Devon......5 P3
Easton Dorset......7 Q8
Easton Hants......9 N2
Easton Lincs......42 D5
Easton Norfk......45 J7
Easton Somset......17 M6
Easton Suffk......35 L5
Easton Wilts......18 D6
Easton Grey Wilts......18 C4
Easton-in-Gordano
    N Som......17 M2
East Maudit Nhants......32 C5
Easton-on-the-Hill Nhants......42 E8
East Norton Wilts......18 H8
East Orchard Dorset......8 C4
East Peckham Kent......12 D1
East Pennar Pembks......24 G8
East Pennard Somset......17 N8
East Perry Cambs......32 G4
East Portlemouth Devon......5 P11
East Prawle Devon......5 Q11
East Preston W Susx......10 H9
East Putford Devon......14 G8
East Quantoxhead
    Somset......16 F7
East Rainton Sundld......73 N10
East Ravendale NE Lin......52 H4
East Raynham Norfk......44 E5
Eastrea Cambs......43 J10
East Riding
    Crematorium E R Yk......60 H1
Eastriggs D & G......71 L3
East Rigton Leeds......59 J5
Eastrington E R Yk......60 D8
Eastrop Swindn......18 H3
East Rounton N York......65 Q6
East Rudham Norfk......44 D5
East Runton Norfk......45 K2
East Ruston Norfk......45 M5
Eastry Kent......23 P11
East Saltoun E Loth......87 J8
East Sheen Gt Lon......21 K8
East Shefford W Berk......19 L6
East Stockwith Lincs......52 B5
East Stoke Dorset......8 C9
East Stoke Notts......51 Q10
East Stour Dorset......8 B4
East Stourmouth Kent......23 N10
East Stowford Devon......15 L6
East Stratton Hants......19 P11
East Studdal Kent......23 P12
East Taphouse Cnwll......4 F7
East-the-Water Devon......14 H6
East Thirston Nthumb......73 L2
East Tilbury Thurr......22 D7
East Tisted Hants......10 B4
East Torrington Lincs......52 G6

East Tuddenham Norfk......44 H7
East Tytherley Hants......9 J3
East Tytherton Wilts......18 E6
East Village Devon......15 P10
Eastville Bristl......17 N2
Eastville Lincs......53 L11
East Walton Norfk......44 C6
East Week Devon......5 N2
East Wellow Hants......9 K4
East Wemyss Fife......86 G3
East Whitburn W Loth......85 Q9
Eastwick Herts......21 N1
East Wickham Gt Lon......21 P7
East Williamston Pembks......25 J7
East Winch Norfk......44 B6
East Winterslow Wilts......9 J1
East Wittering W Susx......10 C9
East Witton N York......65 L9
Eastwood Notts......51 L10
Eastwood Sthend......22 G6
East Woodburn Nthumb......72 G4
East Woodhay Hants......19 L8
East Worldham Hants......10 C3
East Wretham Norfk......44 F11
East Youlstone Devon......14 E8
Eathorpe Warks......31 K1
Eaton Ches E......49 Q3
Eaton Ches W......49 L3
Eaton Leics......42 B4
Eaton Norfk......45 K8
Eaton Oxon......31 K12
Eaton Shrops......39 J4
Eaton Bray C Beds......32 D11
Eaton Constantine
    Shrops......39 L2
Eaton Green C Beds......32 D11
Eaton Hastings Oxon......19 J2
Eaton Mascott Shrops......39 K2
Eaton Socon Cambs......32 G5
Eaton upon Tern Shrops......49 M10
Ebberston N York......67 K10
Ebbesborne Wake Wilts......8 E3
Ebbw Vale Blae G......27 N6
Ebchester Dur......73 K9
Ebford Devon......6 D5
Ebley Gloucs......29 L7
Ebnal Ches W......49 J6
Ebrington Gloucs......30 F6
Ecchinswell Hants......19 N8
Ecclaw Border......87 P8
Ecclefechan D & G......71 K1
Eccles Border......80 G6
Eccles Kent......22 E10
Eccles Salfd......57 P8
Ecclesall Sheff......50 H4
Eccles Crematorium Salfd......57 N8
Ecclesfield Sheff......51 J3
Eccleshall Staffs......49 P9
Eccleshill C Brad......58 F6
Ecclesmachan W Loth......86 C7
Eccles Road Norfk......44 G11
Eccleston Ches W......48 H3
Eccleston Lancs......57 K5
Eccleston St Hel......57 J9
Echt Abers......95 M2
Eckford Border......80 F8
Eckington Derbys......51 K5
Eckington Worcs......29 N1
Ecton Nhants......32 B4
Edale Derbys......50 E4
Eday Ork......111 h1
Eday Airport Ork......111 h1
Edburton W Susx......11 K7
Edderton Highld......107 L5
Eddleston Border......86 F11
Eddlewood S Lans......85 M11
Edenbridge Kent......11 N2
Edenfield Lancs......57 P5
Edenhall Cumb......71 Q8
Edenham Lincs......42 F6
Eden Park Gt Lon......21 M9
Eden Project Cnwll......3 M5
Edensor Derbys......50 G6
Edentaggart Ag & B......84 F4
Edenthorpe Donc......59 N11
Edern Gwynd......46 E4
Edgbaston Birm......40 D9
Edgcott Bucks......31 P9
Edgcott Somset......15 P4
Edge Gloucs......29 L6
Edgefield Norfk......44 H4
Edgefield Green Norfk......44 H4
Edgerton Kirk......58 F10
Edgeworth Gloucs......29 N7
Edgmond Wrekin......49 N10
Edgton Shrops......38 G5
Edgware Gt Lon......21 J5
Edgworth Bl w D......57 N5
Edinbane Highld......104 D11
Edinburgh C Edin......86 F7
Edinburgh Airport
    C Edin......86 D7
Edinburgh Castle
    C Edin......86 F7
Edinburgh Old & New
    Town C Edin......86 F7
Edinburgh Royal
    Botanic Gardens
    C Edin......86 F7
Edinburgh Zoo C Edin......86 E7
Edingale Staffs......40 G4
Edingham D & G......70 D3
Edingley Notts......51 P9
Edingthorpe Norfk......45 M4
Edingthorpe Green
    Norfk......45 M4
Edington Border......81 J3
Edington Nthumb......73 M5
Edington Somset......17 J8
Edington Wilts......18 D9
Edington Burtle Somset......17 K7
Edingworth Somset......17 J5
Edithmead Somset......17 J5
Edith Weston Rutlnd......42 D8
Edlesborough Bucks......32 D11
Edlingham Nthumb......81 M11
Edlington Lincs......52 H8
Edmondsham Dorset......8 F5
Edmondsley Dur......73 M10
Edmondthorpe Leics......42 C6
Edmonton Gt Lon......21 M5
Edmundbyers Dur......72 H10
Ednam Border......80 G6
Ednaston Derbys......50 H11
Edradynate P & K......92 D5
Edrom Border......80 H3

Edstaston Shrops......49 K8
Edstone Warwks......30 F2
Edwalton Notts......41 N1
Edwinstowe Notts......51 N7
Edworth C Beds......32 H8
Edwyn Ralph Herefs......39 M9
Edzell Angus......95 K8
Edzell Woods Abers......95 K7
Efail-fach Neath......26 H11
Efail Isaf Rhondd......27 M11
Efailnewydd Gwynd......46 F4
Efailwen Carmth......25 K4
Efenechtyd Denbgs......48 C4
Effgill D & G......79 L9
Effingham Surrey......21 H11
Efford Crematorium
    C Plym......5 L8
Egerton Bolton......57 N6
Egerton Kent......12 H1
Eggborough N York......59 N8
Eggbuckland C Plym......5 K8
Eggesford Devon......15 M9
Eggington C Beds......32 D10
Egginton Derbys......40 H2
Egglescliffe S on T......65 P5
Eggleston Dur......64 H3
Egham Surrey......20 G8
Egleton Rutlnd......42 C8
Eglingham Nthumb......81 M9
Egloshayle Cnwll......3 M2
Egloskerry Cnwll......4 G3
Eglwys-Brewis V Glam......55 L7
Eglwys Cross Wrexhm......49 J7
Eglwyswrw Pembks......25 K2
Egmanton Notts......51 Q7
Egremont Cumb......70 G12
Egremont Wirral......56 G9
Egton N York......66 H6
Egton Bridge N York......66 H6
Egypt Bucks......20 F6
Eigg Highld......96 F11
Eight Ash Green Essex......34 F10
Eilanreach Highld......97 L6
Eilean Donan Castle
    Highld......97 M5
Elan Valley Powys......37 Q3
Elan Village Powys......37 Q7
Elberton S Glos......28 H10
Elburton C Plym......5 L9
Elcombe Swindn......18 G5
Eldersfield Worcs......29 L3
Elderslie Rens......84 H9
Eldon Dur......65 M2
Elfhill Abers......95 N5
Elford Staffs......40 F5
Elgin Moray......101 J3
Elgol Highld......96 G6
Elham Kent......13 M2
Elie Fife......87 K3
Elim IoA......54 E5
Eling Hants......9 L5
Elkesley Notts......51 P6
Elkstone Gloucs......29 N6
Ella Abers......102 E4
Ellacombe Torbay......6 C9
Elland Calder......58 E9
Ellary Ag & B......83 L7
Ellastone Staffs......50 E11
Ellel Lancs......63 J10
Ellemford Border......87 N9
Ellenabeich Ag & B......89 P11
Ellenhall Staffs......49 Q9
Ellen's Green Surrey......10 H3
Ellerbeck N York......66 B8
Ellerby N York......66 H5
Ellerdine Heath Wrekin......49 L10
Elleric Ag & B......90 E6
Ellerker E R Yk......60 F8
Ellerton E R Yk......60 C6
Ellerton N York......65 M7
Ellesborough Bucks......20 D3
Ellesmere Shrops......48 H8
Ellesmere Port Ches W......56 H12
Ellingham Hants......8 G6
Ellingham Norfk......45 N10
Ellingham Nthumb......81 N8
Ellingstring N York......65 L10
Ellington Cambs......32 G3
Ellington Nthumb......73 M3
Elliots Green Somset......18 B10
Ellisfield Hants......19 Q10
Ellishader Highld......104 G8
Ellistown Leics......41 K5
Ellon Abers......103 K8
Ellonby Cumb......71 N8
Elloughton E R Yk......60 G8
Ellwood Gloucs......28 G7
Elm Cambs......43 M8
Elmbridge Worcs......30 B1
Elmdon Essex......33 M8
Elmdon Solhll......40 F10
Elmers End Gt Lon......21 M9
Elmer's Green Lancs......57 J7
Elmesthorpe Leics......41 L8
Elmhurst Staffs......40 E5
Elmley Castle Worcs......29 N1
Elmley Lovett Worcs......39 Q8
Elmore Gloucs......29 K6
Elmore Back Gloucs......29 K5
Elm Park Gt Lon......21 Q6
Elmsett Suffk......34 H7
Elmstead Market
    Essex......34 H10
Elmsted Kent......13 L2
Elmstone Kent......23 N10
Elmstone Hardwicke
    Gloucs......29 M4
Elmswell E R Yk......60 G3
Elmswell Suffk......34 G4
Elmton Derbys......51 L6
Elphin Highld......108 E12
Elphinstone E Loth......86 H8
Elrick Abers......95 N1
Elrig D & G......69 J9
Elrington Nthumb......72 F8
Elsdon Nthumb......72 H3
Elsecar Barns......51 J2
Elsenham Essex......33 N10
Elsfield Oxon......31 M11
Elsham N Linc......60 H10
Elsing Norfk......44 H6
Elslack N York......58 B4
Elson Hants......9 P7
Elsrickle S Lans......86 C12
Elstead Surrey......10 E2
Elsted W Susx......10 D6
Elsted Lincs......42 F6
Elsthorpe Lincs......42 F6
Elston Notts......51 Q10
Elstow Bed......32 F7

Elstree Herts......21 J4
Elstronwick E R Yk......61 L7
Elswick Lancs......56 H2
Elswick N u Ty......73 M7
Elsworth Cambs......33 K4
Elterwater Cumb......62 G2
Eltham Gt Lon......21 N8
Eltham Crematorium
   Gt Lon......21 N8
Eltisley Cambs......33 J5
Elton Cambs......42 F10
Elton Ches W......49 J1
Elton Derbys......50 G8
Elton Herefs......39 J7
Elton Notts......51 Q11
Elton S on T......65 P4
Eltringham Nthumb......73 J9
Elvanfoot S Lans......78 F5
Elvaston Derbys......41 K2
Elveden Suff......34 D2
Elvetham Heath Hants......20 C11
Elvingston E Loth......87 J7
Elvington E York......60 C5
Elvington Kent......23 P12
Elwick Hartpl......66 C2
Elworth Ches E......49 N3
Elworthy Somset......16 E8
Ely Cambs......33 N11
Ely Cardif......16 F2
Emberton M Keyn......32 C6
Embleton Cumb......71 J9
Embleton Nthumb......81 P9
Embo Highld......107 N6
Emborough Somset......17 N6
Embo Street Highld......107 N4
Embsay N York......58 D4
Emery Down Hants......9 K6
Emley Kirk......58 G10
Emmington Oxon......20 C3
Emneth Norfk......43 M8
Emneth Hungate Norfk......43 N8
Empingham Rutlnd......42 D8
Empshott Hants......10 C4
Emstrey Crematorium
   Shrops......49 K12
Emsworth Hants......10 C8
Enborne W Berk......19 M7
Enborne Row W Berk......19 M7
Enderby Leics......41 M7
Endmoor Cumb......63 K5
Endon Staffs......50 B9
Endon Bank Staffs......50 B9
Enfield Gt Lon......21 M4
Enfield Crematorium
   Gt Lon......21 M4
Enfield Lock Gt Lon......21 M4
Enfield Wash Gt Lon......21 M4
Enford Wilts......18 G9
Engine Common S Glos......29 J11
Englefield W Berk......19 Q6
Englefield Green Surrey......20 F8
English Bicknor Gloucs......28 G5
Englishcombe BaNES......17 Q4
English Frankton Shrops......49 J9
Enham-Alamein Hants......19 L10
Enmore Somset......16 H8
Enmore Green Dorset......8 C3
Ennerdale Bridge
   Cumb......70 H11
Enochdhu P & K......92 F3
Ensay Ag & B......88 H6
Ensbury Bmouth......8 F8
Ensdon Shrops......48 H11
Enstone Oxon......31 J8
Enterkinfoot D & G......78 E7
Enville Staffs......39 P5
Eolaigearraidh W Isls......111 a6
Epney Gloucs......29 K6
Epperstone Notts......51 P10
Epping Essex......21 P3
Epping Green Essex......21 N3
Epping Upland Essex......21 N3
Eppleby N York......65 L5
Epsom Surrey......21 K10
Epwell Oxon......31 J6
Epworth N Linc......52 A3
Erbistock Wrexhm......48 G7
Erdington Birm......40 E8
Eridge Green E Susx......12 B3
Erines Ag & B......83 N7
Eriska Ag & B......90 C7
Eriskay W Isls......111 b6
Eriswell Suffk......34 C2
Erith Gt Lon......21 P7
Erlestoke Wilts......18 E9
Ermington Devon......5 M9
Erpingham Norfk......45 K4
Errogie Highld......98 H5
Errol P & K......93 J10
Erskine Rens......84 H8
Ervie D & G......68 D5
Erwarton Suffk......35 K9
Erwood Powys......38 C12
Eryholme N York......65 N6
Eryrys Denbgs......48 E4
Escomb Dur......65 L2
Escrick N York......59 N5
Esgairgeiliog Powys......47 M9
Esh Dur......73 L11
Esher Surrey......21 J9
Eshott Nthumb......73 L2
Esh Winning Dur......73 L11
Eskadale Highld......98 F2
Eskbank Mdloth......86 G8
Eskdale Green Cumb......62 D3
Eskdalemuir D & G......79 L11
Esprick Lancs......56 H2
Essendine Rutlnd......42 E7
Essendon Herts......21 L2
Essich Highld......99 G1
Essington Staffs......40 C6
Esslemont Abers......103 J8
Eston R & Cl......66 D4
Etal Nthumb......81 K6
Etchilhampton Wilts......18 F8
Etchingham E Susx......12 E5
Etchinghill Kent......13 M3
Etchinghill Staffs......40 D4
Eton W & M......20 F7
Eton Wick W & M......20 F7
Etruria C Stke......49 Q4
Etteridge Highld......99 K9
Ettersgill Dur......64 F2
Ettiley Heath Ches E......49 N3
Ettingshall Wolves......40 B8
Ettington Warwks......30 H4
Etton C Pete......42 G8

Etton E R Yk......60 G5
Ettrick Border......79 L6
Ettrickbridge Border......79 N4
Ettrickhill Border......79 L6
Etwall Derbys......40 H2
Euston Suffk......34 E2
Euxton Lancs......57 K5
Evanton Highld......107 K8
Evedon Lincs......42 F1
Evelix Highld......107 M4
Evenjobb Powys......38 F9
Evenley Nhants......31 N7
Evenlode Gloucs......30 G8
Evenwood Dur......65 K3
Evercreech Somset......17 N8
Everingham E R Yk......60 D6
Everleigh Wilts......18 H9
Eversholt C Beds......32 E9
Evershot Dorset......7 N2
Eversley Hants......20 C10
Eversley Cross Hants......20 C10
Everthorpe E R Yk......60 F7
Everton C Beds......32 H6
Everton Hants......9 K8
Everton Lpool......56 G9
Everton Notts......51 P3
Evertown D & G......71 M1
Evesbatch Herefs......39 M11
Evesham Worcs......30 D5
Evington C Leic......41 N6
Ewden Village Sheff......50 H2
Ewell Surrey......21 K10
Ewell Minnis Kent......13 N2
Ewelme Oxon......19 Q3
Ewen Gloucs......18 E2
Ewenny V Glam......27 J12
Ewerby Lincs......42 G1
Ewhurst Surrey......10 H3
Ewhurst Green E Susx......12 F5
Ewhurst Green Surrey......10 H3
Ewloe Flints......48 F3
Eworthy Devon......5 J2
Ewshot Hants......20 D11
Ewyas Harold Herefs......28 D3
Exbourne Devon......15 K10
Exbury Hants......9 M7
Exebridge Somset......16 C10
Exelby N York......65 N9
Exeter Devon......6 C4
Exeter Airport Devon......6 D4
Exeter & Devon
   Crematorium Devon......6 C5
Exeter Services Devon......6 C4
Exford Somset......15 P5
Exfordsgreen Shrops......39 J2
Exhall Warwks......30 E3
Exhall Warwks......41 J9
Exlade Street Oxon......19 Q4
Exminster Devon......6 C5
Exmoor National Park......15 P4
Exmouth Devon......6 D6
Exning Suffk......33 P4
Exton Devon......6 D5
Exton Hants......9 Q4
Exton Rutlnd......42 D7
Exton Somset......16 C9
Exwick Devon......6 B4
Eyam Derbys......50 G5
Eydon Nhants......31 M4
Eye C Pete......42 H9
Eye Herefs......39 J8
Eye Suffk......35 J3
Eyemouth Border......81 K2
Eyeworth C Beds......33 J7
Eyhorne Street Kent......22 G11
Eyke Suffk......35 M6
Eynesbury Cambs......32 H5
Eynsford Kent......22 B9
Eynsham Oxon......31 K11
Eype Dorset......7 L5
Eyre Highld......104 F10
Eythorne Kent......23 P12
Eyton Herefs......39 J9
Eyton Shrops......48 H10
Eyton on Severn Shrops......39 J2
Eyton upon the Weald
   Moors Wrekin......49 M11

F

Faccombe Hants......19 L8
Faceby N York......66 C7
Fachwen Powys......48 B11
Faddiley Ches E......49 L5
Fadmoor N York......66 F9
Faerdre Swans......26 F8
Faifley W Duns......84 H8
Failand N Som......17 M2
Failford S Ayrs......76 H6
Failsworth Oldham......50 B1
Fairbourne Gwynd......47 K8
Fairburn N York......59 L8
Fairfield Derbys......50 E6
Fairfield Worcs......40 C11
Fairford Gloucs......18 H1
Fairgirth D & G......70 E4
Fair Green Norfk......43 Q6
Fairhaven Lancs......56 G4
Fair Isle Shet......111 m5
Fairlands Surrey......20 F11
Fairlie N Ayrs......84 D11
Fairlight E Susx......12 G7
Fairmile Devon......6 E4
Fairmile Surrey......20 H10
Fairnilee Border......79 P3
Fair Oak Hants......9 N4
Fair Oak Green Hants......19 Q8
Fairseat Kent......22 D10
Fairstead Essex......34 C12
Fairstead Norfk......43 Q6
Fairwarp E Susx......11 P5
Fairwater Cardif......27 N12
Fairy Cross Devon......14 G7
Fakenham Norfk......44 F5
Fakenham Magna Suffk......34 E2
Fala Mdloth......87 J9
Fala Dam Mdloth......87 J9
Faldingworth Lincs......52 F6
Faldouet Jersey......7 c2
Falfield S Glos......29 J9
Falkenham Suffk......35 L8
Falkirk Falk......85 P7
Falkirk Crematorium Falk......85 P7
Falkirk Wheel Falk......85 P7

Falkland Fife......86 F2
Fallburn S Lans......78 F2
Fallin Stirlg......85 N5
Fallodon Nthumb......81 P9
Fallowfield Manch......57 Q9
Fallowfield Nthumb......72 G7
Falls of Blarghour Ag & B......83 Q1
Falmer E Susx......11 M8
Falmouth Cnwll......3 J8
Falnash Border......79 N7
Falnash Border......79 M9
Falsgrave N York......67 M9
Falstone Nthumb......72 D4
Fanagmore Highld......108 D6
Fancott C Beds......32 E10
Fanellan Highld......98 G1
Fangdale Beck N York......66 D8
Fangfoss E R Yk......60 D4
Fanmore Ag & B......89 J7
Fannich Lodge Highld......106 D3
Fans Border......80 E6
Far Bletchley M Keyn......32 C9
Farcet Cambs......42 H10
Far Cotton Nhants......31 Q3
Fareham Hants......9 P6
Far End Cumb......62 F3
Farewell Staffs......40 E5
Faringdon Oxon......19 K2
Farington Lancs......57 K4
Farlam Cumb......71 Q4
Farleigh N Som......17 M3
Farleigh Surrey......21 M10
Farleigh Hungerford
   Somset......18 B8
Farleigh Wallop Hants......19 Q10
Farlesthorpe Lincs......53 M8
Farleton Cumb......63 K6
Farleton Lancs......63 L8
Farley Staffs......50 E11
Farley Wilts......9 J2
Farley Green Surrey......10 G2
Farley Hill Wokham......20 C9
Farleys End Gloucs......29 K6
Farlington C Port......10 B8
Farlington N York......59 N1
Farlow Shrops......39 L6
Farmborough BaNES......17 P4
Farmcote Gloucs......30 D8
Farmers Carmth......37 K10
Farmington Gloucs......30 F10
Farmoor Oxon......31 L11
Far Moor Wigan......57 K7
Farmtown Moray......101 P5
Farnborough Gt Lon......21 N9
Farnborough Hants......20 E11
Farnborough W Berk......19 M4
Farnborough Warwks......31 K4
Farnborough Park Hants......20 E11
Farnborough Street
   Hants......20 E11
Farncombe Surrey......10 F2
Farndish Bed......32 D4
Farndon Ches W......48 H5
Farndon Notts......51 Q9
Farne Islands Nthumb......81 P6
Farnell Angus......93 Q5
Farnham Dorset......8 D4
Farnham Essex......33 M10
Farnham N York......59 J3
Farnham Suffk......35 M5
Farnham Surrey......10 D1
Farnham Common Bucks......20 F6
Farnham Royal Bucks......20 F6
Farningham Kent......22 B9
Farnley Leeds......58 G7
Farnley N York......58 G5
Farnley Tyas Kirk......58 F10
Farnsfield Notts......51 P9
Farnworth Bolton......57 N7
Farnworth Halton......57 K10
Far Oakridge Gloucs......29 N7
Farr Highld......99 K3
Farr Highld......99 M8
Farr Highld......109 M3
Farraline Highld......98 H5
Farringdon Devon......6 D5
Farrington Gurney BaNES......17 P5
Far Sawrey Cumb......62 H3
Farthing Nhants......31 M6
Farthingstone Nhants......31 N3
Fartown Kirk......57 F9
Fartown Leeds......58 G7
Fasnacloich Ag & B......90 D6
Fasnakyle Highld......98 D3
Fassfern Highld......90 D1
Fatfield Sundld......73 N9
Fauldhouse W Loth......85 Q10
Faulkbourne Essex......34 D12
Faulkland Somset......17 Q5
Fauls Shrops......49 L8
Faversham Kent......23 K10
Fawdington N York......66 B11
Fawdon N u Ty......73 M7
Fawkham Green Kent......22 C9
Fawler Oxon......31 J10
Fawley Bucks......20 C6
Fawley Hants......9 M6
Fawley W Berk......19 L5
Faxfleet E R Yk......60 E8
Faygate W Susx......11 K4
Fazakerley Lpool......56 G9
Fazeley Staffs......40 G7
Fearby N York......65 L10
Fearn Highld......107 N7
Fearnan P & K......91 Q7
Fearnbeg Highld......105 L9
Fearnhead Warrtn......57 L9
Fearnmore Highld......105 K9
Fearnoch Ag & B......83 P7
Featherstone Staffs......40 C6
Featherstone Wakefd......59 K9
Feckenham Worcs......30 D2
Feering Essex......34 E11
Feetham N York......64 H7
Felbridge Surrey......11 M3
Felbrigg Norfk......45 K3
Felcourt Surrey......11 M2
Felden Herts......20 H2
Felindre Carmth......25 N2
Felindre Carmth......26 D5
Felindre Carmth......26 D7
Felindre Powys......38 E5
Felindre Swans......26 E8
Felindre Farchog Pembks......24 G3
Felingwm Isaf Carmth......26 C4
Felingwm Uchaf Carmth......26 C4
Felixkirk N York......66 C10
Felixstowe Suffk......35 L9
Felixstowe Ferry Suffk......35 M8
Felling Gatesd......73 M8
Felmersham Bed......32 E5
Felmingham Norfk......45 L5

Felpham W Susx......10 F9
Felsham Suffk......34 F5
Felsted Essex......34 B11
Feltham Gt Lon......20 H8
Felthamhill Surrey......20 H8
Felthorpe Norfk......45 J6
Felton Herefs......39 L11
Felton N Som......17 M3
Felton Nthumb......73 L2
Felton Butler Shrops......48 H11
Feltwell Norfk......44 B11
Fence Lancs......57 P2
Fence Rothm......51 K4
Fencott Oxon......31 M10
Fen Ditton Cambs......33 M5
Fen Drayton Cambs......33 K5
Feniscowles Bl w D......57 M4
Feniton Devon......6 F3
Fenland Crematorium
   Cambs......43 L10
Fenn Green Shrops......39 P5
Fenn Street Medway......22 F8
Fenny Bentley Derbys......50 F10
Fenny Bridges Devon......6 F3
Fenny Compton Warwks......31 K4
Fenny Drayton Leics......41 K3
Fenstanton Cambs......33 K3
Fen Street Norfk......44 G10
Fenton C Stke......50 B11
Fenton Cambs......33 K2
Fenton Cumb......71 Q4
Fenton Lincs......52 B8
Fenton Lincs......52 C12
Fenton Lincs......52 B6
Fenton Nthumb......81 K7
Fenton Barns E Loth......87 K6
Fenwick Donc......59 N10
Fenwick E Ayrs......76 H3
Fenwick Nthumb......73 J6
Fenwick Nthumb......81 M6
Feock Cnwll......3 J7
Feolin Ferry Ag & B......82 F8
Fergushill N Ayrs......76 F3
Feriniquarrie Highld......104 B11
Fern Angus......94 H9
Ferndale Rhondd......27 L9
Ferndown Dorset......8 F7
Ferness Highld......100 E6
Fernham Oxon......19 K3
Fernhill Heath Worcs......39 Q9
Fernhurst W Susx......10 E4
Fernie Fife......93 K11
Ferniegair S Lans......85 M11
Fernilea Highld......96 D3
Fernilee Derbys......50 D5
Fernwood Notts......52 B12
Ferrensby N York......59 J3
Ferrindonald Highld......97 J7
Ferring W Susx......10 H9
Ferrybridge Services
   Wakefd......59 L9
Ferryden Angus......95 M9
Ferryhill Dur......65 M2
Ferry Point Highld......107 M5
Ferryside Carmth......25 N6
Ferrytown Highld......107 M5
Fersfield Norfk......44 H12
Fersit Highld......91 K2
Feshiebridge Highld......99 M8
Fetcham Surrey......21 J11
Fetlar Shet......111 m2
Fetterangus Abers......103 K5
Fettercairn Abers......95 K7
Fewston N York......58 G4
Ffairfach Carmth......26 E5
Ffair Rhos Cerdgn......37 M7
Ffestiniog Gwynd......47 L3
Ffestiniog Railway Gwynd......47 K3
Fforest Carmth......26 D7
Fforest Fach Swans......26 E9
Ffostrasol Cerdgn......36 F10
Ffrith Flints......48 F3
Ffynnongroyw Flints......56 D11
Fiag Lodge Highld......108 H9
Fickleshole Surrey......21 M10
Fiddington Somset......16 G7
Fiddleford Dorset......8 B5
Fiddlers Green Cnwll......3 J5
Field Staffs......40 D2
Field Dalling Norfk......44 G3
Field Head Leics......41 L5
Fifehead Magdalen
   Dorset......8 B3
Fifehead Neville Dorset......8 B5
Fifehead St Quintin
   Dorset......8 B5
Fife Keith Moray......101 M5
Fifield Oxon......30 G9
Fifield W & M......20 E7
Figheldean Wilts......18 H10
Filby Norfk......45 P7
Filey N York......67 N10
Filgrave M Keyn......32 C7
Filkins Oxon......30 G12
Filleigh Devon......15 L6
Fillingham Lincs......52 D6
Fillongley Warwks......40 H9
Filton S Glos......28 H11
Fimber E R Yk......60 F3
Finavon Angus......93 N4
Fincham Norfk......44 B8
Finchampstead Wokham......20 C10
Fincharn Ag & B......83 N3
Finchdean Hants......10 B7
Finchingfield Essex......34 B9
Finchley Gt Lon......21 L5
Findern Derbys......40 H2
Findhorn Moray......100 H4
Findhorn Bridge Highld......99 M4
Findo Gask P & K......92 E10
Findon Abers......95 Q3
Findon W Susx......10 H8
Findon Mains Highld......107 K7
Findrack House Abers......95 K2
Finedon Nhants......32 D3
Fingask P & K......92 H10
Fingest Bucks......20 C5
Finghall N York......65 L9
Fingland D & G......77 M7
Fingringhoe Essex......34 G11
Finlarig Stirlg......91 N8
Finmere Oxon......31 N7
Finnart P & K......91 M5
Finningham Suffk......34 H3

Finningley Donc......51 P2
Finsbay W Isls......111 c4
Finstall Worcs......40 C12
Finsthwaite Cumb......62 G5
Finstock Oxon......31 J10
Finstown Ork......111 h2
Fintry Abers......102 G4
Fintry Stirlg......85 K5
Finzean Abers......95 K4
Fionnphort Ag & B......88 G10
Fionnsbhagh W Isls......111 c4
Firbank Cumb......63 L4
Firbeck Rothm......51 M3
Firby N York......60 C2
Firby N York......65 M9
Firle E Susx......11 P8
Firsby Lincs......53 M10
Fir Tree Dur......65 K1
Fishbourne IoW......9 P8
Fishbourne W Susx......10 D8
Fishburn Dur......65 P2
Fishcross Clacks......85 P4
Fisherford Abers......102 E8
Fisherrow E Loth......86 G7
Fisher's Pond Hants......9 N4
Fisherton Highld......107 M11
Fisherton S Ayrs......76 E7
Fisherton de la Mere
   Wilts......18 E11
Fishguard Pembks......24 G2
Fishlake Donc......59 P10
Fishnish Pier Ag & B......89 N7
Fishponds Brist......17 P2
Fishtoft Lincs......43 L2
Fishtoft Drove Lincs......43 K1
Fiskavaig Highld......96 D3
Fiskerton Lincs......52 F8
Fiskerton Notts......51 Q9
Fittleton Wilts......18 G10
Fittleworth W Susx......10 G6
Fitz Shrops......49 J11
Fitzhead Somset......16 F9
Fitzwilliam Wakefd......59 K10
Five Ash Down E Susx......11 P5
Five Ashes E Susx......12 B5
Fivehead Somset......17 J10
Fivelanes Cnwll......4 F4
Five Oak Green Kent......12 D2
Five Oaks Jersey......7 c2
Five Oaks W Susx......10 H4
Five Roads Carmth......26 C7
Flackwell Heath Bucks......20 E5
Fladbury Worcs......30 C5
Fladdabister Shet......111 k4
Flagg Derbys......50 F7
Flamborough E R Yk......67 Q12
Flamborough Head
   E R Yk......67 Q12
Flamingo Land Theme
   Park N York......66 H10
Flamstead Herts......20 H1
Flansham W Susx......10 F9
Flanshaw Wakefd......58 H9
Flasby N York......58 C3
Flash Staffs......50 D7
Flashader Highld......104 D10
Flaunden Herts......20 G4
Flawborough Notts......42 B2
Flawith N York......59 L2
Flax Bourton N Som......17 M3
Flaxby N York......59 K3
Flaxley Gloucs......29 J6
Flaxpool Somset......16 F8
Flaxton N York......59 P2
Fleckney Leics......41 P8
Flecknoe Warwks......31 L2
Fledborough Notts......52 B8
Fleet Dorset......7 P6
Fleet Hants......20 D11
Fleet Lincs......43 L5
Fleet Hargate Lincs......43 L5
Fleet Services Hants......20 C11
Fleetwood Lancs......62 G11
Flemingston V Glam......16 D3
Flemington S Lans......85 L10
Flempton Suffk......34 D3
Fletchertown Cumb......71 K7
Fletching E Susx......11 N5
Flexbury Cnwll......14 D10
Flexford Surrey......20 E12
Flimby Cumb......70 G8
Flimwell E Susx......12 E4
Flint Flints......48 E2
Flintham Notts......51 Q10
Flinton E R Yk......61 L7
Flitcham Norfk......44 C5
Flitton C Beds......32 F9
Flitwick C Beds......32 E9
Flixborough N Linc......60 E10
Flixborough Stather
   N Linc......60 E10
Flixton N York......67 M10
Flixton Suffk......45 M11
Flixton Traffd......57 N9
Flockton Kirk......58 G10
Flockton Green Kirk......58 G10
Flodigarry Highld......104 F7
Flookburgh Cumb......62 G6
Flordon Norfk......45 K10
Flore Nhants......31 N3
Flowton Suffk......34 H7
Flushing Cnwll......3 J8
Fluxton Devon......6 E4
Flyford Flavell Worcs......30 C3
Fobbing Thurr......22 E6
Fochabers Moray......101 L4
Fochriw Caerph......27 M7
Fockerby N Linc......60 E9
Foddington Somset......17 N9
Foel Powys......48 B12
Foggathorpe E R Yk......60 D6
Fogo Border......80 G5
Fogwatt Moray......101 K4
Foindle Highld......108 D6
Folda Angus......94 D7
Fole Staffs......50 D12
Foleshill Covtry......41 J10
Folke Dorset......17 P12
Folkestone Kent......13 N3
Folkingham Lincs......42 F4
Folkington E Susx......12 C8
Folksworth Cambs......42 G11
Folkton N York......67 M10
Folla Rule Abers......102 F8
Follifoot N York......59 J4
Folly Gate Devon......15 K11
Fonthill Bishop Wilts......8 D2

Fonthill Gifford Wilts....8 D2
Fontmell Magna Dorset....8 C4
Fontmell Parva Dorset....8 C4
Fontwell W Susx....10 F8
Foolow Derbys....50 F5
Forbestown Abers....101 M11
Forcett N York....65 L5
Ford Ag & B....83 N3
Ford Bucks....31 Q11
Ford Derbys....51 K5
Ford Devon....14 G7
Ford Gloucs....30 E8
Ford Nthumb....81 K6
Ford Somset....16 E9
Ford Staffs....50 E9
Ford W Susx....10 F8
Ford Wilts....18 C6
Fordcombe Kent....11 Q3
Fordell Fife....86 D5
Forden Powys....38 E2
Ford End Essex....34 B12
Forder Green Devon....5 Q6
Fordham Cambs....33 Q3
Fordham Essex....34 F10
Fordham Norfk....43 P9
Fordingbridge Hants....8 G5
Fordon E R Yk....67 M11
Fordoun Abers....95 M6
Fordstreet Essex....34 F10
Ford Street Somset....16 F11
Fordwich Kent....23 M10
Fordyce Abers....102 D3
Forebridge Staffs....40 B3
Forest Guern....6 b2
Forest Chapel Ches E....50 C6
Forest Gate Gt Lon....21 N6
Forest Green Surrey....10 H2
Forest Hall N Tyne....73 M6
Forest Hill Gt Lon....21 M8
Forest Hill Oxon....31 N11
Forest Lane Head N York....59 J3
Forest Mill Clacks....85 Q4
Forest of Dean Gloucs....28 H6
Forest Park Crematorium Gt Lon....21 P5
Forest Row E Susx....11 N3
Forestside W Susx....10 C7
Forfar Angus....93 M5
Forgandenny P & K....92 G11
Forge Hammer Torfn....28 C9
Forgie Moray....101 M4
Forgieside Moray....101 M5
Forgue Abers....102 D6
Formby Sefton....56 F7
Forncett End Norfk....45 J10
Forncett St Mary Norfk....45 J10
Forncett St Peter Norfk....45 J10
Fornham All Saints Suffk....34 D4
Fornham St Martin Suffk....34 E4
Fornighty Highld....100 H5
Forres Moray....100 H4
Forsbrook Staffs....50 C11
Forse Highld....110 E8
Forsinard Highld....109 Q7
Fort Augustus Highld....98 E7
Forteviot P & K....92 F11
Forth S Lans....85 Q11
Forthampton Gloucs....29 M3
Fortingall P & K....91 Q6
Forton Hants....19 M11
Forton Lancs....63 J11
Forton Shrops....48 H11
Forton Somset....7 J2
Forton Staffs....49 N10
Fortrie Abers....102 E6
Fortrose Highld....107 M10
Fortuneswell Dorset....7 P7
Fort William Highld....90 F2
Forty Hill Gt Lon....21 M4
Fosbury Wilts....19 K8
Foscot Oxon....30 G9
Fosdyke Lincs....43 K4
Foss P & K....92 B4
Fossebridge Gloucs....30 E11
Foster Street Essex....21 P2
Foston Derbys....40 F2
Foston Leics....41 N8
Foston Lincs....42 C2
Foston N York....59 P2
Foston on the Wolds E R Yk....61 J3
Fotherby Lincs....53 K5
Fotheringhay Nhants....42 F10
Foulden Border....81 K3
Foulden Norfk....44 C9
Foul End Warwks....40 G8
Foulness Island Essex....23 J5
Foulon Vale Crematorium Guern....6 b2
Foulridge Lancs....58 B6
Foulsham Norfk....44 G6
Fountainhall Border....87 J11
Four Ashes Suffk....34 G3
Four Crosses Powys....48 F10
Four Elms Kent....11 P1
Four Forks Somset....16 G8
Four Gotes Cambs....43 M6
Four Lanes Cnwll....2 G7
Four Marks Hants....9 R1
Four Mile Bridge IoA....54 C6
Four Oaks Solhll....40 G10
Fourpenny Highld....107 N4
Four Roads Carmth....25 Q7
Fourstones Nthumb....72 F7
Four Throws Kent....12 F4
Fovant Wilts....8 E3
Foveran Abers....103 K9
Fowey Cnwll....4 D9
Fowlhall Kent....12 E2
Fowlis Angus....93 K8
Fowlis Wester P & K....92 D10
Fowlmere Cambs....33 L7
Fownhope Herefs....28 G3
Foxbar Rens....84 H10
Foxcote Somset....17 Q5
Foxdale IoM....56 b5
Foxearth Essex....34 D7
Foxfield Cumb....62 E5
Foxhole Cnwll....3 L5
Foxholes N York....67 L11
Foxley Norfk....44 H6
Foxt Staffs....50 D10
Foxton Cambs....33 L7
Foxton Leics....41 P9
Foxton N York....65 Q8
Foxwood Shrops....39 L6
Foy Herefs....28 H3

Foyers Highld....98 G5
Foynesfield Highld....100 D5
Fraddon Cnwll....3 K4
Fradley Staffs....40 F5
Fradswell Staffs....40 C2
Fraisthorpe E R Yk....61 K2
Framfield E Susx....11 P6
Framingham Earl Norfk....45 L9
Framingham Pigot Norfk....45 L9
Framlingham Suffk....35 L4
Frampton Dorset....7 P4
Frampton Lincs....43 K3
Frampton Cotterell S Glos....29 J11
Frampton Mansell Gloucs....29 N8
Frampton-on-Severn Gloucs....29 K7
Framsden Suffk....35 K5
Framwellgate Moor Dur....73 M11
Franche Worcs....39 P6
Frankby Wirral....56 E10
Frankley Worcs....40 C10
Frankley Services Worcs....40 C10
Frankton Warwks....41 K12
Frant E Susx....12 C3
Fraserburgh Abers....103 K2
Frating Essex....34 H11
Frating Green Essex....34 H11
Fratton C Port....9 Q7
Freathy Cnwll....5 J9
Freckenham Suffk....33 Q3
Freckleton Lancs....56 H3
Freeby Leics....42 B6
Freefolk Hants....19 N10
Freehay Staffs....40 C12
Freeland Oxon....31 K10
Freethorpe Norfk....45 N8
Freethorpe Common Norfk....45 N8
Freiston Lincs....43 L2
Fremington Devon....15 J6
Fremington N York....65 J7
Frenchay S Glos....28 H12
French Cnwll....92 C4
Frensham Surrey....10 D2
Freshfield Sefton....56 F7
Freshford Wilts....18 B3
Freshwater IoW....9 K9
Fressingfield Suffk....35 L2
Freston Suffk....35 J8
Freswick Highld....110 G3
Fretherne Gloucs....29 K6
Frettenham Norfk....45 L6
Freuchie Fife....86 F2
Freystrop Pembks....24 G6
Friar Park Sandw....40 D8
Friday Bridge Cambs....43 M8
Friday Street Suffk....35 N5
Fridaythorpe E R Yk....60 E3
Friern Barnet Gt Lon....21 L5
Friesthorpe Lincs....52 F6
Frieston Lincs....42 D1
Frieth Bucks....20 C5
Frilford Oxon....19 M2
Frilsham W Berk....19 P6
Frimley Surrey....20 E10
Frindsbury Medway....22 E9
Fring Norfk....44 C3
Fringford Oxon....31 N8
Frinsted Kent....22 H11
Frinton-on-Sea Essex....35 K11
Friockheim Angus....93 Q6
Frisby on the Wreake Leics....41 P4
Friskney Lincs....53 M11
Friston E Susx....12 B9
Friston Suffk....35 N5
Fritchley Derbys....51 J9
Fritham Hants....9 J5
Frithelstock Devon....14 H8
Frithelstock Stone Devon....14 H8
Frithville Lincs....53 K12
Frittenden Kent....12 F2
Frittiscombe Devon....5 Q10
Fritton Norfk....45 K10
Fritton Norfk....45 P9
Fritwell Oxon....31 M8
Frizinghall C Brad....58 F7
Frizington Cumb....70 G11
Frocester Gloucs....29 K8
Frodesley Shrops....39 K2
Frodsham Ches W....57 K12
Frogden Border....80 G8
Frog End Cambs....33 L7
Froggatt Derbys....50 G5
Froghall Staffs....50 D10
Frogmore Devon....5 P10
Frognall Lincs....42 G7
Frog Pool Worcs....39 P8
Frogwell Cnwll....4 H6
Frolesworth Leics....41 L8
Frome Somset....18 B10
Frome St Quintin Dorset....7 N3
Fromes Hill Herefs....39 M11
Froncysyllte Denbgs....48 F7
Fron-goch Gwynd....47 P4
Fron Isaf Wrexhm....48 F7
Frosterley Dur....72 H12
Froxfield Wilts....19 K7
Froxfield Green Hants....10 B5
Fryern Hill Hants....9 M4
Fryerning Essex....22 D4
Fuinary Highld....89 M7
Fulbeck Lincs....52 D12
Fulbourn Cambs....33 N5
Fulbrook Oxon....30 H10
Fulflood Hants....9 M2
Fulford C York....59 N4
Fulford Somset....16 G9
Fulford Staffs....50 C12
Fulham Gt Lon....21 K8
Fulking W Susx....11 K7
Fullarton N Ayrs....76 F4
Fuller Street Essex....34 C12
Fullerton Hants....19 L11
Fulletby Lincs....53 J8
Fullready Warwks....30 H5
Full Sutton E R Yk....60 D3
Fullwood E Ayrs....76 G2
Fulmer Bucks....20 F6
Fulmodeston Norfk....44 G4
Fulnetby Lincs....52 F7
Fulney Lincs....43 J5
Fulstow Lincs....53 K4
Fulwell Sundld....73 P8
Fulwood Lancs....57 K3
Fulwood Sheff....50 H4
Fundenhall Norfk....45 J10
Funtington W Susx....10 C8

Funtullich P & K....92 B9
Furley Devon....6 H3
Furnace Ag & B....83 Q3
Furnace Carmth....26 C8
Furness Vale Derbys....50 D4
Furneux Pelham Herts....33 L10
Furzley Hants....9 K4
Fyfield Essex....22 C3
Fyfield Hants....19 K10
Fyfield Oxon....19 M2
Fyfield Wilts....18 G7
Fyfield Wilts....18 H8
Fylingthorpe N York....67 K6
Fyning W Susx....10 D5
Fyvie Abers....102 G7

G

Gabroc Hill E Ayrs....76 H2
Gaddesby Leics....41 P5
Gaddesden Row Herts....20 G2
Gadgirth S Ayrs....76 G6
Gaer-llwyd Mons....28 E9
Gaerwen IoA....54 F7
Gailes N Ayrs....76 F4
Gailey Staffs....40 B5
Gainford Dur....65 L4
Gainsborough Lincs....52 B5
Gainsford End Essex....34 C9
Gairloch Highld....105 M7
Gairlochy Highld....98 B11
Gairneybridge P & K....86 D3
Gaitsgill Cumb....71 N6
Galashiels Border....80 C7
Galgate Lancs....63 J10
Galhampton Somset....17 P9
Gallanachbeg Ag & B....90 B10
Gallanachmore Ag & B....89 R10
Gallatown Fife....86 G4
Gallovie Highld....98 H10
Galloway Forest Park....69 L3
Gallowfauld Angus....93 M7
Gallowhill P & K....92 H8
Galltair Highld....97 L5
Galmpton Devon....5 N11
Galmpton Torbay....6 B10
Galphay N York....65 M11
Galston E Ayrs....76 H4
Gamblesby Cumb....72 B11
Gamlingay Cambs....33 J6
Gamlingay Great Heath Cambs....32 H6
Gamrie Abers....102 G3
Gamston Notts....51 N12
Gamston Notts....51 P5
Ganavan Bay Ag & B....90 B9
Ganllwyd Gwynd....47 M6
Gannachy Angus....95 K7
Ganstead E R Yk....61 K7
Ganthorpe N York....66 F12
Ganton N York....67 L11
Garbity Moray....101 L5
Garboldisham Norfk....34 G1
Garbole Highld....99 L4
Garchory Abers....101 L12
Gardeners Green Wokham....20 D9
Gardenstown Abers....102 G3
Garden Village Sheff....50 H2
Garderhouse Shet....111 k4
Gare Hill Somset....18 B11
Garelochhead Ag & B....84 D5
Garford Oxon....19 M2
Garforth Leeds....59 K7
Gargrave N York....58 B4
Gargunnock Stirlg....85 M4
Garlic Street Norfk....45 K12
Garlieston D & G....69 L9
Garlinge Kent....23 P9
Garlinge Green Kent....23 L11
Garlogie Abers....95 M2
Garmond Abers....102 G5
Garmouth Moray....101 L3
Garmston Shrops....39 L2
Garn-Dolbenmaen Gwynd....46 H3
Garnkirk N Lans....85 L8
Garrabost W Isls....111 e2
Garrallan E Ayrs....77 J7
Garras Cnwll....2 H10
Garreg Gwynd....47 K3
Garrigill Cumb....72 D11
Garroch D & G....69 N3
Garrochtrie D & G....68 F10
Garrochty Ag & B....84 B11
Garros Highld....104 G9
Garsdale Head Cumb....64 E8
Garsdon Wilts....18 D4
Garshall Green Staffs....40 C1
Garsington Oxon....31 M12
Garstang Lancs....63 J12
Garston Herts....20 H4
Garston Lpool....56 H11
Gartachossan Ag & B....82 E10
Gartcosh N Lans....85 L9
Garth Powys....37 Q10
Garth Wrexhm....48 F7
Garthamlock C Glas....85 L9
Garthmyl Powys....38 E3
Garthorpe Leics....42 B6
Garthorpe N Linc....60 E9
Garth Penrhyncoch Cerdgn....37 K3
Garth Row Cumb....63 K3
Gartly Abers....102 C8
Gartmore Stirlg....85 J4
Gartness N Lans....85 N9
Gartness Stirlg....84 H5
Gartocharn W Duns....84 G6
Garton-on-the-Wolds E R Yk....60 G3
Gartymore Highld....110 C9
Garvald E Loth....87 L7
Garvan Highld....90 D2
Garvard Ag & B....82 E5
Garve Highld....106 G9
Garvellachs Ag & B....83 K2
Garvestone Norfk....44 G8
Garvock Inver....84 E8
Garway Herefs....28 E4
Garyvard W Isls....111 d2
Gasper Wilts....8 B2
Gastard Wilts....18 C7
Gasthorpe Norfk....34 F1
Gaston Green Essex....33 N12
Gatcombe IoW....9 N9

Gate Burton Lincs....52 B7
Gateforth N York....59 M7
Gatehead E Ayrs....76 G4
Gate Helmsley N York....59 P3
Gatehouse Nthumb....72 E3
Gatehouse of Fleet D & G....69 P7
Gateley Norfk....44 F5
Gatenby N York....65 N9
Gateshaw Border....80 G9
Gateshead Gatesd....73 M8
Gateside Abers....93 M6
Gateside E Rens....84 H10
Gateside Fife....86 E1
Gateside N Ayrs....84 F11
Gateslack D & G....78 E8
Gathurst Wigan....57 J7
Gatley Stockp....57 Q10
Gattonside Border....80 D7
Gatwick Airport W Susx....11 L2
Gaulby Leics....41 P7
Gauldry Fife....93 L10
Gauldswell P & K....93 J5
Gautby Lincs....52 H8
Gavinton Border....80 G4
Gawcott Bucks....31 P7
Gawsworth Ches E....50 B6
Gawthrop Cumb....63 M6
Gawthwaite Cumb....62 F5
Gaydon Warwks....31 J4
Gayhurst M Keyn....32 C7
Gayle N York....64 F9
Gayles N York....65 K6
Gayton Nhants....31 P4
Gayton Norfk....44 C6
Gayton Staffs....40 C2
Gayton le Marsh Lincs....53 L6
Gayton Thorpe Norfk....44 C6
Gaywood Norfk....44 Q6
Gazeley Suffk....34 C4
Gearraidh Bhaird W Isls....111 d3
Geary Highld....104 C9
Gedding Suffk....34 F5
Geddington Nhants....42 C12
Gedling Notts....51 N11
Gedney Lincs....43 L5
Gedney Broadgate Lincs....43 L5
Gedney Drove End Lincs....43 M4
Gedney Dyke Lincs....43 L5
Gedney Hill Lincs....43 K7
Geeston Rutlnd....42 E8
Geldeston Norfk....45 N10
Gellifor Denbgs....48 D3
Gelligaer Caerph....27 N9
Gellilydan Gwynd....47 L4
Gellinudd Neath....26 G7
Gellyburn P & K....92 G7
Gellywen Carmth....25 M4
Gelston D & G....70 C4
Gelston Lincs....42 C2
Gembling E R Yk....61 J3
Gentleshaw Staffs....40 D5
Georgefield D & G....79 L9
George Green Bucks....20 F7
Georgeham Devon....14 H4
Georgemas Junction Station Highld....110 D4
George Nympton Devon....15 M7
Georth Ork....111 h2
Germansweek Devon....5 J2
Gerrans Cnwll....3 K8
Gerrards Cross Bucks....20 G6
Gerrick R & Cl....66 G5
Gestingthorpe Essex....34 D8
Geuffordd Powys....48 E11
Gidea Park Gt Lon....21 Q5
Giffnock E Rens....85 J10
Gifford E Loth....87 K8
Giffordtown Fife....93 K12
Giggleswick N York....63 P9
Gigha Ag & B....75 J3
Gilberdyke E R Yk....60 E8
Gilchriston E Loth....87 J8
Gilcrux Cumb....71 H7
Gildersome Leeds....58 H8
Gildingwells Rothm....51 M4
Gilesgate Moor Dur....73 N11
Gileston V Glam....16 D3
Gilfach Caerph....27 N8
Gilfach Goch Brdgnd....27 K10
Gilfachrheda Cerdgn....36 G9
Gilgarran Cumb....70 G10
Gillamoor N York....66 F9
Gillen Highld....104 C9
Gillesbie D & G....79 J9
Gilling East N York....66 E11
Gillingham Dorset....8 B3
Gillingham Medway....22 F9
Gillingham Norfk....45 N10
Gilling West N York....65 L6
Gillock Highld....110 E4
Gills Highld....110 G2
Gilmanscleuch Border....79 M5
Gilmerton C Edin....86 F8
Gilmerton P & K....92 D10
Gilmonby Dur....64 H5
Gilmorton Leics....41 M9
Gilroes Crematorium C Leic....41 M6
Gilsland Nthumb....72 B7
Gilston Border....87 J10
Gilston Herts....21 N2
Gilwern Mons....27 Q6
Gimingham Norfk....45 L3
Gipping Suffk....34 H4
Gipsey Bridge Lincs....53 J12
Girdle Toll N Ayrs....76 F3
Girlsta Shet....111 k4
Girsby N York....65 N6
Girthon D & G....69 N8
Girton Cambs....33 M5
Girton Notts....52 B9
Girvan S Ayrs....68 E3
Gisburn Lancs....63 P11
Gisleham Suffk....45 Q11
Gislingham Suffk....34 H3
Gissing Norfk....45 J11
Gittisham Devon....6 F4
Gladestry Powys....38 E10
Gladsmuir E Loth....87 J7
Glais Swans....26 F8
Glaisdale N York....66 H6
Glamis Angus....93 L6
Glanaman Carmth....26 F6
Glandford Norfk....44 H2
Glandwr Pembks....25 K4
Glandyfi Cerdgn....47 L11
Glanllynfi Brdgnd....27 J10
Glan-rhyd Powys....26 H7

Glanton Nthumb....81 M10
Glanvilles Wootton Dorset....7 P2
Glan-y-don Flints....56 D11
Glapthorn Nhants....42 F11
Glapwell Derbys....51 L7
Glasbury Powys....27 P2
Glascwm Powys....38 D10
Glasfryn Conwy....55 N10
Glasgow C Glas....85 K9
Glasgow Airport Rens....84 H9
Glasgow Science Centre C Glas....85 J9
Glasinfryn Gwynd....54 H7
Glasnacardoch Bay Highld....97 J9
Glasnakille Highld....96 F5
Glassford S Lans....77 M2
Glasshouse Gloucs....29 J5
Glasshouses N York....58 F2
Glasson Cumb....71 L4
Glasson Lancs....63 J10
Glassonby Cumb....72 B12
Glasterlaw Angus....93 Q5
Glaston Rutlnd....42 C9
Glastonbury Somset....17 M8
Glatton Cambs....42 G11
Glazebrook Warrtn....57 M9
Glazebury Warrtn....57 M9
Glazeley Shrops....39 N5
Gleaston Cumb....62 F7
Glebe Highld....98 G5
Gledhow Leeds....58 H6
Gledpark D & G....69 P8
Gledrid Shrops....48 F7
Glemsford Suffk....34 D7
Glenallachie Moray....101 K7
Glenancross Highld....97 J10
Glenaros House Ag & B....89 L7
Glenbarr Ag & B....75 K5
Glenbarry Abers....102 D4
Glenbeg Highld....89 M4
Glenbervie Abers....95 M6
Glenboig N Lans....85 M8
Glenborrodale Highld....89 M4
Glenbranter Ag & B....84 B4
Glenbreck Border....78 H5
Glenbrittle House Highld....96 E5
Glenbuck E Ayrs....77 M5
Glencally Angus....94 F8
Glencaple D & G....70 G2
Glencarron Lodge Highld....105 R11
Glencarse P & K....92 H10
Glen Clunie Lodge Abers....94 C5
Glencoe Highld....90 F5
Glencothe Border....78 H3
Glencraig Fife....86 E4
Glencrosh D & G....78 C10
Glendale Highld....104 B11
Glendaruel Ag & B....83 Q6
Glendevon P & K....86 B2
Glendoe Lodge Highld....98 E7
Glendoick P & K....93 J10
Glenduckie Fife....93 K11
Glenegedale Ag & B....74 D3
Glenelg Highld....97 L6
Glenerney Moray....100 F6
Glenfarg P & K....92 G12
Glenfield Leics....41 M6
Glenfinnan Highld....97 M12
Glenfintaig Lodge Highld....98 C10
Glenfoot P & K....92 H11
Glenfyne Lodge Ag & B....90 H12
Glengarnock N Ayrs....84 F11
Glengolly Highld....110 C3
Glengorm Castle Ag & B....89 K5
Glengrasco Highld....96 E1
Glenholm Border....78 H3
Glenhoul D & G....78 N2
Glenisla Angus....94 D9
Glenkin Ag & B....84 C7
Glenkindie Abers....101 N11
Glenlivet Moray....101 J9
Glenlochar D & G....70 C3
Glenlomond P & K....86 E2
Glenluce D & G....68 G8
Glenmassan Ag & B....84 B5
Glenmavis N Lans....85 M9
Glen Maye IoM....56 b5
Glenmore Highld....96 E2
Glenmore Lodge Highld....99 P7
Glen Nevis House Highld....90 F2
Glenochil Clacks....85 P4
Glen Parva Leics....41 M7
Glenquiech Angus....94 G9
Glenralloch Ag & B....83 M8
Glenridding Cumb....71 N11
Glenrothes Fife....86 F3
Glenshero Lodge Highld....98 H9
Glenstriven Ag & B....84 B7
Glentham Lincs....52 E5
Glen Trool Lodge D & G....69 K3
Glentrool Village D & G....69 J4
Glentruim House Highld....99 K9
Glentworth Lincs....52 D6
Glenuig Highld....89 N2
Glenvarragill Highld....96 F2
Glen Vine IoM....56 c5
Glenwhilly D & G....68 G5
Glespin S Lans....78 D4
Glewstone Herefs....28 G4
Glinton C Pete....42 G8
Glooston Leics....41 Q8
Glossop Derbys....50 D3
Gloster Hill Nthumb....81 Q12
Gloucester Gloucs....29 L5
Gloucester Crematorium Gloucs....29 L5
Gloucester Services Gloucs....29 L6
Gloucestershire Airport Gloucs....29 M5
Glusburn N York....58 D5
Glutt Lodge Highld....110 B8
Glympton Oxon....31 K9
Glyn Ceiriog Wrexhm....48 E7
Glyncorrwg Neath....27 J8
Glynde E Susx....11 P8
Glyndyfrdwy Denbgs....48 D7
Glynneath Neath....27 J7
Glynn Valley Crematorium Cnwll....3 N3
Glyntaff Crematorium Rhondd....27 M10
Glyntawe Powys....26 H6

Glynteg Carmth 25 N2
Gnosall Staffs 49 P10
Gnosall Heath Staffs 49 P10
Goadby Leics 41 Q7
Goadby Marwood Leics 41 R3
Goatacre Wilts 18 F5
Goathill Dorset 17 P11
Goathland N York 67 J7
Goathurst Somset 16 H8
Gobowen Shrops 48 F8
Godalming Surrey 10 F2
Goddard's Green Kent 12 G3
Godmanchester Cambs 33 J3
Godmanstone Dorset 7 P4
Godmersham Kent 23 K12
Godney Somset 17 L7
Godolphin Cross Cnwll 2 F9
Godre'r-graig Neath 26 G7
Godshill IoW 9 N10
Godstone Surrey 21 M11
Goetre Mons 28 C7
Goff's Oak Herts 21 M3
Gofilon Mons 28 B6
Gogar C Edin 86 E7
Goginan Cerdgn 37 L4
Golan Gwynd 46 H3
Golant Cnwll 4 D8
Golberdon Cnwll 4 H6
Golborne Wigan 57 L8
Golcar Kirk 58 E10
Goldcliff Newpt 28 D11
Golden Green Kent 12 D1
Golden Pot Hants 10 B2
Golders Green Gt Lon 21 K6
Golders Green
  Crematorium Gt Lon 21 K6
Goldhanger Essex 22 H2
Goldington Bed 32 F6
Goldsborough N York 59 J3
Goldsborough N York 67 J5
Goldsithney Cnwll 2 E9
Goldsworth Park Surrey 20 F10
Goldthorpe Barns 59 L12
Goldworthy Devon 14 G7
Gollanfield Highld 107 N10
Golspie Highld 107 N3
Gomeldon Wilts 8 H1
Gomshall Surrey 10 H1
Gonalston Notts 51 P10
Gonerby Hill Foot Lincs 42 C3
Gonfirth Shet 111 k3
Good Easter Essex 22 D2
Gooderstone Norfk 44 C9
Goodleigh Devon 15 K5
Goodmanham E R Yk 60 F5
Goodmayes Gt Lon 21 P6
Goodnestone Kent 23 K10
Goodnestone Kent 23 N11
Goodrich Herefs 28 G5
Goodrington Torbay 6 B10
Goodshaw Lancs 57 P4
Goodwick Pembks 24 G3
Goodworth Clatford
  Hants 19 L11
Goole E R Yk 60 C9
Goom's Hill Worcs 30 D3
Goonbell Cnwll 2 G6
Goonhavern Cnwll 2 H5
Goonvrea Cnwll 2 G6
Goosecruives Abers 95 M5
Gooseford Devon 5 N2
Goose Green Essex 35 J10
Goose Green S Glos 17 N2
Gooseham Cnwll 14 E8
Goosey Oxon 19 L3
Goosnargh Lancs 57 K2
Goostrey Ches E 49 P2
Gordano Services N Som 17 M2
Gordon Border 80 E5
Gordon Arms Hotel
  Border 79 L4
Gordonstown Abers 102 D4
Gordonstown Abers 102 F7
Gorebridge Mdloth 86 G9
Gorefield Cambs 43 L7
Gores Wilts 18 G8
Gorey Jersey 7 c2
Goring Oxon 19 Q5
Goring-by-Sea W Susx 10 H9
Gorleston on Sea Norfk 45 Q8
Gornal Wood
  Crematorium Dudley 40 B4
Gorrachie Abers 102 F4
Gorran Churchtown Cnwll 3 M7
Gorran Haven Cnwll 3 M7
Gorsedd Flints 56 D12
Gorse Hill Swindn 18 H4
Gorseinon Swans 26 D8
Gorsgoch Cerdgn 36 H9
Gorslas Carmth 26 D6
Gorsley Gloucs 29 J4
Gorsley Common Herefs 29 J4
Gorstan Highld 106 H9
Gorsty Hill Staffs 40 E2
Gorten Ag & B 89 P9
Gorthleck Highld 98 G4
Gorton Manch 50 B2
Gosbeck Suffk 35 J5
Gosberton Lincs 43 J4
Gosfield Essex 34 D10
Gosforth Cumb 62 C2
Gosforth N u Ty 73 M7
Gospel End Staffs 40 B8
Gosport Hants 9 Q7
Gossington Gloucs 29 K8
Gotham Notts 41 M2
Gotherington Gloucs 29 N3
Gotton Somset 16 H9
Goudhurst Kent 12 E3
Goulceby Lincs 53 J7
Gourdas Abers 102 G7
Gourdie C Dund 93 L8
Gourdon Abers 95 N7
Gourock Inver 84 D7
Govan C Glas 85 J9
Goveton Devon 5 P10
Gowdall E R Yk 59 N9
Gower Highld 106 H10
Gower Swans 26 C10
Gowerton Swans 26 D9
Gowkhall Fife 86 C5
Goxhill E R Yk 61 K5
Goxhill N Linc 61 J7
Grabhair W Isls 111 d3
Graffham W Susx 10 E6
Grafham Cambs 32 G3
Grafham Surrey 10 G2

Grafton N York 59 K2
Grafton Oxon 19 J1
Grafton Shrops 48 H10
Grafton Worcs 29 N2
Grafton Flyford Worcs 30 C3
Grafton Regis Nhants 31 Q5
Grafton Underwood
  Nhants 32 D2
Grafty Green Kent 12 G1
Graig Conwy 55 L7
Graig-fechan Denbgs 48 D5
Grain Medway 22 H7
Grainsby Lincs 53 J4
Grainthorpe Lincs 53 L4
Grampound Cnwll 3 L6
Grampound Road Cnwll 3 K5
Gramsdal W Isls 111 b5
Gramsdale W Isls 111 b5
Granborough Bucks 31 Q8
Granby Notts 41 Q1
Grandborough Warwks 31 L2
Grand Chemins Jersey 7 c2
Grandes Rocques Guern 6 b1
Grandtully P & K 92 D5
Grange Cumb 71 L11
Grange Medway 22 F9
Grange P & K 93 K10
Grange Crossroads Moray 101 N4
Grange Hall Moray 100 E3
Grangehall S Lans 78 F1
Grange Hill Essex 21 N5
Grangemill Derbys 50 G8
Grange Moor Kirk 58 G10
Grangemouth Falk 85 Q6
Grange of Lindores Fife 93 J11
Grange-over-Sands Cumb 62 H6
Grangepans Falk 86 B6
Grangetown R & Cl 66 D4
Grangetown Sundld 73 P9
Grange Villa Dur 73 M9
Gransmoor E R Yk 61 J3
Granston Pembks 24 F2
Grantchester Cambs 33 M6
Grantham Lincs 42 D3
Grantham
  Crematorium Lincs 42 D3
Granton C Edin 86 F6
Grantown-on-Spey
  Highld 100 H9
Grantshouse Border 87 P8
Grasby Lincs 52 F3
Grasmere Cumb 62 G1
Grasscroft Oldham 58 C12
Grassendale Lpool 56 H10
Grassington N York 58 D2
Grassmoor Derbys 51 K7
Grassthorpe Notts 52 B9
Grateley Hants 19 J11
Graveley Cambs 33 J4
Graveley Herts 32 H10
Graveney Kent 23 K10
Gravesend Kent 22 D8
Gravir W Isls 111 d3
Grayingham Lincs 52 D4
Grayrigg Cumb 63 L3
Grays Thurr 22 D7
Grayshott Hants 10 E3
Grayswood Surrey 10 E3
Greasbrough Rothm 51 K2
Greasby Wirral 56 F10
Great Abington Cambs 33 N7
Great Addington Nhants 32 D2
Great Alne Warwks 30 E3
Great Altcar Lancs 56 G7
Great Amwell Herts 21 M2
Great Asby Cumb 64 C5
Great Ashfield Suffk 34 G4
Great Ayton N York 66 D5
Great Baddow Essex 22 E3
Great Badminton S Glos 18 B4
Great Bardfield Essex 34 B10
Great Barford Bed 32 G6
Great Barr Sandw 40 D8
Great Barrington Gloucs 30 G10
Great Barrow Ches W 49 J2
Great Barton Suffk 34 E4
Great Barugh N York 66 G10
Great Bavington Nthumb 72 H5
Great Bealings Suffk 35 K7
Great Bedwyn Wilts 19 J7
Great Bentley Essex 35 J11
Great Billing Nhants 32 B4
Great Bircham Norfk 44 C4
Great Blakenham Suffk 35 J6
Great Blencow Cumb 71 P8
Great Bolas Wrekin 49 M10
Great Bookham Surrey 21 J11
Great Bourton Oxon 31 L5
Great Bowden Leics 41 Q9
Great Bradley Suffk 34 B6
Great Braxted Essex 22 G1
Great Bricett Suffk 34 G6
Great Brickhill Bucks 32 C10
Great Bridgeford Staffs 40 B3
Great Brington Nhants 31 P2
Great Bromley Essex 34 H10
Great Broughton Cumb 70 H8
Great Broughton N York 66 E6
Great Budworth Ches W 57 M12
Great Burdon Darltn 65 N4
Great Burstead Essex 22 D5
Great Busby N York 66 D6
Great Carlton Lincs 53 L6
Great Casterton Rutlnd 42 E8
Great Chalfield Wilts 18 C7
Great Chart Kent 13 J2
Great Chatwell Staffs 49 P11
Great Cheverell Wilts 18 E8
Great Chishill Cambs 33 L8
Great Clacton Essex 35 K12
Great Clifton Cumb 70 G9
Great Coates NE Lin 61 L11
Great Comberton Worcs 29 N1
Great Corby Cumb 71 P5
Great Cornard Suffk 34 E8
Great Cowden E R Yk 61 L6
Great Coxwell Oxon 19 J3
Great Cransley Nhants 32 B2
Great Cressingham Norfk 44 E9
Great Crosthwaite Cumb 71 L10
Great Cubley Derbys 50 F12
Great Cumbrae Island
  N Ayrs 84 C10
Great Dalby Leics 41 Q5
Great Doddington Nhants 32 C4
Great Dunham Norfk 44 E7

Great Dunmow Essex 33 Q11
Great Durnford Wilts 18 G12
Great Easton Essex 33 P10
Great Easton Leics 42 C10
Great Eccleston Lancs 56 H2
Great Ellingham Norfk 44 G10
Great Elm Somset 17 Q6
Great Everdon Nhants 31 N3
Great Eversden Cambs 33 K6
Great Fencote N York 65 M8
Great Finborough Suffk 34 G5
Greatford Lincs 42 F7
Great Fransham Norfk 44 E7
Great Gaddesden Herts 20 G2
Greatgate Staffs 50 D11
Great Gidding Cambs 42 G2
Great Givendale E R Yk 60 E4
Great Glemham Suffk 35 M4
Great Glen Leics 41 P7
Great Gonerby Lincs 42 C3
Great Gransden Cambs 33 J5
Great Green Cambs 33 J7
Great Green Suffk 34 G4
Great Habton N York 66 G11
Great Hale Lincs 42 G2
Great Hallingbury Essex 33 N11
Great Hampden Bucks 20 D3
Great Harrowden Nhants 32 C3
Great Harwood Lancs 57 N3
Great Haseley Oxon 19 Q1
Great Haywood Staffs 40 D3
Great Heck N York 59 N9
Great Henny Essex 34 E8
Great Hinton Wilts 18 D8
Great Hockham Norfk 44 F10
Great Holland Essex 35 K11
Great Hollands Br For 20 D9
Great Horkesley Essex 34 F9
Great Hormead Herts 33 L10
Great Horton C Brad 58 F7
Great Horwood Bucks 31 Q7
Great Houghton Barns 59 K11
Great Houghton Nhants 32 B5
Great Hucklow Derbys 50 F5
Great Kelk E R Yk 61 J3
Great Kimble Bucks 20 D3
Great Kingshill Bucks 20 E4
Great Langdale Cumb 62 F2
Great Langton N York 65 M7
Great Leighs Essex 34 C12
Great Limber Lincs 52 G2
Great Linford M Keyn 32 C8
Great Livermere Suffk 34 E3
Great Longstone Derbys 50 G6
Great Lumley Dur 73 N10
Great Malvern Worcs 39 P11
Great Maplestead Essex 34 D9
Great Marton Bpool 56 G2
Great Massingham Norfk 44 D5
Great Milton Oxon 19 Q1
Great Missenden Bucks 20 E3
Great Mitton Lancs 57 N2
Great Mongeham Kent 23 Q12
Great Moulton Norfk 45 J11
Great Musgrave Cumb 64 D5
Great Ness Shrops 48 H11
Great Notley Essex 34 C11
Great Oak Mons 28 D6
Great Oakley Essex 35 K10
Great Oakley Nhants 42 C11
Great Offley Herts 32 G10
Great Ormside Cumb 64 C4
Great Orton Cumb 71 M5
Great Ouseburn N York 59 K2
Great Oxendon Nhants 41 Q10
Great Oxney Green Essex 22 D3
Great Paxton Cambs 32 H4
Great Plumpton Lancs 56 H3
Great Plumstead Norfk 45 L7
Great Ponton Lincs 42 D3
Great Preston Leeds 59 K8
Great Raveley Cambs 33 J1
Great Rissington Gloucs 30 G10
Great Rollright Oxon 31 J7
Great Ryburgh Norfk 44 F5
Great Ryton Shrops 39 J2
Great Saling Essex 34 B10
Great Salkeld Cumb 71 Q8
Great Sampford Essex 33 Q9
Great Saughall Ches W 48 G2
Great Shefford W Berk 19 L6
Great Shelford Cambs 33 M6
Great Smeaton N York 65 N6
Great Snoring Norfk 44 F4
Great Somerford Wilts 18 E4
Great Soudley Shrops 49 N9
Great Stainton Darltn 65 N3
Great Stambridge Essex 22 H5
Great Staughton Cambs 32 G4
Great Steeping Lincs 53 M9
Great Stoke S Glos 28 H11
Greatstone-on-Sea Kent 13 K5
Great Strickland Cumb 71 Q10
Great Stukeley Cambs 32 H2
Great Sturton Lincs 53 J7
Great Swinburne Nthumb 72 G6
Great Tew Oxon 31 K8
Great Tey Essex 34 E10
Great Thurlow Suffk 34 B6
Great Torrington Devon 15 J8
Great Tosson Nthumb 72 H2
Great Totham Essex 22 G1
Great Totham Essex 22 G1
Great Urswick Cumb 62 F7
Great Wakering Essex 22 H6
Great Waldingfield Suffk 34 F7
Great Walsingham Norfk 44 F4
Great Waltham Essex 22 D2
Great Warley Essex 22 C5
Great Washbourne Gloucs 29 N2
Great Weeke Devon 5 P4
Great Weldon Nhants 42 D11
Great Wenham Suffk 34 H8
Great Whittington
  Nthumb 72 H6
Great Wigborough Essex 23 J1
Great Wilbraham Cambs 33 N5
Great Wishford Wilts 8 F1
Great Witcombe Gloucs 29 M6
Great Witley Worcs 39 N8
Great Wolford Warwks 30 G7
Greatworth Nhants 31 M5
Great Wratting Suffk 34 B7

Great Wymondley Herts 32 H10
Great Wyrley Staffs 40 C6
Great Yarmouth Norfk 45 Q8
Great Yarmouth
  Crematorium Norfk 45 Q8
Great Yeldham Essex 34 C8
Greenburn W Loth 85 Q10
Green End Herts 33 K11
Green End Herts 33 K9
Greenfield Ag & B 84 D5
Greenfield C Beds 32 F9
Greenfield Flints 56 E12
Greenfield Highld 98 B8
Greenfield Oldham 58 C12
Greenford Gt Lon 21 J7
Greengairs N Lans 85 N8
Greengates C Brad 58 G6
Greenham Somset 16 E11
Green Hammerton N York 59 L3
Greenhaugh Nthumb 72 C4
Greenhead Nthumb 72 C7
Green Heath Staffs 40 C5
Greenhill D & G 78 H11
Greenhill Falk 85 N7
Greenhill Kent 23 M9
Greenhill S Lans 78 F3
Greenhithe Kent 22 C8
Greenholm E Ayrs 77 J4
Greenhouse Border 80 D9
Greenhow Hill N York 58 E2
Greenland Highld 110 E3
Greenland Sheff 51 K3
Greenlaw Border 80 F5
Greenlea D & G 70 G1
Greenloaning P & K 85 N2
Greenmount Bury 57 P6
Greenock Inver 84 E7
Greenock Crematorium
  Inver 84 E7
Greenodd Cumb 62 G6
Green Ore Somset 17 N6
Green Quarter Cumb 63 J2
Greenshields S Lans 86 B12
Greenside Gatesd 73 K8
Greenside Kirk 58 F10
Greens Norton Nhants 31 P4
Greenstead Green Essex 34 D10
Green Street Herts 21 J4
Green Street Herts 33 M11
Green Street Green Kent 22 C8
Green Tye Herts 33 M11
Greenway Somset 17 J10
Greenwich Gt Lon 21 M7
Greenwich Maritime
  Gt Lon 21 M7
Greet Gloucs 30 D7
Greete Shrops 39 L7
Greetham Lincs 53 K8
Greetham Rutlnd 42 D7
Greetland Calder 58 E9
Greinton Somset 17 K8
Grenaby IoM 56 b6
Grendon Nhants 32 C5
Grendon Warwks 40 H7
Grendon Underwood
  Bucks 31 P9
Grenoside Sheff 51 J3
Grenoside
  Crematorium Sheff 51 J3
Greosabhagh W Isls 111 c3
Gresford Wrexhm 48 G5
Gresham Norfk 45 J3
Greshornish House
  Hotel Highld 104 D10
Gressenhall Norfk 44 F7
Gressenhall Green Norfk 44 F6
Gressingham Lancs 63 K8
Greta Bridge Dur 65 J5
Gretna D & G 71 M3
Gretna Green D & G 71 M2
Gretna Services D & G 71 L2
Gretton Gloucs 30 D7
Gretton Nhants 42 C10
Gretton Shrops 39 K3
Grewelthorpe N York 65 M11
Greyrigg D & G 78 H10
Greys Green Oxon 20 B6
Greysouthen Cumb 70 H9
Greystoke Cumb 71 P8
Greystone Angus 93 P7
Greywell Hants 20 B12
Griff Warwks 41 J9
Griffithstown Torfn 28 C8
Grimeford Village Lancs 57 L6
Grimesthorpe Sheff 51 J3
Grimethorpe Barns 59 K11
Grimley Worcs 39 Q9
Grimmet S Ayrs 76 F8
Grimoldby Lincs 53 L6
Grimpo Shrops 48 G9
Grimsargh Lancs 57 L3
Grimsby NE Lin 61 M11
Grimsby Crematorium
  NE Lin 53 J3
Grimscote Nhants 31 P4
Grimscott Cnwll 14 E10
Grimshader W Isls 111 d2
Grimsthorpe Lincs 42 F5
Grimston Leics 41 P3
Grimston Norfk 44 C5
Grimstone Dorset 7 P4
Grimstone End Suffk 34 F3
Grindale E R Yk 67 N12
Grindleford Derbys 50 H5
Grindleton Lancs 63 N11
Grindley Brook Shrops 49 K7
Grindlow Derbys 50 F5
Grindon S on T 65 P3
Grindon Staffs 50 E9
Gringley on the Hill Notts 51 Q3
Grinsdale Cumb 71 M4
Grinshill Shrops 49 K10
Grinton N York 65 J7
Griomaisiader W Isls 111 d2
Griomsaigh W Isls 111 b5
Grishipoll Ag & B 88 F5
Gristhorpe N York 67 M10
Criston Norfk 44 F9
Gritley Ork 111 h2
Grittenham Wilts 18 F4
Grittleton Wilts 18 C5
Grizebeck Cumb 62 E5
Grizedale Cumb 62 G3
Groby Leics 41 M6
Groes Conwy 55 Q8
Groes-faen Rhondd 27 M11
Groeslon Gwynd 54 F9
Groes-Wen Caerph 27 N10

Grogarry W Isls 111 a5
Grogport Ag & B 75 M4
Groigearraidh W Isls 111 a5
Gronant Flints 56 C11
Groombridge E Susx 11 Q3
Grosebay W Isls 111 c3
Grosmont Mons 28 E4
Grosmont N York 67 J6
Groton Suffk 34 F8
Grouville Jersey 7 c2
Grove Notts 51 Q5
Grove Oxon 19 L3
Grove Green Kent 22 F11
Grove Park Gt Lon 21 N8
Grovesend Swans 26 D8
Gruinard Highld 105 P4
Gruinart Ag & B 82 D9
Grula Highld 96 D4
Gruline Ag & B 89 L8
Grundisburgh Suffk 35 K6
Gruting Shet 111 j4
Gualachulain Highld 90 F7
Guardbridge Fife 93 M11
Guarlford Worcs 39 P11
Guay P & K 92 E6
Guernsey Guern 6 b2
Guernsey Airport Guern 6 b2
Guestling Green E Susx 12 G7
Guestling Thorn E Susx 12 G6
Guestwick Norfk 44 H5
Guide Post Nthumb 73 M4
Guilden Morden Cambs 33 J7
Guilden Sutton Ches W 49 J2
Guildford Surrey 20 F12
Guildford Crematorium
  Surrey 10 F2
Guildtown P & K 92 G8
Guilsborough Nhants 41 P11
Guilsfield Powys 48 E12
Guiltreehill S Ayrs 76 F8
Guineaford Devon 15 J5
Guisborough R & Cl 66 E4
Guiseley Leeds 58 G6
Guist Norfk 44 G5
Guiting Power Gloucs 30 E8
Gullane E Loth 87 J5
Gulval Cnwll 2 D9
Gulworthy Devon 5 K5
Gumfreston Pembks 25 J8
Gumley Leics 41 P9
Gunby Lincs 42 D6
Gunby Lincs 53 M9
Gundleton Hants 9 Q2
Gun Hill E Susx 12 C7
Gunn Devon 15 L5
Gunnerside N York 64 G7
Gunnerton Nthumb 72 G6
Gunness N Linc 60 E11
Gunnislake Cnwll 5 J6
Gunnista Shet 111 k4
Gunthorpe N Linc 52 B4
Gunthorpe Norfk 44 G4
Gunthorpe Notts 51 P11
Gunwalloe Cnwll 2 F10
Gurnard IoW 9 N8
Gurney Slade Somset 17 N6
Gurnos Powys 26 G7
Gussage All Saints Dorset 8 E5
Gussage St Andrew
  Dorset 8 E5
Gussage St Michael
  Dorset 8 E5
Guston Kent 13 P2
Gutcher Shet 111 k2
Guthrie Angus 93 P5
Guyhirn Cambs 43 L8
Guyzance Nthumb 81 P12
Gwaenysgor Flints 56 C11
Gwalchmai IoA 54 E6
Gwaun-Cae-Gurwen
  Carmth 26 F6
Gweek Cnwll 2 G9
Gwenddwr Powys 38 C12
Gwennap Cnwll 2 H7
Gwennap Mining
  District Cnwll 2 H7
Gwent Crematorium
  Mons 28 C8
Gwernaffield Flints 48 E3
Gwernesney Mons 28 E8
Gwernogle Carmth 26 D3
Gwernymynydd Flints 48 E3
Gwespyr Flints 56 C11
Gwinear Cnwll 2 E8
Gwithian Cnwll 2 E7
Gwyddelwern Denbgs 48 C6
Gwyddgrug Carmth 26 C3
Gwytherin Conwy 55 N8

H

Habberley Shrops 38 H2
Habberley Worcs 39 P6
Habergham Lancs 57 P3
Habertoft Lincs 53 N9
Habrough NE Lin 61 K10
Hacconby Lincs 42 F5
Haceby Lincs 42 E3
Hacheston Suffk 35 M5
Hackbridge Gt Lon 21 L9
Hackenthorpe Sheff 51 K4
Hackford Norfk 44 H9
Hackforth N York 65 M8
Hackland Ork 111 h2
Hackleton Nhants 32 B6
Hacklinge Kent 23 Q11
Hackness N York 67 L9
Hackney Gt Lon 21 M6
Hackthorn Lincs 52 F7
Hackthorpe Cumb 71 Q10
Hadden Border 80 G7
Haddenham Bucks 20 C3
Haddenham Cambs 33 M2
Haddington E Loth 87 K7
Haddiscoe Norfk 45 P10
Haddo Abers 102 H7
Haddon Cambs 42 G10
Hadfield Derbys 50 D3
Hadham Ford Herts 33 M11
Hadleigh Essex 22 F6
Hadleigh Suffk 34 G8
Hadley Worcs 39 Q8
Hadley Wrekin 49 M12
Hadley End Staffs 40 F4

Hadley Wood Gt Lon....21 L4
Hadlow Kent....22 D12
Hadlow Down E Susx....11 Q5
Hadnall Shrops....49 K10
Hadrian's Wall Nthumb....72 G6
Hadstock Essex....33 N7
Hadzor Worcs....30 B2
Haggersta Shet....111 k4
Haggerston Nthumb....81 L5
Haggs Falk....85 N7
Hagley Herefs....28 G1
Hagley Worcs....40 B10
Hagworthingham Lincs....53 K9
Haile Cumb....62 B1
Hailey Oxon....31 J10
Hailsham E Susx....12 C8
Hail Weston Cambs....32 G4
Hainault Gt Lon....21 P5
Hainford Norfk....45 K6
Hainton Lincs....52 H6
Haisthorpe E R Yk....61 J2
Hakin Pembks....24 F7
Halam Notts....51 P9
Halbeath Fife....86 D5
Halberton Devon....6 D1
Halcro Highld....110 E4
Hale Cumb....63 J6
Hale Halton....57 J11
Hale Hants....8 H4
Hale Surrey....10 D1
Hale Traffd....57 P10
Halebarns Traffd....57 P10
Hales Norfk....45 N10
Hales Staffs....49 N8
Halesowen Dudley....40 C10
Hales Place Kent....23 M10
Hale Street Kent....22 D12
Halesworth Suffk....35 N2
Halewood Knows....57 J10
Halford Devon....5 Q5
Halford Warwks....30 H5
Halfpenny Green Staffs....39 P4
Halfway House Shrops....48 G12
Halfway Houses Kent....22 H8
Halifax Calder....58 E8
Halket E Ayrs....84 G11
Halkirk Highld....110 D4
Halkyn Flints....48 E2
Hall E Rens....84 G11
Halland E Susx....11 P6
Hallaton Leics....42 B10
Hallatrow BaNES....17 P5
Hallbankgate Cumb....72 B8
Hall Dunnerdale Cumb....62 E3
Hallen S Glos....28 G11
Hallgarth Dur....73 N11
Hall Glen Falk....85 P7
Hall Green Birm....40 E10
Hallin Highld....104 C9
Halling Medway....22 E10
Hallington Lincs....53 K6
Hallington Nthumb....72 H6
Halliwell Bolton....57 M6
Halloughton Notts....51 P9
Hallow Worcs....39 P9
Hall's Green Herts....33 J10
Hallyne Border....79 K2
Halmore Gloucs....29 J8
Halnaker W Susx....10 E8
Halsall Lancs....56 G6
Halse Nhants....31 M6
Halse Somset....16 F9
Halsetown Cnwll....2 D7
Halsham E R Yk....61 M8
Halstead Essex....34 D10
Halstead Kent....21 P10
Halstead Leics....41 Q6
Halstock Dorset....7 M2
Haltemprice Crematorium E R Yk....60 H7
Haltham Lincs....53 J10
Halton Bucks....20 E2
Halton Halton....57 K11
Halton Lancs....63 J8
Halton Leeds....59 J7
Halton Nthumb....72 H7
Halton Wrexhm....48 F7
Halton East N York....58 D4
Halton Gill N York....64 F11
Halton Holegate Lincs....53 L9
Halton Lea Gate Nthumb....72 C8
Halton Shields Nthumb....72 H7
Halton West N York....63 Q10
Haltwhistle Nthumb....72 D7
Halvergate Norfk....45 N8
Halwell Devon....5 Q8
Halwill Devon....14 H11
Halwill Junction Devon....14 H11
Ham Devon....6 H3
Ham Gloucs....29 J8
Ham Gt Lon....21 J8
Ham Kent....23 P11
Ham Somset....16 H10
Ham Wilts....19 K8
Hambleden Bucks....20 C6
Hambledon Hants....9 Q4
Hambledon Surrey....10 F3
Hamble-le-Rice Hants....9 N6
Hambleton Lancs....56 G1
Hambleton N York....59 M7
Hambridge Somset....17 K10
Hambrook W Susx....10 C8
Hameringham Lincs....53 K9
Hamerton Cambs....32 F1
Ham Green Worcs....30 D2
Hamilton S Lans....85 M11
Hamilton Services S Lans....85 M10
Hamlet Dorset....7 N2
Hammersmith Gt Lon....21 K7
Hammerwich Staffs....40 E6
Hammoon Dorset....8 B5
Hamnavoe Shet....111 k4
Hampden Park E Susx....12 C9
Hampnett Gloucs....30 E10
Hampole Donc....59 L11
Hampreston Dorset....8 F7
Hampstead Gt Lon....21 L6
Hampstead Norreys W Berk....19 N5
Hampsthwaite N York....58 H3
Hampton C Pete....42 G10
Hampton Gt Lon....21 J9
Hampton Kent....23 M9
Hampton Shrops....39 N5
Hampton Swindn....18 H3
Hampton Worcs....30 D5
Hampton Bishop Herefs....28 G2

Hampton Court Palace Gt Lon....21 J9
Hampton Heath Ches W....49 J5
Hampton in Arden Solhll....40 G10
Hampton Lovett Worcs....30 B2
Hampton Lucy Warwks....30 G3
Hampton Magna Warwks....30 H2
Hampton Poyle Oxon....31 L10
Hampton Wick Gt Lon....21 J9
Hamptworth Wilts....9 J4
Hamsey E Susx....11 N7
Hamstall Ridware Staffs....40 E4
Hamstead Marshall W Berk....19 M7
Hamsterley Dur....65 K2
Hamsterley Dur....73 K9
Hamstreet Kent....13 J4
Ham Street Somset....17 M8
Hanbury Staffs....40 F2
Hanbury Worcs....30 C2
Hanchurch Staffs....49 Q7
Handa Island Highld....108 C6
Hand and Pen Devon....6 E4
Handbridge Ches W....48 H3
Handcross W Susx....11 L4
Handforth Ches E....57 Q11
Handley Ches W....49 J4
Handley Derbys....51 J8
Handsworth Birm....40 D9
Handsworth Sheff....51 K4
Hanging Heaton Kirk....58 G9
Hanging Houghton Nhants....41 Q11
Hanging Langford Wilts....18 F12
Hangleton Br & H....11 L8
Hanham S Glos....17 P2
Hankelow Ches E....49 M6
Hankerton Wilts....29 N9
Hanley C Stke....50 B10
Hanley Castle Worcs....39 Q12
Hanley Child Worcs....39 M8
Hanley Swan Worcs....39 P12
Hanley William Worcs....39 M8
Hanlith N York....58 B2
Hanmer Wrexhm....49 J7
Hannaford Devon....15 K6
Hannington Hants....19 N9
Hannington Nhants....32 B3
Hannington Swindn....18 H3
Hannington Wick Swindn....18 H2
Hanslope M Keyn....32 B7
Hanthorpe Lincs....42 F5
Hanwell Gt Lon....21 J7
Hanwell Oxon....31 K5
Hanwood Shrops....49 J12
Hanworth Gt Lon....20 H8
Hanworth Norfk....45 K3
Happendon S Lans....78 E3
Happendon Services S Lans....78 D3
Happisburgh Norfk....45 N4
Happisburgh Common Norfk....45 N4
Hapsford Ches W....49 J1
Hapton Lancs....57 P3
Hapton Norfk....45 K10
Harberton Devon....5 Q8
Harbertonford Devon....5 Q8
Harbledown Kent....23 L10
Harborne Birm....40 D10
Harborough Magna Warwks....41 L10
Harbottle Nthumb....81 K12
Harbourneford Devon....5 P7
Harbury Warwks....31 J3
Harby Leics....41 Q2
Harby Notts....52 C8
Harcombe Devon....6 B6
Harcombe Devon....6 F5
Harcombe Bottom Devon....7 J4
Harden C Brad....58 E6
Harden Wsall....40 D7
Hardenhuish Wilts....18 D6
Hardgate Abers....95 N2
Hardgate D & G....70 D3
Hardgate W Duns....84 H8
Hardham W Susx....10 H6
Hardingham Norfk....44 H8
Hardingstone Nhants....31 Q3
Hardington Somset....17 Q5
Hardington Mandeville Somset....7 M1
Hardington Marsh Somset....7 M2
Hardington Moor Somset....7 M1
Hardisworthy Devon....14 E7
Hardley Hants....9 M6
Hardley Street Norfk....45 N8
Hardraw N York....64 F8
Hardstoft Derbys....51 K8
Hardway Hants....9 Q7
Hardway Somset....17 Q8
Hardwick Bucks....32 B11
Hardwick Cambs....33 L5
Hardwick Nhants....32 C3
Hardwick Norfk....45 K11
Hardwick Oxon....31 J11
Hardwick Oxon....31 M7
Hardwicke Gloucs....29 L6
Hardwicke Gloucs....29 M4
Hardwick Hall Dur....65 N2
Hardy's Green Essex....34 F11
Hare Croft C Brad....58 E7
Harefield Gt Lon....20 G5
Hare Green Essex....34 H10
Hare Hatch Wokham....20 C7
Harehill Derbys....40 F1
Harehills Leeds....59 J7
Harelaw Border....80 C9
Harelaw D & G....79 N12
Harescombe Gloucs....29 L6
Haresfield Gloucs....29 L6
Harestock Hants....9 M2
Hare Street Essex....21 L6
Hare Street Herts....33 L10
Harewood Leeds....58 H5
Harewood End Herefs....28 F4
Harford Devon....5 M8
Hargrave Ches W....49 J3
Hargrave Nhants....32 E3
Hargrave Suffk....34 C5
Harker Cumb....71 M3
Harkstead Suffk....35 K9
Harlaston Staffs....40 G5
Harlaxton Lincs....42 C4
Harlech Gwynd....47 J5
Harlech Castle Gwynd....47 J5

Harlescott Shrops....49 J11
Harlesden Gt Lon....21 K6
Harlesthorpe Derbys....51 L5
Harleston Devon....5 Q10
Harleston Norfk....45 L12
Harleston Suffk....34 G5
Harlestone Nhants....31 P2
Harle Syke Lancs....57 Q2
Harley Rothm....51 J2
Harley Shrops....39 L2
Harlington C Beds....32 E10
Harlington Donc....51 L1
Harlington Gt Lon....20 H7
Harlosh Highld....96 C2
Harlow Essex....21 N2
Harlow Carr RHS N York....58 H4
Harlow Hill Nthumb....73 J7
Harlthorpe E R Yk....60 C6
Harlton Cambs....33 L6
Harlyn Cnwll....3 K1
Harman's Cross Dorset....8 E10
Harmby N York....65 K9
Harmer Green Herts....33 J12
Harmer Hill Shrops....49 J10
Harmston Lincs....52 D10
Harnage Shrops....39 K2
Harnhill Gloucs....18 F1
Harold Hill Gt Lon....21 Q5
Haroldston West Pembks....24 F6
Haroldswick Shet....111 m2
Harold Wood Gt Lon....22 B5
Harome N York....66 F10
Harpenden Herts....21 J1
Harpford Devon....6 E5
Harpham E R Yk....61 J2
Harpley Norfk....44 D5
Harpley Worcs....39 M9
Harpole Nhants....31 P2
Harpsdale Highld....110 D5
Harpswell Lincs....52 D5
Harpurhey Manch....57 Q8
Harraby Cumb....71 N5
Harracott Devon....15 K6
Harrapool Highld....97 J5
Harrietfield P & K....92 E9
Harrietsham Kent....22 G11
Harringay Gt Lon....21 L6
Harrington Cumb....70 G9
Harrington Lincs....53 L8
Harrington Nhants....41 Q10
Harringworth Nhants....42 D10
Harris W Isls....111 c3
Harrogate N York....58 H3
Harrogate Crematorium N York....58 J4
Harrold Bed....32 D5
Harrow Gt Lon....21 J6
Harrowbarrow Cnwll....5 J6
Harrow Green Suffk....34 E6
Harrow on the Hill Gt Lon....21 J6
Harrow Weald Gt Lon....21 J6
Harston Cambs....33 L6
Harston Leics....42 B4
Harswell E R Yk....60 E6
Hart Hartpl....66 C1
Hartburn Nthumb....73 J4
Hartest Suffk....34 D6
Hartfield E Susx....11 P3
Hartford Cambs....33 J3
Hartford Ches W....49 L2
Hartfordbridge Hants....20 C10
Hartford End Essex....34 B12
Hartforth N York....65 L6
Hartgrove Dorset....8 C4
Harthill Ches W....49 J4
Harthill N Lans....85 Q9
Harthill Rothm....51 L5
Hartington Derbys....50 F8
Hartland Devon....14 E7
Hartland Quay Devon....14 D7
Hartlebury Worcs....39 Q7
Hartlepool Hartpl....66 C2
Hartlepool Crematorium Hartpl....66 C2
Hartley Cumb....64 E6
Hartley Kent....12 F3
Hartley Kent....22 C9
Hartley Wespall Hants....20 B10
Hartley Wintney Hants....20 C11
Hartlip Kent....22 G9
Harton N York....60 C2
Harton S Tyne....73 P7
Hartpury Gloucs....29 L4
Hartshead N York....58 F9
Hartshead Moor Services Calder....58 F8
Hartshill C Stke....49 Q6
Hartshill Warwks....41 J8
Hartshorne Derbys....41 J4
Hartwell Nhants....32 B6
Hartwith N York....58 G2
Hartwood N Lans....85 P10
Hartwoodmyres Border....79 N9
Harvel Kent....22 D10
Harvington Worcs....30 D4
Harvington Worcs....39 Q7
Harwell Notts....51 P3
Harwell Oxon....19 N3
Harwich Essex....35 L9
Harwood Dale N York....67 J7
Harwood Park Crematorium Herts....33 J11
Harworth Notts....51 N3
Hasbury Dudley....40 C10
Hascombe Surrey....10 G3
Haselbech Nhants....41 P11
Haselbury Plucknett Somset....7 L1
Haseley Warwks....30 H2
Haselor Warwks....30 E3
Hasfield Gloucs....29 L4
Haskayne Lancs....56 G7
Hasketon Suffk....35 L6
Haslemere Surrey....10 E4
Haslingden Lancs....57 N4
Haslingfield Cambs....33 L6
Haslington Ches E....49 N4
Hassingham Norfk....45 N8
Hassocks W Susx....11 L6
Hassop Derbys....50 G6
Haster Highld....110 G5
Hastingleigh Kent....13 L2
Hastings E Susx....12 G7
Hastings Borough Crematorium E Susx....12 G7
Hastingwood Essex....21 N2
Hastoe Herts....20 E2

Haswell Dur....73 P11
Haswell Plough Dur....73 P11
Hatch Beauchamp Somset....17 J11
Hatch End Gt Lon....21 J5
Hatchmere Ches W....49 K2
Hatcliffe NE Lin....52 H4
Hatfield Donc....59 P11
Hatfield Herefs....39 L9
Hatfield Herts....21 K2
Hatfield Broad Oak Essex....33 N12
Hatfield Heath Essex....21 Q1
Hatfield Peverel Essex....22 F2
Hatfield Woodhouse Donc....59 P11
Hatford Oxon....19 K2
Hatherden Hants....19 K10
Hatherleigh Devon....15 J10
Hathern Leics....41 L3
Hatherop Gloucs....30 F11
Hathersage Derbys....50 G5
Hathersage Booths Derbys....50 G5
Hatherton Ches E....49 M6
Hatherton Staffs....40 C5
Hatley St George Cambs....33 J6
Hatt Cnwll....5 J7
Hattersley Tamesd....50 C2
Hatton Abers....103 L7
Hatton Angus....93 N7
Hatton Derbys....40 G2
Hatton Gt Lon....20 H8
Hatton Lincs....52 H7
Hatton Shrops....39 J4
Hatton Warrtn....57 L11
Hatton Warwks....30 G1
Hatton of Fintray Abers....102 H11
Haugh E Ayrs....76 H6
Haugham Lincs....53 K7
Haughhead E Duns....85 K7
Haughley Suffk....34 G4
Haughley Green Suffk....34 G4
Haugh of Glass Moray....101 M7
Haugh of Urr D & G....70 D3
Haughs of Kinnaird Angus....93 Q4
Haughton Shrops....49 H9
Haughton Staffs....49 Q10
Haughton le Skerne Darltn....65 N4
Haughton Moss Ches E....49 L4
Haultwick Herts....33 K11
Haunton Staffs....40 G5
Hauxton Cambs....33 M6
Havant Hants....10 B8
Havant Crematorium Hants....10 B8
Havenstreet IoW....9 P8
Havercroft Wakefd....59 K10
Haverfordwest Pembks....24 G6
Haverhill Suffk....33 Q7
Haverigg Cumb....62 D6
Havering-atte-Bower Gt Lon....21 P5
Haversham M Keyn....32 B8
Haverthwaite Cumb....62 G5
Havyat N Som....17 L4
Hawarden Flints....48 G3
Hawbush Green Essex....34 D11
Hawen Cerdgn....36 F10
Hawes N York....64 F9
Hawe's Green Norfk....45 L9
Hawford Worcs....39 Q9
Hawick Border....80 C10
Hawkchurch Devon....7 J3
Hawkedon Suffk....34 D6
Hawkeridge Wilts....18 C9
Hawkesbury S Glos....18 B4
Hawkesbury Upton S Glos....18 B4
Hawkhurst Kent....12 F4
Hawkinge Kent....13 N3
Hawkinge Crematorium Kent....13 M3
Hawkley Hants....10 C4
Hawkridge Somset....15 P6
Hawkshead Cumb....62 G3
Hawkshead Hill Cumb....62 G3
Hawksland S Lans....78 D2
Hawkstone Shrops....49 L9
Hawkswick N York....64 G12
Hawksworth Leeds....58 F6
Hawksworth Notts....51 Q11
Hawkwell Essex....22 G5
Hawley Hants....20 D10
Hawling Gloucs....30 E9
Hawnby N York....66 D9
Haworth C Brad....58 D6
Hawstead Suffk....34 D5
Hawthorn Dur....73 P10
Hawthorn Hill Lincs....52 H11
Hawton Notts....52 B12
Haxby C York....59 N3
Haxey N Linc....51 Q2
Haycombe Crematorium BaNES....17 Q4
Haydock St Hel....57 K9
Haydon Bridge Nthumb....72 F7
Haydon Wick Swindn....18 G4
Hayes Gt Lon....20 H7
Hayes Gt Lon....21 N9
Hayes End Gt Lon....20 H7
Hayfield Ag & B....90 E10
Hayfield Derbys....50 D4
Hayhillock Angus....93 N7
Hayle Cnwll....2 E8
Hayle Port Cnwll....2 E8
Hayley Green Dudley....40 C10
Hayling Island Hants....10 B9
Hayne Devon....6 P3
Haynes (Church End) C Beds....32 F8
Haynes (Northwood End) C Beds....32 F8
Haynes (Silver End) C Beds....32 F8
Haynes (West End) C Beds....32 F8
Hay-on-Wye Powys....27 L2
Hayscastle Pembks....24 F4
Hayscastle Cross Pembks....24 G4
Hay Street Herts....33 L10
Hayton Cumb....70 H7
Hayton Cumb....71 Q4
Hayton E R Yk....60 E5
Hayton Notts....51 Q4
Haytor Vale Devon....5 P5
Haytown Devon....14 G9
Haywards Heath W Susx....11 M5

Haywood Donc....59 N10
Hazelbank S Lans....77 P3
Hazelbury Bryan Dorset....7 Q2
Hazeleigh Essex....22 G3
Hazel Grove Stockp....50 B4
Hazelton Walls Fife....93 J10
Hazelwood Derbys....51 J10
Hazlemere Bucks....20 E4
Hazlerigg N u Ty....73 M6
Hazleton Gloucs....30 E9
Heacham Norfk....44 B3
Headbourne Worthy Hants....9 N2
Headcorn Kent....12 G2
Headingley Leeds....58 H7
Headington Oxon....31 M11
Headlam Dur....65 L4
Headlesscross N Lans....85 Q10
Headless Cross Worcs....30 D2
Headley Hants....10 D3
Headley Hants....19 N8
Headley Surrey....21 K11
Headley Down Hants....10 D3
Headon Notts....51 Q5
Heads Nook Cumb....71 P5
Heage Derbys....51 J10
Healaugh N York....59 L5
Healaugh N York....64 H7
Heald Green Stockp....57 Q10
Heale Somset....16 H11
Heale Somset....17 K10
Healey N York....65 L10
Healeyfield Dur....73 J10
Healing NE Lin....61 L11
Heamoor Cnwll....2 C9
Heanor Derbys....51 K10
Heanton Punchardon Devon....15 J5
Heapham Lincs....52 C6
Heart of England Crematorium Warwks....41 J8
Heart of Scotland Services N Lans....85 Q9
Heasley Mill Devon....15 M6
Heast Highld....96 H6
Heath Derbys....51 K7
Heath Wakefd....59 J9
Heath and Reach C Beds....32 D10
Heathcote Derbys....50 F8
Heather Leics....41 K5
Heathfield E Susx....12 C6
Heathfield Somset....16 F10
Heath Green Worcs....40 E12
Heath Hall D & G....78 G11
Heath Hayes & Wimblebury Staffs....40 D5
Heath Hill Shrops....49 N11
Heathrow Airport Gt Lon....20 H8
Heathton Shrops....39 P4
Heath Town Wolves....40 B7
Heatley Warrtn....57 N10
Heaton C Brad....58 F7
Heaton N u Ty....73 M7
Heaton Staffs....50 C8
Heaton's Bridge Lancs....56 H6
Heaverham Kent....22 C10
Heavitree Devon....6 C4
Hebburn S Tyne....73 N7
Hebden N York....58 D2
Hebden Bridge Calder....58 C8
Hebing End Herts....33 K11
Hebron Carmth....25 L4
Hebron Nthumb....73 L4
Heckfield Hants....20 B10
Heckfield Green Suffk....35 K2
Heckfordbridge Essex....34 F11
Heckington Lincs....42 G2
Heckmondwike Kirk....58 G9
Heddington Wilts....18 E7
Heddon-on-the-Wall Nthumb....73 K7
Hedenham Norfk....45 M10
Hedge End Hants....9 N5
Hedgerley Bucks....20 F6
Hedging Somset....17 J9
Hedley on the Hill Nthumb....73 J8
Hednesford Staffs....40 D5
Hedon E R Yk....61 K8
Hedsor Bucks....20 E6
Heglibister Shet....111 k4
Heighington Darltn....65 M3
Heighington Lincs....52 E9
Heightington Worcs....39 N7
Heiton Border....80 F7
Hele Devon....6 D3
Hele Devon....15 J3
Helensburgh Ag & B....84 E6
Helenton S Ayrs....76 G5
Helford Cnwll....2 H9
Helford Passage Cnwll....2 H9
Helhoughton Norfk....44 E5
Helions Bumpstead Essex....33 Q8
Helland Cnwll....4 N2
Hellescott Cnwll....4 G3
Hellesdon Norfk....45 K7
Hellidon Nhants....31 M3
Hellifield N York....63 Q10
Hellingly E Susx....12 C7
Helmdon Nhants....31 N5
Helme Kirk....58 E10
Helmingham Suffk....35 K5
Helmsdale Highld....110 B11
Helmshore Lancs....57 P5
Helmsley N York....66 E10
Helperby N York....59 K1
Helperthorpe N York....67 K12
Helpringham Lincs....42 G2
Helpston C Pete....42 G9
Helsby Ches W....49 J1
Helston Cnwll....2 G9
Helstone Cnwll....4 D4
Helton Cumb....71 Q10
Hemel Hempstead Herts....20 G2
Hemerdon Devon....5 L8
Hemingbrough N York....59 P7
Hemingby Lincs....53 J8
Hemingford Abbots Cambs....33 J3
Hemingford Grey Cambs....33 J3
Hemingstone Suffk....35 J6
Hemington Leics....41 L2
Hemington Nhants....42 F12
Hemington Somset....17 Q5
Hemley Suffk....35 L8
Hemlington Middsb....66 C5
Hempnall Norfk....45 L10

80 Hempnall Green - Horrocksford

Hempnall Green Norfk 45 L10
Hempriggs Moray 100 H3
Hempstead Essex 33 Q8
Hempstead Norfk 44 H3
Hempstead Norfk 45 N5
Hempton Norfk 44 E4
Hempton Oxon 31 K7
Hemsby Norfk 45 P6
Hemswell Lincs 52 D5
Hemswell Cliff Lincs 52 D5
Hemsworth Wakefd 59 K10
Hemyock Devon 16 F12
Hendon Gt Lon 21 K5
Hendon Sundld 73 P9
Hendon Crematorium Gt Lon 21 K5
Hendy Carmth 26 D7
Henfield W Susx 11 K6
Hengoed Caerph 27 N9
Hengoed Powys 38 E10
Hengrave Suffk 34 D3
Henham Essex 33 N10
Heniarth Powys 38 D1
Henlade Somset 16 H10
Henley Dorset 7 Q2
Henley Somset 17 L9
Henley Suffk 35 J6
Henley W Susx 10 E5
Henley-in-Arden Warwks 30 F2
Henley-on-Thames Oxon 20 C6
Henley's Down E Susx 12 E7
Henllan Cerdgn 36 F11
Henllan Denbgs 55 Q7
Henllys Torfn 28 B9
Henlow C Beds 32 H8
Hennock Devon 5 Q4
Henny Street Essex 34 E8
Henryd Conwy 55 L6
Henry's Moat (Castell Hendre) Pembks 24 H4
Hensall N York 59 N9
Henshaw Nthumb 72 D7
Hensingham Cumb 70 G11
Henstead Suffk 45 P11
Hensting Hants 9 N3
Henstridge Somset 17 Q11
Henstridge Ash Somset 17 Q11
Henton Oxon 20 C3
Henton Somset 17 L7
Henwick Worcs 39 Q10
Henwood Cnwll 4 G5
Heol-y-Cyw Brdgnd 27 K11
Hepple Nthumb 72 H1
Hepscott Nthumb 73 L4
Heptonstall Calder 58 C8
Hepworth Kirk 58 F11
Hepworth Suffk 34 G2
Herbrandston Pembks 24 F7
Hereford Herefs 28 F2
Hereford Crematorium Herefs 28 F2
Hereson Kent 23 Q9
Heribusta Highld 104 E8
Heriot Border 86 H10
Hermiston C Edin 86 E8
Hermitage Border 79 P9
Hermitage Dorset 7 P2
Hermitage W Berk 19 N6
Hermon Carmth 25 N3
Hermon Pembks 25 L3
Herne Kent 23 M9
Herne Bay Kent 23 M9
Herne Hill Gt Lon 21 L8
Herne Pound Kent 22 D11
Hernhill Kent 23 K10
Herodsfoot Cnwll 4 F7
Heronsford S Ayrs 68 F3
Herriard Hants 19 Q10
Herringfleet Suffk 45 P9
Herringswell Suffk 34 C3
Herringthorpe Rothm 51 K3
Herrington Sundld 73 P9
Hersden Kent 23 M10
Hersham Surrey 20 H9
Herstmonceux E Susx 12 D7
Herston Ork 111 h3
Hertford Herts 21 M2
Hertford Heath Herts 21 M2
Hertingfordbury Herts 21 L2
Hesketh Bank Lancs 57 J4
Hesketh Lane Lancs 57 L1
Hesket Newmarket Cumb 71 M7
Hesleden Dur 73 Q12
Heslington C York 59 N4
Hessay C York 59 M4
Hessenford Cnwll 4 G8
Hessett Suffk 34 F4
Hessle E R Yk 60 H8
Hessle Wakefd 59 K10
Hest Bank Lancs 63 J8
Heston Gt Lon 20 H7
Heston Services Gt Lon 20 H7
Hestwall Ork 111 g2
Heswall Wirral 56 F11
Hethe Oxon 31 N8
Hethersett Norfk 45 J8
Hethersgill Cumb 71 P3
Hett Dur 73 M12
Hetton N York 58 C3
Hetton-le-Hole Sundld 73 N10
Heugh Nthumb 73 J6
Heughhead Abers 101 M11
Heugh Head Border 87 Q9
Heveningham Suffk 35 M3
Hever Kent 11 P2
Heversham Cumb 63 J5
Hevingham Norfk 45 K6
Hewas Water Cnwll 3 L6
Hewelsfield Gloucs 28 G8
Hewish Somset 7 K2
Hewood Dorset 7 J3
Hexham Nthumb 72 G7
Hextable Kent 21 P8
Hexthorpe Donc 51 M1
Hexton Herts 32 F10
Hexworthy Cnwll 4 H4
Hexworthy Devon 5 N6
Heybridge Essex 22 D4
Heybridge Essex 22 G2
Heybrook Bay Devon 5 K9
Heydon Cambs 33 M8
Heydon Norfk 45 J5
Heydour Lincs 42 E3
Heylipoll Ag & B 88 B7
Heylor Shet 111 j3
Heysham Lancs 62 H9
Heyshott W Susx 10 E6
Heytesbury Wilts 18 D11
Heythrop Oxon 31 J8
Heywood Rochdl 57 Q6
Heywood Wilts 18 C9
Hibaldstow N Linc 52 D3
Hickleton Donc 59 L12
Hickling Norfk 45 N5
Hickling Notts 41 P2
Hickling Green Norfk 45 N5
Hickstead W Susx 11 L6
Hidcote Bartrim Gloucs 30 F5
Hidcote Boyce Gloucs 30 F6
High Ackworth Wakefd 59 K9
Higham Barns 58 H11
Higham Derbys 51 K8
Higham Kent 12 C1
Higham Kent 22 E8
Higham Lancs 57 P2
Higham Suffk 34 C4
Higham Suffk 34 G9
Higham Ferrers Nhants 32 D3
Higham Gobion C Beds 32 F9
Higham Hill Gt Lon 21 M5
Higham on the Hill Leics 41 J8
Highampton Devon 14 H10
Highams Park Gt Lon 21 M5
High Ardwell D & G 68 E9
High Auldgirth D & G 78 E10
High Bankhill Cumb 71 Q7
High Beach Essex 21 N4
High Bentham N York 63 M8
High Bickington Devon 15 K7
High Biggins Cumb 63 L6
High Blantyre S Lans 85 L10
High Bonnybridge Falk 85 N7
High Bray Devon 15 M5
Highbridge Somset 17 J6
Highbrook W Susx 11 M4
High Brooms Kent 12 C2
Highburton Kirk 58 F10
Highbury Gt Lon 21 L6
Highbury Somset 17 Q6
High Casterton Cumb 63 L6
High Catton E R Yk 60 C4
Highclere Hants 19 M8
Highcliffe Dorset 8 H8
High Coniscliffe Darltn 65 M5
High Crosby Cumb 71 P4
High Cross E Ayrs 76 G3
High Cross Hants 10 B5
High Cross Herts 33 K11
High Cross Warwks 30 G1
High Drummore D & G 68 F11
High Easter Essex 22 C1
High Ellington N York 65 L10
Higher Ansty Dorset 8 B6
Higher Bartle Lancs 57 J3
Higher Bockhampton Dorset 7 Q4
Higher Brixham Torbay 6 C10
High Ercall Wrekin 49 L11
Higher Chillington Somset 7 K2
Higher Folds Wigan 57 M8
Higher Gabwell Devon 6 C8
Higher Heysham Lancs 62 H9
Higher Irlam Salfd 57 N9
Higher Kinnerton Flints 48 G4
Higher Muddiford Devon 15 K5
Higher Penwortham Lancs 57 K3
Higher Prestacott Devon 14 G11
Higher Town Cnwll 3 J6
Higher Town Cnwll 3 M4
Higher Town IoS 2 c1
Higher Walton Lancs 57 L4
Higher Walton Warrtn 57 L10
Higher Wambrook Somset 6 H2
Higher Waterston Dorset 7 Q4
Higher Wheelton Lancs 57 L4
Higher Whitley Ches W 57 L11
Higher Wincham Ches W 57 M12
Higher Wraxhall Dorset 7 N3
Higher Wych Ches W 49 J6
High Etherley Dur 65 L2
Highfield Gatesd 73 K8
Highfield N Ayrs 76 E2
High Garrett Essex 34 C10
Highgate Gt Lon 21 L6
High Grantley N York 65 M12
High Green Norfk 45 J11
High Green Norfk 45 J8
High Green Sheff 51 J2
High Halden Kent 12 H3
High Halstow Medway 22 F8
High Ham Somset 17 K9
High Harrogate N York 58 H3
High Hatton Shrops 49 L9
High Hauxley Nthumb 73 M1
High Hawsker N York 67 K6
High Hesket Cumb 71 P6
High Hoyland Barns 58 H11
High Hurstwood E Susx 11 P5
High Hutton N York 60 D1
High Ireby Cumb 71 K7
High Kilburn N York 66 D10
High Lands Dur 65 K3
Highlane Derbys 51 K4
High Lane Stockp 50 C4
High Lanes Cnwll 2 E8
Highleadon Gloucs 29 K4
High Legh Ches E 57 M11
Highleigh W Susx 10 D9
High Leven S on T 66 C5
Highley Shrops 39 N5
High Littleton BaNES 17 P5
High Lorton Cumb 71 J9
High Marnham Notts 52 B9
High Melton Donc 51 L1
High Mickley Nthumb 73 J8
Highmoor Oxon 20 B6
Highmoor Cross Oxon 20 B6
Highnam Gloucs 29 K5
High Newport Sundld 73 P9
High Newton Cumb 62 H5
High Nibthwaite Cumb 62 F4
High Offley Staffs 49 P9
High Ongar Essex 22 C3
High Onn Staffs 49 P11
High Park Corner Essex 34 G11
High Pennyvenie E Ayrs 76 H9
High Roding Essex 33 P12
High Salvington W Susx 10 H8
High Spen Gatesd 73 K8
Highsted Kent 22 H10
High Street Cnwll 3 L5
Highstreet Kent 23 L10
Highstreet Green Surrey 10 F3
Hightae D & G 78 H11
Hightown Sefton 56 F7
Hightown Green Suffk 34 F5
High Toynton Lincs 53 J9
High Valleyfield Fife 86 B5
Highweek Devon 6 B8
Highwood Hill Gt Lon 21 K5
Highworth Swindn 18 H3
High Wray Cumb 62 G3
High Wych Herts 21 P1
High Wycombe Bucks 20 D5
Hilborough Norfk 44 D9
Hilcott Wilts 18 G8
Hildenborough Kent 12 C1
Hilden Park Kent 12 C1
Hildersham Cambs 33 N7
Hilderstone Staffs 40 C1
Hilderthorpe E R Yk 61 K2
Hilgay Norfk 43 P9
Hill S Glos 28 H9
Hill Warwks 31 L2
Hillam N York 59 L8
Hill Brow Hants 10 C5
Hillbutts Dorset 8 E7
Hill Chorlton Staffs 49 P7
Hillcliffane Derbys 50 H10
Hill Common Somset 16 F10
Hilldyke Lincs 43 K1
Hill End Fife 86 C3
Hillend Fife 86 D5
Hill End Gloucs 29 M2
Hillend Mdloth 86 F8
Hillend N Lans 85 N9
Hillesden Bucks 31 P8
Hillesley Gloucs 29 K10
Hillfarrance Somset 16 F10
Hill Green Kent 22 G10
Hillhead Abers 102 D8
Hill Head Hants 9 P6
Hillhead S Lans 78 F2
Hillhead of Cocklaw Abers 103 M6
Hilliclay Highld 110 D3
Hillingdon Gt Lon 20 H6
Hillington C Glas 85 J9
Hillington Norfk 44 C5
Hillmorton Warwks 41 M11
Hill of Beath Fife 86 D4
Hill of Fearn Highld 107 N6
Hillowton D & G 70 C3
Hill Ridware Staffs 40 E4
Hillside Abers 95 Q3
Hillside Angus 95 L9
Hill Side Kirk 58 F10
Hills Town Derbys 51 L6
Hillstreet Hants 9 K4
Hillswick Shet 111 j3
Hill Top Wakefd 59 J10
Hillwell Shet 111 k5
Hilmarton Wilts 18 E6
Hilperton Wilts 18 C8
Hilsea C Port 9 Q6
Hilston E R Yk 61 M7
Hilton Border 81 J4
Hilton Cambs 33 J4
Hilton Cumb 64 D4
Hilton Derbys 40 G2
Hilton Dorset 8 B6
Hilton Dur 65 L3
Hilton Highld 107 P7
Hilton S on T 66 C5
Hilton Shrops 39 P3
Hilton Park Services Staffs 40 C6
Himbleton Worcs 30 C3
Himley Staffs 39 Q4
Hincaster Cumb 63 K5
Hinchley Wood Surrey 21 J9
Hinckley Leics 41 K8
Hinderclay Suffk 34 G2
Hinderwell N York 66 H4
Hindhead Surrey 10 E3
Hindley Wigan 57 L7
Hindlip Worcs 39 Q9
Hindolveston Norfk 44 G4
Hindon Wilts 8 D2
Hindringham Norfk 44 G3
Hingham Norfk 44 G9
Hinstock Shrops 49 M9
Hintlesham Suffk 34 H7
Hinton Herefs 28 D2
Hinton S Glos 17 Q2
Hinton Shrops 38 H1
Hinton Ampner Hants 9 P2
Hinton Blewett BaNES 17 N5
Hinton Charterhouse BaNES 18 B8
Hinton-in-the-Hedges Nhants 31 M6
Hinton Martell Dorset 8 E6
Hinton on the Green Worcs 30 D6
Hinton Parva Swindn 19 J4
Hinton St George Somset 7 K1
Hinton St Mary Dorset 8 B4
Hinton Waldrist Oxon 19 L2
Hints Staffs 40 F6
Hinwick Bed 32 D5
Hinxhill Kent 13 K2
Hinxton Cambs 33 M7
Hinxworth Herts 32 H8
Hipperholme Calder 58 E8
Hipswell N York 65 L7
Hirn Abers 95 M2
Hirnant Powys 48 B10
Hirst Nthumb 73 M4
Hirst Courtney N York 59 N8
Hirwaun Rhondd 27 K7
Hiscott Devon 15 J7
Histon Cambs 33 M4
Hitcham Suffk 34 G6
Hitcham Causeway Suffk 34 G6
Hitcham Street Suffk 34 G6
Hitchin Herts 32 H10
Hither Green Gt Lon 21 M8
Hittisleigh Devon 5 P2
Hive E R Yk 60 E7
Hixon Staffs 40 D3
Hoaden Kent 23 N10
Hoar Cross Staffs 40 F3
Hoarwithy Herefs 28 G3
Hoath Kent 23 M9
Hobarris Shrops 38 F6
Hobkirk Border 80 D11
Hobson Dur 73 L9
Hoby Leics 41 P4
Hockering Norfk 44 H7
Hockerton Notts 51 Q9
Hockley Essex 22 G5
Hockley Heath Solhll 40 F11
Hockliffe C Beds 32 D10
Hockwold cum Wilton Norfk 44 C11
Hockworthy Devon 16 D11
Hoddesdon Herts 21 M2
Hoddlesden Bl w D 57 N4
Hoddom Cross D & G 71 J2
Hoddom Mains D & G 71 J2
Hodgeston Pembks 24 H8
Hodnet Shrops 49 L9
Hodsock Notts 51 N4
Hodsoll Street Kent 22 D10
Hodson Swindn 18 H5
Hodthorpe Derbys 51 M5
Hoe Norfk 44 G6
Hogben's Hill Kent 23 K11
Hoggeston Bucks 32 B10
Hoggrill's End Warwks 40 G8
Hoghton Lancs 57 L4
Hognaston Derbys 50 G10
Hogsthorpe Lincs 53 N8
Holbeach Lincs 43 K5
Holbeach Bank Lincs 43 K5
Holbeach Clough Lincs 43 K5
Holbeach Drove Lincs 43 K7
Holbeach Hurn Lincs 43 L5
Holbeach St Johns Lincs 43 K6
Holbeach St Mark's Lincs 43 L4
Holbeach St Matthew Lincs 43 L4
Holbeck Notts 51 M6
Holberrow Green Worcs 30 D3
Holbeton Devon 5 M9
Holborn Gt Lon 21 L7
Holbrook Derbys 51 J11
Holbrook Suffk 35 J9
Holbrooks Covtry 41 J10
Holbury Hants 9 M6
Holcombe Devon 6 C7
Holcombe Somset 17 P6
Holcombe Rogus Devon 16 E11
Holcot Nhants 32 B3
Holden Lancs 63 P11
Holdenby Nhants 31 P1
Holder's Green Essex 33 Q10
Holdgate Shrops 39 K4
Holdingham Lincs 42 F1
Holditch Dorset 7 J3
Holemoor Devon 14 H10
Holford Somset 16 F7
Holgate C York 59 N4
Holker Cumb 62 G6
Holkham Norfk 44 E2
Hollacombe Devon 14 G10
Holland Fen Lincs 52 H12
Holland-on-Sea Essex 35 K12
Hollandstoun Ork 111 i1
Hollee D & G 71 L2
Hollesley Suffk 35 M7
Hollicombe Torbay 6 B9
Hollingbourne Kent 22 G11
Hollingbury Br & H 11 L8
Hollingdon Bucks 32 C10
Hollington Derbys 50 G11
Hollington Staffs 50 D11
Hollingworth Tamesd 50 D2
Hollinsclough Staffs 50 E7
Hollins End Sheff 51 J4
Hollins Green Warrtn 57 M10
Hollinswood Wrekin 39 N1
Hollinwood Crematorium Oldham 50 B1
Hollocombe Devon 15 L9
Holloway Derbys 51 J9
Holloway Gt Lon 21 L6
Hollowell Nhants 41 P11
Hollowmoor Heath Ches W 49 J2
Hollows D & G 79 N12
Hollybush Caerph 27 N7
Hollybush E Ayrs 76 G8
Hollybush Herefs 29 K2
Hollym E R Yk 61 N8
Holmbridge Kirk 58 E11
Holmbury St Mary Surrey 10 H2
Holmbush Cnwll 3 M5
Holmcroft Staffs 40 B3
Holme Cambs 42 H11
Holme Cumb 63 K6
Holme Kirk 58 E11
Holme N York 65 P10
Holme Notts 52 B10
Holme Chapel Lancs 57 Q3
Holme Hale Norfk 44 E8
Holme Lacy Herefs 28 G2
Holme Marsh Herefs 38 G10
Holme next the Sea Norfk 44 B2
Holme on the Wolds E R Yk 60 G5
Holme Pierrepont Notts 51 N11
Holmer Herefs 28 F1
Holmer Green Bucks 20 E4
Holme St Cuthbert Cumb 70 H6
Holmes Chapel Ches E 49 N3
Holmesfield Derbys 50 H5
Holmeswood Lancs 56 H5
Holmethorpe Surrey 21 L12
Holme upon Spalding Moor E R Yk 60 D6
Holmewood Derbys 51 K7
Holmfirth Kirk 58 F11
Holmhead E Ayrs 77 J7
Holmpton E R Yk 61 N9
Holmrook Cumb 62 C3
Holmsford Bridge Crematorium N Ayrs 76 F4
Holmside Dur 73 L10
Holne Devon 5 N6
Holnicote Somset 16 C6
Holsworthy Devon 14 F10
Holsworthy Beacon Devon 14 G9
Holt Dorset 8 F6
Holt Norfk 44 H3
Holt Wilts 18 C8
Holt Worcs 39 P9
Holt Wrexhm 48 H5
Holtby C York 59 P4
Holt End Worcs 40 E12
Holt Heath Worcs 39 P9
Holton Oxon 31 N11
Holton Somset 17 P10
Holton Suffk 35 N2
Holton cum Beckering Lincs 52 G7
Holton le Clay Lincs 53 J3
Holton le Moor Lincs 52 F4
Holton St Mary Suffk 34 H8
Holwell Dorset 7 Q1
Holwell Herts 32 G9
Holwell Leics 41 Q3
Holwell Oxon 30 G11
Holwick Dur 64 G3
Holybourne Hants 10 B2
Holyhead IoA 54 C5
Holy Island IoA 54 C5
Holy Island Nthumb 81 N5
Holy Island Nthumb 81 N6
Holymoorside Derbys 51 J7
Holyport W & M 20 E7
Holystone Nthumb 72 G1
Holytown N Lans 85 M10
Holytown Crematorium N Lans 85 N10
Holywell C Beds 32 E12
Holywell Cambs 33 K3
Holywell Cnwll 2 H4
Holywell Dorset 7 N2
Holywell Flints 48 E1
Holywell Green Calder 58 E9
Holywell Lake Somset 16 F11
Holywell Row Suffk 34 B2
Holywood D & G 78 F11
Holywood Village D & G 78 F11
Homer Shrops 39 L2
Homer Green Sefton 56 G8
Homersfield Suffk 45 L11
Homington Wilts 8 G3
Honeybourne Worcs 30 E5
Honeychurch Devon 15 L10
Honeystreet Wilts 18 G8
Honey Tye Suffk 34 F9
Honiley Warwks 40 G11
Honing Norfk 45 M5
Honingham Norfk 44 H7
Honington Lincs 42 D2
Honington Suffk 34 E2
Honington Warwks 30 H5
Honiton Devon 6 F3
Honley Kirk 58 F10
Honor Oak Crematorium Gt Lon 21 M8
Hooe C Plym 5 K9
Hooe E Susx 12 E7
Hoo Green Ches E 57 N11
Hoohill Bpool 56 G2
Hook E R Yk 60 D8
Hook Gt Lon 21 J9
Hook Hants 20 B11
Hook Pembks 24 G6
Hook Wilts 18 F4
Hooke Dorset 7 M3
Hook Green Kent 12 D3
Hook Green Kent 22 C8
Hook Norton Oxon 31 J7
Hookway Devon 15 P11
Hooley Surrey 21 L11
Hoo St Werburgh Medway 22 F8
Hooton Levitt Rothm 51 M3
Hooton Pagnell Donc 59 L11
Hooton Roberts Rothm 51 L2
Hope Derbys 50 F4
Hope Devon 5 N11
Hope Flints 48 F4
Hope Staffs 50 E9
Hope Bagot Shrops 39 L7
Hope Bowdler Shrops 39 J4
Hopehouse Border 79 L5
Hopeman Moray 100 H2
Hope Mansell Herefs 28 H5
Hopesay Shrops 38 H5
Hope under Dinmore Herefs 39 K10
Hopgrove C York 59 N3
Hopperton N York 59 K3
Hopstone Shrops 39 P4
Hopton Derbys 50 H9
Hopton Staffs 40 C3
Hopton Suffk 34 G2
Hopton Cangeford Shrops 39 K6
Hopton Castle Shrops 38 G6
Hoptonheath Shrops 38 H6
Hopton on Sea Norfk 45 Q9
Hopton Wafers Shrops 39 M6
Hopwas Staffs 40 F6
Hopwood Worcs 40 D11
Hopwood Park Services Worcs 40 D11
Horam E Susx 12 C6
Horbling Lincs 42 G3
Horbury Wakefd 58 H9
Horden Dur 73 Q11
Hordle Hants 9 J8
Hordley Shrops 48 H8
Horfield Bristl 17 N2
Horham Suffk 35 K3
Horkesley Heath Essex 34 G10
Horkstow N Linc 60 G9
Horley Oxon 31 K5
Horley Surrey 11 L2
Hornblotton Green Somset 17 N9
Hornby Lancs 63 L8
Hornby N York 65 L8
Hornby N York 65 P6
Horncastle Lincs 53 J9
Hornchurch Gt Lon 21 Q6
Horncliffe Nthumb 81 K4
Horndean Border 81 J4
Horndean Hants 10 B7
Horndon Devon 5 L4
Horndon on the Hill Thurr 22 D6
Horne Surrey 11 M2
Horner Somset 16 B7
Horning Norfk 45 M6
Horninghold Leics 42 B10
Horninglow Staffs 40 G3
Horningsea Cambs 33 M4
Horningsham Wilts 18 B11
Horningtoft Norfk 44 F5
Horns Cross Devon 14 G7
Hornsea E R Yk 61 K5
Hornsey Gt Lon 21 L5
Hornton Oxon 31 K5
Horra Shet 111 k2
Horrabridge Devon 5 K6
Horringer Suffk 34 D4
Horrocksford Lancs 63 N12

Horsebridge - Kelmscott 181

Horsebridge Devon 5 J5
Horsebridge E Susx 12 C7
Horsebridge Hants 9 L2
Horsehay Wrekin 39 M1
Horseheath Cambs 33 P7
Horsehouse N York 65 J10
Horsell Surrey 20 F10
Horseman's Green Wrexhm 49 J7
Horsey Norfk 45 P5
Horsey Somset 17 J8
Horsford Norfk 45 K6
Horsforth Leeds 58 G6
Horsham W Susx 11 J4
Horsham Worcs 39 N9
Horsham St Faith Norfk 45 K7
Horsington Lincs 52 H9
Horsington Somset 17 Q10
Horsley Derbys 51 J11
Horsley Gloucs 29 L8
Horsley Nthumb 72 F2
Horsley Nthumb 73 J7
Horsleycross Street Essex 35 J10
Horsleyhill Border 80 C9
Horsley Woodhouse Derbys 51 K11
Horsmonden Kent 12 E2
Horspath Oxon 31 M12
Horstead Norfk 45 L6
Horsted Keynes W Susx 11 M5
Horton Bucks 32 D11
Horton Dorset 8 F6
Horton Lancs 63 Q11
Horton Nhants 32 B6
Horton S Glos 18 A4
Horton Somset 17 J12
Horton Staffs 50 C8
Horton Swans 26 C10
Horton W & M 20 G8
Horton Wilts 18 F7
Horton Wrekin 49 M11
Horton-cum-Studley Oxon 31 N10
Horton Green Ches W 49 J5
Horton-in-Ribblesdale N York 64 E12
Horton Kirby Kent 22 C9
Horwich Bolton 57 M6
Horwood Devon 15 J6
Hoscote Border 79 N6
Hose Leics 41 Q2
Hosh P & K 92 C10
Hoswick Shet 111 k5
Hotham E R Yk 60 F7
Hothfield Kent 13 J2
Hoton Leics 41 M3
Hough Ches E 49 N5
Hougham Lincs 42 C2
Hough Green Halton 57 J10
Hough-on-the-Hill Lincs 42 D2
Houghton Cambs 33 J3
Houghton Hants 9 K2
Houghton Pembks 24 H7
Houghton W Susx 10 G7
Houghton Conquest C Beds 32 F8
Houghton Green E Susx 12 H5
Houghton-le-Spring Sundld 73 N10
Houghton on the Hill Leics 41 P6
Houghton Regis C Beds 32 E11
Houghton St Giles Norfk 44 F3
Hound Green Hants 20 B10
Houndslow Border 80 E5
Houndwood Border 87 Q9
Hounslow Gt Lon 21 J8
Househill Highld 100 D4
Houses Hill Kirk 58 G10
Housieside Abers 103 J9
Houston Rens 84 G9
Houstry Highld 110 D8
Houton Ork 111 g2
Hove Br & H 11 L8
Hoveringham Notts 51 P10
Hoveton Norfk 45 M6
Hovingham N York 66 F11
How Caple Herefs 28 H3
Howden E R Yk 60 D8
Howden-le-Wear Dur 65 L2
Howe Highld 110 F4
Howe N York 65 P10
Howe Norfk 45 L9
Howe Bridge Crematorium Wigan 57 M8
Howe Green Essex 22 E3
Howegreen Essex 22 G3
Howell Lincs 42 G2
Howe of Teuchar Abers 102 G6
Howes D & G 71 K3
Howe Street Essex 22 E1
Howe Street Essex 34 B9
Howey Powys 38 C9
Howgate Cumb 70 G10
Howgate Mdloth 86 F10
Howick Nthumb 81 Q10
Howlett End Essex 33 P9
Howley Somset 6 H2
How Mill Cumb 71 Q4
Howmore W Isls 111 a5
Hownam Border 80 G9
Howsham N Linc 52 E3
Howsham N York 60 C2
Howtel Nthumb 81 J7
Howwood Rens 84 G10
Hoxne Suffk 35 K2
Hoy Ork 111 g3
Hoylake Wirral 56 E10
Hoyland Nether Barns 51 J1
Hoyland Swaine Barns 58 H12
Hubberston Pembks 24 F7
Huby N York 58 H5
Huby N York 59 M2
Hucclecote Gloucs 29 M5
Hucking Kent 22 G10
Hucknall Notts 51 M10
Huddersfield Kirk 58 F10
Huddersfield Crematorium Kirk 58 F9
Huddington Worcs 30 C3
Hudswell N York 65 K7
Huggate E R Yk 60 F3
Hughenden Valley Bucks 20 D4
Hughley Shrops 39 K3
Hugh Town IoS 2 c2
Huish Devon 15 J9
Huish Wilts 18 G7
Huish Champflower Somset 16 E9
Huish Episcopi Somset 17 L10
Hulcott Bucks 32 C12
Hulham Devon 6 D6
Hulland Derbys 50 G10
Hulland Ward Derbys 50 G10
Hullavington Wilts 18 D4
Hullbridge Essex 22 F4
Hull, Kingston upon C KuH 61 J8
Hulme Manch 57 Q9
Hulme Staffs 50 C10
Hulme Warrtn 57 L9
Hulme End Staffs 50 E8
Hulme Walfield Ches E 49 Q3
Hulverstone IoW 9 L9
Hulver Street Suffk 45 P11
Humberside Airport N Linc 61 J11
Humberston NE Lin 53 K3
Humberstone C Leic 41 N6
Humbie E Loth 87 J9
Humbleton E R Yk 61 L7
Humby Lincs 42 E4
Hume Border 80 F6
Humshaugh Nthumb 72 G6
Huna Highld 110 G2
Huncote Leics 41 M7
Hundalee Border 80 E9
Hunderthwaite Dur 64 H4
Hundleby Lincs 53 L9
Hundleton Pembks 24 G8
Hundon Suffk 34 C7
Hundred House Powys 38 C10
Hungarton Leics 41 P6
Hungerford Somset 16 E7
Hungerford W Berk 19 K7
Hungerford Newtown W Berk 19 L6
Hungerstone Herefs 28 E2
Hunmanby N York 67 N11
Hunningham Warwks 31 J1
Hunsbury Hill Nhants 31 Q3
Hunsdon Herts 21 N1
Hunsingore N York 59 K4
Hunslet Leeds 58 H7
Hunsonby Cumb 64 B1
Hunstanton Norfk 43 Q3
Hunstanworth Dur 72 G10
Hunsterson Ches E 49 M6
Hunston Suffk 34 F3
Hunston W Susx 10 D9
Hunstrete BaNES 17 P4
Hunsworth Kirk 58 F8
Hunter's Quay Ag & B 84 C7
Huntham Somset 17 J10
Hunthill Lodge Angus 94 H7
Huntingdon Cambs 33 J3
Huntingfield Suffk 35 M2
Huntington C York 59 N3
Huntington Ches W 48 H3
Huntington E Loth 87 J7
Huntington Herefs 38 F10
Huntington Staffs 40 C5
Huntley Gloucs 29 J5
Huntly Abers 102 C7
Hunton Kent 22 E12
Hunton N York 65 L8
Huntscott Somset 16 C7
Huntsham Devon 16 D11
Huntshaw Devon 15 J7
Huntspill Somset 17 J7
Huntstile Somset 16 H9
Huntworth Somset 17 J8
Hunwick Dur 65 L2
Hunworth Norfk 44 H3
Hurdcott Wilts 8 H1
Hurdsfield Ches E 50 B6
Hurley W & M 20 D6
Hurley Warwks 40 G8
Hurley Common Warwks 40 G7
Hurlford E Ayrs 76 H4
Hurn Dorset 8 G7
Hursley Hants 9 M3
Hurst Wokham 20 C8
Hurstbourne Priors Hants 19 M10
Hurstbourne Tarrant Hants 19 L9
Hurst Green E Susx 12 E5
Hurst Green Essex 34 H12
Hurst Green Lancs 57 M2
Hurst Green Surrey 21 N12
Hurstpierpoint W Susx 11 L6
Hurstwood Lancs 57 Q3
Hurtiso Ork 111 h2
Hurworth-on-Tees Darltn 65 N5
Hurworth Place Darltn 65 N5
Husbands Bosworth Leics 41 N10
Husborne Crawley C Beds 32 D9
Husthwaite N York 66 D11
Hutcliffe Wood Crematorium Sheff 51 J4
Huthwaite Notts 51 L8
Huttoft Lincs 53 N8
Hutton Border 81 J4
Hutton E R Yk 60 H4
Hutton Essex 22 D4
Hutton Lancs 57 J4
Hutton N Som 17 J4
Hutton Buscel N York 67 L10
Hutton Conyers N York 65 N11
Hutton Cranswick E R Yk 60 H4
Hutton End Cumb 71 P7
Hutton Henry Dur 65 Q1
Hutton-le-Hole N York 66 G9
Hutton Lowcross R & Cl 66 E5
Hutton Magna Dur 65 K5
Hutton Roof Cumb 63 K6
Hutton Roof Cumb 71 M8
Hutton Rudby N York 66 C6
Hutton Sessay N York 66 C11
Hutton Wandesley N York 59 L4
Huxham Devon 6 C4
Huxley Ches W 49 K3
Huyton Knows 57 J10
Hycemoor Cumb 62 C4
Hyde Tamesd 50 C2
Hyde Heath Bucks 20 E4
Hyde Lea Staffs 40 B4
Hylands House & Park Essex 22 D3
Hyndford Bridge S Lans 78 E1
Hynish Ag & B 88 C8
Hyssington Powys 38 F4
Hythe Essex 34 G10
Hythe Hants 9 M6
Hythe Kent 13 M3
Hythe End W & M 20 G8

I

Ibberton Dorset 8 B6
Ible Derbys 50 G9
Ibsley Hants 8 H5
Ibstock Leics 41 K5
Ibstone Bucks 20 C5
Ibthorpe Hants 19 L9
Iburndale N York 67 J6
Ibworth Hants 19 P9
Ichrachan Ag & B 90 D9
Ickburgh Norfk 44 D10
Ickenham Gt Lon 20 H6
Ickford Bucks 31 N11
Ickham Kent 23 N10
Ickleford Herts 32 H9
Icklesham E Susx 12 G6
Ickleton Cambs 33 M7
Icklingham Suffk 34 C3
Ickornshaw N York 58 C5
Ickwell Green C Beds 32 G7
Icomb Gloucs 30 G9
Idbury Oxon 30 G9
Iddesleigh Devon 15 K9
Ide Devon 6 B5
Ideford Devon 6 B7
Ide Hill Kent 21 P11
Iden E Susx 12 H5
Iden Green Kent 12 E3
Iden Green Kent 12 F4
Idle C Brad 58 F6
Idless Cnwll 3 J6
Idlicote Warwks 30 H5
Idmiston Wilts 18 H12
Idole Carmth 25 P6
Idridgehay Derbys 50 H10
Idrigill Highld 104 E9
Idstone Oxon 19 J4
Iffley Oxon 31 M12
Ifield W Susx 11 K3
Ifold W Susx 10 G4
Iford Bmouth 8 G8
Iford E Susx 11 N8
Ifton Mons 28 F10
Ightfield Shrops 49 L7
Ightham Kent 22 C11
Ilam Staffs 50 F10
Ilchester Somset 17 M10
Ilderton Nthumb 81 L9
Ilford Gt Lon 21 N6
Ilford Somset 17 K11
Ilfracombe Devon 15 J3
Ilkeston Derbys 51 L11
Ilketshall St Andrew Suffk 45 N11
Ilketshall St Margaret Suffk 45 M11
Ilkley C Brad 58 E5
Illand Cnwll 4 G5
Illey Dudley 40 C10
Illogan Cnwll 2 G7
Illston on the Hill Leics 41 P7
Ilmer Bucks 20 C3
Ilmington Warwks 30 G5
Ilminster Somset 17 J12
Ilsington Devon 5 Q5
Ilston Swans 26 D10
Ilton N York 65 L11
Ilton Somset 17 J11
Imachar N Ayrs 75 N4
Immingham NE Lin 61 K10
Immingham Dock NE Lin 61 K10
Impington Cambs 33 M4
Ince Ches W 57 J12
Ince Blundell Sefton 56 G8
Ince-in-Makerfield Wigan 57 L7
Inchbae Lodge Hotel Highld 106 G8
Inchbare Angus 95 K8
Inchberry Moray 101 L4
Incheril Highld 105 Q9
Inchinnan Rens 84 H8
Inchlaggan Highld 98 B8
Inchmichael P & K 93 J9
Inchnacardoch Hotel Highld 98 E6
Inchnadamph Highld 108 E10
Inchture P & K 93 K9
Inchvuilt Highld 98 C2
Inchyra P & K 92 H10
Indian Queens Cnwll 3 K4
Ingatestone Essex 22 D4
Ingbirchworth Barns 58 G11
Ingestre Staffs 40 C3
Ingham Lincs 52 D6
Ingham Norfk 45 N5
Ingham Suffk 34 E3
Ingham Corner Norfk 45 N5
Ingleby Derbys 41 J3
Ingleby Arncliffe N York 66 C7
Ingleby Barwick S on T 66 C5
Ingleby Greenhow N York 66 E6
Ingleigh Green Devon 15 K10
Inglesbatch BaNES 17 Q4
Inglesham Swindn 18 H2
Ingleston D & G 70 F3
Ingleton Dur 65 L4
Ingleton N York 63 M7
Inglewhite Lancs 57 K2
Ingoe Nthumb 73 J6
Ingol Lancs 57 K3
Ingoldisthorpe Norfk 44 B4
Ingoldmells Lincs 53 N9
Ingoldsby Lincs 42 E4
Ingram Nthumb 81 L10
Ingrave Essex 22 D5
Ingrow C Brad 58 D6
Ings Cumb 63 J3
Ingst S Glos 28 G10
Ingthorpe Rutlnd 42 E8
Ingworth Norfk 45 K4
Inkberrow Worcs 30 D3
Inkhorn Abers 103 J7
Inkpen W Berk 19 L7
Inkstack Highld 110 F2
Innellan Ag & B 84 C8
Innerleithen Border 79 M2
Innerleven Fife 86 H3
Innermessan D & G 68 E6
Innerwick E Loth 87 N7
Innesmill Moray 101 K3
Insch Abers 102 E9
Insh Highld 99 M8
Inskip Lancs 57 J2
Instow Devon 14 H6
Intake Sheff 51 K4
Inver Abers 94 D4
Inver Highld 107 P6
Inver P & K 92 F7
Inverailort Highld 97 K12
Inveralligin Highld 105 M10
Inverallochy Abers 103 L3
Inveran Highld 107 J3
Inveraray Ag & B 84 B2
Inverarish Highld 96 G3
Inverarity Angus 93 M6
Inverarnan Stirlg 91 J11
Inverasdale Highld 105 M5
Inverbeg Ag & B 84 F4
Inverbervie Abers 95 N7
Inver-boyndie Abers 102 E3
Invercreran House Hotel Ag & B 90 D7
Inverdruie Highld 99 N6
Inveresk E Loth 86 G7
Inveresragan Ag & B 90 D8
Inverey Abers 94 B4
Inverfarigaig Highld 98 G4
Inverfolla Ag & B 90 C7
Invergarry Highld 98 D8
Invergeldie P & K 91 Q10
Invergloy Highld 98 C10
Invergordon Highld 107 L8
Invergowrie P & K 93 L9
Inverguseran Highld 97 K8
Inverhadden P & K 91 P5
Inverherive Hotel Stirlg 91 K10
Inverie Highld 97 K9
Inverinan Ag & B 90 D11
Inverinate Highld 97 N5
Inverkeilor Angus 93 R6
Inverkeithing Fife 86 D5
Inverkeithny Abers 102 E6
Inverkip Inver 84 D8
Inverkirkaig Highld 108 B10
Inverlael Highld 106 C5
Inverlair Highld 98 D11
Inverliever Lodge Ag & B 83 N2
Inverlochy Ag & B 90 G10
Invermark Angus 94 G6
Invermoriston Highld 98 F5
Invernaver Highld 109 M4
Inverness Highld 107 L12
Inverness Airport Highld 107 M11
Inverness Crematorium Highld 99 J1
Invernoaden Ag & B 84 C4
Inveroran Hotel Ag & B 90 H7
Inverquharity Angus 93 M4
Inverquhomery Abers 103 L6
Inverroy Highld 98 C11
Inversanda Highld 90 C4
Invershiel Highld 97 N6
Invershin Highld 107 J3
Invershore Highld 110 F8
Inversnaid Hotel Stirlg 84 F2
Inverugie Abers 103 M6
Inveruglas Ag & B 84 F2
Inveruglass Highld 99 M8
Inverurie Abers 102 G10
Inwardleigh Devon 15 K11
Inworth Essex 34 E12
Iochdar W Isls 111 a5
Iona Ag & B 88 G10
Iping W Susx 10 D5
Ipplepen Devon 5 Q7
Ipsden Oxon 19 Q4
Ipstones Staffs 50 D10
Ipswich Suffk 35 J7
Ipswich Crematorium Suffk 35 K7
Irby Wirral 56 F11
Irby in the Marsh Lincs 53 M10
Irby upon Humber NE Lin 52 H3
Irchester Nhants 32 D4
Ireby Cumb 71 K7
Ireby Lancs 63 M7
Ireleth Cumb 62 E6
Ireshopeburn Dur 72 F12
Irlam Salfd 57 N9
Irnham Lincs 42 E5
Iron Acton S Glos 29 J11
Ironbridge Wrekin 39 M2
Ironbridge Gorge Wrekin 39 M2
Ironmacannie D & G 69 P4
Ironville Derbys 51 K9
Irstead Norfk 45 M6
Irthington Cumb 71 P4
Irthlingborough Nhants 32 D3
Irton N York 67 L10
Irvine N Ayrs 76 F4
Isauld Highld 110 A3
Isbister Shet 111 k2
Isbister Shet 111 m3
Isfield E Susx 11 N6
Isham Nhants 32 C3
Isington Hants 10 C2
Islay Ag & B 82 E7
Islay Airport Ag & B 74 D3
Isle Abbotts Somset 17 J11
Isle Brewers Somset 17 K11
Isleham Cambs 33 Q2
Isle of Dogs Gt Lon 21 M7
Isle of Grain Medway 22 G7
Isle of Lewis W Isls 111 d2
Isle of Man IoM 56 c4
Isle of Man Ronaldsway Airport IoM 56 b7
Isle of Mull Ag & B 89 M8
Isle of Purbeck Dorset 8 E10
Isle of Sheppey Kent 23 J9
Isle of Skye Highld 96 E3
Isle of Thanet Kent 23 P9
Isle of Walney Cumb 62 E8
Isle of Whithorn D & G 69 L10
Isle of Wight IoW 9 N9
Isle of Wight Crematorium IoW 9 N8
Isleornsay Highld 97 J7
Isles of Scilly IoS 2 c2
Isles of Scilly St Mary's Airport IoS 2 c2
Islesteps D & G 70 F2
Isleworth Gt Lon 21 J8
Isley Walton Leics 41 K3
Islibhig W Isls 111 b2
Islington Gt Lon 21 L6
Islip Nhants 32 E2
Islip Oxon 31 M10
Islivig W Isls 111 b2
Isombridge Wrekin 49 L11
Itchen Abbas Hants 9 N2
Itchen Stoke Hants 9 P2
Itchingfield W Susx 11 J4
Itteringham Norfk 45 J4
Itton Mons 28 F9
Itton Common Mons 28 F9
Ivegill Cumb 71 N6
Iver Bucks 20 G7
Iver Heath Bucks 20 G6
Iveston Dur 73 K10
Ivinghoe Bucks 32 D12
Ivinghoe Aston Bucks 32 D12
Ivington Herefs 39 J10
Ivybridge Devon 5 M8
Ivychurch Kent 13 K5
Ivy Hatch Kent 22 C11
Iwade Kent 22 H9
Iwerne Courtney or Shroton Dorset 8 C5
Iwerne Minster Dorset 8 C5
Ixworth Suffk 34 F3
Ixworth Thorpe Suffk 34 F3

J

Jack-in-the-Green Devon 6 D4
Jackton S Lans 85 K11
Jacobstow Cnwll 4 F2
Jacobstowe Devon 15 K10
Jameston Pembks 25 J8
Jamestown Highld 106 H10
Jamestown W Duns 84 G6
Janetstown Highld 110 E8
Janetstown Highld 110 G5
Jardine Hall D & G 78 H10
Jarrow S Tyne 73 N7
Jasper's Green Essex 34 C10
Jawcraig Falk 85 P7
Jaywick Essex 23 M1
Jedburgh Border 80 E9
Jeffreyston Pembks 25 J7
Jemimaville Highld 107 M8
Jerbourg Guern 6 c2
Jersey Jersey 7 b1
Jersey Airport Jersey 7 a2
Jersey Crematorium Jersey 7 b2
Jesmond N u Ty 73 M7
Jevington E Susx 12 C9
Jockey End Herts 20 G1
Johnby Cumb 71 N8
John Lennon Airport Lpool 56 H11
John o' Groats Highld 110 H2
Johnshaven Abers 95 N8
Johnston Pembks 24 G6
Johnstone D & G 79 L8
Johnstone Rens 84 G9
Johnstonebridge D & G 78 H9
Johnstown Carmth 25 P5
Johnstown Wrexhm 48 F6
Joppa C Edin 86 G7
Joppa Cerdgn 37 J7
Joppa S Ayrs 76 G7
Jordanston Pembks 24 G3
Joyden's Wood Kent 21 P8
Juniper Nthumb 72 G8
Juniper Green C Edin 86 E8
Jura Ag & B 82 G6
Jurassic Coast Devon 7 J5
Jurby IoM 56 c2

K

Kaber Cumb 64 E5
Kaimend S Lans 86 B11
Kames Ag & B 83 P8
Kames E Ayrs 77 L6
Kea Cnwll 3 J7
Keadby N Linc 60 E10
Keal Cotes Lincs 53 K10
Kearsley Bolton 57 N7
Kearsney Kent 13 P2
Kearstwick Cumb 63 L6
Kedington Suffk 34 B7
Kedleston Derbys 50 H11
Keelby Lincs 61 K11
Keele Staffs 49 P6
Keele Services Staffs 49 P6
Keelham C Brad 58 E7
Keeston Pembks 24 F5
Keevil Wilts 18 D8
Kegworth Leics 41 L3
Kehelland Cnwll 2 F7
Keig Abers 102 D10
Keighley C Brad 58 D6
Keighley Crematorium C Brad 58 D6
Keilarsbrae Clacks 85 P4
Keillour P & K 92 E9
Keiloch Abers 94 C4
Keils Ag & B 82 G8
Keinton Mandeville Somset 17 M9
Keir Mill D & G 78 E9
Keisley Cumb 64 D3
Keiss Highld 110 G4
Keith Moray 101 N5
Keithick P & K 93 J7
Keithock Angus 95 K8
Keithtown Highld 106 H10
Kelbrook Lancs 58 B5
Kelby Lincs 42 E2
Keld N York 64 F7
Kelfield N York 59 N6
Kelham Notts 51 Q9
Kelhead D & G 71 J2
Kellamergh Lancs 56 H3
Kellas Angus 93 M8
Kellas Moray 101 J5
Kellaton Devon 5 Q11
Kelling Norfk 44 H2
Kellington N York 59 M8
Kelloe Dur 73 N12
Kelloholm D & G 77 M8
Kelly Devon 5 J4
Kelmarsh Nhants 41 Q10
Kelmscott Oxon 19 J2

Kelsale Suffk 35 N4
Kelsall Ches W 49 K2
Kelshall Herts 33 K9
Kelsick Cumb 71 K5
Kelso Border 80 G7
Kelstedge Derbys 51 J7
Kelstern Lincs 53 J5
Kelston BaNES 17 Q3
Keltneyburn P & K 92 B6
Kelton D & G 70 G2
Kelty Fife 86 D4
Kelvedon Essex 34 E11
Kelvedon Hatch Essex 22 C4
Kelynack Cnwll 2 B9
Kemback Fife 93 M11
Kemberton Shrops 39 N2
Kempley Gloucs 29 J3
Kemble Gloucs 29 P8
Kemerton Worcs 29 N2
Kemeys Commander Mons 28 D7
Kemnay Abers 102 F11
Kempley Gloucs 29 J3
Kempley Green Gloucs 29 J3
Kempsey Worcs 39 Q11
Kempsford Gloucs 18 H2
Kempshott Hants 19 P10
Kempston Bed 32 E7
Kempton Shrops 38 G5
Kemp Town Br & H 11 M8
Kemsing Kent 22 B10
Kemsley Kent 23 ...
Kenardington Kent 13 J4
Kenchester Herefs 38 H12
Kencot Oxon 30 G12
Kendal Cumb 63 K4
Kenfig Brdgnd 26 H11
Kenilworth Warwks 40 H12
Kenley Gt Lon 21 L10
Kenley Shrops 39 K3
Kenmore Highld 105 L10
Kenmore P & K 92 B6
Kenn Devon 6 C6
Kenn N Som 17 K3
Kennacraig Ag & B 83 M9
Kennall Vale Cnwll 2 H8
Kennerleigh Devon 15 P10
Kennessee Green Sefton 56 H8
Kennet Clacks 85 Q5
Kennethmont Abers 102 C9
Kennett Cambs 34 B3
Kennford Devon 6 C5
Kenninghall Norfk 44 G11
Kennington Kent 13 K2
Kennington Oxon 19 N1
Kennoway Fife 86 G2
Kenny Somset 17 J11
Kennyhill Suffk 33 Q2
Kennythorpe N York 60 D2
Kenovay Ag & B 88 C7
Kensaleyre Highld 104 F11
Kensington Gt Lon 21 K7
Kensington Palace Gt Lon 21 K7
Kensworth C Beds 32 E12
Kensworth Common C Beds 32 E12
Kentallen Highld 90 D5
Kent and Sussex Crematorium Kent 12 C3
Kentchurch Herefs 28 E4
Kentford Suffk 34 B4
Kent International Airport Kent 23 P9
Kentisbeare Devon 6 E2
Kentisbury Devon 15 L4
Kentish Town Gt Lon 21 L6
Kentmere Cumb 63 J2
Kenton Devon 6 C6
Kenton Gt Lon 21 J6
Kenton N u Ty 73 L7
Kenton Suffk 35 K4
Kentra Highld 89 N3
Kent's Green Gloucs 29 K4
Kent's Oak Hants 9 K3
Kenwyn Cnwll 3 J6
Keoldale Highld 108 G3
Keppoch Highld 97 M5
Kepwick N York 66 C8
Keresley Covtry 40 H10
Kerrera Ag & B 89 Q10
Kerris Cnwll 2 C9
Kerry Powys 38 D4
Kerrycroy Ag & B 84 B10
Kersall Notts 51 Q8
Kersbrook Devon 6 E6
Kersey Suffk 34 G7
Kershader W Isls 111 d2
Kerswell Devon 6 E2
Kerswell Green Worcs 39 Q11
Kesgrave Suffk 35 K7
Kessingland Suffk 45 Q11
Kestle Cnwll 3 L6
Kestle Mill Cnwll 3 J4
Keston Gt Lon 21 N9
Keswick Cumb 71 L10
Keswick Norfk 45 K8
Kettering Nhants 32 C2
Kettering Crematorium Nhants 32 C2
Ketteringham Norfk 45 J9
Kettins P & K 93 J7
Kettlebaston Suffk 34 F6
Kettlebridge Fife 86 G2
Kettlebrook Staffs 40 G6
Kettleburgh Suffk 35 L5
Kettleholm D & G 79 J12
Kettleshulme Ches E 50 C5
Kettlesing N York 58 G3
Kettlesing Bottom N York 58 G3
Kettlestone Norfk 44 F4
Kettlethorpe Lincs 52 C8
Kettletoft Ork 111 i1
Kettlewell N York 64 H11
Ketton Rutlnd 42 E8
Kew Gt Lon 21 J7
Kew Royal Botanic Gardens Gt Lon 21 J7
Kewstoke N Som 17 J4
Kexby York 60 C4
Kexby Lincs 52 C6
Key Green Ches E 50 B7
Keyham Leics 41 P6
Keyhaven Hants 9 K8
Keyingham E R Yk 61 L8
Keymer W Susx 11 L7
Keynsham BaNES 17 P3
Keysoe Bed 32 F4
Keysoe Row Bed 32 F4
Keyston Cambs 32 F2
Keyworth Notts 41 N2

Kibblesworth Gatesd 73 M9
Kibworth Beauchamp Leics 41 P8
Kibworth Harcourt Leics 41 P8
Kidbrooke Gt Lon 21 N7
Kidderminster Worcs 39 Q6
Kidlington Oxon 31 L10
Kidmore End Oxon 20 B7
Kidsdale D & G 69 L10
Kidsgrove Staffs 49 Q5
Kidwelly Carmth 25 P7
Kiel Crofts Ag & B 90 C8
Kielder Nthumb 72 B3
Kiells Ag & B 82 F8
Kilbarchan Rens 84 G9
Kilbeg Highld 97 J8
Kilberry Ag & B 83 K9
Kilbirnie N Ayrs 84 E11
Kilbride Ag & B 83 L7
Kilbride Ag & B 83 Q9
Kilbuiack Moray 100 G4
Kilburn Derbys 51 J10
Kilburn Gt Lon 21 K6
Kilburn N York 66 D10
Kilby Leics 41 N8
Kilchamaig Ag & B 83 M10
Kilchattan Ag & B 82 E4
Kilchattan Ag & B 84 B11
Kilcheran Ag & B 89 Q8
Kilchoan Highld 89 K4
Kilchoman Ag & B 82 C9
Kilchrenan Ag & B 90 E10
Kilconquhar Fife 87 J2
Kilcot Gloucs 29 J4
Kilcoy Highld 107 J11
Kilcreggan Ag & B 84 D6
Kildale N York 66 E5
Kildalloig Ag & B 75 L8
Kildary Highld 107 M7
Kildavaig Ag & B 83 Q9
Kildavanan Ag & B 83 Q9
Kildonan Highld 109 Q10
Kildonan N Ayrs 75 Q8
Kildonan Lodge Highld 109 Q10
Kildonnan Highld 96 F11
Kildrochet House D & G 68 E7
Kildrummy Abers 101 N10
Kildwick N York 58 D5
Kilfinan Ag & B 83 P7
Kilfinnan Highld 98 C9
Kilgetty Pembks 25 K7
Kilgrammie S Ayrs 76 E10
Kilgwrrwg Common Mons 28 F8
Kilham E R Yk 60 H2
Kilkenneth Ag & B 88 B7
Kilkenzie Ag & B 75 K7
Kilkerran Ag & B 75 L8
Kilkhampton Cnwll 14 E9
Killamarsh Derbys 51 L5
Killay Swans 26 E9
Killearn Stirlg 85 J6
Killen Highld 107 L10
Killerby Darltn 65 L4
Killerton Devon 6 D3
Killichonan P & K 91 M5
Killiechonate Highld 98 C11
Killiechronan Ag & B 89 L7
Killiecrankie P & K 92 D3
Killilan Highld 97 N4
Killimster Highld 110 G4
Killin Stirlg 91 N9
Killinghall N York 58 H3
Killington Cumb 63 L5
Killingworth N Tyne 73 M6
Killochyett Border 87 J12
Kilmacolm Inver 84 F8
Kilmahog Stirlg 85 K2
Kilmahumaig Ag & B 83 L4
Kilmaluag Highld 104 F7
Kilmany Fife 93 L10
Kilmarnock E Ayrs 76 G4
Kilmartin Ag & B 83 M3
Kilmaurs E Ayrs 76 G3
Kilmelford Ag & B 83 M1
Kilmersdon Somset 17 Q6
Kilmeston Hants 9 P3
Kilmichael Ag & B 75 K7
Kilmichael Glassary Ag & B 83 N4
Kilmichael of Inverlussa Ag & B 83 L6
Kilmington Devon 6 H4
Kilmington Wilts 18 B12
Kilmington Common Wilts 8 B1
Kilmington Street Wilts 8 B1
Kilmorack Highld 106 H12
Kilmore Ag & B 90 B10
Kilmore Highld 97 J8
Kilmory Ag & B 83 K7
Kilmory Highld 89 L3
Kilmory N Ayrs 75 P7
Kilmuir Highld 104 C11
Kilmuir Highld 104 E8
Kilmuir Highld 107 L11
Kilmuir Highld 107 M7
Kilmun Ag & B 84 C6
Kilncadzow S Lans 77 P2
Kilndown Kent 12 E3
Kilninver Ag & B 89 Q11
Kilnsea E R Yk 61 P10
Kilnsey N York 58 C1
Kilnwick E R Yk 60 G4
Kiloran Ag & B 82 E4
Kilpatrick N Ayrs 75 N7
Kilpeck Herefs 28 E3
Kilpin E R Yk 60 D8
Kilrenny Fife 87 L2
Kilsby Nhants 41 M12
Kilspindie P & K 93 J9
Kilstay D & G 68 F10
Kilsyth N Lans 85 M7
Kiltarlity Highld 98 G3
Kilton R & Cl 66 F4
Kilton Thorpe R & Cl 66 F4
Kilvaxter Highld 104 E8
Kilve Somset 16 F7
Kilvington Notts 51 B2
Kilwinning N Ayrs 76 E3
Kimberley Norfk 44 H8
Kimberley Notts 51 L11
Kimberworth Rothm 51 K3
Kimblesworth Dur 73 M10

Kimbolton Cambs 32 F4
Kimbolton Herefs 39 K9
Kimcote Leics 41 N9
Kimmeridge Dorset 8 D10
Kimpton Hants 19 J10
Kimpton Herts 32 H11
Kinbrace Highld 109 Q8
Kinbuck Stirlg 85 N3
Kincaple Fife 93 M11
Kincardine Fife 85 Q5
Kincardine Highld 107 K6
Kincardine O'Neil Abers 95 K3
Kinclaven P & K 92 H7
Kincorth C Aber 95 Q2
Kincorth House Moray 100 F3
Kincraig Highld 99 M7
Kincraigie P & K 92 E6
Kindallachan P & K 92 E6
Kinerarach Ag & B 75 J2
Kineton Gloucs 30 D4
Kineton Warwks 31 J4
Kinfauns P & K 92 H10
Kingarth Ag & B 84 B10
Kingcausie Abers 95 P3
Kingcoed Mons 28 E7
Kingerby Lincs 52 F5
Kingham Oxon 30 H8
Kingholm Quay D & G 70 F2
Kinghorn Fife 86 F5
Kinglassie Fife 86 E3
Kingoldrum Angus 93 L5
Kingoodie P & K 93 L9
Kingsand Cnwll 5 J9
Kingsbarns Fife 93 Q12
Kingsbridge Devon 5 P10
Kingsbridge Somset 16 D8
King's Bromley Staffs 40 E4
Kingsburgh Highld 104 E10
Kingsbury Gt Lon 21 J5
Kingsbury Warwks 40 G8
Kingsbury Episcopi Somset 17 L11
King's Caple Herefs 28 G3
Kingsclere Hants 19 N8
King's Cliffe Nhants 42 E10
Kingscote Gloucs 29 L9
Kingscott Devon 15 J8
King's Coughton Warwks 30 E3
Kingscross N Ayrs 75 Q6
Kingsdon Somset 17 M10
Kingsdown Kent 13 Q1
Kingsdown Swindn 18 H3
Kingsdown Wilts 18 B7
Kingsdown Crematorium Swindn 18 H3
Kingseat Fife 86 D4
Kingsey Bucks 20 C3
Kingsfold W Susx 11 J3
Kingsford C Aber 95 P1
Kingsford E Ayrs 76 H2
Kingsgate Kent 23 Q8
Kingshall Street Suffk 34 F4
King's Heath Birm 40 E10
Kings Hill Kent 22 D11
King's Hill Wsall 40 C8
Kings House Hotel Highld 90 H5
Kingshouse Hotel Stirlg 91 N11
Kingskerswell Devon 6 B8
Kingskettle Fife 86 G1
Kingsland Herefs 38 J9
Kingsland IoA 54 C5
Kings Langley Herts 20 H3
King's Lynn Norfk 43 P6
Kings Meaburn Cumb 64 B4
King's Mills Guern 6 b2
Kingsmuir Angus 93 N6
Kingsmuir Fife 87 K1
Kings Muir Border 79 L2
Kingsnorth Kent 13 J3
King's Norton Birm 40 D10
King's Norton Leics 41 P7
Kings Nympton Devon 15 M8
King's Pyon Herefs 38 H11
Kings Ripton Cambs 33 J2
King's Somborne Hants 9 L2
King's Stag Dorset 7 Q1
King's Stanley Gloucs 29 L7
King's Sutton Nhants 31 L6
Kingstanding Birm 40 E8
Kingsteignton Devon 6 B8
Kingsthorne Herefs 28 F3
Kingsthorpe Nhants 31 Q2
Kingston Cambs 33 K6
Kingston Cnwll 4 H5
Kingston Devon 5 M10
Kingston Dorset 7 Q2
Kingston Dorset 8 E10
Kingston E Loth 87 K6
Kingston IoW 9 N10
Kingston Kent 23 M12
Kingston Bagpuize Oxon 19 L2
Kingston Blount Oxon 20 B4
Kingston Deverill Wilts 18 C12
Kingstone Herefs 28 E2
Kingstone Somset 17 K12
Kingstone Staffs 40 D2
Kingston Lacy House & Gardens Dorset 8 E7
Kingston Lisle Oxon 19 K4
Kingston near Lewes E Susx 11 N8
Kingston on Soar Notts 41 L2
Kingston on Spey Moray 101 L3
Kingston Russell Dorset 7 N5
Kingston St Mary Somset 16 G9
Kingston Seymour N Som 17 K3
Kingston upon Hull C KuH 61 J8
Kingston upon Thames Gt Lon 21 J9
Kingston upon Thames Crematorium Gt Lon 21 J9
King's Walden Herts 32 G11
Kingswear Devon 6 B11
Kingswells C Aber 95 P1
Kings Weston Bristl 28 G12
Kingswinford Dudley 40 B9
Kingswood Bucks 31 Q9
Kingswood Gloucs 29 K9
Kingswood S Glos 17 P2
Kingswood Somset 16 F8
Kingswood Surrey 21 K11
Kingswood Warwks 40 F12

Kingswood Common Staffs 39 Q2
Kings Worthy Hants 9 N2
Kingthorpe Lincs 52 G8
Kington Herefs 38 F10
Kington S Glos 28 H10
Kington Worcs 30 C3
Kington Langley Wilts 18 D5
Kington Magna Dorset 8 B3
Kington St Michael Wilts 18 D5
Kingussie Highld 99 L8
Kingweston Somset 17 M9
Kinharrachie Abers 103 J8
Kinharvie D & G 70 F3
Kinkell Bridge P & K 92 D11
Kinknockie Abers 103 L8
Kinleith C Edin 86 E8
Kinlet Shrops 39 N6
Kinloch Highld 96 E9
Kinloch Highld 108 G8
Kinloch Highld 109 K5
Kinloch P & K 92 H6
Kinlochard Stirlg 84 H3
Kinlochbervie Highld 108 E4
Kinlocheil Highld 90 D1
Kinlochewe Highld 105 Q9
Kinloch Hourn Highld 97 N8
Kinlochlaggan Highld 98 G10
Kinlochleven Highld 90 G4
Kinlochmoidart Highld 89 P2
Kinlochnanuagh Highld 97 K11
Kinloch Rannoch P & K 91 P5
Kinloss Moray 100 G3
Kinmel Bay Conwy 55 P5
Kinmuck Abers 102 H10
Kinmundy Abers 103 J10
Kinnabus Ag & B 74 D4
Kinnadie Abers 103 K6
Kinnaird P & K 92 E4
Kinneff Abers 95 N6
Kinnelhead D & G 78 G8
Kinnell Angus 93 Q5
Kinnerley Shrops 48 G10
Kinnersley Herefs 38 G11
Kinnersley Worcs 39 Q12
Kinnerton Powys 38 E9
Kinnesswood P & K 86 E2
Kinnordy Angus 93 L5
Kinoulton Notts 41 P2
Kinross P & K 86 D2
Kinrossie P & K 92 H8
Kinross Services P & K 86 D2
Kinsham Herefs 38 G8
Kinsham Worcs 29 N2
Kinsley Wakefd 59 K10
Kinson Bmouth 8 F7
Kintail Highld 97 P6
Kintbury W Berk 19 L7
Kintessack Moray 100 F4
Kintillo P & K 92 G11
Kinton Herefs 38 H7
Kinton Shrops 48 G10
Kintore Abers 102 G11
Kintour Ag & B 74 F3
Kintra Ag & B 74 D3
Kintra Ag & B 88 H10
Kintraw Ag & B 83 M3
Kintyre Ag & B 75 L5
Kinveachy Highld 99 N5
Kinver Staffs 39 Q5
Kippax Leeds 59 K7
Kippen Stirlg 85 L4
Kippford or Scaur D & G 70 D5
Kipping's Cross Kent 12 D3
Kirbister Ork 111 h2
Kirby Bedon Norfk 45 L8
Kirby Bellars Leics 41 Q4
Kirby Cane Norfk 45 N10
Kirby Cross Essex 35 K11
Kirby Fields Leics 41 M6
Kirby Grindalythe N York 60 F1
Kirby Hill N York 59 K1
Kirby Hill N York 65 K6
Kirby Knowle N York 66 C9
Kirby le Soken Essex 35 K11
Kirby Misperton N York 66 H10
Kirby Muxloe Leics 41 M6
Kirby Underdale E R Yk 60 D3
Kirby Wiske N York 65 P9
Kirdford W Susx 10 G5
Kirk Highld 110 F4
Kirkabister Shet 111 k4
Kirkandrews D & G 69 N9
Kirkandrews upon Eden Cumb 71 M4
Kirkbampton Cumb 71 L4
Kirkbean D & G 70 F4
Kirk Bramwith Donc 59 N10
Kirkbride Cumb 71 K4
Kirkbuddo Angus 93 N7
Kirkburn Border 79 L2
Kirkburn E R Yk 60 G3
Kirkburton Kirk 58 G10
Kirkby Knows 56 H8
Kirkby Lincs 52 F5
Kirkby N York 66 D6
Kirkby Fleetham N York 65 M8
Kirkby Green Lincs 52 F11
Kirkby in Ashfield Notts 51 L9
Kirkby-in-Furness Cumb 62 E6
Kirkby la Thorpe Lincs 42 F2
Kirkby Lonsdale Cumb 63 L6
Kirkby Malham N York 58 B3
Kirkby Mallory Leics 41 L7
Kirkby Malzeard N York 65 M11
Kirkbymoorside N York 66 F9
Kirkby on Bain Lincs 53 J10
Kirkby Overblow N York 59 J4
Kirkby Stephen Cumb 64 E6
Kirkby Thore Cumb 64 B3
Kirkby Underwood Lincs 42 F5
Kirkby Wharf N York 59 L6
Kirkcaldy Fife 86 F4
Kirkcaldy Crematorium Fife 86 F4
Kirkcambeck Cumb 71 Q2
Kirkchrist D & G 69 P8
Kirkcolm D & G 68 D5
Kirkconnel D & G 77 M8
Kirkconnell D & G 70 F2
Kirkcowan D & G 69 J7
Kirkcudbright D & G 69 P8
Kirkdale Lpool 56 G9
Kirk Deighton N York 59 K4
Kirk Ella E R Yk 60 H8
Kirkfieldbank S Lans 77 P3
Kirkgunzeon D & G 70 E3

Kirk Hallam Derbys 51 L11
Kirkham Lancs 56 H3
Kirkham N York 60 C2
Kirkhamgate Wakefd 58 H9
Kirk Hammerton N York 59 L3
Kirkhaugh Nthumb 72 C10
Kirkheaton Kirk 58 F9
Kirkheaton Nthumb 72 H5
Kirkhill Highld 107 J12
Kirkhope S Lans 78 F7
Kirkibost Highld 96 G6
Kirkinch P & K 93 K6
Kirkinner D & G 69 K8
Kirkintilloch E Duns 85 L8
Kirk Ireton Derbys 50 H10
Kirkland Cumb 70 H11
Kirkland Cumb 77 M8
Kirkland D & G 78 D10
Kirkland D & G 78 C10
Kirkland D & G 78 G10
Kirk Langley Derbys 50 H11
Kirkleatham R & Cl 66 E3
Kirklevington S on T 66 B5
Kirkley Suffk 45 Q10
Kirklington N York 65 N10
Kirklington Notts 51 N8
Kirklinton Cumb 71 N3
Kirkliston C Edin 86 D7
Kirkmabreck D & G 69 L7
Kirkmaiden D & G 68 F10
Kirk Merrington Dur 65 M2
Kirk Michael IoM 56 C4
Kirkmichael P & K 92 B9
Kirkmichael S Ayrs 76 F9
Kirkmuirhill S Lans 77 N3
Kirknewton Nthumb 81 J8
Kirknewton W Loth 86 D8
Kirkney Abers 101 P8
Kirk of Shotts N Lans 85 P9
Kirkoswald Cumb 71 Q7
Kirkoswald S Ayrs 76 D9
Kirkpatrick D & G 78 E10
Kirkpatrick Durham D & G 70 C2
Kirkpatrick-Fleming D & G 71 L2
Kirk Sandall Donc 59 N11
Kirksanton Cumb 62 D6
Kirk Smeaton N York 59 M10
Kirkstall Leeds 58 H7
Kirkstile Abers 102 C8
Kirkstile D & G 79 M10
Kirkstyle Highld 110 G2
Kirkthorpe Wakefd 59 J9
Kirkton Abers 102 E9
Kirkton D & G 78 F11
Kirkton Fife 93 L10
Kirkton Highld 97 L4
Kirkton Highld 97 N2
Kirkton P & K 92 E11
Kirkton Manor Border 79 K2
Kirkton of Airlie Angus 93 K5
Kirkton of Auchterhouse Angus 93 L7
Kirkton of Barevan Highld 107 L4
Kirkton of Collace P & K 92 H8
Kirkton of Glenbuchat Abers 101 M11
Kirkton of Logie Buchan Abers 103 K8
Kirkton of Menmuir Angus 95 J8
Kirkton of Monikie Angus 93 N7
Kirkton of Rayne Abers 102 F8
Kirkton of Skene Abers 95 N1
Kirkton of Strathmartine Angus 93 L8
Kirkton of Tealing Angus 93 M7
Kirkton of Tough Abers 102 D11
Kirktown Abers 103 K3
Kirktown Abers 103 M3
Kirktown of Alvah Abers 102 E4
Kirktown of Bourtie Abers 102 G9
Kirktown of Fetteresso Abers 95 P5
Kirktown of Mortlach Moray 101 L7
Kirktown of Slains Abers 103 L9
Kirkurd Border 86 D12
Kirkwall Ork 111 h2
Kirkwall Airport Ork 111 h2
Kirkwhelpington Nthumb 72 H4
Kirk Yetholm Border 80 H8
Kirmington N Linc 61 J11
Kirmond le Mire Lincs 52 H5
Kirn Ag & B 84 C7
Kirriemuir Angus 93 L5
Kirstead Green Norfk 45 L10
Kirtlebridge D & G 71 K2
Kirtling Cambs 34 B5
Kirtling Green Cambs 34 B5
Kirtlington Oxon 31 L9
Kirtomy Highld 109 N3
Kirton Lincs 43 K3
Kirton Notts 51 P7
Kirton Suffk 35 L8
Kirtonhill W Duns 84 G7
Kirton in Lindsey N Linc 52 D4
Kirwaugh D & G 69 K8
Kishorn Highld 97 L2
Kislingbury Nhants 31 P3
Kittisford Somset 16 E10
Kittybrewster C Aber 95 Q1
Kivernoll Herefs 28 F3
Kiveton Park Rothm 51 L4
Knaith Lincs 52 B6
Knap Corner Dorset 8 B3
Knaphill Surrey 20 F10
Knapp Somset 17 J10
Knapton C York 59 M4
Knapton N York 67 J11
Knapton Norfk 45 M4
Knapwell Cambs 33 K4
Knaresborough N York 59 J3
Knarsdale Nthumb 72 C9
Knaven Abers 103 J6
Knayton N York 66 B9
Knebworth Herts 33 J11
Knedlington E R Yk 60 C8
Kneesall Notts 51 P7
Kneesworth Cambs 33 K7
Kneeton Notts 51 P10
Knelston Swans 26 C10
Knenhall Staffs 50 B12
Knightcote Warwks 31 K4
Knightley Staffs 49 P9

Knighton - Linton-on-Ouse 183

Knighton C Leic 41 N7
Knighton Dorset 7 N1
Knighton Powys 38 F7
Knighton Somset 16 G7
Knighton Staffs 49 N7
Knighton Staffs 49 N9
Knighton on Teme Worcs 39 L7
Knightwick Worcs 39 N10
Knill Herefs 38 F9
Knipton Leics 42 B4
Kniveton Derbys 50 G10
Knock Cumb 64 C3
Knock Highld 97 J7
Knock Moray 102 C5
Knock W Isls 111 d2
Knockally Highld 110 D9
Knockan Highld 106 D1
Knockando Moray 101 J7
Knockbain Highld 98 H1
Knockbain Highld 107 K10
Knock Castle N Ayrs 84 D9
Knockdee Highld 110 D4
Knockdow Ag & B 84 B8
Knockdown Wilts 18 C3
Knockeen S Ayrs 76 E11
Knockenkelly N Ayrs 75 Q7
Knockentiber E Ayrs 76 G4
Knockholt Kent 21 P10
Knockholt Pound Kent 21 P10
Knockin Shrops 48 G10
Knockinlaw E Ayrs 76 G4
Knocknain D & G 68 C6
Knockrome Ag & B 82 H8
Knocksharry IoM 56 b4
Knocksheen D & G 69 N3
Knockvennie Smithy D & G 70 C2
Knodishall Suffk 35 N4
Knodishall Common Suffk 35 P5
Knole Somset 17 L10
Knolls Green Ches E 57 P11
Knolton Wrexhm 48 H7
Knook Wilts 18 D11
Knossington Leics 42 B8
Knott End-on-Sea Lancs 62 G11
Knotting Bed 32 E4
Knotting Green Bed 32 E4
Knottingley Wakefd 59 L9
Knotty Ash Lpool 56 H9
Knowbury Shrops 39 L7
Knowe D & G 69 J5
Knowehead D & G 69 N2
Knoweside S Ayrs 76 E8
Knowle Bristl 17 N3
Knowle Devon 6 D2
Knowle Devon 6 E6
Knowle Devon 15 J5
Knowle Devon 15 N10
Knowle Shrops 39 L7
Knowle Solhll 40 F11
Knowle Somset 16 C7
Knowlefield Cumb 71 N4
Knowle Green Lancs 57 L2
Knowle St Giles Somset 7 J1
Knowl Hill W & M 20 D7
Knowsley Knows 56 H9
Knowsley Safari Park Knows 57 J9
Knowstone Devon 15 P7
Knox Bridge Kent 12 F2
Knucklas Powys 38 F7
Knuston Nhants 32 D4
Knutsford Ches E 57 N12
Knutsford Services Ches E 57 N12
Krumlin Calder 58 D9
Kuggar Cnwll 2 G11
Kyleakin Highld 97 K4
Kyle of Lochalsh Highld 97 K4
Kylerhea Highld 97 L5
Kylesku Highld 108 E8
Kylesmorar Highld 97 L10
Kyles Scalpay W Isls 111 c3
Kylestrome Highld 108 E8
Kynnersley Wrekin 49 M11
Kyrewood Worcs 39 L8

L

Lacasaigh W Isls 111 d2
Lacasdal W Isls 111 d2
Laceby NE Lin 52 H3
Lacey Green Bucks 20 D4
Lach Dennis Ches W 49 N2
Lackford Suffk 34 D3
Lackford Green Suffk 34 D3
Lacock Wilts 18 D7
Ladbroke Warwks 31 K3
Laddingford Kent 12 E1
Ladock Cnwll 3 K5
Lady Ork 111 i1
Ladybank Fife 93 K12
Ladygill S Lans 78 F4
Lady Hall Cumb 62 E5
Ladykirk Border 81 J5
Ladywood Birm 40 D9
Ladywood Worcs 39 Q9
La Fontenelle Guern 6 c1
Lag D & G 78 E10
Laga Highld 89 N4
Lagavulin Ag & B 74 F4
Lagg N Ayrs 75 P7
Laggan Highld 98 D9
Laggan Highld 99 J9
Lagganlia Highld 99 M8
La Greve de Lecq Jersey 7 a1
Laid Highld 108 H4
Laide Highld 105 N4
Laig Highld 96 F11
Laigh Clunch E Ayrs 76 H2
Laigh Fenwick E Ayrs 76 H3
Laigh Glenmuir E Ayrs 77 K7
Laighstonehall S Lans 85 M11
Laindon Essex 22 D5
Lairg Highld 107 J2
Laisterdyke C Brad 58 F7
Lake IoW 9 P10
Lake Wilts 18 G11
Lake District National Park Cumb 62 E1
Lakenheath Suffk 44 B12
Lakesend Norfk 43 N10
Laleston Brdgnd 27 J11
Lamarsh Essex 34 E9
Lamas Norfk 45 L5
Lambden Border 80 G5
Lamberhurst Kent 12 D3
Lamberhurst Down Kent 12 D3
Lamberton Border 81 K3
Lambeth Gt Lon 21 L7
Lambeth Crematorium Gt Lon 21 L8
Lambfair Green Suffk 34 B6
Lambley Notts 51 N10
Lambley Nthumb 72 C8
Lambourn W Berk 19 K5
Lambourne End Essex 21 P5
Lambs Green W Susx 11 K3
Lamerton Devon 5 K5
Lamesley Gatesd 73 M8
Lamington S Lans 78 F3
Lamlash N Ayrs 75 Q6
Lamonby Cumb 71 N8
Lamorna Cnwll 2 C10
Lamorran Cnwll 3 K7
Lampeter Cerdgn 37 J10
Lampeter Velfrey Pembks 25 K6
Lamphey Pembks 24 H8
Lamplugh Cumb 70 H10
Lamport Nhants 41 Q11
Lamyatt Somset 17 P8
Lanark S Lans 77 P3
Lancaster Lancs 63 J9
Lancaster & Morecambe Crematorium Lancs 63 J9
Lancaster Services Lancs 63 J10
Lanchester Dur 73 L10
Lancing W Susx 11 J8
L'Ancresse Guern 6 c1
Landbeach Cambs 33 M4
Landcross Devon 14 H7
Landerberry Abers 95 M2
Landford Wilts 9 J4
Land-hallow Highld 110 E8
Landican Crematorium Wirral 56 F10
Landimore Swans 26 C9
Landkey Devon 15 K6
Landore Swans 26 F9
Landrake Cnwll 4 H7
Land's End Airport Cnwll 2 B9
Landulph Cnwll 5 J7
Lane Cnwll 3 J4
Laneast Cnwll 4 F4
Lane End Bucks 20 D5
Lane End Wilts 18 B10
Lane Ends Derbys 40 G1
Laneham Notts 52 B8
Lane Head Dur 65 K5
Lanehead Dur 72 F11
Langaller Somset 16 H10
Langar Notts 41 Q1
Langbank Rens 84 F8
Langbar N York 58 E4
Langcliffe N York 63 P8
Langdale End N York 67 K8
Langdown Hants 9 M6
Langdyke Fife 86 G2
Langenhoe Essex 34 G11
Langford C Beds 32 H8
Langford Devon 6 D3
Langford Essex 22 G2
Langford Notts 52 B10
Langford Oxon 30 G12
Langford Budville Somset 16 F10
Langham Essex 34 G9
Langham Norfk 44 G2
Langham Rutlnd 42 B7
Langham Suffk 34 F3
Langho Lancs 57 N3
Langholm D & G 79 M11
Langlee Border 80 C7
Langley Hants 9 M7
Langley Herts 32 H11
Langley Kent 22 F11
Langley Nthumb 72 E8
Langley Slough 20 G7
Langley Somset 16 E9
Langley W Susx 10 D4
Langley Warwks 30 F2
Langley Burrell Wilts 18 D6
Langley Green Essex 34 E11
Langley Marsh Somset 16 E9
Langley Park Dur 73 L11
Langley Street Norfk 45 N9
Langley Upper Green Essex 33 M9
Langney E Susx 12 D9
Langold Notts 51 N4
Langore Cnwll 4 G3
Langport Somset 17 K10
Langrick Lincs 43 J1
Langridge BaNES 17 Q3
Langrigg Cumb 71 J6
Langrish Hants 10 B5
Langsett Barns 50 G2
Langside P & K 92 B11
Langstone Hants 10 B8
Langthorne N York 65 M8
Langthorpe N York 59 K1
Langthwaite N York 64 H7
Langtoft E R Yk 60 H2
Langtoft Lincs 42 G7
Langton Dur 65 L4
Langton Lincs 52 H9
Langton Lincs 53 L9
Langton N York 60 D2
Langton by Wragby Lincs 52 G7
Langton Green Kent 12 B3
Langton Herring Dorset 7 N6
Langton Matravers Dorset 8 E10
Langtree Devon 14 H8
Langwathby Cumb 71 R8
Langwell House Highld 110 D10
Langwith Derbys 51 M6
Langwith Junction Derbys 51 L7
Langworth Lincs 52 F8
Lanhydrock House & Gardens Cnwll 3 N3
Lanivet Cnwll 3 M3
Lanlivery Cnwll 3 N4
Lanner Cnwll 2 G7
Lanreath Cnwll 4 E8
Lansallos Cnwll 4 E9
Lanteglos Cnwll 4 D4
Lanteglos Highway Cnwll 4 E9
Lanton Border 80 E9
Lanton Nthumb 81 K7
Lapford Devon 15 M9
Laphroaig Ag & B 74 E4
Lapley Staffs 49 Q11
Lapworth Warwks 40 F12
Larachbeg Highld 89 N6
Larbert Falk 85 P6
Largie Abers 102 D8
Largiemore Ag & B 83 P6
Largoward Fife 87 J1
Largs N Ayrs 84 D10
Largybeg N Ayrs 75 Q7
Largymore N Ayrs 75 Q7
Larkfield Inver 84 D7
Larkfield Kent 22 E10
Larkhall S Lans 77 M2
Larkhill Wilts 18 G11
Larling Norfk 44 G11
La Rocque Jersey 7 c2
Lartington Dur 64 H4
Lasham Hants 10 A2
Lasswade Mdloth 86 G8
Lastingham N York 66 G9
Latchingdon Essex 22 G4
Latchley Cnwll 5 J5
Lathbury M Keyn 32 C7
Latheron Highld 110 E8
Latheronwheel Highld 110 E8
Lathones Fife 87 J1
Latimer Bucks 20 G4
Latteridge S Glos 29 J10
Lattiford Somset 17 Q10
Latton Wilts 18 G2
Lauder Border 80 C5
Laugharne Carmth 25 M6
Laughterton Lincs 52 B8
Laughton E Susx 11 P7
Laughton Leics 41 P9
Laughton Lincs 42 F4
Laughton Lincs 52 B4
Laughton-en-le-Morthen Rothm 51 M4
Launcells Cnwll 14 E10
Launceston Cnwll 4 H4
Launton Oxon 31 N9
Laurencekirk Abers 95 L7
Laurieston D & G 69 P6
Laurieston Falk 85 Q7
Lavendon M Keyn 32 D6
Lavenham Suffk 34 F7
Lavernock V Glam 16 G3
Laversdale Cumb 71 P3
Laverstock Wilts 8 H2
Laverstoke Hants 19 N10
Laverton Gloucs 30 E7
Laverton N York 65 M11
Laverton Somset 18 B9
La Villette Guern 6 b2
Lavister Wrexhm 48 G4
Law S Lans 85 N11
Lawers P & K 91 Q8
Lawford Essex 34 H9
Lawford Somset 16 F8
Law Hill S Lans 85 N11
Lawhitton Cnwll 4 H4
Lawkland N York 63 P8
Lawns Wood Crematorium Leeds 58 H6
Lawrenny Pembks 24 H7
Lawshall Suffk 34 E6
Laxay W Isls 111 d2
Laxdale W Isls 111 d2
Laxey IoM 56 d4
Laxfield Suffk 35 L3
Laxford Bridge Highld 108 E6
Laxo Shet 111 k3
Laxton E R Yk 60 D8
Laxton Nhants 42 D10
Laxton Notts 51 Q7
Laycock C Brad 58 D6
Layer Breton Essex 34 F12
Layer-de-la-Haye Essex 34 F11
Layer Marney Essex 34 F12
Layham Suffk 34 G8
Laymore Dorset 7 K2
Laytham E R Yk 60 D6
Lazonby Cumb 71 Q7
Lea Derbys 51 J8
Lea Herefs 28 H4
Lea Lincs 52 B6
Lea Shrops 38 G4
Lea Wilts 18 E4
Leachkin Highld 107 K12
Leadburn Border 86 F10
Leadenham Lincs 52 D11
Leaden Roding Essex 22 C1
Leadgate Dur 73 K9
Leadhills S Lans 78 E6
Leafield Oxon 30 H10
Leagrave Luton 32 F11
Leake Common Side Lincs 53 L11
Lealholm N York 66 G6
Lealt Highld 104 G9
Lea Marston Warwks 40 G8
Leamington Hastings Warwks 31 K1
Leamington Spa Warwks 30 H2
Leap Cross E Susx 12 C7
Leasgill Cumb 63 J5
Leasingham Lincs 42 F1
Leasingthorne Dur 65 M2
Leatherhead Surrey 21 J11
Leathley N York 58 G5
Leaton Shrops 49 J10
Leaveland Kent 23 J11
Leavenheath Suffk 34 F8
Leavening N York 60 D2
Leaves Green Gt Lon 21 N10
Lebberston N York 67 M10
Le Bourg Guern 6 b2
Lechlade on Thames Gloucs 18 H2
Lecht Gruinart Ag & B 82 D8
Leck Lancs 63 M6
Leckbuie P & K 91 Q8
Leckford Hants 19 L12
Leckhampstead Bucks 31 Q6
Leckhampstead W Berk 19 M5
Leckhampstead Thicket W Berk 19 M5
Leckhampton Gloucs 29 N5
Leckmelm Highld 106 C4
Leconfield E R Yk 60 H5
Ledaig Ag & B 90 C8
Ledburn Bucks 32 C11
Ledbury Herefs 29 J2
Ledgemoor Herefs 38 H11
Ledmore Junction Highld 108 E12
Ledsham Leeds 59 L8
Ledston Leeds 59 K8
Ledwell Oxon 31 K8
Lee Devon 14 H3
Lee Gt Lon 21 M8
Leebotwood Shrops 39 J3
Lee Brockhurst Shrops 49 K9
Leece Cumb 62 E8
Lee Chapel Essex 22 E6
Lee Clump Bucks 20 E3
Leeds Kent 22 G11
Leeds Leeds 58 H7
Leeds Bradford Airport Leeds 58 G6
Leeds Castle Kent 22 G11
Leedstown Cnwll 2 E8
Leek Staffs 50 C9
Leek Wootton Warwks 30 H1
Lee Mill Devon 5 M8
Leeming N York 65 N9
Leeming Bar N York 65 M9
Lee-on-the-Solent Hants 9 P7
Lees Derbys 50 H12
Lees Oldham 58 C12
Lees Green Derbys 50 H12
Leesthorpe Leics 42 B7
Leeswood Flints 48 F4
Leetown P & K 93 J10
Leftwich Ches W 49 M2
Legbourne Lincs 53 L6
Legerwood Border 80 D5
Legoland W & M 20 F8
Legsby Lincs 52 G6
Leicester C Leic 41 N6
Leicester Forest East Leics 41 M6
Leicester Forest East Services Leics 41 M7
Leigh Dorset 7 N2
Leigh Gloucs 29 M4
Leigh Kent 12 B2
Leigh Surrey 11 K1
Leigh Wigan 57 M8
Leigh Wilts 18 F3
Leigh Worcs 39 P10
Leigh Beck Essex 22 F6
Leigh Delamere Wilts 18 C5
Leigh Delamere Services Wilts 18 D5
Leigh Green Kent 12 H4
Leigh Knoweglass S Lans 77 K2
Leigh-on-Sea Sthend 22 G6
Leigh Park Dorset 8 F7
Leigh Sinton Worcs 39 P11
Leighswood Wsall 40 D7
Leighterton Gloucs 29 L9
Leighton Powys 38 E2
Leighton Shrops 39 L2
Leighton Bromswold Cambs 32 G2
Leighton Buzzard C Beds 32 D10
Leigh upon Mendip Somset 17 Q6
Leigh Woods N Som 17 N2
Leinthall Earls Herefs 39 J8
Leinthall Starkes Herefs 38 H8
Leintwardine Herefs 38 H7
Leire Leics 41 M9
Leiston Suffk 35 P4
Leith C Edin 86 F7
Leitholm Border 80 G5
Lelant Cnwll 2 E8
Lelley E R Yk 61 L7
Lempitlaw Border 80 G7
Lemreway W Isls 111 d3
Lemsford Herts 21 K2
Lenchwick Worcs 30 D5
Lendalfoot S Ayrs 68 F2
Lendrick Stirlg 85 J2
Lendrum Terrace Abers 103 M7
Lenham Kent 22 H11
Lenham Heath Kent 22 H12
Lenie Highld 98 G4
Lennel Border 80 H6
Lennox Plunton D & G 69 N8
Lennoxtown E Duns 85 K7
Lenton C Nott 51 M11
Lenton Lincs 42 E4
Lenwade Norfk 44 H6
Lenzie E Duns 85 L8
Leochel-Cushnie Abers 102 C12
Leominster Herefs 39 J9
Leonard Stanley Gloucs 29 L7
Lephin Highld 104 B11
Leppington N York 60 D2
Lepton Kirk 58 G10
Lerags Ag & B 90 B10
L'Erée Guern 6 a2
Lerryn Cnwll 4 E8
Lerwick Shet 111 k4
Lesbury Nthumb 81 P10
Leslie Abers 102 D9
Leslie Fife 86 F2
Lesmahagow S Lans 78 D2
Lesnewth Cnwll 4 E3
Les Quartiers Guern 6 c1
Les Quennevais Jersey 7 a2
Lessingham Norfk 45 N5
Lessonhall Cumb 71 K5
Leswalt D & G 68 D6
L'Etacq Jersey 7 a1
Letchmore Heath Herts 21 J4
Letchworth Garden City Herts 32 H9
Letcombe Bassett Oxon 19 L4
Letcombe Regis Oxon 19 L4
Letham Angus 93 P6
Letham Border 80 F11
Letham Falk 85 P6
Letham Fife 93 K11
Letham Grange Angus 93 Q6
Lethendy P & K 92 G7
Lethenty Abers 102 D10
Lethenty Abers 102 H7
Letheringham Suffk 35 L5
Letheringsett Norfk 44 H3
Letterewe Highld 105 P7
Letterfearn Highld 97 M5
Letterfinlay Lodge Hotel Highld 98 C10
Lettermorar Highld 97 K10
Letters Highld 106 C5
Lettershaw S Lans 78 E5
Letterston Pembks 24 G3
Lettoch Highld 99 Q5
Lettoch Highld 100 H8
Letton Herefs 38 G11
Letty Green Herts 21 L2
Letwell Rothm 51 M4
Leuchars Fife 93 M10
Leumrabhagh W Isls 111 d3
Leurbost W Isls 111 d2
Levedale Staffs 40 B4
Leven E R Yk 61 J5
Leven Fife 86 H3
Levens Cumb 63 J5
Levens Green Herts 33 K11
Levenshulme Manch 57 Q9
Levenwick Shet 111 k5
Leverburgh W Isls 111 c4
Leverington Cambs 43 M7
Leverstock Green Herts 20 H3
Leverton Lincs 43 L1
Le Villocq Guern 6 b1
Levington Suffk 35 K8
Levisham N York 67 J8
Lew Oxon 31 J11
Lewannick Cnwll 4 G4
Lewdown Devon 5 K3
Lewes E Susx 11 N7
Leweston Pembks 24 G4
Lewisham Gt Lon 21 M8
Lewisham Crematorium Gt Lon 21 N8
Lewiston Highld 98 G4
Lewistown Brdgnd 27 K10
Lewknor Oxon 20 B4
Lewson Street Kent 23 J10
Lewtrenchard Devon 5 K3
Lexden Essex 34 F10
Lexworthy Somset 16 H8
Leybourne Kent 22 D10
Leyburn N York 65 K9
Leygreen Herts 32 G10
Ley Hill Bucks 20 F3
Leyland Lancs 57 K4
Leylodge Abers 102 G11
Leys Abers 103 K5
Leys P & K 93 J7
Leysdown-on-Sea Kent 23 K8
Leysmill Angus 93 Q6
Leys of Cossans Angus 93 L6
Leysters Herefs 39 K8
Leyton Gt Lon 21 M6
Leytonstone Gt Lon 21 N6
Lezant Cnwll 4 H4
Lhanbryde Moray 101 K3
Libanus Powys 27 L4
Libberton S Lans 78 G1
Liberton C Edin 86 F8
Lichfield Staffs 40 E5
Lickey Worcs 40 C11
Lickey End Worcs 40 C11
Lickfold W Susx 10 E5
Liddesdale Highld 89 Q4
Liddington Swindn 18 H5
Lidgate Suffk 34 C5
Lidlington C Beds 32 E8
Liff Angus 93 L8
Lifford Birm 40 D10
Lifton Devon 5 J3
Liftondown Devon 4 H3
Lighthorne Warwks 31 J3
Lighthorne Heath Warwks 31 J3
Lightwater Surrey 20 E10
Lightwater Valley Theme Park N York 65 M11
Lilbourne Nhants 41 M11
Lilleshall Wrekin 49 N11
Lilley Herts 32 G10
Lilliesleaf Border 80 C8
Lillingstone Dayrell Bucks 31 P6
Lillingstone Lovell Bucks 31 P6
Lillington Dorset 7 P1
Lilliput Poole 8 F9
Lilstock Somset 16 F7
Limbury Luton 32 F11
Limekilnburn S Lans 77 M2
Limekilns Fife 86 C5
Limerigg Falk 85 P8
Limerstone IoW 9 M10
Lime Street Worcs 29 L3
Limington Somset 17 M10
Limmerhaugh E Ayrs 77 K6
Limpenhoe Norfk 45 N8
Limpley Stoke Wilts 18 B8
Limpsfield Surrey 21 N11
Limpsfield Chart Surrey 21 N11
Linby Notts 51 M9
Linchmere W Susx 10 D4
Lincluden D & G 78 F12
Lincoln Lincs 52 D8
Lincoln Crematorium Lincs 52 E9
Lincomb Worcs 39 P8
Lindale Cumb 62 H6
Lindal in Furness Cumb 62 F7
Lindfield W Susx 11 M5
Lindford Hants 10 D3
Lindley Kirk 58 E9
Lindores Fife 93 K11
Lindridge Worcs 39 M8
Lindsell Essex 33 Q10
Lindsey Suffk 34 G7
Lindsey Tye Suffk 34 G7
Lingdale R & Cl 66 F4
Lingen Herefs 38 G8
Lingfield Surrey 11 M2
Lingwood Norfk 45 M8
Linicro Highld 104 E8
Linkend Worcs 29 L3
Linkenholt Hants 19 L8
Linkinhorne Cnwll 4 G5
Linktown Fife 86 F4
Linkwood Moray 101 K3
Linley Shrops 38 G4
Linley Green Herefs 39 M10
Linlithgow W Loth 86 B6
Linsidemore Highld 107 J3
Linslade C Beds 32 C10
Linstead Parva Suffk 35 M2
Linstock Cumb 71 N4
Linthurst Worcs 40 D11
Linthwaite Kirk 58 E10
Lintlaw Border 87 Q9
Lintmill Moray 101 P3
Linton Border 80 G8
Linton Cambs 33 P7
Linton Derbys 40 H4
Linton Herefs 28 H4
Linton Kent 22 F12
Linton Leeds 59 K5
Linton N York 58 C2
Linton Hill Herefs 29 J4
Linton-on-Ouse N York 59 L3

Linwood Lincs....52 G6
Linwood Rens....84 G9
Lionacleit W Isls....111 b5
Lional W Isls....111 e1
Liphook Hants....10 D4
Liscard Wirral....56 F9
Liscombe Somset....15 P5
Liskeard Cnwll....4 F7
Lismore Ag & B....90 B7
Liss Hants....10 C5
Lissett E R Yk....61 K3
Lissington Lincs....52 G6
Lisvane Cardif....27 P11
Liswerry Newpt....28 D10
Litcham Norfk....44 E6
Litchborough Nhants....31 N4
Litchfield Hants....19 M9
Litherland Sefton....56 G8
Litlington Cambs....33 K8
Litlington E Susx....11 Q9
Little Abington Cambs....33 N7
Little Addington Nhants....32 D3
Little Airies D & G....69 K9
Little Alne Warwks....30 F2
Little Altcar Sefton....56 F7
Little Amwell Herts....21 M2
Little Aston Staffs....40 E7
Little Ayton N York....66 D5
Little Baddow Essex....22 F2
Little Badminton S Glos....18 B4
Little Bampton Cumb....71 L5
Little Bardfield Essex....33 Q9
Little Barford Bed....32 H5
Little Barningham Norfk....45 J4
Little Barrington Gloucs....30 G10
Little Barrow Ches W....49 J2
Little Bavington Nthumb....72 H5
Little Bedwyn Wilts....19 K7
Little Bentley Essex....35 J10
Little Berkhamsted Herts....21 L2
Little Billing Nhants....32 B4
Little Billington C Beds....32 D11
Little Birch Herefs....28 F3
Little Blakenham Suffk....34 H7
Little Blencow Cumb....71 P8
Little Bognor W Susx....10 G6
Little Bollington Ches E....57 N10
Little Bookham Surrey....20 H11
Littleborough Notts....52 B7
Littleborough Rochdl....58 C10
Littlebourne Kent....23 N11
Little Bourton Oxon....31 L5
Little Braxted Essex....22 G1
Little Brechin Angus....95 J9
Littlebredy Dorset....7 N5
Little Brickhill M Keyn....32 C9
Little Brington Nhants....31 P2
Little Bromley Essex....34 H10
Little Budworth Ches W....49 L3
Littleburn Highld....107 K10
Little Burstead Essex....22 D5
Littlebury Essex....33 N8
Littlebury Green Essex....33 M8
Little Bytham Lincs....42 E6
Little Carlton Lincs....53 L6
Little Casterton Rutlnd....42 E8
Little Cawthorpe Lincs....53 K6
Little Chalfont Bucks....20 F4
Little Chart Kent....12 H2
Little Chesterford Essex....33 N8
Little Cheverell Wilts....18 E9
Little Chishill Cambs....33 L8
Little Clacton Essex....35 J11
Little Clifton Cumb....70 H9
Little Comberton Worcs....30 C5
Little Common E Susx....12 E8
Little Compton Warwks....30 H7
Little Cornard Suffk....34 E8
Little Coxwell Oxon....19 K3
Little Crakehall N York....65 M9
Little Cressingham Norfk....44 E9
Little Crosby Sefton....56 G8
Little Cubley Derbys....50 F12
Little Dalby Leics....41 Q5
Littledean Gloucs....29 J6
Little Dewchurch Herefs....28 F3
Little Ditton Cambs....33 Q5
Little Downham Cambs....43 N12
Little Driffield E R Yk....60 H3
Little Dunham Norfk....44 E7
Little Dunkeld P & K....92 F7
Little Dunmow Essex....33 Q11
Little Durnford Wilts....8 G1
Little Easton Essex....33 P11
Little Eaton Derbys....51 J11
Little Ellingham Norfk....44 G9
Little Everdon Nhants....31 N3
Little Eversden Cambs....33 L6
Little Faringdon Oxon....19 J1
Little Fencote N York....65 M8
Little Fenton N York....59 M7
Little Fransham Norfk....44 E7
Little Gaddesden Herts....20 F2
Little Glemham Suffk....35 M5
Little Gorsley Herefs....29 J4
Little Gransden Cambs....33 J6
Little Green Somset....17 Q6
Little Hadham Herts....33 M11
Little Hale Lincs....42 G2
Little Hallam Derbys....51 L11
Little Hallingbury Essex....33 N12
Littleham Devon....6 D6
Littleham Devon....14 H7
Littlehampton W Susx....10 G9
Little Harrowden Nhants....32 C3
Little Haseley Oxon....19 Q1
Little Haven Pembks....24 F6
Littlehaven W Susx....11 J4
Little Hay Staffs....40 E7
Little Haywood Staffs....40 D3
Littlehempston Devon....5 Q7
Little Hereford Herefs....39 K8
Little Horkesley Essex....34 F9
Little Hormead Herts....33 L10
Little Horsted E Susx....11 P6
Little Horton C Brad....58 F7
Little Horwood Bucks....32 B9
Little Houghton Barns....59 K11
Little Houghton Nhants....32 B5
Little Hucklow Derbys....50 F5
Little Hutton N York....66 C11
Little Irchester Nhants....32 C4
Little Keyford Somset....18 B10
Little Kimble Bucks....20 D3
Little Kineton Warwks....30 J4
Little Kingshill Bucks....20 E4

Little Knox D & G....70 D4
Little Langdale Cumb....62 G2
Little Langford Wilts....18 F12
Little Leigh Ches W....49 L1
Little Leighs Essex....34 C12
Little Lever Bolton....57 N7
Little Linford M Keyn....32 B7
Little Load Somset....17 L10
Little London E Susx....12 C6
Little London Hants....19 L10
Little London Hants....19 Q8
Little Longstone Derbys....50 F6
Little Maplestead Essex....34 D9
Little Marcle Herefs....29 J2
Little Marlow Bucks....20 E6
Little Massingham Norfk....44 D5
Little Melton Norfk....45 J8
Littlemill Abers....94 E3
Littlemill Highld....100 E5
Little Mill Mons....28 C8
Little Milton Oxon....19 Q1
Little Missenden Bucks....20 E4
Littlemore Oxon....31 M12
Little Musgrave Cumb....64 D5
Little Ness Shrops....48 H10
Little Newcastle Pembks....24 G3
Little Newsham Dur....65 K4
Little Norton Somset....17 L11
Little Oakley Essex....35 K10
Little Oakley Nhants....42 C11
Little Orton Cumb....71 M5
Littleover C Derb....41 J1
Little Packington Warwks....40 G9
Little Paxton Cambs....32 H4
Little Petherick Cnwll....3 K2
Little Plumstead Norfk....45 M7
Little Ponton Lincs....42 D4
Littleport Cambs....43 P11
Little Preston Nhants....31 N4
Little Raveley Cambs....33 J2
Little Reedness E R Yk....60 D9
Little Ribston N York....59 J4
Little Rissington Gloucs....30 F9
Little Rollright Oxon....30 H7
Little Ryburgh Norfk....44 F5
Little Salkeld Cumb....71 Q8
Little Sampford Essex....33 Q9
Little Saughall Ches W....48 G2
Little Saxham Suffk....34 D4
Little Scatwell Highld....106 F10
Little Shelford Cambs....33 M6
Little Singleton Lancs....56 G2
Little Skipwith N York....59 P6
Little Smeaton N York....59 M10
Little Snoring Norfk....44 F4
Little Sodbury S Glos....18 A4
Little Somborne Hants....9 L2
Little Somerford Wilts....18 E4
Little Soudley Shrops....49 N9
Little Stainton Darltn....65 N4
Little Stanney Ches W....48 H1
Little Staughton Bed....32 F4
Little Steeping Lincs....53 M10
Littlestone-on-Sea Kent....13 L5
Little Stonham Suffk....35 J5
Little Stretton Leics....41 P7
Little Stretton Shrops....39 J4
Little Strickland Cumb....71 Q10
Little Stukeley Cambs....32 H2
Little Sugnall Staffs....49 P8
Little Swinburne Nthumb....72 G5
Little Sypland D & G....70 B5
Little Tew Oxon....31 J8
Little Tey Essex....34 E11
Little Thetford Cambs....33 N2
Little Thorpe Dur....73 Q11
Littlethorpe Leics....41 M7
Littlethorpe N York....59 J1
Little Thurlow Suffk....33 Q6
Little Thurrock Thurr....22 D7
Littleton Angus....93 L5
Littleton Ches W....48 H3
Littleton D & G....69 P7
Littleton Hants....9 M2
Littleton Somset....17 L9
Littleton Surrey....20 H9
Littleton Drew Wilts....18 C5
Littleton-on-Severn S Glos....28 H10
Littleton Pannell Wilts....18 E9
Little Torrington Devon....15 J8
Littletown Dur....73 N11
Little Town Lancs....57 M2
Little Urswick Cumb....62 F7
Little Wakering Essex....22 H6
Little Walden Essex....33 N8
Little Waldingfield Suffk....34 F7
Little Walsingham Norfk....44 F3
Little Waltham Essex....22 E2
Little Weighton E R Yk....60 G7
Little Weldon Nhants....42 D11
Little Wenlock Wrekin....39 M2
Little Weston Somset....17 N10
Little Whitefield IoW....9 P9
Littlewick Green W & M....20 D7
Little Wilbraham Cambs....33 N5
Little Witcombe Gloucs....29 M6
Little Witley Worcs....39 P8
Little Wittenham Oxon....19 P3
Little Wolford Warwks....30 H7
Little Woodcote Gt Lon....21 L10
Littleworth Oxon....19 K2
Littleworth Staffs....40 C3
Littleworth Worcs....30 B4
Little Wymington Bed....32 D4
Little Wymondley Herts....32 H10
Little Wyrley Staffs....40 D6
Little Yeldham Essex....34 C8
Littley Green Essex....34 B12
Litton Derbys....50 F6
Litton N York....64 G11
Litton Cheney Dorset....7 M5
Liurbost W Isls....111 d2
Liverpool Lpool....56 G10
Liverpool Maritime Mercantile City Lpool....56 G10
Liversedge Kirk....58 G9
Liverton Devon....5 Q5
Liverton R & Cl....66 G4
Liverton Village W Loth....86 C8
Livingston W Loth....86 C8
Livingston Village W Loth....86 C8
Lixwm Flints....48 D2
Lizard Cnwll....2 G12
Llanaelhaearn Gwynd....46 F3
Llanafan Cerdgn....37 L6

Llanafan-Fawr Powys....37 Q9
Llanaligo IoA....54 G5
Llanarmon Dyffryn Ceiriog Wrexhm....48 D8
Llanarmon-yn-Ial Denbgs....48 E4
Llanarth Cerdgn....36 G8
Llanarth Mons....28 D6
Llanarthne Carmth....26 D5
Llanasa Flints....56 C11
Llanbadarn Fawr Cerdgn....37 K4
Llanbadarn Fynydd Powys....38 C6
Llanbadoc Mons....28 D8
Llanbeder Newpt....28 D10
Llanbedr Gwynd....47 J6
Llanbedr Powys....27 P5
Llanbedr-Dyffryn-Clwyd Denbgs....48 D4
Llanbedrgoch IoA....54 G5
Llanbedr-y-Cennin Conwy....55 L7
Llanberis Gwynd....54 H9
Llanbethery V Glam....16 D3
Llanbister Powys....38 C7
Llanblethian V Glam....16 D2
Llanboidy Carmth....25 L4
Llanbradach Caerph....27 N10
Llanbrynmair Powys....47 P10
Llancadle V Glam....16 D3
Llancarfan V Glam....16 E3
Llancloudy Herefs....28 F5
Llandaff Cardif....27 N12
Llandanwg Gwynd....47 J5
Llanddaniel Fab IoA....54 G7
Llanddarog Carmth....26 C5
Llanddeiniol Cerdgn....37 J6
Llanddeiniolen Gwynd....54 G8
Llandderfel Gwynd....47 R4
Llanddeusant Carmth....26 D5
Llanddeusant IoA....54 D5
Llanddew Powys....27 M3
Llanddewi Swans....26 B10
Llanddewi Brefi Cerdgn....37 L9
Llanddewi Rhydderch Mons....28 D6
Llanddewi Velfrey Pembks....25 K5
Llanddewi Ystradenni Powys....38 C8
Llanddoget Conwy....55 L8
Llanddona IoA....54 H5
Llanddowror Carmth....25 M6
Llanddulas Conwy....55 N6
Llanddwywe Gwynd....47 J6
Llanddyfnan IoA....54 G6
Llandefaelog-Tre'r-Graig Powys....27 N3
Llandefalle Powys....27 M2
Llandegfan IoA....54 H6
Llandegla Denbgs....48 E5
Llandegley Powys....38 D9
Llandegveth Mons....28 D9
Llandeilo Carmth....26 E4
Llandeilo Graban Powys....38 C12
Llandeloy Pembks....24 F4
Llandenny Mons....28 E7
Llandevaud Newpt....28 E10
Llandevenny Mons....28 E10
Llandinam Powys....38 B5
Llandissilio Pembks....25 K5
Llandogo Mons....28 F7
Llandough V Glam....16 D2
Llandough V Glam....16 F2
Llandovery Carmth....26 G2
Llandow V Glam....16 C2
Llandre Carmth....37 L11
Llandre Cerdgn....37 K4
Llandre Isaf Pembks....25 K3
Llandrillo Denbgs....48 B7
Llandrillo-yn-Rhos Conwy....55 M5
Llandrindod Wells Powys....38 C9
Llandrinio Powys....48 F11
Llandudno Conwy....55 L5
Llandudno Junction Conwy....55 L6
Llandulas Powys....37 P11
Llandwrog Gwynd....54 F9
Llandybie Carmth....26 E6
Llandyfaelog Carmth....25 P6
Llandyfriog Cerdgn....36 F11
Llandygai Gwynd....54 H7
Llandygwydd Cerdgn....36 D11
Llandyrnog Denbgs....48 C3
Llandyssil Powys....38 E3
Llandysul Cerdgn....36 G11
Llanedeyrn Cardif....27 P11
Llaneglwys Powys....27 M2
Llanegryn Gwynd....47 K9
Llanegwad Carmth....26 C5
Llaneilian IoA....54 F3
Llanelian-yn-Rhôs Conwy....55 M6
Llanelidan Denbgs....48 C5
Llanelieu Powys....27 P3
Llanellen Mons....28 C6
Llanelli Carmth....26 C8
Llanelli Crematorium Carmth....26 D8
Llanelltyd Gwynd....47 L7
Llanelwedd Powys....38 B10
Llanenddwyn Gwynd....47 J6
Llanengan Gwynd....46 E6
Llanerchymedd IoA....54 F5
Llanerfyl Powys....48 B12
Llanfachraeth IoA....54 D5
Llanfachreth Gwynd....47 M6
Llanfaelog IoA....54 D7
Llanfaelrhys Gwynd....46 D6
Llanfaethlu IoA....54 D4
Llanfair Gwynd....47 J5
Llanfair Caereinion Powys....38 C2
Llanfair Clydogau Cerdgn....37 K9
Llanfair Dyffryn Clwyd Denbgs....48 D4
Llanfairfechan Conwy....55 K6
Llanfairpwllgwyngyll IoA....54 G7
Llanfair Talhaiarn Conwy....55 N7
Llanfair Waterdine Shrops....38 E6
Llanfairynghornwy IoA....54 D4
Llanfair-yn-Neubwll IoA....54 D5
Llanfallteg Carmth....25 K5
Llanfallteg West Carmth....25 K5
Llanfarian Cerdgn....37 J5
Llanfechain Powys....48 E10
Llanfechell IoA....54 E4
Llanferres Denbgs....48 D4
Llanfihangel-ar-arth Carmth....36 G11

Llanfihangel Glyn Myfyr Conwy....55 P10
Llanfihangel Nant Bran Powys....27 K2
Llanfihangel Rhydithon Powys....38 D7
Llanfihangel Rogiet Mons....28 E10
Llanfihangel-Creuddyn Cerdgn....37 L5
Llanfihangel-yng-Ngwynfa Powys....48 C11
Llanfihangel yn Nhowyn IoA....54 D6
Llanfihangel-y-traethau Gwynd....47 K4
Llanfilo Powys....27 N3
Llanfoist Mons....28 C6
Llanfor Gwynd....47 Q4
Llanfrechfa Torfn....28 C9
Llanfrynach Powys....27 M4
Llanfwrog Denbgs....48 D4
Llanfwrog IoA....54 D5
Llanfyllin Powys....48 D10
Llanfynydd Carmth....26 D4
Llanfynydd Flints....48 F4
Llanfyrnach Pembks....25 L3
Llangadfan Powys....48 B12
Llangadog Carmth....26 F3
Llangadwaladr IoA....54 E7
Llangaffo IoA....54 F7
Llangammarch Wells Powys....37 Q10
Llangan V Glam....27 K12
Llangarron Herefs....28 F5
Llangathen Carmth....26 D4
Llangattock Powys....27 P5
Llangattock Lingoed Mons....28 D5
Llangedwyn Powys....48 E10
Llangefni IoA....54 F6
Llangeinor Brdgnd....27 J10
Llangeitho Cerdgn....37 K8
Llangeler Carmth....36 F11
Llangelynin Gwynd....47 J9
Llangendeirne Carmth....26 B6
Llangennech Carmth....26 D8
Llangennith Swans....25 P9
Llangenny Powys....27 N7
Llangernyw Conwy....55 N7
Llangian Gwynd....46 E5
Llangloffan Pembks....24 F3
Llanglydwen Carmth....25 L4
Llangoed IoA....54 H6
Llangollen Denbgs....48 E7
Llangolman Pembks....25 K4
Llangors Powys....27 N4
Llangower Gwynd....47 P5
Llangranog Cerdgn....36 E9
Llangristiolus IoA....54 F6
Llangrove Herefs....28 F5
Llangunllo Powys....38 E7
Llangunnor Carmth....25 P5
Llangurig Powys....37 P5
Llangwm Conwy....47 Q3
Llangwm Mons....28 E8
Llangwm Pembks....24 H6
Llangwnnadl Gwynd....46 D5
Llangwyryfon Cerdgn....37 K6
Llangybi Cerdgn....37 K9
Llangybi Gwynd....46 G3
Llangybi Mons....28 D9
Llangynhafal Denbgs....48 D3
Llangynidr Powys....27 N5
Llangynin Carmth....25 M5
Llangynog Carmth....25 N6
Llangynog Powys....48 B9
Llangynwyd Brdgnd....27 J10
Llanhamlach Powys....27 M4
Llanharan Rhondd....27 L11
Llanharry Rhondd....27 L11
Llanhennock Mons....28 D9
Llanhilleth Blae G....27 P8
Llanidloes Powys....37 Q4
Llaniestyn Gwynd....46 E5
Llanigon Powys....27 P2
Llanilar Cerdgn....37 K5
Llanilid Rhondd....27 K11
Llanina Cerdgn....36 G8
Llanishen Cardif....27 N11
Llanishen Mons....28 F7
Llanllechid Conwy....55 J7
Llanllowell Mons....28 D8
Llanllugan Powys....38 C2
Llanllwch Carmth....25 P5
Llanllwchaiarn Powys....38 D4
Llanllwni Carmth....36 H11
Llanllyfni Gwynd....54 F10
Llanmadoc Swans....25 Q9
Llanmaes V Glam....16 D3
Llanmartin Newpt....28 D10
Llanmiloe Carmth....25 M7
Llannefydd Conwy....55 P7
Llannon Carmth....26 D7
Llannor Gwynd....46 F4
Llanon Cerdgn....36 H7
Llanover Mons....28 C7
Llanpumsaint Carmth....25 P5
Llanrhaeadr-ym-Mochnant Powys....48 D9
Llanrhian Pembks....24 E3
Llanrhidian Swans....26 C9
Llanrhychwyn Conwy....55 L8
Llanrhyddlad IoA....54 D4
Llanrhystud Cerdgn....37 J6
Llanrug Gwynd....54 G8
Llanrumney Cardif....27 P11
Llanrwst Conwy....55 L8
Llansadurnen Carmth....25 M6
Llansadwrn Carmth....26 F3
Llansadwrn IoA....54 H6
Llansaint Carmth....25 P7
Llansamlet Swans....26 F8
Llansanffraid Glan Conwy Conwy....55 L6
Llansannan Conwy....55 N8
Llansannor Powys....27 N4
Llansantffraed-Cwmdeuddwr Powys....37 Q7
Llansantffraed-in-Elvel Powys....38 C10
Llansantffraid Cerdgn....36 H7
Llansantffraid-ym-Mechain Powys....48 E10
Llansawel Carmth....26 E2
Llansilin Powys....48 E9
Llansoy Mons....28 E8
Llanspyddid Powys....27 L3
Llanstadwell Pembks....24 G7

Llansteffan Carmth....25 N6
Llantarnam Torfn....28 C9
Llanteg Pembks....25 L6
Llanthewy Skirrid Mons....28 D5
Llanthony Mons....28 C4
Llantilio-Crossenny Mons....28 D5
Llantilio Pertholey Mons....28 C5
Llantrisant Mons....28 D9
Llantrisant Rhondd....27 L11
Llantrithyd V Glam....16 E2
Llantwit Fardre Rhondd....27 M10
Llantwit Major V Glam....16 C3
Llanuwchllyn Gwynd....47 P5
Llanvaches Newpt....28 E9
Llanvair Discoed Mons....28 E9
Llanvapley Mons....28 D6
Llanvetherine Mons....28 D5
Llanvihangel Crucorney Mons....28 C5
Llanwddyn Powys....48 B10
Llanwenog Cerdgn....36 H10
Llanwern Newpt....28 D10
Llanwinio Carmth....25 M4
Llanwnda Gwynd....54 F9
Llanwnda Pembks....24 G2
Llanwnnen Cerdgn....37 J10
Llanwnog Powys....38 B4
Llanwrda Carmth....26 F3
Llanwrin Powys....47 M9
Llanwrthwl Powys....37 Q7
Llanwrtyd Wells Powys....37 P10
Llanwyddelan Powys....38 C2
Llanyblodwel Shrops....48 E10
Llanybri Carmth....25 N6
Llanybydder Carmth....36 H10
Llanycefn Pembks....25 J4
Llanychaer Bridge Pembks....24 H2
Llanymawddwy Gwynd....47 P7
Llanymynech Powys....48 F10
Llanynghenedl IoA....54 D5
Llanynys Denbgs....48 C3
Llanyre Powys....38 B9
Llanystumdwy Gwynd....46 H4
Llanywern Powys....27 M3
Llawhaden Pembks....25 J5
Llawryglyn Powys....37 Q3
Llay Wrexhm....48 G4
Llechrhyd Caerph....27 M7
Llechryd Cerdgn....36 D11
Lledrod Cerdgn....37 K6
Lleyn Peninsula Gwynd....46 E4
Llithfaen Gwynd....46 F3
Lloc Flints....56 D12
Llowes Powys....27 P1
Llwydcoed Rhondd....27 L7
Llwydcoed Crematorium Rhondd....27 L7
Llwydiarth Powys....48 B11
Llwyncelyn Cerdgn....36 G8
Llwyndafydd Cerdgn....36 F9
Llwyngwril Gwynd....47 J9
Llwynmawr Wrexhm....48 E7
Llwynypia Rhondd....27 L9
Llynclys Shrops....48 F10
Llynfaes IoA....54 E6
Llysfaen Conwy....55 N6
Llyswen Powys....27 N2
Llysworney V Glam....16 C2
Llys-y-frân Pembks....24 H4
Llywel Powys....27 J3
Loan Falk....85 Q7
Loanhead Mdloth....86 F8
Loaningfoot D & G....70 F4
Loans S Ayrs....76 F5
Lobhillcross Devon....5 K3
Lochailort Highld....97 K12
Lochaline Highld....89 N7
Lochans D & G....68 E7
Locharbriggs D & G....78 G11
Lochavich Ag & B....90 C12
Lochawe Ag & B....90 F10
Loch Baghasdail W Isls....111 b6
Lochboisdale W Isls....111 b6
Lochbuie Highld....89 M10
Lochcarron Highld....97 M2
Lochdon Ag & B....89 P9
Lochdonhead Ag & B....89 P9
Lochead Ag & B....83 L7
Lochearnhead Stirlg....91 N10
Lochee C Dund....93 L8
Locheilside Station Highld....90 D1
Lochend Highld....98 H2
Locheport W Isls....111 b4
Loch Euphoirt W Isls....111 b4
Lochfoot D & G....70 E2
Lochgair Ag & B....83 P3
Lochgelly Fife....86 E4
Lochgilphead Ag & B....83 N5
Lochgoilhead Ag & B....84 D3
Lochieheads Fife....93 J11
Lochill Moray....101 K3
Lochindorb Lodge Highld....100 E8
Lochinver Highld....108 C10
Loch Lomond and The Trossachs National Park....84 H1
Lochluichart Highld....106 F9
Lochmaben D & G....78 H11
Lochmaddy W Isls....111 b4
Loch Maree Hotel Highld....105 N8
Loch nam Madadh W Isls....111 b4
Loch Ness Highld....98 G4
Lochore Fife....86 E3
Lochranza N Ayrs....75 P3
Lochside Abers....95 M8
Lochside D & G....78 F12
Lochside Highld....107 N11
Lochslin Highld....107 N6
Lochton S Ayrs....68 H3
Lochty Angus....95 J9
Lochty Fife....87 K1
Lochuisge Highld....89 Q5
Lochwinnoch Rens....84 F10
Lochwood D & G....78 H9
Lockengate Cnwll....3 M4
Lockerbie D & G....79 J11
Lockeridge Wilts....18 G7
Lockerley Hants....9 K3
Locking N Som....17 J4
Locking Stumps Warrtn....57 M9
Lockington E R Yk....60 G5
Lockleywood Shrops....49 M9
Locksbottom Gt Lon....21 N9
Locks Heath Hants....9 N6
Lockton N York....67 J9
Loddington Leics....42 B9

Loddington Nhants.....32 B2
Loddiswell Devon.....5 P9
Loddon Norfk.....45 M9
Lode Cambs.....33 N4
Lode Heath Solhll.....40 F10
Loders Dorset.....7 L4
Lodge Hill Crematorium
  Birm.....40 D10
Lodsworth W Susx.....10 E5
Lofthouse Leeds.....59 J8
Lofthouse N York.....65 K11
Lofthouse Gate Wakefd.....59 J8
Loftus R & Cl.....66 G4
Logan E Ayrs.....77 K7
Loganlea W Loth.....86 B9
Loggerheads Staffs.....49 N8
Logie Angus.....95 L8
Logie Fife.....93 M10
Logie Moray.....100 F5
Logie Coldstone Abers.....94 G2
Logie Newton Abers.....102 F7
Logie Pert Angus.....95 L8
Logierait P & K.....92 E5
Logierieve Abers.....103 J9
Login Carmth.....25 K4
Lolworth Cambs.....33 L4
Lonbain Highld.....105 K10
Londesborough E R Yk.....60 E5
London Gt Lon.....21 L7
London Apprentice Cnwll.....3 M6
London Colney Herts.....21 J3
Londonderry N York.....65 N9
London Gateway
  Services Gt Lon.....21 K5
Londonthorpe Lincs.....42 D3
London Zoo ZSL Gt Lon.....21 L6
Londubh Highld.....105 M6
Lonemore Highld.....105 L6
Long Ashton N Som.....17 M3
Long Bank Worcs.....39 N7
Long Bennington Lincs.....42 B2
Longbenton N Tyne.....73 M7
Longborough Gloucs.....30 F8
Long Bredy Dorset.....7 N5
Longbridge Birm.....40 D10
Longbridge Deverill Wilts.....18 C11
Long Buckby Nhants.....31 N1
Longburton Dorset.....7 P1
Long Clawson Leics.....41 Q3
Longcliffe Derbys.....50 G9
Longcombe Devon.....5 Q8
Long Compton Staffs.....49 Q10
Long Compton Warwks.....30 H7
Longcot Oxon.....19 J3
Long Crendon Bucks.....20 B2
Long Crichel Dorset.....8 E5
Longden Shrops.....38 H2
Long Ditton Surrey.....21 J9
Longdon Staffs.....40 E5
Longdon Worcs.....29 L2
Longdon Green Staffs.....40 E5
Longdon upon Tern
  Wrekin.....49 L11
Longdown Devon.....6 B5
Longdowns Cnwll.....2 H8
Long Duckmanton Derbys.....51 K6
Long Eaton Derbys.....41 L2
Longfield Kent.....22 C9
Longford Covtry.....41 J10
Longford Derbys.....50 G12
Longford Gloucs.....29 L5
Longford Shrops.....49 M8
Longford Wrekin.....49 N10
Longforgan P & K.....93 K9
Longformacus Border.....87 N10
Longframlington Nthumb.....73 K1
Long Green Ches W.....49 J2
Longham Dorset.....8 F7
Longham Norfk.....44 F7
Long Harborough Oxon.....31 K10
Longhaven Abers.....103 M7
Longhirst Nthumb.....73 L3
Longhope Gloucs.....29 J5
Longhope Ork.....111 g3
Longhorsley Nthumb.....73 K2
Longhoughton Nthumb.....81 P10
Long Itchington Warwks.....31 N2
Longlane Derbys.....50 G12
Long Lawford Warwks.....41 L11
Longleat Safari &
  Adventure Park Wilts.....18 B11
Longlevens Gloucs.....29 L5
Longleys P & K.....93 K7
Long Load Somset.....17 L10
Longmanhill Abers.....102 F3
Long Marston Herts.....20 E1
Long Marston N York.....59 L4
Long Marston Warwks.....30 E4
Long Marton Cumb.....64 C3
Long Melford Suffk.....34 E7
Longmoor Camp Hants.....10 C4
Longmorn Moray.....101 K4
Longmoss Ches E.....50 B6
Long Newnton Gloucs.....29 M9
Longnewton Border.....80 D8
Long Newton E Loth.....87 K8
Longnewton S on T.....65 P4
Longney Gloucs.....29 K6
Longniddry E Loth.....87 J7
Longnor Shrops.....39 J3
Longnor Staffs.....50 E7
Longparish Hants.....19 M10
Long Preston N York.....63 Q9
Longridge Lancs.....57 L2
Longridge W Loth.....85 Q9
Longriggend N Lans.....85 N8
Long Riston E R Yk.....61 J6
Longrock Cnwll.....2 D9
Longsdon Staffs.....50 C9
Longside Abers.....103 L6
Longstanton Cambs.....33 L4
Longstock Hants.....19 L12
Longstowe Cambs.....33 K6
Long Stratton Norfk.....45 K10
Long Street M Keyn.....32 B7
Longstreet Wilts.....18 G8
Long Sutton Hants.....10 B1
Long Sutton Lincs.....43 L6
Long Sutton Somset.....17 L10
Longthorpe C Pete.....42 G9
Long Thurlow Suffk.....34 G3
Longthwaite Cumb.....71 N10
Longton C Stke.....50 B11
Longton Lancs.....57 J4
Longtown Cumb.....71 N2
Longtown Herefs.....28 C3
Longueville Jersey.....7 c2

Longville in the Dale
  Shrops.....39 K4
Long Waste Wrekin.....49 L11
Long Whatton Leics.....41 L3
Longwick Bucks.....20 C3
Long Wittenham Oxon.....19 P3
Longwitton Nthumb.....73 J3
Longwood D & G.....70 B4
Longworth Oxon.....19 L2
Longyester E Loth.....87 K8
Lonmay Abers.....103 L4
Lonmore Highld.....104 C12
Looe Cnwll.....4 F8
Loose Kent.....22 F11
Loosley Row Bucks.....20 D4
Lootcherbrae Abers.....102 D5
Lopen Somset.....17 K12
Loppington Shrops.....49 J9
Lords Wood Medway.....22 F10
Lornty P & K.....92 H6
Loscoe Derbys.....51 K10
Lossiemouth Moray.....101 K2
Lostock Gralam Ches W.....49 M2
Lostock Green Ches W.....49 M2
Lostwithiel Cnwll.....4 D8
Lothbeg Highld.....107 Q1
Lothersdale N York.....58 C5
Lothmore Highld.....110 A12
Loudwater Bucks.....20 E5
Loughborough Leics.....41 M4
Loughborough
  Crematorium Leics.....41 M4
Loughor Swans.....26 D8
Loughton Essex.....21 N4
Loughton M Keyn.....32 B8
Lound Lincs.....42 F6
Lound Notts.....51 P4
Lound Suffk.....45 Q9
Lount Leics.....41 K4
Louth Lincs.....53 K6
Lovedean Hants.....10 B7
Lover Wilts.....8 H4
Loversall Donc.....51 M2
Loves Green Essex.....22 D3
Loveston Pembks.....25 J7
Lovington Somset.....17 N9
Low Ackworth Wakefd.....59 K10
Low Barbeth D & G.....68 D6
Low Bentham N York.....63 M8
Low Biggins Cumb.....63 L6
Low Borrowbridge Cumb.....63 L3
Low Bradfield Sheff.....50 H3
Low Bradley N York.....58 D5
Low Burnham N Linc.....52 A4
Lowca Cumb.....70 F10
Low Catton E R Yk.....60 C4
Low Crosby Cumb.....71 P4
Lowdham Notts.....51 P10
Low Dinsdale Darltn.....65 N5
Lower Aisholt Somset.....16 G8
Lower Ansty Dorset.....8 B6
Lower Apperley Gloucs.....29 M4
Lower Ashton Devon.....6 A6
Lower Assendon Oxon.....20 C6
Lower Bartle Lancs.....57 J3
Lower Basildon W Berk.....19 Q5
Lower Beeding W Susx.....11 K5
Lower Benefield Nhants.....42 E11
Lower Bentley Worcs.....30 C2
Lower Boddington
  Nhants.....31 L4
Lower Bourne Surrey.....10 D2
Lower Brailes Warwks.....30 H6
Lower Breakish Highld.....97 J5
Lower Broadheath Worcs.....39 P10
Lower Broxwood Herefs.....38 G10
Lower Bullingham Herefs.....28 F2
Lower Burgate Hants.....8 H4
Lower Caldecote C Beds.....32 H7
Lower Chapel Powys.....27 L2
Lower Chicksgrove Wilts.....8 E2
Lower Chute Wilts.....19 K9
Lower Clapton Gt Lon.....21 M6
Lower Clent Worcs.....40 B10
Lower Cumberworth Kirk.....58 G11
Lower Dean Bed.....32 F3
Lower Diabaig Highld.....105 L9
Lower Dicker E Susx.....12 B7
Lower Down Shrops.....38 G5
Lower Dunsforth N York.....59 K2
Lower Egleton Herefs.....39 L11
Lower End M Keyn.....32 D8
Lower Eythorne Kent.....23 P12
Lower Failand N Som.....17 M2
Lower Farringdon Hants.....10 B3
Lower Feltham Gt Lon.....20 H8
Lower Froyle Hants.....10 C2
Lower Gabwell Devon.....6 C8
Lower Gledfield Highld.....107 K4
Lower Godney Somset.....17 L7
Lower Gravenhurst
  C Beds.....32 G9
Lower Green Kent.....12 C3
Lower Green Kent.....12 D2
Lower Halliford Surrey.....20 H9
Lower Halstow Kent.....22 G9
Lower Hamworthy
  Poole.....8 E8
Lower Hardres Kent.....23 M11
Lower Hartwell Bucks.....20 C2
Lower Hergest Herefs.....38 F10
Lower Heyford Oxon.....31 L8
Lower Houses Kirk.....58 F10
Lower Irlam Salfd.....57 N9
Lower Killeyan Ag & B.....74 D4
Lower Langford N Som.....17 L4
Lower Largo Fife.....86 H2
Lower Leigh Staffs.....40 D1
Lower Loxhore Devon.....15 K5
Lower Lydbrook Gloucs.....28 G5
Lower Lye Herefs.....38 H8
Lower Machen Newpt.....27 P10
Lower Merridge Somset.....16 G8
Lower Middleton
  Cheney Nhants.....31 L6
Lower Moor Worcs.....30 C5
Lower Morton S Glos.....28 H9
Lower Nazeing Essex.....21 N3
Lower Penarth V Glam.....16 F3
Lower Penn Staffs.....39 Q3
Lower Peover Ches E.....49 N1
Lower Quinton Warwks.....30 F5
Lower Raydon Suffk.....34 G8
Lower Roadwater Somset.....16 D8
Lower Seagry Wilts.....18 D5
Lower Shelton C Beds.....32 E8
Lower Shiplake Oxon.....20 C7

Lower Shuckburgh
  Warwks.....31 L2
Lower Slaughter Gloucs.....30 F9
Lower Standen Kent.....13 N3
Lower Stanton St
  Quintin Wilts.....18 D5
Lower Stoke Medway.....22 G8
Lower Stone Gloucs.....29 J9
Lower Stow Bedon Norfk.....44 F10
Lower Street Norfk.....45 L3
Lower Street Suffk.....35 J6
Lower Swanwick Hants.....9 N5
Lower Swell Gloucs.....30 F8
Lower Tean Staffs.....50 D12
Lower Town Devon.....5 P5
Lower Town Pembks.....24 G2
Lower Upcott Devon.....6 B6
Lower Upham Hants.....9 N4
Lower Weare Somset.....17 K5
Lower Welson Herefs.....38 F11
Lower Westmancote
  Worcs.....29 N2
Lower Whatley Somset.....17 Q6
Lower Whitley Ches W.....57 L11
Lower Wield Hants.....19 Q11
Lower Willingdon E Susx.....12 C9
Lower Withington Ches E.....49 P2
Lower Woodford Wilts.....8 G1
Lower Wraxhall Dorset.....7 N3
Lowesby Leics.....41 Q6
Lowestoft Suffk.....45 Q10
Loweswater Cumb.....71 J10
Low Fell Gatesd.....73 M8
Lowfield Heath W Susx.....11 L3
Low Gartachorrans Stirlg.....84 H6
Low Grantley N York.....65 M12
Low Ham Somset.....17 L9
Low Harrogate N York.....58 H3
Low Hesket Cumb.....71 P6
Low Hutton N York.....60 D1
Lowick Nhants.....32 E1
Lowick Nthumb.....81 M5
Lowick Green Cumb.....62 F5
Low Lorton Cumb.....71 J9
Low Marnham Notts.....52 B9
Low Mill N York.....66 F8
Low Moorsley Sundld.....73 N10
Low Moresby Cumb.....70 G10
Low Newton Cumb.....62 H6
Low Row Cumb.....72 B8
Low Row N York.....64 H7
Low Salchrie D & G.....68 D6
Low Santon N Linc.....60 G10
Lowsonford Warwks.....30 F1
Low Tharston Norfk.....45 K10
Lowther Cumb.....71 Q10
Lowthorpe E R Yk.....61 J3
Lowton Somset.....16 G11
Low Torry Fife.....86 B5
Low Worsall N York.....65 P5
Low Wray Cumb.....62 G3
Loxbeare Devon.....16 C11
Loxhill Surrey.....10 G3
Loxhore Devon.....15 K4
Loxley Warwks.....30 H4
Loxton N Som.....17 K5
Loxwood W Susx.....10 G4
Loyal Lodge Highld.....109 L6
Lubenham Leics.....41 P9
Luccombe Somset.....16 C7
Luccombe Village IoW.....9 P10
Lucker Nthumb.....81 N8
Luckett Cnwll.....5 J5
Lucking Street Essex.....34 D9
Luckington Wilts.....18 C4
Lucklawhill Fife.....93 M10
Luckwell Bridge Somset.....16 B8
Lucton Herefs.....38 H8
Ludag W Isls.....111 b6
Ludborough Lincs.....53 J4
Ludbrook Devon.....5 M8
Ludchurch Pembks.....25 K6
Luddenden Calder.....58 D8
Luddenden Foot Calder.....58 D8
Luddesdown Kent.....22 D9
Luddington N Linc.....60 E10
Luddington Warwks.....30 F4
Luddington in the
  Brook Nhants.....42 F12
Ludford Lincs.....52 H5
Ludford Shrops.....39 K7
Ludgershall Bucks.....31 P10
Ludgershall Wilts.....19 J9
Ludgvan Cnwll.....2 D8
Ludham Norfk.....45 N6
Ludlow Shrops.....39 K7
Ludney Somset.....8 D3
Ludwell Wilts.....8 D3
Ludworth Dur.....73 P11
Luffenhall Herts.....33 J10
Luffincott Devon.....5 N2
Luffness E Loth.....87 J6
Lugar E Ayrs.....77 K7
Luggate Burn E Loth.....87 L7
Luggiebank N Lans.....85 M8
Lugton E Ayrs.....84 G11
Lugwardine Herefs.....28 G1
Luib Highld.....96 G4
Luing Ag & B.....83 L2
Lulham Herefs.....28 E1
Lullington Derbys.....40 G5
Lullington Somset.....18 B9
Lulsgate Bottom N Som.....17 M3
Lulsley Worcs.....39 N10
Lumb Calder.....58 D9
Lumby N York.....59 L7
Lumloch E Duns.....85 K8
Lumphanan Abers.....95 J2
Lumphinnans Fife.....86 E4
Lumsden Abers.....101 N10
Lunan Angus.....93 N5
Lunanhead Angus.....93 N5
Luncarty P & K.....92 G9
Lund E R Yk.....60 G5
Lund N York.....59 N7
Lundie Angus.....93 K8
Lundin Links Fife.....86 H2
Lundin Mill Fife.....86 H2
Lundy Devon.....14 C3
Lunga Ag & B.....83 K2
Lunna Shet.....111 k3
Lunsford Kent.....22 E10
Lunsford's Cross E Susx.....12 E7
Lunt Sefton.....56 G8
Luppitt Devon.....6 F3
Lupset Wakefd.....59 H9
Lupton Cumb.....63 K6
Lurgashall W Susx.....10 F5
Lurley Devon.....16 C12

Luscombe Devon.....5 Q8
Luss Ag & B.....84 F4
Lussagiven Ag & B.....83 J6
Lusta Highld.....104 C10
Lustleigh Devon.....5 Q4
Luston Herefs.....39 J9
Luthermuir Abers.....95 L8
Luthrie Fife.....93 K10
Luton Devon.....6 B7
Luton Devon.....6 E3
Luton Luton.....32 F11
Luton Medway.....22 F9
Luton Airport Luton.....32 G11
Lutterworth Leics.....41 M9
Lutton Devon.....5 M8
Lutton Lincs.....43 M5
Lutton Nhants.....42 G11
Luxborough Somset.....16 D8
Luxulyan Cnwll.....3 M4
Luxulyan Valley Cnwll.....3 N4
Lybster Highld.....110 F8
Lydbury North Shrops.....38 G5
Lydd Kent.....13 K6
Lydd Airport Kent.....13 K6
Lydden Kent.....13 N2
Lydden Kent.....23 Q9
Lyddington Rutlnd.....42 C10
Lydeard St Lawrence
  Somset.....16 F9
Lydford Devon.....5 K3
Lydford on Fosse Somset.....17 N9
Lydgate Calder.....58 B8
Lydham Shrops.....38 G4
Lydiard Millicent Wilts.....18 G4
Lydiard Tregoze Swindn.....18 G4
Lydiate Sefton.....56 G7
Lydiate Ash Worcs.....40 C11
Lydlinch Dorset.....17 Q12
Lydney Gloucs.....28 H7
Lydstep Pembks.....25 J8
Lye Dudley.....40 B10
Lye Green E Susx.....11 P4
Lye Green Warwks.....30 G2
Lye's Green Wilts.....18 B10
Lyford Oxon.....19 L2
Lymbridge Green Kent.....13 L2
Lyme Regis Dorset.....7 J4
Lyminge Kent.....13 M2
Lymington Hants.....9 K8
Lyminster W Susx.....10 G8
Lymm Warrtn.....57 M10
Lymm Services Warrtn.....57 M11
Lympne Kent.....13 L3
Lympsham Somset.....17 J5
Lympstone Devon.....6 D6
Lynchat Highld.....99 J8
Lynch Green Norfk.....45 J8
Lyndhurst Hants.....9 K6
Lyndon Rutlnd.....42 C8
Lyne Border.....79 K1
Lyne Surrey.....20 G9
Lyneal Shrops.....49 J8
Lyneham Oxon.....30 H9
Lyneham Wilts.....18 F5
Lynemouth Nthumb.....73 N3
Lyne of Skene Abers.....102 G12
Lyness Ork.....111 g3
Lyng Norfk.....44 H6
Lyng Somset.....17 J9
Lynmouth Devon.....15 M3
Lynsted Kent.....22 H10
Lynton Devon.....15 M3
Lyon's Gate Dorset.....7 P2
Lyonshall Herefs.....38 G10
Lytchett Matravers
  Dorset.....8 D8
Lytchett Minster Dorset.....8 E8
Lyth Highld.....110 F3
Lytham Lancs.....56 G4
Lytham St Anne's Lancs.....56 F4
Lythe N York.....67 J5
Lythmore Highld.....110 C3

M

Mabe Burnthouse Cnwll.....2 H8
Mablethorpe Lincs.....53 N6
Macclesfield Ches E.....50 B6
Macclesfield
  Crematorium Ches E.....50 B6
Macduff Abers.....102 F3
Macharioch Ag & B.....75 L9
Machen Caerph.....27 P10
Machrie N Ayrs.....75 N5
Machrihanish Ag & B.....75 J8
Machrins Ag & B.....82 K4
Machynlleth Powys.....47 M10
Machynys Carmth.....26 C8
Mackworth Derbys.....50 H12
Macmerry E Loth.....87 J7
Madderty P & K.....92 E10
Maddiston Falk.....85 Q7
Madeley Staffs.....49 P6
Madeley Wrekin.....39 M2
Madingley Cambs.....33 L5
Madley Herefs.....28 E2
Madresfield Worcs.....39 P11
Madron Cnwll.....2 C9
Maenclochog Pembks.....25 J4
Maendy V Glam.....16 D2
Maentwrog Gwynd.....47 L3
Maen-y-groes Cerdgn.....36 F8
Maer Staffs.....49 P7
Maerdy Rhondd.....27 K8
Maesbrook Shrops.....48 F10
Maesbury Shrops.....48 F9
Maesbury Marsh Shrops.....48 F10
Maesllyn Cerdgn.....36 G10
Maesteg Brdgnd.....27 J9
Maesybont Carmth.....26 D5
Maesycwmmer Caerph.....27 N9
Maggieknockater Moray.....101 L6
Magham Down E Susx.....12 C7
Maghull Sefton.....56 G7
Magna Park Leics.....41 L9
Magor Mons.....28 E10
Magor Services Mons.....28 E10
Maidenbower W Susx.....11 L3
Maiden Bradley Wilts.....18 B11
Maidencombe Torbay.....6 C8
Maidenhayne Devon.....6 H4
Maiden Head N Som.....17 N3
Maidenhead W & M.....20 E7
Maiden Newton Dorset.....7 N4

Maidens S Ayrs.....76 D9
Maiden's Green Br For.....20 E8
Maiden Wells Pembks.....24 G8
Maidford Nhants.....31 N4
Maids Moreton Bucks.....31 P7
Maidstone Kent.....22 F11
Maidstone Services Kent.....22 G11
Maidwell Nhants.....41 Q11
Mail Shet.....111 k4
Maindee Newpt.....28 C10
Mainland Ork.....111 h2
Mainland Shet.....111 k4
Mainsforth Dur.....65 N2
Mains of Balhall Angus.....94 H8
Mains of Balnakettle
  Abers.....95 K7
Mains of Dalvey Highld.....100 H8
Mains of Haulkerton
  Abers.....95 K7
Mains of Lesmoir Abers.....101 N9
Mains of Melgunds Angus.....93 P5
Mainsriddle D & G.....70 F4
Mainstone Shrops.....38 F5
Maisemore Gloucs.....29 L5
Malborough Devon.....5 P11
Maldon Essex.....22 G3
Malham N York.....58 B2
Maligar Highld.....104 G9
Mallaig Highld.....97 J9
Mallaigvaig Highld.....97 J9
Malleny Mills C Edin.....86 E8
Malltraeth IoA.....54 E7
Mallwyd Gwynd.....47 P8
Malmesbury Wilts.....18 D4
Malmsmead Devon.....15 N3
Malpas Ches W.....49 J6
Malpas Cnwll.....3 J7
Malpas Newpt.....28 C10
Maltby Rothm.....51 M3
Maltby S on T.....66 C5
Maltby le Marsh Lincs.....53 M7
Maltman's Hill Kent.....12 H2
Malton N York.....66 H12
Malvern Hills.....39 P12
Malvern Link Worcs.....39 P11
Malvern Wells Worcs.....29 K1
Mamble Worcs.....39 M7
Mamhilad Mons.....28 C7
Manaccan Cnwll.....2 H10
Manafon Powys.....38 C2
Manais W Isls.....111 c3
Manaton Devon.....5 P4
Manby Lincs.....53 L6
Mancetter Warwks.....40 H7
Manchester Manch.....57 Q8
Manchester Airport
  Manch.....57 P11
Manchester Cathedral
  Salfd.....57 P8
Mancot Flints.....48 G3
Mandally Highld.....98 D8
Manea Cambs.....43 M11
Maney Birm.....40 E8
Manfield N York.....65 L5
Mangotsfield S Glos.....17 P2
Manish W Isls.....111 c3
Manley Ches W.....49 J2
Manmoel Caerph.....27 P7
Mannel Ag & B.....88 C8
Manningford Bohune
  Wilts.....18 G8
Manningford Bruce Wilts.....18 G8
Manningham C Brad.....58 F7
Manning's Heath W Susx.....11 K4
Mannington Dorset.....8 F6
Manningtree Essex.....34 H9
Mannofield C Aber.....95 Q2
Manorbier Pembks.....25 J8
Manorbier Newton
  Pembks.....25 H8
Manorhill Border.....80 F7
Manorowen Pembks.....24 G2
Manor Park Gt Lon.....21 N6
Manor Park
  Crematorium Gt Lon.....21 N6
Mansell Gamage Herefs.....38 H12
Mansell Lacy Herefs.....38 H11
Mansfield E Ayrs.....77 K8
Mansfield Notts.....51 M8
Mansfield & District
  Crematorium Notts.....51 M8
Mansfield Woodhouse
  Notts.....51 M7
Manston Dorset.....8 B4
Manston Kent.....23 Q9
Manston Leeds.....59 J7
Manswood Dorset.....8 E6
Manthorpe Lincs.....42 F7
Manton N Linc.....52 D3
Manton Rutlnd.....42 C8
Manton Wilts.....18 H7
Manuden Essex.....33 M10
Maperton Somset.....17 P10
Maplebeck Notts.....51 P8
Mapledurham Oxon.....19 R5
Mapledurwell Hants.....20 B12
Maplehurst W Susx.....11 J5
Maplescombe Kent.....22 C9
Mapleton Derbys.....50 F10
Mapperley Derbys.....51 K11
Mapperley Park C Nott.....51 M11
Mapperton Dorset.....7 M3
Mappleborough Green
  Warwks.....30 E2
Mappleton E R Yk.....61 L5
Mapplewell Barns.....59 J11
Mappowder Dorset.....7 Q2
Marazanvose Cnwll.....2 H6
Marazion Cnwll.....2 D9
Marbury Ches E.....49 K6
March Cambs.....43 L10
March S Lans.....78 G6
Marcham Oxon.....19 M2
Marchamley Shrops.....49 L9
Marchington Staffs.....40 F2
Marchros Gwynd.....46 E6
Marchwiel Wrexhm.....48 G6
Marchwood Hants.....9 L5
Marcross V Glam.....16 C3
Marden Herefs.....39 K11
Marden Kent.....12 E2
Marden Wilts.....18 F8
Marden Thorn Kent.....12 F2
Mardy Mons.....28 C5
Mareham le Fen Lincs.....53 J10
Mareham on the Hill Lincs.....53 J9
Marehill W Susx.....10 G6

186 Maresfield - Molland

Maresfield E Susx 11 P5
Marfleet C KuH 61 K8
Marford Wrexhm 48 G4
Margam Neath 26 G10
Margam Crematorium Neath 26 H10
Margaret Marsh Dorset 8 B4
Margaretting Essex 22 D3
Margaretting Tye Essex 22 D4
Margate Kent 23 Q8
Margnaheglish N Ayrs 75 Q6
Margrie D & G 69 N8
Margrove Park R & Cl 66 F4
Marham Norfk 44 B7
Marhamchurch Cnwll 14 D10
Marholm C Pete 42 G9
Mariansleigh Devon 15 M7
Marine Town Kent 22 H8
Marionburgh Abers 95 L1
Marishader Highld 104 G9
Maristow Devon 5 K7
Marjoriebanks D & G 78 H11
Mark Somset 17 K6
Markbeech Kent 11 P2
Markby Lincs 53 M7
Mark Cross E Susx 12 C4
Markeaton Crematorium C Derb 51 J12
Market Bosworth Leics 41 K6
Market Deeping Lincs 42 G7
Market Drayton Shrops 49 M8
Market Harborough Leics 41 Q9
Market Lavington Wilts 18 E9
Market Overton Rutlnd 42 C6
Market Rasen Lincs 52 G5
Market Stainton Lincs 52 H7
Market Warsop Notts 51 M7
Market Weighton E R Yk 60 F6
Market Weston Suffk 34 G2
Markfield Leics 41 L5
Markham Caerph 27 N8
Markham Moor Notts 51 Q6
Markinch Fife 86 G2
Markington N York 58 H2
Markle E Loth 87 L6
Marksbury BaNES 17 P4
Marks Tey Essex 34 E11
Markyate Herts 32 F12
Marlborough Wilts 18 H7
Marlcliff Warwks 30 E4
Marldon Devon 6 B9
Marlesford Suffk 35 M5
Marlingford Norfk 45 J8
Marloes Pembks 24 E7
Marlow Bucks 20 D6
Marlow Bottom Bucks 20 D6
Marlpit Hill Kent 11 N1
Marnhull Dorset 8 B4
Marple Stockp 50 C3
Marr Donc 59 L12
Marrick N York 65 J7
Marsden Kirk 58 D10
Marsden S Tyne 73 P7
Marshalswick Herts 21 J2
Marsham Norfk 45 K5
Marsh Baldon Oxon 19 P2
Marshborough Kent 23 P11
Marshbrook Shrops 38 H4
Marshchapel Lincs 53 K4
Marsh Farm Luton 32 F10
Marshfield Newpt 28 B11
Marshfield S Glos 18 B6
Marshgate Cnwll 4 E2
Marsh Gibbon Bucks 31 N9
Marsh Green Devon 6 E4
Marsh Green Kent 11 N2
Marshland St James Norfk 43 N8
Marsh Lane Derbys 51 K5
Marsh Street Somset 16 D7
Marshwood Dorset 7 K3
Marske N York 65 K7
Marske-by-the-Sea R & Cl 66 E3
Marston Herefs 38 G10
Marston Lincs 42 C2
Marston Oxon 31 M11
Marston Staffs 40 B3
Marston Wilts 18 E9
Marston Green Solhll 40 F9
Marston Magna Somset 17 N10
Marston Meysey Wilts 18 G2
Marston Montgomery Derbys 50 F12
Marston Moretaine C Beds 32 E8
Marston on Dove Derbys 40 G2
Marston St Lawrence Nhants 31 M6
Marston Trussell Nhants 41 P9
Marstow Herefs 28 G5
Marsworth Bucks 20 E1
Marten Wilts 19 K8
Martham Norfk 45 P6
Martin Hants 8 F4
Martin Kent 13 Q1
Martin Lincs 52 G10
Martinhoe Devon 15 L3
Martin Hussingtree Worcs 39 Q9
Martinstown Dorset 7 P5
Martlesham Suffk 35 L7
Martlesham Heath Suffk 35 L7
Martletwy Pembks 24 H6
Martley Worcs 39 N9
Martock Somset 17 L11
Marton Ches E 49 Q2
Marton E R Yk 61 K6
Marton Lincs 52 B7
Marton Middsb 66 D4
Marton N York 59 K2
Marton N York 66 G10
Marton Shrops 38 F2
Marton Warwks 31 K1
Marton-le-Moor N York 65 P12
Martyr Worthy Hants 9 N2
Marwell Wildlife Hants 9 N3
Marwick Ork 111 g2
Marwood Devon 15 J5
Marybank Highld 106 H10
Maryburgh Highld 107 J10
Maryculter Abers 95 P3
Marygold Border 87 P9
Maryhill C Glas 85 J8
Maryhill Crematorium C Glas 85 J8
Marykirk Abers 95 L8
Marylebone Gt Lon 21 L7
Marylebone Wigan 57 L7
Marypark Moray 101 J7
Maryport Cumb 70 G8
Maryport D & G 68 F11
Marystow Devon 5 J4
Mary Tavy Devon 5 K4
Maryton Angus 95 L10
Marywell Abers 95 J3
Marywell Abers 95 Q3
Marywell Angus 93 Q6
Masham N York 65 L10
Masongill N York 63 M7
Masonhill Crematorium S Ayrs 76 F7
Mastin Moor Derbys 51 L5
Matching Green Essex 21 Q2
Matching Tye Essex 21 P2
Matfen Nthumb 73 J6
Matfield Kent 12 D2
Mathern Mons 28 F9
Mathon Herefs 39 N11
Mathry Pembks 24 F3
Matlask Norfk 45 J3
Matlock Derbys 50 H8
Matlock Bath Derbys 50 H8
Matson Gloucs 29 L5
Mattersey Notts 51 P3
Mattingley Hants 20 B10
Mattishall Norfk 44 H7
Mattishall Burgh Norfk 44 H7
Mauchline E Ayrs 76 H6
Maud Abers 103 J6
Maufant Jersey 7 c1
Maugersbury Gloucs 30 G8
Maughold IoM 56 e3
Mauld Highld 98 E2
Maulden C Beds 32 F8
Maulds Meaburn Cumb 64 B4
Maunby N York 65 N9
Maundown Somset 16 E9
Mautby Norfk 45 P7
Mavesyn Ridware Staffs 40 E4
Mavis Enderby Lincs 53 K9
Mawbray Cumb 70 H6
Mawdesley Lancs 57 J6
Mawdlam Brdgnd 26 H11
Mawgan Cnwll 2 G10
Mawgan Porth Cnwll 3 J3
Mawla Cnwll 2 G6
Mawnan Cnwll 2 H9
Mawnan Smith Cnwll 2 H9
Mawsley Nhants 32 B2
Maxey C Pete 42 G8
Maxstoke Warwks 40 G9
Maxton Border 80 E7
Maxton Kent 13 P2
Maxwell Town D & G 70 F1
Maxworthy Cnwll 4 G2
May Bank Staffs 49 Q6
Maybole S Ayrs 76 E8
Maybury Surrey 20 G10
Mayfield E Susx 12 C5
Mayfield Mdloth 86 G8
Mayfield Staffs 50 F10
Mayford Surrey 20 F11
May Hill Gloucs 29 J5
Mayland Essex 22 H3
Maylandsea Essex 22 H3
Maynard's Green E Susx 12 C6
Maypole Green Norfk 45 N10
Maypole Green Suffk 34 F5
Meadgate BaNES 17 P5
Meadle Bucks 20 C3
Meadowfield Dur 73 M11
Meadwell Devon 5 J4
Meanwood Leeds 58 H6
Meare Somset 17 L7
Meare Green Somset 16 H10
Meare Green Somset 17 J10
Mearns E Rens 85 J11
Mears Ashby Nhants 32 B4
Measham Leics 41 J5
Meathop Cumb 62 H6
Meavy Devon 5 L6
Medbourne Leics 42 B10
Meddon Devon 14 E8
Meden Vale Notts 51 M6
Medmenham Bucks 20 D6
Medomsley Dur 73 K9
Medstead Hants 19 Q12
Medway Crematorium Kent 22 E10
Medway Services Medway 22 G10
Meerbrook Staffs 50 C8
Meesden Herts 33 L9
Meeth Devon 15 J9
Meeting House Hill Norfk 45 M5
Meidrim Carmth 25 M5
Meifod Powys 48 D11
Meigle P & K 93 K6
Meikle Carco D & G 77 N8
Meikle Earnock S Lans 85 M11
Meikle Kilmory Ag & B 83 R10
Meikle Obney P & K 92 F8
Meikleour P & K 92 H7
Meikle Wartle Abers 102 F8
Meinciau Carmth 26 B6
Meir C Stke 50 C11
Melbourn Cambs 33 L7
Melbourne Derbys 41 J3
Melbourne E R Yk 60 D5
Melbury Abbas Dorset 8 C4
Melbury Bubb Dorset 7 N2
Melbury Osmond Dorset 7 N2
Melchbourne Bed 32 E4
Melcombe Bingham Dorset 8 B6
Meldon Devon 5 L2
Meldon Nthumb 73 K4
Meldreth Cambs 33 L7
Meldrum Stirlg 85 M3
Melfort Ag & B 90 B12
Meliden Denbgs 56 C11
Melin-y-wig Denbgs 48 B6
Melkinthorpe Cumb 71 Q9
Melkridge Nthumb 72 D7
Melksham Wilts 18 D7
Melling Lancs 63 L7
Melling Sefton 56 H8
Mellis Suffk 34 H2
Mellon Charles Highld 105 M4
Mellon Udrigle Highld 105 N3
Mellor Lancs 57 M3
Mellor Stockp 50 C3
Mellor Brook Lancs 57 M3
Mells Somset 17 Q6
Melmerby Cumb 72 B12
Melmerby N York 65 J9
Melmerby N York 65 N11
Melness Highld 109 K4
Melplash Dorset 7 L3
Melrose Border 80 D7
Melsetter Ork 111 g3
Melsonby N York 65 L6
Meltham Kirk 58 E11
Melton E R Yk 60 G8
Melton Suffk 35 L6
Melton Constable Norfk 44 H4
Melton Mowbray Leics 41 Q4
Melton Ross N Linc 60 H11
Melvaig Highld 105 L5
Melverley Shrops 48 G11
Melvich Highld 109 Q3
Membury Devon 6 H3
Membury Services W Berk 19 K5
Memsie Abers 103 K3
Memus Angus 93 M4
Menai Bridge IoA 54 H7
Mendham Suffk 45 L12
Mendip Crematorium Somset 17 N7
Mendip Hills 17 M5
Mendlesham Suffk 34 H4
Mendlesham Green Suffk 34 H4
Menheniot Cnwll 4 G7
Mennock D & G 77 N9
Menston C Brad 58 F5
Menstrie Clacks 85 P4
Mentmore Bucks 32 C11
Meoble Highld 97 L11
Meole Brace Shrops 49 J12
Meonstoke Hants 9 Q4
Meopham Kent 22 D9
Mepal Cambs 33 M1
Meppershall C Beds 32 G9
Mere Ches E 57 N11
Mere Wilts 8 B2
Mere Brow Lancs 56 H5
Mereclough Lancs 57 Q3
Mereworth Kent 22 D11
Meriden Solhll 40 G10
Merkadale Highld 96 D4
Merley Poole 8 F7
Merrion Pembks 24 G8
Merriott Somset 7 L1
Merrow Surrey 20 G12
Merry Hill Herts 21 J5
Merryhill Wolves 40 B7
Merrymeet Cnwll 4 G7
Mersea Island Essex 23 K1
Mersham Kent 13 K3
Merstham Surrey 21 L11
Merston W Susx 10 E9
Merstone IoW 9 N9
Merthyr Cynog Powys 27 L2
Merthyr Mawr Brdgnd 27 J12
Merthyr Tydfil Myr Td 27 M7
Merthyr Vale Myr Td 27 M8
Merton Devon 15 J9
Merton Gt Lon 21 K9
Merton Norfk 44 E9
Merton Oxon 31 M9
Meshaw Devon 15 N8
Messing Essex 34 E11
Messingham N Linc 52 C3
Metfield Suffk 35 L1
Metherell Cnwll 5 J6
Metheringham Lincs 52 F10
Methil Fife 86 H3
Methilhill Fife 86 G3
Methlick Abers 102 H7
Methven P & K 92 F9
Methwold Norfk 44 C10
Methwold Hythe Norfk 44 B10
Mettingham Suffk 45 M11
Metton Norfk 45 K3
Mevagissey Cnwll 3 M6
Mexborough Donc 51 L2
Mey Highld 110 F2
Meyllteyrn Gwynd 46 D5
Meysey Hampton Gloucs 18 G1
Miabhig W Isls 111 c2
Miavaig W Isls 111 c2
Michaelchurch Herefs 28 F4
Michaelchurch Escley Herefs 28 C3
Michaelstone-y-Fedw Newpt 27 P11
Michaelston-le-Pit V Glam 16 F2
Michaelstow Cnwll 4 D4
Michaelwood Services Gloucs 29 J9
Micheldever Hants 19 N11
Micheldever Station Hants 19 N11
Michelmersh Hants 9 L3
Mickfield Suffk 35 J4
Micklebring Donc 51 L2
Mickleby N York 66 H5
Micklefield Leeds 59 K7
Mickleham Surrey 21 J11
Mickleover C Derb 40 H1
Mickleton Dur 64 H3
Mickleton Gloucs 30 F5
Mickletown Leeds 59 K8
Mickle Trafford Ches W 49 J2
Mickley N York 65 M11
Mickley Square Nthumb 73 J8
Mid Ardlaw Abers 103 K3
Midbea Ork 111 h1
Mid Beltie Abers 95 K2
Mid Calder W Loth 86 C8
Mid Clyth Highld 110 F8
Mid Culbeuchly Abers 102 E3
Middle Aston Oxon 31 L8
Middle Barton Oxon 31 K8
Middlebie D & G 71 K1
Middlebridge P & K 92 D3
Middle Chinnock Somset 17 L12
Middle Claydon Bucks 31 Q8
Middleham N York 65 K9
Middle Handley Derbys 51 K5
Middlehill Wilts 18 B7
Middlehope Shrops 39 J4
Middle Kames Ag & B 83 N5
Middle Littleton Worcs 30 E5
Middlemarsh Dorset 7 P2
Middle Mayfield Staffs 50 F10
Middle Rasen Lincs 52 F5
Middle Rocombe Devon 6 B8
Middlesbrough Middsb 66 C4
Middleshaw Cumb 63 K4
Middlesmoor N York 65 J11
Middle Stoke Medway 22 G8
Middlestone Dur 65 M2
Middlestown Wakefd 58 H10
Middlethird Border 80 F5
Middleton Ag & B 88 B7
Middleton Derbys 50 G8
Middleton Derbys 50 H9
Middleton Essex 34 E8
Middleton Hants 19 M11
Middleton Herefs 39 K8
Middleton Leeds 58 H8
Middleton N York 58 E4
Middleton N York 66 H9
Middleton Nhants 42 B11
Middleton Norfk 43 Q6
Middleton Nthumb 73 J4
Middleton P & K 86 D2
Middleton Rochdl 57 Q7
Middleton Shrops 39 K6
Middleton Suffk 35 N3
Middleton Swans 25 P10
Middleton Warwks 40 F7
Middleton Cheney Nhants 31 L6
Middleton Crematorium Rochdl 58 B11
Middleton-in-Teesdale Dur 64 G3
Middleton Moor Suffk 35 N4
Middleton One Row Darltn 65 P5
Middleton-on-Sea W Susx 10 F9
Middleton on the Hill Herefs 39 K8
Middleton on the Wolds E R Yk 60 G4
Middleton Park C Aber 103 J11
Middleton Quernhow N York 65 N10
Middleton St George Darltn 65 N5
Middleton Scriven Shrops 39 M5
Middleton Stoney Oxon 31 M9
Middleton Tyas N York 65 M6
Middle Town IoS 2 b3
Middletown Powys 48 F11
Middle Tysoe Warwks 31 J5
Middle Wallop Hants 19 K12
Middlewich Ches E 49 N3
Middle Winterslow Wilts 9 J2
Middlewood Cnwll 4 G5
Middle Woodford Wilts 18 G12
Middlewood Green Suffk 34 H5
Middleyard E Ayrs 77 J5
Middlezoy Somset 17 K9
Midford BaNES 18 B8
Midgham W Berk 19 P7
Midgley Calder 58 D8
Midgley Wakefd 58 H10
Midhopestones Sheff 50 G2
Midhurst W Susx 10 E6
Mid Lavant W Susx 10 D8
Midlem Border 80 C8
Mid Mains Highld 98 F2
Midpark Ag & B 83 Q10
Midsomer Norton BaNES 17 P5
Midtown Highld 109 K4
Mid Warwickshire Crematorium Warwks 30 H3
Mid Yell Shet 111 k2
Migvie Abers 94 G1
Milborne Port Somset 17 P11
Milborne St Andrew Dorset 8 B7
Milborne Wick Somset 17 P11
Milbourne Nthumb 73 K6
Milbourne Wilts 18 D4
Milburn Cumb 64 C2
Milbury Heath S Glos 29 J10
Milby N York 59 K1
Milcombe Oxon 31 K7
Milden Suffk 34 F7
Mildenhall Suffk 34 B2
Mildenhall Wilts 18 H6
Mileham Norfk 44 F6
Mile Oak Br & H 11 K8
Milesmark Fife 86 C5
Miles Platting Manch 57 Q8
Mile Town Kent 22 H8
Milfield Nthumb 81 K7
Milford Derbys 51 J10
Milford Devon 14 E7
Milford Staffs 40 C4
Milford Surrey 10 F2
Milford Haven Pembks 24 F7
Milford on Sea Hants 9 K8
Milkwall Gloucs 28 G7
Milland W Susx 10 D4
Mill Bank Calder 58 D9
Millbreck Abers 103 K6
Millbridge Surrey 10 D2
Millbrook C Beds 32 E8
Millbrook C Sotn 9 L5
Millbrook Cnwll 5 J9
Millbrook Jersey 7 b2
Mill Brow Stockp 50 C3
Millbuie Abers 102 G12
Millbuie Highld 107 J11
Millcorner E Susx 12 G5
Millcraig Highld 107 L7
Milldale Staffs 50 F9
Mill End Bucks 20 C6
Mill End Herts 33 K9
Millerhill Mdloth 86 G8
Miller's Dale Derbys 50 F6
Millerston C Glas 85 L9
Mill Green Cambs 33 P7
Mill Green Essex 22 D3
Mill Green Lincs 42 H5
Mill Green Suffk 34 F8
Mill Green Suffk 34 G5
Mill Green Suffk 35 J5
Millhalf Herefs 38 F11
Millheugh S Lans 77 M2
Mill Hill Gt Lon 21 K5
Millhouse Ag & B 83 P8
Millhousebridge D & G 78 H10
Millhouse Green Barns 58 G12
Millhouses Sheff 51 J4
Milliken Park Rens 84 G9
Millington E R Yk 60 E4
Millmeece Staffs 49 Q8
Mill of Drummond P & K 92 C11
Mill of Haldane W Duns 84 G6
Millom Cumb 62 D6
Millport N Ayrs 84 C11
Mill Street Suffk 34 H3
Millthrop Cumb 63 M4
Milltimber C Aber 95 P2
Milltown Abers 101 K12
Milltown Abers 101 N11
Milltown D & G 71 M1
Milltown Devon 15 K4
Milltown of Campfield Abers 95 L2
Milltown of Edinvillie Moray 101 K7
Milltown of Learney Abers 95 K2
Milnathort P & K 86 D2
Milngavie E Duns 85 J7
Milnrow Rochdl 58 B10
Milnthorpe Cumb 63 J6
Milovaig Highld 104 B11
Milson Shrops 39 M7
Milstead Kent 22 H10
Milston Wilts 18 H10
Milthorpe Nhants 31 N5
Milton Cambs 33 M4
Milton Cumb 71 Q4
Milton D & G 68 G8
Milton D & G 70 D2
Milton Derbys 40 H3
Milton Highld 97 J2
Milton Highld 98 G3
Milton Highld 107 J11
Milton Highld 107 M7
Milton Highld 110 G5
Milton Inver 84 F8
Milton Kent 22 D8
Milton Moray 101 J10
Milton Moray 101 P3
Milton N Som 17 J4
Milton Notts 51 P6
Milton Oxon 19 N3
Milton Oxon 31 L7
Milton P & K 94 B9
Milton Pembks 24 H8
Milton Somset 17 L10
Milton Stirlg 84 H3
Milton W Duns 84 G7
Milton Abbas Dorset 8 B7
Milton Abbot Devon 5 J4
Milton Bridge Mdloth 86 F9
Milton Bryan C Beds 32 D10
Milton Clevedon Somset 17 P8
Milton Combe Devon 5 K7
Milton Damerel Devon 14 G9
Milton Ernest Bed 32 E5
Milton Green Ches W 49 J4
Milton Hill Oxon 19 M3
Milton Keynes M Keyn 32 C8
Milton Lilbourne Wilts 18 H8
Milton Malsor Nhants 31 Q3
Milton Morenish P & K 91 P8
Milton of Auchinhove Abers 95 J2
Milton of Balgonie Fife 86 G3
Milton of Buchanan Stirlg 84 G5
Milton of Campsie E Duns 85 L7
Milton of Leys Highld 99 K1
Milton of Murtle C Aber 95 P2
Milton of Tullich Abers 94 F3
Milton on Stour Dorset 8 B2
Milton Regis Kent 22 H9
Milton-under-Wychwood Oxon 30 H9
Milverton Somset 16 F10
Milverton Warwks 30 H2
Milwich Staffs 40 C2
Minard Ag & B 83 P4
Minchinhampton Gloucs 29 M8
Minehead Somset 16 C6
Minera Wrexhm 48 F5
Minety Wilts 18 F3
Minffordd Gwynd 47 J4
Mingarrypark Highld 89 N3
Miningsby Lincs 53 K10
Minions Cnwll 4 G6
Minishant S Ayrs 76 F8
Minllyn Gwynd 47 P8
Minnigaff D & G 69 K6
Minnonie Abers 102 G4
Minskip N York 59 K2
Minstead Hants 9 K5
Minsted W Susx 10 D6
Minster Kent 23 J8
Minster Kent 23 P9
Minsterley Shrops 38 G2
Minster Lovell Oxon 30 H10
Minsterworth Gloucs 29 K5
Minterne Magna Dorset 7 P2
Minting Lincs 52 H8
Mintlaw Abers 103 K6
Mintlyn Crematorium Norfk 43 Q6
Minto Border 80 D9
Minton Shrops 38 H4
Mirehouse Cumb 70 F11
Mireland Highld 110 G4
Mirfield Kirk 58 G9
Miserden Gloucs 29 N7
Miskin Rhondd 27 L11
Misson Notts 51 P2
Misterton Leics 41 M10
Misterton Notts 51 Q2
Misterton Somset 7 L2
Mistley Essex 35 J9
Mitcham Gt Lon 21 L9
Mitcheldean Gloucs 29 J5
Mitchell Cnwll 3 J5
Mitchellslacks D & G 78 F9
Mitchel Troy Mons 28 F6
Mitford Nthumb 73 L4
Mithian Cnwll 2 H5
Mixbury Oxon 31 N7
Mobberley Ches E 57 P11
Mobberley Staffs 50 D11
Mochdre Powys 38 C4
Mochrum D & G 69 J9
Mockbeggar Kent 12 E1
Mockerkin Cumb 70 H10
Modbury Devon 5 N9
Moddershall Staffs 50 B12
Moelfre IoA 54 G4
Moelfre Powys 48 E9
Moffat D & G 78 H7
Moggerhanger C Beds 32 G6
Moira Leics 40 H4
Molash Kent 23 K11
Mol-chadh Highld 96 E7
Mold Flints 48 E3
Moldgreen Kirk 58 F10
Molehill Green Essex 33 P10
Molescroft E R Yk 60 H6
Molesworth Cambs 32 F2
Molland Devon 15 N6

Mollington Ches W 48 H2
Mollington Oxon 31 K5
Mollinsburn N Lans 85 M8
Mondynes Abers 95 M6
Monewden Suffk 35 L5
Moneydie P & K 92 F9
Monifieth Angus 93 M8
Monikie Angus 93 N7
Monimail Fife 93 K11
Monken Hadley Gt Lon 21 K4
Monk Fryston N York 59 L8
Monkhide Herefs 39 L12
Monkhill Cumb 71 M4
Monkhopton Shrops 39 L4
Monkland Herefs 39 J10
Monkleigh Devon 14 H7
Monknash V Glam 16 C3
Monkokehampton Devon 15 K10
Monkseaton N Tyne 73 N6
Monks Eleigh Suffk 34 F7
Monk's Gate W Susx 11 K5
Monks Heath Ches E 49 Q1
Monk Sherborne Hants 19 Q9
Monksilver Somset 16 E8
Monks Kirby Warwks 41 L10
Monk Soham Suffk 35 K4
Monks Risborough Bucks ..20 D4
Monksthorpe Lincs 53 M9
Monk Street Essex 33 P10
Monkswood Mons 28 D8
Monkton Devon 6 C4
Monkton Kent 23 P9
Monkton S Ayrs 76 F6
Monkton N Tyne 73 N8
Monkton Combe BaNES 18 B8
Monkton Deverill Wilts ..18 C12
Monkton Farleigh Wilts ..18 B7
Monkton Heathfield
    Somset 16 H10
Monkton Wyld Dorset 7 J4
Monkwearmouth Sundld ..73 P8
Monkwood Hants 9 Q2
Monmore Green Wolves ..40 B7
Monmouth Mons 28 F6
Monnington on Wye
    Herefs 38 G12
Monreith D & G 69 J10
Montacute Somset 17 M11
Montford Shrops 48 H11
Montford Bridge Shrops ..48 H11
Montgarrie Abers 102 D10
Montgomery Powys 38 E3
Montrose Angus 95 L9
Mont Saint Guern 6 b2
Monxton Hants 19 K11
Monyash Derbys 50 F7
Monymusk Abers 102 F11
Monzie P & K 92 C9
Moodiesburn N Lans 85 L8
Moonzie Fife 93 L11
Moor Allerton Leeds 58 H6
Moorby Lincs 53 J10
Moor Crichel Dorset 8 G8
Moordown Bmouth 8 G8
Moore Halton 57 L11
Moor End Calder 58 D8
Moorends Donc 59 P10
Moorhead C Brad 58 F6
Moorhouse Cumb 71 M4
Moorhouse Notts 51 Q7
Moorhouse Bank Surrey ..21 N11
Moorlinch Somset 17 K8
Moor Monkton N York 59 L3
Moorsholm R & Cl 66 F5
Moorside Dorset 8 B4
Moorswater Cnwll 4 F7
Moorthorpe Wakefd 59 L11
Moortown Leeds 58 H6
Moortown Lincs 52 F4
Morangie Highld 107 M5
Morar Highld 97 J10
Moray Crematorium
    Moray 101 M3
Morborne Cambs 42 G10
Morchard Bishop Devon ..15 N10
Morcombelake Dorset 7 K4
Morcott Rutlnd 42 D9
Morda Shrops 48 F9
Morden Dorset 8 D8
Morden Gt Lon 21 K9
Mordiford Herefs 28 G2
Mordon Dur 65 N3
More Shrops 38 G4
Morebath Devon 16 C10
Morebattle Border 80 G8
Morecambe Lancs 62 H8
Moredon Swindn 18 G4
Morefield Highld 106 B4
Morehall Kent 13 N3
Moreleigh Devon 5 P7
Morenish P & K 91 N8
Morestead Hants 9 N3
Moreton Dorset 8 B9
Moreton Essex 21 Q3
Moreton Herefs 39 J8
Moreton Oxon 20 B3
Moreton Wirral 56 F10
Moreton Corbet Shrops ..49 K10
Moretonhampstead
    Devon 5 P3
Moreton-in-Marsh Gloucs ..30 G7
Moreton Jeffries Herefs ..39 L11
Moreton Morrell Warwks ..30 H3
Moreton on Lugg Herefs ..39 J11
Moreton Pinkney Nhants ..31 M4
Moreton Say Shrops 49 L8
Moreton Valence Gloucs ..29 K6
Morfa Nefyn Gwynd 46 E4
Morham E Loth 87 K7
Morland Cumb 64 B3
Morley Ches E 57 P11
Morley Derbys 51 K11
Morley Leeds 58 H8
Morley Green Ches E 57 P11
Morley St Botolph Norfk ..44 H9
Morningside C Edin 86 F7
Morningside N Lans 85 N11
Morningthorpe Norfk 45 K10
Morpeth Nthumb 73 L4
Morphie Abers 95 K8
Morrey Staffs 40 E4
Morriston Swans 26 F8
Mortehoe Devon 14 H3
Morthen Rothm 51 L3
Mortimer W Berk 19 Q7

Mortimer West End Hants ..19 Q7
Mortlake Gt Lon 21 K8
Mortlake Crematorium
    Gt Lon 21 K8
Morton Cumb 71 N5
Morton Derbys 51 K8
Morton Lincs 42 F5
Morton Lincs 52 B5
Morton Notts 51 Q9
Morton Shrops 48 F9
Mortonhall
    Crematorium C Edin 86 F8
Morton-on-Swale N York ..65 N8
Morton on the Hill Norfk ..45 J6
Morvah Cnwll 2 B8
Morvich Highld 97 N5
Morville Shrops 39 M4
Morwenstow Cnwll 14 D8
Moscow E Ayrs 76 H4
Mosborough Sheff 51 K5
Moseley Birm 40 E10
Moseley Wolves 40 C7
Moseley Worcs 39 P9
Moss Ag & B 88 B7
Moss Donc 59 N10
Mossat Abers 101 N10
Mossbank Shet 111 k3
Moss Bank St Hel 57 K8
Mossbay Cumb 70 G9
Mossblown S Ayrs 76 G6
Mossburnford Border 80 F10
Mossdale D & G 69 P5
Mossdale E Ayrs 76 H4
Moss Edge Lancs 62 H12
Mossend N Lans 85 M10
Mosser Cumb 70 H10
Mossley Tamesd 50 C1
Mosspaul Hotel Border ..79 N8
Moss-side Highld 100 D4
Mosstodloch Moray 101 L4
Mossyard D & G 69 M8
Mossy Lea Lancs 57 K6
Mosterton Dorset 7 K3
Moston Manch 57 Q8
Mostyn Flints 56 D11
Motcombe Dorset 8 C3
Mothecombe Devon 5 M10
Motherby Cumb 71 N9
Motherwell N Lans 85 M10
Motspur Park Gt Lon 21 K9
Mottingham Gt Lon 21 N8
Mottisfont Hants 9 K3
Mottistone IoW 9 M9
Mottram in
    Longdendale Tamesd ..50 C2
Mottram St Andrew
    Ches E 57 Q12
Mouldsworth Ches W 49 J2
Moulin P & K 92 E4
Moulsecoomb Br & H 11 M8
Moulsford Oxon 19 P4
Moulsoe M Keyn 32 C8
Moulton Ches W 49 M2
Moulton Lincs 43 K5
Moulton N York 65 M6
Moulton Nhants 32 B4
Moulton Suffk 34 B4
Moulton V Glam 16 E3
Moulton Chapel Lincs 43 J6
Moulton St Mary Norfk ..45 N8
Moulton Seas End Lincs ..43 K5
Mount Cnwll 4 E5
Mount C Brad 58 E7
Mountain Ash Rhondd 27 L7
Mountain Cross Border ..86 D11
Mount Ambrose Cnwll 2 G7
Mount Bures Essex 34 E9
Mountfield E Susx 12 E6
Mountgerald House
    Highld 107 J9
Mount Hawke Cnwll 2 G6
Mountjoy Cnwll 3 K4
Mount Lothian Mdloth ..86 F10
Mountnessing Essex 22 D4
Mounton Mons 28 F9
Mount Pleasant Derbys ..51 J10
Mount Pleasant Suffk 34 C7
Mountsett
    Crematorium Dur 73 L9
Mountsorrel Leics 41 M5
Mount Tabor Calder 58 D8
Mousehill Surrey 10 F2
Mousehole Cnwll 2 C9
Mouswald D & G 70 H2
Mow Cop Ches E 49 Q4
Mowhaugh Border 80 H9
Mowsley Leics 41 N9
Moy Highld 98 F11
Moy Highld 99 L3
Moyle Highld 97 M6
Moylegrove Pembks 36 B10
Muasdale Ag & B 75 K4
Muchalls Abers 95 P4
Much Birch Herefs 28 F3
Much Cowarne Herefs 39 L11
Much Dewchurch Herefs ..28 F3
Muchelney Somset 17 K10
Muchelney Ham Somset ..17 L10
Much Hadham Herts 33 M11
Much Hoole Lancs 57 J4
Muchlarnick Cnwll 4 F8
Much Marcle Herefs 28 H3
Much Wenlock Shrops 39 L3
Muck Highld 89 J1
Muckleburgh Collection
    Norfk 44 H2
Mucklestone Staffs 49 N7
Muckton Lincs 53 L7
Muddiford Devon 15 K5
Muddles Green E Susx 12 B7
Mudeford Dorset 8 H8
Mudford Somset 17 N11
Mudford Sock Somset 17 M11
Mugdock Stirlg 85 J7
Mugeary Highld 96 E2
Muggington Derbys 50 H11
Muggleswick Dur 73 J10
Muirden Abers 102 F5
Muirdrum Angus 93 N8
Muiresk Abers 102 F5
Muirhead Angus 93 L8
Muirhead Fife 86 F3
Muirhead N Lans 85 L8
Muirkirk E Ayrs 77 L6
Muirmill Stirlg 85 M6
Muir of Fowlis Abers 102 D11
Muir of Miltonduff Moray ..101 J4
Muir of Ord Highld 107 J11

Muirshearlich Highld 98 A11
Muirtack Abers 103 K7
Muirton P & K 85 Q1
Muirton Mains Highld ..106 H10
Muirton of Ardblair P & K ..92 H7
Muker N York 64 G7
Mulbarton Norfk 45 K9
Mullion Cnwll 2 G11
Mullion Cove Cnwll 2 F11
Mumby Lincs 53 N8
Munderfield Row Herefs ..39 M10
Munderfield Stocks
    Herefs 39 M11
Mundesley Norfk 45 M3
Mundford Norfk 44 D10
Mundham Norfk 45 M9
Mundon Hill Essex 22 G3
Mungrisdale Cumb 71 M9
Munlochy Highld 107 K10
Munnoch N Ayrs 76 E2
Munsley Herefs 29 J1
Munslow Shrops 39 K5
Murchington Devon 5 N3
Murcott Oxon 31 N10
Murkle Highld 110 D3
Murlaggan Highld 97 P10
Murroes Angus 93 N8
Murrow Cambs 43 L8
Mursley Bucks 32 B10
Murthill Angus 93 N4
Murthly P & K 92 G8
Murton C York 59 P4
Murton Cumb 64 D3
Murton Dur 73 P10
Murton Nthumb 81 K5
Musbury Devon 6 H4
Musselburgh E Loth 86 G7
Muston Leics 42 B3
Muston N York 67 N10
Muswell Hill Gt Lon 21 L5
Mutehill D & G 69 P8
Mutford Suffk 45 P11
Muthill P & K 92 C11
Mybster Highld 110 D5
Myddfai Carmth 26 G3
Myddle Shrops 49 J10
Mydroilyn Cerdgn 36 G9
Mylor Cnwll 3 J8
Mylor Bridge Cnwll 3 J8
Mynachlog ddu Pembks ..25 K3
Mynydd-bach Mons 28 F9
Mynydd-bach Swans 26 E8
Mynyddgarreg Carmth ..25 P7
Mynydd Isa Flints 48 F3
Mytchett Surrey 20 E11
Mytholm Calder 58 C8
Mytholmroyd Calder 58 D8
Myton-on-Swale N York ..59 K2

N

Naast Highld 105 M6
Na Buirgh W Isls 111 c3
Naburn C York 59 N5
Nab Wood
    Crematorium C Brad ..58 E6
Nackington Kent 23 M11
Nacton Suffk 35 K8
Nafferton E R Yk 60 H3
Nailbourne Somset 16 G9
Nailsea N Som 17 L3
Nailstone Leics 41 K6
Nailsworth Gloucs 29 L8
Nairn Highld 100 D4
Nannerch Flints 48 D2
Nanpantan Leics 41 L4
Nanpean Cnwll 3 L5
Nanstallon Cnwll 3 M3
Nanternis Cerdgn 36 F8
Nantgaredig Carmth 26 C5
Nantglyn Denbgs 55 Q8
Nantmel Powys 38 B8
Nantmor Gwynd 47 K3
Nant Peris Gwynd 54 H9
Nantwich Ches E 49 M5
Nantyglo Blae G 27 P6
Nant-y-moel Brdgnd 27 K9
Naphill Bucks 20 D4
Napton on the Hill
    Warwks 31 L2
Narberth Pembks 25 J6
Narborough Leics 41 M7
Narborough Norfk 44 C7
Nasareth Gwynd 54 F10
Naseby Nhants 41 P10
Nash Bucks 32 B9
Nash Newpt 28 D11
Nash Shrops 39 L7
Nassington Nhants 42 F10
Nateby Cumb 64 D6
Nateby Lancs 63 J12
National Memorial
    Arboretum Staffs 40 F5
National Motor
    Museum (Beaulieu)
    Hants 9 L6
National Space Science
    Centre C Leic 41 N6
Natland Cumb 63 K4
Naughton Suffk 34 G7
Naunton Gloucs 30 E9
Naunton Worcs 29 M2
Naunton Beauchamp
    Worcs 30 C4
Navenby Lincs 52 E10
Navestock Essex 21 Q4
Navestock Side Essex 22 C4
Navidale House Hotel
    Highld 110 B11
Navity Highld 107 N8
Nawton N York 66 F9
Nayland Suffk 34 F9
Nazeing Essex 21 N3
Neap Shet 111 k4
Near Cotton Staffs 50 E10
Near Sawrey Cumb 62 G3
Neasden Gt Lon 21 K6
Neasham Darltn 65 N5
Neath Neath 26 G8
Neatham Hants 10 C3
Neatishead Norfk 45 M6

Nebo Cerdgn 37 J7
Nebo Conwy 55 M9
Nebo Gwynd 54 F10
Nebo IoA 54 F4
Necton Norfk 44 E8
Nedd Highld 108 C8
Nedging Suffk 34 G7
Nedging Tye Suffk 34 G6
Needham Norfk 35 K1
Needham Lake &
    Nature Reserve Suffk ..34 H6
Needham Market Suffk ..34 H6
Needingworth Cambs 33 K3
Neen Savage Shrops 39 M6
Neen Sollars Shrops 39 M7
Neenton Shrops 39 M5
Nefyn Gwynd 46 E4
Neilston E Rens 84 H10
Nelson Caerph 27 M9
Nelson Lancs 57 Q2
Nemphlar S Lans 77 P3
Nempnett Thrubwell
    BaNES 17 M4
Nenthead Cumb 72 E11
Nenthorn Border 80 F6
Nercwys Flints 48 E4
Nereabolls Ag & B 82 C11
Nerston S Lans 85 L10
Nesbit Nthumb 81 K7
Nesfield N York 58 E4
Nesscliffe Shrops 48 H11
Neston Ches W 56 F12
Neston Wilts 18 C7
Netchwood Shrops 39 L4
Nether Alderley Ches E ..49 Q1
Netheravon Wilts 18 G10
Nether Blainslie Border ..80 D5
Netherbrae Abers 102 G4
Nether Broughton Leics ..41 P3
Netherburn S Lans 77 N2
Netherbury Dorset 7 L3
Netherby N York 59 J5
Nether Cerne Dorset 7 P3
Nethercleuch D & G 79 J10
Nether Compton Dorset ..17 N11
Nether Crimond Abers ..102 H10
Nether Dallachy Moray ..101 M3
Netherend Gloucs 28 G8
Netherfield E Susx 12 E6
Nether Fingland S Lans ..78 F6
Netherhampton Wilts 8 G2
Nether Handwick Angus ..93 L7
Nether Haugh Rothm 51 K2
Netherhay Dorset 7 K2
Nether Headon Notts 51 Q5
Nether Heage Derbys 51 J10
Nether Heyford Nhants ..31 P3
Nether Howcleugh S Lans ..78 G6
Nether Kellet Lancs 63 J8
Nether Kinmundy Abers ..103 L6
Nether Langwith Notts ..51 M6
Netherlaw D & G 70 C6
Netherley Abers 95 P4
Nethermill D & G 78 G10
Nethermuir Abers 103 J6
Netherne-on-the-Hill
    Surrey 21 L11
Netheroyd Hill Kirk 58 F9
Nether Padley Derbys 50 G5
Netherplace E Rens 85 J11
Nether Poppleton C York ..59 M4
Netherseal Derbys 40 H5
Nether Silton N York 66 C8
Nether Stowey Somset ..16 G9
Netherthong Kirk 58 F11
Netherthird E Ayrs 77 L6
Netherton Angus 93 P4
Netherton Devon 6 B8
Netherton Dudley 40 C9
Netherton Kirk 58 F10
Netherton N Lans 85 N11
Netherton Nthumb 81 K11
Netherton P & K 92 H5
Netherton Stirlg 85 J7
Netherton Wakefd 58 H10
Nethertown Cumb 62 B1
Nethertown Highld 110 G1
Nethertown Staffs 40 E4
Netherurd Border 86 D12
Nether Wallop Hants 19 K12
Nether Wasdale Cumb ..62 D2
Nether Westcote Gloucs ..30 G9
Nether Whitacre Warwks ..40 G8
Nether Whitecleuch
    S Lans 78 D5
Nether Winchendon
    Bucks 31 Q10
Netherwitton Nthumb ..73 K3
Nethy Bridge Highld 99 Q5
Netley Hants 9 M6
Netley Marsh Hants 9 K5
Nettlebed Oxon 20 B6
Nettlebridge Somset 17 P6
Nettlecombe Dorset 7 M4
Nettleden Herts 20 G2
Nettleham Lincs 52 E8
Nettlestead Kent 22 D11
Nettlestead Green Kent ..22 D12
Nettlestone IoW 9 Q8
Nettlesworth Dur 73 M10
Nettleton Lincs 52 G4
Nettleton Wilts 18 B5
Netton Wilts 18 G12
Nevern Pembks 36 B11
Nevill Holt Leics 42 B10
New Abbey D & G 70 F3
New Aberdour Abers 103 J3
New Addington Gt Lon ..21 M10
Newall Leeds 58 G5
New Alresford Hants 9 P2
New Alyth P & K 93 J6
Newark Ork 111 i1
Newark-on-Trent Notts ..52 B11
Newarthill N Lans 85 N10
New Ash Green Kent 22 C9
New Balderton Notts 52 B11
New Barn Kent 22 C9
New Barnet Gt Lon 21 L4
Newbattle Mdloth 86 G8
New Bewick Nthumb 81 M9
Newbie D & G 71 K3
Newbiggin Cumb 64 B2
Newbiggin Cumb 71 P9
Newbiggin Cumb 71 Q7
Newbiggin Dur 64 G3
Newbiggin N York 64 G7
Newbiggin-by-the-Sea
    Nthumb 73 N4

Nebo Cerdgn 37 J7
Newbigging Angus 93 K7
Newbigging Angus 93 M8
Newbigging Angus 93 N8
Newbigging S Lans 86 B11
Newbiggin-on-Lune
    Cumb 63 N2
New Bilton Warwks 41 L11
Newbold Derbys 51 J6
Newbold on Avon Warwks ..41 L11
Newbold on Stour
    Warwks 30 G5
Newbold Pacey Warwks ..30 H3
Newbold Verdon Leics ..41 K6
New Bolingbroke Lincs ..53 K11
Newborough C Pete 42 H8
Newborough IoA 54 F8
Newborough Staffs 40 F3
New Boultham Lincs 52 D8
Newbourne Suffk 35 L8
New Bradwell M Keyn ..32 B8
New Brampton Derbys ..51 J6
New Brancepeth Dur 73 M11
Newbridge C Edin 86 D7
Newbridge Caerph 27 P8
Newbridge Cnwll 2 C9
Newbridge D & G 78 F11
Newbridge Hants 9 K4
Newbridge IoW 9 M9
Newbridge Green Worcs ..29 L2
Newbridge on Wye
    Powys 38 B9
New Brighton Wirral 56 F9
New Brinsley Nthumb 72 F7
New Buckenham Norfk ..44 H11
Newbuildings Devon 15 N10
Newburgh Abers 103 K4
Newburgh Abers 103 K9
Newburgh Fife 93 J11
Newburgh Lancs 57 J6
Newburgh Priory N York ..66 D11
Newburn N u Ty 73 L7
Newbury Somset 17 Q6
Newbury W Berk 19 M7
Newbury Park Gt Lon ..21 N6
Newby Cumb 64 B4
Newby Lancs 63 P11
Newby N York 63 N8
Newby N York 66 C5
Newby Bridge Cumb 62 G5
Newby East Cumb 71 P4
Newby West Cumb 71 M5
New Byth Abers 102 H5
Newcastle Mons 28 E5
Newcastle Shrops 38 F5
Newcastle Airport
    Nthumb 73 L6
Newcastle Emlyn Carmth ..36 E11
Newcastleton Border 79 P10
Newcastle-under-Lyme
    Staffs 49 Q6
Newcastle upon Tyne
    N u Ty 73 M7
Newchapel Pembks 36 D11
Newchapel Surrey 11 M2
Newchurch IoW 9 P9
Newchurch Kent 13 K4
Newchurch Mons 28 E8
Newchurch Powys 38 E11
Newchurch Staffs 40 F3
New Costessey Norfk 45 K7
Newcraighall C Edin 86 G7
New Crofton Wakefd 59 K10
New Cross Gt Lon 21 M7
New Cross Somset 17 K11
New Cumnock E Ayrs ..77 K8
New Deer Abers 103 J6
New Denham Bucks 20 G6
Newdigate Surrey 11 K2
New Duston Nhants 31 Q2
New Earswick C York 59 N3
New Edlington Donc 51 M2
New Elgin Moray 101 J3
New Ellerby E R Yk 61 K6
Newell Green Br For 20 E8
New Eltham Gt Lon 21 N8
New End Worcs 30 D3
Newenden Kent 12 G5
New England C Pete 42 H9
Newent Gloucs 29 J4
Newfield Dur 65 L2
Newfield Highld 107 N7
New Fletton C Pete 42 H9
New Forest National Park ..9 K6
Newgale Pembks 24 E4
New Galloway D & G 69 P4
Newgate Street Herts ..21 L3
New Gilston Fife 87 J1
New Grimsby IoS 2 b1
Newhall Ches E 49 L6
New Hartley Nthumb 73 N5
Newhaven C Edin 86 F7
Newhaven E Susx 11 N9
New Haw Surrey 20 G10
New Hedges Pembks 25 K8
New Holland N Linc 61 J5
Newholm N York 67 J5
New Houghton Derbys ..51 L7
New Houghton Norfk 44 D5
Newhouse N Lans 85 N10
New Hutton Cumb 63 K4
Newick E Susx 11 N6
Newington Kent 13 M3
Newington Kent 22 G9
Newington Oxon 19 Q2
New Inn Carmth 26 C2
New Inn Torfn 28 C8
New Invention Shrops ..38 F6
New Lakenham Norfk ..45 K8
New Lanark S Lans 78 E1
New Lanark Village S Lans ..78 E1
Newland C KuH 61 J7
Newland Gloucs 28 G6
Newland N York 59 P8
Newland Somset 15 P5
Newland Worcs 39 P11
Newlandrig Mdloth 86 H9
Newlands Border 79 Q9
Newlands Nthumb 73 J9
Newlands of
    Dundurcas Moray 101 L5
New Langholm D & G ..79 M11
New Leake Lincs 53 L11
New Leeds Abers 103 K4
New Lodge Barns 59 J11
New Longton Lancs 57 K4
New Luce D & G 68 G6
Newlyn Cnwll 2 C9

188 Newmachar - Old Catton

Newmachar Abers 103 J10
Newmains N Lans 85 N10
New Malden Gt Lon 21 K9
Newman's Green Suffk 34 E7
Newmarket Suffk 33 Q4
Newmarket W Isls 111 d2
New Marske R & Cl 66 E4
New Marston Oxon 31 M11
New Mill Abers 95 N5
Newmill Border 79 P6
New Mill Cnwll 2 C8
New Mill Kirk 58 F11
Newmill Moray 101 N5
Newmillerdam Wakefd 59 J10
Newmill of Inshewan Angus 94 G9
Newmills C Edin 86 E8
New Mills Derbys 50 D4
Newmills Fife 86 B5
Newmills Mons 28 F7
New Mills Powys 38 C2
Newmiln P & K 92 G9
Newmilns E Ayrs 77 J4
New Milton Hants 9 J8
New Mistley Essex 35 J9
New Moat Pembks 25 J4
Newney Green Essex 22 D3
Newnham Gloucs 29 J6
Newnham Hants 20 B11
Newnham Herts 33 J8
Newnham Kent 23 J11
Newnham Nhants 31 M3
Newnham Worcs 39 M8
New Ollerton Notts 51 P7
New Pitsligo Abers 103 J4
Newport Cnwll 4 H3
Newport E R Yk 60 E7
Newport Essex 33 N9
Newport Gloucs 29 J8
Newport Highld 110 D10
Newport IoW 9 N9
Newport Newpt 28 C10
Newport Pembks 25 J2
Newport Wrekin 49 N10
Newport-on-Tay Fife 93 M9
Newport Pagnell M Keyn 32 C7
Newport Pagnell Services M Keyn 32 C7
New Prestwick S Ayrs 76 F6
New Quay Cerdgn 36 F8
Newquay Cnwll 3 J4
Newquay Airport Cnwll 3 K3
New Rackheath Norfk 45 L7
New Radnor Powys 38 E9
New Ridley Nthumb 73 J8
New Romney Kent 13 K5
New Rossington Donc 51 N2
New Sauchie Clacks 85 P4
Newseat Abers 102 F8
Newsham Lancs 57 K2
Newsham N York 65 K5
Newsham N York 65 P9
Newsham Nthumb 73 N5
New Sharlston Wakefd 59 J9
Newsholme E R Yk 60 C8
New Silksworth Sundld 73 P9
Newsome Kirk 58 F10
New Somerby Lincs 42 D3
New Southgate Crematorium Gt Lon 21 L5
Newstead Border 80 D7
Newstead Notts 51 L9
Newstead Nthumb 81 N8
New Stevenston N Lans 85 M10
Newthorpe Notts 51 L10
Newton Ag & B 83 Q4
Newton Border 80 E9
Newton Brdgnd 26 H12
Newton C Beds 32 H7
Newton Cambs 33 M6
Newton Cambs 43 M7
Newton Ches W 48 H2
Newton Ches W 49 J4
Newton Cumb 62 E7
Newton Derbys 51 K8
Newton Herefs 28 D3
Newton Herefs 39 K10
Newton Highld 107 J11
Newton Highld 107 M11
Newton Highld 107 M8
Newton Highld 110 G6
Newton Lincs 42 F3
Newton Mdloth 86 G8
Newton Moray 100 H3
Newton Moray 101 L3
Newton Nhants 42 C12
Newton Norfk 44 D7
Newton Notts 51 P11
Newton Nthumb 73 J7
Newton S Lans 78 F3
Newton S Lans 85 L10
Newton Staffs 40 D3
Newton Suffk 34 F8
Newton W Loth 86 C6
Newton Warwks 41 M10
Newton Abbot Devon 6 B8
Newton Arlosh Cumb 71 K5
Newton Aycliffe Dur 65 M3
Newton Bewley Hartpl 66 C3
Newton Blossomville M Keyn 32 D6
Newton Bromswold Nhants 32 E4
Newton Burgoland Leics 41 J6
Newton-by-the-Sea Nthumb 81 P8
Newton by Toft Lincs 52 F6
Newton Ferrers Devon 5 L9
Newton Ferry W Isls 111 b4
Newton Flotman Norfk 45 K9
Newtongrange Mdloth 86 G8
Newton Green Mons 28 F9
Newton Harcourt Leics 41 N7
Newton Heath Manch 57 Q8
Newtonhill Abers 95 P4
Newton-in-Bowland Lancs 63 M11
Newton Kyme N York 59 L5
Newton-le-Willows N York 65 L9
Newton-le-Willows St Hel 57 L9
Newtonloan Mdloth 86 G9
Newton Longville Bucks 32 C9
Newton Mearns E Rens 85 J11
Newtonmill Angus 95 K8
Newtonmore Highld 99 K8
Newton Morrell N York 65 M5
Newton of Balcanquhal P & K 92 H12
Newton of Balcormo Fife 87 K2
Newton on Ouse N York 59 L3
Newton-on-Rawcliffe N York 66 H9
Newton-on-the-Moor Nthumb 81 N12
Newton on Trent Lincs 52 B8
Newton Poppleford Devon 6 E5
Newton Purcell Oxon 31 N7
Newton Regis Warwks 40 H6
Newton Reigny Cumb 71 P8
Newton St Cyres Devon 15 Q11
Newton St Faith Norfk 45 K6
Newton St Loe BaNES 17 Q3
Newton St Petrock Devon 14 G9
Newton Solney Derbys 40 H3
Newton Stacey Hants 19 M11
Newton Stewart D & G 69 K6
Newton Tony Wilts 19 J11
Newton Tracey Devon 15 J6
Newton under Roseberry R & Cl 66 D5
Newton upon Derwent E R Yk 60 C4
Newton Valence Hants 10 B4
Newton Wamphray D & G 78 H9
Newton with Scales Lancs 57 J3
Newtown Cumb 70 H6
Newtown Cumb 71 P3
Newtown D & G 77 N8
Newtown Devon 6 E3
Newtown Devon 15 N7
New Town Dorset 8 D4
New Town Dorset 8 E4
New Town E Susx 11 P6
Newtown Gloucs 29 J8
Newtown Hants 9 Q5
Newtown Herefs 29 J2
Newtown Herefs 39 L12
Newtown Highld 98 E7
Newtown IoW 9 M8
Newtown Nthumb 81 L8
Newtown Poole 8 F8
Newtown Powys 38 C4
Newtown Shrops 48 H10
Newtown Shrops 49 J8
Newtown Somset 6 H1
Newtown Staffs 50 B8
Newtown Wigan 57 K7
Newtown Worcs 39 Q10
Newtown Linford Leics 41 M5
Newtown of Beltrees Rens 84 F10
Newtown St Boswells Border 80 D7
New Tredegar Caerph 27 N7
New Trows S Lans 77 N4
Newtyle Angus 93 K7
New Walsoken Cambs 43 M8
New Waltham NE Lin 53 J3
New Winton E Loth 87 J7
Newyork Ag & B 83 P2
New York Lincs 53 J11
Neyland Pembks 24 G7
Nicholashayne Devon 16 E11
Nicholaston Swans 26 C10
Nidd N York 58 H3
Nigg C Aber 95 Q2
Nigg Highld 107 N7
Nigg Ferry Highld 107 N8
Ninebanks Nthumb 72 E9
Nine Elms Swindn 18 G4
Ninfield E Susx 12 E7
Ningwood IoW 9 L9
Nisbet Border 80 F8
Nisbet Hill Border 80 H4
Niton IoW 9 N11
Nitshill C Glas 85 J10
Nocton Lincs 52 F10
Noke Oxon 31 M10
Nolton Pembks 24 F5
Nolton Haven Pembks 24 F5
No Man's Heath Ches W 49 K6
No Man's Heath Warwks 40 H6
Nomansland Devon 15 P9
Nomansland Wilts 9 J4
Noneley Shrops 49 J9
Nonington Kent 23 N11
Nook Cumb 63 K6
Norbiton Gt Lon 21 K9
Norbury Ches E 49 K6
Norbury Derbys 50 F11
Norbury Gt Lon 21 L9
Norbury Shrops 38 G4
Norbury Staffs 49 P10
Norchard Worcs 39 Q8
Nordelph Norfk 43 N9
Nordley Shrops 39 M3
Norfolk Broads Norfk 45 P8
Norham Nthumb 81 J5
Norley Ches W 49 K2
Norleywood Hants 9 L7
Normanby Lincs 52 E6
Normanby N Linc 60 F10
Normanby N York 66 G10
Normanby R & Cl 66 D4
Normanby le Wold Lincs 52 G5
Normandy Surrey 20 E11
Norman's Green Devon 6 E3
Normanton C Derb 41 J2
Normanton Leics 42 B2
Normanton Lincs 42 D2
Normanton Notts 51 P9
Normanton Wakefd 59 J9
Normanton le Heath Leics 41 J5
Normanton on Soar Notts 41 L3
Normanton on the Wolds Notts 41 N2
Normanton on Trent Notts 52 B9
Norris Green Lpool 56 H9
Norris Hill Leics 41 J4
Norristhorpe Kirk 58 G9
Northall Bucks 32 D11
Northallerton N York 65 P8
Northam C Sotn 9 M5
Northam Devon 14 H6
Northampton Nhants 31 Q2
Northampton Worcs 39 Q8
Northampton Services Nhants 31 Q3
North Anston Rothm 51 M4
North Ascot Br For 20 E9
North Aston Oxon 31 L8
Northaw Herts 21 L3
Northay Somset 6 H1
North Baddesley Hants 9 L4
North Ballachulish Highld 90 E4
North Barrow Somset 17 N9
North Barsham Norfk 44 F3
North Benfleet Essex 22 F5
North Bersted W Susx 10 E9
North Berwick E Loth 87 K5
North Boarhunt Hants 9 P5
Northborough C Pete 42 G8
Northbourne Kent 23 P11
North Bovey Devon 5 P4
North Bradley Wilts 18 C9
North Brentor Devon 5 K4
North Brewham Somset 17 Q8
Northbrook Hants 19 N11
North Buckland Devon 14 H4
North Burlingham Norfk 45 N7
North Cadbury Somset 17 P10
North Carlton Lincs 52 D7
North Carlton Notts 51 N4
North Cave E R Yk 60 F7
North Cerney Gloucs 30 D11
North Chailey E Susx 11 N6
Northchapel W Susx 10 F4
North Charford Hants 8 H4
North Charlton Nthumb 81 N9
North Cheam Gt Lon 21 K9
North Cheriton Somset 17 Q10
North Chideock Dorset 7 K4
Northchurch Herts 20 F2
North Cliffe E R Yk 60 E6
North Clifton Notts 52 B8
North Cockerington Lincs 53 L5
North Connel Ag & B 90 C9
North Cornelly Brdgnd 26 H11
North Cotes Lincs 53 K4
Northcott Devon 4 H2
Northcourt Oxon 19 N2
North Cove Suffk 45 P11
North Cowton N York 65 M6
North Crawley M Keyn 32 D7
North Creake Norfk 44 E3
North Curry Somset 17 J10
North Dalton E R Yk 60 F4
North Deighton N York 59 K4
North Devon Crematorium Devon 15 J6
Northdown Kent 23 Q8
North Downs 22 H11
North Duffield N York 59 P6
North Duntulm Highld 104 F7
North East Surrey Crematorium Gt Lon 21 K9
North Elmham Norfk 44 G6
North Elmsall Wakefd 59 L10
North End C Port 9 Q7
North End Essex 33 Q11
North End Hants 8 G4
North End Nhants 32 D3
North End W Susx 10 F8
Northend Warwks 31 K4
Northenden Manch 57 P10
North Erradale Highld 105 L6
North Evington C Leic 41 N6
North Fambridge Essex 22 G4
North Ferriby E R Yk 60 G8
Northfield Birm 40 D10
Northfield C Aber 103 J12
Northfield E R Yk 60 H8
Northfields Lincs 42 E8
Northfleet Kent 22 D8
North Frodingham E R Yk 61 J4
North Gorley Hants 8 H5
North Green Suffk 35 M4
North Greetwell Lincs 52 E8
North Grimston N York 60 E1
North Haven Shet 111 m5
North Hayling Hants 10 B9
North Hill Cnwll 4 G5
North Hillingdon Gt Lon 20 H6
North Hinksey Village Oxon 31 L11
North Holmwood Surrey 11 J1
North Huish Devon 5 P8
North Hykeham Lincs 52 D9
Northiam E Susx 12 G5
Northill C Beds 32 G7
Northington Hants 19 P12
North Kelsey Lincs 52 F3
North Kessock Highld 107 L11
North Killingholme N Linc 61 K10
North Kilvington N York 65 Q9
North Kilworth Leics 41 N10
North Kyme Lincs 52 G11
North Landing E R Yk 67 Q12
Northlands Lincs 53 K11
Northleach Gloucs 30 E10
North Lee Bucks 20 D2
Northleigh Devon 6 G4
North Leigh Oxon 31 K10
North Leverton with Habblesthorpe Notts 52 B7
Northlew Devon 15 J11
North Littleton Worcs 30 E5
North Lopham Norfk 44 G12
North Luffenham Rutlnd 42 D9
North Marden W Susx 10 D6
North Marston Bucks 31 Q9
North Middleton Mdloth 86 G9
North Millbrex Abers 102 H6
North Milmain D & G 68 E8
North Molton Devon 15 M6
Northmoor Oxon 31 K12
North Moreton Oxon 19 P3
Northmuir Angus 93 L5
North Mundham W Susx 10 E9
North Muskham Notts 52 B10
North Newbald E R Yk 60 F6
North Newington Oxon 31 K6
North Newnton Wilts 18 G8
North Newton Somset 17 J9
Northney Hants 10 B8
North Nibley Gloucs 29 K9
Northolt Gt Lon 21 J6
Northop Flints 48 E2
Northop Hall Flints 48 F2
North Ormesby Middsb 66 D4
North Ormsby Lincs 53 J5
Northorpe Kirk 58 G9
Northorpe Lincs 42 H3
Northorpe Lincs 52 C4
North Otterington N York 65 P9
North Owersby Lincs 52 F5
Northowram Calder 58 E8
North Perrott Somset 7 L2
North Petherton Somset 16 H9
North Petherwin Cnwll 4 G3
North Pickenham Norfk 44 E8
North Piddle Worcs 30 C3
North Poorton Dorset 7 M3
Northport Dorset 8 D9
North Queensferry Fife 86 D6
North Rauceby Lincs 42 E2
Northrepps Norfk 45 L3
North Reston Lincs 53 L6
North Rigton N York 58 H4
North Rode Ches E 50 B7
North Ronaldsay Ork 111 i1
North Ronaldsay Airport Ork 111 i1
North Runcton Norfk 43 Q6
North Scarle Lincs 52 C9
North Shian Ag & B 90 C7
North Shields N Tyne 73 N7
North Shoebury Sthend 22 H6
North Shore Bpool 56 F2
North Side C Pete 43 J9
North Somercotes Lincs 53 L4
North Stainley N York 65 M11
North Stifford Thurr 22 C7
North Stoke BaNES 17 Q3
North Stoke Oxon 19 Q4
North Stoke W Susx 10 G7
North Street Kent 23 K10
North Street W Berk 19 Q6
North Sunderland Nthumb 81 P7
North Tamerton Cnwll 14 F11
North Tawton Devon 15 L10
North Third Stirlg 85 M5
North Thoresby Lincs 53 J4
Northton W Isls 111 b3
North Town Devon 15 J9
North Town Somset 17 N7
North Town W & M 20 E7
North Tuddenham Norfk 44 G7
North Uist W Isls 111 a4
Northumberland National Park Nthumb 72 F1
North Walsham Norfk 45 L4
North Waltham Hants 19 P10
North Warnborough Hants 20 B12
North Weald Bassett Essex 21 P3
North Wheatley Notts 51 Q4
Northwich Ches W 49 M2
Northwick Worcs 39 Q9
North Widcombe BaNES 17 N5
North Willingham Lincs 52 G6
North Wingfield Derbys 51 K7
North Witham Lincs 42 D6
Northwold Norfk 44 C10
Northwood Gt Lon 20 H5
Northwood IoW 9 N8
Northwood Shrops 49 J8
Northwood Green Gloucs 29 J5
North Wootton Dorset 17 P12
North Wootton Norfk 43 Q5
North Wootton Somset 17 N7
North Wraxall Wilts 18 B6
North York Moors National Park 66 G7
Norton Donc 59 M10
Norton E Susx 11 P9
Norton Gloucs 29 M4
Norton Halton 57 K11
Norton Nhants 31 N2
Norton Notts 51 M6
Norton Powys 38 F8
Norton S on T 66 C3
Norton Shrops 39 N3
Norton Suffk 34 F4
Norton W Susx 10 E8
Norton Wilts 18 C4
Norton Worcs 30 D5
Norton Worcs 39 Q11
Norton Bavant Wilts 18 D11
Norton Bridge Staffs 49 Q9
Norton Canes Staffs 40 D6
Norton Canes Services Staffs 40 D6
Norton Canon Herefs 38 H11
Norton Disney Lincs 52 C10
Norton Fitzwarren Somset 16 G10
Norton Green IoW 9 K9
Norton Hawkfield BaNES 17 N4
Norton Heath Essex 22 C3
Norton in Hales Shrops 49 N7
Norton-Juxta-Twycross Leics 41 J6
Norton-le-Clay N York 65 P12
Norton Lindsey Warwks 30 G2
Norton Little Green Suffk 34 F4
Norton Malreward BaNES 17 N3
Norton-on-Derwent N York 66 H12
Norton St Philip Somset 18 B9
Norton Subcourse Norfk 45 N9
Norton sub Hamdon Somset 17 L11
Norwell Notts 51 Q8
Norwell Woodhouse Notts 51 Q8
Norwich Norfk 45 K8
Norwich Airport Norfk 45 K7
Norwich (St Faith) Crematorium Norfk 45 K7
Norwick Shet 111 m2
Norwood Clacks 85 P4
Norwood Green Gt Lon 21 J7
Norwood Hill Surrey 11 K2
Noss Mayo Devon 5 L10
Nosterfield N York 65 M10
Nostie Highld 97 M4
Notgrove Gloucs 30 E9
Nottage Brdgnd 26 H12
Nottingham C Nott 51 M11
Notton Wakefd 59 J10
Notton Wilts 18 D6
Noutard's Green Worcs 39 P8
Nuffield Oxon 19 Q4
Nunburnholme E R Yk 60 E5
Nuneaton Warwks 41 J8
Nunhead Gt Lon 21 M8
Nun Monkton N York 59 L3
Nunney Somset 17 Q7
Nunnington N York 66 F10
Nunsthorpe NE Lin 53 J2
Nunthorpe C York 59 N4
Nunthorpe Middsb 66 D5
Nunthorpe Village Middsb 66 D5
Nunton Wilts 8 H3
Nunwick N York 65 N11
Nursling Hants 9 L4
Nutbourne W Susx 10 C8
Nutbourne W Susx 10 H6
Nutfield Surrey 21 L12
Nuthall Notts 51 M11
Nuthampstead Herts 33 L9
Nuthurst W Susx 11 J5
Nutley E Susx 11 N5
Nuttall Bury 57 P5
Nybster Highld 110 G3
Nyetimber W Susx 10 E9
Nyewood W Susx 10 C6
Nymans W Susx 11 L4
Nymet Rowland Devon 15 M9
Nymet Tracey Devon 15 M11
Nympsfield Gloucs 29 L8
Nynehead Somset 16 F10
Nyton W Susx 10 E8

O

Oadby Leics 41 N7
Oad Street Kent 22 G10
Oakamoor Staffs 50 D11
Oakbank W Loth 86 C8
Oak Cross Devon 15 J11
Oakdale Caerph 27 P8
Oake Somset 16 F10
Oaken Staffs 39 Q2
Oakenclough Lancs 63 K11
Oakengates Wrekin 49 M12
Oakenshaw Dur 73 L12
Oakenshaw Kirk 58 F8
Oakford Cerdgn 36 G8
Oakford Devon 16 C11
Oakham Rutlnd 42 C8
Oakhanger Hants 10 C3
Oakhill Somset 17 P6
Oakington Cambs 33 L4
Oakle Street Gloucs 29 K5
Oakley Bed 32 E6
Oakley Bucks 31 N10
Oakley Fife 86 B4
Oakley Hants 19 P9
Oakley Suffk 35 J2
Oakridge Lynch Gloucs 29 M7
Oaksey Wilts 29 P9
Oakthorpe Leics 40 H5
Oakwood C Derb 51 J12
Oakworth C Brad 58 D6
Oare Kent 23 J10
Oare Somset 15 N3
Oare Wilts 18 H7
Oasby Lincs 42 E3
Oath Somset 17 K10
Oathlaw Angus 93 N4
Oatlands Park Surrey 20 H9
Oban Ag & B 90 B9
Oban Airport Ag & B 90 C8
Obley Shrops 38 G6
Obney P & K 92 F8
Oborne Dorset 17 P11
Occold Suffk 35 J3
Occumster Highld 110 F8
Ochiltree E Ayrs 76 H7
Ockbrook Derbys 41 K1
Ockham Surrey 20 H11
Ockle Highld 89 L3
Ockley Surrey 11 J3
Ocle Pychard Herefs 39 L11
Odcombe Somset 17 M11
Odd Down BaNES 17 Q4
Oddingley Worcs 30 B3
Oddington Gloucs 30 G8
Oddington Oxon 31 M10
Odell Bed 32 D5
Odiham Hants 20 C12
Odsal C Brad 58 F8
Odsey Cambs 33 J8
Odstock Wilts 8 G3
Odstone Leics 41 K6
Offchurch Warwks 31 J2
Offenham Worcs 30 D5
Offerton Stockp 50 B3
Offham E Susx 11 N7
Offham Kent 22 D11
Offham W Susx 10 G8
Offord Cluny Cambs 32 H4
Offord D'Arcy Cambs 32 H4
Offton Suffk 34 H6
Offwell Devon 6 G3
Ogbourne Maizey Wilts 18 H6
Ogbourne St Andrew Wilts 18 H6
Ogbourne St George Wilts 18 H6
Ogle Nthumb 73 K5
Oglet Lpool 56 H11
Ogmore V Glam 16 B2
Ogmore-by-Sea V Glam 16 B2
Ogmore Vale Brdgnd 27 K10
Okeford Fitzpaine Dorset 8 B5
Okehampton Devon 5 M2
Oker Side Derbys 50 H8
Okewood Hill Surrey 11 J3
Old Nhants 32 B3
Old Aberdeen C Aber 95 Q1
Old Alresford Hants 9 P1
Oldany Highld 108 C8
Old Auchenbrack D & G 77 M11
Old Basford C Nott 51 M11
Old Basing Hants 19 Q9
Old Beetley Norfk 44 F6
Oldberrow Warwks 30 E2
Old Bewick Nthumb 81 M9
Old Bolingbroke Lincs 53 K9
Old Bramhope Leeds 58 G5
Old Brampton Derbys 51 J6
Old Bridge of Urr D & G 70 C3
Old Buckenham Norfk 44 H10
Old Burghclere Hants 19 M8
Oldbury Sandw 40 C9
Oldbury Shrops 39 N4
Oldbury Warwks 40 H8
Oldbury-on-Severn S Glos 28 H9
Oldbury on the Hill Gloucs 18 B3
Old Byland N York 66 D9
Old Cantley Donc 51 N1
Oldcastle Mons 28 C4
Old Catton Norfk 45 K7

Old Clee NE Lin........53 J2
Old Cleeve Somset.......16 E7
Old Clipstone Notts......51 N7
Old Colwyn Conwy.......55 M8
Oldcotes Notts..........51 N3
Old Dailly S Ayrs........76 D10
Old Dalby Leics..........41 P3
Old Deer Abers.........103 K6
Old Edlington Donc......51 M2
Old Ellerby E R Yk.......61 K6
Old Felixstowe Suffk....35 M9
Oldfield Worcs..........39 Q8
Old Fletton C Pete.......42 H10
Oldford Somset.........18 B10
Old Forge Herefs........28 G5
Old Grimsby IoS..........2 b1
Old Hall Green Herts.....33 L11
Oldham Oldham.........58 B12
Oldhamstocks E Loth.....87 N7
Old Harlow Essex........21 P2
Old Hunstanton Norfk....44 B2
Old Hurst Cambs.........33 J2
Old Hutton Cumb........63 K5
Old Inns Services N Lans..85 N7
Old Kilpatrick W Duns...84 H8
Old Knebworth Herts....32 H11
Oldland S Glos.............17 P2
Old Langho Lancs........57 M2
Old Leake Lincs..........53 L12
Old Malton N York.......66 H11
Oldmeldrum Abers.....102 H9
Oldmill Cnwll.............4 H5
Old Milverton Warwks...30 H1
Oldmixon N Som.........17 J5
Old Newton Suffk........34 H4
Old Radnor Powys.......38 F9
Old Rayne Abers........102 E9
Old Romney Kent........13 K5
Old Shoreham W Susx...11 K8
Oldshoremore Highld...108 D4
Old Sodbury S Glos.......29 K11
Old Somerby Lincs.......42 D4
Oldstead N York.........66 D10
Old Stratford Nhants....31 Q6
Old Struan P & K.........92 C3
Old Swinford Dudley.....40 B3
Old Thirsk N York.......66 B10
Old Town Cumb...........63 L5
Old Town E Susx..........12 C9
Old Town IoS..............2 c2
Old Trafford Traffd.......57 P9
Oldwall Cumb............71 P4
Oldwalls Swans..........26 C9
Old Warden C Beds.......32 G7
Old Weston Cambs.......32 F2
Old Wick Highld........110 G6
Old Windsor W & M.......20 F8
Old Wives Lees Kent.....23 K11
Old Woking Surrey.......20 G11
Olgrinmore Highld......110 C5
Olive Green Staffs.......40 E4
Oliver's Battery Hants....9 M2
Ollaberry Shet..........111 k3
Ollach Highld............96 H3
Ollerton Ches E..........57 P12
Ollerton Notts...........51 P7
Ollerton Shrops.........49 M9
Olney M Keyn............32 C6
Olrig House Highld.....110 E3
Olton Solhll...............40 F10
Olveston S Glos...........28 H10
Ombersley Worcs........39 Q8
Ompton Notts...........51 P7
Onchan IoM...............56 d5
Onecote Staffs...........50 D9
Onibury Shrops..........39 J6
Onich Highld.............90 E4
Onllwyn Neath...........26 H6
Onneley Staffs...........49 N6
Onslow Green Essex.....33 Q12
Onslow Village Surrey...20 F12
Onston Ches W...........49 L1
Opinan Highld...........105 L7
Orbliston Moray........101 L4
Orbost Highld............96 B2
Orby Lincs................53 M9
Orchard Portman Somset..16 H10
Orcheston Wilts.........18 F10
Orcop Herefs.............28 F4
Orcop Hill Herefs........28 F4
Ord Abers...............102 E4
Ordhead Abers.........102 E12
Ordie Abers..............94 G2
Ordiequish Moray......101 L4
Ordsall Notts............51 P5
Ore E Susx................12 G7
Orford Suffk.............35 N6
Orford Warrtn...........57 L10
Organford Dorset.........8 D8
Orkney Islands Ork.....111 h2
Orkney Neolithic Ork...111 g2
Orlestone Kent..........13 J3
Orleton Herefs...........39 J8
Orleton Worcs...........39 M8
Orlingbury Nhants......32 C3
Ormesby R & Cl..........66 D4
Ormesby St Margaret
  Norfk...................45 P7
Ormesby St Michael
  Norfk...................45 P7
Ormiscaig Highld.......105 M4
Ormiston E Loth........86 H8
Ormsaigmore Highld....89 K4
Ormsary Ag & B..........83 L8
Ormskirk Lancs..........56 H7
Oronsay Ag & B..........82 E5
Orphir Ork...............111 h2
Orpington Gt Lon.......21 P9
Orrell Sefton.............56 G9
Orrell Wigan.............57 K7
Orroland D & G...........70 C7
Orsett Thurr.............22 D7
Orslow Staffs............49 P11
Orston Notts.............51 Q11
Orton Cumb..............63 L1
Orton Nhants.............32 B2
Orton Staffs..............39 Q3
Orton Longueville C Pete..42 G10
Orton-on-the-Hill Leics..40 H6
Orton Waterville C Pete..42 G10
Orwell Cambs.............33 K6
Osbaldeston Lancs......57 M3
Osbaldwick C York.......59 N4
Osbaston Leics..........41 K6
Osbaston Shrops.........48 G10
Osborne House IoW.......9 N8

Osbournby Lincs........42 F3
Oscroft Ches W..........49 J3
Ose Highld................96 C2
Osgathorpe Leics........41 K4
Osgodby Lincs...........52 F5
Osgodby N York..........59 N7
Osgodby N York..........67 M9
Oskaig Highld...........96 G3
Oskamull Ag & B.........89 M7
Osmaston Derbys........50 G11
Osmington Dorset........7 Q6
Osmington Mills Dorset...7 Q6
Osmondthorpe Leeds....59 J7
Osmotherley N York......66 C7
Osney Oxon..............31 L11
Ospringe Kent...........23 J10
Ossett Wakefd..........58 H9
Ossington Notts.........51 Q7
Osterley Gt Lon..........21 J7
Oswaldkirk N York.......66 E10
Oswaldtwistle Lancs.....57 N4
Oswestry Shrops.........48 F9
Otford Kent..............21 Q10
Otham Kent..............22 F11
Othery Somset...........17 K9
Otley Leeds...............58 G5
Otley Suffk...............35 K5
Otterbourne Hants........9 M2
Otterburn N York.........63 Q9
Otterburn Nthumb.......72 F3
Otter Ferry Ag & B.......83 P6
Otterham Cnwll...........4 E3
Otterhampton Somset....16 H7
Otternish W Isls.........111 b4
Ottershaw Surrey........20 G9
Otterswick Shet.........111 k3
Otterton Devon...........6 E5
Ottery St Mary Devon.....6 E4
Ottinge Kent.............13 M2
Ottringham E R Yk.......61 M8
Oughterby Cumb.........71 J7
Oughterside Cumb.......71 J7
Oughtibridge Sheff......50 H3
Oughtrington Warrtn....57 M10
Oulston N York...........66 D11
Oulton Cumb.............71 K5
Oulton Norfk.............45 J4
Oulton Staffs.............40 B1
Oulton Suffk..............45 Q10
Oulton Broad Suffk......45 Q10
Oulton Street Norfk......45 J5
Oundle Nhants...........42 E11
Ounsdale Staffs..........39 Q4
Our Dynamic Earth C Edin..86 F7
Ousby Cumb..............64 B1
Ousden Suffk.............34 C5
Ousefleet E R Yk.........60 E9
Ouston Dur...............73 M9
Outgate Cumb............62 G3
Outhgill Cumb............64 E7
Outhill Warwks...........30 E2
Outlane Kirk.............58 E9
Out Rawcliffe Lancs.....56 H1
Outwell Norfk............43 N8
Outwood Surrey..........11 L2
Outwoods Staffs.........49 P11
Ouzlewell Green Leeds...59 J8
Over Cambs..............33 L3
Overbury Worcs..........29 N2
Overcombe Dorset........7 Q6
Over Compton Dorset....17 N11
Overdale Crematorium
  Bolton..................57 M7
Over Haddon Derbys.....50 G7
Over Kellet Lancs........63 K8
Over Kiddington Oxon...31 K9
Overleigh Somset........17 L8
Over Norton Oxon........30 H8
Over Peover Ches E.......49 P1
Overpool Ches W.........56 H12
Overscaig Hotel Highld..108 H10
Overseal Derbys..........40 H4
Over Silton N York.......66 C18
Oversland Kent..........23 K11
Overstone Nhants.......32 B4
Over Stowey Somset.....16 G8
Overstrand Norfk........45 L3
Over Stratton Somset....17 L11
Overthorpe Nhants......31 L6
Overton C Aber.........102 H11
Overton Hants...........19 N10
Overton Lancs............62 H9
Overton N York...........59 M3
Overton Shrops..........39 J7
Overton Swans...........26 B10
Overton Wakefd.........58 H10
Overton Wrexhm.........48 G7
Overtown N Lans.........85 N11
Over Wallop Hants.......19 K11
Over Whitacre Warwks...40 G8
Over Worton Oxon.......31 K8
Oving Bucks.............32 A11
Oving W Susx.............10 E8
Ovingdean Br & H........11 M8
Ovingham Nthumb.......73 J7
Ovington Dur............65 K5
Ovington Essex..........34 C8
Ovington Hants...........9 P2
Ovington Norfk...........44 F9
Ovington Nthumb........73 J7
Ower Hants................9 K4
Owermoigne Dorset......8 B9
Owlerton Sheff...........51 J3
Owlsmoor Br For.........20 D10
Owlswick Bucks..........20 C3
Owmby Lincs.............52 F6
Owmby Lincs.............52 F3
Owslebury Hants..........9 N3
Owston Donc.............59 M11
Owston Leics.............41 Q6
Owston Ferry N Linc.....52 B4
Owthorne E R Yk........61 N8
Owthorpe Notts.........41 N2
Owton Manor Hartpl.....66 C2
Oxborough Norfk.........44 C9
Oxcombe Lincs...........53 K7
Oxenhope C Brad.........58 D7
Oxen Park Cumb.........62 G5
Oxenpill Somset..........17 L7
Oxenton Gloucs..........29 N3
Oxenwood Wilts..........19 K8
Oxford Oxon..............31 L11
Oxford Airport Oxon.....31 L10
Oxford Crematorium
  Oxon...................31 M11
Oxford Services Oxon....31 N12

Oxhey Herts.............20 H4
Oxhill Warwks...........30 H5
Oxley Wolves............40 B7
Oxley Green Essex.......22 H1
Oxlode Cambs...........43 M11
Oxnam Border...........80 F9
Oxnead Norfk............45 K5
Oxshott Surrey..........21 J10
Oxspring Barns..........50 H1
Oxted Surrey............21 M11
Oxton Border............80 C4
Oxton N York............59 L5
Oxton Notts.............51 N9
Oxwich Swans...........26 C10
Oxwich Green Swans....26 C10
Oykel Bridge Hotel Highld..106 F3
Oyne Abers.............102 E9
Oystermouth Swans.....26 E10

P

Pabail W Isls...........111 e2
Packington Leics........41 J5
Padanaram Angus.......93 M5
Padbury Bucks...........31 Q9
Paddington Gt Lon......21 L7
Paddlesworth Kent.......13 M3
Paddlesworth Kent.......22 D10
Paddock Wood Kent......12 D2
Padiham Lancs...........57 P3
Padside N York...........58 F3
Padstow Cnwll............3 K1
Padworth W Berk........19 Q7
Pagham W Susx..........10 E9
Paglesham Essex.........22 H5
Paignton Torbay..........6 B10
Pailton Warwks...........41 L10
Painscastle Powys.......38 D11
Painshawfield Nthumb...73 J8
Painsthorpe E R Yk.......60 E3
Painswick Gloucs........29 M6
Painter's Forstal Kent....23 J10
Paisley Rens.............84 H9
Paisley Woodside
  Crematorium Rens....84 H9
Pakefield Suffk..........45 Q11
Pakenham Suffk.........34 F4
Paley Street W & M......20 E7
Palfrey Wsall............40 D7
Palgrave Suffk...........35 J2
Pallington Dorset.........8 B8
Palmerston E Ayrs.......76 H7
Palnackie D & G..........70 D4
Palnure D & G.............69 L6
Palterton Derbys.........51 L7
Pamber End Hants.......19 Q8
Pamber Green Hants.....19 Q8
Pamber Heath Hants.....19 Q8
Pamington Gloucs.......29 N3
Pamphill Dorset...........8 E7
Pampisford Cambs.......33 N7
Panbride Angus..........93 P8
Pancrasweek Devon......14 F10
Pandy Mons.............28 D4
Pandy Tudur Conwy......55 M8
Panfield Essex...........34 C10
Pangbourne W Berk......19 Q5
Pangdean W Susx........11 L7
Pannal N York............58 H4
Pannal Ash N York........58 H4
Pannanich Wells Hotel
  Abers...................94 G3
Pant Shrops..............48 F10
Pantasaph Flints.........48 D1
Pant-ffrwyth Brdgnd....27 K11
Pant Glas Gwynd.........46 H2
Pantglas Powys..........47 M10
Panton Lincs.............52 H7
Pant-y-dwr Powys.......37 R6
Pant-y-mwyn Flints......48 E3
Panxworth Norfk........45 M7
Papa Westray Airport Ork..111 h1
Papcastle Cumb..........70 H4
Papigoe Highld.........110 H5
Papple E Loth............87 L7
Papplewick Notts........51 M9
Papworth Everard Cambs..33 J4
Papworth St Agnes
  Cambs..................33 J4
Par Cnwll.................3 N5
Parbold Lancs............57 J6
Parbrook Somset.........17 N8
Parc Gwynd..............47 P5
Parc Gwyn
  Crematorium Pembks..25 K6
Parc Seymour Newpt......28 D9
Pardshaw Cumb.........70 H9
Parham Suffk............35 M5
Park D & G...............78 E10
Park Nthumb.............72 C8
Park Corner Oxon........20 B6
Park Crematorium Lancs..56 G3
Parkend Gloucs..........28 H7
Parkers Green Kent......12 C1
Park Farm Kent...........13 J3
Parkgate Ches W.........56 F12
Parkgate D & G...........78 G10
Park Gate Hants...........9 N6
Park Gate Leeds..........58 F6
Parkgate Surrey..........11 K2
Parkgrove
  Crematorium Angus...93 Q6
Parkhall W Duns.........84 H8
Parkham Devon...........14 G7
Parkmill Swans..........26 D10
Park Royal Gt Lon........21 K7
Parkside Dur..............73 P11
Parkside N Lans..........85 N10
Parkstone Poole...........8 F8
Park Street Herts.........21 J3
Park Wood
  Crematorium Calder...58 E9
Parndon Essex...........21 N2
Parndon Wood
  Crematorium Essex....21 N3
Parracombe Devon.......15 L3
Parson Drove Cambs.....43 J9
Parson's Heath Essex....34 G10
Partick C Glas............85 J9
Partington Traffd........57 N9
Partney Lincs.............53 L9
Parton Cumb..............70 F10
Partridge Green W Susx..11 J6
Parwich Derbys..........50 F9
Passenham Nhants.......32 A8

Paston Norfk.............45 M4
Patcham Br & H..........11 L8
Patching W Susx..........10 H8
Patchway S Glos.........28 H11
Pateley Bridge N York...58 F2
Pathhead Fife............86 F4
Pathhead Mdloth........86 H9
Path of Condie P & K.....92 G12
Patna E Ayrs.............76 G8
Patney Wilts.............18 F8
Patrick IoM...............56 b5
Patrick Brompton N York..65 L8
Patricroft Salfd..........57 N8
Patrington E R Yk........61 N9
Patrington Haven E R Yk..61 N9
Patrixbourne Kent.......23 M11
Patterdale Cumb.........71 N11
Pattingham Staffs........39 P3
Pattishall Nhants........31 P4
Pattiswick Green Essex...34 D11
Paul Cnwll.................2 C9
Paulerspury Nhants......31 Q5
Paull E R Yk..............61 K8
Paul's Dene Wilts.........8 G2
Paulton BaNES...........17 P5
Pauperhaugh Nthumb...73 K2
Pavenham Bed...........32 E5
Pawlett Somset..........16 H7
Paxford Gloucs..........30 F6
Paxton Border...........81 K4
Payhembury Devon.......6 E3
Paythorne Lancs.........63 P10
Peacehaven E Susx.......11 N9
Peak District National
  Park...............50 F3
Peak Forest Derbys......50 E5
Peakirk C Pete...........42 G8
Peasedown St John
  BaNES.................17 Q5
Peaseland Green Norfk...44 H6
Peasemore W Berk.......19 M5
Peasenhall Suffk.........35 M3
Pease Pottage W Susx...11 L4
Peaslake Surrey..........10 H2
Peasley Cross St Hel......57 K9
Peasmarsh E Susx........12 H5
Peathill Abers...........103 J3
Peat Inn Fife.............87 J1
Peatling Magna Leics....41 N8
Peatling Parva Leics......41 N9
Pebmarsh Essex.........34 E9
Pebworth Worcs.........30 F5
Pecket Well Calder.......58 C8
Peckforton Ches E........49 K4
Peckham Gt Lon.........21 M8
Peckleton Leics..........41 L7
Pedlinge Kent............13 L3
Pedmore Dudley.........40 B10
Pedwell Somset..........17 K8
Peebles Border...........79 L2
Peel IoM..................56 b4
Peene Kent...............13 M3
Pegsdon C Beds..........32 G9
Pegswood Nthumb.......73 M4
Pegwell Kent.............23 Q9
Peinchorran Highld......96 G3
Peinlich Highld.........104 F10
Peldon Essex............34 G12
Pelsall Wsall.............40 D6
Pelton Dur...............73 M9
Pelynt Cnwll...............4 F8
Pemberton Carmth.......26 D8
Pemberton Wigan........57 K7
Pembrey Carmth.........25 P8
Pembridge Herefs........38 H9
Pembroke Pembks........24 H8
Pembroke Dock Pembks..24 G7
Pembrokeshire Coast
  National Park Pembks..24 E5
Pembury Kent............12 D2
Pen-allt Herefs..........28 G5
Penallt Mons............28 G7
Penally Pembks..........25 K8
Penarth V Glam..........16 G2
Pen-bont
  Rhydybeddau Cerdgn..37 L4
Penbryn Cerdgn.........36 E9
Pencader Carmth........25 Q2
Pencaitland E Loth.......87 J8
Pencarnisiog IoA..........54 D6
Pencarreg Carmth.......37 J10
Pencelli Powys...........27 M4
Penclawdd Swans........26 D9
Pencoed Brdgnd.........27 K11
Pencombe Herefs........39 L10
Pencraig Herefs..........28 G5
Pencraig Powys..........48 B9
Pendeen Cnwll............2 B8
Penderyn Rhondd........27 K7
Pendine Carmth.........25 L7
Pendlebury Salfd.........57 P8
Pendleton Lancs.........57 N2
Pendock Worcs..........29 K3
Pendoggett Cnwll.........3 M1
Pendomer Somset.........7 M1
Pendoylan V Glam........16 E2
Penegoes Powys.........47 M10
Pen-ffordd Pembks.......24 H4
Pengam Caerph..........27 N8
Pengam Cardif...........27 P12
Penge Gt Lon............21 M8
Pengelly Cnwll............4 D4
Penhallow Cnwll..........2 H5
Penhalvean Cnwll.........2 G8
Penhill Swindn...........18 H3
Penhow Newpt...........28 E10
Penhurst E Susx..........12 D6
Peniarth Gwynd..........47 L9
Penicuik Mdloth.........86 F9
Peniel Carmth............25 P5
Penifiler Highld..........96 F2
Peninver Ag & B..........75 L7
Penistone Barns.........50 H1
Penjerrick Cnwll..........2 H8
Penketh Warrtn..........57 K10
Penkill S Ayrs...........76 D9
Penkridge Staffs.........40 B5
Penley Wrexhm..........48 H7
Penllyn V Glam...........16 C2
Penmachno Conwy.......55 L10
Penmaen Caerph.........27 P8
Penmaen Swans.........26 D10
Penmaenmawr Conwy...55 K6
Penmaenpool Gwynd....47 L7
Penmark V Glam..........16 E3
Penmount
  Crematorium Cnwll.....3 J6
Penmynydd IoA..........54 G6
Penn Bucks..............20 E4
Penn Wolves.............40 B7
Pennal Gwynd...........47 L10
Pennan Abers...........102 H3
Pennant Powys...........47 P10

Pennerley Shrops.........38 G3
Pennines................58 C7
Pennington Cumb.........62 F6
Pennorth Powys..........27 M4
Penn Street Bucks........20 E4
Penny Bridge Cumb.......62 F5
Pennycross Ag & B.......89 L10
Pennyghael Ag & B......89 L10
Pennyglen S Ayrs........76 E8
Pennymoor Devon........15 P9
Pennywell Sundld........73 P9
Penparc Cerdgn.........36 D10
Penperlleni Mons.........28 C7
Penpoll Cnwll..............4 F7
Penponds Cnwll...........2 F7
Penpont D & G............78 D9
Pen-rhiw Pembks.........36 D11
Penrhiwceiber Rhondd...27 M8
Pen Rhiwfawr Neath.....26 G6
Penrhiw-llan Cerdgn.....36 F11
Penrhiw-pal Cerdgn......36 F10
Penrhos Gwynd..........46 F5
Penrhos Mons...........28 E6
Penrhyn Bay Conwy......55 M5
Penrhyndeudraeth
  Gwynd..................47 K4
Penrice Swans...........26 C10
Penrioch N Ayrs.........75 N4
Penrith Cumb............71 Q9
Penrose Cnwll.............3 K2
Penruddock Cumb........71 N9
Penryn Cnwll.............2 H8
Pensarn Conwy..........55 P6
Pensax Worcs............39 N8
Penselwood Somset......17 R9
Pensford BaNES..........17 N4
Pensham Worcs..........30 C5
Penshaw Sundld.........73 N9
Penshurst Kent..........11 Q2
Pensilva Cnwll.............4 G6
Pentewan Cnwll...........3 M6
Pentir Gwynd............54 H8
Pentire Cnwll.............2 H4
Pentlow Essex............34 D7
Pentney Norfk...........44 B7
Pentonbridge Cumb......79 P12
Penton Mewsey Hants...19 K10
Pentraeth IoA............54 G6
Pentre Mons.............28 E8
Pentre Rhondd...........27 K9
Pentre Shrops...........48 G11
Pentrebach Myr Td.......27 M7
Pentre-bach Powys.......27 J3
Pentre Berw IoA..........54 F7
Pentrebychan
  Crematorium Wrexhm..48 F6
Pentre-celyn Denbgs.....48 D5
Pentre-celyn Powys.......47 P9
Pentre-chwyth Swans...26 F9
Pentre-cwrt Carmth......25 P2
Pentredwr Denbgs.......48 E6
Pentrefelin Gwynd.......47 J4
Pentrefoelas Conwy......55 M10
Pentregat Cerdgn........36 F9
Pentre-Gwenlais Carmth..26 E5
Pentre Hodrey Shrops....38 G6
Pentre Llanrhaeadr
  Denbgs..................48 C3
Pentre Meyrick V Glam...16 C2
Pentre-tafarn-y-fedw
  Conwy..................55 M8
Pentrich Derbys..........51 J9
Pentridge Dorset..........8 F4
Pen-twyn Mons..........28 F7
Pentwynmaur Caerph....27 P9
Pentyrch Cardif.........27 M11
Penwithick Cnwll.........3 M5
Penybanc Carmth........26 E4
Penybont Powys.........38 C8
Pen-y-bont Powys.......48 E10
Pen-y-bont-fawr Powys..48 C9
Pen-y-bryn Pembks.......36 C11
Penycae Wrexhm.........48 F6
Pen-y-clawdd Mons......28 E7
Pen-y-coedcae Rhondd...27 M10
Pen-y-cwn Pembks........24 E4
Pen-y-felin Flints.........48 D2
Penyffordd Flints.........48 F4
Pen-y-Garnedd Powys...48 C10
Pen-y-graig Gwynd.......46 C5
Penygraig Rhondd........27 L10
Penygroes Carmth........26 D6
Penygroes Gwynd........54 F10
Pen-y-Mynydd Carmth...26 C7
Penymynydd Flints.......48 F3
Penysarn IoA.............54 F4
Pen-y-stryt Denbgs.......48 E5
Penywaun Rhondd........27 K7
Penzance Cnwll............2 D9
Peopleton Worcs.........30 C4
Peplow Shrops...........49 L9
Perceton N Ayrs..........76 F3
Percyhorner Abers.......103 K3
Perham Down Wilts......19 J10
Periton Somset...........16 C7
Perivale Gt Lon...........21 J6
Perkins Village Devon......6 D5
Perlethorpe Notts........51 N6
Perranarworthal Cnwll...2 H7
Perranporth Cnwll........2 H5
Perranuthnoe Cnwll.......2 D9
Perranwell Cnwll..........2 H7
Perranzabuloe Cnwll......2 H5
Perry Barr Birm..........40 E8
Perry Barr
  Crematorium Birm.....40 E8
Perry Green Wilts........18 E3
Pershall Staffs............49 P9
Pershore Worcs..........30 C5
Pertenhall Bed...........32 F4
Perth P & K................92 G9
Perth Crematorium P & K..92 G9
Perthy Shrops............48 G8
Perton Herefs............28 H2
Perton Staffs.............39 Q3
Peterborough C Pete.....42 H9
Peterborough
  Crematorium C Pete...42 G10
Peterborough Services
  Cambs..................42 G10
Peterchurch Herefs......28 D2
Peterculter C Aber........95 N2
Peterhead Abers.........103 M6
Peterlee Dur.............73 Q11
Petersfield Hants.........10 C5
Peter's Green Herts......32 G11
Petersham Gt Lon........21 J8

Peters Marland Devon 14 H9
Peterstone Wentlooge
  Newpt.....................28 B11
Peterston-super-Ely
  V Glam....................16 E2
Peterstow Herefs..........28 G4
Peter Tavy Devon...........5 K5
Petham Kent...............23 L12
Petherwin Gate Cnwll.......4 G3
Petrockstow Devon.........15 J9
Pett E Susx...............12 G7
Pettaugh Suffk............35 J5
Petterden Angus...........93 M7
Pettinain S Lans..........78 F1
Pettistree Suffk..........35 L6
Petton Devon..............16 D10
Petts Wood Gt Lon.........21 N9
Pettycur Fife.............86 F5
Pettymuk Abers...........103 J9
Petworth W Susx...........10 F6
Pevensey E Susx...........12 D8
Pevensey Bay E Susx.......12 D8
Pewsey Wilts..............18 H8
Phepson Worcs.............30 C3
Philham Devon.............14 E7
Philiphaugh Border........79 N4
Phillack Cnwll.............2 E7
Philleigh Cnwll............3 K7
Philpstoun W Loth.........86 C6
Phoenix Green Hants.......20 C10
Phones Highld.............99 K9
Pibsbury Somset...........17 L10
Pickburn Donc.............59 L11
Pickering N York..........66 H10
Pickford Covtry...........40 H10
Pickhill N York...........65 N10
Picklescott Shrops........38 H3
Pickmere Ches E...........57 M12
Pickney Somset............16 G9
Pickwell Leics............42 B7
Pickworth Lincs...........42 F4
Pickworth Rutlnd..........42 E7
Picton Ches W.............48 H2
Picton N York.............65 P6
Piddinghoe E Susx.........11 N9
Piddington Nhants.........32 B6
Piddington Oxon...........31 N10
Piddlehinton Dorset........7 Q4
Piddletrenthide Dorset.....7 Q3
Pidley Cambs..............33 K2
Piercebridge Darltn.......65 L4
Pierowall Ork............111 h1
Pilgrims Hatch Essex......22 C4
Pilham Lincs..............52 C5
Pillaton Cnwll.............4 H7
Pillerton Hersey Warwks...30 H4
Pillerton Priors Warwks...30 H5
Pilley Barns..............51 J1
Pilley Hants...............9 K7
Pilling Lancs.............62 H11
Pilning Glos..............28 G10
Pilsbury Derbys...........50 E7
Pilsdon Dorset.............7 K3
Pilsley Derbys............50 G6
Pilsley Derbys............51 K8
Pilson Green Norfk........45 N7
Piltdown E Susx...........11 N5
Pilton Devon..............15 K5
Pilton Nhants.............42 E12
Pilton Rutlnd.............42 D9
Pilton Somset.............17 N7
Pimperne Dorset............8 D5
Pinchbeck Lincs...........43 J5
Pin Green Herts...........33 J10
Pinhoe Devon...............6 C4
Pinley Green Warwks.......30 G2
Pinminnoch S Ayrs.........76 D11
Pinmore S Ayrs............76 D11
Pinn Devon.................6 E5
Pinner Gt Lon.............20 H5
Pinner Green Gt Lon.......20 H5
Pinvin Worcs..............30 C4
Pinwherry S Ayrs..........68 G2
Pinxton Derbys............51 L9
Pipe and Lyde Herefs......39 J12
Pipe Aston Herefs.........39 J7
Pipe Gate Shrops..........49 N9
Piperhill Highld.........100 D5
Pipewell Nhants...........42 B11
Pirbright Surrey..........20 F11
Pirnie Border.............80 E8
Pirnmill N Ayrs...........75 N4
Pirton Herts..............32 G9
Pishill Oxon..............20 B5
Pistyll Gwynd.............46 E3
Pitagowan P & K...........92 C3
Pitblae Abers............103 K3
Pitcairngreen P & K.......92 H7
Pitcalnie Highld.........107 N7
Pitcaple Abers...........102 F9
Pitcarity Angus...........94 F8
Pitchcombe Gloucs.........29 L7
Pitchcott Bucks...........31 Q9
Pitchford Shrops..........39 K2
Pitch Green Bucks.........20 C3
Pitchroy Moray...........101 J7
Pitcombe Somset...........17 P9
Pitcox E Loth.............87 M7
Pitfichie Abers..........102 E11
Pitglassie Abers.........102 F6
Pitgrudy Highld..........107 N4
Pitlessie Fife............86 G1
Pitlochry P & K...........92 D4
Pitmachie Abers..........102 E9
Pitmain Highld............99 L8
Pitmedden Abers..........103 J9
Pitmedden Garden Abers...103 J8
Pitminster Somset.........16 G11
Pitmuies Angus............93 P6
Pitmunie Abers...........102 E11
Pitney Somset.............17 L9
Pitroddie P & K...........93 J10
Pitscottie Fife...........93 M11
Pitsea Essex..............22 E6
Pitsford Nhants...........31 Q1
Pitstone Bucks............20 F1
Pittarrow Abers...........95 M7
Pittenweem Fife...........87 K2
Pitteuchar Fife...........86 F3
Pittington Dur............73 N11
Pittodrie House Hotel
  Abers...................102 F9
Pitton Wilts...............8 H2
Pittulie Abers...........103 K2
Pity Me Dur...............73 M10
Pixham Surrey.............21 J12
Plains N Lans.............85 N9

Plaish Shrops.............39 K3
Plaistow Gt Lon...........21 N6
Plaistow W Susx...........10 G4
Plaitford Hants............9 J4
Platt Kent................22 D11
Plawsworth Dur............73 M10
Plaxtol Kent..............22 C11
Playden E Susx............12 H6
Playford Suffk............35 K7
Play Hatch Oxon...........20 B7
Playing Place Cnwll........3 J7
Playley Green Gloucs......29 K3
Plealey Shrops............38 H2
Plean Stirlg..............85 P5
Pleasance Fife............93 J12
Pleasington Bl w D........57 M4
Pleasley Derbys...........51 L7
Plemstall Ches W..........49 J2
Pleshey Essex.............22 D1
Plockton Highld...........97 L3
Plowden Shrops............38 H5
Pluckley Kent.............12 H2
Pluckley Thorne Kent......12 H2
Plumbland Cumb............71 J7
Plumley Ches E............49 N1
Plumpton Cumb.............71 P7
Plumpton E Susx...........11 M6
Plumpton Nhants...........31 N5
Plumpton Green E Susx.....11 M6
Plumstead Gt Lon..........21 N7
Plumstead Norfk...........45 J3
Plumtree Notts............41 N2
Plungar Leics.............41 Q1
Plurenden Kent............12 H3
Plush Dorset...............7 Q3
Plwmp Cerdgn..............36 F9
Plymouth C Plym............5 K8
Plymouth Airport C Plym....5 K8
Plympton C Plym............5 L9
Plymstock C Plym...........5 L9
Plymtree Devon.............6 E3
Pockley N York............66 F9
Pocklington E R Yk........60 D4
Podimore Somset...........17 M10
Podington Bed.............32 D4
Podmore Staffs............49 P8
Pointon Lincs.............42 G4
Pokesdown Bmouth...........8 G8
Polbain Highld...........105 Q1
Polbathic Cnwll............4 H8
Polbeth W Loth............86 B9
Poldark Mine Cnwll.........2 F9
Polebrook Nhants..........42 F11
Polegate E Susx...........12 C8
Polesden Lacey Surrey.....21 J11
Polesworth Warwks.........40 H7
Polglass Highld..........105 Q2
Polgooth Cnwll.............3 M5
Polgown D & G.............77 M9
Poling W Susx.............10 G8
Poling Corner W Susx......10 G8
Polkerris Cnwll............4 D9
Pollington E R Yk.........59 N9
Polloch Highld............89 Q3
Pollokshaws C Glas........85 J10
Pollokshields C Glas......85 J9
Polmassick Cnwll...........3 L6
Polmont Falk..............85 Q7
Polnish Highld............97 K12
Polperro Cnwll.............4 F9
Polruan Cnwll..............4 E9
Polstead Suffk............34 G8
Poltalloch Ag & B.........83 M4
Poltimore Devon............6 C4
Polton Mdloth.............86 F8
Polwarth Border...........80 G4
Polyphant Cnwll............4 G4
Polzeath Cnwll.............3 K1
Pomathorn Mdloth..........86 F9
Pondersbridge Cambs.......43 J10
Ponders End Gt Lon........21 M4
Ponsanooth Cnwll...........2 H8
Ponsworthy Devon...........5 N5
Pont Abraham Services
  Carmth..................26 D7
Pontantwn Carmth..........25 Q6
Pontardawe Neath..........26 F7
Pontarddulais Swans.......26 D7
Pont-ar-gothi Carmth......26 C5
Pontarsais Carmth.........25 Q3
Pontblyddyn Flints........48 F4
Pontcysyllte Aqueduct
  Wrexhm..................48 F7
Pontefract Wakefd.........59 L9
Pontefract
  Crematorium Wakefd.....59 K9
Ponteland Nthumb..........73 L6
Ponterwyd Cerdgn..........37 M4
Pontesbury Shrops.........38 H2
Pontesford Shrops.........38 H2
Pontfadog Wrexhm..........48 E7
Pontfaen Pembks...........24 H3
Pont-faen Powys...........27 L3
Pontgarreg Cerdgn.........36 F9
Ponthenry Carmth..........26 C7
Ponthir Torfn.............28 C9
Ponthirwaun Cerdgn........36 D10
Pontllanfraith Caerph.....27 P9
Pontlliw Swans............26 E8
Pontlottyn Caerph.........27 N7
Pontlyfni Gwynd...........54 F10
Pontneddfechan Neath......27 J7
Pontnewydd Torfn..........28 C9
Pontrhydfendigaid
  Cerdgn..................37 M7
Pont-rhyd-y-fen Neath.....26 H9
Pontrhydygroes Cerdgn.....37 M6
Pontrilas Herefs..........28 D4
Pont Robert Powys.........48 C11
Pontshaen Cerdgn..........36 G10
Pontsticill Myr Td........27 M6
Pontwelly Carmth..........36 G11
Pontyates Carmth..........26 C7
Pontyberem Carmth.........26 C6
Pontybodkin Flints........48 F4
Pontyclun Rhondd..........27 L11
Pontycymer Brdgnd.........27 J9
Pont-y-pant Conwy.........55 N10
Pontypool Torfn...........28 C8
Pontypridd Rhondd.........27 M10
Pontywaun Caerph..........27 P9
Pool Cnwll.................2 G7
Pool Leeds................58 G5
Poole Poole................8 E8
Poole Crematorium Poole....8 E8

Poole Keynes Gloucs.......18 E2
Poolewe Highld...........105 M6
Pooley Bridge Cumb........71 P10
Poolfold Staffs...........50 B8
Poolhill Gloucs...........29 K3
Pool of Muckhart Clacks...86 B3
Pool Street Essex.........34 C8
Poplar Gt Lon.............21 M7
Porchfield IoW.............9 M8
Poringland Norfk..........45 L9
Porkellis Cnwll............2 G8
Porlock Somset............15 Q3
Porlock Weir Somset.......15 P3
Portachoillan Ag & B......83 L10
Port-an-Eorna Highld......97 L3
Port Appin Ag & B.........90 C7
Port Askaig Ag & B........82 F8
Portavadie Ag & B.........83 P8
Port Bannatyne Ag & B.....84 B9
Portbury N Som............17 M2
Port Carlisle Cumb........71 K3
Port Charlotte Ag & B.....82 C10
Portchester Hants..........9 Q6
Portchester
  Crematorium Hants.......9 Q6
Port Driseach Ag & B......83 Q8
Port Ellen Ag & B.........74 E4
Port Elphinstone Abers...102 G10
Portencalzie D & G........68 D5
Portencross N Ayrs........76 C2
Port Erin IoM.............56 a6
Portesham Dorset...........7 N5
Portessie Moray..........101 N3
Port Eynon Swans..........26 C11
Portfield Gate Pembks.....24 G6
Portgate Devon.............5 J5
Port Gaverne Cnwll.........4 C4
Port Glasgow Inver........84 F7
Portgordon Moray.........101 M3
Portgower Highld.........110 B11
Porth Cnwll................3 J4
Porth Rhondd.............27 L9
Porthallow Cnwll...........3 J9
Porthallow Cnwll...........4 F9
Porthcawl Brdgnd..........26 H12
Porthcothan Cnwll..........3 K2
Porthcurno Cnwll...........2 B10
Port Henderson Highld....105 L7
Porthgain Pembks..........24 E3
Porthgwarra Cnwll..........2 B10
Porthkerry V Glam.........16 E3
Porthleven Cnwll...........2 F9
Porthmadog Gwynd..........47 J4
Porth Navas Cnwll..........3 J9
Porthoustock Cnwll.........3 J10
Porthpean Cnwll............3 M5
Porthtowan Cnwll...........2 G6
Porthyrhyd Carmth.........26 C5
Portincaple Ag & B........84 D4
Portington E R Yk.........60 D7
Portinnisherrich Ag & B...83 P2
Portinscale Cumb..........71 L10
Port Isaac Cnwll...........4 C4
Portishead N Som..........17 L2
Portknockie Moray........101 N2
Portland Dorset............7 P8
Portling D & G............70 E5
Portloe Cnwll..............3 L7
Port Logan D & G..........68 E10
Portmahomack Highld......107 Q5
Portmeirion Gwynd.........47 J4
Portmellon Cnwll...........3 M7
Port Mor Highld...........89 J1
Portnacroish Ag & B.......90 C6
Portnaguran W Isls.......111 e2
Portnahaven Ag & B........74 B2
Portnalong Highld.........96 D3
Port nan Giuran W Isls...111 e2
Port nan Long W Isls.....111 b4
Port Nis W Isls..........111 e1
Portobello C Edin.........86 G7
Portobello Wolves.........40 C7
Port of Menteith Stirlg...85 K3
Port of Ness W Isls......111 e1
Portpatrick D & G.........68 D8
Port Quin Cnwll............4 B4
Port Ramsay Ag & B........90 B7
Portreath Cnwll............2 F6
Portreath Harbour Cnwll....2 F6
Portree Highld............96 F2
Port St Mary IoM..........56 b7
Portscatho Cnwll...........3 K8
Portsea C Port.............9 Q7
Portskerra Highld........109 Q3
Portskewett Mons..........28 F10
Portslade Br & H..........11 K8
Portslade-by-Sea Br & H...11 L8
Portslogan D & G..........68 D7
Portsmouth C Port..........9 Q7
Portsmouth Calder.........58 B8
Portsmouth Dockyard
  C Port...................9 Q7
Port Soderick IoM.........56 c6
Portsonachan Hotel
  Ag & B..................90 E11
Portsoy Abers............102 D3
Port Sunlight Wirral......56 G11
Portswood C Sotn...........9 M5
Port Talbot Neath.........26 G10
Portuairk Highld..........89 K3
Portway Worcs.............40 E11
Port Wemyss Ag & B........74 B3
Port William D & G........69 J9
Portwrinkle Cnwll..........4 H9
Portyerrock D & G.........69 L10
Poslingford Suffk.........34 C7
Posso Border..............79 K3
Postbridge Devon...........5 N4
Postcombe Oxon............20 B4
Postling Kent.............13 M3
Postwick Norfk............45 L8
Potarch Abers.............95 K3
Potten End Herts..........20 G2
Potter Brompton N York....67 L11
Potterhanworth Lincs......52 F9
Potterhanworth
  Booths Lincs............52 F9
Potter Heigham Norfk......45 N6
Potterne Wilts............18 E8
Potterne Wick Wilts.......18 E8
Potters Bar Herts.........21 K3
Potters Crouch Herts......20 H3
Potters Green Covtry......41 J10
Potters Marston Leics.....41 L8
Potterspury Nhants........31 Q5

Potterton Abers..........103 K11
Potto N York..............66 C6
Potton C Beds.............32 H6
Pott Shrigley Ches E......50 C5
Poughill Cnwll............14 D11
Poughill Devon............15 P9
Poulner Hants..............8 H6
Poulshot Wilts............18 E8
Poulton Gloucs............18 G1
Poulton-le-Fylde Lancs....56 G2
Poundbury Dorset...........7 P5
Poundffald Swans..........26 D9
Pound Green E Susx........11 P5
Pound Green Suffk.........34 C6
Pound Hill W Susx.........11 L3
Poundon Bucks.............31 N9
Poundsgate Devon...........5 N6
Poundstock Cnwll..........14 D11
Pouton D & G..............69 L9
Povey Cross Surrey........11 L2
Powburn Nthumb............81 M10
Powderham Devon............6 C6
Powerstock Dorset..........7 M4
Powfoot D & G.............71 J3
Powick Worcs..............39 Q10
Powmill P & K.............86 B3
Poxwell Dorset.............7 Q6
Poyle Slough..............20 G7
Poynings W Susx...........11 L7
Poyntington Dorset........17 P11
Poynton Ches E............50 B4
Poynton Green Wrekin......49 K10
Praa Sands Cnwll...........2 E9
Pratt's Bottom Gt Lon.....21 P10
Praze-an-Beeble Cnwll......2 F8
Prees Shrops..............49 K8
Preesall Lancs............62 G11
Prees Green Shrops........49 K8
Prees Heath Shrops........49 K7
Prees Higher Heath
  Shrops..................49 K8
Pren-gwyn Cerdgn..........36 G10
Prenteg Gwynd.............47 J3
Prescot Knows.............57 J9
Prescott Devon............16 E12
Presnerb Angus............94 C8
Prestatyn Denbgs..........56 C11
Prestbury Ches E..........50 B5
Prestbury Gloucs..........29 N4
Presteigne Powys..........38 G8
Prestleigh Somset.........17 P7
Preston Border............87 P10
Preston Br & H............11 L8
Preston Devon..............6 B7
Preston Dorset............7 Q6
Preston E R Yk............61 K7
Preston Gloucs............18 F1
Preston Herts.............32 H10
Preston Kent.............23 K10
Preston Kent.............23 N10
Preston Lancs.............57 K3
Preston Nthumb............81 P8
Preston Rutlnd............42 C9
Preston Somset............16 E8
Preston Suffk.............34 F6
Preston Torbay.............6 B9
Preston Wilts.............18 F5
Preston Bagot Warwks......30 F2
Preston Bissett Bucks.....31 P8
Preston Bowyer Somset.....16 F10
Preston Brockhurst
  Shrops..................49 K9
Preston Brook Halton......57 K11
Preston Candover Hants....19 Q11
Preston Capes Nhants......31 M3
Preston Crematorium
  Lancs...................57 L3
Preston Green Warwks......30 F2
Preston Gubbals Shrops....49 J10
Preston on Stour Warwks...30 G4
Preston on the Hill Halton.57 K11
Preston on Wye Herefs.....28 D1
Prestonpans E Loth........86 H7
Preston Patrick Cumb......63 K5
Preston Plucknett
  Somset..................17 M11
Preston-under-Scar
  N York..................65 J8
Preston upon the
  Weald Moors Wrekin......49 M11
Preston Wynne Herefs......39 K11
Prestwich Bury............57 P7
Prestwick S Ayrs..........76 F6
Prestwick Airport S Ayrs..76 F6
Prestwood Bucks...........20 E4
Prickwillow Cambs.........33 P1
Priddy Somset.............17 M6
Priest Hutton Lancs.......63 K7
Priestland E Ayrs.........77 J4
Priest Weston Shrops......38 F3
Primrosehill Border.......87 P10
Primsidemill Border.......80 H8
Princes Risborough Bucks..20 D3
Princethorpe Warwks.......41 K12
Princetown Devon...........5 M5
Priors Hardwick Warwks....31 L3
Priorslee Wrekin..........49 N12
Priors Marston Warwks.....31 L3
Priors Norton Gloucs......29 M4
Priory Vale Swindn........18 G3
Priston BaNES.............17 Q4
Prittlewell Sthend........22 G6
Privett Hants.............10 B5
Prixford Devon............15 J5
Probus Cnwll...............3 K6
Prora E Loth..............87 K6
Prospect Cumb.............71 J7
Prospidnick Cnwll..........2 F9
Protstonhill Abers.......102 H3
Prudhoe Nthumb............73 J8
Publow BaNES..............17 P4
Puckeridge Herts..........33 L11
Puckington Somset.........17 K11
Pucklechurch S Glos.......17 Q2
Puddington Ches W.........48 G2
Puddington Devon..........15 P9
Puddletown Dorset..........7 Q4
Pudsey Leeds..............58 G7
Pulborough W Susx........10 G6
Pulford Ches W...........48 G4
Pulham Dorset.............7 Q2
Pulham Market Norfk......45 K11
Pulham St Mary Norfk.....45 K11
Pulloxhill C Beds........32 F9
Pumpherston W Loth.......86 C8
Pumsaint Carmth..........37 K11
Puncheston Pembks........24 H3

Puncknowle Dorset..........7 M5
Punnett's Town E Susx.....12 C6
Purbrook Hants............10 A8
Purfleet Thurr............22 B7
Puriton Somset............17 J7
Purleigh Essex............22 G3
Purley Gt Lon.............21 L10
Purley W Berk.............19 Q5
Purse Caundle Dorset......17 Q11
Purtington Somset..........7 K2
Purton Gloucs.............29 J7
Purton Gloucs.............29 J7
Purton Wilts..............18 G4
Purton Stoke Wilts........18 G3
Pury End Nhants...........31 P5
Pusey Oxon................19 L2
Putley Herefs.............28 H2
Putley Green Herefs.......28 H2
Putney Gt Lon.............21 K8
Putney Vale
  Crematorium Gt Lon......21 K8
Puttenham Surrey..........10 E1
Puxley Nhants.............31 Q6
Puxton N Som..............17 K4
Pwll Carmth...............26 C8
Pwll-glâs Denbgs..........48 C5
Pwllgloyw Powys...........27 L3
Pwllheli Gwynd............46 F4
Pwllmeyric Mons...........28 F9
Pwll Trap Carmth..........25 M5
Pwll-y-glaw Neath.........26 H9
Pye Bridge Derbys.........51 K9
Pyecombe W Susx...........11 L7
Pyle Brdgnd...............26 H11
Pyleigh Somset............16 F9
Pylle Somset..............17 N8
Pymoor Cambs.............43 M11
Pymore Dorset..............7 L4
Pyrford Surrey............20 G10
Pyrton Oxon...............20 B4
Pytchley Nhants...........32 C2
Pyworthy Devon............14 F10

Q

Quadring Lincs............42 H4
Quadring Eaudike Lincs....43 J4
Quainton Bucks............31 Q9
Quantock Hills Somset.....16 G8
Quarff Shet..............111 k4
Quarley Hants.............19 J11
Quarndon Derbys...........51 J11
Quarrier's Village Inver..84 F9
Quarrington Lincs.........42 F2
Quarrington Hill Dur......73 N12
Quarry Bank Dudley........40 B9
Quarrywood Moray.........101 J3
Quarter N Ayrs............84 D10
Quarter S Lans............85 M11
Quatford Shrops...........39 N5
Quatt Shrops..............39 N5
Quebec Dur................73 L11
Quedgeley Gloucs..........29 L6
Queen Adelaide Cambs......33 P1
Queenborough Kent.........22 H8
Queen Camel Somset........17 N10
Queen Charlton BaNES......17 P3
Queen Elizabeth Forest
  Park Stirlg.............84 H3
Queenhill Worcs...........29 M2
Queen Oak Dorset...........8 B2
Queen's Bower IoW..........9 P9
Queensbury C Brad.........58 E7
Queensferry Flints........48 G2
Queenslie C Glas..........85 L9
Queenzieburn N Lans.......85 L9
Quendon Essex.............33 N10
Queniborough Leics........41 N5
Quenington Gloucs.........30 F12
Queslett Birm.............40 E8
Quethiock Cnwll............4 G7
Quidenham Norfk...........44 G11
Quidhampton Wilts..........8 G2
Quinton Nhants............31 R4
Quintrell Downs Cnwll......3 K4
Quixwood Border...........87 P9
Quoig P & K...............92 C10
Quorn Leics...............41 M4
Quothquan S Lans..........78 G2
Quoyburray Ork...........111 h2
Quoyloo Ork..............111 g2

R

Raasay Highld.............96 G2
Rachan Mill Border........79 J3
Rachub Gwynd..............55 J7
Rackenford Devon..........15 P8
Rackham W Susx............10 G7
Rackheath Norfk...........45 L7
Racks D & G...............70 G1
Rackwick Ork.............111 g3
Radbourne Derbys..........40 H1
Radcliffe Bury............57 P7
Radcliffe on Trent Notts..51 N12
Radclive Bucks............31 P7
Raddery Highld...........107 L3
Radernie Fife.............87 J1
Radford Covtry............41 J10
Radford Semele Warwks.....31 J2
Radlett Herts.............21 J4
Radley Oxon...............19 N2
Radley Green Essex........22 D3
Radnage Bucks.............20 C4
Radstock BaNES............17 P5
Radstone Nhants...........31 N5
Radway Warwks.............31 J5
Radwell Bed...............32 E5
Radwell Herts.............32 H9
Radwinter Essex...........33 P8
Radyr Cardif..............27 N11
Rafford Moray............100 G4
RAF Museum Cosford
  Shrops..................39 P2
RAF Museum Hendon
  Gt Lon..................21 K5
Ragdale Leics.............41 P4
Raglan Mons...............28 E7
Ragnall Notts.............52 B8
Raigbeg Highld............99 M4
Rainbow Hill Worcs........39 Q10
Rainford St Hel...........57 J8
Rainham Gt Lon............21 P6

Rainham Medway............22 F9
Rainhill St Hel..............57 J10
Rainhill Stoops St Hel.....57 J10
Rainow Ches E..............50 C6
Rainsbrook
  Crematorium Warwks.....41 L11
Rainton N York.............65 P11
Rainworth Notts............51 N8
Rait P & K.................93 J9
Raithby Lincs..............53 K6
Raithby Lincs..............53 L9
Rake Hants.................10 C5
Ralia Highld...............99 K9
Ramasaig Highld............96 A2
Rame Cnwll.................2 G8
Rame Cnwll.................5 J9
Rampisham Dorset..........7 N3
Rampside Cumb.............62 E8
Rampton Cambs.............33 L3
Rampton Notts.............52 B7
Ramsbottom Bury...........57 P5
Ramsbury Wilts............19 J6
Ramscraigs Highld.........110 D9
Ramsdean Hants............10 B5
Ramsdell Hants............19 P8
Ramsden Oxon..............31 J10
Ramsden Bellhouse Essex...22 E5
Ramsey Cambs..............43 J11
Ramsey Essex..............35 K10
Ramsey IoM................56 e3
Ramsey Forty Foot
  Cambs...................43 K11
Ramsey Heights Cambs......43 J12
Ramsey Island Essex.......23 J3
Ramsey Island Pembks......24 C4
Ramsey Mereside Cambs.....43 J11
Ramsey St Mary's Cambs....43 J11
Ramsgate Kent.............23 Q9
Ramsgill N York...........65 K12
Ramshope Nthumb...........80 G12
Ramshorn Staffs...........50 E10
Ramsnest Common
  Surrey..................10 F4
Ranby Lincs...............52 H7
Ranby Notts...............51 P5
Rand Lincs................52 G7
Randalls Park
  Crematorium Surrey......21 J11
Randwick Gloucs...........29 L7
Ranfurly Rens.............84 G9
Rangemore Staffs..........40 F3
Rangeworthy S Glos........29 J10
Rankinston E Ayrs.........76 H8
Rannoch Station P & K.....91 J1
Ranscombe Somset..........16 C7
Ranskill Notts............51 P4
Ranton Staffs.............49 Q10
Ranton Green Staffs.......49 Q10
Ranworth Norfk............45 M7
Raploch Stirlg............85 N4
Rapness Ork...............111 h1
Rascarrel D & G...........70 D6
Rashfield Ag & B..........84 C6
Rashwood Worcs............30 B2
Raskelf N York............66 C12
Rastrick Calder...........58 F9
Ratagan Highld............97 N6
Ratby Leics...............41 L6
Ratcliffe Culey Leics.....41 J7
Ratcliffe on Soar Notts...41 L2
Ratcliffe on the Wreake
  Leics...................41 N5
Rathen Abers..............103 K3
Rathillet Fife............93 L10
Rathmell N York...........63 P9
Ratho C Edin..............86 D7
Ratho Station C Edin......86 D7
Rathven Moray.............101 N3
Ratley Warwks.............31 J5
Ratling Kent..............23 N11
Ratlinghope Shrops........38 H3
Rattar Highld.............110 F2
Rattery Devon.............5 P7
Rattlesden Suffk..........34 F5
Ratton Village E Susx.....12 C9
Rattray P & K.............92 H6
Raunds Nhants.............32 E3
Ravenfield Rothm..........51 L2
Ravenglass Cumb...........62 C3
Raveningham Norfk.........45 N10
Ravenscar N York..........67 L7
Ravenscraig N Lans........85 N10
Ravensden Bed.............32 F6
Ravenshead Notts..........51 M9
Ravensthorpe Kirk.........58 G9
Ravensthorpe Nhants.......41 P12
Ravenstone Leics..........41 K5
Ravenstone M Keyn.........32 C6
Ravenstonedale Cumb.......63 N2
Ravenstruther S Lans......77 Q3
Ravensworth N York........65 K6
Rawcliffe E R Yk..........59 M4
Rawcliffe E R Yk..........59 P9
Rawdon Leeds..............58 G6
Rawdon Crematorium
  Leeds...................58 G6
Rawling Street Kent.......22 H10
Rawmarsh Rothm............51 K2
Rawreth Essex.............22 F5
Rawridge Devon............6 G2
Rawtenstall Lancs.........57 P4
Raydon Suffk..............34 H8
Rayleigh Essex............22 F5
Rayne Essex...............34 C11
Raynes Park Gt Lon........21 K9
Reach Cambs...............33 N4
Read Lancs................57 P2
Reading Readg.............20 B8
Reading Crematorium
  Readg...................20 B8
Reading Services W Berk...20 A9
Reading Street Kent.......12 H4
Reading Street Kent.......23 Q9
Reagill Cumb..............64 B4
Realwa Cnwll..............2 F8
Rearquhar Highld..........107 M4
Rearsby Leics.............41 P5
Reay Highld...............110 A3
Reculver Kent.............23 N9
Red Ball Devon............16 E11
Redberth Pembks...........25 J7
Redbourn Herts............21 H2
Redbourne N Linc..........52 F4
Redbrook Gloucs...........28 G6
Redbrook Wrexhm...........49 K7
Redbrook Street Kent......12 H3
Redburn Highld............100 E10

Redcar R & Cl.............66 E3
Redcastle D & G...........70 D13
Redcastle Highld..........107 J11
Redding Falk..............85 Q7
Reddingmuirhead Falk......85 Q7
Redditch Worcs............30 D1
Redditch Crematorium
  Worcs...................30 D1
Rede Suffk................34 D5
Redenhall Norfk...........45 L12
Redesmouth Nthumb.........72 F5
Redford Abers.............95 M7
Redford Angus.............93 P6
Redford W Susx............10 D5
Redfordgreen Border.......79 M6
Redgorton P & K...........92 G9
Redgrave Suffk............34 H2
Redhill Abers.............95 M2
Red Hill Bmouth...........8 G8
Redhill Herts.............33 J9
Redhill N Som.............17 M4
Redhill Surrey............21 L12
Redisham Suffk............45 N12
Redland Bristl............17 N2
Redland Ork...............111 h2
Redlingfield Suffk........35 K3
Redlingfield Green Suffk..35 K3
Red Lodge Suffk...........34 B3
Redlynch Somset...........17 Q9
Redlynch Wilts............8 H3
Redmarley Worcs...........39 N8
Redmarley D'Abitot
  Gloucs..................29 K3
Redmarshall S on T........65 P4
Redmile Leics.............42 B3
Redmire N York............65 J8
Redmyre Abers.............95 M6
Rednal Shrops.............48 H9
Redpoint Highld...........105 K4
Red Roses Carmth..........25 L6
Red Row Nthumb............73 M2
Redruth Cnwll.............2 G7
Redstone P & K............92 H8
Red Wharf Bay IoA.........54 G5
Redwick Newpt.............28 E11
Redwick S Glos............28 G10
Redworth Darltn...........65 M3
Reed Herts................33 K9
Reedham Norfk.............45 N9
Reedness E R Yk...........60 D9
Reeds Holme Lancs.........57 P4
Reepham Lincs.............52 E8
Reepham Norfk.............44 H5
Reeth N York..............65 J7
Reeves Green Solhll.......40 H11
Regil N Som...............17 M4
Reiff Highld..............108 A11
Reigate Surrey............21 K12
Reisque Abers.............103 J10
Reiss Highld..............110 G5
Relubbus Cnwll............2 F8
Relugas Moray.............100 F5
Remenham Wokham...........20 C6
Remenham Hill Wokham......20 C6
Rempstone Notts...........41 M3
Rendcomb Gloucs...........30 D5
Rendham Suffk.............35 M4
Rendlesham Suffk..........35 M6
Renfrew Rens..............84 H9
Renhold Bed...............32 F6
Renishaw Derbys...........51 K5
Rennington Nthumb.........81 P9
Renton W Duns.............84 G7
Renwick Cumb..............72 B11
Repps Norfk...............45 N6
Repton Derbys.............40 H3
Resaurie Highld...........107 L12
Resipole Highld...........89 P4
Reskadinnick Cnwll........2 F7
Resolis Highld............107 L8
Resolven Neath............26 H8
Rest and be thankful
  Ag & B..................84 D2
Reston Border.............87 R9
Reswallie Angus...........93 P5
Retford Notts.............51 P5
Rettendon Essex...........22 F4
Revesby Lincs.............53 J10
Rewe Devon................6 C3
Rew Street IoW............9 M8
Reydon Suffk..............35 P2
Reymerston Norfk..........44 G8
Reynalton Pembks..........25 J7
Reynoldston Swans.........26 C10
Rezare Cnwll..............4 H5
Rhandirmwyn Carmth........37 M11
Rhayader Powys............37 Q7
Rheindown Highld..........106 H11
Rhes-y-cae Flints.........48 E2
Rhewl Denbgs..............48 C4
Rhewl Denbgs..............48 D6
Rhicarn Highld............108 C10
Rhiconich Highld..........108 F5
Rhicullen Highld..........107 L7
Rhigos Rhondd.............27 K7
Rhireavach Highld.........105 Q4
Rhives Highld.............107 N3
Rhiwbina Cardif...........27 N11
Rhiwderyn Newpt...........28 B10
Rhiwlas Gwynd.............54 H8
Rhiwlas Gwynd.............47 N5
Rhoden Green Kent.........12 D2
Rhodes Minnis Kent........13 M2
Rhodiad-y-brenin
  Pembks..................24 D4
Rhonehouse D & G..........70 C4
Rhoose V Glam.............16 E3
Rhos Carmth...............25 P2
Rhos Neath................26 G8
Rhoscolyn IoA.............54 C6
Rhoscrowther Pembks.......24 F6
Rhosesmor Flints..........48 E2
Rhosgoch Powys............38 E11
Rhoshill Pembks...........36 C11
Rhoshirwaun Gwynd.........46 C5
Rhoslefain Gwynd..........47 J9
Rhosllanerchrugog
  Wrexhm..................48 F6
Rhosmeirch IoA............54 F6
Rhosneigr IoA.............54 D7
Rhosnesni Wrexhm..........48 G5
Rhôs-on-Sea Conwy.........55 M5
Rhossili Swans............26 P10
Rhostryfan Gwynd..........54 F9
Rhostyllen Wrexhm.........48 F6
Rhosybol IoA..............54 F4

Rhos-y-gwaliau Gwynd......47 Q4
Rhosymedre Wrexhm.........48 F7
Rhu Ag & B................84 E6
Rhuallt Denbgs............55 C1
Rhubodach Ag & B..........83 Q8
Rhuddlan Denbgs...........55 Q6
Rhyd Gwynd................47 K3
Rhydargaeau Carmth........25 Q4
Rhydcymerau Carmth........26 D2
Rhyd-Ddu Gwynd............54 H10
Rhydlewis Cerdgn..........36 F10
Rhydowen Cerdgn...........36 G10
Rhyd-uchaf Gwynd..........47 P4
Rhyd-y-clafdy Gwynd.......46 E4
Rhyd-y-foel Conwy.........55 N6
Rhydyfro Neath............26 F7
Rhyd-y-groes Gwynd........54 H8
Rhyd-y pennau Cerdgn......37 K4
Rhyl Denbgs...............55 Q5
Rhymney Caerph............27 N7
Rhynd P & K...............92 H10
Rhynie Abers..............101 P9
Rhynie Highld.............107 P6
Ribbesford Worcs..........39 P7
Ribbleton Lancs...........57 K3
Ribchester Lancs..........57 M2
Riby Lincs................52 H3
Riccall N York............59 N6
Riccarton Border..........79 Q9
Riccarton E Ayrs..........76 G4
Richards Castle Herefs....39 J8
Richmond Gt Lon...........21 J8
Richmond N York...........65 L7
Richmond Sheff............51 K4
Rickerscote Staffs........40 B4
Rickford N Som............17 L4
Rickham Devon.............5 P11
Rickinghall Suffk.........34 H2
Rickling Green Essex......33 N10
Rickmansworth Herts.......20 G5
Riddell Border............80 C8
Riddlecombe Devon.........15 K8
Riddlesden C Brad.........58 E5
Ridge Dorset..............8 D9
Ridge Herts...............21 K4
Ridge Wilts...............8 D2
Ridge Lane Warwks.........40 H8
Ridgeway Derbys...........51 K5
Ridgewell Essex...........34 C8
Ridgewood E Susx..........11 P6
Ridgmont C Beds...........32 D9
Riding Mill Nthumb........72 H8
Ridlington Norfk..........45 M4
Ridlington Rutlnd.........42 C9
Ridsdale Nthumb...........72 G4
Rievaulx N York...........66 E9
Rigg D & G................71 L3
Riggend N Lans............85 M8
Righoul Highld............100 D5
Rigsby Lincs..............53 L8
Rigside S Lans............78 E2
Riley Green Lancs.........57 L4
Rilla Mill Cnwll..........4 G5
Rillington N York.........67 J11
Rimington Lancs...........63 P11
Rimpton Somset............17 N10
Rimswell E R Yk...........61 M8
Rinaston Pembks...........24 H4
Rindleford Shrops.........39 N3
Ringford D & G............69 Q7
Ringland Norfk............45 J7
Ringmer E Susx............11 P7
Ringmore Devon............5 N10
Ringmore Devon............6 C8
Ringorm Moray.............101 K6
Ringsfield Suffk..........45 N11
Ringsfield Corner Suffk...45 N11
Ringshall Herts...........20 F1
Ringshall Suffk...........34 G6
Ringshall Stocks Suffk....34 H6
Ringstead Nhants..........32 E2
Ringstead Norfk...........44 B3
Ringwood Hants............8 H6
Ringwould Kent............13 Q1
Ripe E Susx...............11 P7
Ripley Derbys.............51 K10
Ripley Hants..............8 H7
Ripley N York.............58 H3
Ripley Surrey.............20 G11
Riplington Hants..........9 Q2
Ripon N York..............65 N12
Rippingale Lincs..........42 F5
Ripple Kent...............23 Q12
Ripple Worcs..............29 M2
Ripponden Calder.........58 D9
Risabus Ag & B............74 D4
Risbury Herefs............39 K10
Risby Suffk...............34 D4
Risca Caerph..............27 P9
Rise E R Yk...............61 K6
Risegate Lincs............42 H4
Riseley Bed...............32 F4
Riseley Wokham............20 B10
Rishangles Suffk..........35 J3
Rishton Lancs.............57 N3
Rishworth Calder.........58 D9
Risley Derbys.............41 L1
Risley Warrtn.............57 M9
Risplith N York...........58 G1
River Kent................13 P2
River W Susx..............10 F5
Riverford Highld..........107 J10
Riverhead Kent............21 P11
Rivington Lancs...........57 L6
Rivington Services Lancs..57 L6
Roade Nhants..............31 Q4
Roadmeetings S Lans.......77 P2
Roadside E Ayrs...........77 K7
Roadside Highld...........110 D4
Roadwater Somset..........16 D8
Roag Highld...............96 C2
Roan of Craigoch S Ayrs...76 E9
Roath Cardif..............27 P12
Roberton Border...........79 N6
Roberton S Lans...........78 F3
Robertsbridge E Susx......12 E5
Robertstown Rhondd........27 K7
Robeston Wathen
  Pembks..................25 J5
Rogbill Tower D & G.......71 J3
Robin Hood
  Crematorium Solhll......40 E10
Robin Hood Doncaster
  Sheffield Airport Donc..51 P2
Robin Hood's Bay N York...67 K6
Roborough Devon...........5 K7

Roborough Devon...........15 K8
Roby Knows................56 H10
Rocester Staffs...........50 E11
Roch Pembks...............24 F5
Rochdale Rochdl...........58 B10
Rochdale Crematorium
  Rochdl..................57 Q6
Roche Cnwll...............3 L4
Rochester Medway..........22 E9
Rochester Nthumb..........72 E2
Rochford Essex............22 G5
Rochford Worcs............39 L8
Rock Cnwll................3 L1
Rock Nthumb...............81 P9
Rock Worcs................39 N7
Rockbeare Devon...........6 D4
Rockbourne Hants..........8 G4
Rockcliffe Cumb...........71 M4
Rockcliffe D & G..........70 D5
Rockend Torbay............6 C9
Rock Ferry Wirral.........56 G10
Rockfield Highld..........107 Q6
Rockfield Mons............28 F6
Rockford Devon............15 N3
Rockhampton S Glos........28 H9
Rockhill Shrops...........38 F6
Rockingham Nhants.........42 C10
Rockland All Saints Norfk.44 G10
Rockland St Mary Norfk....45 M8
Rockland St Peter Norfk...44 G9
Rockley Notts.............51 Q6
Rockville Ag & B..........84 D5
Rockwell End Bucks........20 C6
Rodborough Gloucs.........29 L7
Rodbourne Swindn..........18 G4
Rodbourne Wilts...........18 D4
Rodden Dorset.............7 N6
Rode Somset...............18 B9
Rode Heath Ches E.........49 P4
Rodel W Isls..............111 c4
Roden Wrekin..............49 L11
Rodhuish Somset...........16 D8
Rodington Wrekin..........49 L11
Rodington Heath Wrekin....49 L11
Rodley Gloucs.............29 K6
Rodmarton Gloucs..........29 N8
Rodmell E Susx............11 N8
Rodmersham Kent...........22 H10
Rodmersham Green Kent.....22 H10
Rodney Stoke Somset.......17 L6
Rodsley Derbys............50 G11
Roecliffe N York..........59 J2
Roe Green Herts...........21 K2
Roe Green Herts...........33 K9
Roehampton Gt Lon.........21 K8
Roffey W Susx.............11 K4
Rogart Highld.............107 M2
Rogate W Susx.............10 D5
Rogerstone Newpt..........28 C10
Roghadal W Isls...........111 c4
Rogiet Mons...............28 E10
Roke Oxon.................19 Q3
Roker Sundld..............73 P8
Rollesby Norfk............45 P7
Rolleston Leics...........41 Q7
Rolleston Notts...........51 Q9
Rolleston on Dove Staffs..40 G3
Rolston E R Yk............61 L5
Rolvenden Kent............12 G4
Rolvenden Layne Kent......12 G4
Romaldkirk Dur............65 J3
Romanby N York............65 P8
Romanno Bridge Border.....86 D11
Romansleigh Devon.........15 M7
Romesdal Highld...........104 E10
Romford Dorset............8 F5
Romford Gt Lon............21 P5
Romiley Stockp............50 C3
Romsey Hants..............9 L3
Romsley Shrops............39 P5
Romsley Worcs.............40 C10
Rona Highld...............105 J10
Ronachan Ag & B...........83 L11
Rookhope Dur..............72 G11
Rookley IoW...............9 N9
Rooks Bridge Somset.......17 K5
Rooks Nest Somset.........16 E9
Rookwith N York...........65 L9
Roos E R Yk...............61 M7
Roothams Green Bed........32 F5
Ropley Hants..............9 Q2
Ropley Dean Hants.........9 Q2
Ropsley Lincs.............42 E4
Rora Abers................103 L5
Rorrington Shrops.........38 F3
Rosarie Moray.............101 M5
Rose Cnwll................3 J5
Rose Ash Devon............15 N7
Rosebank S Lans...........77 N2
Rosebush Pembks...........25 J3
Rosedale Abbey N York.....66 G8
Rose Green Essex..........34 E10
Rose Green Suffk..........34 F7
Rose Green Suffk..........34 F8
Rose Green W Susx.........10 E9
Rosehall Highld...........108 H2
Rosehearty Abers..........103 J2
Rose Hill Lancs...........57 P3
Roseisle Moray............100 H2
Roselands E Susx..........12 C9
Rosemarket Pembks.........24 G7
Rosemarkie Highld.........107 M10
Rosemary Lane Devon.......16 F12
Rosemount P & K...........92 H7
Rosenannon Cnwll..........3 L3
Rosewell Mdloth...........86 F9
Roseworth S on T..........65 Q3
Rosgill Cumb..............71 Q10
Roskhill Highld...........96 C2
Rosley Cumb...............71 M6
Roslin Mdloth.............86 F9
Rosliston Derbys..........40 G4
Rosneath Ag & B...........84 E6
Ross D & G................69 P9
Rossett Wrexhm............48 G4
Rossett Green N York......58 H4
Rossington Donc..........51 N3
Ross-on-Wye Herefs........28 H4
Roster Highld.............110 F7
Rostherne Ches E..........57 N11
Rosthwaite Cumb...........71 L11
Roston Derbys.............50 F11
Rosyth Fife...............86 D5
Rothbury Nthumb...........73 J1
Rotherby Leics............41 P4
Rotherfield E Susx........12 C4

Rotherfield Greys Oxon....20 B7
Rotherfield Peppard
  Oxon...................20 B7
Rotherham Rothm...........51 K3
Rotherham
  Crematorium Rothm......51 L3
Rothersthorpe Nhants......31 Q3
Rotherwick Hants..........20 B11
Rothes Moray..............101 K5
Rothesay Ag & B...........84 B9
Rothiebrisbane Abers......102 G7
Rothiemay Moray...........102 D5
Rothiemurchus Lodge
  Highld.................99 P7
Rothiemurchus Visitor
  Centre Highld..........99 N6
Rothienorman Abers........102 F7
Rothley Leics.............41 N5
Rothmaise Abers...........102 F8
Rothwell Leeds............59 J8
Rothwell Lincs............52 G4
Rothwell Nhants...........32 B1
Rottal Lodge Angus........94 F7
Rottingdean Br & H........11 M9
Rottington Cumb...........70 F11
Roucan D & G..............78 G12
Roucan Loch
  Crematorium D & G......78 G12
Rougham Norfk.............44 D6
Rougham Suffk.............34 E4
Rough Common Kent.........23 L10
Roughpark Abers...........101 L11
Roughton Lincs............53 J9
Roughton Norfk............45 K3
Roughton Shrops...........39 N4
Roundbush Green Essex.....22 C1
Round Green Luton.........32 F11
Roundham Somset...........7 K2
Roundhay Leeds............59 J6
Roundway Wilts............18 E7
Roundyhill Angus..........93 L5
Rousay Ork................111 h1
Rousdon Devon.............6 H5
Rousham Oxon..............31 L8
Rous Lench Worcs..........30 D4
Routenburn N Ayrs.........84 D10
Routh E R Yk..............61 J6
Row Cumb..................63 J4
Rowanburn D & G...........79 N12
Rowardennan Stirlg........84 F4
Rowarth Derbys............50 D3
Rowberrow Somset..........17 L5
Rowde Wilts...............18 E8
Rowen Conwy...............55 L7
Rowfoot Nthumb............72 C8
Rowhedge Essex............34 G11
Rowington Warwks..........40 G12
Rowland Derbys............50 G6
Rowland's Castle Hants....10 B7
Rowland's Gill Gatesd.....73 L8
Rowledge Surrey...........10 D2
Rowley Dur................73 J10
Rowley Regis Sandw........40 C9
Rowley Regis
  Crematorium Sandw......40 C9
Rowlstone Herefs..........28 D4
Rowly Surrey..............10 G2
Rowner Hants..............9 P7
Rowney Green Worcs........40 D12
Rownhams Hants............9 L4
Rownhams Services
  Hants..................9 L4
Rowrah Cumb...............70 H10
Rowsham Bucks.............32 C12
Rowsley Derbys............50 G7
Rowston Lincs.............52 F11
Rowton Ches W.............49 J3
Rowton Wrekin.............49 L10
Roxburgh Border...........80 F7
Roxby N Linc..............60 F10
Roxton Bed................32 G6
Roxwell Essex.............22 D2
Royal Leamington Spa
  Warwks.................30 H2
Royal Sutton Coldfield
  Birm...................40 E8
Royal Tunbridge Wells
  Kent...................12 C3
Royal Wootton Bassett
  Wilts..................18 F4
Royal Yacht Britannia
  C Edin.................86 F6
Roy Bridge Highld.........98 C10
Roydon Essex..............21 N2
Roydon Norfk..............44 H1
Roydon Norfk..............44 B5
Roydon Hamlet Essex.......21 N2
Royston Barns.............59 J11
Royston Herts.............33 K8
Royton Oldham............58 B11
Rozel Jersey..............7 c1
Ruabon Wrexhm.............48 F6
Ruaig Ag & B..............88 D6
Ruan Lanihorne Cnwll......3 K7
Ruan Major Cnwll..........2 G11
Ruan Minor Cnwll..........2 G11
Ruardean Gloucs...........28 H5
Ruardean Hill Gloucs......28 H5
Ruardean Woodside
  Gloucs.................28 H5
Rubery Birm...............40 C11
Rubha Ban W Isls..........111 b6
Ruckhall Herefs...........28 E2
Ruckinge Kent.............13 K4
Ruckley Shrops............39 K3
Rudby N York..............66 C6
Rudchester Nthumb.........73 K7
Ruddington Notts..........41 M2
Rudge Somset..............18 B8
Rudgeway S Glos...........28 H10
Rudgwick W Susx...........10 H4
Rudheath Ches W...........49 M2
Rudley Green Essex........22 G3
Rudloe Wilts..............18 C6
Rudry Caerph..............27 P10
Rudston E R Yk............61 J1
Rudyard Staffs............50 C8
Ruecastle Border.........80 E8
Rufford Lancs.............57 J6
Rufford Abbey Notts.......51 N7
Rufforth C York...........59 M4
Rugby Warwks..............41 L11
Rugeley Staffs............40 D4
Ruishton Somset...........16 H10
Ruislip Gt Lon............20 H6
Rùm Highld................96 D9
Rumbach Moray.............101 M5

Rumbling Bridge P & K....86 B3
Rumburgh Suffk....35 M1
Rumford Cnwll....3 K2
Rumford Falk....85 Q7
Rumney Cardif....27 P11
Runcorn Halton....57 K11
Runcton W Susx....10 E9
Runcton Holme Norfk....43 P8
Runfold Surrey....10 D1
Runhall Norfk....44 H8
Runham Norfk....45 P7
Runnington Somset....16 F10
Runswick N York....66 H4
Runtaleave Angus....94 E8
Runway Visitor Park
  Manch....57 P11
Runwell Essex....22 F5
Ruscombe Wokham....20 C8
Rushall Herefs....28 H2
Rushall Norfk....45 K12
Rushall Wilts....18 G9
Rushbrooke Suffk....34 E5
Rushbury Shrops....39 K4
Rushden Herts....33 K9
Rushden Nhants....32 D4
Rushenden Kent....22 H8
Rushford Norfk....34 F1
Rush Green Essex....23 M1
Rush Green Gt Lon....21 P6
Rush Green Warrtn....57 M10
Rushlake Green E Susx....12 D6
Rushmere Suffk....45 P11
Rushmoor Surrey....10 E3
Rushock Worcs....40 B12
Rusholme Manch....57 Q9
Rushton Nhants....42 B12
Rushton Spencer Staffs....50 C8
Rushwick Worcs....39 P10
Rushyford Dur....65 M2
Ruskie Stirlg....85 K3
Ruskington Lincs....52 F12
Rusland Cross Cumb....62 G5
Rusper W Susx....11 K3
Ruspidge Gloucs....29 J6
Russell's Water Oxon....20 B5
Russ Hill Surrey....11 K3
Rusthall Kent....12 C3
Rustington W Susx....10 G9
Ruston N York....67 K10
Ruston Parva E R Yk....60 H2
Ruswarp N York....67 J5
Rutherford Border....80 E7
Rutherglen S Lans....85 K10
Ruthernbridge Cnwll....3 M3
Ruthin Denbgs....48 D4
Ruthrieston C Aber....95 Q2
Ruthven Abers....101 P6
Ruthven Angus....93 K6
Ruthven Highld....99 L8
Ruthvoes Cnwll....3 K4
Ruthwell D & G....70 H3
Ruyton-XI-Towns Shrops....48 H10
Ryal Nthumb....72 H6
Ryall Dorset....7 K4
Ryall Worcs....29 M1
Ryarsh Kent....22 D10
Rydal Cumb....62 G2
Ryde IoW....9 P8
Rye E Susx....12 H6
Rye Foreign E Susx....12 H5
Rye Street Worcs....29 K2
Ryhall Rutlnd....42 E7
Ryhill Wakefd....59 J10
Ryhope Sundld....73 P9
Ryland Lincs....52 E7
Rylands Notts....41 M1
Rylstone N York....58 C3
Ryme Intrinseca Dorset....7 N1
Ryther N York....59 M6
Ryton Gatesd....73 K7
Ryton Shrops....39 N2
Ryton-on-Dunsmore
  Warwks....41 J11

S

Sabden Lancs....57 P2
Sacombe Herts....33 K11
Sacriston Dur....73 M10
Sadberge Darltn....65 N4
Saddell Ag & B....75 L6
Saddington Leics....41 P8
Saddle Bow Norfk....43 P7
Saddlescombe W Susx....11 L7
Saffron Walden Essex....33 N8
Sageston Pembks....25 J7
Saham Hills Norfk....44 E9
Saham Toney Norfk....44 E9
Saighton Ches W....49 J3
St Abbs Border....81 J1
St Agnes Border....87 M9
St Agnes Cnwll....2
St Agnes IoS....2 b3
St Agnes Mining District
  Cnwll....2 G6
St Albans Herts....21 J2
St Allen Cnwll....3 J5
St Andrew Guern....6 b2
St Andrews Fife....93 N11
St Andrews Botanic
  Garden Fife....93 N11
St Andrew's Major V Glam....16 F2
St Andrews Well Dorset....7 L4
St Anne's Lancs....56 G3
St Ann's D & G....78 H9
St Ann's Chapel Cnwll....5 J6
St Ann's Chapel Devon....5 L8
St Anthony Cnwll....2 H10
St Anthony's Hill E Susx....12 D9
St Arvans Mons....28 H3
St Asaph Denbgs....48 B3
St Athan V Glam....16 D3
St Aubin Jersey....7 b2
St Austell Cnwll....3 M5
St Bees Cumb....70 F12
St Blazey Cnwll....3 M5
St Boswells Border....80 D7
St Brelade Jersey....7 a2
St Brelade's Bay Jersey....7 a2
St Breock Cnwll....3 L3
St Breward Cnwll....4 D5
St Briavels Gloucs....28 G7
St Bride's Major V Glam....16 B2
St Brides-super-Ely
  V Glam....27 M12

St Brides Wentlooge
  Newpt....28 C11
St Budeaux C Plym....5 K8
Saintbury Gloucs....30 E6
St Buryan Cnwll....2 C9
St Catherines Ag & B....84 C2
St Chloe Gloucs....29 L8
St Clears Carmth....25 M5
St Cleer Cnwll....4 F6
St Clement Cnwll....3 J7
St Clement Jersey....7 c2
St Clether Cnwll....4 F4
St Colmac Ag & B....83 Q9
St Columb Major Cnwll....3 K3
St Columb Minor Cnwll....3 J4
St Columb Road Cnwll....3 K4
St Combs Abers....103 L3
St Cross South Elmham
  Suffk....45 L12
St Cyrus Abers....95 M8
St David's P & K....92 E10
St Davids Pembks....24 D4
St David's Cathedral
  Pembks....24 D4
St Day Cnwll....2 G7
St Dennis Cnwll....3 L4
St Dogmaels Pembks....36 C10
St Dominick Cnwll....5 J6
St Donats V Glam....16 C3
St Endellion Cnwll....4 C5
St Enoder Cnwll....3 K4
St Erme Cnwll....3 J6
St Erney Cnwll....4 H8
St Erth Cnwll....2 E8
St Erth Praze Cnwll....2 E8
St Ervan Cnwll....3 K2
St Eval Cnwll....3 K3
St Ewe Cnwll....3 L6
St Fagans Cardif....27 N12
St Fagans: National
  History Museum
  Cardif....27 N12
St Fergus Abers....103 M5
St Fillans P & K....91 Q10
St Florence Pembks....25 J8
St Gennys Cnwll....14 C11
St George Conwy....55 P6
St Georges N Som....17 K4
St George's V Glam....16 E2
St Germans Cnwll....4 H8
St Giles in the Wood
  Devon....15 J8
St Giles-on-the-Heath
  Devon....4 H3
St Harmon Powys....38 B7
St Helen Auckland Dur....65 L3
St Helens IoW....9 Q9
St Helens St Hel....57 K9
St Helens Crematorium
  St Hel....57 J9
St Helier Gt Lon....21 L9
St Helier Jersey....7 b2
St Hilary Cnwll....2 E9
St Hilary V Glam....16 D2
St Ippollitts Herts....32 H10
St Ishmael's Pembks....24 F7
St Issey Cnwll....3 L2
St Ive Cnwll....4 G6
St Ives Cambs....33 K3
St Ives Cnwll....2 D7
St James's End Nhants....31 Q3
St James South
  Elmham Suffk....35 M1
St Jidgey Cnwll....3 L2
St John Cnwll....5 J9
St John Jersey....7 b1
St John's IoM....56 b5
St John's Kent....21 Q11
St Johns Surrey....20 F10
St Johns Worcs....39 Q10
St John's Chapel Devon....15 J6
St John's Chapel Dur....72 F12
St John's Fen End Norfk....43 N7
St John's Kirk S Lans....78 F2
St John's Town of Dalry
  D & G....69 N3
St John's Wood Gt Lon....21 L6
St Jude's IoM....56 d3
St Just Cnwll....2 B9
St Just-in-Roseland
  Cnwll....3 J8
St Just Mining District
  Cnwll....2 B8
St Katherines Abers....102 H8
St Keverne Cnwll....2 H10
St Kew Cnwll....3 M1
St Kew Highway Cnwll....3 M1
St Keyne Cnwll....4 F7
St Lawrence Essex....23 J3
St Lawrence IoW....9 N11
St Lawrence Jersey....7 b1
St Lawrence Kent....23 Q9
St Leonards Bucks....20 E3
St Leonards Dorset....8 G6
St Leonards E Susx....12 F8
St Levan Cnwll....2 B10
St Lythans V Glam....16 F2
St Mabyn Cnwll....3 M1
St Madoes P & K....92 H10
St Margarets Herefs....28 D3
St Margarets Herts....21 M2
St Margaret's at Cliffe
  Kent....13 Q2
St Margaret South
  Elmham Suffk....45 M12
St Marks IoM....56 c6
St Martin Cnwll....2 H10
St Martin Cnwll....4 G8
St Martin Guern....6 b2
St Martin Jersey....7 c1
St Martin's IoS....2 c1
St Martin's P & K....92 H9
St Martins Shrops....48 H8
St Mary Jersey....7 a1
St Mary Bourne Hants....19 M10
St Marychurch Torbay....6 C9
St Mary Church V Glam....16 D2
St Mary Cray Gt Lon....21 P9
St Mary in the Marsh Kent....13 K5
St Marylebone
  Crematorium Gt Lon....21 L6
St Mary's IoS....2 c2
St Mary's Ork....111 h2
St Mary's Bay Kent....13 L5
St Mary's Hoo Medway....22 F7
St Maughans Green Mons....28 F5

St Mawes Cnwll....3 J8
St Mawgan Cnwll....3 K3
St Mellion Cnwll....5 J7
St Mellons Cardif....27 P11
St Merryn Cnwll....3 K2
St Michael Caerhays Cnwll....3 L7
St Michael Church Somset....17 J9
St Michael Penkevil Cnwll....3 J7
St Michaels Kent....12 H3
St Michaels Worcs....39 L8
St Michael's Mount Cnwll....2 D9
St Michael's on Wyre
  Lancs....57 J1
St Minver Cnwll....3 L1
St Monans Fife....87 K2
St Neot Cnwll....4 E6
St Neots Cambs....32 H5
St Newlyn East Cnwll....3 J5
St Nicholas Pembks....24 F2
St Nicholas V Glam....16 E2
St Nicholas at Wade Kent....23 N9
St Ninians Stirlg....85 N5
St Olaves Norfk....45 P9
St Osyth Essex....23 L1
St Ouen Jersey....7 a1
St Owens Cross Herefs....28 G4
St Paul's Cray Gt Lon....21 P9
St Paul's Walden Herts....32 H11
St Peter Jersey....7 a1
St Peter Port Guern....6 b2
St Peter's Guern....6 a2
St Peter's Kent....23 Q9
St Pinnock Cnwll....4 F7
St Quivox S Ayrs....76 F6
St Sampson Guern....6 c1
St Saviour Guern....6 b2
St Saviour Jersey....7 b2
St Stephen Cnwll....3 L5
St Stephens Cnwll....4 H3
St Stephens Cnwll....5 J8
St Teath Cnwll....4 D4
St Tudy Cnwll....3 N1
St Twynnells Pembks....24 G8
St Veep Cnwll....4 E8
St Vigeans Angus....93 Q7
St Wenn Cnwll....3 L3
St Weonards Herefs....28 F4
Salcey Forest Nhants....32 B6
Salcombe Devon....5 P11
Salcombe Regis Devon....6 F5
Salcott-cum-Virley Essex....23 J1
Sale Traffd....57 P9
Saleby Lincs....53 M6
Sale Green Worcs....30 B3
Salehurst E Susx....12 E5
Salem Cerdgn....37 L4
Salen Ag & B....89 M7
Salen Highld....89 N4
Salford C Beds....32 D8
Salford Oxon....30 H8
Salford Salfd....57 P8
Salford Priors Warwks....30 D4
Salfords Surrey....11 L2
Salhouse Norfk....45 M7
Saline Fife....86 B4
Salisbury Wilts....8 G2
Salisbury Crematorium
  Wilts....8 H2
Salisbury Plain Wilts....18 F10
Salkeld Dykes Cumb....71 Q7
Salle Norfk....45 J5
Salmonby Lincs....53 K8
Salperton Gloucs....30 E9
Salsburgh N Lans....85 N9
Salt Staffs....40 C2
Saltaire C Brad....58 F6
Saltaire C Brad....58 F6
Saltash Cnwll....5 J8
Saltburn Highld....107 M8
Saltburn-by-the-Sea
  R & Cl....66 F4
Saltby Leics....42 C5
Saltcoats N Ayrs....76 D3
Saltdean Br & H....11 M9
Salterbeck Cumb....70 G9
Salterforth Lancs....58 B5
Salterton Wilts....18 G12
Saltfleet Lincs....53 M5
Saltfleetby All Saints
  Lincs....53 M5
Saltfleetby St Clement
  Lincs....53 M5
Saltfleetby St Peter Lincs....53 M5
Saltford BaNES....17 P3
Salthouse Norfk....44 H2
Saltmarshe E R Yk....60 D8
Saltney Flints....48 H3
Salton N York....66 G10
Saltrens Devon....14 H7
Saltwell Crematorium
  Gatesd....73 M8
Saltwood Kent....13 M3
Salvington W Susx....10 H8
Salwarpe Worcs....39 Q8
Salway Ash Dorset....7 L4
Sambourne Warwks....30 D2
Sambrook Wrekin....49 N9
Sampford Arundel
  Somset....16 F11
Sampford Brett Somset....16 E7
Sampford Courtenay
  Devon....15 L11
Sampford Moor Somset....16 F11
Sampford Peverell Devon....16 D12
Sampford Spiney Devon....5 L6
Samsonlane Ork....111 i2
Samuelston E Loth....87 J7
Sanaigmore Ag & B....82 C8
Sancreed Cnwll....2 C9
Sancton E R Yk....60 G6
Sandaig Highld....97 K6
Sandal Magna Wakefd....59 J9
Sandavore Highld....96 F11
Sanday Ork....111 i1
Sanday Airport Ork....111 i1
Sandbach Ches E....49 N4
Sandbach Services Ches E....49 P4
Sandbank Ag & B....84 C6
Sandbanks Poole....8 F9
Sandend Abers....102 D3
Sanderstead Gt Lon....21 M10
Sandford Cumb....64 C4
Sandford Devon....15 P10
Sandford Dorset....8 D9
Sandford Hants....8 H7
Sandford IoW....9 N10
Sandford N Som....17 K4

Sandford S Lans....77 M3
Sandford-on-Thames
  Oxon....19 N1
Sandford Orcas Dorset....17 P11
Sandford St Martin Oxon....31 K8
Sandgate Kent....13 M3
Sandhaven Abers....103 K2
Sandhead D & G....68 E8
Sand Hills Leeds....59 J6
Sandhills Oxon....31 M11
Sandhills Surrey....10 F3
Sandhoe Nthumb....72 H7
Sandhole Ag & B....83 Q4
Sand Hole E R Yk....60 D6
Sandholme E R Yk....60 E7
Sandhurst Br For....20 D10
Sandhurst Gloucs....29 L4
Sandhurst Kent....12 F4
Sand Hutton N York....59 P3
Sandhutton N York....65 P10
Sandiacre Derbys....51 L12
Sandilands Lincs....53 N7
Sandleheath Hants....8 G4
Sandleigh Oxon....19 M1
Sandley Dorset....8 C2
Sandness Shet....111 j4
Sandon Essex....22 E3
Sandon Herts....33 K9
Sandon Staffs....40 C2
Sandon Bank Staffs....40 C2
Sandown IoW....9 P9
Sandplace Cnwll....4 F8
Sandridge Herts....21 J2
Sandringham Norfk....44 B4
Sandsend N York....67 J4
Sandtoft N Linc....60 D11
Sandway Kent....22 H12
Sandwich Kent....23 P10
Sandwick Shet....111 k5
Sandwick W Isls....111 d2
Sandwith Cumb....70 F11
Sandy C Beds....32 G7
Sandyford D & G....79 K9
Sandygate Devon....6 B7
Sandygate IoM....56 d3
Sandyhills D & G....70 E5
Sandylands Lancs....62 H9
Sandy Lane Wilts....18 E7
Sandy Park Devon....5 P3
Sangobeg Highld....108 H3
Sangomore Highld....108 H3
Sankyn's Green Worcs....39 P8
Sanna Bay Highld....89 K3
Sanndabhaig W Isls....111 d2
Sannox N Ayrs....75 Q4
Sanquhar D & G....77 N8
Santon Bridge Cumb....62 C2
Santon Downham Suffk....44 D11
Sapcote Leics....41 L8
Sapey Common Herefs....39 M8
Sapiston Suffk....34 F2
Sapperton Gloucs....29 N7
Sapperton Lincs....42 E4
Saracen's Head Lincs....43 K5
Sarclet Highld....110 G7
Sarisbury Hants....9 N5
Sarn Gwynd....46 D5
Sarn Powys....38 E4
Sarn Powys....47 Q10
Sarnau Cerdgn....36 E9
Sarnau Powys....48 E11
Sarn Park Services
  Brdgnd....27 J11
Saron Carmth....26 E6
Saron Gwynd....54 G4
Sarratt Herts....20 G4
Sarre Kent....23 N9
Sarsden Oxon....30 H9
Satley Dur....73 K11
Satterleigh Devon....15 L8
Satterthwaite Cumb....62 G4
Sauchen Abers....102 F11
Saucher P & K....92 H8
Sauchieburn Abers....95 L1
Saul Gloucs....29 K7
Saundby Notts....52 B8
Saundersfoot Pembks....25 K7
Saunderton Bucks....20 C4
Saunton Devon....14 H5
Sausthorpe Lincs....53 L9
Savile Town Kirk....58 G9
Sawbridge Warwks....31 L2
Sawbridgeworth Herts....21 P2
Sawdon N York....67 K9
Sawley Derbys....51 L1
Sawley Lancs....63 P11
Sawley N York....58 G1
Sawston Cambs....33 M7
Sawtry Cambs....42 G12
Saxby Leics....42 B6
Saxby Lincs....52 E6
Saxby All Saints N Linc....60 G8
Saxelbye Leics....41 P4
Saxham Street Suffk....34 H5
Saxilby Lincs....52 C8
Saxlingham Norfk....44 H4
Saxlingham Green Norfk....45 L10
Saxlingham Nethergate
  Norfk....45 K10
Saxlingham Thorpe Norfk....45 K9
Saxmundham Suffk....35 N4
Saxondale Notts....51 P11
Saxon Street Cambs....34 B5
Saxtead Suffk....35 L4
Saxtead Green Suffk....35 L4
Saxtead Little Green Suffk....35 L4
Saxthorpe Norfk....45 J4
Saxton N York....59 L7
Sayers Common W Susx....11 L6
Scackleton N York....66 F11
Scafell Pike Cumb....62 D2
Scaftworth Notts....51 P3
Scagglethorpe N York....67 J11
Scalasaig Ag & B....82 E4
Scalby E R Yk....60 E8
Scalby N York....67 L9
Scaldwell Nhants....41 Q12
Scaleby Cumb....71 P3
Scalebyhill Cumb....71 P3
Scales Cumb....62 H2
Scales Cumb....71 M9
Scalford Leics....41 Q3
Scaling N York....66 H5
Scalloway Shet....111 k4
Scalpay Highld....96 H4
Scamblesby Lincs....53 J7
Scamodale Highld....90 B2
Scampston N York....67 J11

Scampton Lincs....52 D7
Scaniport Highld....99 J2
Scapegoat Hill Kirk....58 E10
Scarba Ag & B....83 K3
Scarborough N York....67 M9
Scarcewater Cnwll....3 K5
Scarcliffe Derbys....51 L7
Scarcroft Leeds....59 J6
Scarfskerry Highld....110 F2
Scarinish Ag & B....88 C7
Scarisbrick Lancs....56 H6
Scarning Norfk....44 F7
Scarrington Notts....51 Q11
Scartho NE Lin....53 J3
Scatsta Airport Shet....111 k3
Scawby Lincs....52 G3
Scawsby Donc....59 M12
Scawthorpe Donc....59 M11
Scawton N York....66 D10
Scayne's Hill W Susx....11 M5
Scethrog Powys....27 M4
Scholar Green Ches E....49 Q4
Scholemoor
  Crematorium C Brad....58 F7
Scholes Kirk....58 F11
Scholes Leeds....59 J6
Scholes Rothm....51 K2
Scholes Wigan....57 L7
Scissett Kirk....58 G11
Scleddau Pembks....24 G2
Scofton Notts....51 N5
Scole Norfk....35 J2
Scone P & K....92 H9
Sconser Highld....96 F4
Scoonie Fife....86 H2
Scopwick Lincs....52 F11
Scoraig Highld....105 Q3
Scorborough E R Yk....60 H5
Scorrier Cnwll....2 G7
Scorton Lancs....63 J11
Scorton N York....65 M7
Scotby Cumb....71 P5
Scotch Corner N York....65 L6
Scotforth Lancs....63 J9
Scothern Lincs....52 E7
Scotland P & K....52 E7
Scotlandwell P & K....86 E2
Scotscalder Station
  Highld....110 C5
Scot's Gap Nthumb....73 J4
Scotsmill Abers....102 D10
Scotstoun C Glas....85 J9
Scotswood N u Ty....73 L7
Scotter Lincs....52 C4
Scotterthorpe Lincs....52 C3
Scottish Seabird Centre
  E Loth....87 K5
Scottish Wool Centre
  Stirlg....85 J3
Scotton Lincs....52 C4
Scotton N York....59 J4
Scotton N York....65 L8
Scoulton Norfk....44 G9
Scourie Highld....108 D6
Scourie More Highld....108 D6
Scousburgh Shet....111 k5
Scrabster Highld....110 C2
Scraesburgh Border....80 F9
Scrane End Lincs....43 L2
Scraptoft Leics....41 P6
Scratby Norfk....45 Q7
Scrayingham N York....60 C2
Scredington Lincs....42 F2
Scremby Lincs....53 M9
Scremerston Nthumb....81 L4
Screveton Notts....51 Q11
Scriven N York....59 J3
Scrooby Notts....51 N3
Scropton Derbys....40 G2
Scrub Hill Lincs....52 H11
Scruton N York....65 N8
Scullomie Highld....109 L4
Sculthorpe Norfk....44 E4
Scunthorpe N Linc....60 F11
Seaborough Dorset....7 L2
Seabrook Kent....13 M3
Seaburn Sundld....73 Q8
Seacroft Leeds....59 J7
Seafield Highld....96 G5
Seafield W Loth....86 B8
Seafield Crematorium
  C Edin....86 F7
Seaford E Susx....11 N9
Seaforth Sefton....56 G9
Seagrave Leics....41 N4
Seaham Dur....73 P10
Seahouses Nthumb....81 P7
Seal Kent....22 B11
Sealand Flints....48 G2
Seale Surrey....10 E1
Seamer N York....65 C5
Seamer N York....67 L10
Seamill N Ayrs....76 D2
Sea Palling Norfk....45 N5
Searby Lincs....52 G3
Seasalter Kent....23 L9
Seascale Cumb....62 B3
Seathwaite Cumb....62 F4
Seatoller Cumb....71 L11
Seaton Cnwll....4 G8
Seaton Cumb....70 H8
Seaton Devon....6 H5
Seaton E R Yk....61 K5
Seaton Kent....23 N10
Seaton Nthumb....73 N5
Seaton Rutlnd....42 C9
Seaton Carew Hartpl....66 D2
Seaton Delaval Nthumb....73 N5
Seaton Ross E R Yk....60 D6
Seaton Sluice Nthumb....73 N5
Seatown Dorset....7 K4
Seave Green N York....66 E6
Seaview IoW....9 Q8
Seaville Cumb....71 J5
Seavington St Mary
  Somset....17 K12
Seavington St Michael
  Somset....17 K12
Sebergham Cumb....71 M7
Seckington Warwks....40 H6
Sedbergh Cumb....63 M4
Sedbury Gloucs....28 G9
Sedbusk N York....64 G8
Sedgeberrow Worcs....30 D6
Sedgebrook Lincs....42 C3
Sedgefield Dur....65 P2
Sedgeford Norfk....44 B3
Sedgehill Wilts....8 C2

Sedgemoor Services - South Bank 193

Sedgemoor Services Somset 17 J5
Sedgley Dudley 40 B8
Sedgwick Cumb 63 K5
Sedlescombe E Susx 12 F6
Sedrup Bucks 20 C2
Seend Wilts 18 D8
Seend Cleeve Wilts 18 D8
Seer Green Bucks 20 F5
Seething Norfk 45 M9
Sefton Sefton 56 G8
Seighford Staffs 49 Q9
Seion Gwynd 54 H8
Seisdon Staffs 39 Q3
Selattyn Shrops 48 F8
Selborne Hants 10 C4
Selby N York 59 N7
Selham W Susx 10 E6
Selhurst Gt Lon 21 M9
Selkirk Border 79 P3
Sellack Herefs 28 G4
Sellafirth Shet 111 k2
Sellindge Kent 13 L3
Selling Kent 23 K11
Sells Green Wilts 18 D8
Selly Oak Birm 40 D10
Selmeston E Susx 11 P8
Selsdon Gt Lon 21 M10
Selsey Gloucs 29 L7
Selsey W Susx 10 D10
Selside N York 64 E11
Selsted Kent 13 N2
Selston Notts 51 L9
Selworthy Somset 16 C6
Semer Suffk 34 G7
Semington Wilts 18 D8
Semley Wilts 8 D3
Send Surrey 20 G11
Senghenydd Caerph 27 N10
Sennen Cnwll 2 B10
Sennen Cove Cnwll 2 B9
Sennybridge Powys 27 K3
Sessay N York 66 C11
Setchey Norfk 43 Q7
Seton Mains E Loth 87 J7
Settle N York 63 P9
Settrington N York 67 J12
Sevenhampton Gloucs 30 D9
Sevenhampton Swindn 18 H3
Seven Hills Crematorium Suffk 35 K8
Seven Kings Gt Lon 21 P6
Sevenoaks Kent 21 Q11
Sevenoaks Weald Kent 21 Q12
Seven Sisters Neath 26 H7
Seven Star Green Essex 34 F10
Severn Beach S Glos 28 G10
Severn Stoke Worcs 39 Q12
Severn View Services S Glos 28 G10
Sevington Kent 13 K2
Sewards End Essex 33 P8
Sewell C Beds 32 E11
Sewerby E R Yk 61 L1
Seworgan Cnwll 2 G9
Sewstern Leics 42 C6
Sgiogarstaigh W Isls 111 e1
Shabbington Bucks 31 P11
Shackerstone Leics 41 J6
Shackleford Surrey 10 E2
Shader W Isls 111 d1
Shadforth Dur 73 N11
Shadingfield Suffk 45 P12
Shadoxhurst Kent 13 J3
Shadwell Norfk 44 F12
Shaftenhoe End Herts 33 L8
Shaftesbury Dorset 8 C3
Shafton Barns 59 K11
Shakerley Wigan 57 M8
Shalbourne Wilts 19 K7
Shalden Hants 10 B2
Shaldon Devon 6 C8
Shalfleet IoW 9 M9
Shalford Essex 34 C10
Shalford Surrey 10 G1
Shalford Green Essex 34 B10
Shalmsford Street Kent 23 L11
Shalstone Bucks 31 N6
Shamley Green Surrey 10 G2
Shandford Angus 94 H9
Shandon Ag & B 84 E6
Shandwick Highld 107 P7
Shangton Leics 41 Q8
Shanklin IoW 9 P10
Shap Cumb 71 Q11
Shapinsay Ork 111 h2
Shapwick Dorset 8 D7
Shapwick Somset 17 K8
Shardlow Derbys 41 K2
Shareshill Staffs 40 C6
Sharlston Wakefd 59 K9
Sharnbrook Bed 32 E5
Sharnford Leics 41 L8
Sharoe Green Lancs 57 K3
Sharow N York 65 N12
Sharpenhoe C Beds 32 F10
Sharperton Nthumb 81 K12
Sharpness Gloucs 29 J8
Sharrington Norfk 44 G3
Shatterford Worcs 39 P6
Shaugh Prior Devon 5 L7
Shavington Ches E 49 M5
Shaw Oldham 58 C11
Shaw W Berk 19 N7
Shaw Wilts 18 D7
Shawbirch Wrekin 49 M11
Shawbost W Isls 111 d1
Shawbury Shrops 49 K10
Shawell Leics 41 M10
Shawford Hants 9 M3
Shawhead D & G 70 E1
Shaw Mills N York 58 G2
Shawsburn S Lans 77 N2
Shearington D & G 70 G3
Shearsby Leics 41 N8
Shearston Somset 16 H9
Shebbear Devon 14 H9
Shebdon Staffs 49 N9
Shebster Highld 110 B3
Sheddens E Rens 85 J10
Shedfield Hants 9 P5
Sheen Staffs 50 E8
Sheepridge Kirk 58 F9
Sheepscar Leeds 58 H7
Sheepscombe Gloucs 29 M6
Sheepstor Devon 5 L6
Sheepwash Devon 14 H10
Sheepy Magna Leics 41 J7
Sheepy Parva Leics 41 J7
Sheering Essex 21 P1
Sheerness Kent 22 H8
Sheerwater Surrey 20 G10
Sheet Hants 10 C5
Sheffield Sheff 51 J4
Sheffield City Road Crematorium Sheff 51 J4
Sheffield Park E Susx 11 N5
Shefford C Beds 32 G8
Sheigra Highld 108 D4
Sheinton Shrops 39 L2
Shelderton Shrops 38 H6
Sheldon Birm 40 F9
Sheldon Derbys 50 F7
Sheldon Devon 6 F2
Sheldwich Kent 23 K11
Shelfanger Norfk 45 J12
Shelford Notts 51 P11
Shelley Kirk 58 G11
Shelley Suffk 34 G8
Shellingford Oxon 19 K3
Shellow Bowells Essex 22 C2
Shelsley Beauchamp Worcs 39 N9
Shelsley Walsh Worcs 39 N9
Shelton Bed 32 E3
Shelton Norfk 45 K11
Shelton Notts 42 B2
Shelton Under Harley Staffs 49 P7
Shelve Shrops 38 G3
Shelwick Herefs 39 K12
Shenfield Essex 22 C4
Shenington Oxon 31 J5
Shenley Herts 21 J4
Shenley Brook End M Keyn 32 B9
Shenley Church End M Keyn 32 B9
Shenmore Herefs 28 D2
Shennanton D & G 69 J6
Shenstone Staffs 40 E6
Shenstone Worcs 39 Q7
Shenton Leics 41 J7
Shenval Moray 101 J8
Shephall Herts 33 J11
Shepherd's Bush Gt Lon 21 K7
Shepherdswell Kent 13 N1
Shepley Kirk 58 G11
Shepperton Surrey 20 H9
Shepreth Cambs 33 L7
Shepshed Leics 41 L4
Shepton Beauchamp Somset 17 K11
Shepton Mallet Somset 17 N7
Shepton Montague Somset 17 P9
Shepway Kent 22 F11
Sheraton Dur 66 C1
Sherborne Dorset 17 P11
Sherborne Gloucs 30 F10
Sherborne Somset 17 N5
Sherborne St John Hants 19 Q9
Sherbourne Warwks 30 H2
Sherburn Dur 73 N11
Sherburn N York 67 K11
Sherburn Hill Dur 73 N11
Sherburn in Elmet N York 59 L7
Shere Surrey 10 H1
Shereford Norfk 44 E4
Sherfield English Hants 9 K3
Sherfield on Loddon Hants 20 B10
Sherford Devon 5 Q10
Sheriffhales Shrops 49 N11
Sheriff Hutton N York 59 P2
Sheringham Norfk 45 J2
Sherington M Keyn 32 C7
Shernborne Norfk 44 B4
Sherrington Wilts 18 E11
Sherston Wilts 18 C4
Sherwood C Nott 51 M11
Sherwood Forest Notts 51 N8
Sherwood Forest Crematorium Notts 51 P7
Shetland Islands Shet 111 k4
Shettleston C Glas 85 L9
Shevington Wigan 57 K7
Sheviock Cnwll 4 H8
Shibden Head C Brad 58 E8
Shide IoW 9 N9
Shidlaw Nthumb 80 H6
Shiel Bridge Highld 97 N6
Shieldaig Highld 105 M10
Shieldhill D & G 78 G11
Shieldhill Falk 85 P7
Shieldhill House Hotel S Lans 78 G2
Shields N Lans 85 N11
Shielfoot Highld 89 N3
Shielhill Angus 93 M4
Shielhill Inver 84 D8
Shifnal Shrops 39 N1
Shilbottle Nthumb 81 P11
Shildon Dur 65 M3
Shillford E Rens 84 H10
Shillingford Devon 16 D10
Shillingford Oxon 19 P3
Shillingford Abbot Devon 6 B5
Shillingford St George Devon 6 B5
Shillingstone Dorset 8 C5
Shillington C Beds 32 G9
Shilton Oxon 30 H11
Shilton Warwks 41 K9
Shimpling Norfk 45 J12
Shimpling Suffk 34 E6
Shimpling Street Suffk 34 E6
Shincliffe Dur 73 N11
Shiney Row Sundld 73 N9
Shinfield Wokham 20 B9
Shinness Highld 109 J11
Shipbourne Kent 22 C11
Shipdham Norfk 44 F8
Shipham Somset 17 L5
Shiphay Torbay 6 B9
Shiplake Oxon 20 C7
Shipley C Brad 58 F6
Shipley W Susx 11 J6
Shipley Bridge Surrey 11 L3
Shipmeadow Suffk 45 N11
Shippon Oxon 19 N2
Shipston-on-Stour Warwks 30 G6
Shipton Gloucs 30 D9
Shipton N York 59 M3
Shipton Shrops 39 K4
Shipton Bellinger Hants 19 J10
Shipton Gorge Dorset 7 M5
Shipton Green W Susx 10 C9
Shipton Moyne Gloucs 29 M10
Shipton-on-Cherwell Oxon 31 L10
Shiptonthorpe E R Yk 60 E5
Shipton-under-Wychwood Oxon 30 H9
Shirburn Oxon 20 B4
Shirdley Hill Lancs 56 G6
Shirebrook Derbys 51 M7
Shiregreen Sheff 51 J3
Shirehampton Bristl 28 G12
Shiremoor N Tyne 73 N6
Shirenewton Mons 28 F9
Shireoaks Notts 51 M5
Shirland Derbys 51 K8
Shirley C Sotn 9 L5
Shirley Derbys 50 G11
Shirley Gt Lon 21 M9
Shirley Solhll 40 E10
Shirrell Heath Hants 9 P5
Shirvan Ag & B 83 N6
Shirwell Devon 15 K5
Shiskine N Ayrs 75 N6
Shobdon Herefs 38 H9
Shobrooke Devon 15 P11
Shoby Leics 41 P4
Shocklach Ches W 48 H5
Shoeburyness Sthend 22 H6
Sholden Kent 23 Q11
Sholing C Sotn 9 M5
Shop Cnwll 14 E8
Shoreditch Gt Lon 21 M6
Shoreditch Somset 16 H10
Shoreham Kent 21 P10
Shoreham Airport W Susx 11 K8
Shoreham-by-Sea W Susx 11 K8
Shorley Hants 9 P3
Shorne Kent 22 E8
Shortgate E Susx 11 P7
Shortlanesend Cnwll 3 J6
Shortlees E Ayrs 76 G4
Shortstown Bed 32 F7
Shorwell IoW 9 M10
Shoscombe BaNES 17 Q5
Shotesham Norfk 45 L9
Shotgate Essex 22 F5
Shotley Suffk 35 K9
Shotley Bridge Dur 73 J9
Shotley Gate Suffk 35 L9
Shotley Street Suffk 35 K9
Shottenden Kent 23 K11
Shottery Warwks 30 F3
Shotteswell Warwks 31 K5
Shottisham Suffk 35 M7
Shottlegate Derbys 50 H10
Shotton Dur 73 P11
Shotton Flints 48 F2
Shotton Colliery Dur 73 P11
Shotts N Lans 85 P10
Shotwick Ches W 48 G2
Shougle Moray 101 J4
Shouldham Norfk 44 B8
Shouldham Thorpe Norfk 43 Q8
Shoulton Worcs 39 P9
Shrawardine Shrops 48 H11
Shrawley Worcs 39 P8
Shrewley Warwks 30 G1
Shrewsbury Shrops 49 J11
Shrewton Wilts 18 F11
Shripney W Susx 10 F9
Shrivenham Oxon 19 J3
Shropham Norfk 44 G10
Shucknall Herefs 28 G1
Shudy Camps Cambs 33 P7
Shuna Ag & B 83 L2
Shurdington Gloucs 29 N5
Shurlock Row W & M 20 D8
Shurrery Highld 110 B4
Shurrery Lodge Highld 110 B4
Shurton Somset 16 G7
Shustoke Warwks 40 G8
Shute Devon 6 H4
Shute Devon 15 Q11
Shutford Oxon 31 J6
Shut Heath Staffs 49 Q10
Shuthonger Gloucs 29 M2
Shutlanger Nhants 31 Q4
Shuttington Warwks 40 G6
Shuttlewood Derbys 51 L6
Shuttleworth Bury 57 P5
Siabost W Isls 111 d1
Siadar W Isls 111 d1
Sibbertoft Nhants 41 P10
Sibford Ferris Oxon 31 J6
Sibford Gower Oxon 31 J6
Sible Hedingham Essex 34 C9
Sibley's Green Essex 33 P10
Sibsey Lincs 53 K12
Sibson Cambs 42 F10
Sibson Leics 41 J7
Sibster Highld 110 G5
Sibthorpe Notts 51 Q10
Sibthorpe Notts 51 Q6
Sibton Suffk 35 M3
Sicklesmere Suffk 34 E5
Sicklinghall N York 59 J5
Sidbury Devon 6 F4
Sidbury Shrops 39 M5
Sidcot N Som 17 K5
Sidcup Gt Lon 21 P8
Siddington Ches E 49 Q2
Siddington Gloucs 18 F2
Sidestrand Norfk 45 L3
Sidford Devon 6 F5
Sidlesham W Susx 10 D9
Sidley E Susx 12 E8
Sidmouth Devon 6 F5
Sigglesthorne E R Yk 61 K5
Sigingstone V Glam 16 C2
Silchester Hants 19 Q8
Sileby Leics 41 N5
Silecroft Cumb 62 D6
Silfield Norfk 45 J9
Silkstone Barns 58 H11
Silkstone Common Barns 58 H12
Silk Willoughby Lincs 42 F2
Silloth Cumb 70 H5
Silpho N York 67 L8
Silsden C Brad 58 D5
Silsoe C Beds 32 F9
Silton Dorset 8 B2
Silverburn Mdloth 86 E9
Silverdale Lancs 63 J7
Silverdale Staffs 49 P6
Silver End Essex 34 D11
Silverford Abers 102 G3
Silverstone Nhants 31 P5
Silverton Devon 6 C3
Silvington Shrops 39 L6
Simonburn Nthumb 72 F6
Simonsbath Somset 15 N4
Simonstone Lancs 57 P3
Simprim Border 80 H5
Simpson M Keyn 32 C9
Simpson Cross Pembks 24 F5
Sinclair's Hill Border 80 H4
Sinclairston E Ayrs 76 H7
Sinderby N York 65 N10
Sinderland Green Traffd 57 N10
Sindlesham Wokham 20 C9
Sinfin C Derb 41 J2
Singleton Kent 13 J2
Singleton Lancs 56 H2
Singleton W Susx 10 E7
Singlewell Kent 22 D8
Sinnarhard Abers 101 N11
Sinnington N York 66 G9
Sinton Worcs 39 P9
Sinton Worcs 39 Q9
Sinton Green Worcs 39 P9
Sissinghurst Kent 12 F3
Siston S Glos 17 P2
Sithney Cnwll 2 F9
Sittingbourne Kent 22 H10
Six Ashes Shrops 39 P4
Sixhills Lincs 52 G6
Six Mile Bottom Cambs 33 P5
Sixpenny Handley Dorset 8 E4
Skaill Ork 111 h2
Skara Brae Ork 111 g2
Skares E Ayrs 77 J7
Skateraw Abers 95 P4
Skateraw E Loth 87 N7
Skeabost Highld 104 F11
Skeeby N York 65 L7
Skeffington Leics 41 Q7
Skeffling E R Yk 61 N9
Skegby Notts 51 L8
Skegby Notts 52 B9
Skegness Lincs 53 P10
Skelbo Highld 107 N4
Skelbo Street Highld 107 N4
Skelbrooke Donc 59 L10
Skeldyke Lincs 43 K3
Skellingthorpe Lincs 52 D8
Skellow Donc 59 M11
Skelmanthorpe Kirk 58 G11
Skelmersdale Lancs 57 J7
Skelmorlie N Ayrs 84 D9
Skelpick Highld 109 M5
Skelston D & G 78 D10
Skelton C York 59 M3
Skelton Cumb 71 N8
Skelton E R Yk 60 D8
Skelton N York 59 J1
Skelton R & Cl 66 F4
Skelwith Bridge Cumb 62 G2
Skendleby Lincs 53 M9
Skene House Abers 102 G12
Skenfrith Mons 28 E5
Skerne E R Yk 60 H3
Skerray Highld 109 L3
Skerricha Highld 108 E5
Skerton Lancs 63 J9
Sketchley Leics 41 K8
Sketty Swans 26 E9
Skewsby N York 66 E12
Skiall Highld 110 B3
Skidby E R Yk 60 H7
Skigersta W Isls 111 e1
Skilgate Somset 16 D10
Skillington Lincs 42 C5
Skinburness Cumb 71 J4
Skinflats Falk 85 Q6
Skinidin Highld 104 C11
Skipness Ag & B 83 N10
Skipper's Bridge D & G 79 M11
Skipsea E R Yk 61 K3
Skipton N York 58 C4
Skipton-on-Swale N York 65 P10
Skipwith N York 59 P6
Skirlaugh E R Yk 61 K6
Skirling Border 78 H2
Skirmett Bucks 20 C5
Skirpenbeck E R Yk 60 D3
Skirwith Cumb 64 B2
Skirza Highld 110 H3
Skokholm Island Pembks 24 D7
Skomer Island Pembks 24 D7
Skulamus Highld 97 J5
Skye Green Essex 34 E11
Skye of Curr Highld 99 P4
Slack Calder 58 C8
Slacks of Cairnbanno Abers 102 H6
Slad Gloucs 29 M7
Slade Devon 15 J3
Slade Green Gt Lon 21 Q7
Slade Hooton Rothm 51 M3
Slaggyford Nthumb 72 C9
Slaidburn Lancs 63 N10
Slaithwaite Kirk 58 E10
Slaley Nthumb 72 H8
Slamannan Falk 85 P8
Slapton Bucks 32 D11
Slapton Devon 5 Q10
Slapton Nhants 31 N5
Slaugham W Susx 11 K5
Slaughterford Wilts 18 C6
Slawston Leics 41 R8
Sleaford Hants 10 C3
Sleaford Lincs 42 F2
Sleagill Cumb 64 B4
Sleapford Wrekin 49 L11
Sleasdairidh Highld 107 K3
Sledmere E R Yk 60 F2
Sleetbeck Cumb 79 P12
Sleights N York 67 J6
Slickly Highld 110 F3
Sliddery N Ayrs 75 P7
Sligachan Highld 96 F4
Sligrachan Ag & B 84 C5
Slimbridge Gloucs 29 K7
Slimbridge Wetland Centre Gloucs 29 J7
Slindon Staffs 49 P8
Slindon W Susx 10 F8
Slinfold W Susx 10 H4
Slingsby N York 66 F11
Slip End C Beds 32 F11
Slip End Herts 33 J8
Slipton Nhants 32 D2
Slitting Mill Staffs 40 D4
Slockavullin Ag & B 83 M4
Sloncombe Devon 5 P3
Sloothby Lincs 53 M8
Slough Slough 20 F7
Slough Crematorium Bucks 20 F7
Slough Green Somset 16 H11
Slumbay Highld 97 M2
Slyne Lancs 63 J8
Smailholm Border 80 E7
Smallburgh Norfk 45 M5
Small Dole W Susx 11 K7
Smalley Derbys 51 K11
Smallfield Surrey 11 L2
Small Heath Birm 40 E9
Small Hythe Kent 12 H4
Smallridge Devon 7 J3
Smallworth Norfk 34 G1
Smannell Hants 19 L10
Smarden Kent 12 G2
Smarden Bell Kent 12 G2
Smart's Hill Kent 11 Q2
Smearisary Highld 89 N2
Smeatharpe Devon 6 G1
Smeeth Kent 13 K3
Smeeton Westerby Leics 41 P8
Smerral Highld 110 D8
Smestow Staffs 39 Q4
Smethwick Sandw 40 D9
Smisby Derbys 41 J4
Smithfield Cumb 71 P3
Smith's Green Essex 33 Q8
Smithstown Highld 105 L6
Smithton Highld 107 L12
Smoo Highld 108 H3
Smythe's Green Essex 34 F11
Snade D & G 78 D10
Snailbeach Shrops 38 G2
Snailwell Cambs 33 Q4
Snainton N York 67 K10
Snaith E R Yk 59 N9
Snape N York 65 M10
Snape Suffk 35 N5
Snape Street Suffk 35 N5
Snaresbrook Gt Lon 21 N5
Snarestone Leics 41 J5
Snarford Lincs 52 F7
Snargate Kent 13 J4
Snave Kent 13 K4
Sneaton N York 67 J6
Snelland Lincs 52 F7
Snelston Derbys 50 F11
Snetterton Norfk 44 G11
Snettisham Norfk 44 B4
Snitter Nthumb 81 L12
Snitterby Lincs 52 E5
Snitterfield Warwks 30 G3
Snitton Shrops 39 K7
Snodland Kent 22 E10
Snowdon Gwynd 54 H10
Snowdonia National Park 47 N5
Snow End Herts 33 L9
Snowshill Gloucs 30 E7
Soake Hants 9 Q5
Soay Highld 96 E7
Soberton Hants 9 Q4
Soberton Heath Hants 9 P5
Sockburn Darltn 65 N6
Soham Cambs 33 P3
Solas W Isls 111 b4
Soldridge Hants 9 Q1
Sole Street Kent 22 D9
Sole Street Kent 23 L12
Solihull Solhll 40 F10
Sollers Dilwyn Herefs 38 H10
Sollers Hope Herefs 28 H3
Solva Pembks 24 E4
Solwaybank D & G 79 L12
Somerby Leics 41 R5
Somerby Lincs 52 F3
Somercotes Derbys 51 K9
Somerford Dorset 8 H8
Somerford Keynes Gloucs 18 E2
Somerley W Susx 10 D9
Somerleyton Suffk 45 P10
Somersal Herbert Derbys 40 F1
Somersby Lincs 53 K8
Somersham Cambs 33 K2
Somersham Suffk 34 H7
Somerton Oxon 31 L8
Somerton Somset 17 L9
Somerton Suffk 34 D6
Sompting W Susx 11 J8
Sonning Wokham 20 C8
Sonning Common Oxon 20 B7
Sopley Hants 8 H7
Sopworth Wilts 18 C4
Sorbie D & G 69 L9
Sordale Highld 110 D4
Sorisdale Ag & B 88 G4
Sorn E Ayrs 77 J6
Sortat Highld 110 F3
Sotby Lincs 52 H7
Sotterley Suffk 45 P12
Soughton Flints 48 E3
Soulbury Bucks 32 C10
Soulby Cumb 64 D5
Souldern Oxon 31 M7
Souldrop Bed 32 E4
Sound Ches E 49 L6
Sound Muir Moray 101 M5
Soundwell S Glos 17 P2
Sourton Devon 5 L3
Soutergate Cumb 62 E6
South Acre Norfk 44 D7
South Alkham Kent 13 N2
Southall Gt Lon 20 H7
South Allington Devon 5 Q11
South Alloa Falk 85 P5
Southam Gloucs 29 N4
Southam Warwks 31 K2
South Ambersham W Susx 10 E6
Southampton C Sotn 9 M5
Southampton Airport Hants 9 M4
Southampton Crematorium Hants 9 M4
South Anston Rothm 51 L4
South Ashford Kent 13 J2
South Baddesley Hants 9 L7
South Ballachulish Highld 90 E5
South Bank C York 59 N4

South Barrow Somset	17	N9
South Beddington Gt Lon	21	L10
South Benfleet Essex	22	F6
South Bersted W Susx	10	F9
Southborough Gt Lon	21	N9
Southborough Kent	12	C2
Southbourne Bmouth	8	C8
Southbourne W Susx	10	C8
South Bramwith Donc	59	N11
South Brent Devon	5	N2
South Brewham Somset	17	Q8
South Bristol Crematorium Bristl	17	N3
South Broomhill Nthumb	73	M2
Southburgh Norfk	44	G8
South Burlingham Norfk	45	N8
Southburn E R Yk	60	G4
South Cadbury Somset	17	P10
South Carlton Lincs	52	D8
South Carlton Notts	51	N4
South Cave E R Yk	60	F7
South Cerney Gloucs	18	F2
South Chailey E Susx	11	N6
South Charlton Nthumb	81	N10
South Cheriton Somset	17	Q10
South Church Dur	65	L2
Southchurch Sthend	22	H6
South Cliffe E R Yk	60	E7
South Clifton Notts	52	B9
South Cockerington Lincs	53	L8
South Cornelly Brdgnd	26	H11
Southcott Cnwll	4	F2
Southcott Devon	5	P4
Southcourt Bucks	20	D2
South Cove Suffk	35	P1
South Creake Norfk	44	E3
South Croxton Leics	41	P5
South Dalton E R Yk	60	G5
South Darenth Kent	22	C9
South Downs National Park	11	M8
South Duffield N York	59	P7
Southease E Susx	11	N8
South Elkington Lincs	53	J6
South Elmsall Wakefd	59	L11
Southend Ag & B	75	K10
Southend Airport Essex	22	G5
Southend Crematorium Sthend	22	H6
Southend-on-Sea Sthend	22	H6
Southerndown V Glam	16	B2
Southerness D & G	70	F5
South Erradale Highld	105	L7
Southerton Devon	6	E5
Southery Norfk	43	P10
South Essex Crematorium Gt Lon	22	C6
South Fambridge Essex	22	G4
South Ferriby N Linc	60	G9
South Field E R Yk	60	H8
Southfield Falk	85	P8
Southfleet Kent	22	C8
Southgate Gt Lon	21	L5
Southgate Swans	26	D10
South Gorley Hants	8	H5
South Gosforth N u Ty	73	M7
South Green Essex	22	D5
South Green Kent	22	G10
South Green Norfk	44	H7
South Gyle C Edin	86	E7
South Hanningfield Essex	22	E4
South Harting W Susx	10	C6
South Hayling Hants	10	B9
South Heath Bucks	20	E3
South Heighton E Susx	11	N9
South Hetton Dur	73	P10
South Hiendley Wakefd	59	K10
South Hill Cnwll	4	H5
South Hinksey Oxon	31	L12
South Holmwood Surrey	11	J2
South Hornchurch Gt Lon	21	P6
South Huish Devon	5	N11
South Hykeham Lincs	52	D9
South Hylton Sundld	73	P9
Southill C Beds	32	G8
Southington Hants	19	N10
South Kelsey Lincs	52	E4
South Kessock Highld	107	L11
South Killingholme N Linc	61	K10
South Kilvington N York	65	Q10
South Kilworth Leics	41	N10
South Kirkby Wakefd	59	K11
South Kyme Lincs	52	G12
South Lanarkshire Crematorium S Lans	85	N12
Southleigh Devon	6	G4
South Leigh Oxon	31	K12
South Leverton Notts	52	A7
South Littleton Worcs	30	E5
South London Crematorium Gt Lon	21	L9
South Lopham Norfk	34	G4
South Luffenham Rutlnd	42	D9
South Malling E Susx	11	N7
South Marston Swindn	18	H3
South Merstham Surrey	21	L11
South Milford N York	59	L7
South Milton Devon	5	N11
South Mimms Herts	21	K3
South Mimms Services Herts	21	K4
Southminster Essex	23	J4
South Molton Devon	15	N7
South Moor Dur	73	L9
Southmoor Oxon	19	L2
South Moreton Oxon	19	P3
Southmuir Angus	93	L5
South Mundham W Susx	10	E9
South Newbald E R Yk	60	F7
South Newington Oxon	31	K7
South Newton Wilts	8	F2
South Normanton Derbys	51	K9
South Norwood Gt Lon	21	M9
South Ockendon Thurr	22	C6
Southoe Cambs	32	H4
Southolt Suffk	35	K3
South Ormsby Lincs	53	L8
Southorpe C Pete	42	F9
South Otterington N York	65	P9
Southover Dorset	7	N4
South Owersby Lincs	52	F5
Southowram Calder	58	G8
South Park Surrey	11	K1
South Perrott Dorset	7	L3
South Petherton Somset	17	L11
South Petherwin Cnwll	4	G4
South Pickenham Norfk	44	E8

South Pill Cnwll	5	J8
South Pool Devon	5	Q11
South Poorton Dorset	7	M4
Southport Sefton	56	G5
Southport Crematorium Lancs	56	G6
South Queensferry C Edin	86	D6
South Rauceby Lincs	42	E2
South Raynham Norfk	44	E5
Southrepps Norfk	45	L3
South Reston Lincs	53	L6
Southrey Lincs	52	G9
South Ronaldsay Ork	111	h3
Southrop Gloucs	30	G12
Southrope Hants	19	Q10
South Runcton Norfk	43	Q8
South Scarle Notts	52	B10
Southsea C Port	9	Q7
South Shian Ag & B	90	C7
South Shields S Tyne	73	P7
South Shields Crematorium S Tyne	73	N8
South Shore Bpool	56	F3
Southside Dur	65	K3
South Stainley N York	58	H2
South Stoke BaNES	17	Q4
South Stoke Oxon	19	P4
South Stoke W Susx	10	G7
South Street Kent	23	K10
South Street Kent	23	L9
South Tarbrax S Lans	86	B10
South Tawton Devon	5	N2
South Tehidy Cnwll	2	F7
South Thoresby Lincs	53	L7
Southtown Norfk	45	Q8
South Uist W Isls	111	b6
Southwaite Cumb	71	P6
Southwaite Services Cumb	71	P6
South Walsham Norfk	45	M7
Southwark Gt Lon	21	L7
South Warnborough Hants	10	B1
Southwater W Susx	11	J5
South Weald Essex	22	C5
Southwell Notts	51	P9
South West Middlesex Crematorium Gt Lon	20	H8
South Weston Oxon	20	B4
Southwick Hants	9	Q6
Southwick Nhants	42	E10
Southwick Sundld	73	P9
Southwick W Susx	11	K8
Southwick Wilts	18	C9
South Widcombe BaNES	17	N5
South Wigston Leics	41	N7
South Willesborough Kent	13	K2
South Willingham Lincs	52	H6
South Wingfield Derbys	51	J9
South Witham Lincs	42	D6
Southwold Suffk	35	Q2
South Woodham Ferrers Essex	22	F4
South Wootton Norfk	43	Q5
South Wraxall Wilts	18	C7
South Zeal Devon	5	N2
Sowerby Calder	58	D9
Sowerby N York	66	B10
Sowerby Bridge Calder	58	D9
Sowood Calder	58	E9
Sowton Devon	6	K7
Sowton Devon	6	D4
Soyland Town Calder	58	D9
Spain's End Essex	33	Q8
Spalding Lincs	43	J5
Spaldington E R Yk	60	C7
Spaldwick Cambs	32	G3
Spalford Notts	52	B9
Spanby Lincs	42	F3
Sparham Norfk	44	H6
Spark Bridge Cumb	62	F5
Sparkford Somset	17	N10
Sparkhill Birm	40	E10
Sparkwell Devon	5	M8
Sparrowpit Derbys	50	E5
Sparrows Green E Susx	12	D4
Sparsholt Hants	9	M2
Sparsholt Oxon	19	L4
Spaunton N York	66	G8
Spaxton Somset	16	G8
Spean Bridge Highld	98	C11
Spearywell Hants	9	K2
Speen Bucks	20	D4
Speen W Berk	19	M7
Speeton N York	67	N11
Speke Lpool	56	H11
Speldhurst Kent	12	B2
Spellbrook Herts	33	M12
Spencers Wood Wokham	20	B9
Spen Green Ches E	49	P3
Spennithorne N York	65	K9
Spennymoor Dur	65	M2
Spetchley Worcs	30	B4
Spetisbury Dorset	8	D7
Spexhall Suffk	35	N2
Spey Bay Moray	101	L3
Speybridge Highld	100	E9
Speyview Moray	101	K6
Spilsby Lincs	53	L9
Spinkhill Derbys	51	L5
Spinningdale Highld	107	L12
Spital Hill Donc	51	N3
Spittal E Loth	87	J6
Spittal Highld	110	D5
Spittal Nthumb	81	N1
Spittal Pembks	24	G4
Spittalfield P & K	92	G7
Spittal of Glenmuick Abers	94	E5
Spittal of Glenshee P & K	92	B7
Spittal-on-Rule Border	80	D7
Spixworth Norfk	45	L7
Splatt Devon	15	K10
Splayne's Green E Susx	11	N5
Splottlands Cardif	27	P12
Spofforth N York	59	J4
Spondon C Derb	41	K1
Spooner Row Norfk	44	H10
Sporle Norfk	44	E7
Spott E Loth	87	N7
Spottiswoode Border	80	E4
Spratton Nhants	41	Q12
Spreakley Surrey	10	D2
Spreyton Devon	15	M11
Spriddlestone Devon	5	L9
Spridlington Lincs	52	E6

Springburn C Glas	85	K8
Springfield D & G	71	M2
Springfield Essex	22	E2
Springfield Fife	93	L12
Springholm D & G	70	D2
Springside N Ayrs	76	F4
Springthorpe Lincs	52	C5
Springwell Sundld	73	M8
Springwood Crematorium Lpool	56	H10
Sproatley E R Yk	61	K7
Sproston Green Ches W	49	N3
Sprotbrough Donc	51	M1
Sproughton Suffk	35	J7
Sprouston Border	80	G7
Sprowston Norfk	45	L7
Sproxton Leics	42	C5
Sproxton N York	66	E10
Spurstow Ches E	49	K4
Spyway Dorset	7	M4
Stableford Shrops	39	N3
Stacey Bank Sheff	50	H3
Stackhouse N York	63	P8
Stackpole Pembks	24	H9
Staddiscombe C Plym	5	K9
Stadhampton Oxon	19	Q2
Stadhlaigearraidh W Isls	111	a5
Staffield Cumb	71	Q7
Staffin Highld	104	G8
Stafford Staffs	40	B3
Stafford Crematorium Staffs	40	C3
Stafford Services (Northbound) Staffs	40	B2
Stafford Services (Southbound) Staffs	40	B2
Stagsden Bed	32	E7
Stainburn Cumb	70	G9
Stainby Lincs	42	C5
Staincross Barns	59	J11
Staindrop Dur	65	K4
Staines-upon-Thames Surrey	20	G8
Stainforth Donc	59	N10
Stainforth N York	63	P8
Staining Lancs	56	G2
Stainland Calder	58	E9
Stainsacre N York	67	K6
Stainton Cumb	63	K5
Stainton Cumb	71	P9
Stainton Donc	51	M3
Stainton Dur	65	J4
Stainton Middsb	66	C5
Stainton by Langworth Lincs	52	F7
Staintondale N York	67	L7
Stainton le Vale Lincs	52	H5
Stainton with Adgarley Cumb	62	F7
Stair E Ayrs	76	G6
Stairhaven D & G	68	G8
Staithes N York	66	H4
Stakeford Nthumb	73	M4
Stakes Hants	10	B8
Stalbridge Dorset	17	Q11
Stalbridge Weston Dorset	17	Q11
Stalham Norfk	45	N5
Stalisfield Green Kent	23	J11
Stallen Dorset	17	N11
Stallingborough NE Lin	61	K11
Stalmine Lancs	62	G12
Stalybridge Tamesd	50	C2
Stambourne Essex	34	C8
Stambourne Green Essex	34	B8
Stamford Lincs	42	E8
Stamford Nthumb	81	P9
Stamford Bridge Ches W	49	J3
Stamford Bridge E R Yk	60	C3
Stamfordham Nthumb	73	J6
Stamford Hill Gt Lon	21	M6
Stanbridge C Beds	32	D11
Stanbury C Brad	58	D6
Stand N Lans	85	M8
Standburn Falk	85	Q7
Standeford Staffs	40	B6
Standen Kent	12	G3
Standerwick Somset	18	B10
Standford Hants	10	D3
Standingstone Cumb	70	H8
Standish Wigan	57	K6
Standlake Oxon	31	K12
Standon Hants	9	M3
Standon Herts	33	L11
Standon Staffs	49	P8
Stane N Lans	85	P10
Stanfield Norfk	44	F6
Stanford C Beds	32	G8
Stanford Kent	13	L3
Stanford Bishop Herefs	39	N10
Stanford Bridge Worcs	39	N8
Stanford Dingley W Berk	19	P6
Stanford in the Vale Oxon	19	K3
Stanford le Hope Thurr	22	D7
Stanford on Avon Nhants	41	N10
Stanford on Soar Notts	41	M3
Stanford on Teme Worcs	39	N8
Stanfree Derbys	51	L6
Stanghow R & Cl	66	F4
Stanground C Pete	42	H10
Stanhoe Norfk	44	D3
Stanhope Border	79	J3
Stanhope Dur	72	H11
Stanhope Kent	13	J2
Stanion Nhants	42	D11
Stanley Derbys	51	K11
Stanley Dur	73	L9
Stanley P & K	92	G8
Stanley Staffs	50	B9
Stanley Crook Dur	73	L12
Stanley Pontlarge Gloucs	30	D7
Stanmer Br & H	11	M7
Stanmore Gt Lon	21	J5
Stanmore Hants	9	M2
Stannersburn Nthumb	72	E3
Stanningfield Suffk	34	E5
Stannington Nthumb	73	L5
Stannington Sheff	50	H4
Stannington Station Nthumb	73	L5
Stansbatch Herefs	38	G9
Stansfield Suffk	34	C6
Stanstead Suffk	34	D6
Stanstead Abbotts Herts	21	N2
Stansted Kent	22	C9
Stansted Airport Essex	33	N11
Stansted Mountfitchet Essex	33	N10

Stanton Gloucs	30	E7
Stanton Nthumb	73	K3
Stanton Staffs	50	E10
Stanton Suffk	34	F3
Stanton by Bridge Derbys	41	J3
Stanton by Dale Derbys	51	L12
Stanton Drew BaNES	17	N4
Stanton Fitzwarren Swindn	18	H3
Stanton Harcourt Oxon	31	K11
Stanton in Peak Derbys	50	G7
Stanton Lacy Shrops	39	J6
Stanton Lees Derbys	50	G8
Stanton Long Shrops	39	L4
Stanton on the Wolds Notts	41	N2
Stanton Prior BaNES	17	P4
Stanton St Bernard Wilts	18	G8
Stanton St John Oxon	31	M11
Stanton St Quintin Wilts	18	D5
Stanton Street Suffk	34	F4
Stanton under Bardon Leics	41	L5
Stanton upon Hine Heath Shrops	49	K9
Stanton Wick BaNES	17	N4
Stanway Essex	34	F11
Stanway Gloucs	30	D7
Stanwell Surrey	20	G8
Stanwick Nhants	32	E3
Stanwix Cumb	71	N4
Staoinebrig W Isls	111	a5
Stape N York	66	H8
Stapeley Ches E	49	M5
Stapenhill Staffs	40	G3
Staple Kent	23	P11
Staple Cross Devon	16	D11
Staple Cross E Susx	12	F5
Staplefield W Susx	11	L5
Staple Fitzpaine Somset	16	H11
Stapleford Cambs	33	M6
Stapleford Herts	33	K10
Stapleford Leics	42	B6
Stapleford Lincs	52	C11
Stapleford Notts	51	L12
Stapleford Wilts	18	F12
Stapleford Abbotts Essex	21	P5
Staplegrove Somset	16	G10
Staplehay Somset	16	G10
Staplehurst Kent	12	F2
Staplestreet Kent	23	K10
Stapleton Herefs	38	G8
Stapleton Leics	41	K7
Stapleton N York	65	M5
Stapleton Shrops	39	J2
Stapleton Somset	17	L11
Stapley Somset	16	G12
Staploe Bed	32	G5
Staplow Herefs	29	J1
Star Fife	86	G2
Star Pembks	25	M2
Star Somset	17	L5
Starbeck N York	59	J3
Starbotton N York	64	C11
Starcross Devon	6	C6
Stareton Warwks	41	J12
Starlings Green Essex	33	M9
Starston Norfk	45	K12
Startforth Dur	65	J4
Startley Wilts	18	D4
Statenborough Kent	23	P11
Statham Warrtn	57	M10
Stathe Somset	17	K9
Stathern Leics	41	Q2
Staughton Green Cambs	32	G4
Staunton Gloucs	28	G6
Staunton Gloucs	29	K3
Staunton on Arrow Herefs	38	G9
Staunton on Wye Herefs	38	G12
Staveley Cumb	62	H5
Staveley Cumb	63	J3
Staveley Derbys	51	K6
Staveley N York	59	J2
Staverton Devon	5	Q7
Staverton Gloucs	29	M4
Staverton Nhants	31	M2
Staverton Wilts	18	C8
Stawell Somset	17	K8
Stawley Somset	16	E10
Staxigoe Highld	110	H5
Staxton N York	67	L10
Staynall Lancs	62	G12
Stean N York	65	J11
Stearsby N York	66	E12
Steart Somset	16	H7
Stebbing Essex	33	Q11
Stedham W Susx	10	D5
Steelend Fife	86	B4
Steele Road Border	79	Q9
Steen's Bridge Herefs	39	K10
Steep Hants	10	C5
Steep Lane Calder	58	D9
Steeple Essex	22	H3
Steeple Ashton Wilts	18	D9
Steeple Aston Oxon	31	L8
Steeple Bumpstead Essex	34	B8
Steeple Claydon Bucks	31	P8
Steeple Gidding Cambs	32	G1
Steeple Langford Wilts	18	F12
Steeple Morden Cambs	33	J8
Steeton C Brad	58	D5
Stein Highld	104	C10
Stelling Minnis Kent	13	M1
Stembridge Somset	17	K11
Stenalees Cnwll	3	M4
Stenhouse D & G	77	N11
Stenhousemuir Falk	85	P6
Stenscholl Highld	104	F8
Stenson Fields Derbys	41	J2
Stenton E Loth	87	M7
Stenton D & G	11	H7
Steornabhagh W Isls	111	d2
Stepaside Pembks	25	K6
Stepford D & G	78	E11
Stepney Gt Lon	21	M7
Steppingley C Beds	32	E8
Stepps N Lans	85	K8
Sternfield Suffk	35	M5
Stert Wilts	18	F8
Stetchworth Cambs	33	Q5
Stevenage Herts	32	H10
Stevenston N Ayrs	76	E3
Steventon Hants	19	P10
Steventon Oxon	19	M3
Steventon End Essex	33	P8
Stevington Bed	32	E6
Stewartby Bed	32	E8

Stewartfield S Lans	85	K11
Stewarton E Ayrs	76	G3
Stewkley Bucks	32	C10
Stewley Somset	17	J11
Steyning W Susx	11	J7
Steynton Pembks	24	G7
Stibb Cnwll	14	D9
Stibbard Norfk	44	G4
Stibb Cross Devon	14	H8
Stibb Green Wilts	18	J8
Stibbington Cambs	42	F9
Stichill Border	80	F6
Sticker Cnwll	3	L6
Stickford Lincs	53	K10
Sticklepath Devon	5	M2
Stickney Lincs	53	K11
Stiffkey Norfk	44	F2
Stilligarry W Isls	111	a5
Stillingfleet N York	59	N6
Stillington N York	59	N1
Stillington S on T	65	P3
Stilton Cambs	42	G11
Stinchcombe Gloucs	29	K8
Stinsford Dorset	7	Q5
Stiperstones Shrops	38	G3
Stirchley Wrekin	39	M1
Stirling Abers	103	M6
Stirling Stirlg	85	N4
Stirling Castle Stirlg	85	N4
Stirling Services Stirlg	85	N5
Stirtloe Cambs	32	H4
Stirton N York	58	C4
Stisted Essex	34	D10
Stithians Cnwll	2	G8
Stivichall Covtry	41	J11
Stixwould Lincs	52	H9
Stoak Ches W	48	H2
Stobo Border	79	K2
Stoborough Dorset	8	D9
Stobs Castle Border	80	C11
Stobswood Nthumb	73	L2
Stock Essex	22	E4
Stock N Som	17	L4
Stockbridge Hants	9	L1
Stockbriggs S Lans	77	N4
Stockbury Kent	22	G10
Stockcross W Berk	19	M7
Stockerston Leics	42	B9
Stock Green Worcs	30	C3
Stocking Herefs	28	H3
Stockingford Warwks	41	J8
Stocking Pelham Herts	33	M10
Stockland Devon	6	H4
Stockland Bristol Somset	16	H7
Stockleigh English Devon	15	P10
Stockleigh Pomeroy Devon	15	P10
Stockley Wilts	18	E7
Stocklinch Somset	17	K11
Stockport Stockp	50	B3
Stockport Crematorium Stockp	50	B3
Stocksbridge Sheff	50	H2
Stocksfield Nthumb	73	J8
Stockton Herefs	39	K9
Stockton Norfk	45	N10
Stockton Shrops	39	N3
Stockton Warwks	31	K2
Stockton Wilts	18	E12
Stockton Wrekin	49	P11
Stockton Heath Warrtn	57	L10
Stockton-on-Tees S on T	66	C4
Stockton on Teme Worcs	39	N8
Stockton on the Forest C York	59	P3
Stockwood Bristl	17	P3
Stockwood Dorset	7	N2
Stock Wood Worcs	30	D3
Stodmarsh Kent	23	N10
Stody Norfk	44	H3
Stoer Highld	108	B9
Stoford Somset	17	N12
Stoford Wilts	8	F1
Stogumber Somset	16	E8
Stogursey Somset	16	G7
Stoke Covtry	41	J10
Stoke Devon	14	E7
Stoke Hants	10	B8
Stoke Hants	19	L9
Stoke Medway	22	G8
Stoke Abbott Dorset	7	L3
Stoke Albany Nhants	42	B11
Stoke Ash Suffk	35	J3
Stoke Bardolph Notts	51	N11
Stoke Bliss Worcs	39	M9
Stoke Bruerne Nhants	31	Q4
Stoke by Clare Suffk	34	C8
Stoke-by-Nayland Suffk	34	G9
Stoke Canon Devon	6	C3
Stoke Charity Hants	19	N11
Stoke Climsland Cnwll	4	H5
Stoke Cross Herefs	39	L11
Stoke D'Abernon Surrey	20	H10
Stoke Doyle Nhants	42	E11
Stoke Dry Rutlnd	42	C10
Stoke Edith Herefs	28	H3
Stoke Farthing Wilts	8	F3
Stoke Ferry Norfk	44	B8
Stoke Fleming Devon	6	B11
Stokeford Dorset	8	C9
Stoke Gabriel Devon	6	B10
Stoke Gifford S Glos	28	H11
Stoke Golding Leics	41	K7
Stoke Goldington M Keyn	32	B7
Stokeham Notts	52	A7
Stoke Hammond Bucks	32	C10
Stoke Holy Cross Norfk	45	L9
Stokeinteignhead Devon	6	C7
Stoke Lacy Herefs	39	L11
Stoke Lyne Oxon	31	M8
Stoke Mandeville Bucks	20	D2
Stokenchurch Bucks	20	C4
Stoke Newington Gt Lon	21	M6
Stokenham Devon	5	Q10
Stoke-on-Trent C Stke	50	B10
Stoke Orchard Gloucs	29	M3
Stoke Poges Bucks	20	F6
Stoke Prior Herefs	39	K9
Stoke Prior Worcs	30	C1
Stoke Rivers Devon	15	L5
Stoke Rochford Lincs	42	D4
Stoke Row Oxon	20	B6
Stoke St Gregory Somset	17	J10
Stoke St Mary Somset	16	H10
Stoke St Michael Somset	17	P6
Stoke St Milborough Shrops	39	K5

Stokesby - Telscombe 195

Stokesby Norfk 45 N7
Stokesley N York 66 D6
Stoke sub Hamdon Somset 17 L11
Stoke Talmage Oxon 20 B4
Stoke Trister Somset 17 Q9
Stoke upon Tern Shrops 49 M9
Stoke-upon-Trent C Stke 49 Q6
Stolford Somset 16 G7
Stondon Massey Essex 22 C4
Stone Bucks 20 C2
Stone Gloucs 29 J9
Stone Rothm 51 M3
Stone Staffs 40 B1
Stone Worcs 39 Q7
Stone Allerton Somset 17 K6
Ston Easton Somset 17 N5
Stonebridge N Som 17 K4
Stonebridge Warwks 40 G10
Stonebroom Derbys 51 K8
Stone Cross Kent 23 P11
Stonecrouch Kent 12 E4
Stoneferry C KuH 61 J7
Stonefield Castle Hotel Ag & B 83 N8
Stonegate E Susx 12 D4
Stonegrave N York 66 F11
Stonehaven Abers 95 P5
Stonehenge Wilts 18 G11
Stonehouse C Plym 5 K9
Stonehouse Gloucs 29 L7
Stonehouse S Lans 77 M3
Stone in Oxney Kent 12 H5
Stoneleigh Warwks 41 J11
Stonesby Leics 42 B5
Stonesfield Oxon 31 K10
Stones Green Essex 35 J10
Stone Street Kent 22 C11
Stone Street Suffk 35 N1
Stonewells Moray 101 K3
Stoneybridge W Isls 111 a5
Stoneyburn W Loth 86 B9
Stoneygate C Leic 41 N7
Stoneykirk D & G 68 E8
Stoney Middleton Derbys 50 G6
Stoney Stanton Leics 41 L8
Stoney Stoke Somset 17 Q9
Stoney Stratton Somset 17 P8
Stoneywood C Aber 103 J11
Stoneywood Falk 85 N6
Stonham Aspal Suffk 35 J5
Stonnall Staffs 40 E6
Stonor Oxon 20 B6
Stonton Wyville Leics 41 Q8
Stony Houghton Derbys 51 L7
Stony Stratford M Keyn 32 B8
Stoodleigh Devon 15 L6
Stoodleigh Devon 16 C11
Stop 24 Services Kent 13 L3
Stopham W Susx 10 G6
Stopsley Luton 32 F11
Stornoway W Isls 111 d2
Stornoway Airport W Isls 111 d2
Storrington W Susx 10 H7
Storth Cumb 63 J6
Storwood E R Yk 60 C5
Stotfield Moray 101 J2
Stotfold C Beds 32 H9
Stottesdon Shrops 39 M5
Stoughton Leics 41 N7
Stoughton Surrey 20 F12
Stoughton W Susx 10 C7
Stoulton Worcs 30 B4
Stourbridge Dudley 40 B10
Stourbridge Crematorium Dudley 40 B10
Stourhead Wilts 8 B1
Stourpaine Dorset 8 C5
Stourport-on-Severn Worcs 39 P7
Stour Provost Dorset 8 B3
Stour Row Dorset 8 B3
Stourton Staffs 39 Q5
Stourton Warwks 30 H6
Stourton Wilts 8 B1
Stourton Caundle Dorset 17 Q12
Stove Shet 111 k5
Stoven Suffk 35 P1
Stow Border 87 J12
Stow Lincs 52 C7
Stow Bardolph Norfk 43 P8
Stow Bedon Norfk 44 F10
Stowbridge Norfk 43 P8
Stow-cum-Quy Cambs 33 N5
Stowe Shrops 38 F7
Stowe by Chartley Staffs 40 D3
Stowell Somset 17 P10
Stowey BaNES 17 N4
Stowford Devon 5 J3
Stowlangtoft Suffk 34 F3
Stow Longa Cambs 32 G3
Stow Maries Essex 22 G4
Stowmarket Suffk 34 H5
Stow-on-the-Wold Gloucs 30 F8
Stowting Kent 13 L2
Stowting Common Kent 13 L2
Stowupland Suffk 34 H5
Straanruie Highld 99 P6
Strachan Abers 95 L4
Strachur Ag & B 84 B3
Stradbroke Suffk 35 K3
Stradishall Suffk 34 C6
Stradsett Norfk 43 Q8
Stragglethorpe Lincs 52 C11
Straiton Mdloth 86 F8
Straiton S Ayrs 76 G9
Straloch Abers 102 H10
Straloch P & K 92 F3
Stramshall Staffs 40 E1
Strang IoM 56 c5
Strangeways Salfd 57 P8
Strangford Herefs 28 G4
Stranraer D & G 68 E7
Stratfield Mortimer W Berk 19 Q7
Stratfield Saye Hants 20 B10
Stratfield Turgis Hants 20 B10
Stratford Gt Lon 21 M6
Stratford St Andrew Suffk 35 M5
Stratford St Mary Suffk 34 H9
Stratford Tony Wilts 8 G3
Stratford-upon-Avon Warwks 30 G3
Strath Highld 105 L6
Strathan Highld 108 C10
Strathan Highld 109 K3
Strathaven S Lans 77 L3
Strathblane Stirlg 85 J7
Strathcanaird Highld 106 C3
Strathcarron Highld 97 N2
Strathcoil Ag & B 89 N9
Strathdon Abers 101 L11
Strathkinness Fife 93 M11
Strathloanhead W Loth 85 Q8
Strathmashie House Highld 98 H10
Strathmiglo Fife 86 E1
Strathpeffer Highld 106 H10
Strathtay P & K 92 D5
Strathwhillan N Ayrs 75 Q5
Strathy Highld 109 P3
Strathy Inn Highld 109 P3
Strathyre Stirlg 91 N11
Stratton Cnwll 14 E10
Stratton Dorset 7 P4
Stratton Gloucs 30 D12
Stratton Audley Oxon 31 N8
Stratton-on-the-Fosse Somset 17 P6
Stratton St Margaret Swindn 18 H4
Stratton St Michael Norfk 45 K10
Stratton Strawless Norfk 45 K6
Streat E Susx 11 M7
Streatham Gt Lon 21 L8
Streatley C Beds 32 F10
Streatley W Berk 19 P5
Street Devon 6 G5
Street Somset 17 L8
Street Ashton Warwks 41 L10
Street Dinas Shrops 48 G7
Street End Kent 23 M11
Street End W Susx 10 D9
Streethay Staffs 40 F5
Streetlam N York 65 N7
Streetly Crematorium Wsall 40 E7
Streetly End Cambs 33 P7
Street on the Fosse Somset 17 N8
Strelitz P & K 92 H8
Strelley Notts 51 L11
Strensall C York 59 N3
Strensham Services (northbound) Worcs 29 M1
Strensham Services (southbound) Worcs 29 M2
Stretcholt Somset 16 H7
Strete Devon 5 R10
Stretford Traffd 57 P9
Strethall Essex 33 M8
Stretham Cambs 33 N2
Strettington W Susx 10 E8
Stretton Derbys 51 K8
Stretton Rutlnd 42 D7
Stretton Staffs 40 B5
Stretton Staffs 40 G3
Stretton Warrtn 57 L11
Stretton Grandison Herefs 39 L12
Stretton-on-Dunsmore Warwks 41 K11
Stretton on Fosse Warwks 30 G6
Stretton Sugwas Herefs 28 E1
Stretton under Fosse Warwks 41 L10
Stretton Westwood Shrops 39 L3
Strichen Abers 103 K4
Stringston Somset 16 G7
Strixton Nhants 32 C4
Stroat Gloucs 28 G8
Stroma Highld 110 G1
Stromeferry Highld 97 M3
Stromness Ork 111 g2
Stronachlachar Stirlg 84 G2
Stronafian Ag & B 83 Q6
Stronchrubie Highld 108 E11
Strone Ag & B 84 D6
Strone Highld 98 A11
Strone Highld 98 G4
Stronenaba Highld 98 B11
Stronmilchan Ag & B 90 F10
Stronsay Ork 111 i2
Stronsay Airport Ork 111 i2
Strontian Highld 89 Q4
Strood Medway 22 E9
Stroud Gloucs 29 L7
Stroud Hants 10 B5
Stroud Green Gloucs 29 L7
Stroxton Lincs 42 C4
Struan Highld 96 D3
Struan P & K 92 B3
Strumpshaw Norfk 45 M8
Strutherhill S Lans 77 M2
Struthers Fife 86 H1
Struy Highld 98 E2
Stuartfield Abers 103 K6
Stubbington Hants 9 P6
Stubbins Lancs 57 P5
Stubton Lincs 42 C1
Stuckton Hants 8 H5
Studham C Beds 32 E12
Studland Dorset 8 F10
Studley Warwks 30 E2
Studley Wilts 18 E6
Studley Roger N York 65 N12
Studley Royal N York 65 M12
Studley Royal Park & Fountains Abbey N York 58 H1
Stuntney Cambs 33 N2
Sturmer Essex 34 B7
Sturminster Common Dorset 8 B5
Sturminster Marshall Dorset 8 D7
Sturminster Newton Dorset 8 B5
Sturry Kent 23 M10
Sturton N Linc 52 D3
Sturton by Stow Lincs 52 C7
Sturton le Steeple Notts 52 B6
Stuston Suffk 35 J2
Stutton N York 59 L6
Stutton Suffk 35 J9
Styal Ches E 57 Q11
Stynie Moray 101 L3
Styrrup Notts 51 N3
Succoth Ag & B 84 E2
Suckley Worcs 39 N10
Sudborough Nhants 32 D1
Sudbourne Suffk 35 N6
Sudbrook Lincs 42 D2
Sudbrook Mons 28 F10
Sudbrooke Lincs 52 E8
Sudbury Derbys 40 F2
Sudbury Gt Lon 21 J6
Sudbury Suffk 34 E8
Suffield N York 67 L8
Suffield Norfk 45 K4
Sugnall Staffs 49 P8
Sugwas Pool Herefs 28 E1
Suisnish Highld 96 H6
Sulby IoM 56 d3
Sulgrave Nhants 31 M5
Sulham W Berk 19 Q6
Sulhamstead W Berk 19 Q7
Sullom Shet 111 k3
Sullom Voe Shet 111 k3
Sully V Glam 16 F3
Sumburgh Airport Shet 111 k5
Summerbridge N York 58 G2
Summercourt Cnwll 3 K5
Summerfield Norfk 44 C3
Summerhill Pembks 25 K7
Summerhouse Darltn 65 L4
Summersdale W Susx 10 D8
Summerseat Bury 57 P6
Summertown Oxon 31 L11
Sunbury-on-Thames Surrey 20 H9
Sundaywell D & G 78 D11
Sunderland Ag & B 82 C9
Sunderland Cumb 71 J8
Sunderland Lancs 62 H10
Sunderland Sundld 73 P9
Sunderland Bridge Dur 73 M12
Sunderland Crematorium Sundld 73 P9
Sundhope Border 79 M4
Sundon Park Luton 32 F10
Sundridge Kent 21 P11
Sunningdale W & M 20 F9
Sunninghill W & M 20 F9
Sunningwell Oxon 19 N1
Sunniside Dur 73 K12
Sunniside Gatesd 73 L8
Sunnyhill C Derb 41 J2
Sunnyhurst Bl w D 57 M4
Sunnylaw Stirlg 85 N4
Sunnymead Oxon 31 L11
Surbiton Gt Lon 21 J9
Surfleet Lincs 43 J5
Surlingham Norfk 45 M8
Surrex Essex 34 E11
Surrey & Sussex Crematorium W Susx 11 L3
Sustead Norfk 45 K3
Susworth Lincs 52 B3
Sutcombe Devon 14 F9
Sutcombemill Devon 14 F9
Sutterby Lincs 53 L8
Sutterton Lincs 43 J3
Sutton C Beds 32 H7
Sutton C Pete 42 F9
Sutton Cambs 33 M2
Sutton Devon 5 N10
Sutton E Susx 11 P9
Sutton Gt Lon 21 K9
Sutton Kent 23 P12
Sutton N York 59 L8
Sutton Norfk 45 N5
Sutton Notts 51 Q12
Sutton Oxon 31 K11
Sutton Shrops 39 N5
Sutton Staffs 49 N10
Sutton Suffk 35 M7
Sutton W Susx 10 F7
Sutton at Hone Kent 22 B9
Sutton Bassett Nhants 41 Q9
Sutton Benger Wilts 18 D5
Sutton Bonington Notts 41 L3
Sutton Bridge Lincs 43 M6
Sutton Cheney Leics 41 K7
Sutton Coldfield Birm 40 E8
Sutton Coldfield Crematorium Birm 40 F7
Sutton Courtenay Oxon 19 N2
Sutton cum Lound Notts 51 P4
Sutton Green Surrey 20 G11
Sutton Howgrave N York 65 N10
Sutton in Ashfield Notts 51 L8
Sutton-in-Craven N York 58 D5
Sutton Maddock Shrops 39 N2
Sutton Mallet Somset 17 K8
Sutton Mandeville Wilts 8 E2
Sutton Montis Somset 17 P10
Sutton-on-Hull C KuH 61 J7
Sutton on Sea Lincs 53 N7
Sutton-on-the-Forest N York 59 M2
Sutton on the Hill Derbys 40 G2
Sutton on Trent Notts 52 B9
Sutton St Edmund Lincs 43 L7
Sutton St James Lincs 43 L6
Sutton St Nicholas Herefs 39 K11
Sutton Scotney Hants 19 M11
Sutton-under-Brailes Warwks 30 H6
Sutton-under-Whitestonecliffe N York 66 C10
Sutton upon Derwent E R Yk 60 C5
Sutton Valence Kent 12 F1
Sutton Veny Wilts 18 D11
Sutton Waldron Dorset 8 C4
Sutton Weaver Ches W 57 K11
Sutton Wick BaNES 17 N4
Sutton Wick Oxon 19 N2
Swaby Lincs 53 L7
Swadlincote Derbys 40 H4
Swaffham Norfk 44 D8
Swaffham Bulbeck Cambs 33 N4
Swaffham Prior Cambs 33 P4
Swafield Norfk 45 L4
Swainby N York 66 C7
Swainsthorpe Norfk 45 K9
Swainswick BaNES 18 B7
Swalcliffe Oxon 31 J6
Swalecliffe Kent 23 L9
Swallow Lincs 52 H3
Swallow Beck Lincs 52 D9
Swallowcliffe Wilts 8 E3
Swallowfield Wokham 20 B9
Swanage Dorset 8 F10
Swanbourne Bucks 32 B10
Swan Green Ches W 49 N2
Swanland E R Yk 60 G8
Swanley Kent 21 P9
Swanley Village Kent 21 Q9
Swanmore Hants 9 P4
Swannington Leics 41 K4
Swannington Norfk 45 J6
Swanpool Garden Suburb Lincs 52 D9
Swanscombe Kent 22 C8
Swansea Swans 26 E9
Swansea Airport Swans 26 D9
Swansea Crematorium Swans 26 E8
Swansea West Services Swans 26 E8
Swanton Abbot Norfk 45 L5
Swanton Morley Norfk 44 G6
Swanton Novers Norfk 44 G4
Swanwick Derbys 51 K9
Swanwick Hants 9 N5
Swanwick Crematorium Derbys 51 K9
Swarby Lincs 42 F3
Swardeston Norfk 45 K9
Swarkestone Derbys 41 J2
Swarland Nthumb 81 N12
Swarraton Hants 19 P12
Swarthmoor Cumb 62 F6
Swaton Lincs 42 G3
Swavesey Cambs 33 K3
Sway Hants 9 J7
Swayfield Lincs 42 E5
Swaythling C Sotn 9 M4
Sweetham Devon 15 Q11
Sweethaws E Susx 11 P4
Sweets Cnwll 4 E2
Sweetshouse Cnwll 3 N4
Swefling Suffk 35 M4
Swepstone Leics 41 J5
Swerford Oxon 31 J7
Swettenham Ches E 49 P3
Swilland Suffk 35 K6
Swillington Leeds 59 J7
Swimbridge Devon 15 L6
Swimbridge Newland Devon 15 K6
Swinbrook Oxon 30 H10
Swincliffe N York 58 G3
Swinderby Lincs 52 C10
Swindon Gloucs 29 N4
Swindon Staffs 39 Q4
Swindon Swindn 18 G4
Swine E R Yk 61 K7
Swinefleet E R Yk 60 D9
Swineshead Bed 32 F4
Swineshead Lincs 43 J3
Swiney Highld 110 E8
Swinford Leics 41 M10
Swingfield Minnis Kent 13 N2
Swingfield Street Kent 13 N2
Swingleton Green Suffk 34 F7
Swinhoe Nthumb 81 P8
Swinithwaite N York 65 J9
Swinside Cumb 71 K10
Swinstead Lincs 42 E5
Swinton Border 80 H5
Swinton N York 65 L10
Swinton N York 66 G11
Swinton Rothm 51 K2
Swinton Salfd 57 P8
Swithland Leics 41 M5
Swordale Highld 107 J8
Swordland Highld 97 L10
Swordly Highld 109 N3
Swynnerton Staffs 49 Q8
Swyre Dorset 7 M5
Sychtyn Powys 38 B1
Syde Gloucs 29 N6
Sydenham Gt Lon 21 M8
Sydenham Oxon 20 B3
Sydenham Damerel Devon 5 J5
Syderstone Norfk 44 D4
Sydling St Nicholas Dorset 7 P3
Sydmonton Hants 19 N8
Syerston Notts 51 Q10
Sykehouse Donc 59 N10
Symbister Shet 111 k3
Symington S Ayrs 76 G5
Symington S Lans 78 G2
Symondsbury Dorset 7 L4
Symonds Yat Herefs 28 G5
Syre Highld 109 M7
Syreford Gloucs 30 D9
Syresham Nhants 31 N6
Syston Leics 41 N5
Syston Lincs 42 D2
Sytchampton Worcs 39 Q8
Sywell Nhants 32 B4

T

Tackley Oxon 31 L9
Tacolneston Norfk 45 J10
Tadcaster N York 59 L5
Taddington Derbys 50 F6
Tadley Hants 19 P8
Tadlow Cambs 33 J7
Tadmarton Oxon 31 K6
Tadworth Surrey 21 K11
Taff's Well Rhondd 27 N11
Taibach Neath 26 G10
Tain Highld 107 M6
Tain Highld 110 E3
Tairbeart W Isls 111 c3
Takeley Essex 33 P11
Takeley Street Essex 33 N11
Talaton Devon 6 E3
Talbenny Pembks 24 E6
Taleford Devon 6 E4
Talerddig Powys 47 Q10
Talgarreg Cerdgn 36 G9
Talgarth Powys 27 N3
Talisker Highld 96 D4
Talke Staffs 49 P5
Talkin Cumb 71 Q4
Talladale Highld 105 N8
Talla Linnfoots Border 79 J5
Tallaminnock S Ayrs 76 G10
Tallarn Green Wrexhm 49 J6
Tallentire Cumb 70 H8
Talley Carmth 26 E3
Tallington Lincs 42 F8
Talmine Highld 109 K3
Talog Carmth 25 N4
Talsarn Cerdgn 37 J9
Talsarnau Gwynd 47 K4
Talskiddy Cnwll 3 K3
Talwrn IoA 54 G6
Tal-y-bont Cerdgn 37 K3
Tal-y-Bont Conwy 55 L7
Tal-y-bont Gwynd 47 J7
Tal-y-bont Gwynd 54 H7
Talybont-on-Usk Powys 27 N4
Tal-y-Cafn Conwy 55 L7
Tal-y-coed Mons 28 E6
Talysarn Gwynd 54 G10
Tamar Valley Mining District Devon 5 J7
Tamerton Foliot C Plym 5 K7
Tamworth Staffs 40 G6
Tamworth Services Warwks 40 G7
Tandridge Surrey 21 M12
Tanfield Dur 73 L9
Tanfield Lea Dur 73 L9
Tangley Hants 19 K9
Tangmere W Susx 10 E8
Tangusdale W Isls 111 a7
Tankerness Ork 111 h2
Tankersley Barns 51 J2
Tankerton Kent 23 L9
Tannach Highld 110 G6
Tannachie Abers 95 N5
Tannadice Angus 93 N4
Tanner's Green Worcs 40 E11
Tannington Suffk 35 L4
Tannochside N Lans 85 L10
Tansley Derbys 51 J8
Tansor Nhants 42 F11
Tantobie Dur 73 L9
Tanworth in Arden Warwks 40 E12
Tan-y-groes Cerdgn 36 E10
Taobh Tuath W Isls 111 b3
Taplow Bucks 20 E7
Tarbert Ag & B 75 J3
Tarbert Ag & B 83 N8
Tarbert W Isls 111 c3
Tarbet Ag & B 84 F3
Tarbet Highld 97 L10
Tarbet Highld 108 D6
Tarbolton S Ayrs 76 G6
Tarbrax S Lans 86 B10
Tardebigge Worcs 30 D1
Tarfside Angus 94 H6
Tarland Abers 94 H2
Tarleton Lancs 57 J5
Tarlton Gloucs 29 N8
Tarnock Somset 17 K5
Tarporley Ches W 49 K3
Tarrant Crawford Dorset 8 D6
Tarrant Gunville Dorset 8 D5
Tarrant Hinton Dorset 8 D5
Tarrant Keyneston Dorset 8 D6
Tarrant Launceston Dorset 8 D5
Tarrant Monkton Dorset 8 D6
Tarrant Rawston Dorset 8 D6
Tarrant Rushton Dorset 8 D6
Tarring Neville E Susx 11 N8
Tarrington Herefs 28 H1
Tarskavaig Highld 96 H7
Tarves Abers 102 H8
Tarvin Ches W 49 J3
Tasburgh Norfk 45 K10
Tatenhill Staffs 40 G3
Tathwell Lincs 53 K6
Tatsfield Surrey 21 N11
Tattenhall Ches W 49 J4
Tatterford Norfk 44 E5
Tattersett Norfk 44 E4
Tattershall Lincs 52 H11
Tattershall Thorpe Lincs 52 H10
Tattingstone Suffk 35 J8
Tattingstone White Horse Suffk 35 J8
Tatton Park Ches E 57 N11
Tatworth Somset 7 J2
Tauchers Moray 101 M5
Taunton Somset 16 G10
Taunton Deane Crematorium Somset 16 G10
Taunton Deane Services Somset 16 G11
Taverham Norfk 45 J7
Tavernspite Pembks 25 L6
Tavistock Devon 5 K5
Tavistock Devon 5 K5
Taw Green Devon 15 L11
Tawstock Devon 15 K6
Taxal Derbys 50 D5
Taychreggan Hotel Ag & B 90 E11
Tay Forest Park P & K 92 B4
Tayinloan Ag & B 75 K4
Taynton Gloucs 29 J4
Taynton Oxon 30 G10
Taynuilt Ag & B 90 D9
Tayport Fife 93 M9
Tayvallich Ag & B 83 L5
Tealby Lincs 52 G5
Tealing Angus 93 M7
Team Valley Gatesd 73 M8
Teangue Highld 97 J7
Teanord Highld 107 K9
Tebay Cumb 63 L2
Tebay Services Cumb 63 L2
Tebworth C Beds 32 E10
Tedburn St Mary Devon 5 Q2
Teddington Gloucs 29 N3
Teddington Gt Lon 21 J8
Tedstone Delamere Herefs 39 M9
Tedstone Wafer Herefs 39 M9
Teesside Crematorium Middsb 66 C4
Teeton Nhants 41 P12
Teffont Evias Wilts 8 E2
Teffont Magna Wilts 8 E2
Tegryn Pembks 25 L3
Teigh Rutlnd 42 C7
Teigngrace Devon 6 B7
Teignmouth Devon 6 C8
Teindside Border 79 P7
Telford Wrekin 39 M1
Telford Crematorium Wrekin 49 N12
Telford Services Shrops 39 N1
Tellisford Somset 18 B9
Telscombe E Susx 11 N8

6 Tempar - Trealaw

Tempar P & K 91 Q5
Templand D & G 78 H10
Temple Cnwll 4 E5
Temple Mdloth 86 G9
Temple Bar Cerdgn 37 J9
Temple Cloud BaNES 17 P5
Templecombe Somset 17 Q10
Temple Ewell Kent 13 P2
Temple Grafton Warwks 30 E3
Temple Guiting Gloucs 30 E8
Temple Hirst N York 59 N8
Temple Normanton Derbys 51 K7
Temple of Fiddes Abers 95 N6
Temple Sowerby Cumb 64 B3
Templeton Devon 15 Q9
Templeton Pembks 25 K6
Templetown Dur 73 K10
Tempsford C Beds 32 G6
Tenbury Wells Worcs 39 L8
Tenby Pembks 25 K8
Tendring Essex 35 J11
Tendring Green Essex 35 J10
Tendring Heath Essex 35 J10
Ten Mile Bank Norfk 43 P10
Tenterden Kent 12 H4
Terling Essex 22 F1
Ternhill Shrops 49 L8
Terregles D & G 78 F12
Terrington N York 66 F12
Terrington St Clement Norfk 43 N6
Terrington St John Norfk 43 N7
Teston Kent 22 E11
Testwood Hants 9 L5
Tetbury Gloucs 29 M9
Tetchill Shrops 48 H8
Tetcott Devon 14 F11
Tetford Lincs 53 K8
Tetney Lincs 53 K4
Tetsworth Oxon 20 B3
Tettenhall Wolves 40 B7
Teversal Notts 51 L8
Teversham Cambs 33 M5
Teviothead Border 79 N7
Tewin Herts 21 L1
Tewkesbury Gloucs 29 M3
Teynham Kent 23 J10
Thackley C Brad 58 F6
Thainstone Abers 102 G10
Thakeham W Susx 10 H6
Thame Oxon 20 B3
Thames Ditton Surrey 21 J9
Thamesmead Gt Lon 21 P7
Thamesport Medway 22 G8
Thanet Crematorium Kent 23 Q9
Thanington Kent 23 L11
Thankerton S Lans 78 F2
Tharston Norfk 45 K10
Thatcham W Berk 19 N7
Thaxted Essex 33 P9
Theakston N York 65 N9
Thealby N Linc 60 F9
Theale Somset 17 L7
Theale W Berk 19 Q6
Thearne E R Yk 61 J6
The Beeches Gloucs 18 F1
Theberton Suffk 35 P4
The Braes Highld 96 G3
The Brunt E Loth 87 M7
The Bungalow IoM 56 d4
The Burf Worcs 39 P8
The Butts Gloucs 29 M5
The City Bucks 20 C4
The Common Wilts 9 J2
The Counties Crematorium Nhants 31 Q3
Theddingworth Leics 41 P9
Theddlethorpe All Saints Lincs 53 M6
Theddlethorpe St Helen Lincs 53 M6
The Den N Ayrs 76 F2
The Forest of Dean Crematorium Gloucs 28 H6
The Forstal Kent 13 K3
The Garden of England Crematorium Kent 22 H9
The Green Cumb 62 D5
The Green Essex 34 C11
The Green N York 66 H6
The Green Wilts 8 C2
The Headland Hartpl 66 D1
The Hill Cumb 62 D5
The Lee Bucks 20 E3
The Lhen IoM 56 d2
The Linn Crematorium E Rens 85 K10
Thelnetham Suffk 34 G2
The Lochs Moray 101 L3
Thelveton Norfk 35 J1
Thelwall Warrtn 57 M10
The Manchester Crematorium Manch 57 P9
Themelthorpe Norfk 44 H5
The Moor Kent 12 F4
The Mumbles Swans 26 E10
The Murray S Lans 85 K11
The Neuk Abers 95 M3
Thenford Nhants 31 M6
The Park Crematorium Hants 10 E1
The Reddings Gloucs 29 M5
Therfield Herts 33 K8
The Rose Hill Crematorium Donc 51 N1
The Ross P & K 92 B10
The Stocks Kent 12 H5
The Strand Wilts 18 D8
Thetford Norfk 44 E12
Thetford Forest Park 44 D11
The Vale Crematorium Luton 32 G10
Theydon Bois Essex 21 N4
Thickwood Wilts 18 C6
Thimbleby Lincs 53 J9
Thimbleby N York 66 C8
Thingwall Wirral 56 F11
Thirkleby N York 66 C10
Thirlby N York 66 C10
Thirlestane Border 80 D5
Thirn N York 65 L9
Thirsk N York 65 Q10
Thistleton Lancs 56 H2
Thistleton Rutlnd 42 D6
Thistley Green Suffk 33 Q2
Thixendale N York 60 E3
Thockrington Nthumb 72 G5
Tholomas Drove Cambs 43 L8
Tholthorpe N York 59 L2
Thomastown Abers 102 D7
Thompson Norfk 44 F10
Thoralby N York 64 H9
Thoresway Lincs 52 G4
Thorganby Lincs 52 H4
Thorganby N York 59 P6
Thorgill N York 66 G7
Thorington Suffk 35 N2
Thorington Street Suffk 34 G9
Thorlby N York 58 C4
Thorley Herts 33 M11
Thorley Street IoW 9 L9
Thormanby N York 66 C11
Thornaby-on-Tees S on T 66 C4
Thornage Norfk 44 H3
Thornborough Bucks 31 Q7
Thornborough N York 65 N10
Thornbury C Brad 58 G7
Thornbury Devon 14 G9
Thornbury Herefs 39 L9
Thornbury S Glos 28 H10
Thornby Nhants 41 P11
Thorncliff Staffs 50 D8
Thorncliffe Crematorium Cumb 62 E7
Thorncombe Dorset 7 K3
Thorndon Suffk 35 J3
Thorndon Cross Devon 5 L2
Thorne Donc 59 P10
Thorner Leeds 59 J6
Thorne St Margaret Somset 16 E11
Thorney C Pete 43 J8
Thorney Notts 52 C8
Thorney Somset 17 K10
Thorney Hill Hants 8 H7
Thorney Island W Susx 10 C9
Thornfalcon Somset 16 H10
Thornford Dorset 17 N12
Thorngrafton Nthumb 72 E7
Thorngumbald E R Yk 61 L8
Thornham Norfk 44 C2
Thornham Magna Suffk 34 H3
Thornham Parva Suffk 35 J3
Thornhaugh C Pete 42 F9
Thornhill C Sotn 9 M5
Thornhill Cumb 62 B1
Thornhill D & G 78 E9
Thornhill Derbys 50 G4
Thornhill Kirk 58 G9
Thornhill Stirlg 85 L3
Thornhill Crematorium Cardif 27 N11
Thornholme E R Yk 61 J2
Thornicombe Dorset 8 C6
Thornington Nthumb 81 J7
Thornley Dur 73 K12
Thornley Dur 73 P11
Thornliebank E Rens 85 J10
Thorns Suffk 34 C6
Thornsett Derbys 50 D4
Thornthwaite Cumb 71 K9
Thornthwaite N York 58 F3
Thornton Angus 93 M6
Thornton Bucks 31 Q7
Thornton C Brad 58 E7
Thornton E R Yk 60 D5
Thornton Fife 86 F3
Thornton Lancs 56 G1
Thornton Leics 41 L6
Thornton Middsb 66 C5
Thornton Nthumb 81 K5
Thornton Curtis N Linc 61 J9
Thornton Garden of Rest Crematorium Sefton 56 G8
Thorntonhall S Lans 85 K11
Thornton Heath Gt Lon 21 L9
Thornton Hough Wirral 56 F11
Thornton-in-Craven N York 58 B5
Thornton in Lonsdale N York 63 M7
Thornton-le-Beans N York 65 P9
Thornton-le-Clay N York 59 P2
Thornton-le-Dale N York 67 J10
Thornton le Moor Lincs 52 F4
Thornton-le-Moor N York 65 P9
Thornton-le-Moors Ches W 48 H1
Thornton-le-Street N York 65 P9
Thorntonloch E Loth 87 N7
Thornton Rust N York 64 G9
Thornton Steward N York 65 L9
Thornton Watlass N York 65 M9
Thornydykes Border 80 E5
Thornythwaite Cumb 71 N10
Thoroton Notts 51 Q11
Thorp Arch Leeds 59 K5
Thorpe Derbys 50 F10
Thorpe E R Yk 60 G5
Thorpe N York 58 D2
Thorpe Notts 51 Q10
Thorpe Surrey 20 G9
Thorpe Abbotts Norfk 35 K2
Thorpe Arnold Leics 41 Q4
Thorpe Audlin Wakefd 59 L10
Thorpe Bassett N York 67 J11
Thorpe Bay Sthend 22 H6
Thorpe by Water Rutlnd 42 C10
Thorpe Constantine Staffs 40 H6
Thorpe End Norfk 45 L7
Thorpe Green Essex 35 J11
Thorpe Green Suffk 34 F6
Thorpe Hesley Rothm 51 J2
Thorpe in Balne Donc 59 N11
Thorpe Langton Leics 41 Q8
Thorpe Lea Surrey 20 G8
Thorpe-le-Soken Essex 35 K11
Thorpe le Street E R Yk 60 E5
Thorpe Malsor Nhants 32 B2
Thorpe Mandeville Nhants 31 M5
Thorpe Market Norfk 45 L3
Thorpe Marriot Norfk 45 K7
Thorpe Morieux Suffk 34 F6
Thorpeness Suffk 35 P5
Thorpe on the Hill Lincs 52 C9
Thorpe Park Surrey 20 G9
Thorpe St Andrew Norfk 45 L8
Thorpe St Peter Lincs 53 M10
Thorpe Salvin Rothm 51 M5
Thorpe Satchville Leics 41 Q5
Thorpe Thewles S on T 65 P3
Thorpe Tilney Lincs 52 G11
Thorpe Underwood N York 59 L3
Thorpe Waterville Nhants 32 E1
Thorpe Willoughby N York 59 M7
Thorrington Essex 34 H11
Thorverton Devon 6 C3
Thrandeston Suffk 35 J2
Thrapston Nhants 32 E2
Threapwood Ches W 48 H6
Threapwood Staffs 50 D11
Threave S Ayrs 76 F9
Three Bridges W Susx 11 L3
Three Chimneys Kent 12 G3
Three Cocks Powys 27 N2
Three Counties Crematorium Essex 34 D10
Three Crosses Swans 26 D9
Three Cups Corner E Susx 12 D6
Threekingham Lincs 42 F3
Three Leg Cross E Susx 12 D4
Three Legged Cross Dorset 8 F6
Three Mile Cross Wokham 20 B9
Threemilestone Cnwll 2 H6
Three Miletown W Loth 86 C7
Three Oaks E Susx 12 G7
Threlkeld Cumb 71 M9
Threshers Bush Essex 21 P2
Threshfield N York 58 C2
Thrigby Norfk 45 P7
Thringstone Leics 41 K4
Thrintoft N York 65 N8
Thriplow Cambs 33 M7
Throcking Herts 33 K10
Throckley N u Ty 73 K7
Throckmorton Worcs 30 C4
Throop Bmouth 8 G8
Thropton Nthumb 72 H1
Throsk Stirlg 85 P5
Throughgate D & G 78 E11
Throwleigh Devon 5 N3
Throwley Forstal Kent 23 J11
Thrumpton Notts 41 L2
Thrumster Highld 110 G6
Thrunscoe NE Lin 53 K2
Thrupp Gloucs 29 M7
Thrussington Leics 41 P4
Thruxton Hants 19 K10
Thruxton Herefs 28 E2
Thrybergh Rothm 51 L2
Thulston Derbys 41 K2
Thundersley Essex 22 F6
Thurcaston Leics 41 M5
Thurcroft Rothm 51 L3
Thurgarton Norfk 45 K3
Thurgarton Notts 51 P10
Thurgoland Barns 50 H1
Thurlaston Leics 41 L7
Thurlaston Warwks 41 L12
Thurlbear Somset 16 H11
Thurlby Lincs 42 F6
Thurlby Lincs 52 C10
Thurlby Lincs 53 M8
Thurleigh Bed 32 F5
Thurlestone Devon 5 N10
Thurloxton Somset 16 H9
Thurlstone Barns 58 G12
Thurlton Norfk 45 N9
Thurmaston Leics 41 N5
Thurnby Leics 41 N6
Thurne Norfk 45 N7
Thurnham Kent 22 F11
Thurning Nhants 42 F12
Thurning Norfk 44 H4
Thurnscoe Barns 59 L11
Thurrock Services Thurr 22 C7
Thursby Cumb 71 M5
Thursford Norfk 44 G4
Thursley Surrey 10 E3
Thurso Highld 110 D3
Thurstaston Wirral 56 F11
Thurston Suffk 34 F4
Thurstonfield Cumb 71 M4
Thurstonland Kirk 58 F11
Thurton Norfk 45 M9
Thurvaston Derbys 50 G12
Thuxton Norfk 44 G8
Thwaite N York 64 F7
Thwaite Suffk 35 J3
Thwaite Head Cumb 62 G4
Thwaite St Mary Norfk 45 M10
Thwing E R Yk 67 M12
Tibbermore P & K 92 F10
Tibbers D & G 78 E9
Tibberton Gloucs 29 K4
Tibberton Worcs 30 B3
Tibberton Wrekin 49 M10
Tibbie Shiels Inn Border 79 K5
Tibenham Norfk 45 J11
Tibshelf Derbys 51 K8
Tibshelf Services Derbys 51 K8
Tibthorpe E R Yk 60 G3
Ticehurst E Susx 12 E4
Tichborne Hants 9 P2
Tickencote Rutlnd 42 E8
Tickenham N Som 17 L2
Tickhill Donc 51 N3
Ticklerton Shrops 39 J4
Ticknall Derbys 41 J3
Tickton E R Yk 60 H6
Tidcombe Wilts 19 K8
Tiddington Oxon 31 P12
Tiddington Warwks 30 G3
Tidebrook E Susx 12 C4
Tideford Cnwll 4 H8
Tidenham Gloucs 28 G9
Tideswell Derbys 50 F6
Tidmarsh W Berk 19 Q6
Tidmington Warwks 30 H6
Tidworth Wilts 19 J10
Tiers Cross Pembks 24 F6
Tiffield Nhants 31 P4
Tigerton Angus 95 J8
Tigh a Ghearraidh W Isls 111 a4
Tigharry W Isls 111 a4
Tighnabruaich Ag & B 83 P8
Tigley Devon 5 P7
Tilbrook Cambs 32 F3
Tilbury Thurr 22 D8
Tile Hill Covtry 40 H11
Tilehurst Readg 19 Q6
Tilford Surrey 10 E2
Tilgate W Susx 11 L3
Tilham Street Somset 17 M8
Tillicoultry Clacks 85 Q4
Tillietudlem S Lans 77 N3
Tillingham Essex 23 J3
Tillington Herefs 39 J12
Tillington W Susx 10 F6
Tillington Common Herefs 39 J11
Tillybirloch Abers 95 L1
Tillyfourie Abers 102 E11
Tillygreig Abers 103 J10
Tillyrie P & K 86 D2
Tilmanstone Kent 23 P12
Tilney All Saints Norfk 43 P6
Tilney High End Norfk 43 N6
Tilney St Lawrence Norfk 43 N7
Tilshead Wilts 18 F10
Tilstock Shrops 49 K7
Tilston Ches W 49 J5
Tilstone Fearnall Ches W 49 K4
Tilsworth C Beds 32 E11
Tilton on the Hill Leics 41 Q6
Tiltups End Gloucs 29 L8
Timberland Lincs 52 G10
Timbersbrook Ches E 50 B8
Timberscombe Somset 16 C7
Timble N York 58 F4
Timpanheck D & G 71 M1
Timperley Traffd 57 P10
Timsbury BaNES 17 P4
Timsbury Hants 9 L3
Timsgarry W Isls 111 c2
Timsgearraidh W Isls 111 c2
Timworth Suffk 34 E3
Timworth Green Suffk 34 E3
Tincleton Dorset 8 B8
Tindale Cumb 72 B8
Tindale Crescent Dur 65 L3
Tingewick Bucks 31 P7
Tingrith C Beds 32 E9
Tingwall Airport Shet 111 k4
Tingwell Ork 111 h2
Tinhay Devon 5 J3
Tinsley Sheff 51 K3
Tinsley Green W Susx 11 L3
Tintagel Cnwll 4 C3
Tintern Parva Mons 28 F8
Tintinhull Somset 17 M11
Tintwistle Derbys 50 D2
Tinwald D & G 78 G11
Tinwell Rutlnd 42 E8
Tipton Sandw 40 C8
Tipton St John Devon 6 E5
Tiptree Essex 34 E12
Tiptree Heath Essex 22 G1
Tirabad Powys 37 P11
Tiree Ag & B 88 C7
Tiree Airport Ag & B 88 C7
Tiretigan Ag & B 83 K9
Tirley Gloucs 29 L3
Tiroran Ag & B 89 K10
Tirphil Caerph 27 N7
Tirril Cumb 71 P9
Tisbury Wilts 8 D2
Tissington Derbys 50 F9
Titchberry Devon 14 E6
Titchfield Hants 9 P6
Titchmarsh Nhants 32 E2
Titchwell Norfk 44 C2
Tithby Notts 51 P12
Titley Herefs 38 G9
Titsey Surrey 21 N11
Titson Cnwll 14 E10
Tittensor Staffs 49 Q7
Tittleshall Norfk 44 E6
Titton Worcs 39 P7
Tiverton Ches W 49 K4
Tiverton Devon 6 C1
Tivetshall St Margaret Norfk 45 K11
Tivetshall St Mary Norfk 45 J11
Tixall Staffs 40 C3
Tixover Rutlnd 42 D9
Toab Shet 111 k5
Tobermory Ag & B 89 L5
Toberonochy Ag & B 83 L2
Tobha Mor W Isls 111 a5
Tocher Abers 102 F8
Tochieneal Moray 101 P3
Tockenham Wilts 18 F5
Tockholes Bl w D 57 M4
Tockington S Glos 28 H10
Tockwith N York 59 L4
Todber Dorset 8 B4
Toddington C Beds 32 E10
Toddington Gloucs 30 D7
Toddington Services C Beds 32 E10
Todenham Gloucs 30 G7
Todhills Angus 93 M7
Todhills Services Cumb 71 N3
Todmorden Calder 58 C8
Todwick Rothm 51 L4
Toft Cambs 33 K5
Toft Lincs 42 F6
Toft Shet 111 k3
Toft Hill Dur 65 K2
Toft Monks Norfk 45 N10
Toft next Newton Lincs 52 E6
Toftrees Norfk 44 E5
Togston Nthumb 73 M1
Tokavaig Highld 96 H7
Tokers Green Oxon 20 B7
Tolastadh W Isls 111 e1
Tolland Somset 16 E9
Tollard Royal Wilts 8 D4
Toll Bar Donc 59 M11
Toller Fratrum Dorset 7 N4
Toller Porcorum Dorset 7 N3
Tollerton N York 59 L2
Tollerton Notts 41 N1
Tollesbury Essex 23 J2
Tolleshunt D'Arcy Essex 22 H2
Tolleshunt Knights Essex 22 H1
Tolleshunt Major Essex 22 H2
Tolpuddle Dorset 8 B8
Tolsta W Isls 111 e1
Tolworth Gt Lon 21 J9
Tomatin Highld 99 M4
Tomchrasky Highld 98 C6
Tomdoun Highld 98 B8
Tomich Highld 98 D4
Tomich Highld 107 J11
Tomich Highld 107 K2
Tomich Highld 107 L8
Tomintoul Moray 101 J10
Tomnacross Highld 98 G2
Tomnavoulin Moray 101 J9
Tonbridge Kent 12 C2
Tondu Brdgnd 27 J11
Tonedale Somset 16 F11
Tong C Brad 58 G7
Tong Kent 23 J11
Tong Shrops 39 P1
Tonge Leics 41 K3
Tongham Surrey 10 E1
Tongland D & G 69 Q8
Tong Norton Shrops 39 P1
Tongue Highld 109 K4
Tongwynlais Cardif 27 N11
Tonmawr Neath 26 H9
Tonna Neath 26 G8
Tonwell Herts 33 K12
Tonypandy Rhondd 27 L9
Tonyrefail Rhondd 27 L10
Toot Baldon Oxon 19 P1
Toot Hill Essex 21 P3
Toothill Swindn 18 G4
Tooting Gt Lon 21 L8
Tooting Bec Gt Lon 21 L8
Topcliffe N York 65 P11
Topcroft Norfk 45 L10
Topcroft Street Norfk 45 L10
Toppesfield Essex 34 C8
Toprow Norfk 45 J9
Topsham Devon 6 C5
Torbeg N Ayrs 75 N6
Torboll Highld 107 M3
Torbreck Highld 99 J2
Torbryan Devon 5 Q6
Torcastle Highld 90 F1
Torcross Devon 5 Q10
Tore Highld 107 K10
Torinturk Ag & B 83 M9
Torksey Lincs 52 B7
Tormarton S Glos 18 B5
Tormore N Ayrs 75 N6
Tornagrain Highld 107 M11
Tornaveen Abers 95 K2
Torness Highld 98 H4
Toronto Dur 65 L2
Torpenhow Cumb 71 K7
Torphichen W Loth 86 A7
Torphins Abers 95 K2
Torpoint Cnwll 5 J8
Torquay Torbay 6 C9
Torquay Crematorium Torbay 6 B9
Torquhan Border 87 J11
Torran Highld 104 H11
Torrance E Duns 85 K8
Torranyard N Ayrs 76 F3
Torridon Highld 105 N10
Torridon House Highld 105 M10
Torrin Highld 96 G5
Torrisdale Ag & B 75 M5
Torrisdale Highld 109 M4
Torrish Highld 110 A11
Torrisholme Lancs 63 J9
Torrobull Highld 107 K2
Torry C Aber 95 Q2
Torryburn Fife 86 B5
Torteval Guern 6 a2
Torthorwald D & G 78 G12
Tortington W Susx 10 G8
Torton Worcs 39 Q7
Tortworth S Glos 29 J9
Torvaig Highld 96 F2
Torver Cumb 62 F4
Torwood Falk 85 P6
Torwoodlee Border 79 P2
Torworth Notts 51 P4
Toscaig Highld 97 J3
Toseland Cambs 33 J4
Tosside Lancs 63 P10
Tostock Suffk 34 F4
Totaig Highld 104 B11
Tote Highld 104 F11
Tote Highld 104 G9
Totland IoW 9 K9
Totley Sheff 50 H5
Totnes Devon 5 Q7
Toton Notts 41 L1
Totronald Ag & B 88 E5
Totscore Highld 104 E8
Tottenham Gt Lon 21 M5
Tottenhill Norfk 43 Q7
Totteridge Gt Lon 21 K5
Totternhoe C Beds 32 E11
Tottington Bury 57 P6
Totton Hants 9 L5
Toulton Somset 16 G9
Toulvaddie Highld 107 P6
Tovil Kent 22 F11
Toward Ag & B 84 C8
Toward Quay Ag & B 84 B9
Towcester Nhants 31 P4
Towednack Cnwll 2 D7
Tower of London Gt Lon 21 M7
Towersey Oxon 20 B3
Towie Abers 101 N11
Tow Law Dur 73 K11
Town End Cambs 43 L10
Townend W Duns 84 G7
Townhead Barns 50 F1
Townhead D & G 78 G10
Townhead of Greenlaw D & G 70 C3
Townhill Fife 86 D4
Town Littleworth E Susx 11 N6
Towns End Hants 19 P8
Townshend Cnwll 2 E8
Town Street Suffk 44 C11
Town Yetholm Border 80 H8
Towthorpe C York 59 N3
Towton N York 59 L6
Towyn Conwy 55 P6
Toxteth Lpool 56 G10
Toynton All Saints Lincs 53 L10
Toy's Hill Kent 21 P12
Trabboch E Ayrs 76 G7
Trabbochburn E Ayrs 76 H7
Tradespark Highld 100 D4
Trallong Powys 27 K3
Tranent E Loth 86 H7
Tranmere Wirral 56 G10
Trantelbeg Highld 109 Q5
Trantlemore Highld 109 Q5
Trapp Carmth 26 E5
Traprain E Loth 87 L7
Traquair Border 79 M3
Trawden Lancs 58 B6
Trawsfynydd Gwynd 47 L4
Trealaw Rhondd 27 L9

Treales - Walditch 197

Treales Lancs 56 H3
Trearddur Bay IoA 54 C6
Treaslane Highld 104 E10
Trebetherick Cnwll 4 B5
Treborough Somset 16 D8
Trebullett Cnwll 4 H5
Treburley Cnwll 4 H5
Trecastle Powys 27 J3
Trecwn Pembks 24 G3
Trecynon Rhondd 27 L7
Tredegar Blae G 27 N7
Tredington Gloucs 29 M3
Tredington Warwks 30 H5
Tredunnock Mons 28 D9
Treen Cnwll 2 B10
Treeton Rothm 51 K4
Trefasser Pembks 24 F2
Trefecca Powys 27 N3
Trefeglwys Powys 37 Q3
Treffgarne Pembks 24 G4
Treffgarne Owen Pembks 24 F4
Trefforest Rhondd 27 M10
Trefilan Cerdgn 37 J8
Trefin Pembks 24 E3
Trefnant Denbgs 48 B2
Trefonen Shrops 48 F9
Trefor Gwynd 46 F3
Trefriw Conwy 55 L8
Tregadillett Cnwll 4 G4
Tregare Mons 28 E6
Tregaron Cerdgn 37 L8
Tregarth Gwynd 54 H7
Tregeare Cnwll 4 F3
Tregeiriog Wrexhm 48 D8
Tregele IoA 54 E3
Treglemais Pembks 24 E3
Tregonetha Cnwll 3 L3
Tregonning & Gwinear Mining District Cnwll 2 E9
Tregony Cnwll 3 K6
Tregorrick Cnwll 3 M5
Tregoyd Powys 27 P2
Tre-groes Cerdgn 36 G10
Tregynon Powys 38 C3
Tre-gynwr Carmth 25 P5
Trehafod Rhondd 27 L10
Trehan Cnwll 5 J8
Treharris Myr Td 27 M9
Treherbert Rhondd 27 K8
Trekenner Cnwll 4 H5
Treknow Cnwll 4 C3
Trelawnyd Flints 56 C11
Trelech Carmth 25 M3
Treleddyd-fawr Pembks 24 D3
Trelewis Myr Td 27 M9
Trelights Cnwll 4 B4
Trelill Cnwll 4 C5
Trellech Mons 28 F7
Trelogan Flints 56 D11
Tremadog Gwynd 47 J4
Tremail Cnwll 4 E3
Tremain Cerdgn 36 D10
Tremaine Cnwll 4 F3
Tremar Cnwll 4 G6
Trematon Cnwll 5 J8
Tremeirchion Denbgs 48 C2
Trenance Cnwll 3 J3
Trenance Cnwll 3 L2
Trench Wrekin 49 M11
Trenear Cnwll 2 G9
Treneglos Cnwll 4 F3
Trent Dorset 17 N11
Trentham C Stke 49 Q7
Trentishoe Devon 15 L3
Treoes V Glam 27 K12
Treorchy Rhondd 27 K8
Trequite Cnwll 3 M1
Trerhyngyll V Glam 27 L12
Trerulefoot Cnwll 4 H8
Tresaith Cerdgn 36 E9
Tresco IoS 2 b2
Trescowe Cnwll 2 E9
Tresean Cnwll 2 H4
Tresham Gloucs 29 L9
Treshnish Isles Ag & B 88 G7
Tresillian Cnwll 3 K6
Treskinnick Cross Cnwll 14 D11
Tresmeer Cnwll 4 F3
Tresparrett Cnwll 4 E2
Tressait P & K 92 C4
Tresta Shet 111 k4
Tresta Shet 111 m2
Treswell Notts 52 A7
Treswithian Downs Crematorium Cnwll 2 F7
Tre Taliesin Cerdgn 37 L3
Trethevey Cnwll 4 D3
Trethewey Cnwll 2 B10
Trethurgy Cnwll 3 M5
Tretire Herefs 28 F4
Tretower Powys 27 P5
Treuddyn Flints 48 F4
Trevalga Cnwll 4 D3
Trevalyn Wrexhm 48 H4
Trevarrian Cnwll 3 J3
Treveal Cnwll 2 H4
Treveighan Cnwll 4 D4
Trevellas Downs Cnwll 2 H5
Trevelmond Cnwll 4 F7
Treverva Cnwll 2 H9
Trevescan Cnwll 2 B10
Treviscoe Cnwll 3 L5
Trevone Cnwll 3 K1
Trevor Wrexhm 48 F7
Trewalder Cnwll 4 D4
Trewarmett Cnwll 4 D3
Trewavas Mining District Cnwll 2 E9
Trewen Cnwll 4 F4
Trewint Cnwll 4 F4
Trewithian Cnwll 3 K8
Trewoon Cnwll 3 L5
Treyford W Susx 10 D6
Trimdon Dur 65 P1
Trimdon Colliery Dur 65 P1
Trimdon Grange Dur 65 P1
Trimingham Norfk 45 L3
Trimley St Martin Suffk 35 L8
Trimley St Mary Suffk 35 L9
Trimsaran Carmth 26 B7
Trimstone Devon 15 J4
Trinafour P & K 91 Q4
Tring Herts 20 E2
Trinity Angus 95 K9
Trinity Jersey 7 b1
Trinity Gask P & K 92 E11
Triscombe Somset 16 F8
Trislaig Highld 90 E2
Trispen Cnwll 3 J6
Tritlington Nthumb 73 L3
Trochry P & K 92 E7
Troedyraur Cerdgn 36 E10
Troedyrhiw Myr Td 27 M8
Troon Cnwll 2 F8
Troon S Ayrs 76 F5
Tropical World Roundhay Park Leeds 59 J6
Trossachs Stirlg 84 H2
Trossachs Pier Stirlg 84 H2
Troston Suffk 34 E3
Trotshill Worcs 30 B3
Trottiscliffe Kent 22 D10
Trotton W Susx 10 D5
Troutbeck Cumb 62 H2
Troutbeck Bridge Cumb 62 H3
Troway Derbys 51 K5
Trowbridge Wilts 18 C8
Trowell Notts 51 L11
Trowell Services Notts 51 L11
Trowse Newton Norfk 45 L8
Trudoxhill Somset 17 Q7
Trull Somset 16 G10
Trumpan Highld 104 C9
Trumpet Herefs 28 H2
Trumpington Cambs 33 M6
Trunch Norfk 45 L3
Truro Cnwll 3 J6
Trusham Devon 6 B6
Trusley Derbys 40 G1
Trusthorpe Lincs 53 N6
Trysull Staffs 39 Q4
Tubney Oxon 19 M2
Tuckenhay Devon 5 Q8
Tuckhill Shrops 39 P5
Tuckingmill Cnwll 2 F7
Tuckingmill Wilts 8 D2
Tuckton Bmouth 8 G8
Tuddenham Suffk 34 C3
Tuddenham Suffk 35 K7
Tudeley Kent 12 C2
Tudhoe Dur 65 M1
Tudweiliog Gwynd 46 D4
Tuffley Gloucs 29 L6
Tufton Hants 19 M10
Tufton Pembks 24 H3
Tugby Leics 41 Q7
Tugford Shrops 39 K5
Tughall Nthumb 81 P8
Tullibody Clacks 85 P4
Tullich Highld 99 J4
Tullich Highld 107 P7
Tulliemet P & K 92 E5
Tulloch Abers 102 G8
Tullochgorm Ag & B 83 P4
Tulloch Station Highld 98 E11
Tullymurdoch P & K 92 H5
Tullynessle Abers 102 D10
Tulse Hill Gt Lon 21 L8
Tumble Carmth 26 D6
Tumby Lincs 53 J10
Tumby Woodside Lincs 53 J11
Tummel Bridge P & K 92 B4
Tunbridge Wells Kent 12 C3
Tundergarth D & G 79 J11
Tunley BaNES 17 Q4
Tunstall C Stke 49 Q5
Tunstall E R Yk 61 M7
Tunstall Kent 22 H10
Tunstall Lancs 63 L7
Tunstall N York 65 L8
Tunstall Norfk 45 N8
Tunstall Staffs 49 P9
Tunstall Suffk 35 M6
Tunstall Sundld 73 P9
Tunstead Derbys 50 E6
Tunstead Norfk 45 L6
Tunstead Milton Derbys 50 D5
Turgis Green Hants 20 B10
Turkdean Gloucs 30 E9
Tur Langton Leics 41 Q8
Turleigh Wilts 18 B8
Turnastone Herefs 28 D2
Turnberry S Ayrs 76 D9
Turnditch Derbys 50 H10
Turner's Hill W Susx 11 M3
Turnhouse C Edin 86 D7
Turnworth Dorset 8 B6
Turriff Abers 102 F5
Turton Bottoms Bl w D 57 N6
Turves Cambs 43 K10
Turvey Bed 32 D6
Turville Bucks 20 C5
Turweston Bucks 31 N6
Tushielaw Inn Border 79 L5
Tutbury Staffs 40 G2
Tutshill Gloucs 28 G9
Tuttington Norfk 45 K5
Tuxford Notts 51 Q6
Twatt Ork 111 g2
Twatt Shet 111 k4
Twechar E Duns 85 L7
Tweedbank Border 80 C7
Tweedmouth Nthumb 81 L4
Tweedsmuir Border 78 H4
Twelveheads Cnwll 2 H7
Twemlow Green Ches E 49 P2
Twenty Lincs 42 G6
Twerton BaNES 17 Q4
Twickenham Gt Lon 21 J8
Twigworth Gloucs 29 L4
Twineham W Susx 11 K6
Twinstead Essex 34 E9
Twitchen Devon 15 N6
Two Dales Derbys 50 H8
Two Gates Staffs 40 G7
Twycross Leics 41 J6
Twycross Zoo Leics 40 H6
Twyford Bucks 31 P8
Twyford Hants 9 N3
Twyford Leics 41 Q5
Twyford Norfk 44 G5
Twyford Wokham 20 C8
Twynholm D & G 69 P8
Twyning Green Gloucs 29 M2
Twynllanan Carmth 26 G4
Twywell Nhants 32 D2
Tyberton Herefs 28 D2
Tycroes Carmth 26 E6
Tycrwyn Powys 48 C10
Tydd Gote Lincs 43 M6
Tydd St Giles Cambs 43 L6
Tydd St Mary Lincs 43 M6
Tye Green Essex 33 P9
Tyldesley Wigan 57 M8
Tyler Hill Kent 23 L10
Tylorstown Rhondd 27 L9
Ty-nant Conwy 48 B6
Tyndrum Stirlg 91 J9
Ty'n-dwr Denbgs 48 E7
Tynemouth N Tyne 73 P7
Tynemouth Crematorium N Tyne 73 N7
Tyninghame E Loth 87 L6
Tynron D & G 77 N11
Tynygraig Cerdgn 37 L6
Ty'n-y-Groes Conwy 55 L7
Tyn-y-nant Rhondd 27 M10
Tyringham M Keyn 32 C7
Tythegston Brdgnd 27 J11
Tytherington Ches E 50 B6
Tytherington S Glos 29 J10
Tytherington Wilts 18 D11
Tytherleigh Devon 7 J3
Tytherton Lucas Wilts 18 D6
Tywardreath Cnwll 3 N5
Tywyn Gwynd 47 J10

U

Ubbeston Green Suffk 35 M3
Ubley BaNES 17 M5
Uckfield E Susx 11 P6
Uckinghall Worcs 29 M2
Uckington Gloucs 29 M4
Uddingston S Lans 85 L10
Uddington S Lans 78 E3
Udimore E Susx 12 G6
Udny Green Abers 103 J9
Udny Station Abers 103 J9
Uffculme Devon 16 E12
Uffington Lincs 42 F8
Uffington Oxon 19 K3
Uffington Shrops 49 K11
Ufford C Pete 42 F8
Ufford Suffk 35 L6
Ufton Warwks 31 J2
Ufton Nervet W Berk 19 Q7
Ugadale Ag & B 75 L6
Ugborough Devon 5 N8
Uggeshall Suffk 35 P2
Ugglebarnby N York 67 J6
Ughill Sheff 50 G3
Ugley Essex 33 N10
Ugley Green Essex 33 N10
Ugthorpe N York 66 H5
Uibhist A Deas W Isls 111 b6
Uibhist A Tuath W Isls 111 a4
Uig Ag & B 88 E5
Uig Highld 104 B10
Uig Highld 104 E9
Uig W Isls 111 c2
Uigshader Highld 104 F12
Uisken Ag & B 89 J11
Ulbster Highld 110 G7
Ulceby Lincs 53 L8
Ulceby N Linc 61 J10
Ulceby Skitter N Linc 61 J10
Ulcombe Kent 12 G1
Uldale Cumb 71 L7
Uley Gloucs 29 K8
Ulgham Nthumb 73 M3
Ullapool Highld 106 B4
Ullenhall Warwks 30 E1
Ulleskelf N York 59 M6
Ullesthorpe Leics 41 L9
Ulley Rothm 51 L4
Ullingswick Herefs 39 L11
Ullinish Lodge Hotel Highld 96 C3
Ullock Cumb 70 H10
Ullswater Cumb 71 N10
Ullswater Steamers Cumb 71 N11
Ulpha Cumb 62 E4
Ulrome E R Yk 61 K3
Ulsta Shet 111 k3
Ulva Ag & B 89 J8
Ulverston Cumb 62 F6
Ulwell Dorset 8 F10
Ulzieside D & G 77 N9
Umberleigh Devon 15 K7
Unapool Highld 108 E8
Underbarrow Cumb 63 J4
Under Burnmouth Border 79 P11
Undercliffe C Brad 58 F7
Underdale Shrops 49 J11
Under River Kent 22 B11
Underwood Notts 51 L10
Undy Mons 28 E10
Union Mills IoM 56 c5
Unst Shet 111 m2
Unstone Derbys 51 J5
Upavon Wilts 18 G9
Upchurch Kent 22 G9
Upcott Devon 15 N6
Up Exe Devon 6 C3
Upgate Norfk 45 J6
Uphall Dorset 7 M3
Uphall W Loth 86 C7
Upham Devon 15 Q9
Upham Hants 9 N4
Uphampton Herefs 38 H9
Uphampton Worcs 39 Q8
Uphill N Som 17 J5
Up Holland Lancs 57 K7
Uplawmoor E Rens 84 G11
Upleadon Gloucs 29 K4
Upleatham R & Cl 66 E4
Uploders Dorset 7 M4
Uplowman Devon 16 D11
Uplyme Devon 7 J4
Up Marden W Susx 10 C7
Upminster Gt Lon 22 C6
Up Mudford Somset 17 N11
Up Nately Hants 20 B11
Upottery Devon 6 G2
Upper Affcot Shrops 39 J5
Upper Ardchronie Highld 107 K5
Upper Arley Worcs 39 N6
Upper Basildon W Berk 19 P5
Upper Beeding W Susx 11 K7
Upper Benefield Nhants 42 E11
Upper Bentley Worcs 30 C2
Upper Bighouse Highld 109 Q4
Upper Boddington Nhants 31 L4
Upper Brailes Warwks 30 H6
Upper Breakish Highld 97 J5
Upper Broadheath Worcs 39 P10
Upper Broughton Notts 41 P3
Upper Bucklebury W Berk 19 P7
Upper Burgate Hants 8 H4
Upperby Cumb 71 N5
Upper Caldecote C Beds 32 G7
Upper Chapel Powys 27 L1
Upper Chicksgrove Wilts 8 E2
Upper Chute Wilts 19 K9
Upper Clapton Gt Lon 21 M6
Upper Clatford Hants 19 L11
Upper Cound Shrops 39 K2
Upper Cumberworth Kirk 58 G11
Upper Dallachy Moray 101 M3
Upper Deal Kent 23 Q11
Upper Dean Bed 32 F4
Upper Denby Kirk 58 G11
Upper Dicker E Susx 12 B7
Upper Dounreay Highld 110 B3
Upper Dovercourt Essex 35 K9
Upper Drumbane Stirlg 85 L2
Upper Dunsforth N York 59 K2
Upper Eashing Surrey 10 F2
Upper Eathie Highld 107 M9
Upper Egleton Herefs 39 M12
Upper Elkstone Staffs 50 D8
Upper Ellastone Staffs 50 E11
Upper Farringdon Hants 10 B3
Upper Framilode Gloucs 29 K6
Upper Froyle Hants 10 C2
Upperglen Highld 104 D11
Upper Godney Somset 17 L7
Upper Gravenhurst C Beds 32 G9
Upper Green W Berk 19 L7
Upper Grove Common Herefs 28 G4
Upper Hale Surrey 10 D1
Upper Halliford Surrey 20 H9
Upper Hambleton Rutlnd 42 C8
Upper Harbledown Kent 23 L10
Upper Hartfield E Susx 11 P3
Upper Hatherley Gloucs 29 M5
Upper Heaton Kirk 58 F9
Upper Helmsley N York 59 P3
Upper Hergest Herefs 38 F10
Upper Heyford Nhants 31 P3
Upper Heyford Oxon 31 L8
Upper Hill Herefs 39 J10
Upper Hopton Kirk 58 G9
Upper Hulme Staffs 50 D8
Upper Inglesham Swindn 18 H2
Upper Killay Swans 26 D9
Upper Kinchrackine Ag & B 90 G10
Upper Lambourn W Berk 19 K5
Upper Landywood Staffs 40 C6
Upper Langford N Som 17 L4
Upper Langwith Derbys 51 L6
Upper Largo Fife 87 J2
Upper Leigh Staffs 50 D12
Upper Lochton Abers 95 L3
Upper Longdon Staffs 40 D5
Upper & Lower Stondon C Beds 32 G9
Upper Lybster Highld 110 F8
Upper Lydbrook Gloucs 28 H6
Upper Lye Herefs 38 H8
Uppermill Oldham 58 C11
Upper Milton Worcs 39 P7
Upper Minety Wilts 18 E3
Upper Mulben Moray 101 L5
Upper Netchwood Shrops 39 L4
Upper Nobut Staffs 40 D1
Upper Norwood W Susx 10 F6
Upper Poppleton C York 59 M4
Upper Ratley Hants 9 K3
Upper Rissington Gloucs 30 G9
Upper Rochford Worcs 39 L8
Upper Ruscoe D & G 69 N6
Upper Sapey Herefs 39 M8
Upper Seagry Wilts 18 D5
Upper Shelton C Beds 32 E7
Upper Sheringham Norfk 45 J2
Upper Skelmorlie N Ayrs 84 D9
Upper Slaughter Gloucs 30 F9
Upper Soudley Gloucs 28 H6
Upper Standen Kent 13 N3
Upper Stoke Norfk 45 L9
Upper Stowe Nhants 31 N3
Upper Street Hants 8 H4
Upper Street Norfk 45 M6
Upper Street Norfk 45 M6
Upper Street Suffk 34 C6
Upper Street Suffk 34 H6
Upper Sundon C Beds 32 F10
Upper Swell Gloucs 30 F8
Upper Tasburgh Norfk 45 K10
Upper Tean Staffs 50 D11
Upperthong Kirk 58 F11
Upperton W Susx 10 F5
Upper Town Herefs 39 L11
Uppertown Highld 110 G1
Upper Town N Som 17 M3
Upper Town Suffk 34 F4
Upper Tumble Carmth 26 D6
Upper Tysoe Warwks 31 J5
Upper Victoria Angus 93 P8
Upper Wardington Oxon 31 L5
Upper Welland Worcs 29 K1
Upper Wellingham E Susx 11 N7
Upper Weybread Suffk 35 K2
Upper Wield Hants 19 Q11
Upper Winchendon Bucks 31 Q10
Upper Woodford Wilts 18 G12
Upper Wraxall Wilts 18 B6
Uppingham Rutlnd 42 C9
Uppington Shrops 49 L12
Upsall N York 66 C9
Upsettlington Border 81 J5
Upshire Essex 21 N4
Up Somborne Hants 9 L2
Upstreet Kent 23 N10
Upton Bucks 31 Q10
Upton C Pete 42 G9
Upton Cambs 32 H2
Upton Ches W 48 H2
Upton Cnwll 4 G6
Upton Devon 5 N10
Upton Devon 6 E3
Upton Dorset 7 Q6
Upton Dorset 8 E8
Upton Halton 57 J10
Upton Hants 9 L4
Upton Hants 19 L9
Upton Leics 41 J7
Upton Lincs 52 C6
Upton Norfk 45 N7
Upton Notts 51 Q5
Upton Notts 51 Q9
Upton Oxon 19 N4
Upton Slough 20 F7
Upton Somset 16 D9
Upton Somset 17 L10
Upton Wakefd 59 L10
Upton Wirral 56 F10
Upton Bishop Herefs 28 H4
Upton Cheyney S Glos 17 Q3
Upton Cressett Shrops 39 M4
Upton Grey Hants 10 B1
Upton Hellions Devon 15 P10
Upton Lovell Wilts 18 D11
Upton Magna Shrops 49 K11
Upton Noble Somset 17 Q8
Upton Pyne Devon 6 C3
Upton St Leonards Gloucs 29 M6
Upton Scudamore Wilts 18 C10
Upton Snodsbury Worcs 30 C4
Upton-upon-Severn Worcs 29 L1
Upton Warren Worcs 30 B1
Upwaltham W Susx 10 F7
Upwell Norfk 43 N9
Upwood Cambs 43 J12
Urchfont Wilts 18 F8
Urmston Traffd 57 P9
Urquhart Moray 101 K3
Urquhart Castle Highld 98 G4
Urra N York 66 D7
Urray Highld 106 H10
Usan Angus 95 M10
Ushaw Moor Dur 73 M11
Usk Mons 28 D8
Usselby Lincs 52 F5
Usworth Sundld 73 N8
Utkinton Ches W 49 K3
Utley C Brad 58 D5
Uton Devon 15 P11
Utterby Lincs 53 K5
Uttoxeter Staffs 40 E2
Uxbridge Gt Lon 20 G6
Uyeasound Shet 111 m2
Uzmaston Pembks 24 G6

V

Vale Guern 6 c1
Vale of Glamorgan Crematorium V Glam 16 F3
Valley IoA 54 D6
Valtos Highld 104 G9
Valtos W Isls 111 c2
Vange Essex 22 E6
Vatsetter Shet 111 k2
Vatten Highld 96 C2
Vaynor Myr Td 27 L6
Veensgarth Shet 111 k4
Velindre Powys 27 P2
Venngreen Devon 14 G9
Venn Ottery Devon 6 E5
Ventnor IoW 9 P11
Venton Devon 5 M8
Vernham Dean Hants 19 K9
Vernham Street Hants 19 L8
Verwood Dorset 8 G5
Veryan Cnwll 3 K7
Vickerstown Cumb 62 E8
Victoria Cnwll 3 L4
Vidlin Shet 111 k3
Viewfield Moray 101 K3
Viewpark N Lans 85 M10
Vigo Kent 22 D10
Village de Putron Guern 6 c2
Vines Cross E Susx 12 C6
Vinters Park Crematorium Kent 22 F11
Virginia Water Surrey 20 G9
Virginstow Devon 4 H2
Vobster Somset 17 Q6
Voe Shet 111 k3
Vowchurch Herefs 28 D2

W

Waberthwaite Cumb 62 C4
Wackerfield Dur 65 K3
Wacton Norfk 45 K10
Wadborough Worcs 30 B5
Waddesdon Bucks 31 Q10
Waddesdon Manor Bucks 31 Q10
Waddeton Devon 6 B10
Waddingham Lincs 52 E4
Waddington Lancs 63 N12
Waddington Lincs 52 D9
Wadebridge Cnwll 3 L2
Wadeford Somset 7 J1
Wadenhoe Nhants 42 E12
Wadesmill Herts 33 K12
Wadhurst E Susx 12 D4
Wadshelf Derbys 50 H6
Wadworth Donc 51 M2
Wainfleet All Saints Lincs 53 N10
Wainfleet St Mary Lincs 53 M10
Wainhouse Corner Cnwll 4 E2
Wainscott Medway 22 E8
Wainstalls Calder 58 D8
Waitby Cumb 64 D6
Waithe Lincs 53 J4
Wakefield Wakefd 59 J9
Wakefield Crematorium Wakefd 58 H10
Wakehurst Place W Susx 11 M4
Wakerley Nhants 42 D9
Wakes Colne Essex 34 E10
Walberswick Suffk 35 P2
Walberton W Susx 10 F8
Walbutt D & G 70 C2
Walcombe Somset 17 M6
Walcot Lincs 42 F3
Walcot Shrops 49 L11
Walcot Swindn 18 H4
Walcote Leics 41 M10
Walcot Green Norfk 35 J1
Walcott Lincs 52 G11
Walcott Norfk 45 M4
Walden Stubbs N York 59 M10
Walderslade Medway 22 F10
Walderton W Susx 10 C7
Walditch Dorset 7 L4

198 Waldridge - Weston Beggard

Waldridge Dur 73 M10
Waldringfield Suffk 35 L7
Waldron E Susx 12 B6
Wales Rothm 51 L4
Wales Somset 17 N10
Walesby Lincs 52 G5
Walesby Notts 51 P6
Wales Millennium Centre Cardif 16 G2
Walford Herefs 28 G5
Walford Herefs 38 H7
Walford Heath Shrops 49 J10
Walgherton Ches E 49 M6
Walgrave Nhants 32 B3
Walkden Salfd 57 N8
Walker N u Ty 73 M7
Walkerburn Border 79 M2
Walkeringham Notts 51 Q3
Walkerith Lincs 52 B5
Walkern Herts 33 J10
Walkerton Fife 86 F3
Walkford Dorset 8 H8
Walkhampton Devon 5 L6
Walkington E R Yk 60 G6
Walkley Sheff 51 J3
Walk Mill Lancs 57 Q3
Walkwood Worcs 30 D2
Wall Nthumb 72 G7
Wall Staffs 40 E6
Wallacetown S Ayrs 76 E10
Wallacetown S Ayrs 76 F6
Wallands Park E Susx 11 N7
Wallasey Wirral 56 F9
Wallingford Oxon 19 P3
Wallington Gt Lon 21 L9
Wallington Hants 9 P6
Wallington Herts 33 J9
Wallisdown Poole 8 F8
Walls Shet 111 j4
Wallsend N Tyne 73 N7
Wallyford E Loth 86 H7
Walmer Kent 23 Q12
Walmer Bridge Lancs 57 J4
Walmley Birm 40 F8
Walpole Suffk 35 M2
Walpole Cross Keys Norfk 43 N6
Walpole Highway Norfk 43 N7
Walpole St Andrew Norfk 43 N6
Walpole St Peter Norfk 43 N6
Walsall Wsall 40 D7
Walsden Calder 58 C9
Walsgrave on Sowe Covtry 41 J10
Walsham le Willows Suffk 34 G3
Walshford N York 59 K4
Walsoken Norfk 43 M7
Walston S Lans 86 C12
Walsworth Herts 32 H10
Walter's Ash Bucks 20 D4
Waltham Kent 13 L1
Waltham NE Lin 53 J3
Waltham Abbey Essex 21 M4
Waltham Chase Hants 9 P4
Waltham Cross Herts 21 M4
Waltham on the Wolds Leics 42 B5
Waltham St Lawrence W & M 20 D7
Walthamstow Gt Lon 21 M5
Walton Cumb 71 Q3
Walton Derbys 51 J7
Walton Leeds 59 K5
Walton Leics 41 N9
Walton M Keyn 32 C9
Walton Powys 38 F9
Walton Somset 17 L8
Walton Suffk 35 L9
Walton W Susx 10 D8
Walton Wakefd 59 J10
Walton Wrekin 49 L10
Walton Cardiff Gloucs 29 M3
Walton East Pembks 24 H4
Walton-in-Gordano N Som 17 K2
Walton Lea Crematorium Warrtn 57 L10
Walton-le-Dale Lancs 57 K4
Walton-on-Thames Surrey 20 H9
Walton-on-the-Hill Staffs 40 C4
Walton on the Hill Surrey 21 K11
Walton on the Naze Essex 35 L11
Walton on the Wolds Leics 41 N4
Walton-on-Trent Derbys 40 G4
Walton Park N Som 17 K2
Walton West Pembks 24 F6
Waltonwrays Crematorium N York 58 C4
Walworth Darltn 65 M4
Walworth Gt Lon 21 M7
Walwyn's Castle Pembks 24 F6
Wambrook Somset 6 H2
Wanborough Surrey 10 E1
Wanborough Swindn 18 H4
Wandsworth Gt Lon 21 K8
Wangford Suffk 35 P2
Wanlip Leics 41 N5
Wanlockhead D & G 78 E6
Wannock E Susx 12 C8
Wansford C Pete 42 F9
Wansford E R Yk 60 H3
Wanshurst Green Kent 12 F2
Wanstead Gt Lon 21 N6
Wanstrow Somset 17 Q7
Wanswell Gloucs 29 J8
Wantage Oxon 19 L3
Wappenbury Warwks 41 J12
Wappenham Nhants 31 N5
Warbleton E Susx 12 C6
Warborough Oxon 19 P3
Warboys Cambs 33 K2
Warbreck Bpool 56 G2
Warbstow Cnwll 4 F3
Warburton Traffd 57 M10
Warcop Cumb 64 D5
Warden Nthumb 72 G7
Wardington Oxon 31 L5
Wardle Ches E 49 L4
Wardle Rochdl 58 B10
Wardley Gatesd 73 N8
Wardley Rutlnd 42 B9
Wardlow Derbys 50 F6
Wardy Hill Cambs 33 M1
Ware Herts 21 M1
Wareham Dorset 8 D9
Warehorne Kent 13 J4
Warenford Nthumb 81 N8
Wareside Herts 21 N1
Waresley Cambs 33 J6
Warfield Br For 20 E8
Warfleet Devon 6 B11
Wargrave Wokham 20 C7
Warham All Saints Norfk 44 F2
Warham St Mary Norfk 44 F2
Wark Nthumb 72 F5
Wark Nthumb 80 H6
Warkleigh Devon 15 L7
Warkton Nhants 32 C2
Warkworth Nhants 31 L6
Warkworth Nthumb 81 P11
Warlaby N York 65 N8
Warleggan Cnwll 4 E6
Warley Town Calder 58 D8
Warlingham Surrey 21 M10
Warmfield Wakefd 59 J9
Warmingham Ches E 49 N4
Warmington Nhants 42 F11
Warmington Warwks 31 K5
Warminster Wilts 18 C10
Warmley S Glos 17 P2
Warmsworth Donc 51 M1
Warmwell Dorset 7 Q5
Warner Bros Studio Tour Herts 20 H4
Warnford Hants 9 Q3
Warnham W Susx 11 J4
Warningcamp W Susx 10 G8
Warninglid W Susx 11 K5
Warren Ches E 50 B6
Warren Pembks 24 G8
Warrenhill S Lans 78 F2
Warren Row W & M 20 D7
Warren Street Kent 22 H11
Warrington M Keyn 32 C6
Warrington Warrtn 57 L10
Warriston C Edin 86 F7
Warriston Crematorium C Edin 86 F7
Warsash Hants 9 N6
Warslow Staffs 50 E8
Warter E R Yk 60 E4
Warthermaske N York 65 L10
Warthill N York 59 P3
Wartling E Susx 12 D8
Wartnaby Leics 41 P3
Warton Lancs 56 H3
Warton Lancs 63 J7
Warton Warwks 40 H6
Warwick Warwks 30 H2
Warwick Bridge Cumb 71 P4
Warwick Castle Warwks 30 H2
Warwick Services Warwks 31 J3
Wasbister Ork 111 h1
Wasdale Head Cumb 62 E1
Washaway Cnwll 3 M2
Washbourne Devon 5 Q8
Washbrook Suffk 35 J8
Washfield Devon 16 C11
Washford Somset 16 E7
Washford Pyne Devon 15 N9
Washingborough Lincs 52 E8
Washington Sundld 73 N9
Washington W Susx 10 H7
Washington Services Gatesd 73 M9
Wasperton Warwks 30 H3
Wass N York 66 D10
Watchet Somset 16 E7
Watchfield Oxon 19 J3
Watchgate Cumb 63 K3
Water Devon 5 P4
Waterbeach Cambs 33 M4
Waterbeach W Susx 10 E8
Waterbeck D & G 79 L12
Water End E R Yk 60 D6
Waterfall Staffs 50 E9
Waterfoot E Rens 85 J11
Waterford Herts 21 L1
Waterheads Border 86 F11
Waterhouses Staffs 50 E10
Wateringbury Kent 22 E11
Waterloo Highld 97 J5
Waterloo N Lans 85 N11
Waterloo P & K 92 F8
Waterloo Pembks 24 G7
Waterloo Sefton 56 G8
Waterlooville Hants 10 B7
Watermillock Cumb 71 P10
Water Newton Cambs 42 G10
Water Orton Warwks 40 F8
Waterperry Oxon 31 N11
Waterrow Somset 16 E10
Watersfield W Susx 10 G6
Waterside Bl w D 57 N4
Waterside E Ayrs 76 G9
Waterside E Ayrs 76 H3
Waterside E Duns 85 L8
Waterstein Highld 104 A11
Waterstock Oxon 31 N11
Waterston Pembks 24 G7
Water Stratford Bucks 31 P7
Waters Upton Wrekin 49 L10
Watford Herts 20 H4
Watford Nhants 31 N1
Watford Gap Services Nhants 31 N1
Wath N York 58 F1
Wath N York 65 N11
Wath upon Dearne Rothm 51 K1
Watlington Norfk 43 P7
Watlington Oxon 20 B5
Watten Highld 110 F5
Wattisfield Suffk 34 G2
Wattisham Suffk 34 G6
Watton Dorset 7 L4
Watton E R Yk 60 H4
Watton Norfk 44 F9
Watton-at-Stone Herts 33 K11
Wattston N Lans 85 N8
Wattsville Caerph 27 P9
Waulkmill Abers 95 K4
Waunarlwydd Swans 26 E9
Waunfawr Cerdgn 37 K4
Waunfawr Gwynd 54 G9
Wavendon M Keyn 32 C8
Waverbridge Cumb 71 K6
Waverton Ches W 49 J3
Waverton Cumb 71 K6
Wawne E R Yk 61 J6
Waxham Norfk 45 P5
Wayford Somset 7 K2
Waytown Dorset 7 L4
Way Village Devon 15 Q9
Weacombe Somset 16 F7
Weald Oxon 19 K1
Wealdstone Gt Lon 21 J5
Weardley Leeds 58 H5
Weare Somset 17 K5
Weare Giffard Devon 14 H7
Wearhead Dur 72 F11
Wearne Somset 17 K9
Wear Valley Crematorium Dur 65 M2
Weasenham All Saints Norfk 44 E6
Weasenham St Peter Norfk 44 E5
Weaste Salfd 57 P8
Weaverham Ches W 49 L1
Weaverthorpe N York 67 L12
Webheath Worcs 30 D2
Wedderlairs Abers 102 H8
Weddington Warwks 41 J8
Wedhampton Wilts 18 F8
Wedmore Somset 17 L6
Wednesbury Sandw 40 C8
Wednesfield Wolves 40 C7
Weedon Bucks 32 B12
Weedon Nhants 31 N3
Weedon Lois Nhants 31 N5
Weeford Staffs 40 F6
Weeke Hants 9 M2
Weekley Nhants 32 C1
Week St Mary Cnwll 14 E11
Weel E R Yk 60 H6
Weeley Essex 35 J11
Weeley Crematorium Essex 35 J11
Weeley Heath Essex 35 J11
Weem P & K 92 C6
Weethley Warwks 30 D3
Weeting Norfk 44 C11
Weeton E R Yk 61 N9
Weeton Lancs 56 H2
Weeton N York 58 H5
Weetwood Leeds 58 H6
Weir Lancs 57 Q4
Weir Quay Devon 5 J7
Weisdale Shet 111 k4
Welborne Norfk 44 H7
Welbourn Lincs 52 D11
Welburn N York 60 C1
Welbury N York 65 P7
Welby Lincs 42 D3
Welcombe Devon 14 E8
Welford Nhants 41 N10
Welford W Berk 19 L6
Welford-on-Avon Warwks 30 F4
Welham Leics 41 Q8
Welham Notts 51 Q5
Welham Green Herts 21 K3
Well Hants 10 C2
Well Lincs 53 M8
Well N York 65 M10
Welland Worcs 29 L2
Wellbank Angus 93 N8
Wellesbourne Warwks 30 H3
Well Head Herts 32 H10
Welling Gt Lon 21 P8
Wellingborough Nhants 32 C3
Wellingham Norfk 44 E6
Wellingore Lincs 52 E11
Wellington Cumb 62 C2
Wellington Herefs 39 J11
Wellington Somset 16 F11
Wellington Wrekin 49 M12
Wellington Heath Herefs 29 J1
Wellow BaNES 17 Q5
Wellow IoW 9 L9
Wellow Notts 51 P7
Wells Somset 17 M7
Wells-next-the-sea Norfk 44 F2
Wellstye Green Essex 33 Q11
Welltree P & K 92 E10
Wellwood Fife 86 C5
Welney Norfk 43 N10
Welshampton Shrops 48 H8
Welsh Frankton Shrops 48 G8
Welsh Newton Herefs 28 F5
Welshpool Powys 38 E1
Welsh St Donats V Glam 16 D2
Welton Cumb 71 M6
Welton E R Yk 60 G8
Welton Lincs 52 E7
Welton Nhants 31 N2
Welton le Marsh Lincs 53 M9
Welton le Wold Lincs 53 J6
Welwick E R Yk 61 N9
Welwyn Herts 32 H12
Welwyn Garden City Herts 21 K2
Wem Shrops 49 K9
Wembdon Somset 16 H8
Wembley Gt Lon 21 J6
Wembury Devon 5 L9
Wembworthy Devon 15 L9
Wemyss Bay Inver 84 D8
Wendens Ambo Essex 33 N9
Wendlebury Oxon 31 M9
Wendling Norfk 44 F7
Wendover Bucks 20 D2
Wendron Cnwll 2 G9
Wendron Mining District Cnwll 2 G8
Wendy Cambs 33 K7
Wenhaston Suffk 35 N2
Wennington Cambs 33 J2
Wennington Gt Lon 22 B7
Wennington Lancs 63 L8
Wensley Derbys 50 H8
Wensley N York 65 J9
Wentbridge Wakefd 59 L10
Wentnor Shrops 38 H4
Wentworth Cambs 33 M2
Wentworth Rothm 51 J2
Wenvoe V Glam 16 F2
Weobley Herefs 38 H10
Wepham W Susx 10 G8
Wereham Norfk 44 B9
Werrington C Pete 42 G9
Werrington Cnwll 4 H3
Wervin Ches W 48 H2
Wesham Lancs 56 H3
Wessex Vale Crematorium Hants 9 N4
Wessington Derbys 51 J8
West Acre Norfk 44 C7
West Alvington Devon 5 P10
West Anstey Devon 15 P6
West Ashby Lincs 53 J8
West Ashling W Susx 10 D8
West Ashton Wilts 18 C9
West Auckland Dur 65 L3
West Ayton N York 67 L9
West Bagborough Somset 16 G9
West Bank Halton 57 K11
West Barkwith Lincs 52 G7
West Barnby N York 66 H5
West Barns E Loth 87 M6
West Barsham Norfk 44 E4
West Bay Dorset 7 L5
West Beckham Norfk 45 J3
West Bedfont Surrey 20 H8
Westbere Kent 23 M10
West Bergholt Essex 34 F10
West Berkshire Crematorium W Berk 19 P7
West Bexington Dorset 7 M5
West Bilney Norfk 44 B7
West Blatchington Br & H 11 L8
West Boldon S Tyne 73 P8
Westborough Lincs 42 C2
Westbourne Bmouth 8 F8
Westbourne W Susx 10 C8
West Bowling C Brad 58 F7
West Bradenham Norfk 44 F8
West Bradford Lancs 63 N12
West Bradley Somset 17 M8
West Bretton Wakefd 58 H10
West Bridgford Notts 51 N12
West Bromwich Sandw 40 D8
West Bromwich Crematorium Sandw 40 D8
Westbrook Kent 23 Q8
Westbrook W Berk 19 M6
West Buckland Devon 15 L6
West Buckland Somset 16 G11
West Burton N York 64 H9
Westbury Bucks 31 N7
Westbury Shrops 38 G1
Westbury Wilts 18 C9
Westbury Leigh Wilts 18 C10
Westbury on Severn Gloucs 29 J6
Westbury-on-Trym Bristl 28 G12
Westbury-sub-Mendip Somset 17 M6
West Butterwick N Linc 52 B3
Westby Lancs 56 H3
West Byfleet Surrey 20 G10
West Cairngaan D & G 68 F11
West Caister Norfk 45 Q7
West Calder W Loth 86 B9
West Camel Somset 17 N10
West Chaldon Dorset 8 B10
West Challow Oxon 19 L3
West Charleton Devon 5 P10
West Chiltington W Susx 10 H6
West Chinnock Somset 17 L12
West Clandon Surrey 20 G11
West Cliffe Kent 13 Q2
Westcliff-on-Sea Sthend 22 G6
West Coker Somset 17 M12
Westcombe Somset 17 P8
West Compton Somset 17 N7
West Compton Abbas Dorset 7 N4
Westcote Gloucs 30 G9
Westcote Barton Oxon 31 K8
Westcott Bucks 31 Q10
Westcott Devon 6 D2
Westcott Surrey 11 J1
West Cottingwith N York 59 P6
Westcourt Wilts 19 J8
West Cowick E R Yk 59 P9
West Cross Swans 26 E10
West Curthwaite Cumb 71 M6
Westdean E Susx 11 Q9
West Dean W Susx 10 D7
West Dean Wilts 9 J3
West Deeping Lincs 42 G8
West Derby Lpool 56 H9
West Dereham Norfk 43 Q9
West Down Devon 15 J4
Westdowns Cnwll 4 C4
West Drayton Gt Lon 20 G7
West Drayton Notts 51 P6
West Dunnet Highld 110 E2
West Ella E R Yk 60 H8
West End Bed 32 E6
West End Hants 9 M5
West End N Som 17 L3
West End Norfk 45 Q7
West End Surrey 20 F10
West End Wilts 8 E3
West End Green Hants 19 Q8
Wester Aberchalder Highld 98 H5
Westerdale Highld 110 D5
Westerdale N York 66 F6
Westerfield Suffk 35 K7
Westergate W Susx 10 F8
Westerham Kent 21 N11
Westerhope N u Ty 73 L7
Westerland Devon 6 B9
Westerleigh S Glos 29 J11
Westerleigh Crematorium S Glos 29 J12
Western Isles W Isls 111 c3
Wester Ochiltree W Loth 86 B7
Wester Pitkierie Fife 87 K2
Wester Ross Highld 105 P6
Westerton of Rossie Angus 93 R5
Westerwick Shet 111 j4
West Farleigh Kent 22 E11
West Farndon Nhants 31 M4
West Felton Shrops 48 G9
Westfield BaNES 17 P5
Westfield Cumb 70 G9
Westfield E Susx 12 F7
Westfield Highld 110 C3
Westfield N Lans 85 M8
Westfield Norfk 44 G8
Westfield W Loth 85 Q8
Westfields of Rattray P & K 92 H6
Westgate Dur 72 G12
Westgate N Linc 60 D11
Westgate on Sea Kent 23 P8
West Grafton Wilts 19 J8
West Green Hants 20 C11
West Grimstead Wilts 8 H3
West Grinstead W Susx 11 J5
West Haddlesey N York 59 M8
West Haddon Nhants 41 N12
West Hagbourne Oxon 19 N3
West Hagley Worcs 40 B10
Westhall Suffk 35 N1
West Hallam Derbys 51 K11
West Halton N Linc 60 F9
Westham Dorset 7 P7
Westham E Susx 12 D8
West Ham Gt Lon 21 N6
Westham Somset 17 K6
Westhampnett W Susx 10 E8
West Handley Derbys 51 K5
West Hanney Oxon 19 L3
West Hanningfield Essex 22 E4
West Harnham Wilts 8 G2
West Harptree BaNES 17 M5
West Harting W Susx 10 C6
West Hatch Somset 16 H11
West Hatch Wilts 8 D2
West Haven Angus 93 P8
Westhay Somset 17 L7
West Heath Birm 40 D11
West Helmsdale Highld 110 B11
West Hendred Oxon 19 M3
West Hertfordshire Crematorium Herts 20 H3
West Heslerton N York 67 K11
West Hewish N Som 17 K4
Westhide Herefs 39 L12
Westhill Abers 95 N1
West Hill Devon 6 E4
West Hoathly W Susx 11 M4
West Holme Dorset 8 C9
Westhope Herefs 39 J11
Westhope Shrops 39 J5
West Horndon Essex 22 D6
Westhorpe Lincs 42 H4
Westhorpe Suffk 34 H3
West Horrington Somset 17 N6
West Horsley Surrey 20 H11
West Hougham Kent 13 N3
Westhoughton Bolton 57 M7
Westhouse N York 63 M7
Westhouses Derbys 51 K8
West Howe Bmouth 8 F8
Westhumble Surrey 21 J11
West Huntingtower P & K 92 G10
West Huntspill Somset 17 J7
West Hythe Kent 13 L3
West Ilsley W Berk 19 M4
West Itchenor W Susx 10 C9
West Kennett Wilts 18 G7
West Kilbride N Ayrs 76 D2
West Kingsdown Kent 22 C10
West Kington Wilts 18 B5
West Kirby Wirral 56 E10
West Knapton N York 67 J11
West Knighton Dorset 7 Q5
West Knoyle Wilts 8 C2
Westlake Devon 5 M9
West Lambrook Somset 17 K11
West Langdon Kent 13 P1
West Lavington W Susx 10 E6
West Lavington Wilts 18 E9
West Layton N York 65 K5
West Leake Notts 41 M3
Westleigh Devon 14 H6
Westleigh Devon 16 E11
West Leigh Somset 16 F9
Westleton Suffk 35 P3
West Lexham Norfk 44 D6
Westley Suffk 34 D4
Westley Waterless Cambs 33 P5
West Lilling N York 59 P2
Westlington Bucks 31 Q11
West Linton Border 86 D10
Westlinton Cumb 71 N3
West Littleton S Glos 18 B5
West Lockinge Oxon 19 M4
West London Crematorium Gt Lon 21 K7
West Lulworth Dorset 8 B10
West Lutton N York 60 F1
West Lydford Somset 17 N9
West Lyng Somset 17 J9
West Lynn Norfk 43 P6
West Malling Kent 22 D10
West Malvern Worcs 39 N11
West Marden W Susx 10 C7
West Markham Notts 51 Q6
Westmarsh Kent 23 P10
West Marsh NE Lin 61 L11
West Marton N York 58 B4
West Melbury Dorset 8 C4
West Meon Hants 9 Q3
West Mersea Essex 23 J2
Westmeston E Susx 11 M7
West Midland Safari Park Worcs 39 P7
Westmill Herts 33 K10
West Milton Dorset 7 M4
Westminster Gt Lon 21 L7
West Minster Kent 22 H8
Westminster Abbey & Palace Gt Lon 21 L7
West Molesey Surrey 21 J9
West Monkton Somset 16 H9
West Moors Dorset 8 F6
West Morden Dorset 8 D8
West Morriston Border 80 E6
West Mudford Somset 17 N11
Westmuir Angus 93 L5
West Ness N York 66 F10
Westnewton Cumb 71 J6
West Newton E R Yk 61 L6
West Newton Norfk 44 B5
West Newton Somset 16 H9
West Norwood Gt Lon 21 L8
West Norwood Crematorium Gt Lon 21 L8
Westoe S Tyne 73 P7
West Ogwell Devon 5 Q6
Weston BaNES 17 Q3
Weston Ches E 49 N5
Weston Devon 6 F3
Weston Devon 6 F5
Weston Hants 10 B6
Weston Herts 33 J10
Weston Lincs 43 J5
Weston N York 58 F5
Weston Nhants 31 N5
Weston Notts 51 Q7
Weston Shrops 39 L4
Weston Shrops 48 F9
Weston Staffs 40 C3
Weston W Berk 19 L6
Weston Beggard Herefs 28 G1

Westonbirt Gloucs 18 C3
Weston by Welland
   Nhants 41 Q8
Weston Colville Cambs 33 P6
Weston Corbett Hants 10 B1
Weston Coyney C Stke 50 C11
Weston Favell Nhants 32 B4
Weston Green Cambs 33 P6
Weston Heath Shrops 49 P11
Westoning C Beds 32 E9
Weston-in-Gordano
   N Som 17 L2
Weston Jones Staffs 49 N10
Weston Longville Norfk 45 J7
Weston Lullingfields
   Shrops 48 H9
Weston Mill
   Crematorium C Plym 5 K8
Weston-on-the-Green
   Oxon 31 M9
Weston Park Staffs 49 P12
Weston Patrick Hants 10 B1
Weston Rhyn Shrops 48 F8
Weston-sub-Edge Gloucs 30 E6
Weston-super-Mare
   N Som 17 J4
Weston-super-Mare
   Crematorium N Som 17 J4
Weston Turville Bucks 20 D2
Weston-under-Lizard
   Staffs 49 P12
Weston under Penyard
   Herefs 28 H4
Weston-under-
   Redcastle Shrops 49 K9
Weston under
   Wetherley Warwks 41 J12
Weston Underwood
   Derbys 50 H11
Weston Underwood
   M Keyn 32 C6
Weston-upon-Trent
   Derbys 41 K2
Westonzoyland Somset 17 J8
West Orchard Dorset 8 B4
West Overton Wilts 18 G7
Westow N York 60 D2
West Park Abers 95 N3
West Parley Dorset 8 G7
West Peckham Kent 22 D11
West Pelton Dur 73 M9
West Pennard Somset 17 M4
West Pentire Cnwll 2 H4
West Perry Cambs 32 G4
West Porlock Somset 15 P3
Westport Somset 17 K11
West Putford Devon 14 G8
West Quantoxhead
   Somset 16 F7
Westquarter Falk 85 Q7
West Rainton Dur 73 N10
West Rasen Lincs 52 F5
Westray Ork 111 h1
Westray Airport Ork 111 h1
West Raynham Norfk 44 F5
Westrigg W Loth 85 Q9
West Road
   Crematorium N u Ty 73 L7
Westrop Swindn 18 H3
West Rounton N York 65 P6
West Row Suffk 34 B2
West Rudham Norfk 44 D5
West Runton Norfk 45 K2
Westruther Border 80 L4
Westry Cambs 43 L9
West Saltoun E Loth 87 J8
West Sandford Devon 15 N10
West Sandwick Shet 111 k3
West Scrafton N York 65 J10
West Stafford Dorset 7 Q5
West Stockwith Notts 52 B5
West Stoke W Susx 10 D8
West Stour Dorset 8 B3
West Stourmouth Kent 23 N10
West Stow Suffk 34 D3
West Stowell Wilts 18 G8
West Street Suffk 34 G3
West Suffolk
   Crematorium Suffk 34 D4
West Tanfield N York 65 M10
West Taphouse Cnwll 4 E7
West Tarbert Ag & B 83 M9
West Tarring W Susx 10 H8
West Thirston Nthumb 73 L2
West Thorney W Susx 10 C9
West Thorpe Notts 41 N9
West Thurrock Thurr 22 C7
West Tilbury Thurr 22 D7
West Tisted Hants 9 Q2
West Torrington Lincs 52 G7
West Town Hants 10 B9
West Town N Som 17 L3
West Tytherley Hants 9 J2
West Walton Norfk 43 M7
West Walton Highway
   Norfk 43 M7
Westward Cumb 71 L6
Westward Ho! Devon 14 H6
Westwell Kent 13 J1
Westwell Oxon 30 G11
Westwell Leacon Kent 13 J1
West Wellow Hants 9 K4
West Wembury Devon 5 L9
West Wemyss Fife 86 G4
Westwick Cambs 33 L4
West Wickham Cambs 33 P6
West Wickham Gt Lon 21 M9
West Williamston Pembks 24 H7
West Wiltshire
   Crematorium Wilts 18 D8
West Winch Norfk 43 Q6
West Winterslow Wilts 9 J2
West Witton N York 65 J9
Westwood Devon 6 D3
Westwood Kent 23 Q9
Westwood Wilts 18 B8
West Woodburn Nthumb 72 H4
West Woodhay W Berk 19 L8
Westwoodside N Linc 51 Q4
West Worldham Hants 10 C3
West Worthing W Susx 11 J9
West Wratting Cambs 33 P6
Wetheral Cumb 71 P5
Wetherby Leeds 59 K5
Wetherby Services N York 59 K4
Wetherden Suffk 34 G4

Wetheringsett Suffk 35 J4
Wethersfield Essex 34 B9
Wetherup Street Suffk 35 J4
Wetley Rocks Staffs 50 C10
Wettenhall Ches E 49 L4
Wetton Staffs 50 E9
Wetwang E R Yk 60 F3
Wetwood Staffs 49 P8
Wexcombe Wilts 19 J8
Weybourne Norfk 45 J2
Weybourne Surrey 10 D1
Weybread Suffk 35 L1
Weybread Street Suffk 35 L2
Weybridge Surrey 20 H9
Weycroft Devon 7 J3
Weydale Highld 110 D3
Weyhill Hants 19 K10
Weymouth Dorset 7 P7
Weymouth
   Crematorium Dorset 7 P7
Whaddon Bucks 32 B9
Whaddon Cambs 33 K7
Whaddon Gloucs 29 L6
Whaddon Wilts 8 H3
Whaddon Wilts 18 C8
Whaley Derbys 51 L6
Whaley Bridge Derbys 50 D5
Whaley Thorns Derbys 51 M6
Whaligoe Highld 110 G7
Whalley Lancs 57 N2
Whalsay Shet 111 m3
Whalton Nthumb 73 K5
Whaplode Lincs 43 K5
Whaplode Drove Lincs 43 K7
Wharf Warwks 31 K4
Wharfe N York 63 P8
Wharles Lancs 57 J2
Wharley End C Beds 32 D7
Wharncliffe Side Sheff 50 H2
Wharram-le-Street N York 60 E2
Wharton Herefs 39 J10
Whashton N York 65 K6
Whasset Cumb 63 K6
Whatcote Warwks 30 H5
Whatfield Suffk 34 G7
Whatley Somset 7 J2
Whatley Somset 17 Q6
Whatlington E Susx 12 F6
Whatton Notts 51 J10
Whauphill D & G 69 K8
Wheal Peevor Cnwll 2 H6
Wheatacre Norfk 45 P10
Wheathampstead Herts 21 J1
Wheatley Hants 10 C3
Wheatley Oxon 31 N11
Wheatley Hill Dur 73 P11
Wheatley Hills Donc 59 N12
Wheaton Aston Staffs 49 Q11
Wheddon Cross Somset 16 C8
Wheelock Ches E 49 N4
Wheelton Lancs 57 L5
Wheldrake C York 59 P5
Whelford Gloucs 18 H2
Whelpley Hill Bucks 20 F3
Whempstead Herts 33 K11
Whenby N York 66 E12
Whepstead Suffk 34 D5
Wherstead Suffk 35 J8
Wherwell Hants 19 L11
Wheston Derbys 50 F5
Whetsted Kent 12 D2
Whetstone Leics 41 M7
Whicham Cumb 62 D6
Whichford Warwks 30 H7
Whickham Gatesd 73 L8
Whiddon Down Devon 5 N2
Whigstreet Angus 93 N6
Whilton Nhants 31 N2
Whimple Devon 6 E4
Whimpwell Green Norfk 45 N4
Whinburgh Norfk 44 G8
Whinnie Liggate D & G 70 B5
Whinnyfold Abers 103 M8
Whippingham IoW 9 N8
Whipsnade C Beds 32 E12
Whipsnade Zoo ZSL
   C Beds 32 E12
Whipton Devon 6 C4
Whisby Lincs 52 C9
Whissendine Rutlnd 42 B7
Whissonsett Norfk 44 F5
Whistlefield Ag & B 84 D4
Whistlefield Inn Ag & B 84 C4
Whistley Green Wokham 20 C8
Whiston Knows 57 J9
Whiston Nhants 32 C5
Whiston Rothm 51 K3
Whiston Staffs 40 B5
Whiston Staffs 50 D10
Whitbeck Cumb 62 D5
Whitbourne Herefs 39 N10
Whitburn S Tyne 73 P8
Whitburn W Loth 85 Q9
Whitby N York 67 J5
Whitchester Border 87 N9
Whitchurch BaNES 17 N3
Whitchurch Bucks 32 B11
Whitchurch Cardif 27 N11
Whitchurch Devon 5 K5
Whitchurch Hants 19 M10
Whitchurch Herefs 28 G5
Whitchurch Oxon 19 Q5
Whitchurch Pembks 24 E4
Whitchurch Shrops 49 K7
Whitchurch
   Canonicorum Dorset 7 K4
Whitchurch Hill Oxon 19 Q5
Whitcombe Dorset 7 Q5
Whitcott Shrops 38 H4
Whitcott Keysett Shrops 38 F5
Whiteacre Heath Warwks 40 G8
White Ball Somset 16 E11
Whitebridge Highld 98 G5
Whitebrook Mons 28 G7
Whitecairns Abers 103 J10
Whitechapel Gt Lon 21 M7
White Chapel Lancs 57 K1
Whitecliffe Gloucs 28 G6
Whitecraig E Loth 86 G8
Whitecrook D & G 68 F7
White Cross Cnwll 2 H9
Whitecross Falk 85 R7
Whitefarland N Ayrs 75 N4
Whitefaulds S Ayrs 76 E8

Whitefield Bury 57 P7
Whitefield Somset 16 E9
Whiteford Abers 102 H9
Whitegate Ches W 49 L2
Whitehall Ork 111 i2
Whitehaven Cumb 70 F11
Whitehill and Bordon
   Hants 10 C4
Whitehills Abers 102 E3
Whitehouse Abers 102 E11
Whitehouse Ag & B 83 M10
Whitekirk E Loth 87 L6
White Lackington Dorset 7 Q3
White Lackington Somset 17 K11
White Ladies Aston Worcs 30 B4
Whiteleaf Bucks 20 D3
Whiteley Hants 9 N5
Whiteley Bank IoW 9 P10
Whitemire Moray 100 F5
Whitemoor C Nott 51 M11
Whitemoor Cnwll 3 L4
Whiteness Shet 111 k4
White Notley Essex 34 D11
Whiteparish Wilts 9 J3
White Pit Lincs 53 L7
Whiterashes Abers 102 H9
White Roding Essex 22 C1
Whiterow Highld 110 G6
Whiterow Moray 100 F4
Whiteshill Gloucs 29 L7
Whitesmith E Susx 11 Q7
Whitestaunton Somset 6 H1
Whitestone Cross Devon 6 B4
White Waltham W & M 20 D7
Whitewell Lancs 63 M11
Whitfield C Dund 93 M8
Whitfield Kent 13 P2
Whitfield Nhants 31 N6
Whitfield Nthumb 72 E8
Whitfield S Glos 29 J9
Whitford Devon 6 H4
Whitford Flints 56 D12
Whitgift E R Yk 60 E9
Whitgreave Staffs 40 B2
Whithorn D & G 69 L10
Whiting Bay N Ayrs 75 Q7
Whitkirk Leeds 59 J7
Whitland Carmth 25 L5
Whitlaw Border 80 C10
Whitletts S Ayrs 76 F6
Whitley N York 59 M9
Whitley Readg 20 B8
Whitley Sheff 51 J2
Whitley Wilts 18 C7
Whitley Bay N Tyne 73 N6
Whitley Bay
   Crematorium N Tyne 73 N6
Whitley Chapel Nthumb 72 G8
Whitley Lower Kirk 58 G10
Whitminster Gloucs 29 K7
Whitmore Staffs 49 P7
Whitnage Devon 16 D11
Whitnash Warwks 31 J2
Whitney-on-Wye Herefs 38 F11
Whitsbury Hants 8 G4
Whitsome Border 81 J4
Whitson Newpt 28 D11
Whitstable Kent 23 J9
Whitstone Cnwll 14 E11
Whittingham Nthumb 81 M10
Whittingslow Shrops 38 H4
Whittington Derbys 51 J6
Whittington Gloucs 30 D9
Whittington Lancs 63 L7
Whittington Norfk 44 B9
Whittington Shrops 48 G9
Whittington Staffs 39 Q5
Whittington Staffs 40 F6
Whittington Warwks 40 H7
Whittington Worcs 39 Q10
Whittlebury Nhants 31 P5
Whittle-le-Woods Lancs 57 L5
Whittlesey Cambs 43 J10
Whittlesford Cambs 33 M7
Whitton N Linc 60 F8
Whitton Nthumb 73 J1
Whitton Powys 38 F8
Whitton S on T 65 P3
Whitton Shrops 39 L7
Whittonstall Nthumb 73 J9
Whitway Hants 19 M8
Whitwell Derbys 51 M5
Whitwell Herts 32 H11
Whitwell IoW 9 N10
Whitwell N York 65 M7
Whitwell Rutlnd 42 D8
Whitwell-on-the-Hill
   N York 60 C2
Whitwell Street Norfk 44 H6
Whitwick Leics 41 K4
Whitworth Lancs 58 B9
Whixall Shrops 49 K8
Whixley N York 59 K3
Whorlton Dur 65 K5
Whyle Herefs 39 K9
Whyteleafe Surrey 21 M10
Wibsey Brad 58 F7
Wibtoft Warwks 41 L9
Wichenford Worcs 39 P9
Wichling Kent 22 H11
Wick Bmouth 8 H8
Wick Highld 110 G5
Wick S Glos 17 Q2
Wick V Glam 16 C2
Wick W Susx 10 G8
Wick Worcs 30 C5
Wicken Cambs 33 P3
Wicken Nhants 31 Q6
Wicken Bonhunt Essex 33 N9
Wickenby Lincs 52 F7
Wicken Green Village
   Norfk 44 D4
Wickersley Rothm 51 L3
Wicker Street Green Suffk 34 F8
Wickford Essex 22 F3
Wickham Hants 9 P5
Wickham W Berk 19 L6
Wickham Bishops Essex 22 G2
Wickhambreaux Kent 23 N10
Wickhambrook Suffk 34 C6
Wickhamford Worcs 30 D6
Wickham Green Suffk 34 H3
Wickham Market Suffk 35 M5
Wickhampton Norfk 45 N8
Wickham St Paul Essex 34 D9
Wickham Skeith Suffk 34 H3
Wickham Street Suffk 34 H3

Wick John o' Groats
   Airport Highld 110 G5
Wicklewood Norfk 44 H9
Wickmere Norfk 45 J4
Wick St Lawrence N Som 17 K3
Wicksteed Park Nhants 32 C2
Wickwar S Glos 29 J10
Widdington Essex 33 N9
Widdrington Nthumb 73 M2
Widdrington Station
   Nthumb 73 M3
Widecombe in the
   Moor Devon 5 P5
Widegates Cnwll 4 G8
Widemouth Bay Cnwll 14 D10
Wide Open N Tyne 73 M6
Widford Essex 22 E3
Widford Herts 33 L12
Widmer End Bucks 20 E4
Widmerpool Notts 41 N2
Widmore Gt Lon 21 N9
Widnes Halton 57 K11
Widnes Crematorium
   Halton 57 K10
Widworthy Devon 6 G3
Wigan Wigan 57 L7
Wigan Crematorium
   Wigan 57 L7
Wigborough Somset 17 L12
Wiggaton Devon 6 E4
Wiggenhall St Germans
   Norfk 43 P7
Wiggenhall St Mary
   Magdalen Norfk 43 P7
Wiggenhall St Mary the
   Virgin Norfk 43 P7
Wigginton C York 59 N3
Wigginton Herts 20 F2
Wigginton Oxon 31 K7
Wigginton Staffs 40 G6
Wigglesworth N York 63 P10
Wiggonby Cumb 71 L5
Wighill N York 59 L5
Wighton Norfk 44 F3
Wightwick Wolves 39 Q3
Wigley Hants 9 K4
Wigmore Herefs 38 H8
Wigmore Medway 22 F9
Wigsley Notts 52 C9
Wigsthorpe Nhants 32 F1
Wigston Leics 41 N7
Wigston Parva Leics 41 L9
Wigthorpe Notts 51 N4
Wigtoft Lincs 43 J3
Wigton Cumb 71 L6
Wigtown D & G 69 L7
Wike Leeds 59 J5
Wilbarston Nhants 42 B11
Wilberfoss E R Yk 60 C4
Wilburton Cambs 33 M2
Wilby Nhants 32 C4
Wilby Norfk 44 G11
Wilby Suffk 35 L3
Wilcot Wilts 18 G8
Wilcott Shrops 48 H10
Wildboarclough Ches E 50 C7
Wilden Bed 32 F6
Wilden Worcs 39 P7
Wildmanbridge S Lans 85 N11
Wildmoor Worcs 40 C10
Wildsworth Lincs 52 B4
Wilford Hill
   Crematorium Notts 41 M1
Wilkesley Ches E 49 L7
Wilkhaven Highld 107 Q5
Wilkieston W Loth 86 D8
Willand Devon 6 D1
Willaston Ches E 49 M5
Willaston Ches W 56 G12
Willen M Keyn 32 C8
Willenhall Covtry 41 J11
Willenhall Wsall 40 C7
Willerby E R Yk 60 H7
Willerby N York 67 L10
Willersey Gloucs 30 E6
Willersley Herefs 38 G11
Willesborough Kent 13 K2
Willesborough Lees Kent 13 K2
Willesden Gt Lon 21 K6
Willesley Wilts 18 C3
Willett Somset 16 F9
Willey Shrops 39 M3
Willey Warwks 41 L9
Willey Green Surrey 20 F12
Williamscot Oxon 31 L5
Willian Herts 32 H9
Willingale Essex 22 C2
Willingdon E Susx 12 C9
Willingham Cambs 33 L3
Willingham by Stow Lincs 52 C6
Willington Bed 32 G6
Willington Derbys 40 H2
Willington Dur 65 L1
Willington Kent 22 F11
Willington Warwks 30 H6
Willington Quay N Tyne 73 N7
Willitoft E R Yk 60 C7
Williton Somset 16 E7
Willoughby Lincs 53 M8
Willoughby Warwks 31 M1
Willoughby-on-the-
   Wolds Notts 41 N3
Willoughby Waterleys
   Leics 41 M8
Willoughton Lincs 52 D5
Willows Green Essex 34 C11
Willtown Somset 17 K10
Wilmcote Warwks 30 F3
Wilmington Devon 6 G3
Wilmington E Susx 11 Q9
Wilmington Kent 21 Q8
Wilmslow Ches E 57 Q11
Wilpshire Lancs 57 M3
Wilsden C Brad 58 E6
Wilsford Lincs 42 E2
Wilsford Wilts 18 G11
Wilsford Wilts 18 G8
Wilshaw Kirk 58 E11
Wilsill N York 58 F2
Wilsley Green Kent 12 F3
Wilson Herefs 28 H5
Wilson Leics 41 K3
Wilsontown S Lans 85 N10
Wilstead Bed 32 F7
Wilsthorpe Lincs 42 F7
Wilstone Herts 20 E1
Wilton Herefs 28 H5
Wilton N York 67 J10
Wilton R & Cl 66 E4

Wilton Wilts 8 F2
Wilton Wilts 19 J8
Wilton Dean Border 80 C10
Wimbish Green Essex 33 P9
Wimbledon Gt Lon 21 K8
Wimblington Cambs 43 L9
Wimboldsley Ches W 49 M3
Wimborne Minster Dorset 8 E7
Wimborne St Giles Dorset 8 F5
Wimbotsham Norfk 43 P8
Wimpole Cambs 33 K6
Wimpstone Warwks 30 G5
Wincanton Somset 17 Q9
Winchburgh W Loth 86 C7
Winchcombe Gloucs 30 D8
Winchelsea E Susx 12 H6
Winchester Hants 9 N2
Winchester Services
   Hants 9 N1
Winchet Hill Kent 12 E2
Winchfield Hants 20 C11
Winchmore Hill Bucks 20 E4
Winchmore Hill Gt Lon 21 L5
Wincle Ches E 50 C7
Wincobank Sheff 51 J3
Windermere Cumb 62 H3
Windermere
   Steamboats &
   Museum Cumb 62 H3
Winderton Warwks 31 J6
Windhill Highld 107 J11
Windlesham Surrey 20 E9
Windmill Cnwll 3 K2
Windmill Hill E Susx 12 C8
Windmill Hill Somset 17 J11
Windrush Gloucs 30 F10
Windsole Abers 102 D4
Windsor W & M 20 F7
Windsor Castle W & M 20 F7
Windsoredge Gloucs 29 L8
Windsor Green Suffk 34 E6
Windy Arbour Warwks 40 H12
Windygates Fife 86 G3
Wineham W Susx 11 K6
Winestead E R Yk 61 M8
Winfarthing Norfk 45 J11
Winford IoW 9 P9
Winford N Som 17 M3
Winforton Herefs 38 F11
Winfrith Newburgh
   Dorset 8 B9
Wing Bucks 32 C11
Wing Rutlnd 42 C9
Wingate Dur 73 P12
Wingerworth Derbys 51 J7
Wingfield C Beds 32 E10
Wingfield Suffk 35 K2
Wingfield Wilts 18 B9
Wingham Kent 23 N11
Wingrave Bucks 32 C11
Winkburn Notts 51 P8
Winkfield Br For 20 E8
Winkfield Row Br For 20 E8
Winkhill Staffs 50 D9
Winkleigh Devon 15 L9
Winksley N York 65 M12
Winlaton Gatesd 73 L8
Winless Highld 110 G5
Winmarleigh Lancs 63 J11
Winnall Hants 9 N2
Winnersh Wokham 20 C8
Winnington Ches W 49 M1
Winscombe N Som 17 K5
Winsford Ches W 49 M3
Winsford Somset 16 B8
Winsham Somset 7 K2
Winshill Staffs 40 H3
Winshwen Swans 26 F9
Winskill Cumb 64 B1
Winsley Wilts 18 B8
Winslow Bucks 31 Q8
Winson Gloucs 30 E11
Winsor Hants 9 K5
Winster Cumb 62 H4
Winster Derbys 50 G8
Winston Dur 65 K4
Winston Suffk 35 K5
Winstone Gloucs 29 N6
Winswell Devon 15 J9
Winterborne Came
   Dorset 7 Q5
Winterborne Clenston
   Dorset 8 C6
Winterborne Houghton
   Dorset 8 B6
Winterborne Kingston
   Dorset 8 C7
Winterborne Monkton
   Dorset 7 P5
Winterborne Stickland
   Dorset 8 C6
Winterborne
   Whitechurch Dorset 8 C7
Winterborne Zelston
   Dorset 8 D7
Winterbourne S Glos 28 H11
Winterbourne W Berk 19 M6
Winterbourne Abbas
   Dorset 7 N5
Winterbourne Bassett
   Wilts 18 G6
Winterbourne
   Dauntsey Wilts 8 H1
Winterbourne Earls Wilts 8 H1
Winterbourne Gunner
   Wilts 8 H1
Winterbourne Monkton
   Wilts 18 G6
Winterbourne
   Steepleton Dorset 7 P5
Winterbourne Stoke Wilts 18 F11
Winterburn N York 58 C3
Winteringham N Linc 60 F9
Winterley Ches E 49 N4
Winterslow Wilts 9 J2
Winterton N Linc 60 F9
Winterton-on-Sea Norfk 45 P6
Winthorpe Notts 52 B11
Winton Bmouth 8 G8
Winton Cumb 64 E5
Wintringham N York 67 J11
Winwick Cambs 32 F1
Winwick Nhants 41 N11
Winwick Warrtn 57 L9
Wirksworth Derbys 50 H9
Wirral Ches W 56 F10
Wirswall Ches E 49 K6

...M8
...43 L8
...10 G5
...Surrey...20 G10
...25 K7
...51 Q3
...85 N11
...40 F8
...y Garden RHS...20 G10
Wispington Lincs...52 H8
Wissett Suffk...35 M2
Wissington Suffk...34 F9
Wistanstow Shrops...38 H5
Wistanswick Shrops...49 M9
Wistaston Ches E...49 M5
Wiston Pembks...24 H5
Wiston S Lans...78 F3
Wiston W Susx...11 J7
Wistow Cambs...33 J1
Wistow N York...59 N7
Wiswell Lancs...57 N2
Witcham Cambs...33 M2
Witchampton Dorset...8 E6
Witchford Cambs...33 N2
Witcombe Somset...17 L10
Witham Essex...22 G1
Witham Friary Somset...17 Q7
Witham on the Hill Lincs...42 F6
Withcall Lincs...53 J6
Withdean Br & H...11 L8
Witherenden Hill E Susx...12 D5
Witheridge Devon...15 N8
Witherley Leics...41 J7
Withern Lincs...53 L7
Withernsea E R Yk...61 N8
Withernwick E R Yk...61 K6
Withersdale Street Suffk...35 L1
Withersfield Suffk...33 Q7
Witherslack Cumb...62 H5
Withiel Cnwll...3 M3
Withiel Florey Somset...16 D9
Withington Gloucs...30 D10
Withington Herefs...39 K12
Withington Manch...57 Q9
Withington Shrops...49 L11
Withington Staffs...40 D1
Withleigh Devon...6 B1
Withnell Lancs...57 L4
Withybed Green Worcs...40 D11
Withybrook Warwks...41 K10
Withycombe Somset...16 D7
Withyham E Susx...11 P3
Withypool Somset...15 P5
Withywood Bristl...17 N3
Witley Surrey...10 F3
Witnesham Suffk...35 K6
Witney Oxon...31 J11
Wittering C Pete...42 F9
Wittersham Kent...12 H5
Witton Birm...40 E8
Witton Norfk...45 M4
Witton Norfk...45 M8
Witton Gilbert Dur...73 M10
Witton le Wear Dur...65 K2
Witton Park Dur...65 L2
Wiveliscombe Somset...16 E9
Wivelrod Hants...19 R12
Wivelsfield E Susx...11 M6
Wivelsfield Green E Susx...11 M6
Wivenhoe Essex...34 G11
Wiveton Norfk...44 G2
Wix Essex...35 J10
Wixford Warwks...30 E3
Wixoe Suffk...34 C8
Woburn C Beds...32 D9
Woburn Abbey C Beds...32 D9
Woburn Sands M Keyn...32 D9
Woking Surrey...20 G10
Woking Crematorium
  Surrey...20 F11
Wokingham Wokham...20 D9
Woldingham Surrey...21 M11
Wold Newton E R Yk...67 M11
Wold Newton NE Lin...53 J4
Wolfclyde S Lans...78 G2
Wolferton Norfk...43 Q4
Wolfhill P & K...92 H8
Wolf's Castle Pembks...24 G4
Wolfsdale Pembks...24 G5
Wollaston Dudley...40 B9
Wollaston Nhants...32 C4
Wollaston Shrops...48 G10
Wollaton C Nott...51 M11
Wollaton Hall & Park
  C Nott...51 M11
Wollerton Shrops...49 L9
Wollescote Dudley...40 B10
Wolseley Bridge Staffs...40 D4
Wolsingham Dur...73 J12
Wolstanton Staffs...49 Q6
Wolston Warwks...41 K11
Wolvercote Oxon...31 L11
Wolverhampton Wolves...40 B7
Wolverhampton
  Halfpenny Green
  Airport Staffs...39 P4
Wolverley Worcs...39 P6
Wolverton Hants...19 P8
Wolverton M Keyn...32 B8
Wolverton Warwks...30 G2
Wolverton Wilts...8 B2
Wolvesnewton Mons...28 E8
Wolvey Warwks...41 K9
Wolvey Heath Warwks...41 K9
Wolviston S on T...66 C3
Wombleton N York...66 F10
Wombourne Staffs...39 Q4
Wombwell Barns...51 K1
Womenswold Kent...23 N12
Womersley N York...59 M9
Wonersh Surrey...10 G2
Wonford Devon...6 C4
Wonson Devon...5 Q3
Wonston Dorset...7 Q2
Wonston Hants...19 M11
Wooburn Bucks...20 E6
Wooburn Green Bucks...20 E6
Woodacott Devon...14 G9
Woodall Rothm...51 L5
Woodall Services Rothm...51 L5
Woodbastwick Norfk...45 M7
Wood Bevington Warwks...30 D4
Woodborough Notts...51 N10
Woodborough Wilts...18 G8
Woodbridge Suffk...35 L7
Woodbury Devon...6 D5

Woodbury Salterton
  Devon...6 D5
Woodchester Gloucs...29 L8
Woodchurch Kent...12 H3
Woodcombe Somset...16 C6
Woodcote Gt Lon...21 L10
Woodcote Oxon...19 Q4
Woodcote Wrekin...49 P11
Woodcroft Gloucs...28 G9
Wood Dalling Norfk...44 H5
Woodditton Cambs...33 Q5
Woodeaton Oxon...31 M10
Wood End Gt Lon...20 H7
Wood End Herts...33 K10
Woodend Highld...89 Q4
Woodend Nhants...31 N4
Woodend W Loth...85 Q8
Woodend W Susx...10 D8
Wood End Warwks...40 E11
Wood Enderby Lincs...53 J10
Woodfalls Wilts...8 H4
Woodford Cnwll...14 D9
Woodford Gloucs...29 J9
Woodford Gt Lon...21 N5
Woodford Nhants...32 D2
Woodford Stockp...50 B4
Woodford Bridge Gt Lon...21 N5
Woodford Halse Nhants...31 M4
Woodford Wells Gt Lon...21 N5
Woodgate Birm...40 D10
Woodgate Devon...16 E12
Woodgate W Susx...10 F8
Woodgate Worcs...30 C2
Wood Green Gt Lon...21 L5
Woodgreen Hants...8 H4
Woodhall N York...64 H9
Woodhall Spa Lincs...52 H10
Woodham Bucks...31 P9
Woodham Surrey...20 G10
Woodham Ferrers Essex...22 F4
Woodham Mortimer
  Essex...22 F3
Woodham Walter Essex...22 F3
Wood Hayes Wolves...40 C7
Woodhead Abers...102 G7
Woodhill Shrops...39 N5
Woodhill Somset...17 J10
Woodhorn Nthumb...73 N3
Woodhouse Leeds...58 H7
Woodhouse Leics...41 M5
Woodhouse Sheff...51 K4
Woodhouse Wakefd...59 J9
Woodhouse Eaves Leics...41 M5
Woodhouselee Mdloth...86 F8
Woodhouselees D & G...79 N1
Woodhouses Staffs...40 F4
Woodhurst Cambs...33 K2
Woodingdean Br & H...11 M8
Woodkirk Leeds...58 H8
Woodland Abers...103 J9
Woodland Devon...5 M8
Woodland Devon...5 Q6
Woodland Dur...65 J3
Woodland S Ayrs...76 C11
Woodlands Abers...95 N3
Woodlands Donc...59 M11
Woodlands Dorset...8 F5
Woodlands Hants...9 K5
Woodlands N York...59 J3
Woodlands (Coleshill)
  Crematorium Warwks...40 F9
Woodlands Park W & M...20 D7
Woodlands
  (Scarborough)
  Crematorium N York...67 L9
Woodlands
  (Scunthorpe)
  Crematorium N Linc...60 F11
Woodleigh Devon...5 P9
Woodley Wokham...20 C8
Woodmancote Gloucs...29 K8
Woodmancote Gloucs...29 N4
Woodmancote Gloucs...30 D11
Woodmancote W Susx...10 C8
Woodmancote W Susx...11 K7
Woodmancott Hants...19 P11
Woodmansey E R Yk...60 H6
Woodmansgreen
  W Susx...10 D5
Woodmansterne Surrey...21 L10
Woodmanton Devon...6 D5
Woodnesborough Kent...23 P11
Woodnewton Nhants...42 E10
Wood Norton Norfk...44 G5
Woodplumpton Lancs...57 J2
Woodrising Norfk...44 G9
Wood's Corner E Susx...12 D6
Woodseaves Staffs...49 P9
Woodsetts Rothm...51 M4
Woodsford Dorset...8 A8
Wood's Green E Susx...12 D4
Woodside Br For...20 E8
Woodside Fife...86 H1
Woodside Gt Lon...21 M9
Woodside P & K...93 J7
Woodstock Oxon...31 K10
Woodston C Pete...42 H10
Wood Street Norfk...45 N6
Wood Street Village
  Surrey...20 F12
Woodton Norfk...45 L10
Woodtown Devon...14 G7
Woodvale
  Crematorium Br & H...11 L8
Wood Walton Cambs...32 H1
Woofferton Shrops...39 K8
Wookey Somset...17 M7
Wookey Hole Somset...17 M6
Wool Dorset...8 C9
Woolacombe Devon...14 H3
Woolage Green Kent...23 N12
Woolaston Gloucs...28 G8
Woolaston Common
  Gloucs...28 G8
Woolavington Somset...17 J7
Woolbeding W Susx...10 E5
Woolbrook Devon...6 F5
Wooler Nthumb...81 L8
Woolfardisworthy Devon...14 F7
Woolfardisworthy Devon...15 P9
Woolfords S Lans...86 B10
Woolhampton W Berk...19 P7
Woolhope Herefs...28 H2
Woolland Dorset...8 B6
Woolley BaNES...17 Q3
Woolley Cambs...32 G2
Woolley Wakefd...58 H10

Woolley Edge Services
  Wakefd...58 H10
Woolmere Green Worcs...30 C2
Woolmer Green Herts...33 J11
Woolminstone Somset...7 K2
Woolpit Suffk...34 F4
Woolstaston Shrops...39 J3
Woolsthorpe Lincs...42 B4
Woolsthorpe-by-
  Colsterworth Lincs...42 D5
Woolston C Sotn...9 M5
Woolston Shrops...48 G9
Woolston Somset...16 E8
Woolston Somset...17 P9
Woolston Warrtn...57 M10
Woolstone Gloucs...29 N3
Woolstone M Keyn...32 C8
Woolstone Oxon...19 K4
Woolston Green Devon...5 Q7
Woolton Lpool...56 H10
Woolton Hill Hants...19 M8
Woolverstone Suffk...35 K8
Woolverton Somset...18 B9
Woolwich Gt Lon...21 N7
Woonton Herefs...38 G10
Woore Shrops...49 N7
Wootten Green Suffk...35 K3
Wootton Bed...32 E7
Wootton Kent...13 N2
Wootton N Linc...61 J10
Wootton Nhants...31 Q3
Wootton Oxon...19 N1
Wootton Oxon...31 K9
Wootton Staffs...50 E10
Wootton Bassett Wilts...18 F4
Wootton Bridge IoW...9 P8
Wootton Courtenay
  Somset...16 C7
Wootton Fitzpaine
  Dorset...7 K4
Wootton Rivers Wilts...18 H8
Wootton St Lawrence
  Hants...19 P9
Wootton Wawen Warwks...30 F2
Worcester Worcs...39 Q10
Worcester
  Crematorium Worcs...39 Q10
Worcester Park Gt Lon...21 K9
Wordsley Dudley...40 B9
Worfield Shrops...39 N3
Workington Cumb...70 G9
Worksop Notts...51 N5
Worlaby N Linc...60 H10
Worlds End Hants...9 Q5
Worlds End W Susx...11 L6
Worle N Som...17 J4
Worleston Ches E...49 M4
Worlingham Suffk...45 P11
Worlington Devon...15 N9
Worlington Suffk...34 B3
Worlingworth Suffk...35 K3
Wormbridge Herefs...28 E3
Wormegay Norfk...43 Q7
Wormelow Tump Herefs...28 F3
Wormhill Derbys...50 E6
Wormingford Essex...34 F9
Worminghall Bucks...31 N11
Wormington Gloucs...30 D6
Wormit Fife...93 M9
Wormleighton Warwks...31 K4
Wormley Herts...21 M3
Wormley Surrey...10 F3
Wormshill Kent...22 G11
Wormsley Herefs...38 H11
Worplesdon Surrey...20 F11
Worrall Sheff...50 H3
Worsbrough Barns...51 J1
Worsbrough Bridge Barns...59 J12
Worsbrough Dale Barns...59 J12
Worsley Salfd...57 N8
Worstead Norfk...45 M5
Worsthorne Lancs...57 Q3
Worston Devon...5 M9
Worston Lancs...57 P1
Worth Kent...23 P11
Wortham Suffk...34 H2
Worthen Shrops...38 G2
Worthenbury Wrexhm...48 H6
Worthing Norfk...44 G6
Worthing W Susx...11 J9
Worthing Crematorium
  W Susx...10 H8
Worthington Leics...41 K4
Worth Matravers Dorset...8 E11
Wortley Barns...50 H2
Wortley Leeds...58 H7
Worton N York...64 G9
Worton Wilts...18 E8
Wortwell Norfk...45 L12
Wotton-under-Edge
  Gloucs...29 K9
Wotton Underwood
  Bucks...31 P10
Woughton on the
  Green M Keyn...32 C8
Wouldham Kent...22 E9
Wrabness Essex...35 K9
Wrafton Devon...15 J5
Wragby Lincs...52 H6
Wragby Wakefd...59 K10
Wrangaton Devon...5 N8
Wrangle Lincs...53 L12
Wrangway Somset...16 F11
Wrantage Somset...17 J10
Wrawby N Linc...52 E2
Wraxall N Som...17 L2
Wraxall Somset...17 N8
Wray Lancs...63 L8
Wraysbury W & M...20 G8
Wrayton Lancs...63 L7
Wrea Green Lancs...56 H3
Wreay Cumb...71 N6
Wrecclesham Surrey...10 D2
Wrekenton Gatesd...73 M8
Wrelton N York...66 G9
Wrenbury Ches E...49 L6
Wreningham Norfk...45 J9
Wrentham Suffk...35 Q1
Wrentnall Shrops...38 H2
Wressle E R Yk...60 C7
Wressle N Linc...52 D2
Wrestlingworth C Beds...33 J7
Wretton Norfk...44 B9
Wrexham Wrexhm...48 G5
Wribbenhall Worcs...39 P7
Wrinehill Staffs...49 N6
Wrington N Som...17 L4

Writhlington BaNES...17 Q5
Writtle Essex...22 D3
Wrockwardine Wrekin...49 L11
Wroot N Linc...60 C12
Wrose C Brad...58 F6
Wrotham Kent...22 C10
Wroughton Swindn...18 G5
Wroxall IoW...9 P10
Wroxall Warwks...40 G12
Wroxeter Shrops...39 K1
Wroxham Norfk...45 L6
Wroxham Barns Norfk...45 M6
Wroxton Oxon...31 K6
Wyaston Derbys...50 F11
Wyberton East Lincs...43 K3
Wyboston Bed...32 G5
Wybunbury Ches E...49 M5
Wychbold Worcs...30 B2
Wychnor Staffs...40 F4
Wyck Rissington Gloucs...30 F9
Wycliffe Dur...65 K5
Wycoller Lancs...58 C6
Wycomb Leics...41 Q3
Wycombe Marsh Bucks...20 E5
Wyddial Herts...33 L9
Wye Kent...13 K1
Wyke C Brad...58 F8
Wyke Dorset...8 B3
Wyke Champflower
  Somset...17 P8
Wykeham N York...67 L10
Wyken Covtry...41 J10
Wyken Shrops...39 N3
Wyke Regis Dorset...7 P7
Wykey Shrops...48 H9
Wylam Nthumb...73 K7
Wylde Green Birm...40 E8
Wylye Wilts...18 E12
Wymeswold Leics...41 N3
Wymington Bed...32 D4
Wymondham Leics...42 C6
Wymondham Norfk...45 J9
Wynford Eagle Dorset...7 N4
Wyre Forest
  Crematorium Worcs...39 P7
Wyre Piddle Worcs...30 C5
Wysall Notts...41 N3
Wythall Worcs...40 E11
Wytham Oxon...31 L11
Wythenshawe Manch...57 P10
Wyton Cambs...33 J3
Wyton E R Yk...61 K7
Wyverstone Suffk...34 G3
Wyverstone Street Suffk...34 G4

Y

Yaddlethorpe N Linc...52 C3
Yafforth N York...65 N8
Yalberton Torbay...6 B10
Yalding Kent...22 E12
Yanwath Cumb...71 Q9
Yanworth Gloucs...30 E10
Yapham E R Yk...60 D4
Yapton W Susx...10 F9
Yarborough N Som...17 K5
Yarburgh Lincs...53 K5
Yarcombe Devon...6 H2
Yard Devon...15 N7
Yardley Birm...40 F9
Yardley Crematorium
  Birm...40 F9
Yardley Gobion Nhants...31 Q5
Yardley Hastings Nhants...32 C5
Yardley Wood Birm...40 E10
Yarkhill Herefs...28 H1
Yarley Somset...17 M7
Yarlington Somset...17 P9
Yarm S on T...65 P5
Yarmouth IoW...9 L9
Yarnbrook Wilts...18 C9
Yarnfield Staffs...49 Q8
Yarnscombe Devon...15 K7
Yarnton Oxon...31 L10
Yarpole Herefs...39 J8
Yarrow Border...79 M4
Yarrow Feus Border...79 M4
Yarrowford Border...79 N3
Yarwell Nhants...42 F9
Yate S Glos...29 J11
Yateley Hants...20 D10
Yatesbury Wilts...18 F6
Yattendon W Berk...19 P6
Yatton Herefs...38 H8
Yatton N Som...17 L3
Yatton Keynell Wilts...18 C5
Yaverland IoW...9 Q9
Yaxham Norfk...44 G7
Yaxley Cambs...42 H10
Yaxley Suffk...35 J2
Yazor Herefs...38 H11
Yeading Gt Lon...20 H7
Yeadon Leeds...58 G6
Yealand Conyers Lancs...63 J7
Yealand Redmayne Lancs...63 J7
Yealmpton Devon...5 M9
Yearsley N York...66 E11
Yeaton Shrops...48 H10
Yeaveley Derbys...50 F11
Yeavering Nthumb...81 K7
Yedingham N York...67 J10
Yelford Oxon...31 J12
Yell Shet...111 k3
Yelling Cambs...33 J4
Yelvertoft Nhants...41 N11
Yelverton Devon...5 L6
Yelverton Norfk...45 L9
Yenston Somset...17 Q11
Yeoford Devon...15 N11
Yeolmbridge Cnwll...4
Yeovil Somset...17 M11
Yeovil Crematorium
  Somset...17 M11
Yeovil Marsh Somset...17 M11
Yeovilton Somset...17 M10
Yesnaby Ork...111 g2
Yetminster Dorset...7 N1
Yettington Devon...6 E5
Yetts o'Muckhart Clacks...86 B2
Yew Tree Sandw...40 D8
Y Felinheli Gwynd...54 G7
Y Ferwig Cerdgn...36 C10
Y Ffor Gwynd...46 G4
Y Gyffylliog Denbgs...48 C4
Yielden Bed...32 E4

Yieldshields S Lans...77 P2
Yiewsley Gt Lon...20 G7
Y Maerdy Rhondd...48 B6
Ynysboeth Rhondd...27 M9
Ynysddu Caerph...27 P9
Ynyshir Rhondd...27 L9
Ynystawe Swans...26 F8
Ynysybwl Rhondd...27 M9
Yockleton Shrops...48 H12
Yockfleet E R Yk...60 E8
Yoker C Glas...84 H8
York C York...59 N4
York City Crematorium
  C York...59 N5
Yorkletts Kent...23 L10
Yorkley Gloucs...28 H7
Yorkshire Dales National
  Park...64 F11
York Town Surrey...20 D10
Youlgreave Derbys...50 G7
Youlthorpe E R Yk...60 D3
Youlton N York...59 L2
Yoxall Staffs...40 F4
Yoxford Suffk...35 N3
Y Rhiw Gwynd...46 D6
Ysbyty Ifan Conwy...55 M10
Ysbyty Ystwyth Cerdgn...37 M6
Ysceifiog Flints...48 D2
Ystalyfera Neath...26 G7
Ystrad Rhondd...27 L9
Ystrad Aeron Cerdgn...36 H9
Ystradfellte Powys...27 K6
Ystradgynlais Powys...26 H6
Ystrad Meurig Cerdgn...37 L7
Ystrad Mynach Caerph...27 N9
Ystradowen V Glam...27 L12
Ythanbank Abers...103 J8
Ythanwells Abers...102 E7
Ythsie Abers...103 J8

Z

Zeal Monachorum Devon...15 M10
Zeals Wilts...8 B2
Zelah Cnwll...3 J5
Zennor Cnwll...2 C7
Zouch Notts...41 L3
ZSL London Zoo Gt Lon...21 L6
ZSL Whipsnade Zoo
  C Beds...32 E12